SUPERMAN

VOLUME 2

RETURN TO GLORY

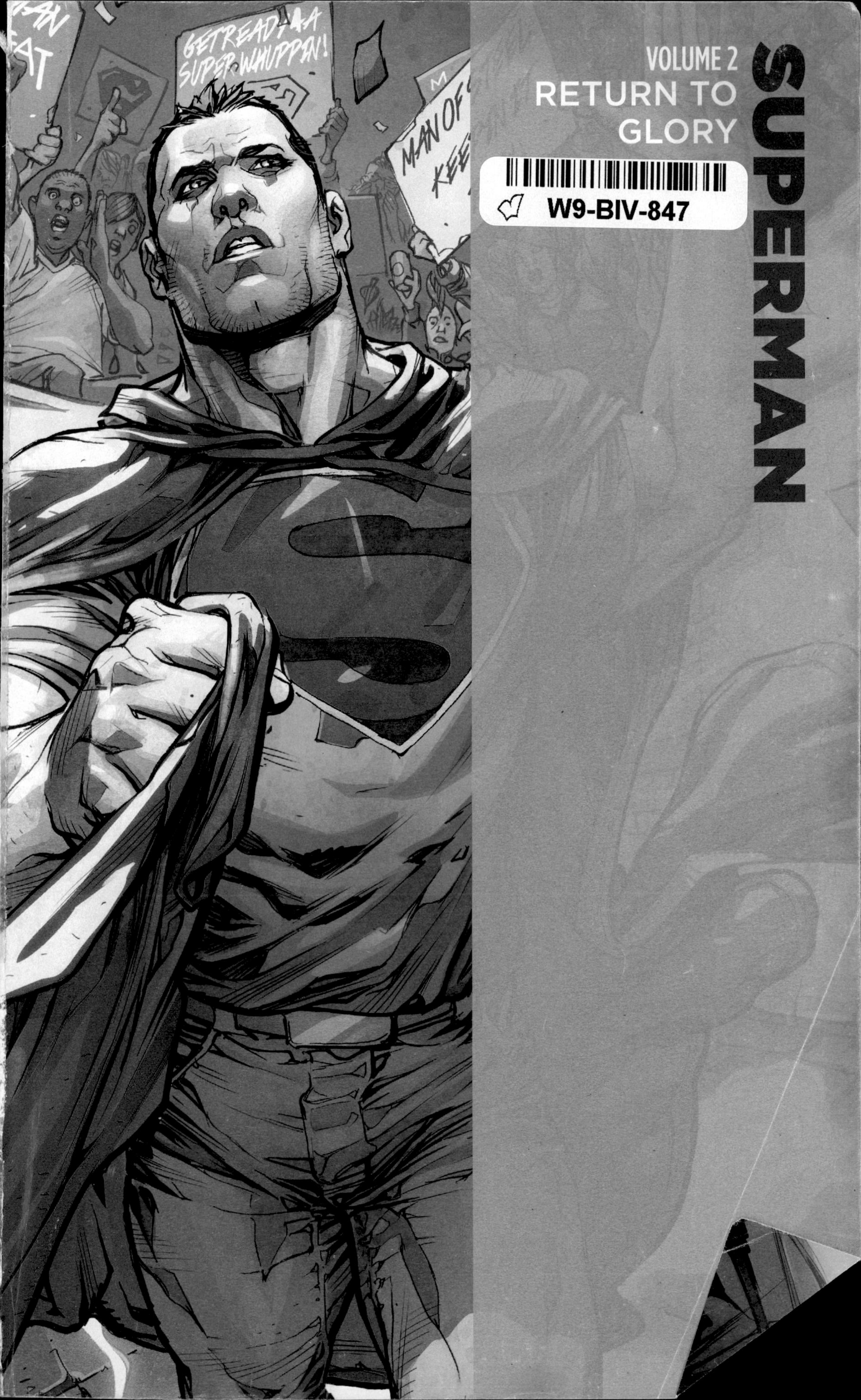
GET READY 4 A SUPER WHUPPIN!

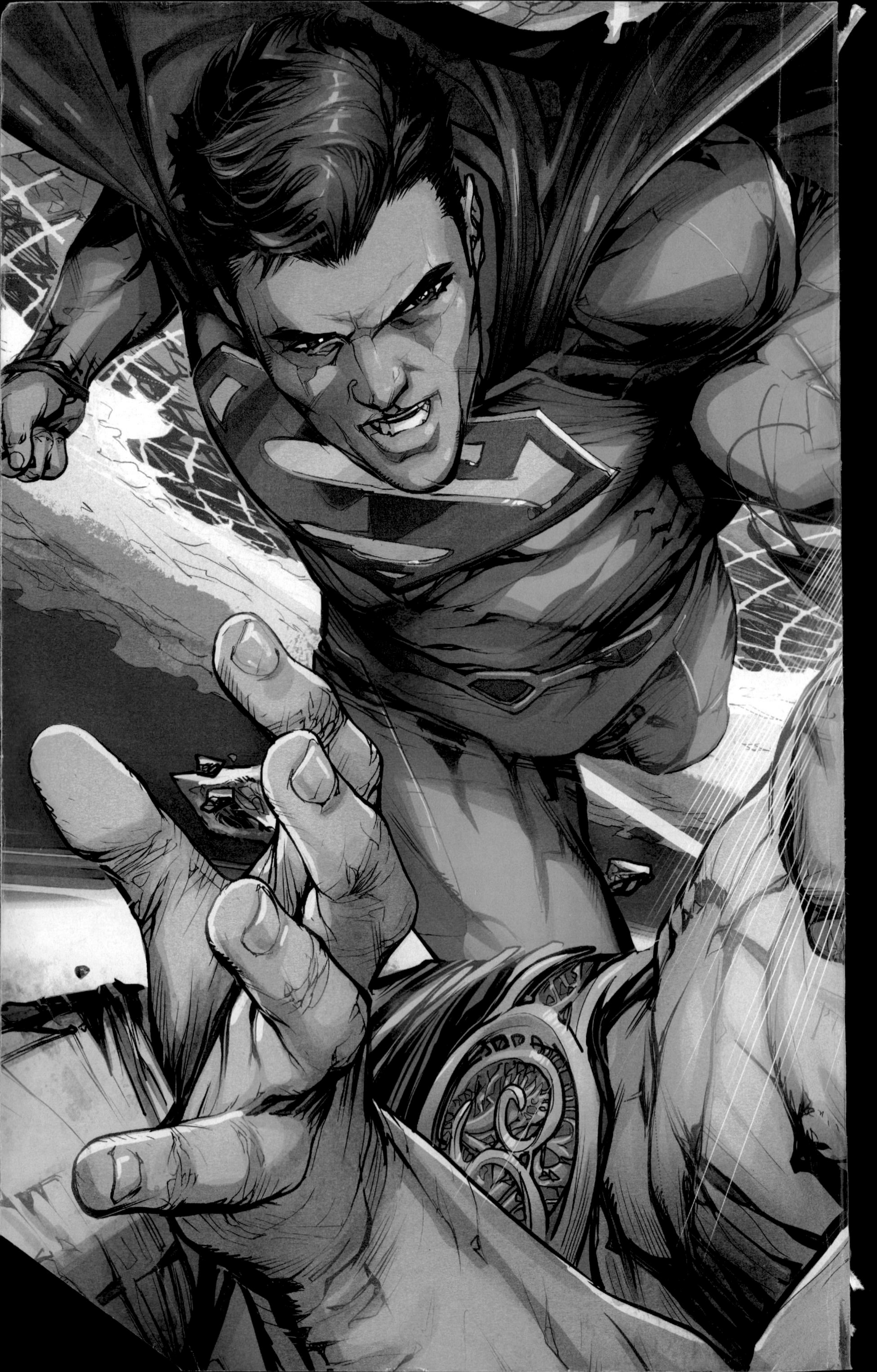

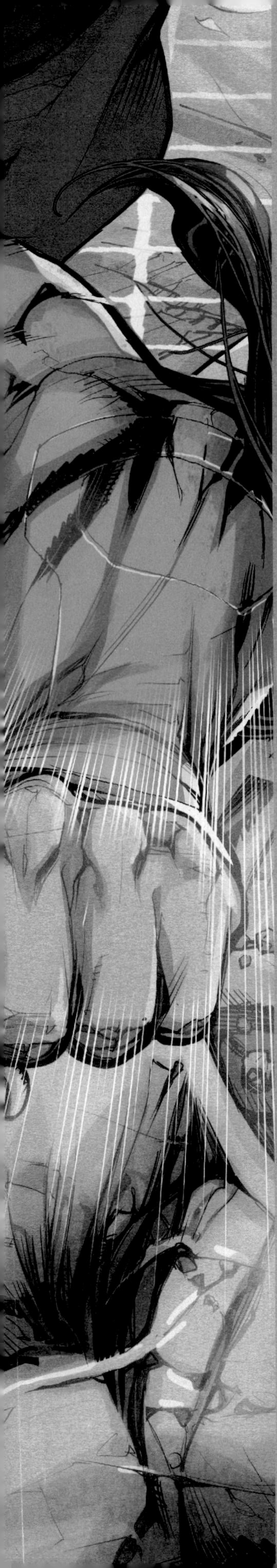

SUPERMAN

VOLUME 2
RETURN TO GLORY

WRITTEN BY
AARON HUDER GREG PAK
PETER J. TOMASI GENE LUEN YANG

PENCILS BY
RAYMUND BERMUDEZ
JON BOGDANOVE TOM DERENICK
JACK HERBERT DAN JURGENS BEN OLIVER
HOWARD PORTER MIKEL JANIN
RAFA SANDOVAL MIGUEL SEPULVEDA
ARDIAN SYAF PATRICK ZIRCHER

INKS BY
RAYMUND BERMUDEZ
JON BOGDANOVE TOM DERENICK
JACK HERBERT DON HO MIKEL JANÍN
HOWARD PORTER JEROME K. MOORE
BEN OLIVER MIGUEL SEPULVEDA
BILL SIENKIEWICZ ARDIAN SYAF
PATRICK ZIRCHER

COLORS BY
BLOND JEROMY COX HI-FI MIKEL JANÍN
TOMEU MOREY TRISH MULVIHILL
LEE LOUGHRIDGE BEN OLIVER

LETTERS BY
A LARGER WORLD STUDIOS
ROB LEIGH STEVE WANDS

COLLECTION COVER ART BY
HOWARD PORTER HI-FI

SUPERMAN CREATED BY
JERRY SIEGEL AND JOE SHUSTER
BY SPECIAL ARRANGEMENT WITH THE JERRY SIEGEL FAMILY.

BATMAN CREATED BY
BOB KANE WITH BILL FINGER

ANDREW MARINO Assistant Editor – Original Series
EDDIE BERGANZA Group Editor – Original Series
JEB WOODARD Group Editor – Collected Editions
SUZANNAH ROWNTREE Editor – Collected Edition
STEVE COOK Design Director – Books
DAMIAN RYLAND Publication Design

BOB HARRAS Senior VP – Editor-in-Chief, DC Comics

DIANE NELSON President
DAN DiDIO Publisher
JIM LEE Publisher
GEOFF JOHNS President & Chief Creative Officer
AMIT DESAI Executive VP – Business & Marketing Strategy, Direct to Consumer & Global Franchise Management
SAM ADES Senior VP – Direct to Consumer
BOBBIE CHASE VP – Talent Development
MARK CHIARELLO Senior VP – Art, Design & Collected Editions
JOHN CUNNINGHAM Senior VP – Sales & Trade Marketing
ANNE DePIES Senior VP – Business Strategy, Finance & Administration
DON FALLETTI VP – Manufacturing Operations
LAWRENCE GANEM VP – Editorial Administration & Talent Relations
ALISON GILL Senior VP – Manufacturing & Operations
HANK KANALZ Senior VP – Editorial Strategy & Administration
JAY KOGAN VP – Legal Affairs
THOMAS LOFTUS VP – Business Affairs
JACK MAHAN VP – Business Affairs
NICK J. NAPOLITANO VP – Manufacturing Administration
EDDIE SCANNELL VP – Consumer Marketing
COURTNEY SIMMONS Senior VP – Publicity & Communications
JIM (SKI) SOKOLOWSKI VP – Comic Book Specialty Sales & Trade Marketing
NANCY SPEARS VP – Mass, Book, Digital Sales & Trade Marketing

SUPERMAN VOLUME 2: RETURN TO GLORY

DC Comics, 2900 West Alameda Ave., Burbank, CA 91505
Printed by LSC Communications, Salem, VA, USA. 2/3/17. First Printing.
ISBN: 978-1-4012-6830-5

Library of Congress Cataloging-in-Publication Data is available.

PEFC Certified

Printed on paper from
sustainably managed
forests, controlled
sources

PEFC
PEFC/29-31-337   www.pefc.org

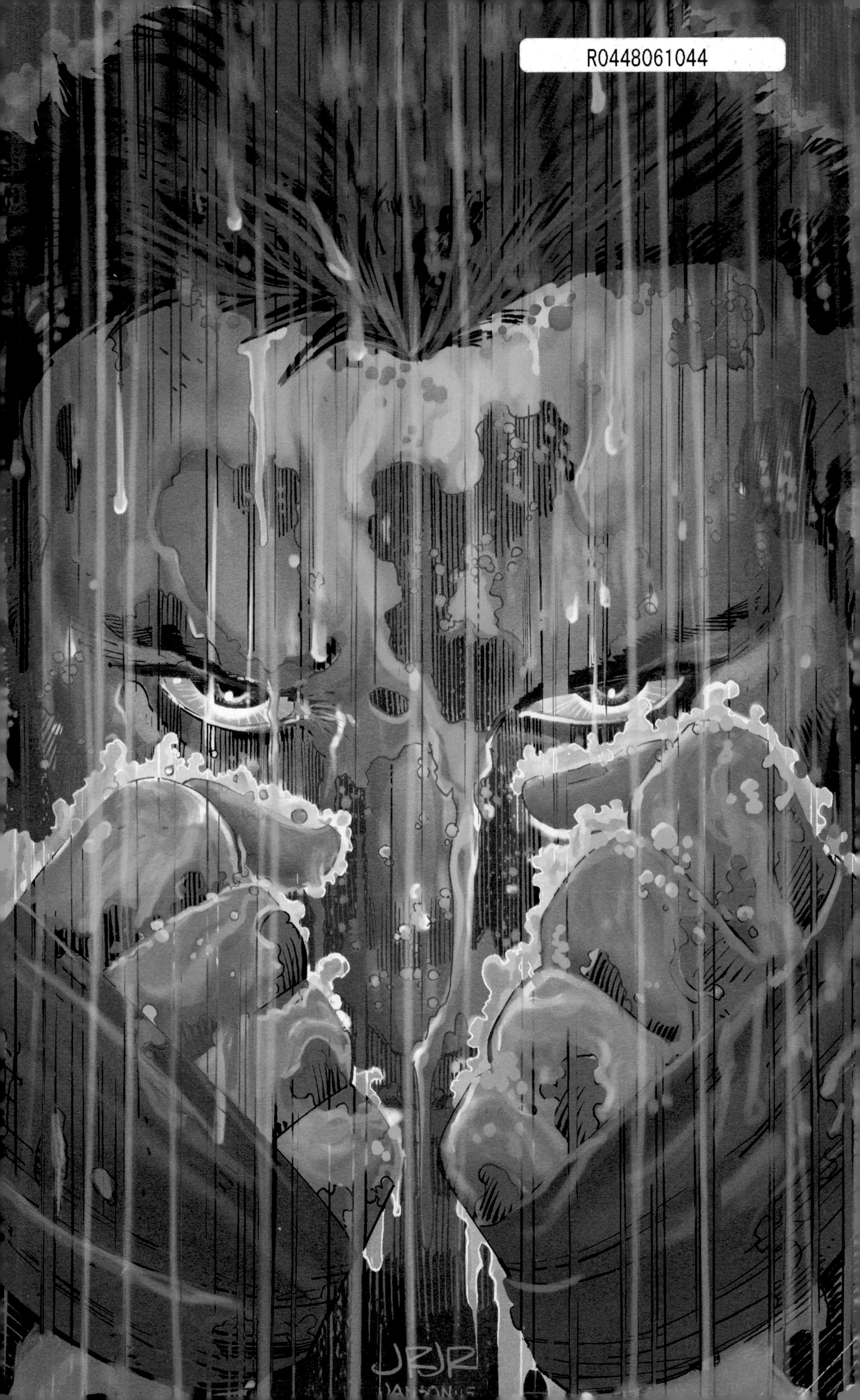

STREET JUSTICE

GENE LUEN YANG writer HOWARD PORTER artist HI-FI colorist ROB LEIGH letterer JOHN ROMITA JR., KLAUS JANSON, DEAN WHITE cover

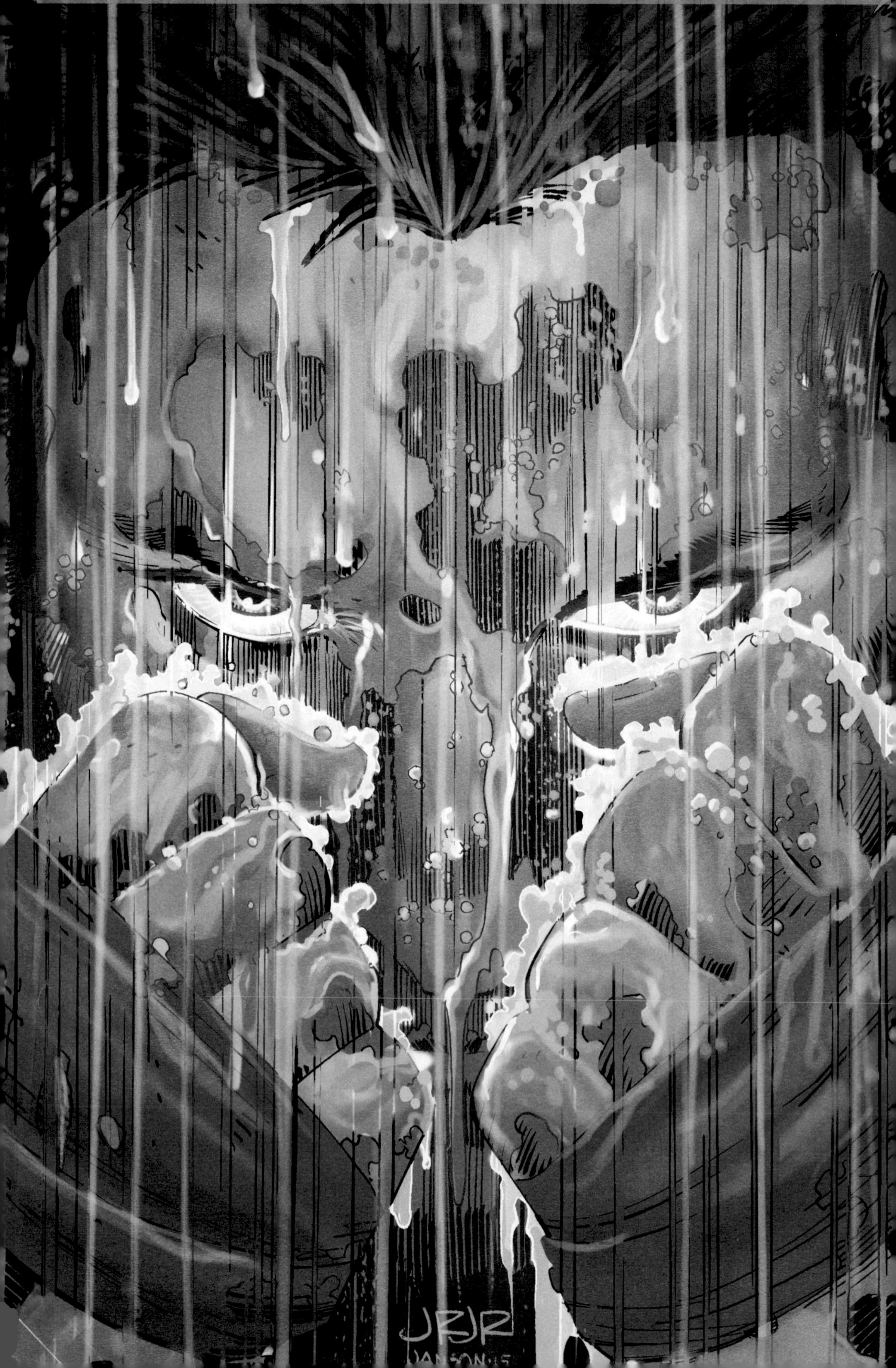

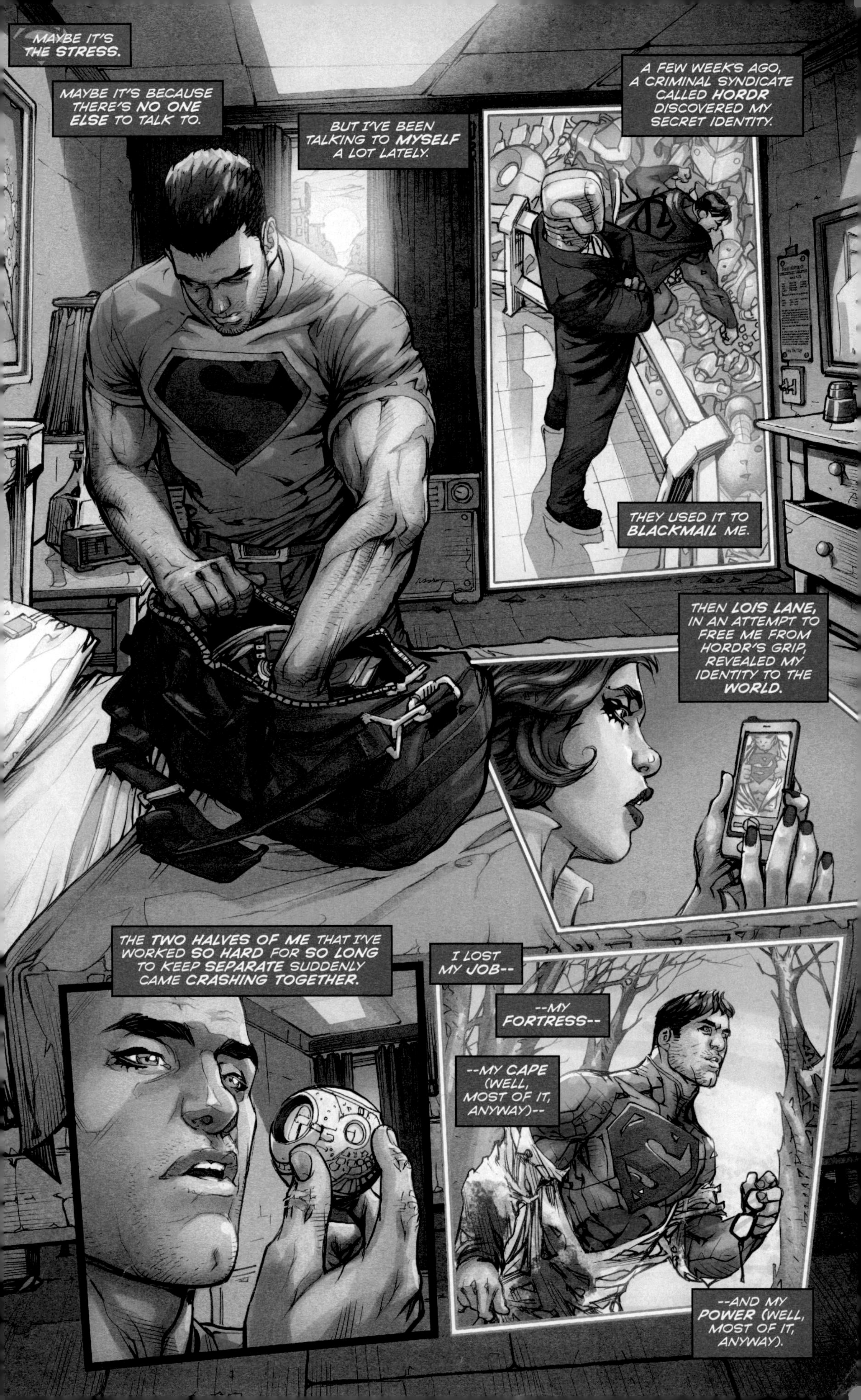
MAYBE IT'S THE STRESS.
MAYBE IT'S BECAUSE THERE'S NO ONE ELSE TO TALK TO.
BUT I'VE BEEN TALKING TO MYSELF A LOT LATELY.
A FEW WEEKS AGO, A CRIMINAL SYNDICATE CALLED HORDR DISCOVERED MY SECRET IDENTITY.
THEY USED IT TO BLACKMAIL ME.
THEN LOIS LANE, IN AN ATTEMPT TO FREE ME FROM HORDR'S GRIP, REVEALED MY IDENTITY TO THE WORLD.
THE TWO HALVES OF ME THAT I'VE WORKED SO HARD FOR SO LONG TO KEEP SEPARATE SUDDENLY CAME CRASHING TOGETHER.
I LOST MY JOB--
--MY FORTRESS--
--MY CAPE (WELL, MOST OF IT, ANYWAY)--
--AND MY POWER (WELL, MOST OF IT, ANYWAY).

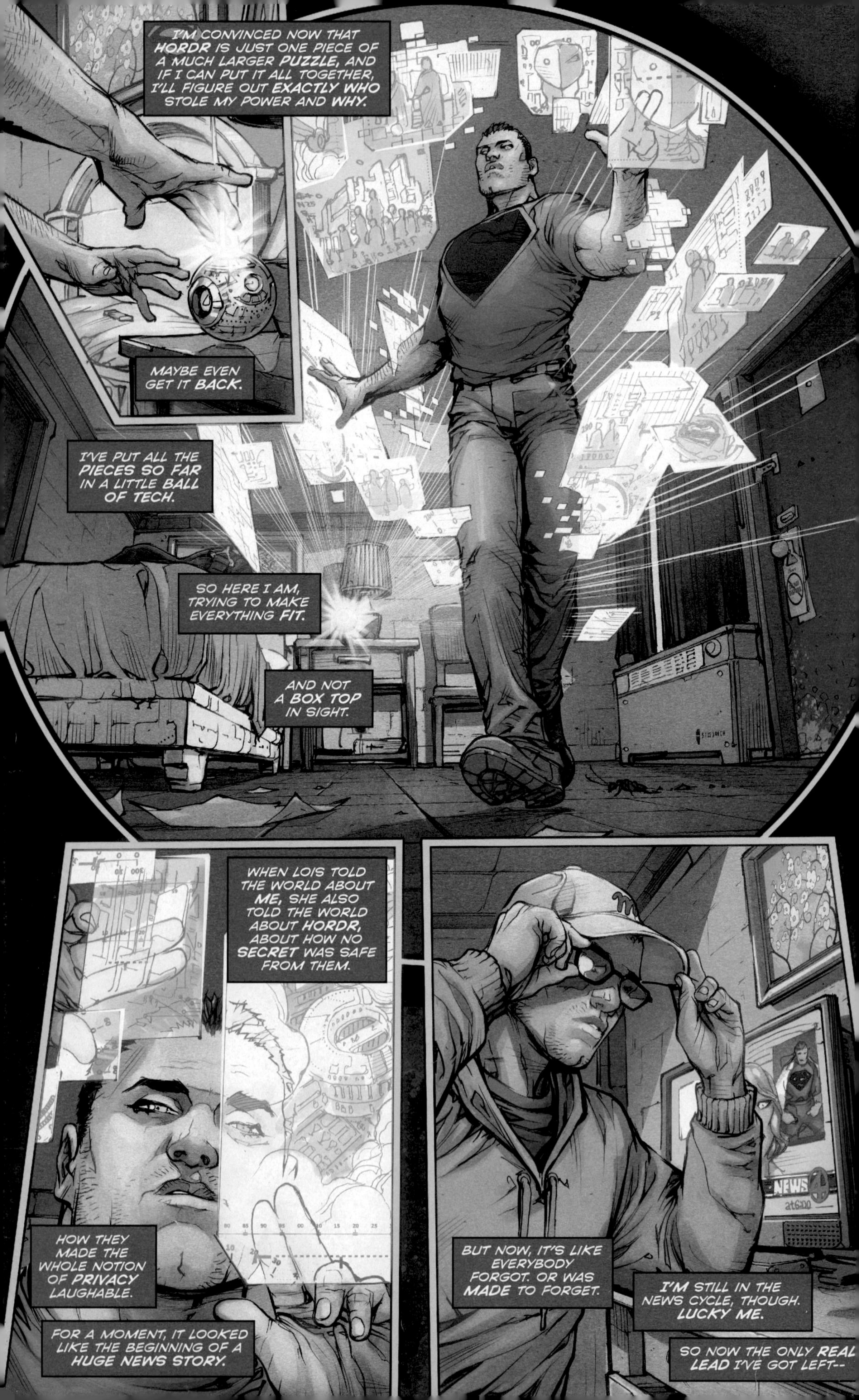
I'M CONVINCED NOW THAT HORDR IS JUST ONE PIECE OF A MUCH LARGER PUZZLE, AND IF I CAN PUT IT ALL TOGETHER, I'LL FIGURE OUT EXACTLY WHO STOLE MY POWER AND WHY.
MAYBE EVEN GET IT BACK.
I'VE PUT ALL THE PIECES SO FAR IN A LITTLE BALL OF TECH.
SO HERE I AM, TRYING TO MAKE EVERYTHING FIT.
AND NOT A BOX TOP IN SIGHT.
WHEN LOIS TOLD THE WORLD ABOUT ME, SHE ALSO TOLD THE WORLD ABOUT HORDR, ABOUT HOW NO SECRET WAS SAFE FROM THEM.
HOW THEY MADE THE WHOLE NOTION OF PRIVACY LAUGHABLE.
FOR A MOMENT, IT LOOKED LIKE THE BEGINNING OF A HUGE NEWS STORY.
BUT NOW, IT'S LIKE EVERYBODY FORGOT. OR WAS MADE TO FORGET.
I'M STILL IN THE NEWS CYCLE, THOUGH. LUCKY ME.
SO NOW THE ONLY REAL LEAD I'VE GOT LEFT--

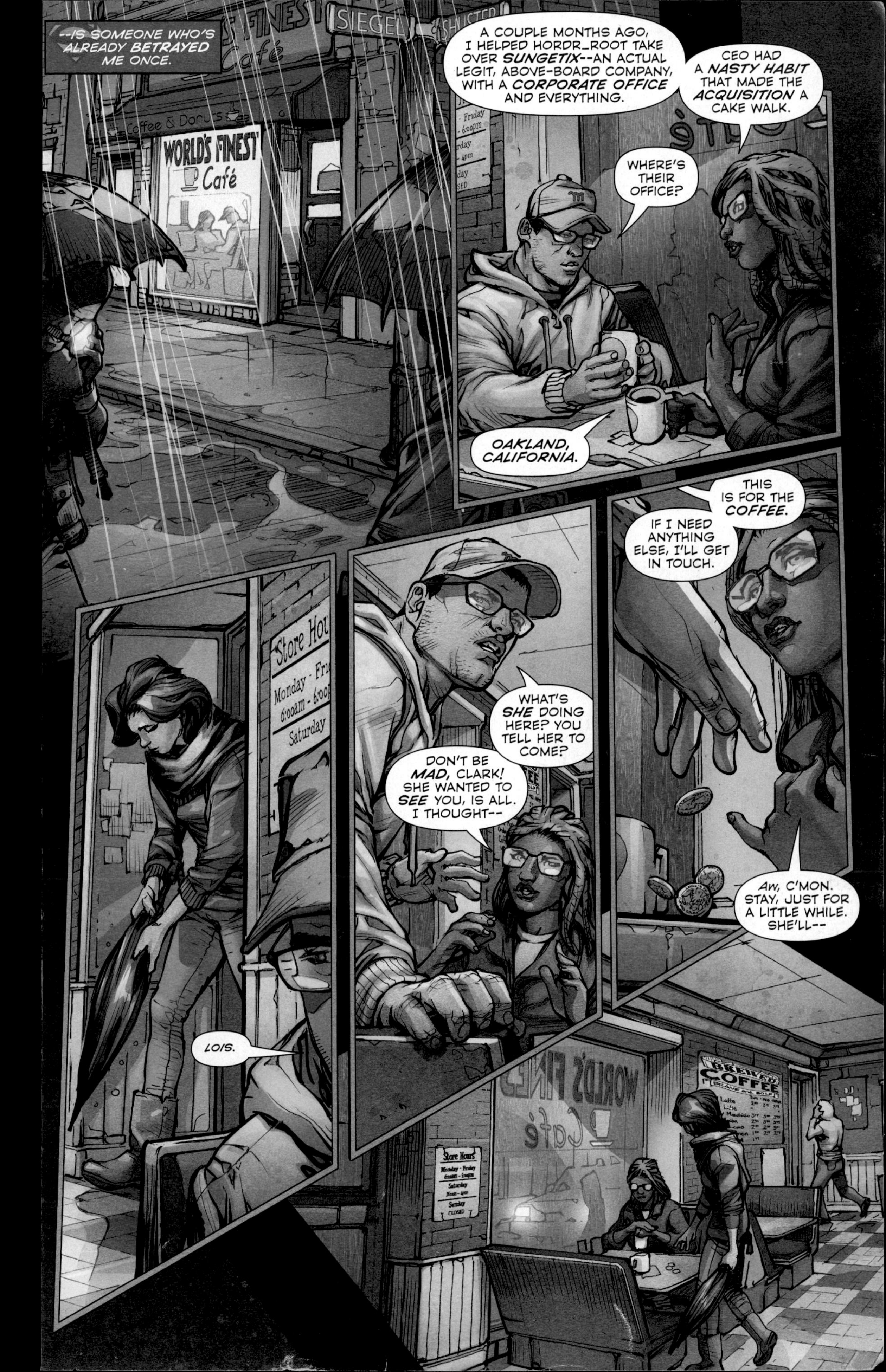
--IS SOMEONE WHO'S ALREADY BETRAYED ME ONCE.
SIEGEL
SHUSTER
WORLD'S FINEST Café
A COUPLE MONTHS AGO, I HELPED HORDR_ROOT TAKE OVER SUNGETIX--AN ACTUAL LEGIT, ABOVE-BOARD COMPANY, WITH A CORPORATE OFFICE AND EVERYTHING.
CEO HAD A NASTY HABIT THAT MADE THE ACQUISITION A CAKE WALK.
WHERE'S THEIR OFFICE?
OAKLAND, CALIFORNIA.
THIS IS FOR THE COFFEE.
IF I NEED ANYTHING ELSE, I'LL GET IN TOUCH.
AW, C'MON. STAY, JUST FOR A LITTLE WHILE. SHE'LL--
WHAT'S SHE DOING HERE? YOU TELL HER TO COME?
DON'T BE MAD, CLARK! SHE WANTED TO SEE YOU, IS ALL. I THOUGHT--
LOIS.
Store Hours
Monday - Friday
Saturday
Sunday
CLOSED
BREWED COFFEE

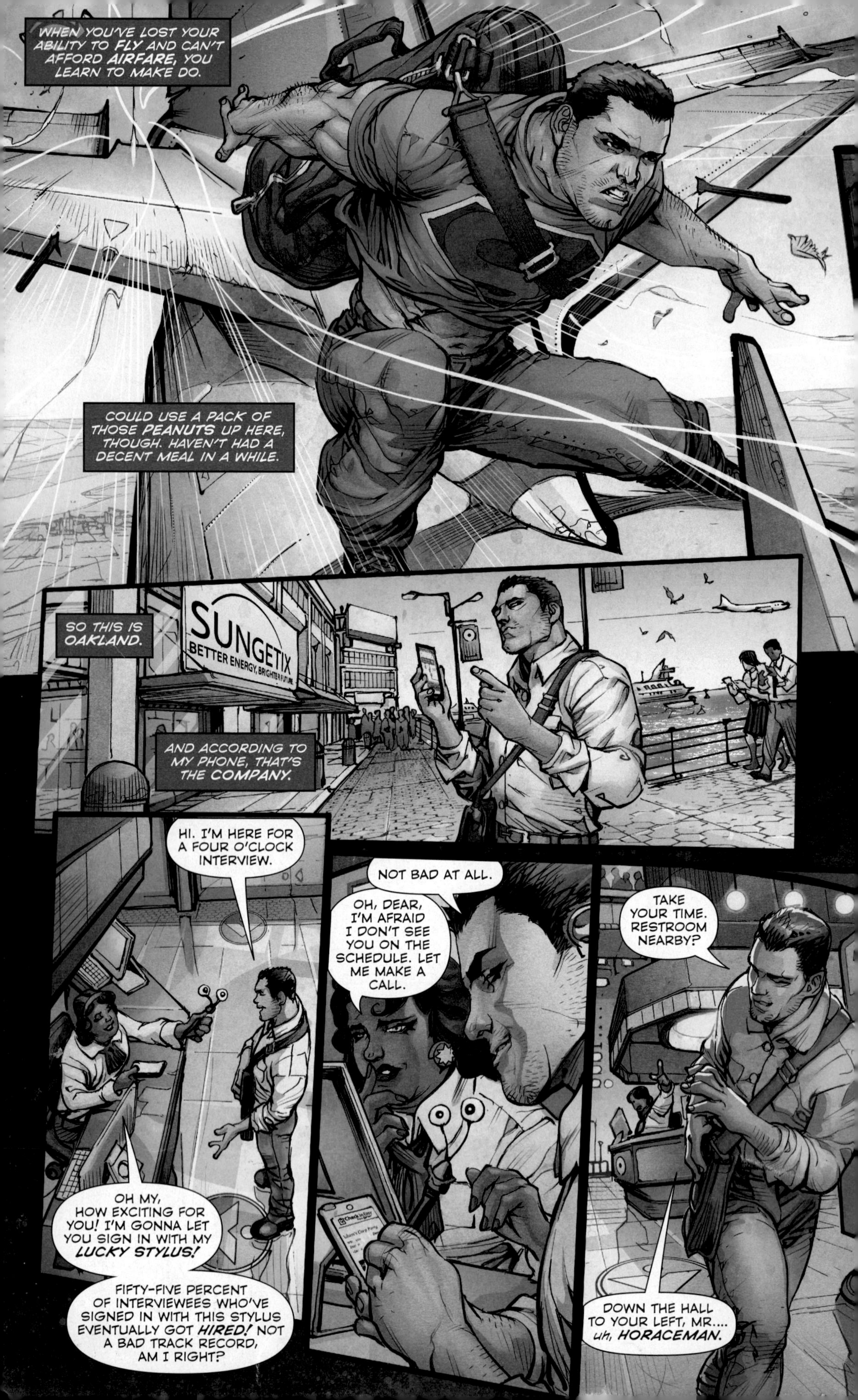
WHEN YOU'VE LOST YOUR ABILITY TO FLY AND CAN'T AFFORD AIRFARE, YOU LEARN TO MAKE DO.
COULD USE A PACK OF THOSE PEANUTS UP HERE, THOUGH. HAVEN'T HAD A DECENT MEAL IN A WHILE.
SO THIS IS OAKLAND.
SUNGETIX BETTER ENERGY, BRIGHTER FUTURE
AND ACCORDING TO MY PHONE, THAT'S THE COMPANY.
HI. I'M HERE FOR A FOUR O'CLOCK INTERVIEW.
OH MY, HOW EXCITING FOR YOU! I'M GONNA LET YOU SIGN IN WITH MY LUCKY STYLUS!
FIFTY-FIVE PERCENT OF INTERVIEWEES WHO'VE SIGNED IN WITH THIS STYLUS EVENTUALLY GOT HIRED! NOT A BAD TRACK RECORD, AM I RIGHT?
NOT BAD AT ALL.
OH, DEAR, I'M AFRAID I DON'T SEE YOU ON THE SCHEDULE. LET ME MAKE A CALL.
TAKE YOUR TIME. RESTROOM NEARBY?
DOWN THE HALL TO YOUR LEFT, MR.... uh, HORACEMAN.

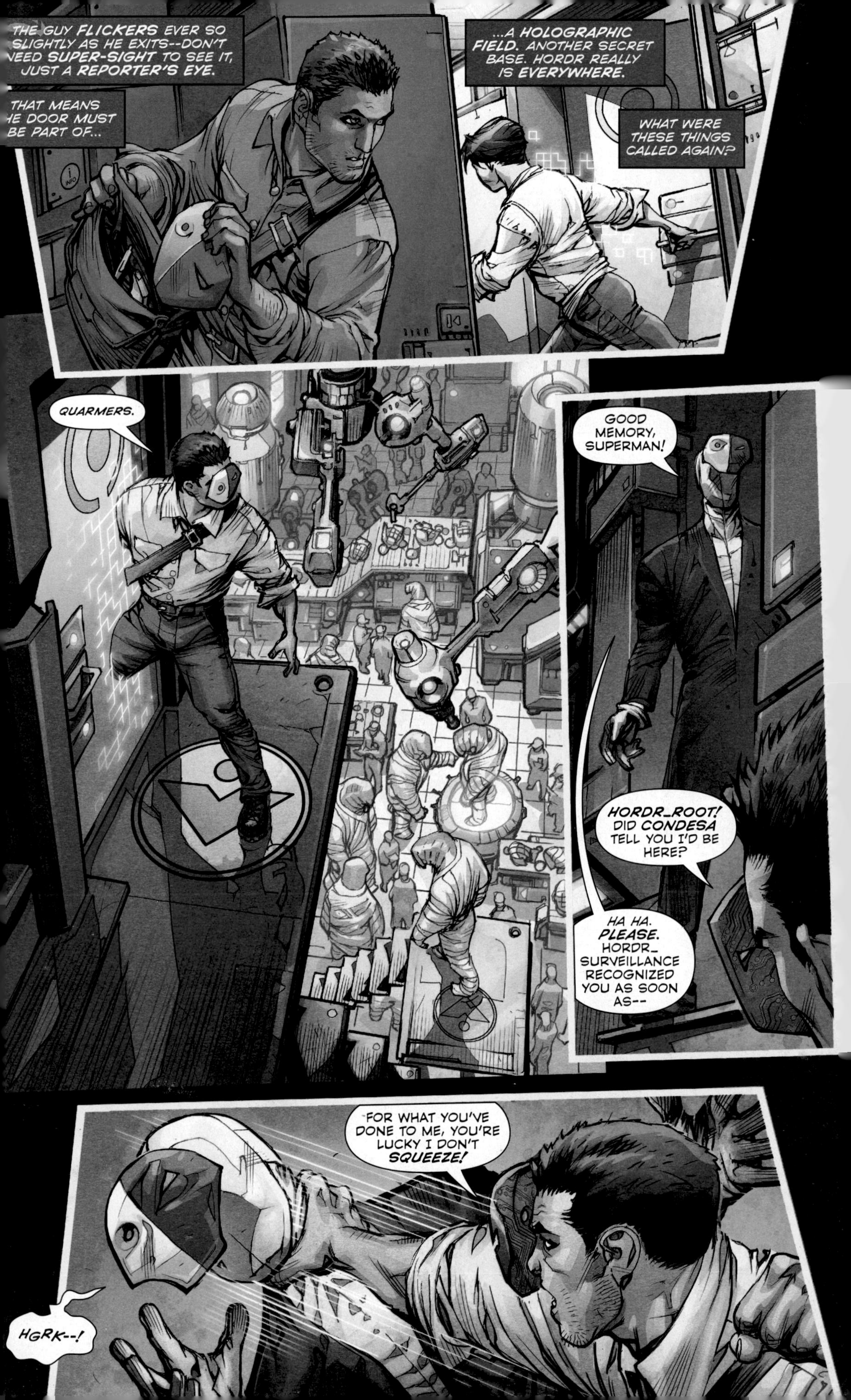
THE GUY FLICKERS EVER SO SLIGHTLY AS HE EXITS--DON'T NEED SUPER-SIGHT TO SEE IT, JUST A REPORTER'S EYE.
THAT MEANS HE DOOR MUST BE PART OF...
...A HOLOGRAPHIC FIELD. ANOTHER SECRET BASE. HORDR REALLY IS EVERYWHERE.
WHAT WERE THESE THINGS CALLED AGAIN?
QUARMERS.
GOOD MEMORY, SUPERMAN!
HORDR_ROOT! DID CONDESA TELL YOU I'D BE HERE?
HA HA. PLEASE. HORDR_ SURVEILLANCE RECOGNIZED YOU AS SOON AS--
FOR WHAT YOU'VE DONE TO ME, YOU'RE LUCKY I DON'T SQUEEZE!
HGRK--!

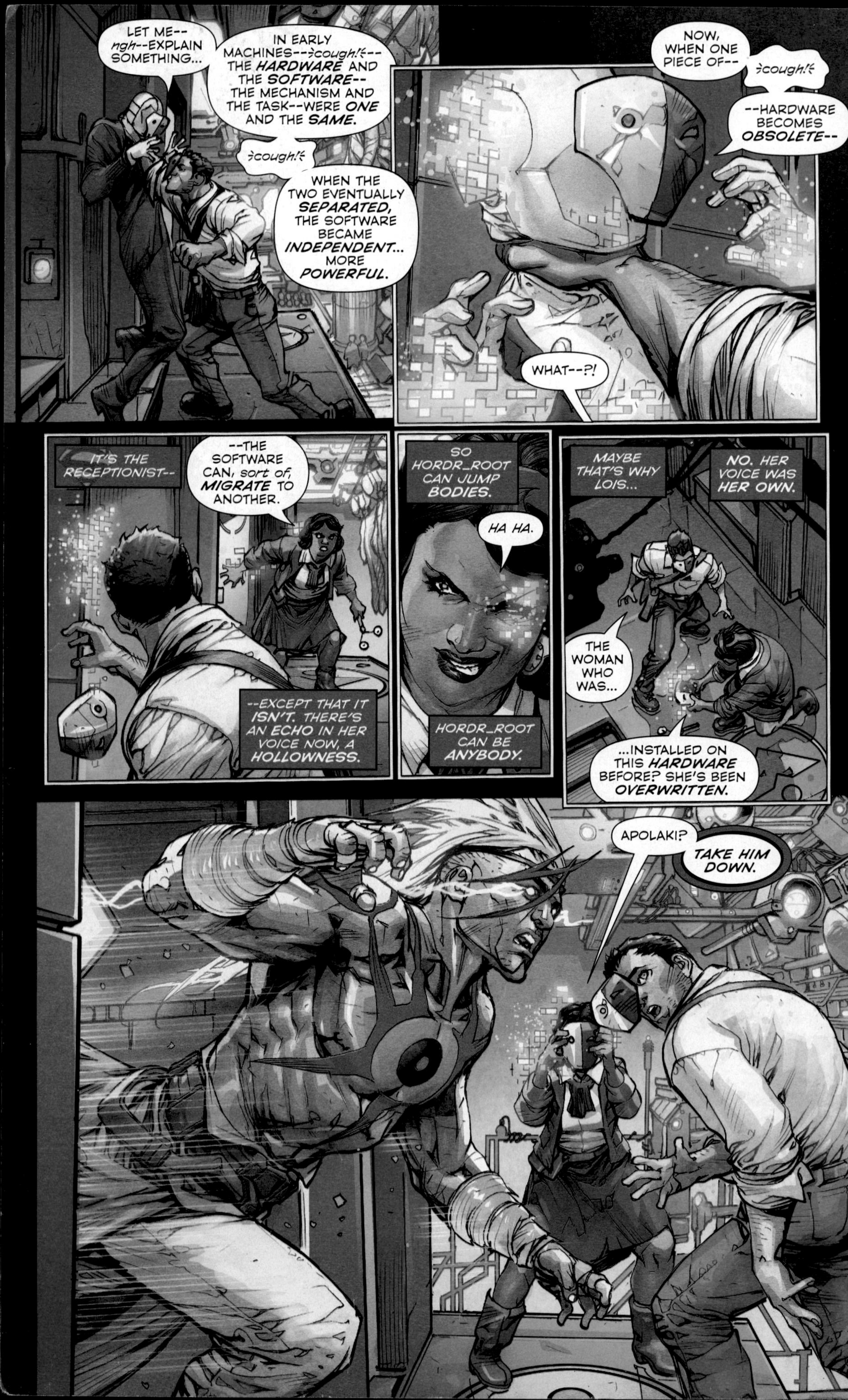

LET ME--ngh--EXPLAIN SOMETHING...
IN EARLY MACHINES--cough!--THE HARDWARE AND THE SOFTWARE--THE MECHANISM AND THE TASK--WERE ONE AND THE SAME.
cough!
WHEN THE TWO EVENTUALLY SEPARATED, THE SOFTWARE BECAME INDEPENDENT... MORE POWERFUL.
NOW, WHEN ONE PIECE OF--
cough!
--HARDWARE BECOMES OBSOLETE--
WHAT--?!
IT'S THE RECEPTIONIST--
--THE SOFTWARE CAN, sort of, MIGRATE TO ANOTHER.
--EXCEPT THAT IT ISN'T. THERE'S AN ECHO IN HER VOICE NOW, A HOLLOWNESS.
SO HORDR_ROOT CAN JUMP BODIES.
HA HA.
HORDR_ROOT CAN BE ANYBODY.
MAYBE THAT'S WHY LOIS...
NO. HER VOICE WAS HER OWN.
THE WOMAN WHO WAS...
...INSTALLED ON THIS HARDWARE BEFORE? SHE'S BEEN OVERWRITTEN.
APOLAKI?
TAKE HIM DOWN.

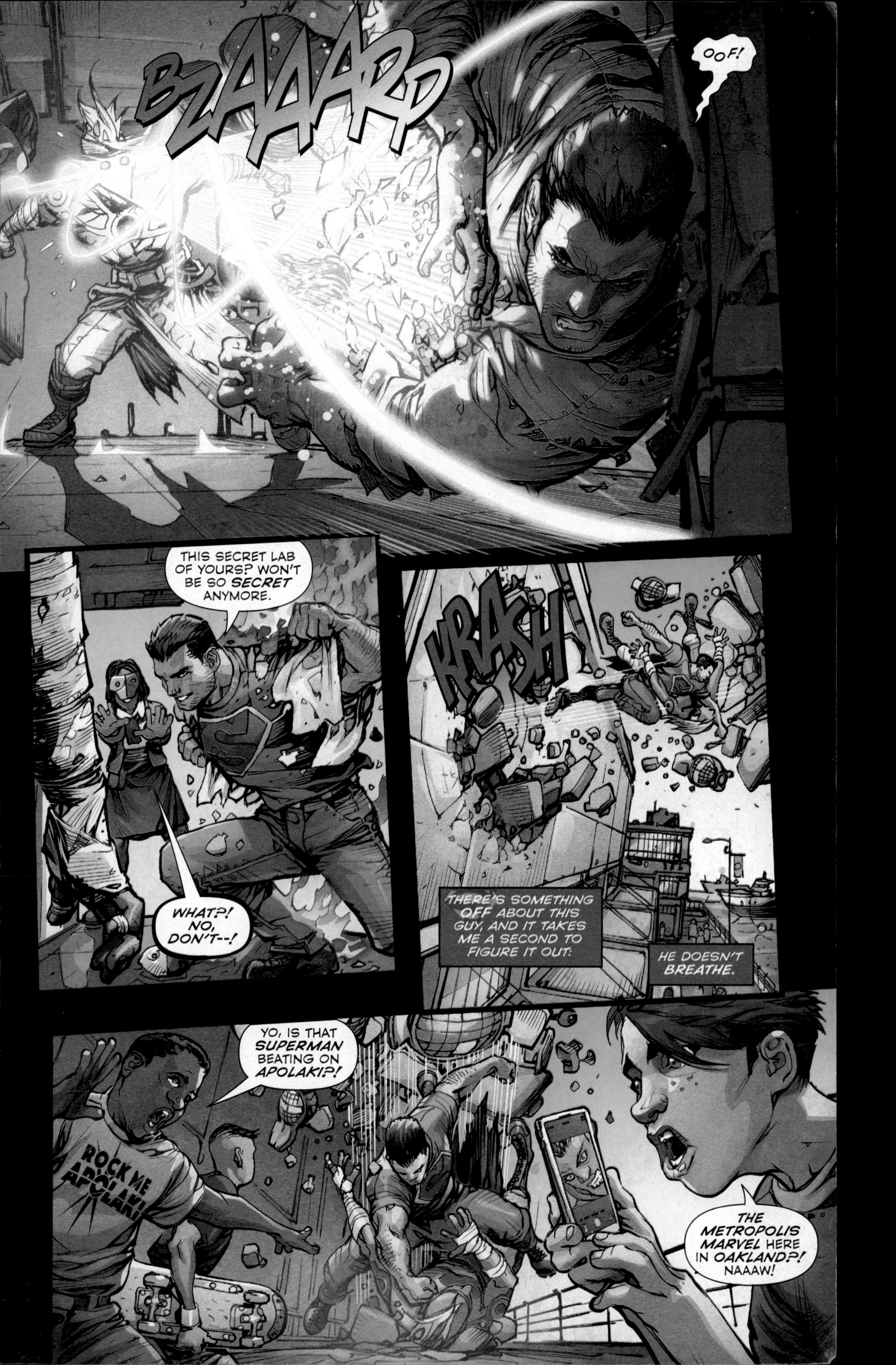
BZAAARD
OOF!
THIS SECRET LAB OF YOURS? WON'T BE SO SECRET ANYMORE.
WHAT?! NO, DON'T--!
KRASH
THERE'S SOMETHING OFF ABOUT THIS GUY, AND IT TAKES ME A SECOND TO FIGURE IT OUT:
HE DOESN'T BREATHE.
YO, IS THAT SUPERMAN BEATING ON APOLAKI?!
ROCK ME APOLAKI
THE METROPOLIS MARVEL HERE IN OAKLAND?! NAAAW!

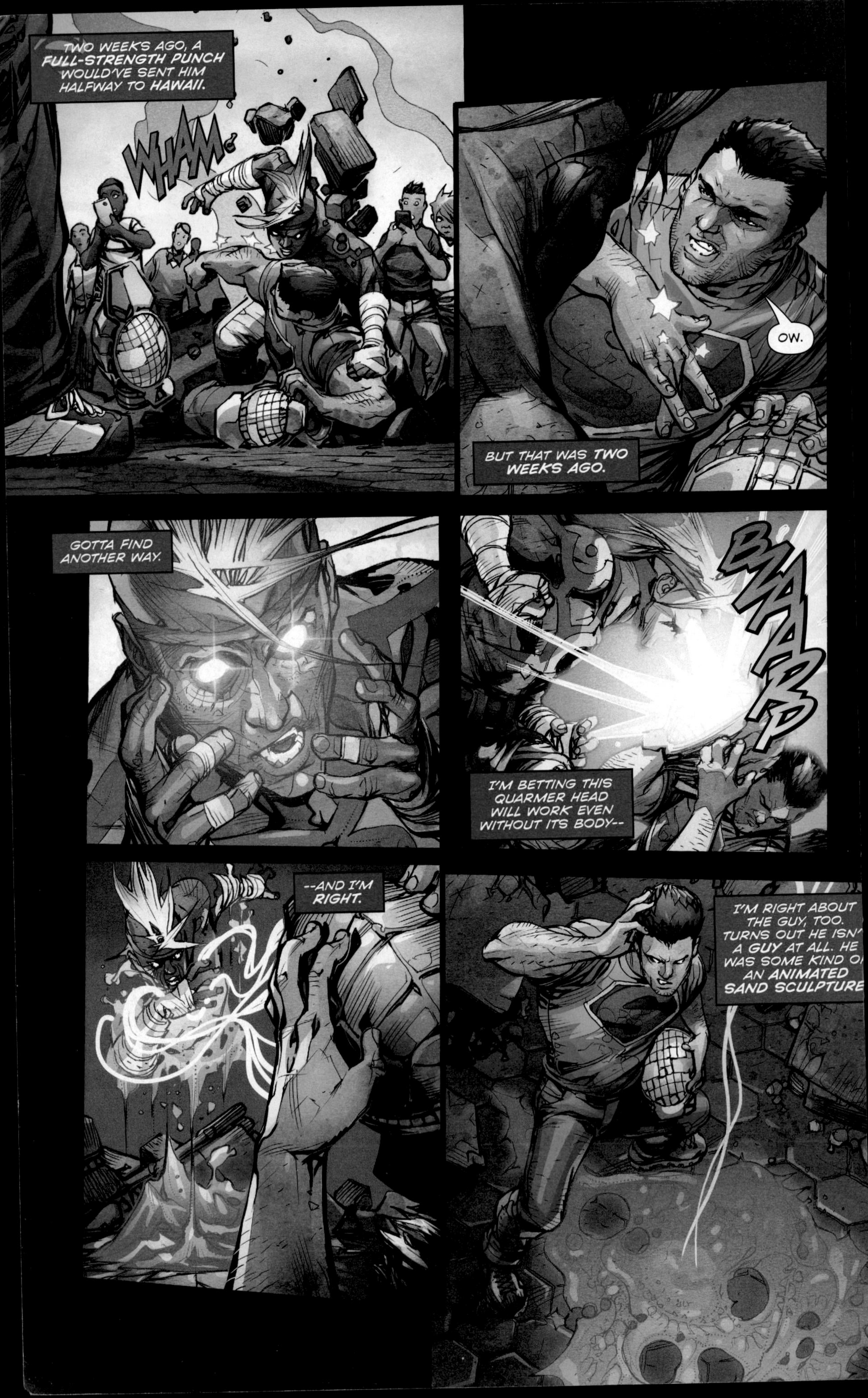
TWO WEEKS AGO, A FULL-STRENGTH PUNCH WOULD'VE SENT HIM HALFWAY TO HAWAII.
WHAM
OW.
BUT THAT WAS TWO WEEKS AGO.
GOTTA FIND ANOTHER WAY.
BRAARRP
I'M BETTING THIS QUARMER HEAD WILL WORK EVEN WITHOUT ITS BODY--
--AND I'M RIGHT.
I'M RIGHT ABOUT THE GUY, TOO. TURNS OUT HE ISN' A GUY AT ALL. HE WAS SOME KIND OF AN ANIMATED SAND SCULPTURE

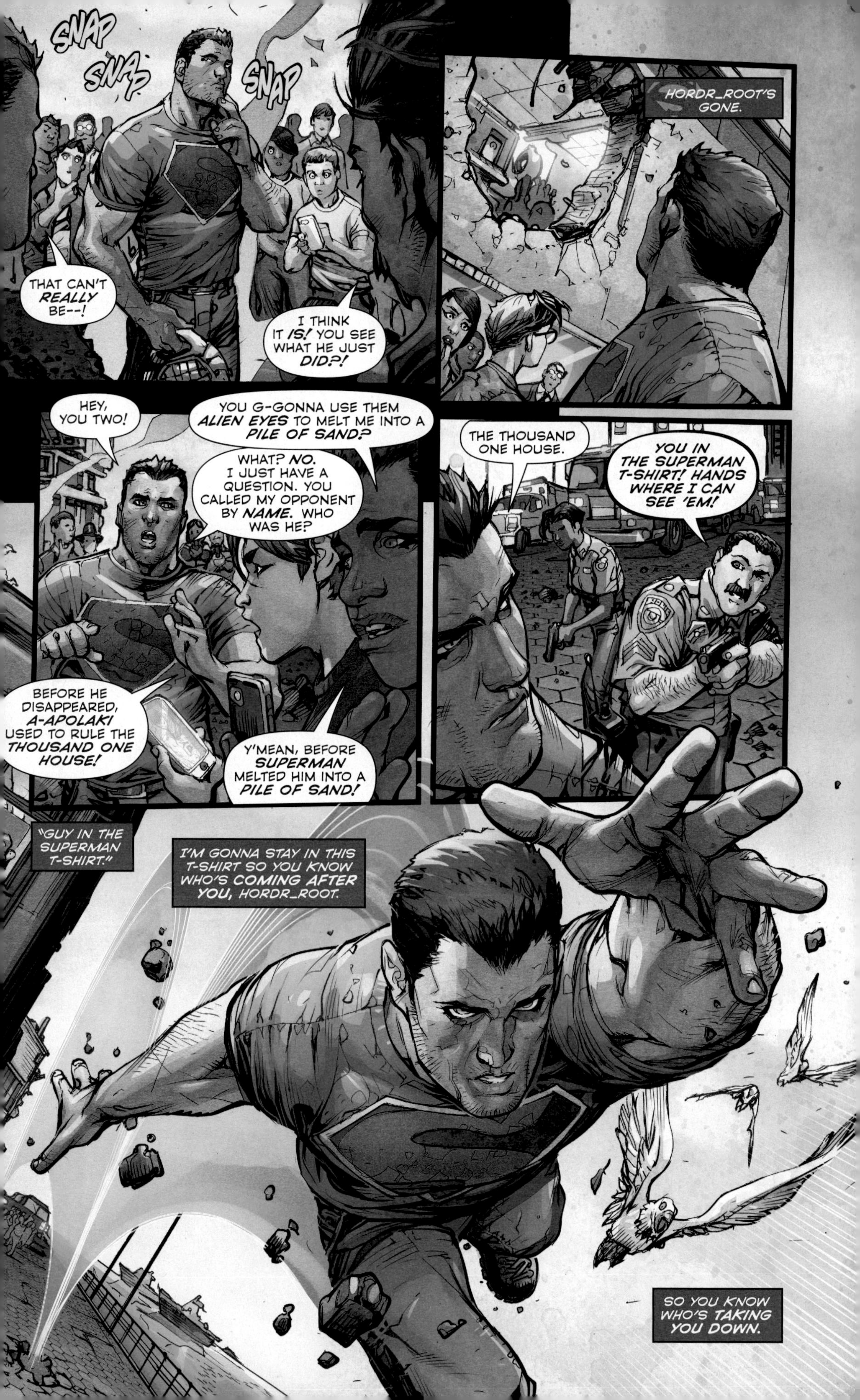
SNAP
SNAP
SNAP
THAT CAN'T REALLY BE--!
I THINK IT IS! YOU SEE WHAT HE JUST DID?!
HORDR_ROOT'S GONE.
HEY, YOU TWO!
YOU G-GONNA USE THEM ALIEN EYES TO MELT ME INTO A PILE OF SAND?
WHAT? NO. I JUST HAVE A QUESTION. YOU CALLED MY OPPONENT BY NAME. WHO WAS HE?
BEFORE HE DISAPPEARED, A-APOLAKI USED TO RULE THE THOUSAND ONE HOUSE!
Y'MEAN, BEFORE SUPERMAN MELTED HIM INTO A PILE OF SAND!
THE THOUSAND ONE HOUSE.
YOU IN THE SUPERMAN T-SHIRT! HANDS WHERE I CAN SEE 'EM!
"GUY IN THE SUPERMAN T-SHIRT."
I'M GONNA STAY IN THIS T-SHIRT SO YOU KNOW WHO'S COMING AFTER YOU, HORDR_ROOT.
SO YOU KNOW WHO'S TAKING YOU DOWN.

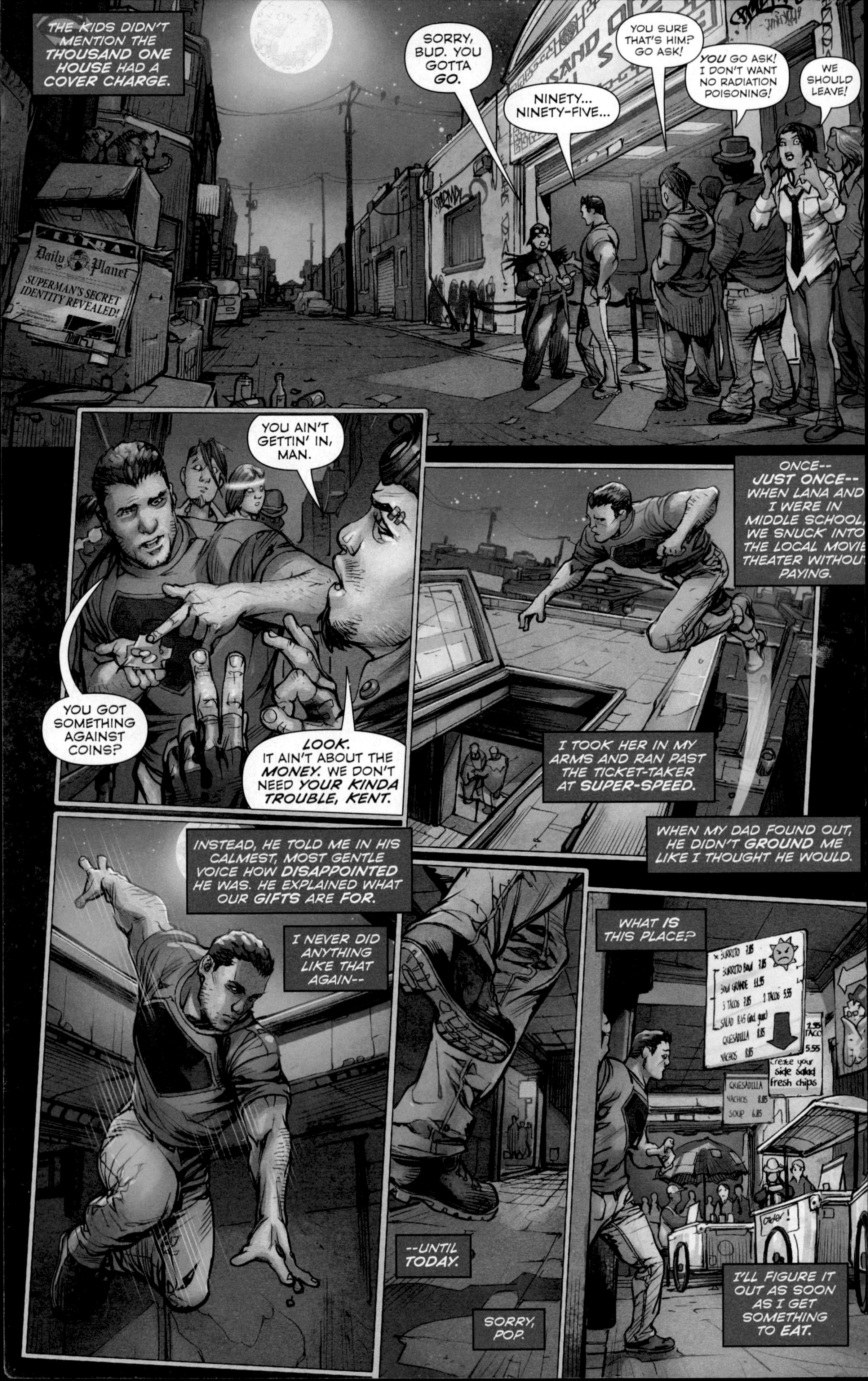
THE KIDS DIDN'T MENTION THE THOUSAND ONE HOUSE HAD A COVER CHARGE.
SORRY, BUD. YOU GOTTA GO.
NINETY... NINETY-FIVE...
YOU SURE THAT'S HIM? GO ASK!
YOU GO ASK! I DON'T WANT NO RADIATION POISONING!
WE SHOULD LEAVE!
EXTRA
Daily Planet
SUPERMAN'S SECRET IDENTITY REVEALED!
YOU AIN'T GETTIN' IN, MAN.
YOU GOT SOMETHING AGAINST COINS?
LOOK. IT AIN'T ABOUT THE MONEY. WE DON'T NEED YOUR KINDA TROUBLE, KENT.
ONCE-- JUST ONCE-- WHEN LANA AND I WERE IN MIDDLE SCHOOL, WE SNUCK INTO THE LOCAL MOVIE THEATER WITHOUT PAYING.
I TOOK HER IN MY ARMS AND RAN PAST THE TICKET-TAKER AT SUPER-SPEED.
WHEN MY DAD FOUND OUT, HE DIDN'T GROUND ME LIKE I THOUGHT HE WOULD.
INSTEAD, HE TOLD ME IN HIS CALMEST, MOST GENTLE VOICE HOW DISAPPOINTED HE WAS. HE EXPLAINED WHAT OUR GIFTS ARE FOR.
I NEVER DID ANYTHING LIKE THAT AGAIN--
--UNTIL TODAY.
SORRY, POP.
WHAT IS THIS PLACE?
I'LL FIGURE IT OUT AS SOON AS I GET SOMETHING TO EAT.

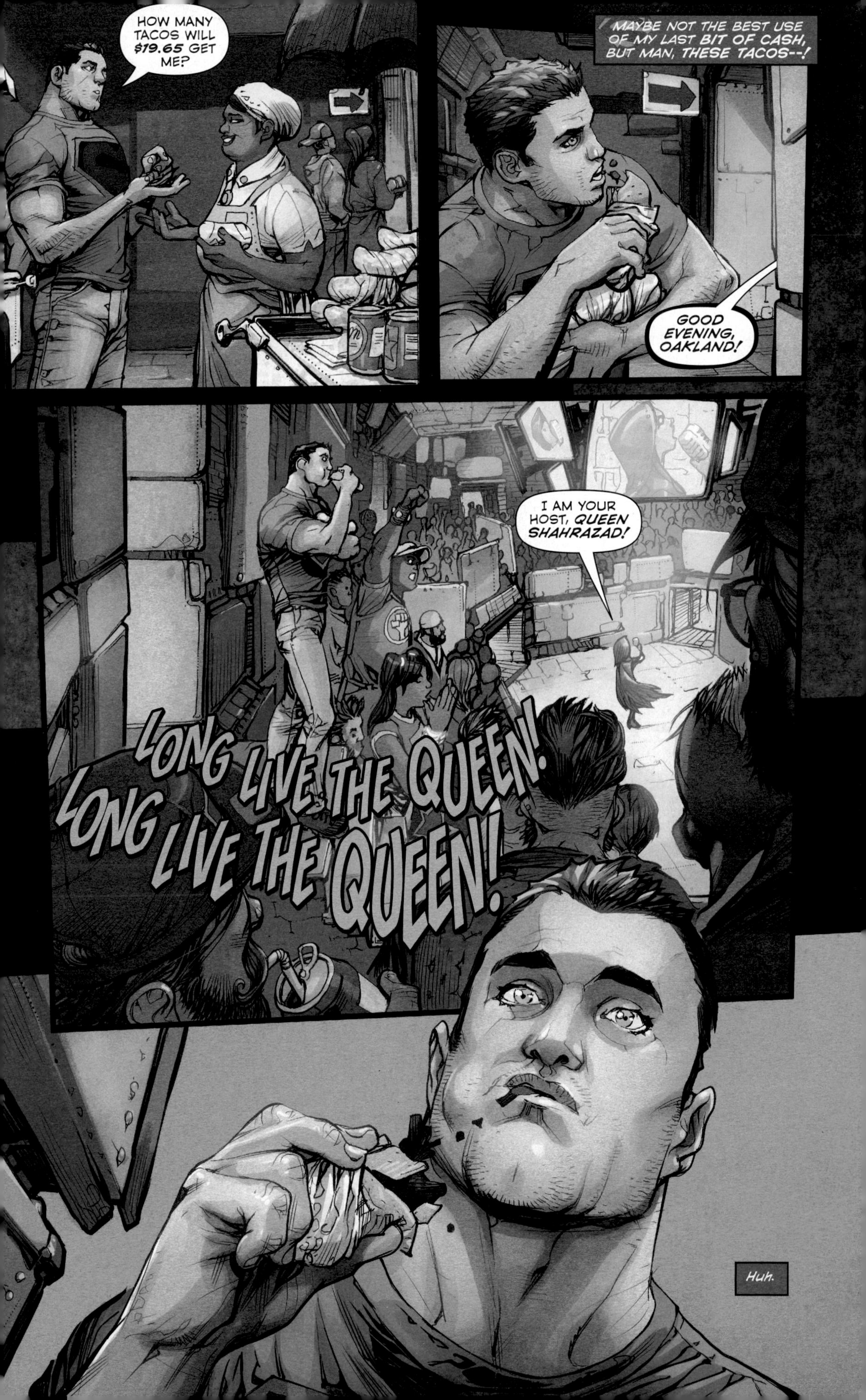
HOW MANY TACOS WILL $19.65 GET ME?
MAYBE NOT THE BEST USE OF MY LAST BIT OF CASH, BUT MAN, THESE TACOS--!
GOOD EVENING, OAKLAND!
I AM YOUR HOST, QUEEN SHAHRAZAD!
LONG LIVE THE QUEEN!
LONG LIVE THE QUEEN!
Huh.

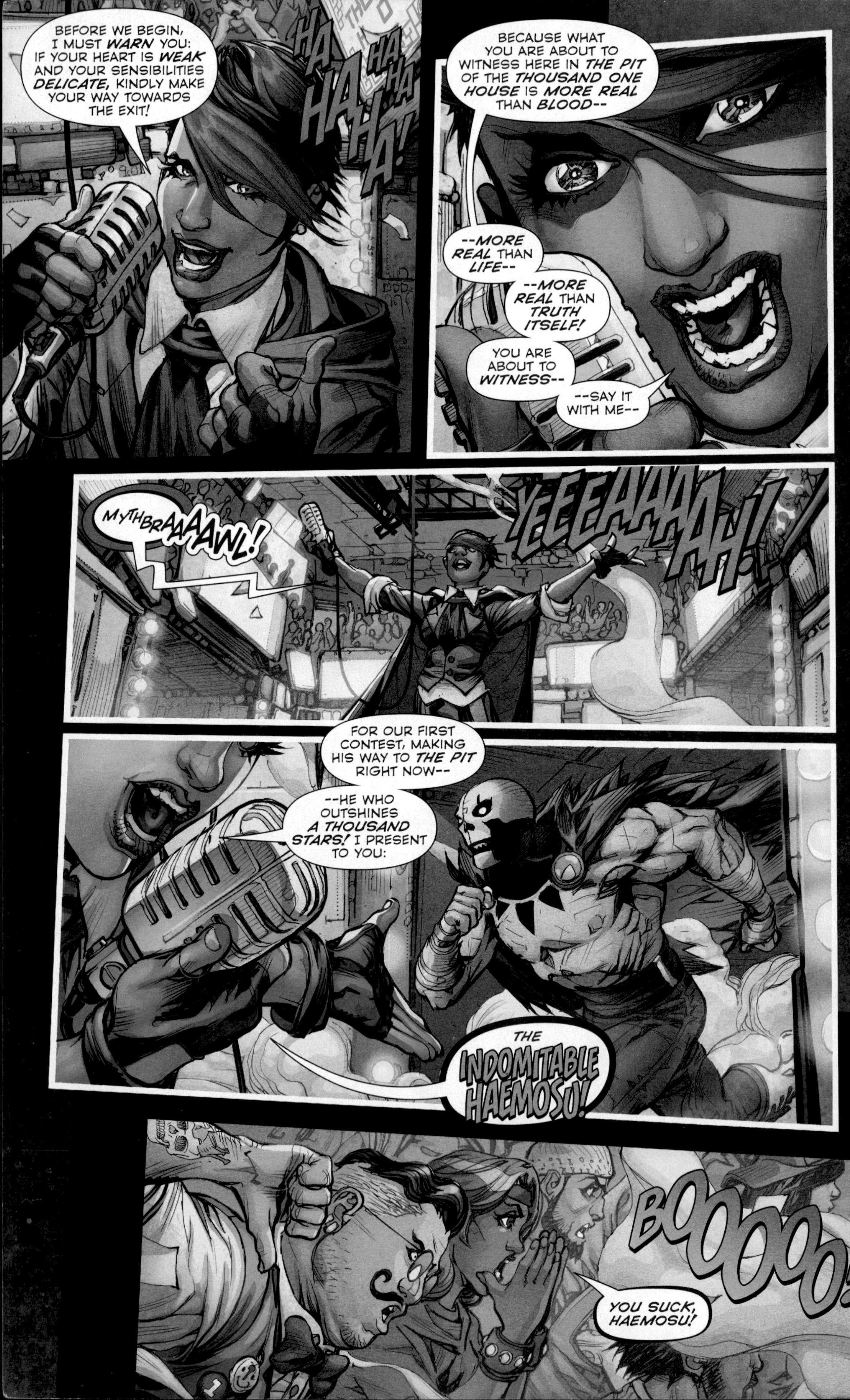
BEFORE WE BEGIN, I MUST *WARN* YOU: IF YOUR HEART IS *WEAK* AND YOUR SENSIBILITIES *DELICATE,* KINDLY MAKE YOUR WAY TOWARDS THE EXIT!
HA HA HA HA HA HA!
BECAUSE WHAT YOU ARE ABOUT TO WITNESS HERE IN *THE PIT* OF THE *THOUSAND ONE HOUSE* IS *MORE REAL* THAN *BLOOD--*
--*MORE REAL* THAN *LIFE--*
--*MORE REAL* THAN *TRUTH ITSELF!*
YOU ARE ABOUT TO *WITNESS--*
--SAY IT WITH ME--
MYTHBRAAAAWL!
YEEEAAAAAH!!
FOR OUR FIRST CONTEST, MAKING HIS WAY TO *THE PIT* RIGHT NOW--
--HE WHO OUTSHINES *A THOUSAND STARS!* I PRESENT TO YOU:
THE INDOMITABLE HAEMOSU!
BOOOOOO!
YOU SUCK, HAEMOSU!

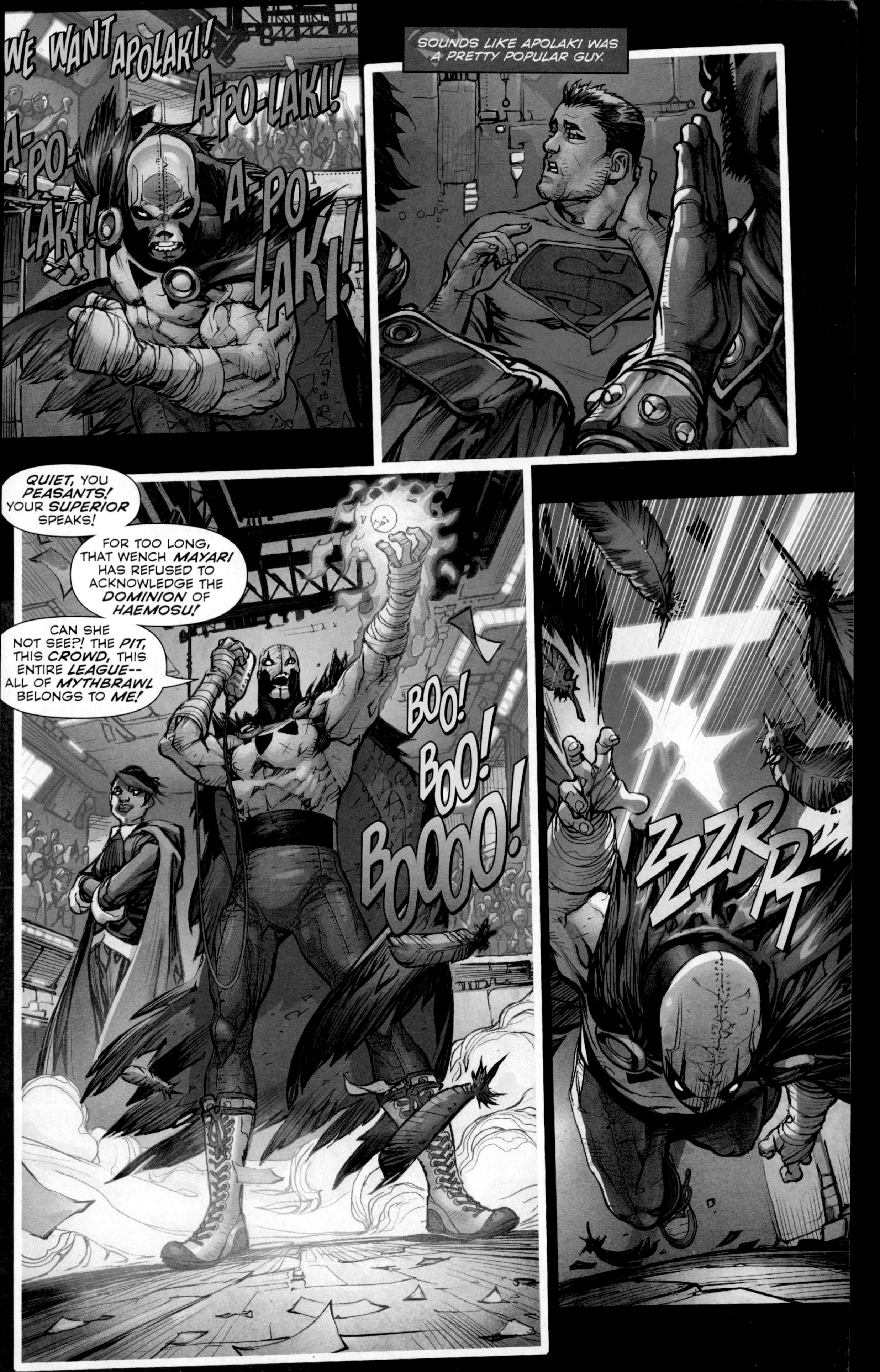
WE WANT APOLAKI!
A-PO-LAKI!
A-PO-LAKI!
A-PO-LAKI!
SOUNDS LIKE APOLAKI WAS A PRETTY POPULAR GUY.
QUIET, YOU PEASANTS! YOUR SUPERIOR SPEAKS!
FOR TOO LONG, THAT WENCH MAYARI HAS REFUSED TO ACKNOWLEDGE THE DOMINION OF HAEMOSU!
CAN SHE NOT SEE?! THE PIT, THIS CROWD, THIS ENTIRE LEAGUE-- ALL OF MYTHBRAWL BELONGS TO ME!
BOO! BOO! BOOOO!
ZZZRRT

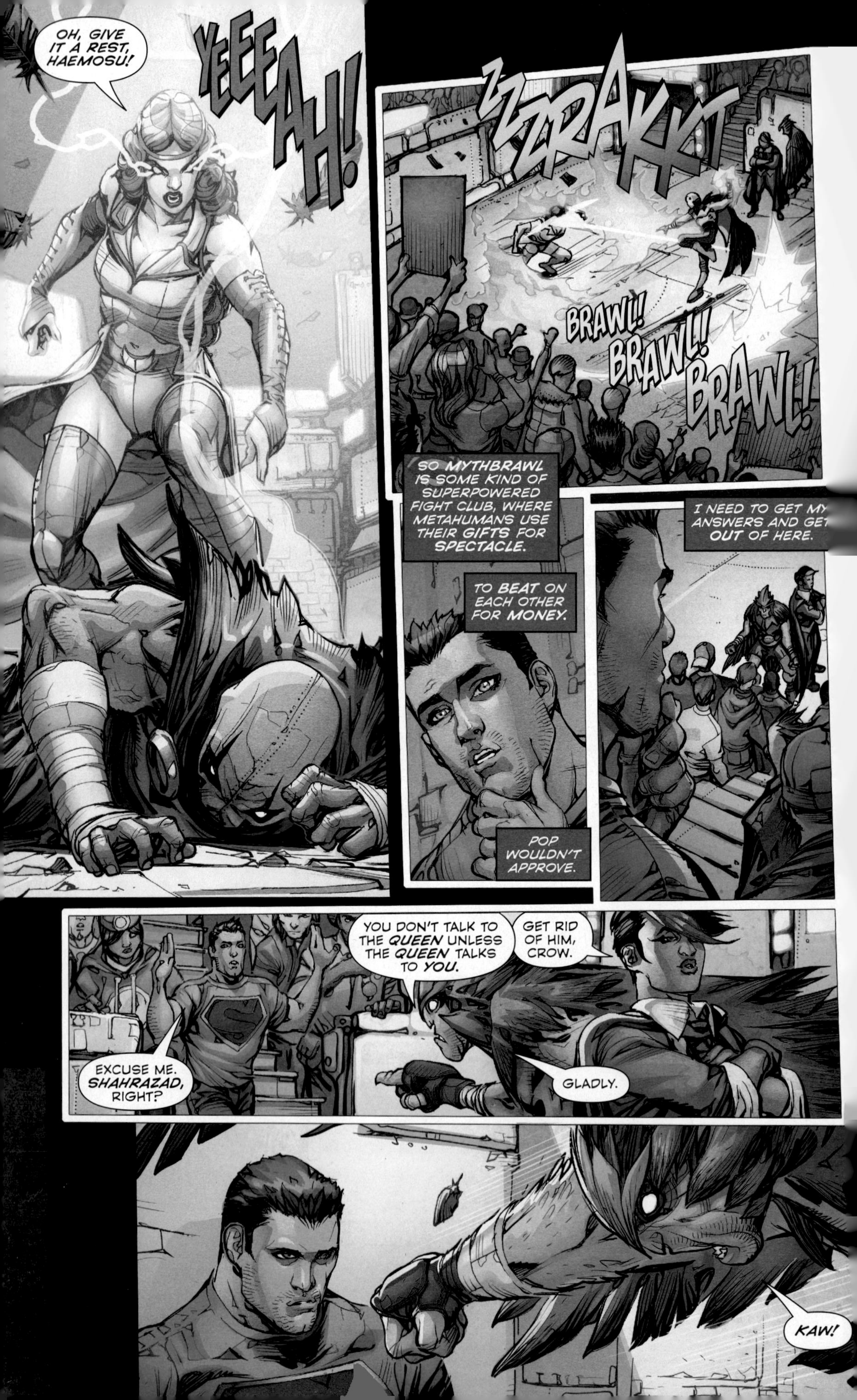
OH, GIVE IT A REST, HAEMOSU!
YEEEAH!
ZZZRAKKT
BRAWL! BRAWL! BRAWL!
SO MYTHBRAWL IS SOME KIND OF SUPERPOWERED FIGHT CLUB, WHERE METAHUMANS USE THEIR GIFTS FOR SPECTACLE.
TO BEAT ON EACH OTHER FOR MONEY.
POP WOULDN'T APPROVE.
I NEED TO GET MY ANSWERS AND GET OUT OF HERE.
EXCUSE ME. SHAHRAZAD, RIGHT?
YOU DON'T TALK TO THE QUEEN UNLESS THE QUEEN TALKS TO YOU.
GET RID OF HIM, CROW.
GLADLY.
KAW!

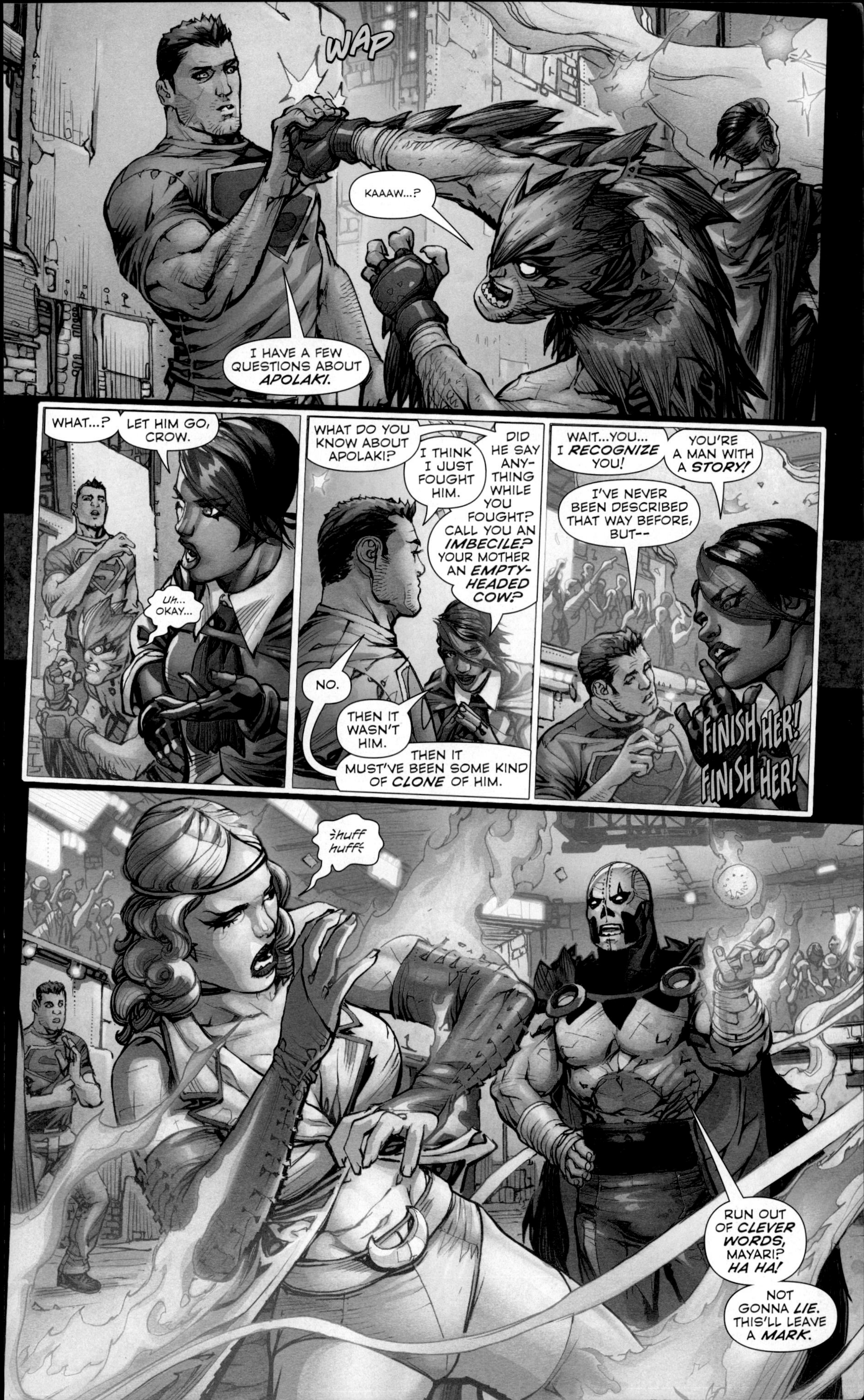
WAP
KAAAW...?
I HAVE A FEW QUESTIONS ABOUT APOLAKI.
WHAT...?
LET HIM GO, CROW.
Uh... OKAY...
WHAT DO YOU KNOW ABOUT APOLAKI?
I THINK I JUST FOUGHT HIM.
DID HE SAY ANYTHING WHILE YOU FOUGHT? CALL YOU AN IMBECILE? YOUR MOTHER AN EMPTY-HEADED COW?
NO.
THEN IT WASN'T HIM.
THEN IT MUST'VE BEEN SOME KIND OF CLONE OF HIM.
WAIT...YOU... I RECOGNIZE YOU!
YOU'RE A MAN WITH A STORY!
I'VE NEVER BEEN DESCRIBED THAT WAY BEFORE, BUT--
FINISH HER! FINISH HER!
huff huff
RUN OUT OF CLEVER WORDS, MAYARI? HA HA!
NOT GONNA LIE. THIS'LL LEAVE A MARK.

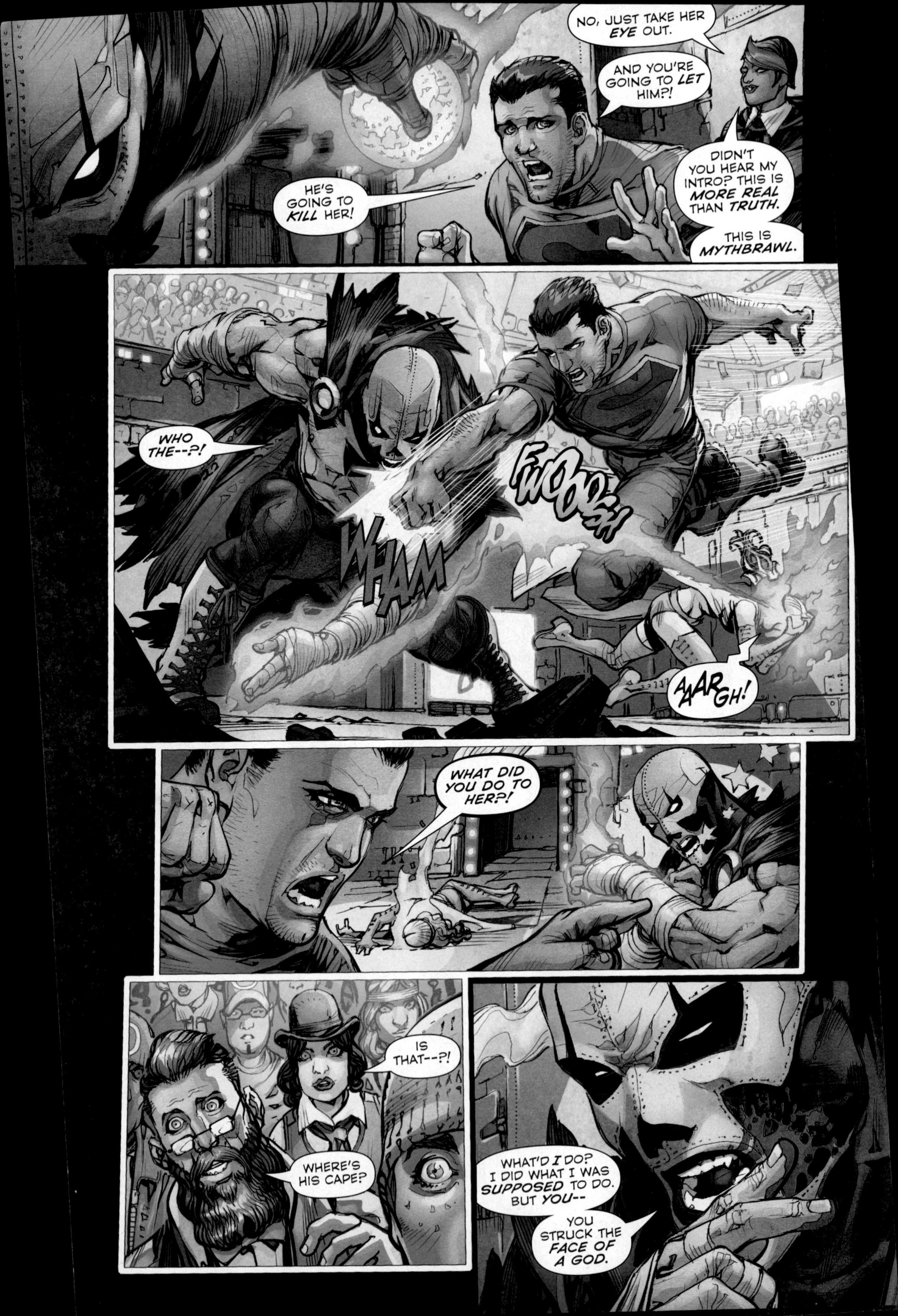

NO, JUST TAKE HER *EYE* OUT.
AND YOU'RE GOING TO *LET* HIM?!
HE'S GOING TO *KILL* HER!
DIDN'T YOU HEAR MY INTRO? THIS IS *MORE REAL* THAN *TRUTH*.
THIS IS *MYTHBRAWL*.
WHO THE--?!
FWOOOSH
WHAM
AAARGH!
WHAT DID YOU DO TO HER?!
IS THAT--?!
WHERE'S HIS CAPE?
WHAT'D *I* DO? I DID WHAT I WAS *SUPPOSED* TO DO. BUT *YOU*--
YOU STRUCK THE *FACE OF A GOD*.

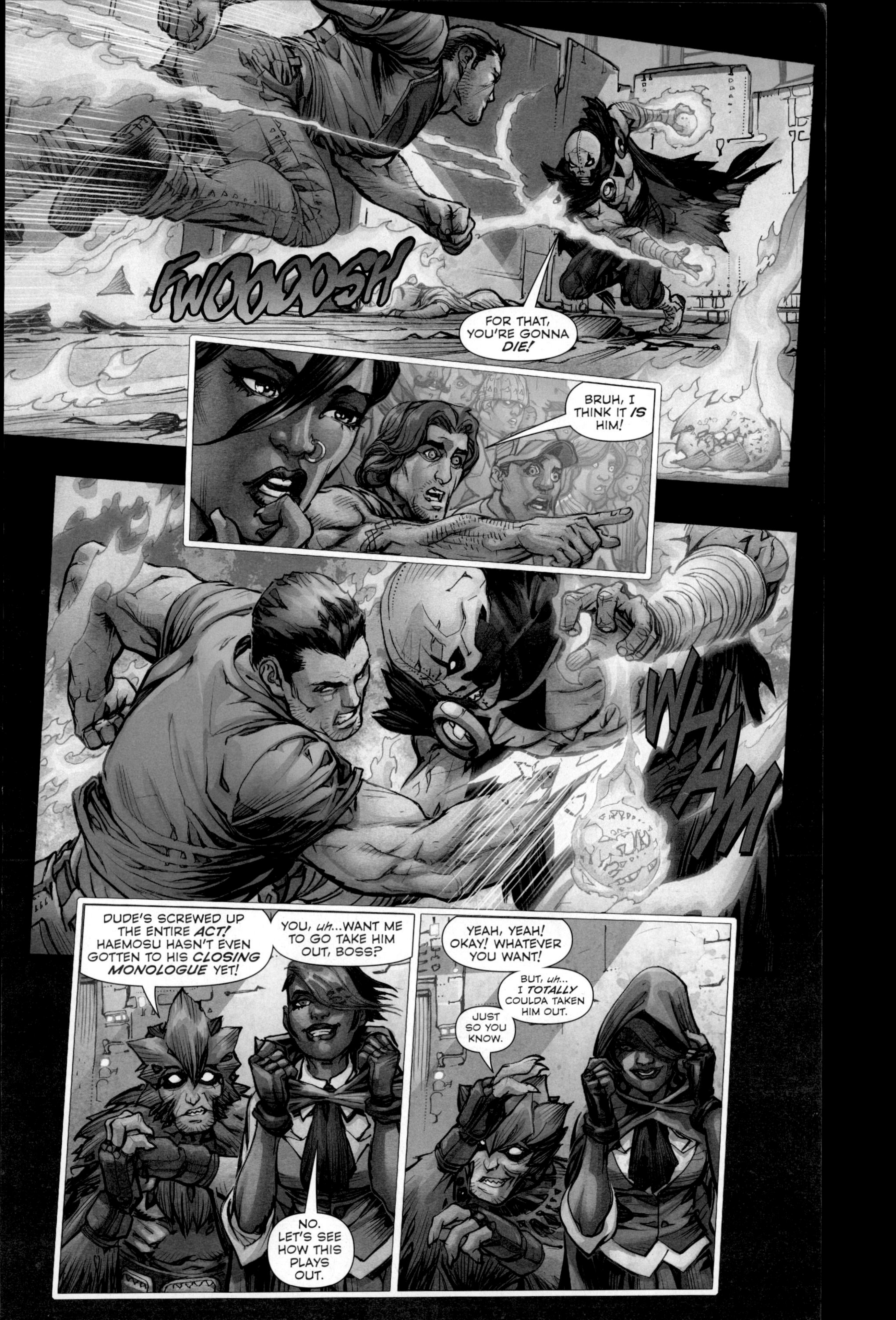
FWOOOOSH
FOR THAT, YOU'RE GONNA *DIE!*
BRUH, I THINK IT *IS* HIM!
WHAM
DUDE'S SCREWED UP THE ENTIRE *ACT!* HAEMOSU HASN'T EVEN GOTTEN TO HIS *CLOSING MONOLOGUE* YET!
YOU, *uh*...WANT ME TO GO TAKE HIM OUT, BOSS?
NO. LET'S SEE HOW THIS PLAYS OUT.
YEAH, YEAH! OKAY! WHATEVER YOU WANT!
BUT, *uh*... I *TOTALLY* COULDA TAKEN HIM OUT.
JUST SO YOU KNOW.

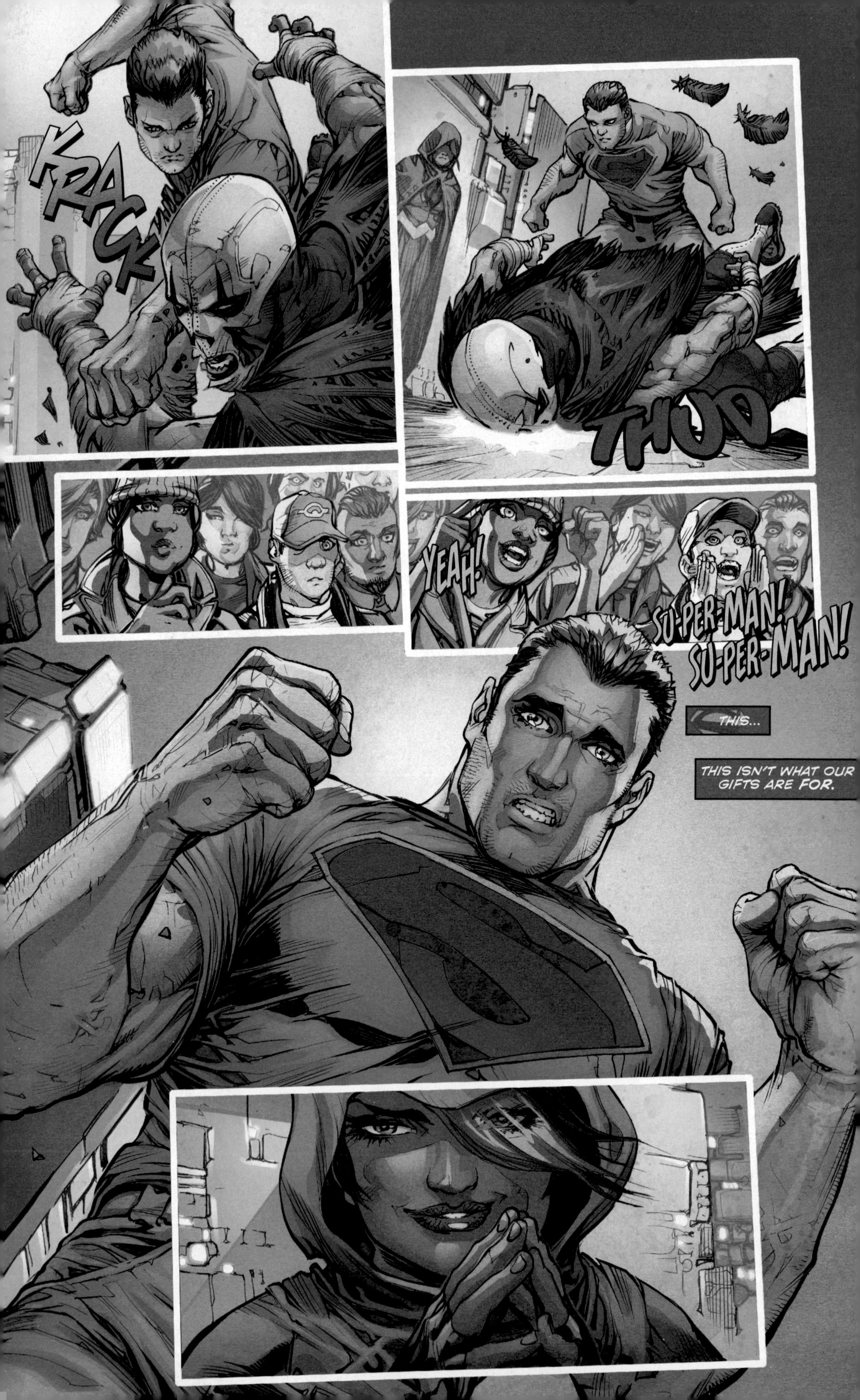
KRACK
THUD
YEAH!
SU-PER-MAN! SU-PER-MAN!
THIS...
THIS ISN'T WHAT OUR GIFTS ARE FOR.

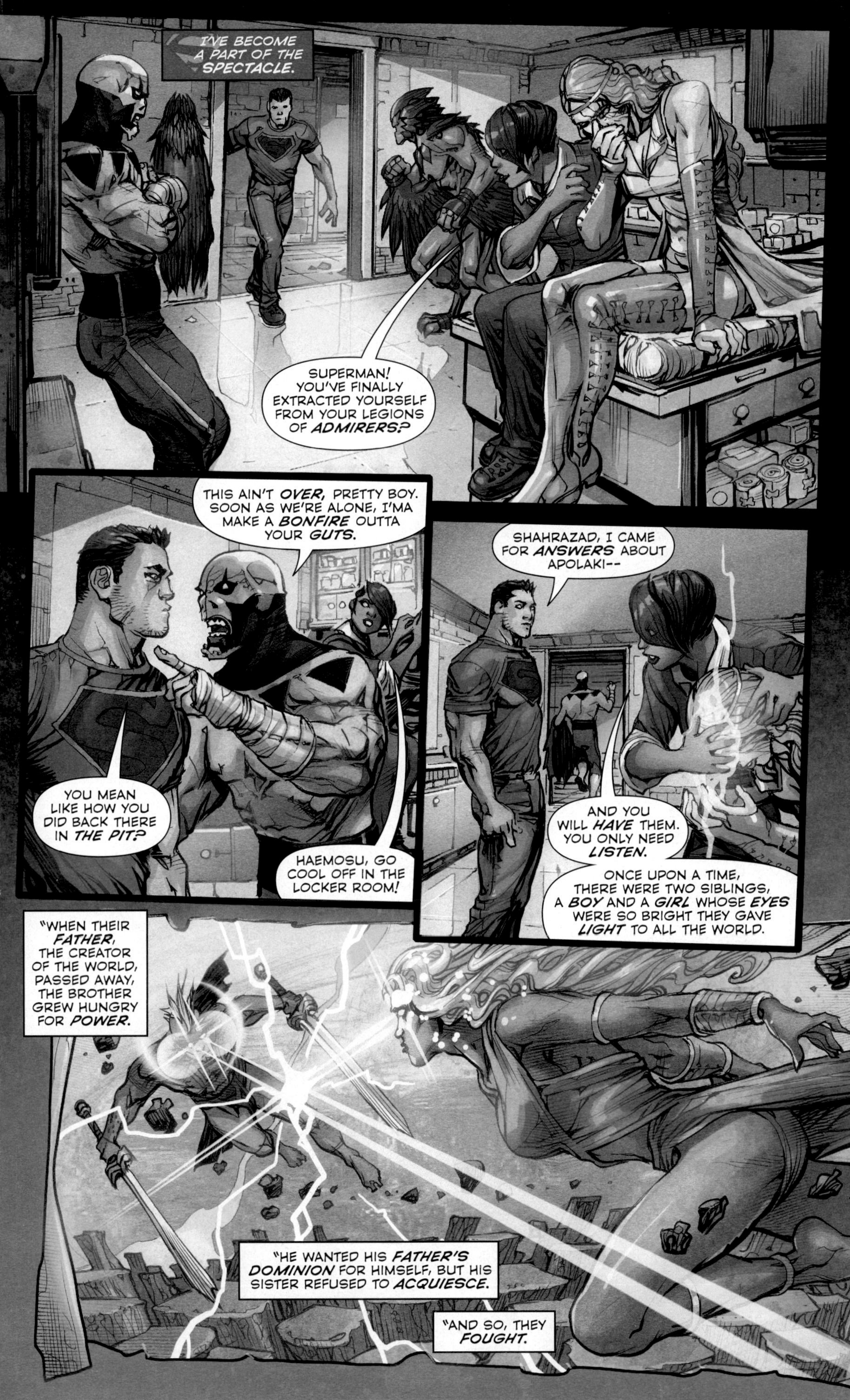
I'VE BECOME A PART OF THE SPECTACLE.
SUPERMAN! YOU'VE FINALLY EXTRACTED YOURSELF FROM YOUR LEGIONS OF ADMIRERS?
THIS AIN'T OVER, PRETTY BOY. SOON AS WE'RE ALONE, I'MA MAKE A BONFIRE OUTTA YOUR GUTS.
YOU MEAN LIKE HOW YOU DID BACK THERE IN THE PIT?
HAEMOSU, GO COOL OFF IN THE LOCKER ROOM!
SHAHRAZAD, I CAME FOR ANSWERS ABOUT APOLAKI--
AND YOU WILL HAVE THEM. YOU ONLY NEED LISTEN.
ONCE UPON A TIME, THERE WERE TWO SIBLINGS, A BOY AND A GIRL WHOSE EYES WERE SO BRIGHT THEY GAVE LIGHT TO ALL THE WORLD.
"WHEN THEIR FATHER, THE CREATOR OF THE WORLD, PASSED AWAY, THE BROTHER GREW HUNGRY FOR POWER.
"HE WANTED HIS FATHER'S DOMINION FOR HIMSELF, BUT HIS SISTER REFUSED TO ACQUIESCE.
"AND SO, THEY FOUGHT.

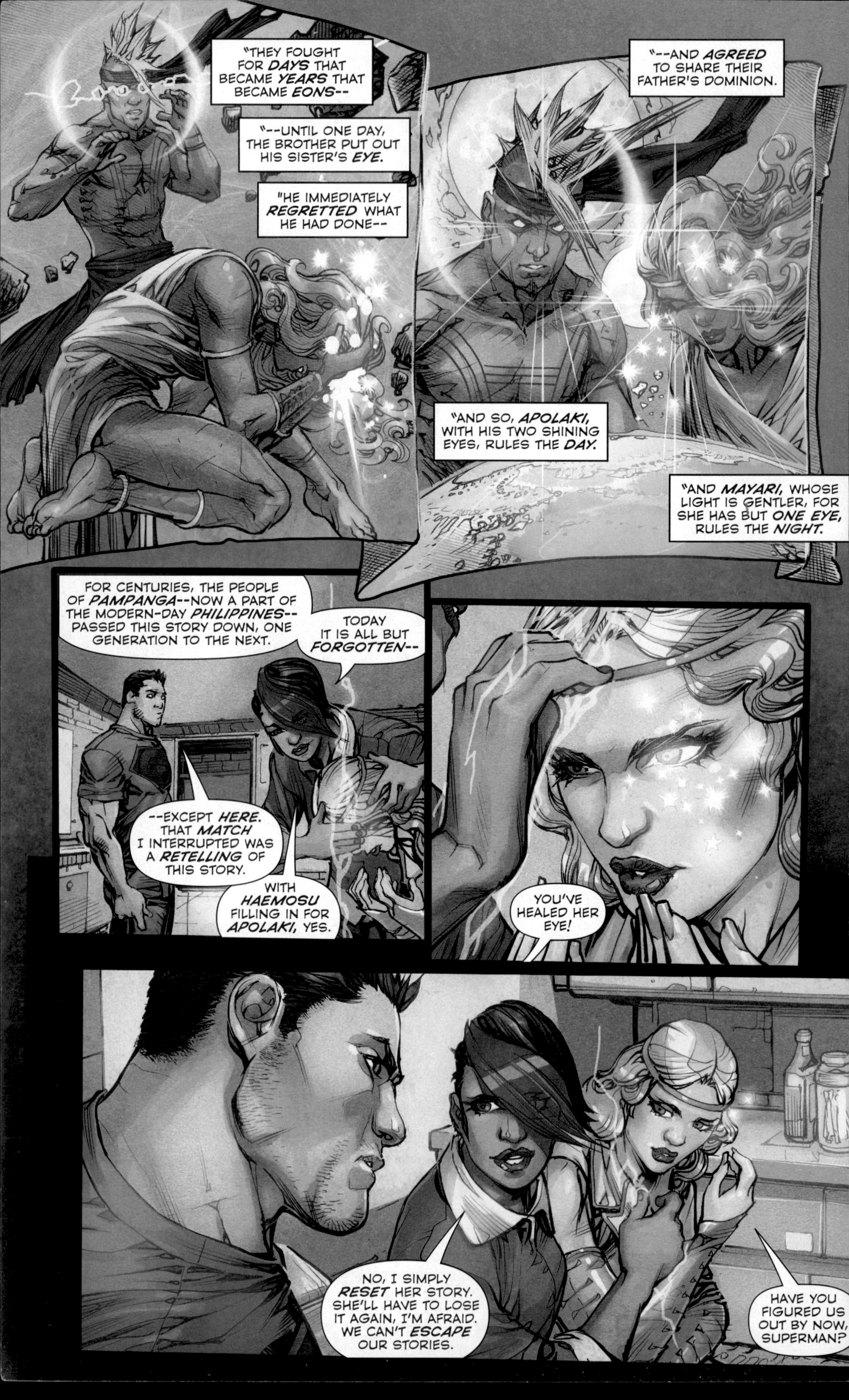
"THEY FOUGHT FOR DAYS THAT BECAME YEARS THAT BECAME EONS--
"--UNTIL ONE DAY, THE BROTHER PUT OUT HIS SISTER'S EYE.
"HE IMMEDIATELY REGRETTED WHAT HE HAD DONE--
"--AND AGREED TO SHARE THEIR FATHER'S DOMINION.
"AND SO, APOLAKI, WITH HIS TWO SHINING EYES, RULES THE DAY.
"AND MAYARI, WHOSE LIGHT IS GENTLER, FOR SHE HAS BUT ONE EYE, RULES THE NIGHT.
FOR CENTURIES, THE PEOPLE OF PAMPANGA--NOW A PART OF THE MODERN-DAY PHILIPPINES--PASSED THIS STORY DOWN, ONE GENERATION TO THE NEXT.
TODAY IT IS ALL BUT FORGOTTEN--
--EXCEPT HERE. THAT MATCH I INTERRUPTED WAS A RETELLING OF THIS STORY.
WITH HAEMOSU FILLING IN FOR APOLAKI, YES.
YOU'VE HEALED HER EYE!
NO, I SIMPLY RESET HER STORY. SHE'LL HAVE TO LOSE IT AGAIN, I'M AFRAID. WE CAN'T ESCAPE OUR STORIES.
HAVE YOU FIGURED US OUT BY NOW, SUPERMAN?

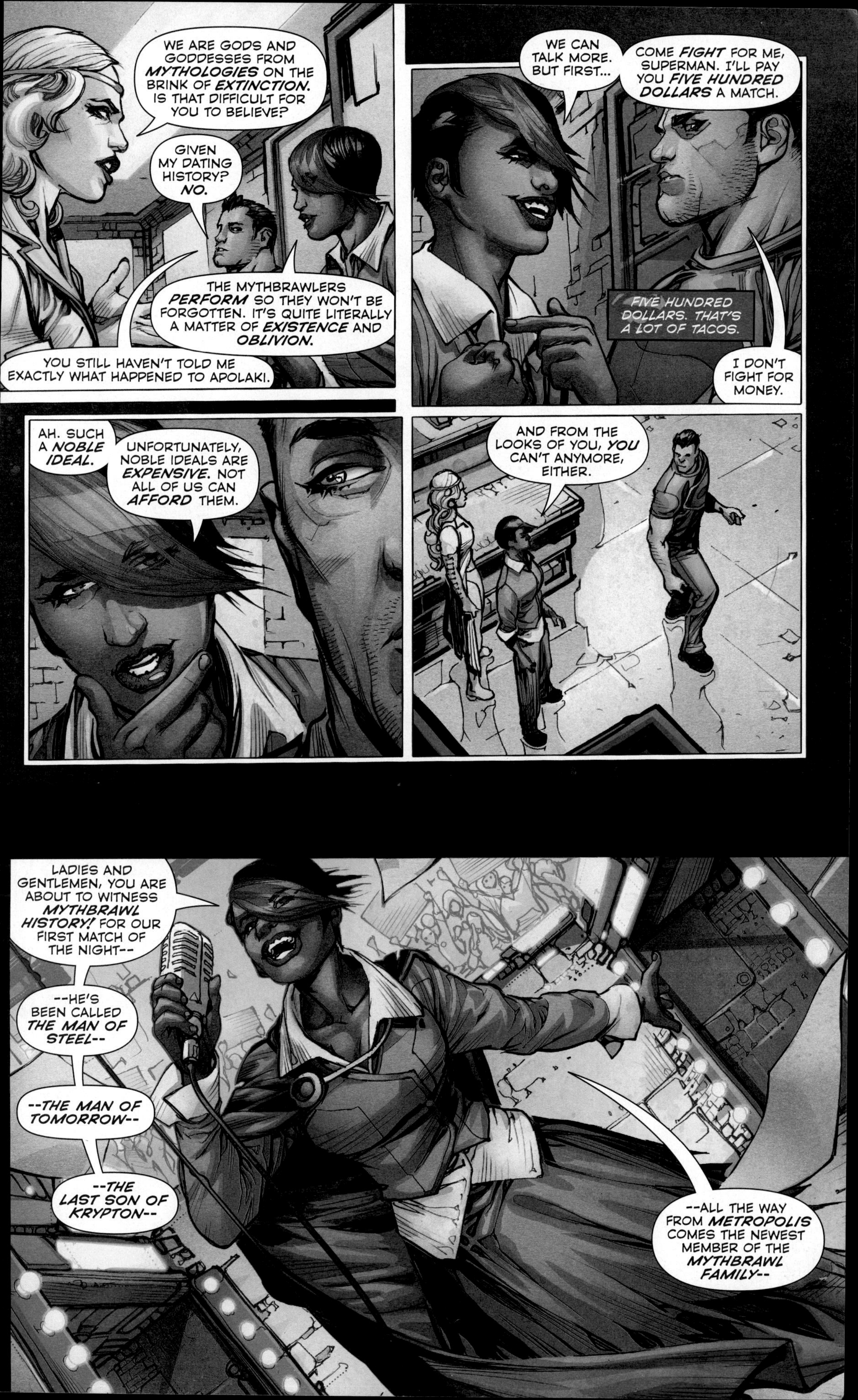
WE ARE GODS AND GODDESSES FROM MYTHOLOGIES ON THE BRINK OF EXTINCTION. IS THAT DIFFICULT FOR YOU TO BELIEVE?
GIVEN MY DATING HISTORY? NO.
THE MYTHBRAWLERS PERFORM SO THEY WON'T BE FORGOTTEN. IT'S QUITE LITERALLY A MATTER OF EXISTENCE AND OBLIVION.
YOU STILL HAVEN'T TOLD ME EXACTLY WHAT HAPPENED TO APOLAKI.
WE CAN TALK MORE. BUT FIRST...
COME FIGHT FOR ME, SUPERMAN. I'LL PAY YOU FIVE HUNDRED DOLLARS A MATCH.
FIVE HUNDRED DOLLARS. THAT'S A LOT OF TACOS.
I DON'T FIGHT FOR MONEY.
AH. SUCH A NOBLE IDEAL.
UNFORTUNATELY, NOBLE IDEALS ARE EXPENSIVE. NOT ALL OF US CAN AFFORD THEM.
AND FROM THE LOOKS OF YOU, YOU CAN'T ANYMORE, EITHER.
LADIES AND GENTLEMEN, YOU ARE ABOUT TO WITNESS MYTHBRAWL HISTORY! FOR OUR FIRST MATCH OF THE NIGHT--
--HE'S BEEN CALLED THE MAN OF STEEL--
--THE MAN OF TOMORROW--
--THE LAST SON OF KRYPTON--
--ALL THE WAY FROM METROPOLIS COMES THE NEWEST MEMBER OF THE MYTHBRAWL FAMILY--

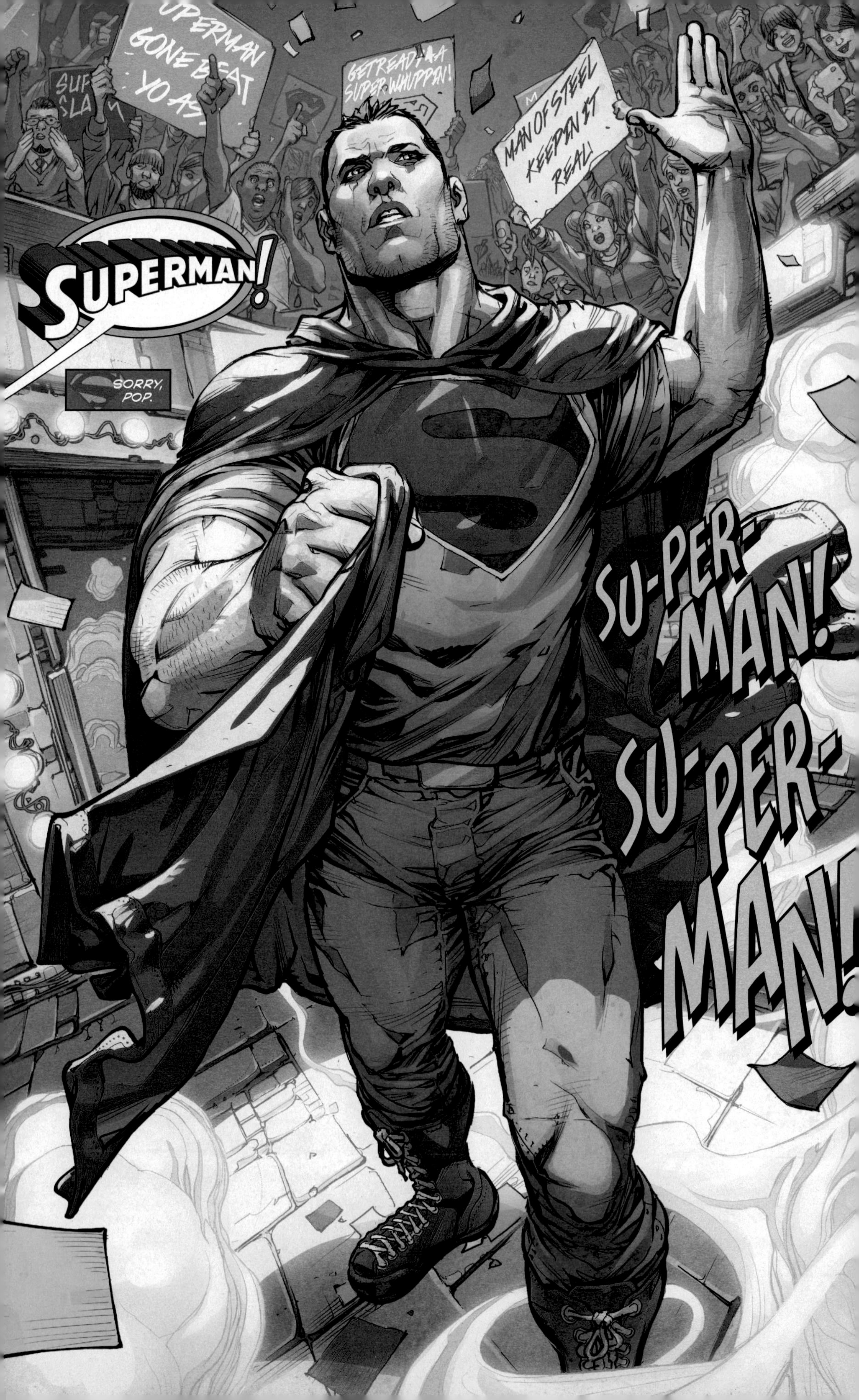

MAN OF STEEL KEEPIN' IT REAL
SUPERMAN!
SORRY, POP.
SU-PER-MAN! SU-PER-MAN!

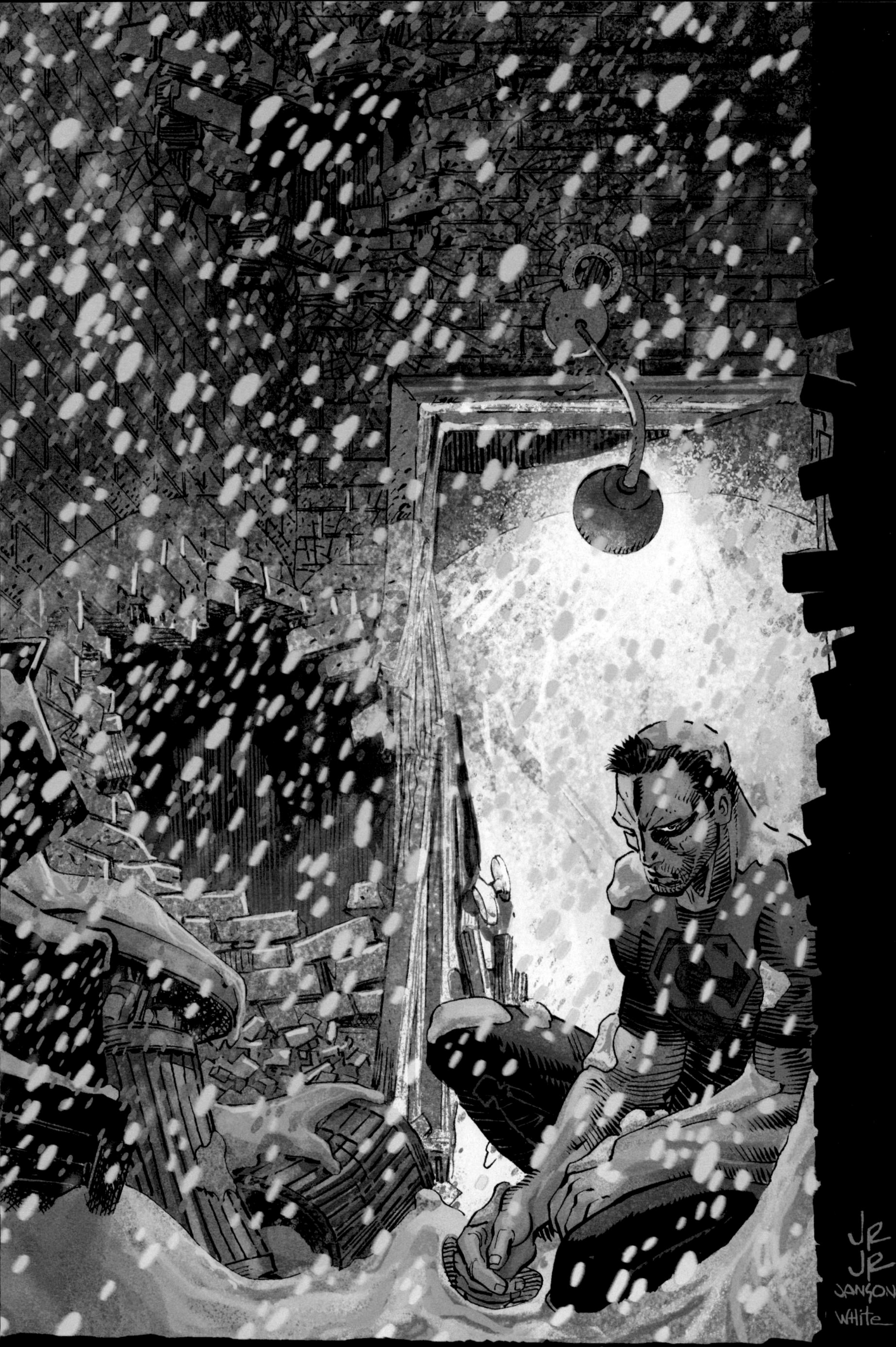
JR JR
JANSON
WHITE

KNOCKED OUT!

GENE LUEN YANG writer HOWARD PORTER artist HI-FI colorist ROB LEIGH letterer JOHN ROMITA JR., KLAUS JANSON, DEAN WHITE cover

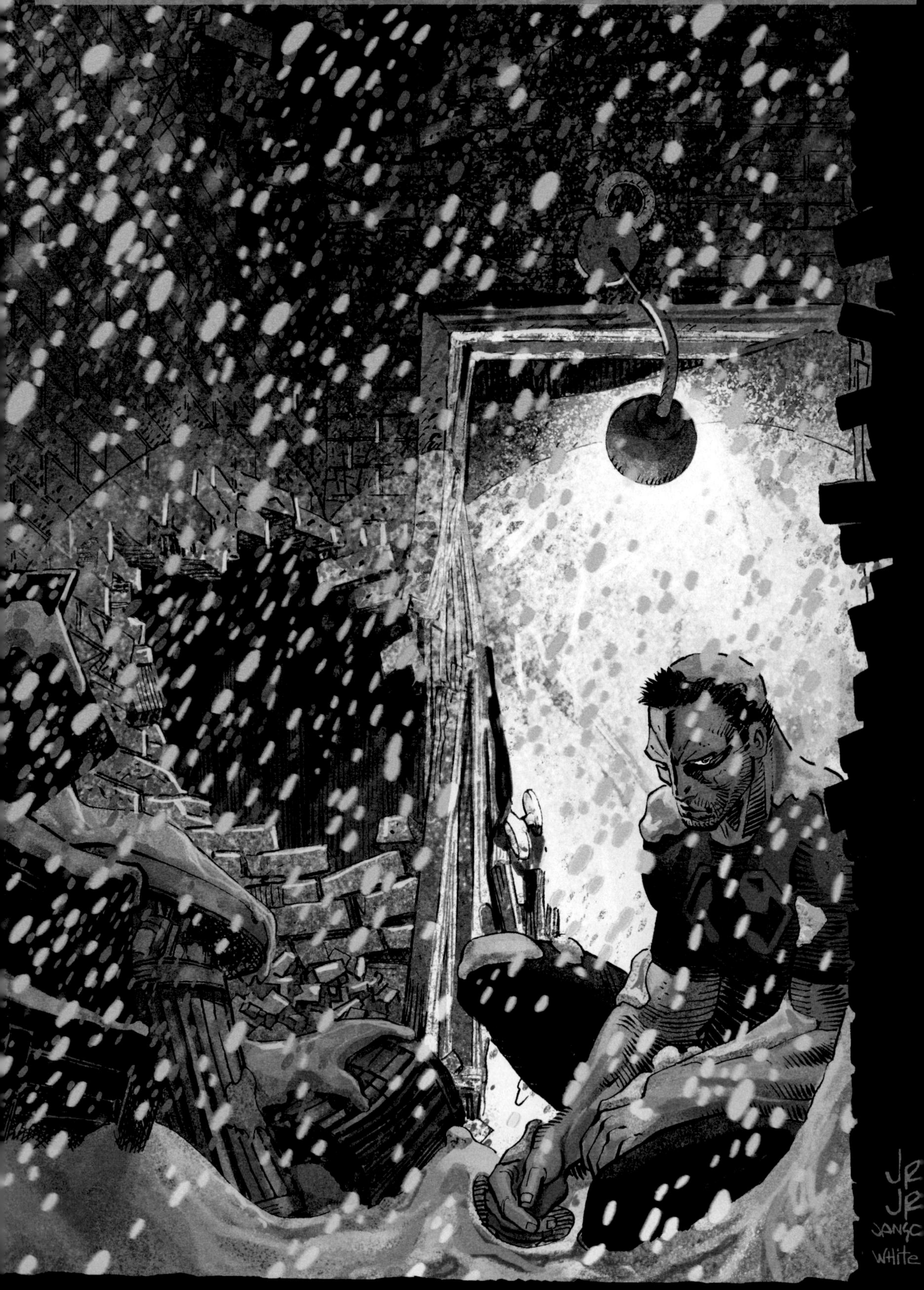

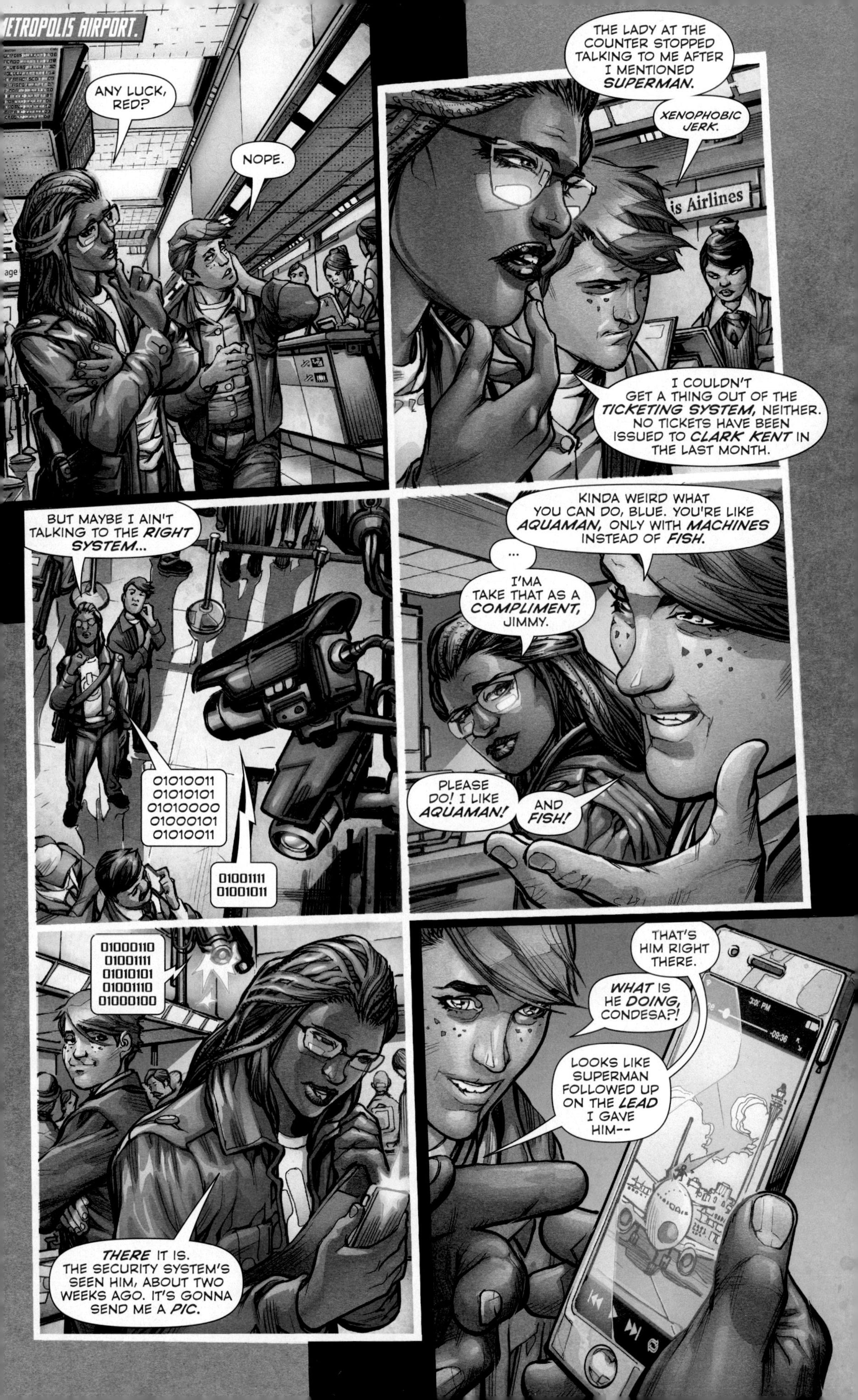
ETROPOLIS AIRPORT.
ANY LUCK, RED?
NOPE.
THE LADY AT THE COUNTER STOPPED TALKING TO ME AFTER I MENTIONED SUPERMAN.
XENOPHOBIC JERK.
is Airlines
I COULDN'T GET A THING OUT OF THE TICKETING SYSTEM, NEITHER. NO TICKETS HAVE BEEN ISSUED TO CLARK KENT IN THE LAST MONTH.
BUT MAYBE I AIN'T TALKING TO THE RIGHT SYSTEM...
01010011 01010101 01010000 01000101 01010011
01001111 01001011
KINDA WEIRD WHAT YOU CAN DO, BLUE. YOU'RE LIKE AQUAMAN, ONLY WITH MACHINES INSTEAD OF FISH.
...
I'MA TAKE THAT AS A COMPLIMENT, JIMMY.
PLEASE DO! I LIKE AQUAMAN!
AND FISH!
01000110 01001111 01010101 01001110 01000100
THERE IT IS. THE SECURITY SYSTEM'S SEEN HIM, ABOUT TWO WEEKS AGO. IT'S GONNA SEND ME A PIC.
THAT'S HIM RIGHT THERE.
WHAT IS HE DOING, CONDESA?!
LOOKS LIKE SUPERMAN FOLLOWED UP ON THE LEAD I GAVE HIM--

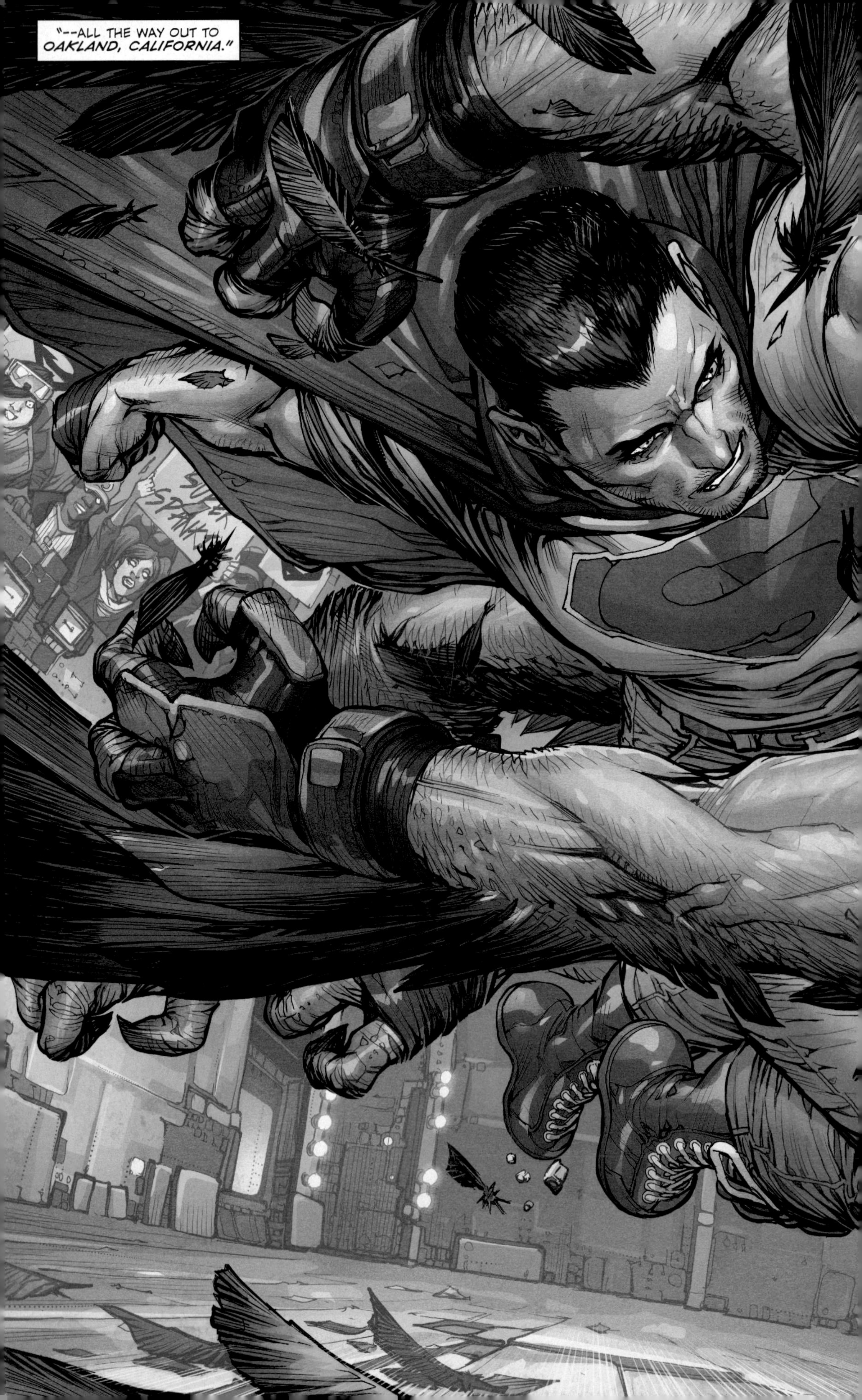
"--ALL THE WAY OUT TO OAKLAND, CALIFORNIA."

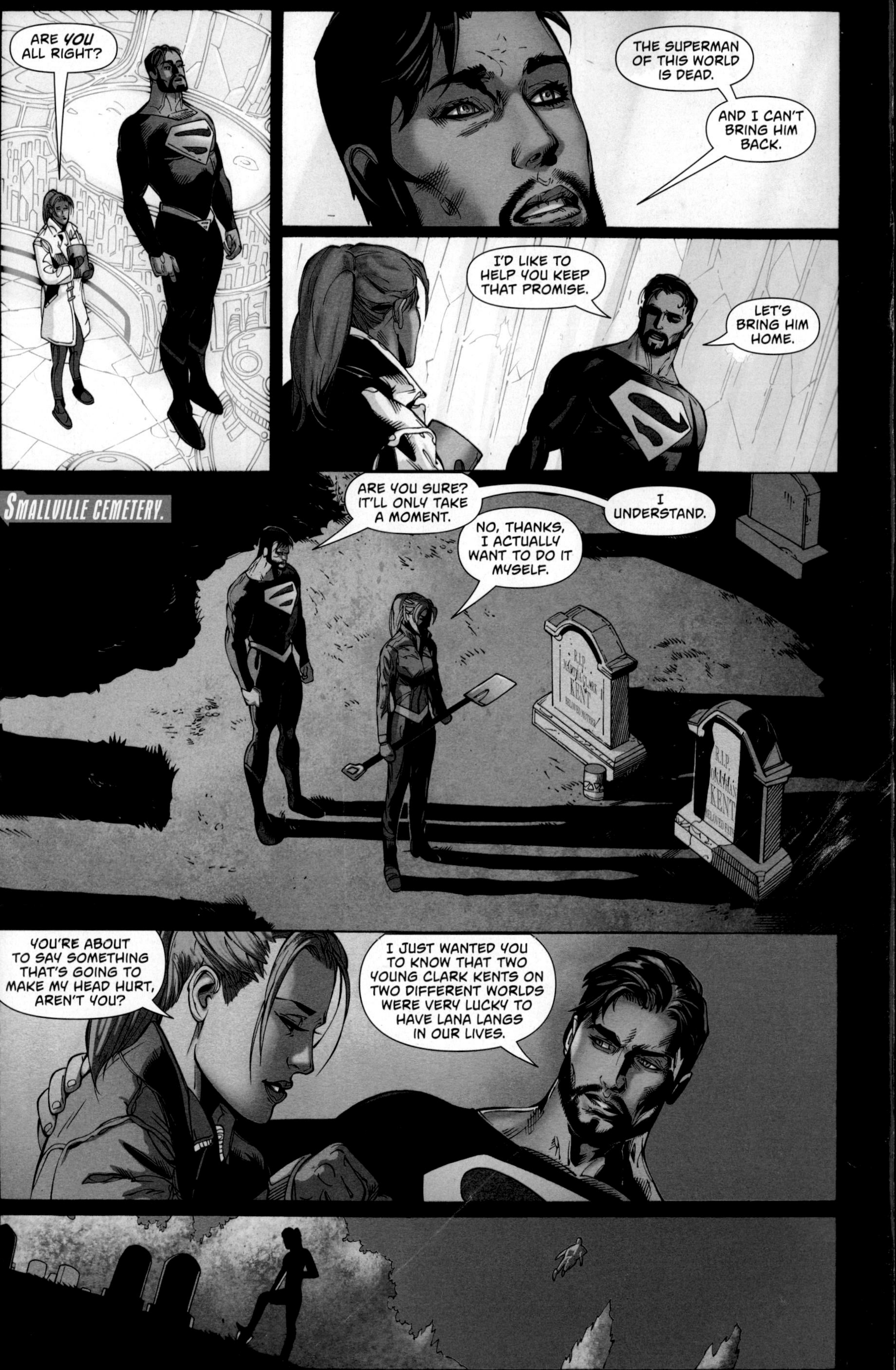
ARE YOU ALL RIGHT?
THE SUPERMAN OF THIS WORLD IS DEAD.
AND I CAN'T BRING HIM BACK.
I'D LIKE TO HELP YOU KEEP THAT PROMISE.
LET'S BRING HIM HOME.
SMALLVILLE CEMETERY.
ARE YOU SURE? IT'LL ONLY TAKE A MOMENT.
NO, THANKS, I ACTUALLY WANT TO DO IT MYSELF.
I UNDERSTAND.
R.I.P.
KENT
BELOVED MOTHER
R.I.P.
KENT
YOU'RE ABOUT TO SAY SOMETHING THAT'S GOING TO MAKE MY HEAD HURT, AREN'T YOU?
I JUST WANTED YOU TO KNOW THAT TWO YOUNG CLARK KENTS ON TWO DIFFERENT WORLDS WERE VERY LUCKY TO HAVE LANA LANGS IN OUR LIVES.

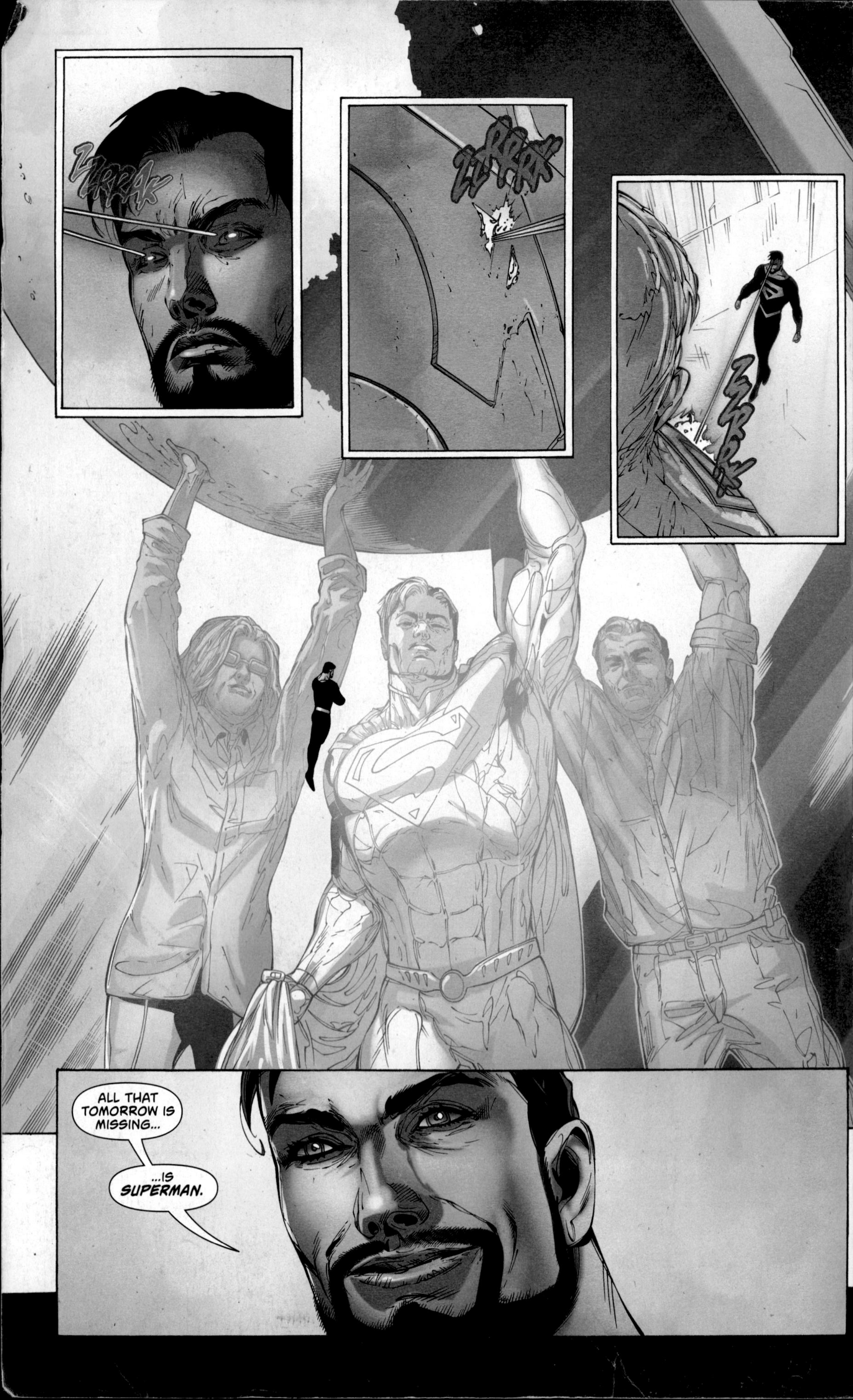
ALL THAT TOMORROW IS MISSING...
...IS SUPERMAN.

START AT THE BEGINNING!

SUPERMAN: ACTION COMICS VOLUME 1:
SUPERMAN AND THE MEN OF STEEL

SUPERMAN: ACTION COMICS VOL. 2: BULLETPROOF

with GRANT MORRISON and RAGS MORALES

SUPERMAN: ACTION COMICS VOL. 3: AT THE END OF DAYS

with GRANT MORRISON and RAGS MORALES

SUPERBOY VOL. 1: INCUBATION

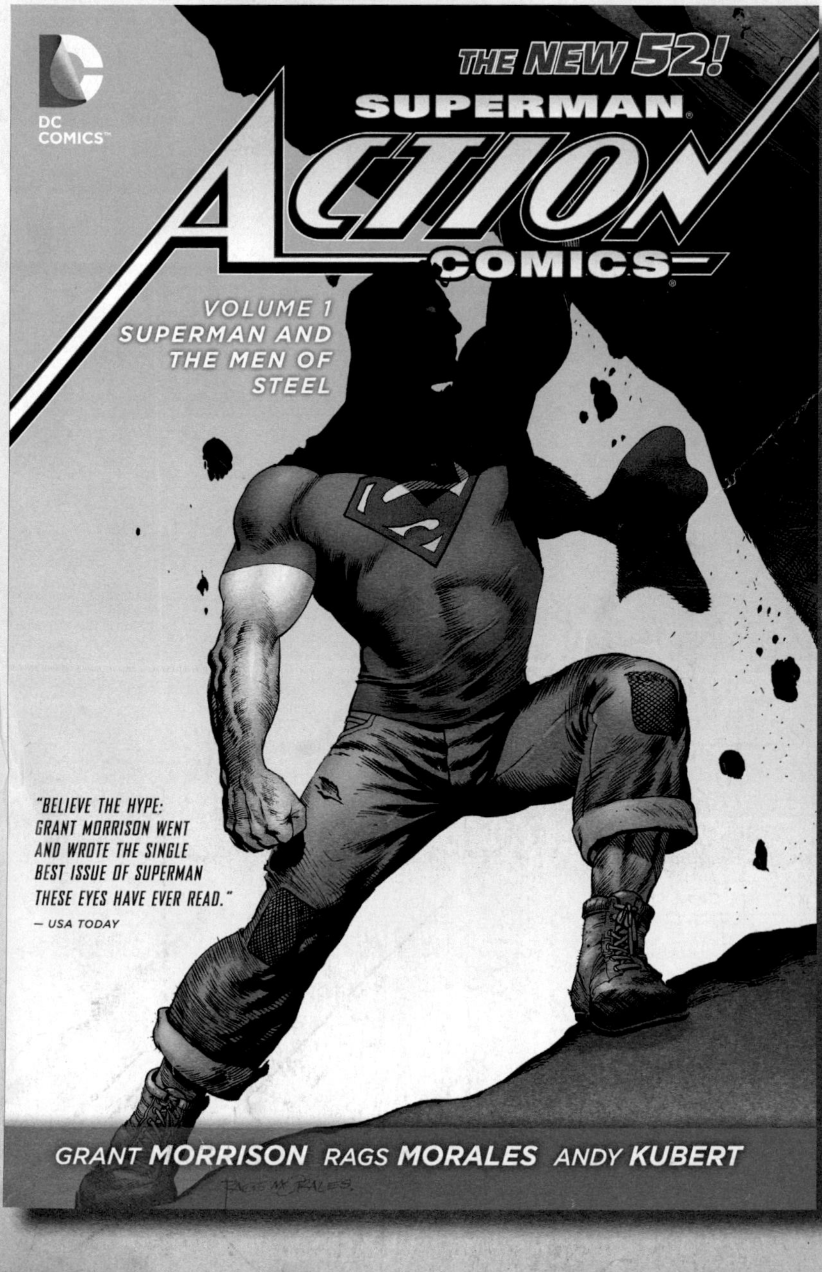

DC COMICS

THE NEW 52!

SUPERMAN

ACTION COMICS

VOLUME 1
SUPERMAN AND THE MEN OF STEEL

"BELIEVE THE HYPE: GRANT MORRISON WENT AND WROTE THE SINGLE BEST ISSUE OF SUPERMAN THESE EYES HAVE EVER READ."
— USA TODAY

GRANT **MORRISON**   RAGS **MORALES**   ANDY **KUBERT**

DC COMICS™

"[A] comic legend." —ROLLING S E

"[Grant Morrison is] comics' high sha ."
—WASHINGTON ST

"[Grant Morrison] is probably my f ite
writer. That guy has more ideas in hi nky
than most people do in a li ne."
—Gerard Way from MY CHEMICAL RO NCE

FROM THE WRITER OF *ALL-STAR SUPERMAN* AND *BATMAN & ROBIN*

GRANT MORRISON

with HOWARD PORTER

JLA VOL. 2

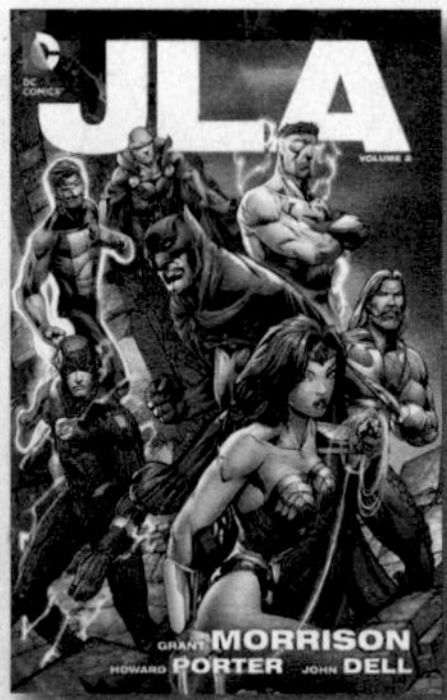

DC COMICS
JLA
GRANT MORRISON
HOWARD PORTER JOHN DELL

with HOWARD PORTER

JLA VOL. 3

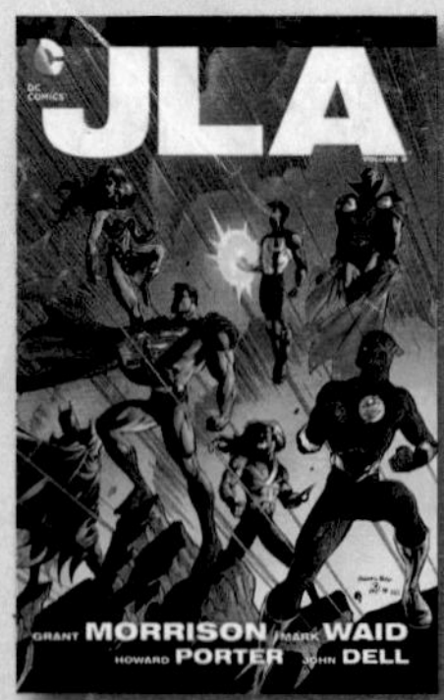

DC COMICS
JLA
GRANT MORRISON MARK WAID
HOWARD PORTER JOHN DELL

with HOWARD PORTER

JLA VOL. 4

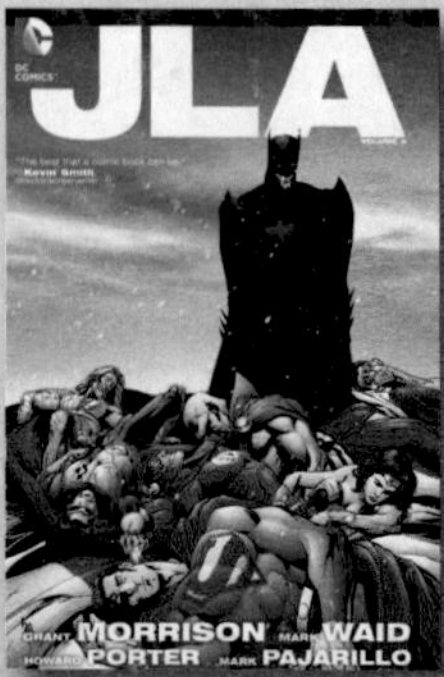

DC COMICS
JLA
GRANT MORRISON MARK WAID
HOWARD PORTER MARK PAJARILLO

with HOWARD PORTER, MARK WAID, and MARK PAJARILLO

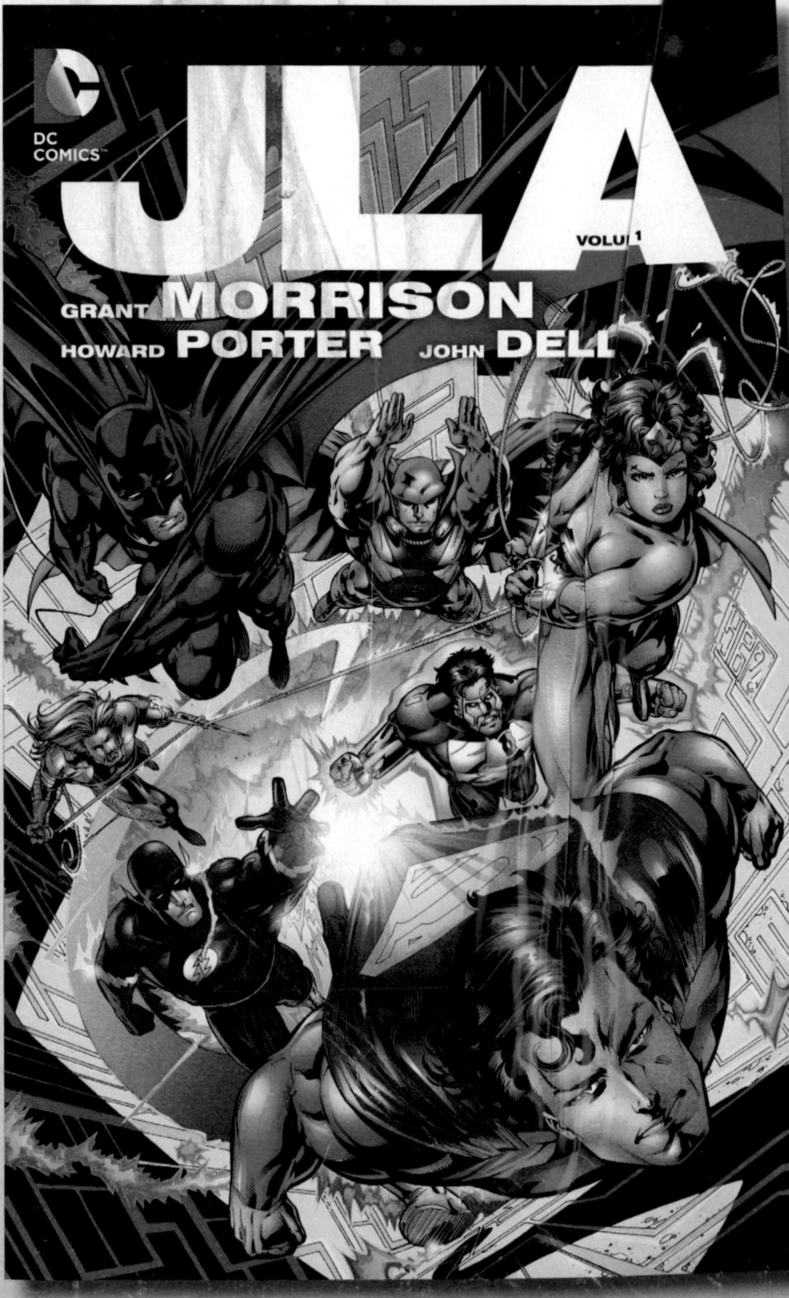

DC COMICS™
JLA
VOLU 1
GRANT MORRISON
HOWARD PORTER JOHN DELL

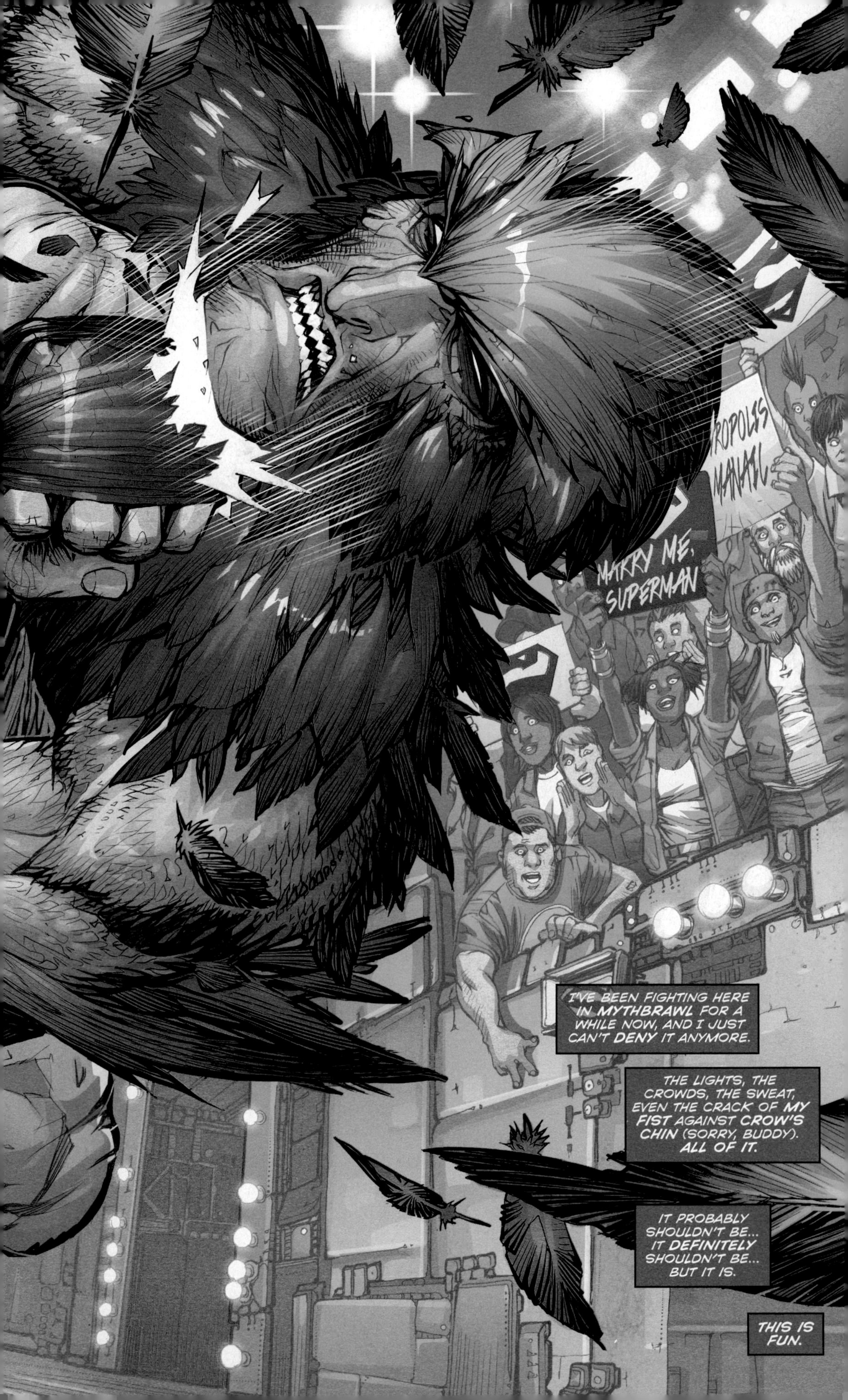

ROPOLIS MANIAC
MARRY ME, SUPERMAN
I'VE BEEN FIGHTING HERE IN MYTHBRAWL FOR A WHILE NOW, AND I JUST CAN'T DENY IT ANYMORE.
THE LIGHTS, THE CROWDS, THE SWEAT, EVEN THE CRACK OF MY FIST AGAINST CROW'S CHIN (SORRY, BUDDY). ALL OF IT.
IT PROBABLY SHOULDN'T BE... IT DEFINITELY SHOULDN'T BE... BUT IT IS.
THIS IS FUN.

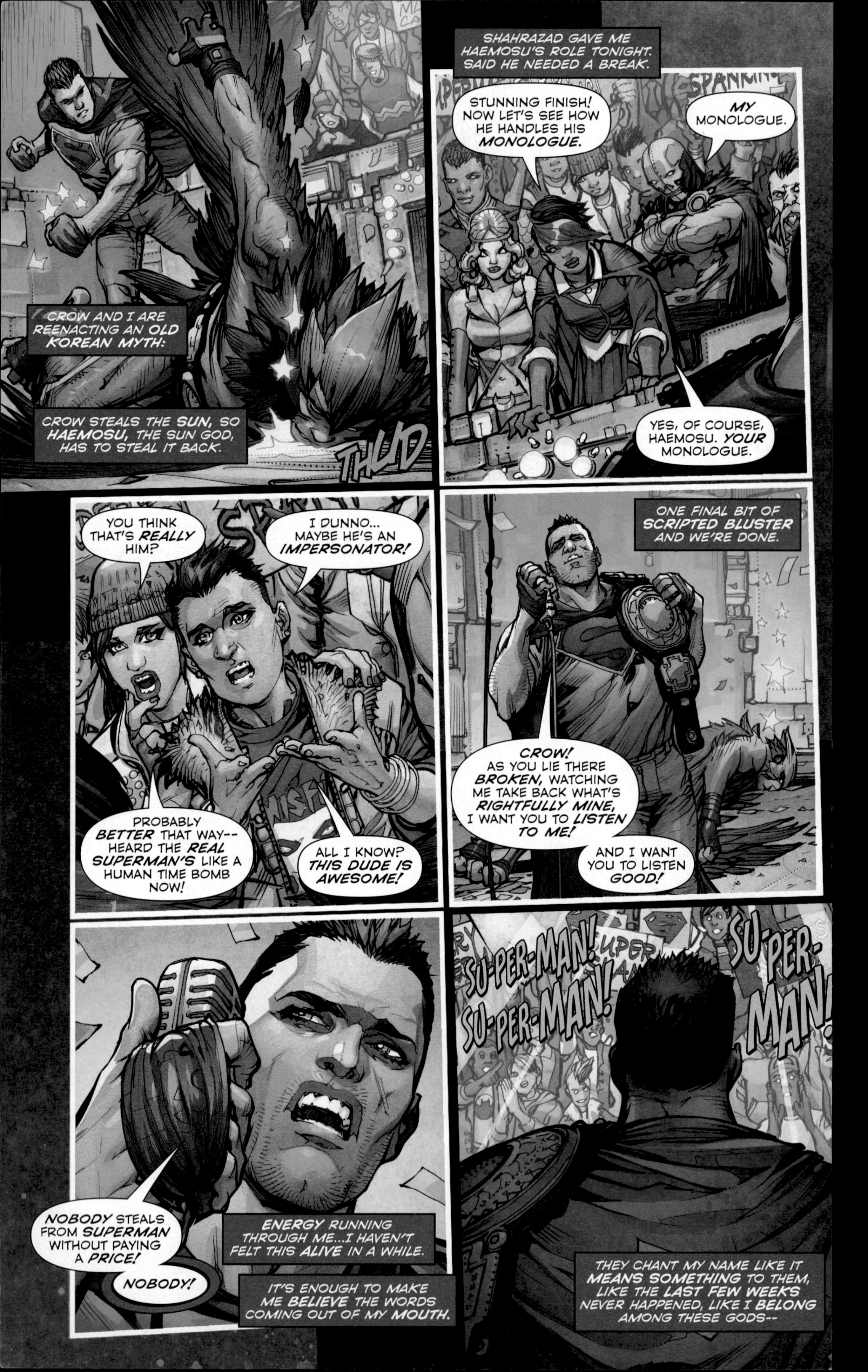
CROW AND I ARE REENACTING AN OLD KOREAN MYTH:
CROW STEALS THE SUN, SO HAEMOSU, THE SUN GOD, HAS TO STEAL IT BACK.
THUD
SHAHRAZAD GAVE ME HAEMOSU'S ROLE TONIGHT. SAID HE NEEDED A BREAK.
STUNNING FINISH! NOW LET'S SEE HOW HE HANDLES HIS MONOLOGUE.
MY MONOLOGUE.
YES, OF COURSE, HAEMOSU. YOUR MONOLOGUE.
YOU THINK THAT'S REALLY HIM?
I DUNNO... MAYBE HE'S AN IMPERSONATOR!
PROBABLY BETTER THAT WAY-- HEARD THE REAL SUPERMAN'S LIKE A HUMAN TIME BOMB NOW!
ALL I KNOW? THIS DUDE IS AWESOME!
ONE FINAL BIT OF SCRIPTED BLUSTER AND WE'RE DONE.
CROW! AS YOU LIE THERE BROKEN, WATCHING ME TAKE BACK WHAT'S RIGHTFULLY MINE, I WANT YOU TO LISTEN TO ME!
AND I WANT YOU TO LISTEN GOOD!
NOBODY STEALS FROM SUPERMAN WITHOUT PAYING A PRICE!
NOBODY!
ENERGY RUNNING THROUGH ME...I HAVEN'T FELT THIS ALIVE IN A WHILE.
IT'S ENOUGH TO MAKE ME BELIEVE THE WORDS COMING OUT OF MY MOUTH.
SU-PER-MAN!
SU-PER-MAN!
SU-PER-MAN!
THEY CHANT MY NAME LIKE IT MEANS SOMETHING TO THEM, LIKE THE LAST FEW WEEKS NEVER HAPPENED, LIKE I BELONG AMONG THESE GODS--

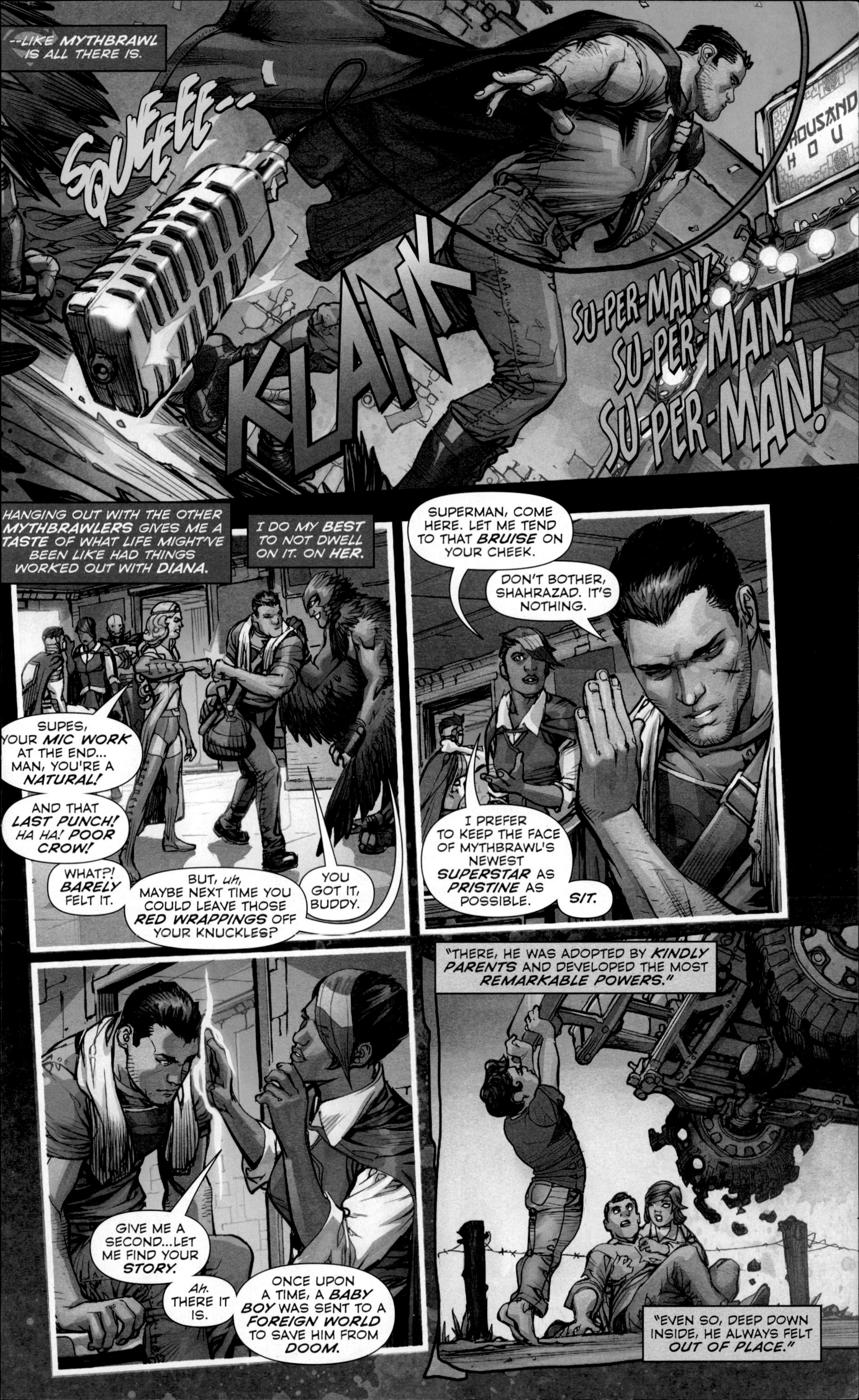
--LIKE MYTHBRAWL IS ALL THERE IS.
SQUEEE--
KLANK
SU-PER-MAN! SU-PER-MAN! SU-PER-MAN!
HANGING OUT WITH THE OTHER MYTHBRAWLERS GIVES ME A TASTE OF WHAT LIFE MIGHT'VE BEEN LIKE HAD THINGS WORKED OUT WITH DIANA.
I DO MY BEST TO NOT DWELL ON IT. ON HER.
SUPES, YOUR MIC WORK AT THE END... MAN, YOU'RE A NATURAL!
AND THAT LAST PUNCH! HA HA! POOR CROW!
WHAT?! BARELY FELT IT.
BUT, uh, MAYBE NEXT TIME YOU COULD LEAVE THOSE RED WRAPPINGS OFF YOUR KNUCKLES?
YOU GOT IT, BUDDY.
SUPERMAN, COME HERE. LET ME TEND TO THAT BRUISE ON YOUR CHEEK.
DON'T BOTHER, SHAHRAZAD. IT'S NOTHING.
I PREFER TO KEEP THE FACE OF MYTHBRAWL'S NEWEST SUPERSTAR AS PRISTINE AS POSSIBLE.
SIT.
GIVE ME A SECOND...LET ME FIND YOUR STORY.
Ah. THERE IT IS.
ONCE UPON A TIME, A BABY BOY WAS SENT TO A FOREIGN WORLD TO SAVE HIM FROM DOOM.
"THERE, HE WAS ADOPTED BY KINDLY PARENTS AND DEVELOPED THE MOST REMARKABLE POWERS."
"EVEN SO, DEEP DOWN INSIDE, HE ALWAYS FELT OUT OF PLACE."

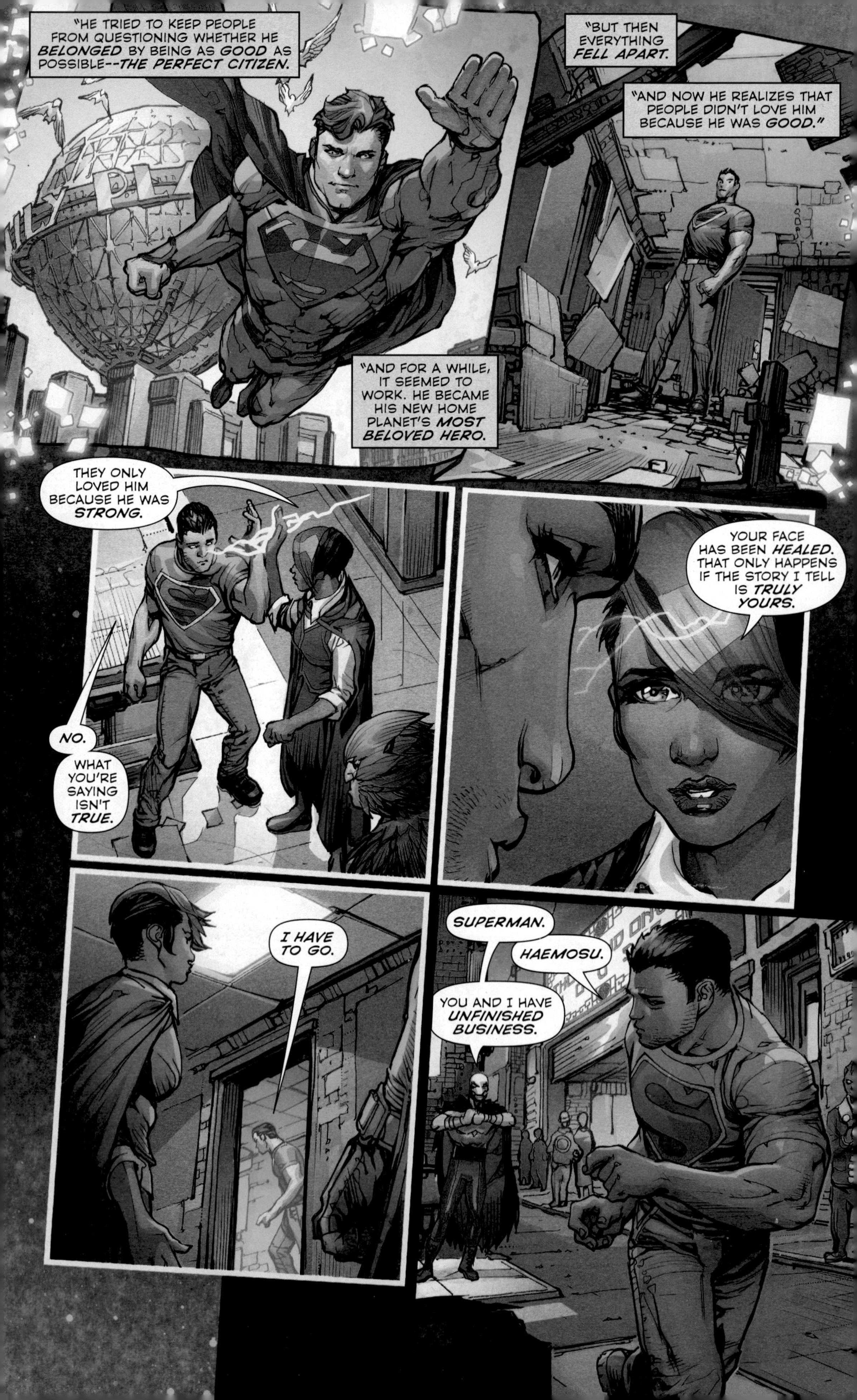
"HE TRIED TO KEEP PEOPLE FROM QUESTIONING WHETHER HE BELONGED BY BEING AS GOOD AS POSSIBLE--THE PERFECT CITIZEN.
"AND FOR A WHILE, IT SEEMED TO WORK. HE BECAME HIS NEW HOME PLANET'S MOST BELOVED HERO.
"BUT THEN EVERYTHING FELL APART.
"AND NOW HE REALIZES THAT PEOPLE DIDN'T LOVE HIM BECAUSE HE WAS GOOD."
THEY ONLY LOVED HIM BECAUSE HE WAS STRONG.
NO.
WHAT YOU'RE SAYING ISN'T TRUE.
YOUR FACE HAS BEEN HEALED. THAT ONLY HAPPENS IF THE STORY I TELL IS TRULY YOURS.
I HAVE TO GO.
SUPERMAN.
HAEMOSU.
YOU AND I HAVE UNFINISHED BUSINESS.

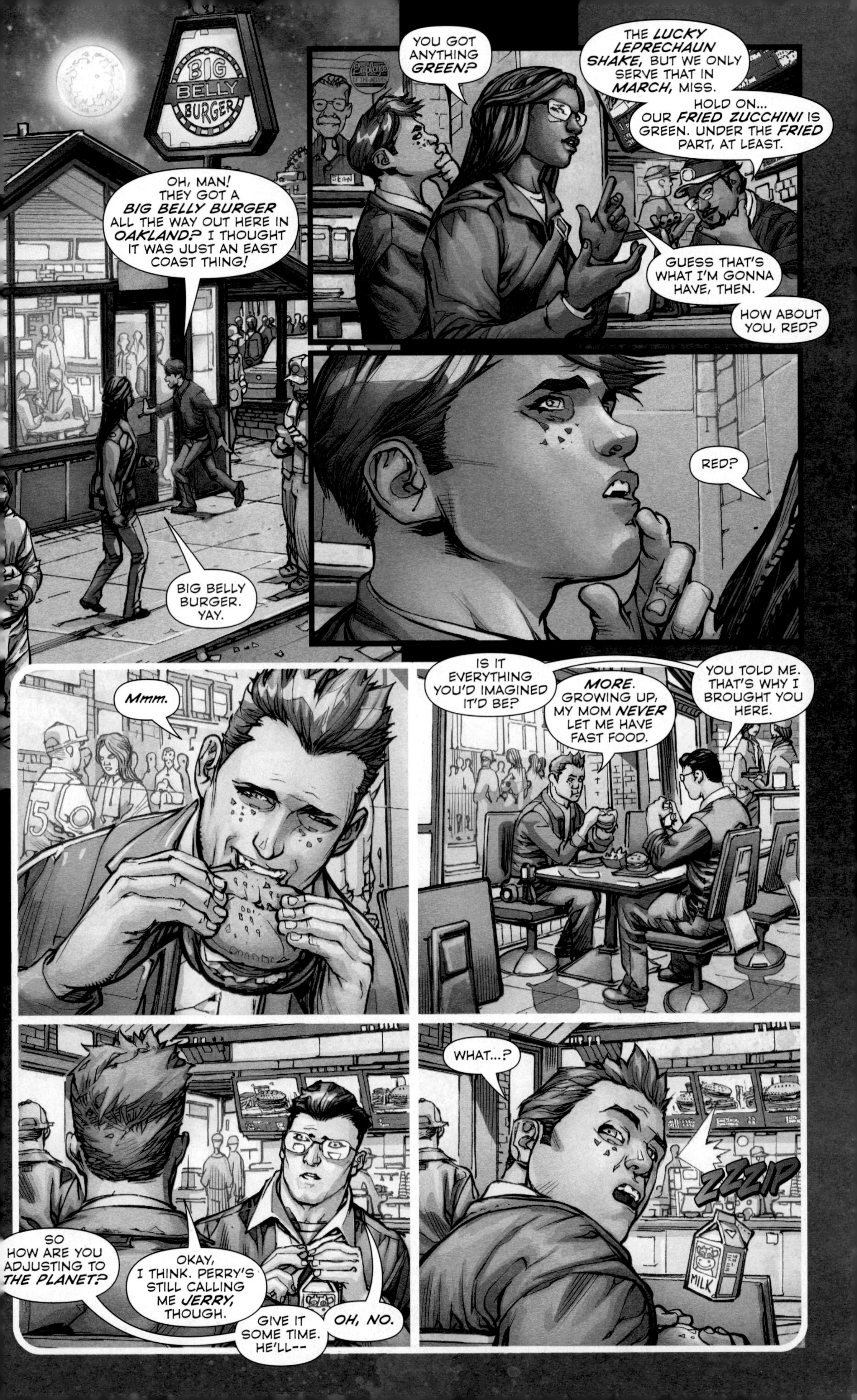
BIG BELLY BURGER
OH, MAN! THEY GOT A BIG BELLY BURGER ALL THE WAY OUT HERE IN OAKLAND? I THOUGHT IT WAS JUST AN EAST COAST THING!
BIG BELLY BURGER. YAY.
YOU GOT ANYTHING GREEN?
THE LUCKY LEPRECHAUN SHAKE, BUT WE ONLY SERVE THAT IN MARCH, MISS.
HOLD ON... OUR FRIED ZUCCHINI IS GREEN. UNDER THE FRIED PART, AT LEAST.
GUESS THAT'S WHAT I'M GONNA HAVE, THEN.
HOW ABOUT YOU, RED?
RED?
Mmm.
IS IT EVERYTHING YOU'D IMAGINED IT'D BE?
MORE. GROWING UP, MY MOM NEVER LET ME HAVE FAST FOOD.
YOU TOLD ME. THAT'S WHY I BROUGHT YOU HERE.
SO HOW ARE YOU ADJUSTING TO THE PLANET?
OKAY, I THINK. PERRY'S STILL CALLING ME JERRY, THOUGH.
GIVE IT SOME TIME. HE'LL--
OH, NO.
WHAT...?
ZZZIP
MILK

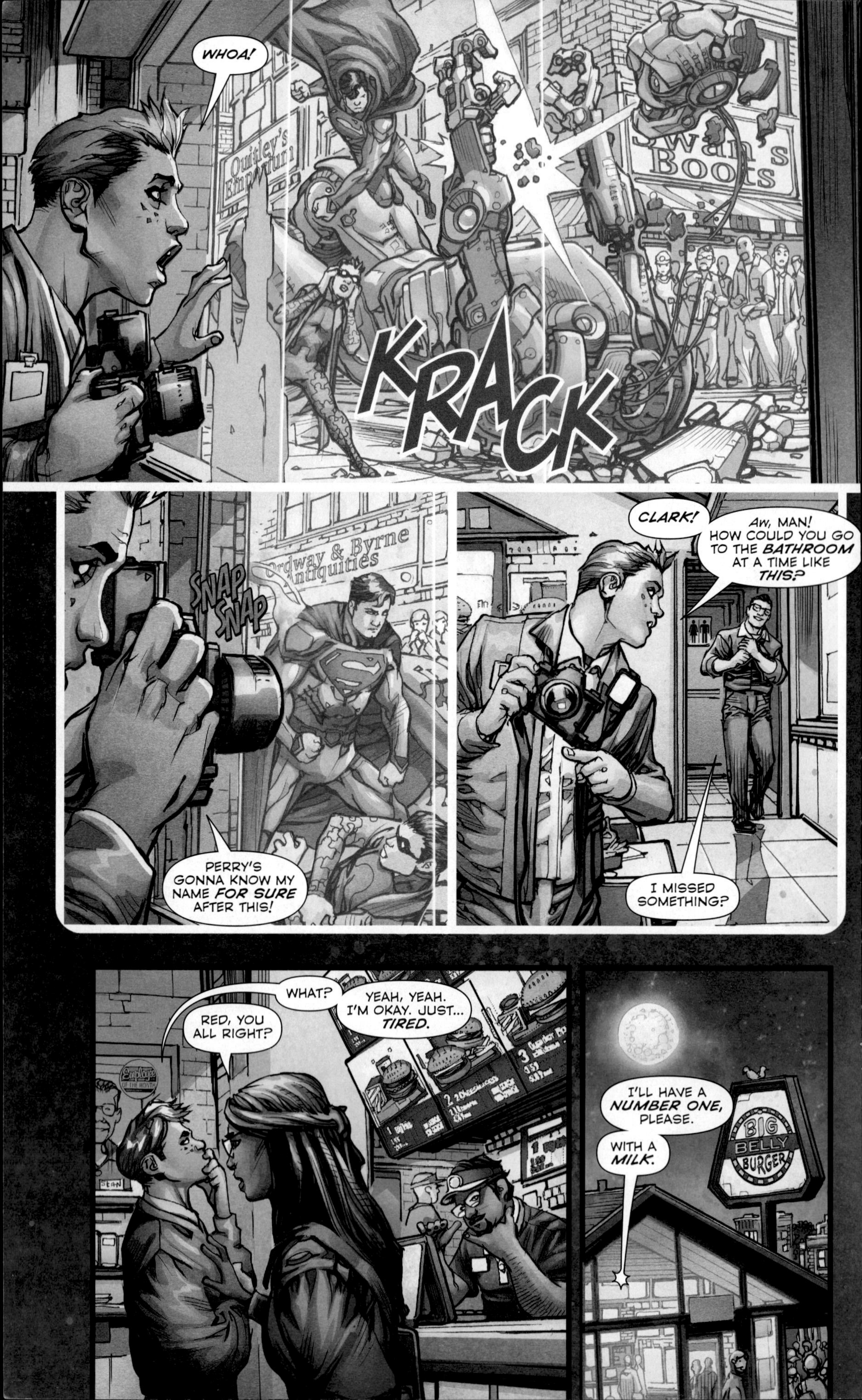
WHOA!
Quitley's Emporium
Swan's Boots
KRACK
Ordway & Byrne Antiquities
SNAP SNAP
PERRY'S GONNA KNOW MY NAME FOR SURE AFTER THIS!
CLARK!
AW, MAN! HOW COULD YOU GO TO THE BATHROOM AT A TIME LIKE THIS?
I MISSED SOMETHING?
RED, YOU ALL RIGHT?
WHAT?
YEAH, YEAH. I'M OKAY. JUST... TIRED.
I'LL HAVE A NUMBER ONE, PLEASE.
WITH A MILK.
BIG BELLY BURGER

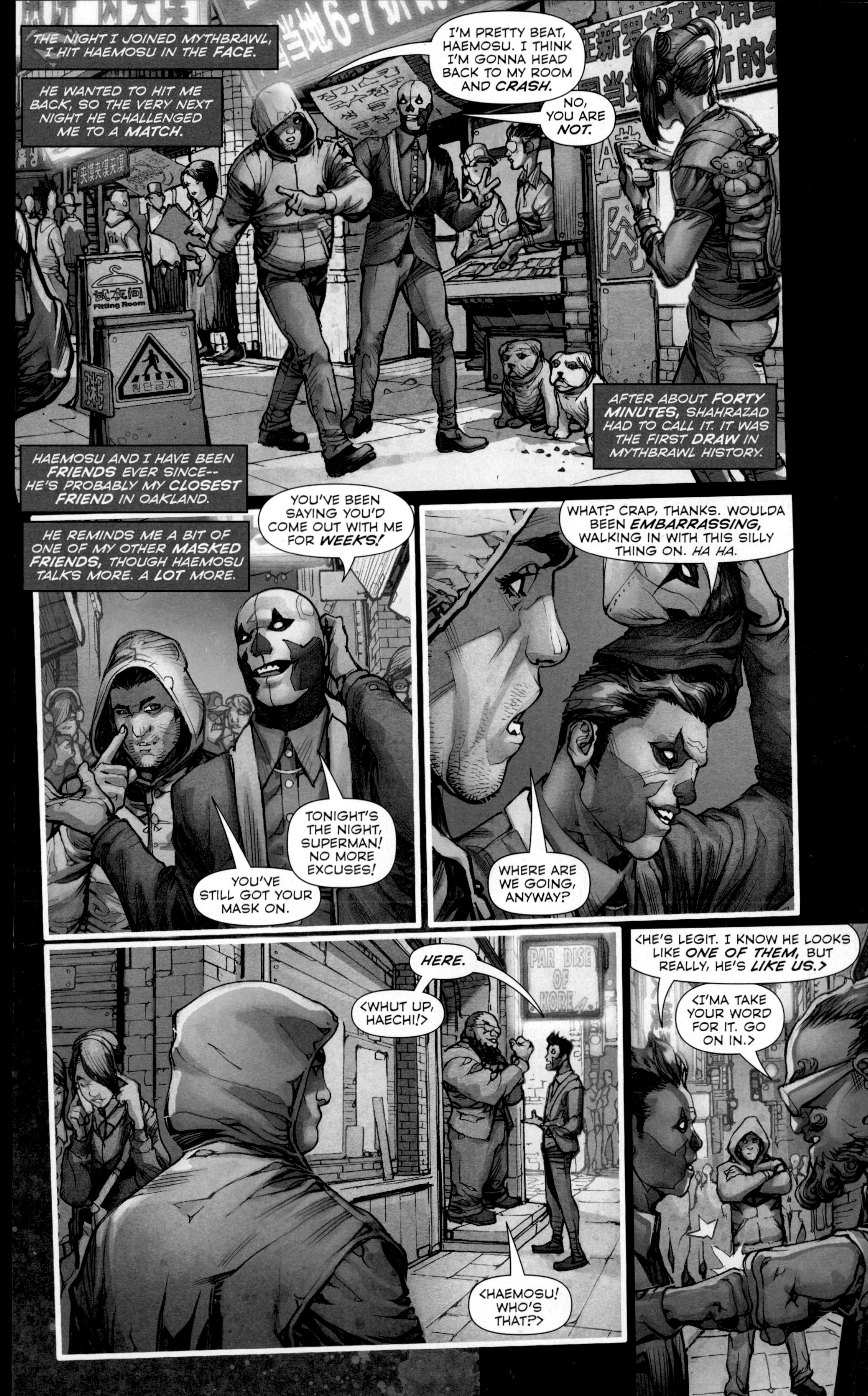
THE NIGHT I JOINED MYTHBRAWL, I HIT HAEMOSU IN THE FACE.
HE WANTED TO HIT ME BACK, SO THE VERY NEXT NIGHT HE CHALLENGED ME TO A MATCH.
I'M PRETTY BEAT, HAEMOSU. I THINK I'M GONNA HEAD BACK TO MY ROOM AND CRASH.
NO, YOU ARE NOT.
Fitting Room
AFTER ABOUT FORTY MINUTES, SHAHRAZAD HAD TO CALL IT. IT WAS THE FIRST DRAW IN MYTHBRAWL HISTORY.
HAEMOSU AND I HAVE BEEN FRIENDS EVER SINCE-- HE'S PROBABLY MY CLOSEST FRIEND IN OAKLAND.
HE REMINDS ME A BIT OF ONE OF MY OTHER MASKED FRIENDS, THOUGH HAEMOSU TALKS MORE. A LOT MORE.
YOU'VE BEEN SAYING YOU'D COME OUT WITH ME FOR WEEKS!
TONIGHT'S THE NIGHT, SUPERMAN! NO MORE EXCUSES!
YOU'VE STILL GOT YOUR MASK ON.
WHAT? CRAP, THANKS. WOULDA BEEN EMBARRASSING, WALKING IN WITH THIS SILLY THING ON. HA HA.
WHERE ARE WE GOING, ANYWAY?
HERE.
<WHUT UP, HAECHI!>
PAR DISE OF KORE
<HAEMOSU! WHO'S THAT?>
<HE'S LEGIT. I KNOW HE LOOKS LIKE ONE OF THEM, BUT REALLY, HE'S LIKE US.>
<I'MA TAKE YOUR WORD FOR IT. GO ON IN.>

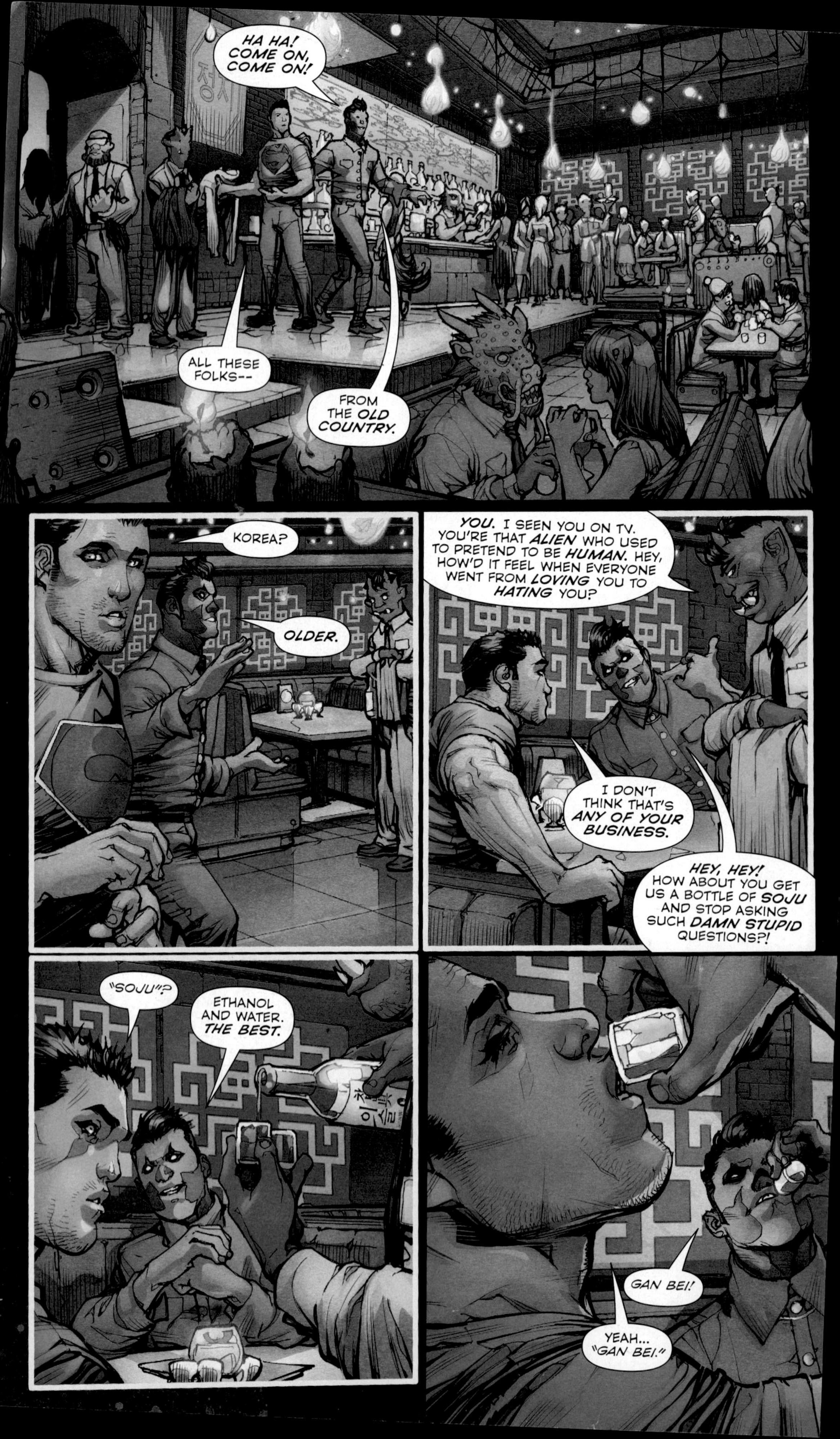
HA HA! COME ON, COME ON!
ALL THESE FOLKS--
FROM THE OLD COUNTRY.
KOREA?
OLDER.
YOU. I SEEN YOU ON TV. YOU'RE THAT ALIEN WHO USED TO PRETEND TO BE HUMAN. HEY, HOW'D IT FEEL WHEN EVERYONE WENT FROM LOVING YOU TO HATING YOU?
I DON'T THINK THAT'S ANY OF YOUR BUSINESS.
HEY, HEY! HOW ABOUT YOU GET US A BOTTLE OF SOJU AND STOP ASKING SUCH DAMN STUPID QUESTIONS?!
"SOJU"?
ETHANOL AND WATER. THE BEST.
GAN BEI!
YEAH... "GAN BEI."

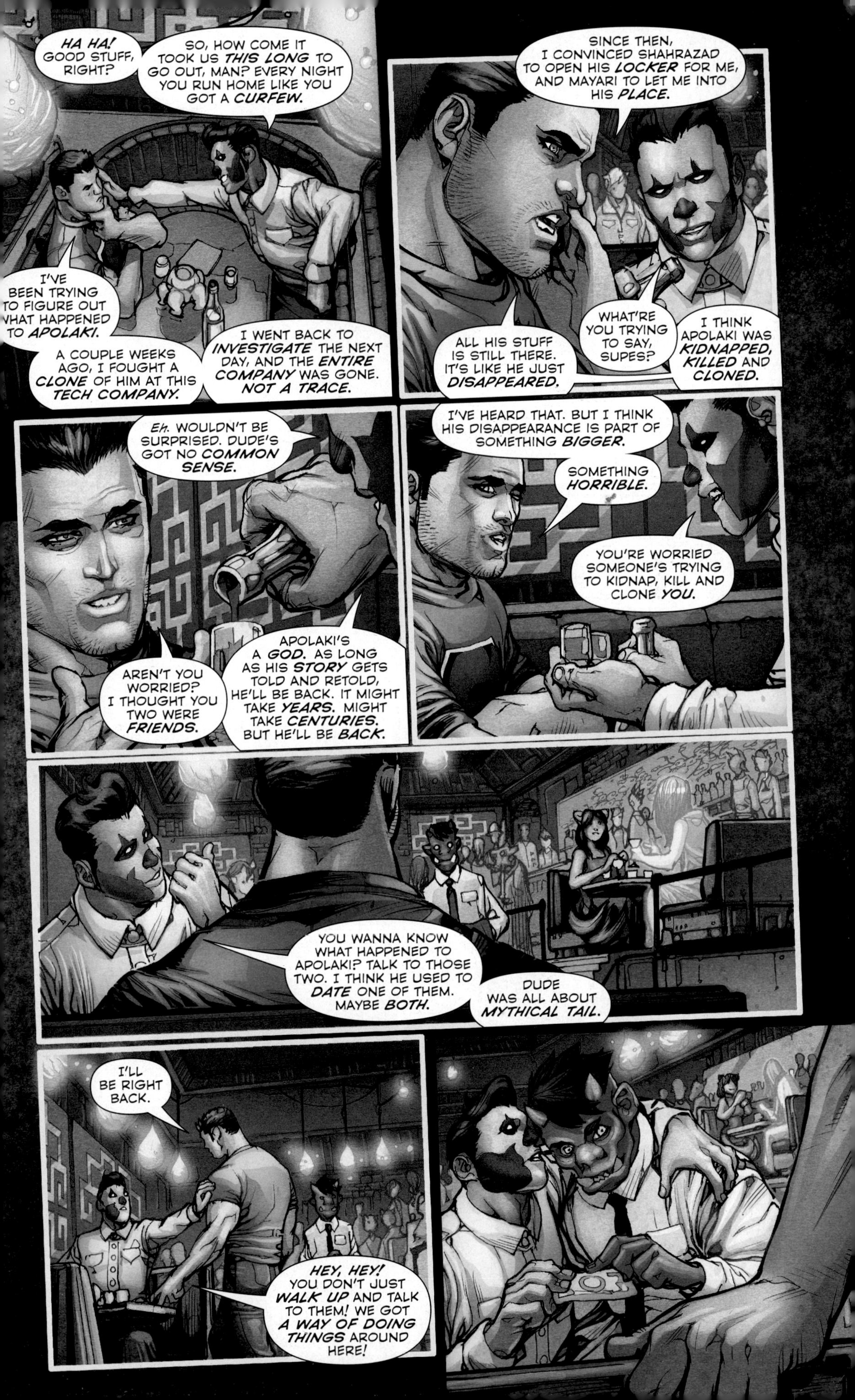
HA HA! GOOD STUFF, RIGHT?
SO, HOW COME IT TOOK US THIS LONG TO GO OUT, MAN? EVERY NIGHT YOU RUN HOME LIKE YOU GOT A CURFEW.
I'VE BEEN TRYING TO FIGURE OUT WHAT HAPPENED TO APOLAKI.
A COUPLE WEEKS AGO, I FOUGHT A CLONE OF HIM AT THIS TECH COMPANY.
I WENT BACK TO INVESTIGATE THE NEXT DAY, AND THE ENTIRE COMPANY WAS GONE. NOT A TRACE.
SINCE THEN, I CONVINCED SHAHRAZAD TO OPEN HIS LOCKER FOR ME, AND MAYARI TO LET ME INTO HIS PLACE.
ALL HIS STUFF IS STILL THERE. IT'S LIKE HE JUST DISAPPEARED.
WHAT'RE YOU TRYING TO SAY, SUPES?
I THINK APOLAKI WAS KIDNAPPED, KILLED AND CLONED.
Eh. WOULDN'T BE SURPRISED. DUDE'S GOT NO COMMON SENSE.
AREN'T YOU WORRIED? I THOUGHT YOU TWO WERE FRIENDS.
APOLAKI'S A GOD. AS LONG AS HIS STORY GETS TOLD AND RETOLD, HE'LL BE BACK. IT MIGHT TAKE YEARS. MIGHT TAKE CENTURIES. BUT HE'LL BE BACK.
I'VE HEARD THAT. BUT I THINK HIS DISAPPEARANCE IS PART OF SOMETHING BIGGER.
SOMETHING HORRIBLE.
YOU'RE WORRIED SOMEONE'S TRYING TO KIDNAP, KILL AND CLONE YOU.
YOU WANNA KNOW WHAT HAPPENED TO APOLAKI? TALK TO THOSE TWO. I THINK HE USED TO DATE ONE OF THEM. MAYBE BOTH.
DUDE WAS ALL ABOUT MYTHICAL TAIL.
I'LL BE RIGHT BACK.
HEY, HEY! YOU DON'T JUST WALK UP AND TALK TO THEM! WE GOT A WAY OF DOING THINGS AROUND HERE!

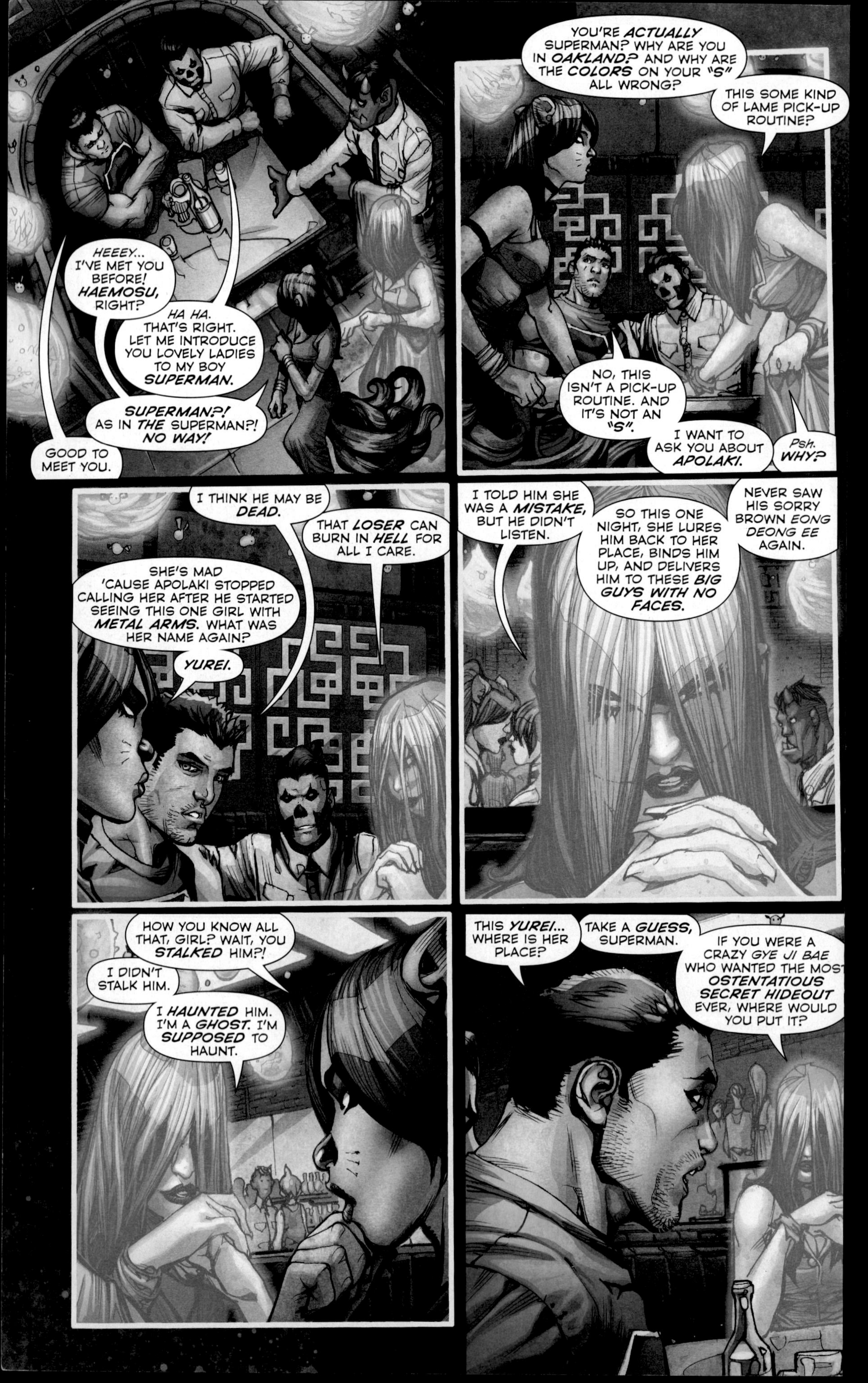
HEEEY... I'VE MET YOU BEFORE! HAEMOSU, RIGHT?
HA HA. THAT'S RIGHT. LET ME INTRODUCE YOU LOVELY LADIES TO MY BOY SUPERMAN.
SUPERMAN?! AS IN THE SUPERMAN?! NO WAY!
GOOD TO MEET YOU.
YOU'RE ACTUALLY SUPERMAN? WHY ARE YOU IN OAKLAND? AND WHY ARE THE COLORS ON YOUR "S" ALL WRONG?
THIS SOME KIND OF LAME PICK-UP ROUTINE?
NO, THIS ISN'T A PICK-UP ROUTINE. AND IT'S NOT AN "S".
I WANT TO ASK YOU ABOUT APOLAKI.
Psh. WHY?
I THINK HE MAY BE DEAD.
THAT LOSER CAN BURN IN HELL FOR ALL I CARE.
SHE'S MAD 'CAUSE APOLAKI STOPPED CALLING HER AFTER HE STARTED SEEING THIS ONE GIRL WITH METAL ARMS. WHAT WAS HER NAME AGAIN?
YUREI.
I TOLD HIM SHE WAS A MISTAKE, BUT HE DIDN'T LISTEN.
SO THIS ONE NIGHT, SHE LURES HIM BACK TO HER PLACE, BINDS HIM UP, AND DELIVERS HIM TO THESE BIG GUYS WITH NO FACES.
NEVER SAW HIS SORRY BROWN EONG DEONG EE AGAIN.
HOW YOU KNOW ALL THAT, GIRL? WAIT, YOU STALKED HIM?!
I DIDN'T STALK HIM.
I HAUNTED HIM. I'M A GHOST. I'M SUPPOSED TO HAUNT.
THIS YUREI... WHERE IS HER PLACE?
TAKE A GUESS, SUPERMAN.
IF YOU WERE A CRAZY GYE JI BAE WHO WANTED THE MOST OSTENTATIOUS SECRET HIDEOUT EVER, WHERE WOULD YOU PUT IT?

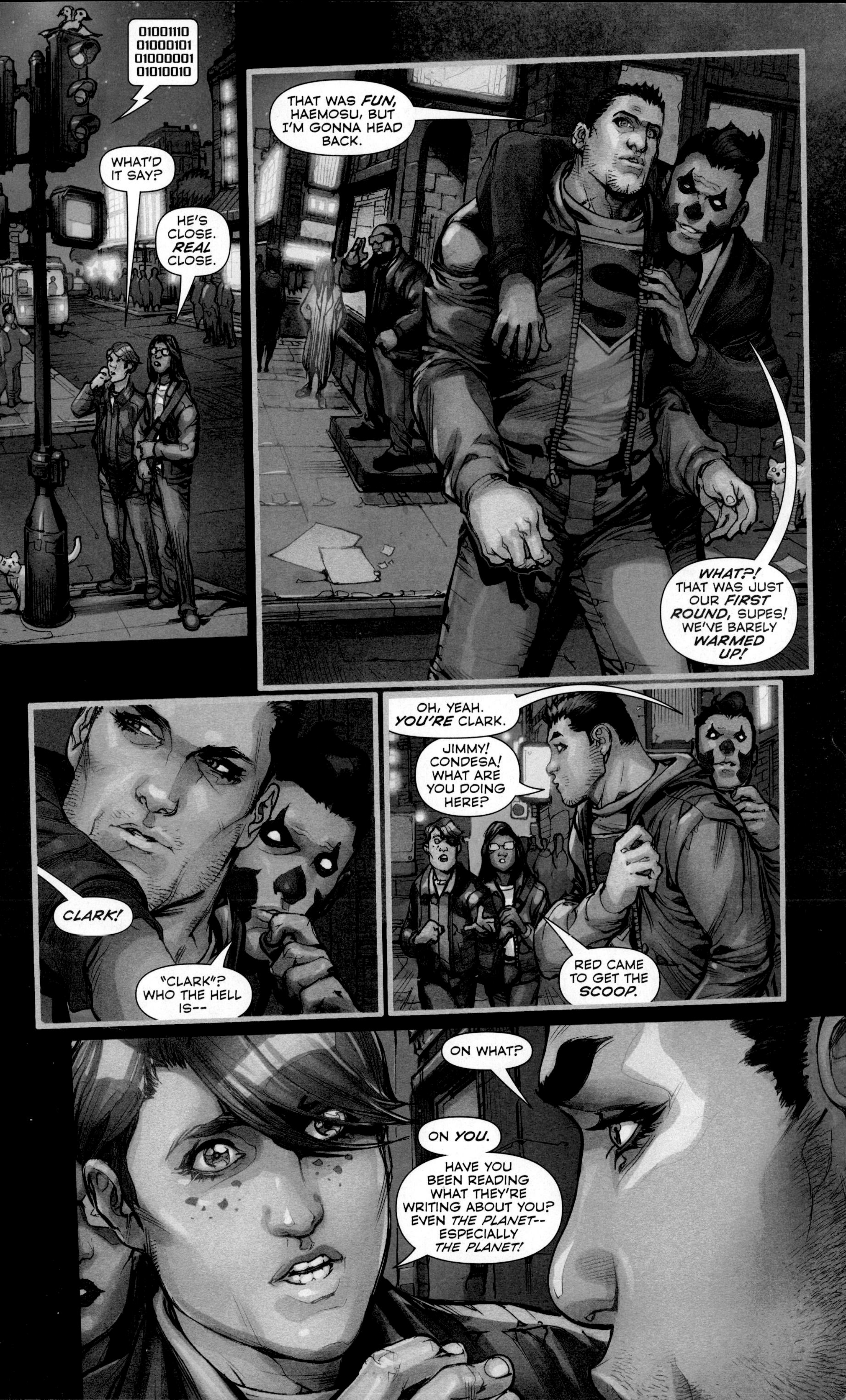

01001110
01000101
01000001
01010010
WHAT'D IT SAY?
HE'S CLOSE. *REAL* CLOSE.
THAT WAS *FUN,* HAEMOSU, BUT I'M GONNA HEAD BACK.
WHAT?! THAT WAS JUST OUR *FIRST ROUND,* SUPES! WE'VE BARELY *WARMED UP!*
CLARK!
"CLARK"? WHO THE HELL IS--
OH, YEAH. *YOU'RE* CLARK.
JIMMY! CONDESA! WHAT ARE YOU DOING HERE?
RED CAME TO GET THE *SCOOP.*
ON WHAT?
ON *YOU.*
HAVE YOU BEEN READING WHAT THEY'RE WRITING ABOUT YOU? EVEN *THE PLANET*-- ESPECIALLY *THE PLANET!*

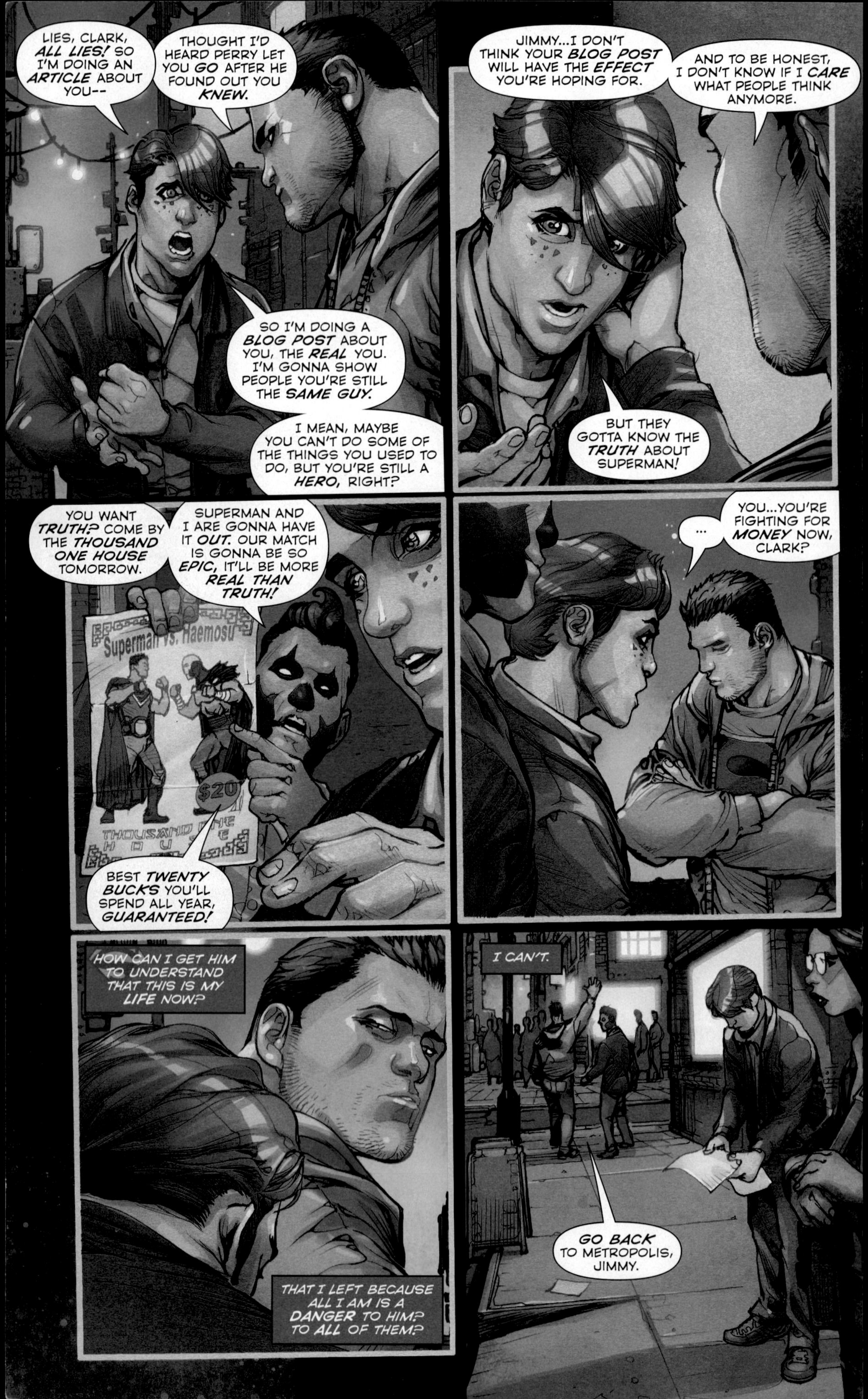
LIES, CLARK, ALL LIES! SO I'M DOING AN ARTICLE ABOUT YOU--
THOUGHT I'D HEARD PERRY LET YOU GO AFTER HE FOUND OUT YOU KNEW.
SO I'M DOING A BLOG POST ABOUT YOU, THE REAL YOU. I'M GONNA SHOW PEOPLE YOU'RE STILL THE SAME GUY.
I MEAN, MAYBE YOU CAN'T DO SOME OF THE THINGS YOU USED TO DO, BUT YOU'RE STILL A HERO, RIGHT?
JIMMY...I DON'T THINK YOUR BLOG POST WILL HAVE THE EFFECT YOU'RE HOPING FOR.
AND TO BE HONEST, I DON'T KNOW IF I CARE WHAT PEOPLE THINK ANYMORE.
BUT THEY GOTTA KNOW THE TRUTH ABOUT SUPERMAN!
YOU WANT TRUTH? COME BY THE THOUSAND ONE HOUSE TOMORROW.
SUPERMAN AND I ARE GONNA HAVE IT OUT. OUR MATCH IS GONNA BE SO EPIC, IT'LL BE MORE REAL THAN TRUTH!
Superman vs. Haemosu
$20
BEST TWENTY BUCKS YOU'LL SPEND ALL YEAR, GUARANTEED!
...
YOU...YOU'RE FIGHTING FOR MONEY NOW, CLARK?
HOW CAN I GET HIM TO UNDERSTAND THAT THIS IS MY LIFE NOW?
THAT I LEFT BECAUSE ALL I AM IS A DANGER TO HIM? TO ALL OF THEM?
I CAN'T.
GO BACK TO METROPOLIS, JIMMY.

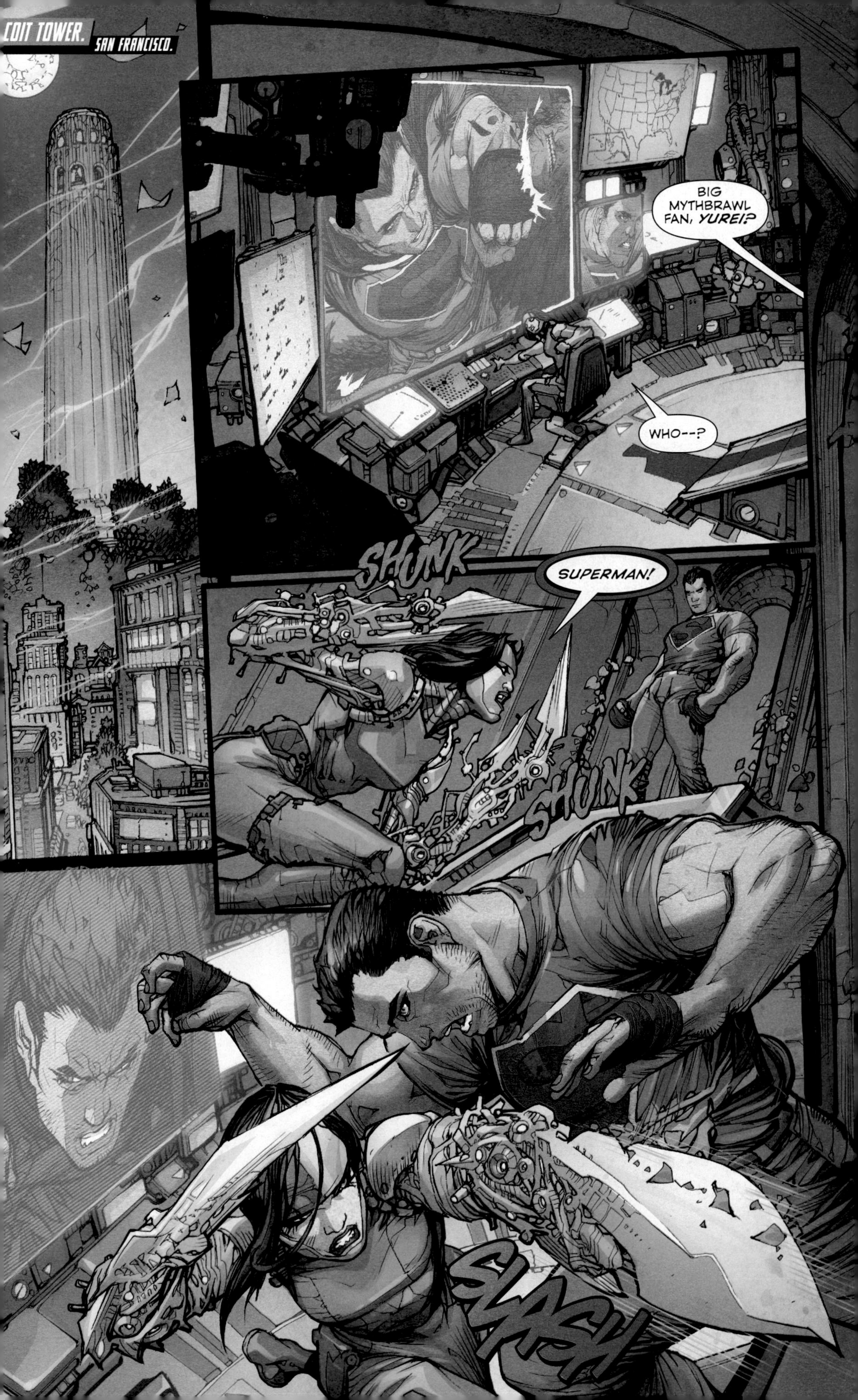
COIT TOWER. SAN FRANCISCO.
BIG MYTHBRAWL FAN, YUREI!?
WHO--?
SHUNK
SUPERMAN!
SHUNK
SLASH

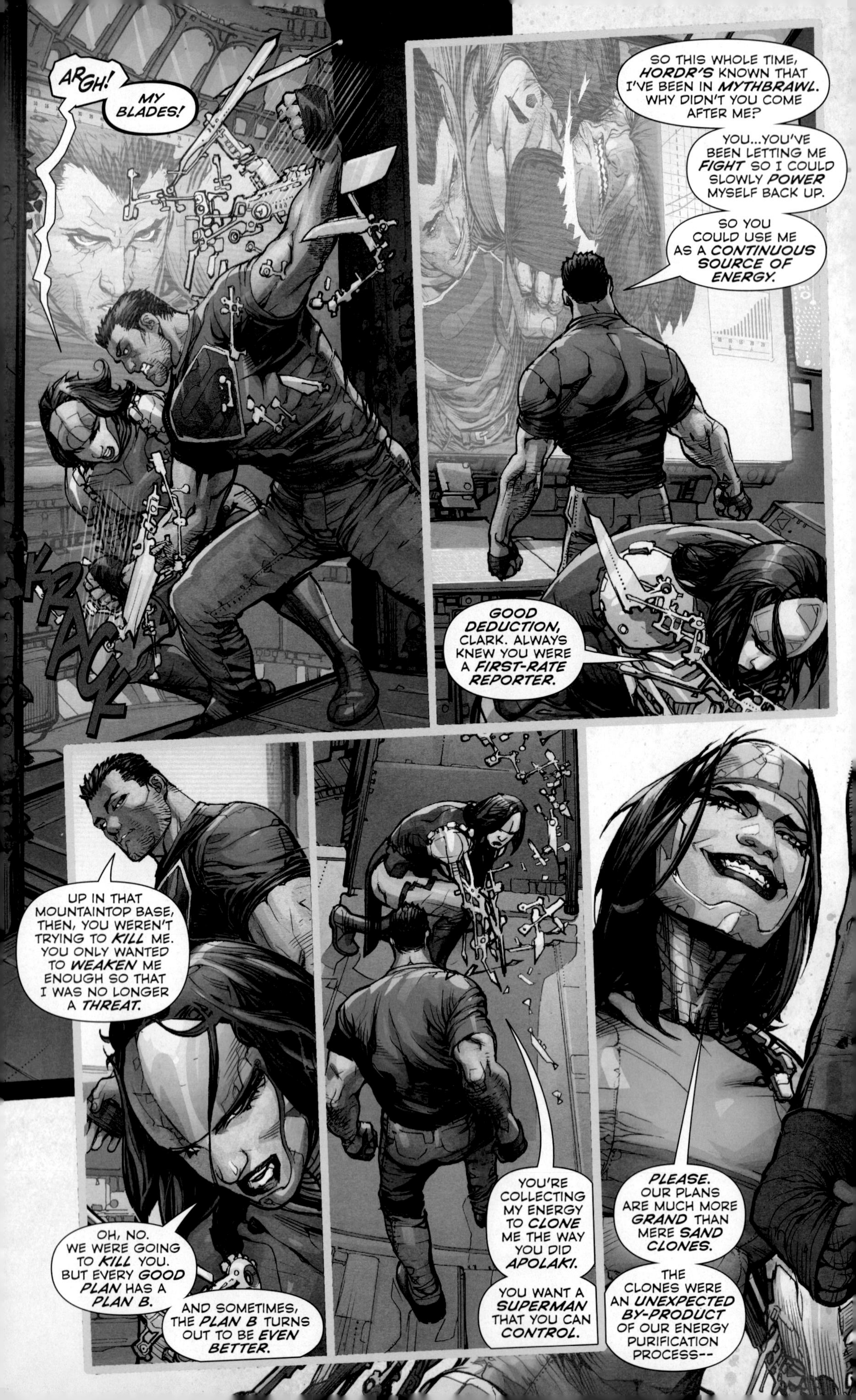
ARGH!
MY BLADES!
KRACK
SO THIS WHOLE TIME, HORDR'S KNOWN THAT I'VE BEEN IN MYTHBRAWL. WHY DIDN'T YOU COME AFTER ME?
YOU...YOU'VE BEEN LETTING ME FIGHT SO I COULD SLOWLY POWER MYSELF BACK UP.
SO YOU COULD USE ME AS A CONTINUOUS SOURCE OF ENERGY.
GOOD DEDUCTION, CLARK. ALWAYS KNEW YOU WERE A FIRST-RATE REPORTER.
UP IN THAT MOUNTAINTOP BASE, THEN, YOU WEREN'T TRYING TO KILL ME. YOU ONLY WANTED TO WEAKEN ME ENOUGH SO THAT I WAS NO LONGER A THREAT.
OH, NO. WE WERE GOING TO KILL YOU. BUT EVERY GOOD PLAN HAS A PLAN B.
AND SOMETIMES, THE PLAN B TURNS OUT TO BE EVEN BETTER.
YOU'RE COLLECTING MY ENERGY TO CLONE ME THE WAY YOU DID APOLAKI.
YOU WANT A SUPERMAN THAT YOU CAN CONTROL.
PLEASE. OUR PLANS ARE MUCH MORE GRAND THAN MERE SAND CLONES.
THE CLONES WERE AN UNEXPECTED BY-PRODUCT OF OUR ENERGY PURIFICATION PROCESS--

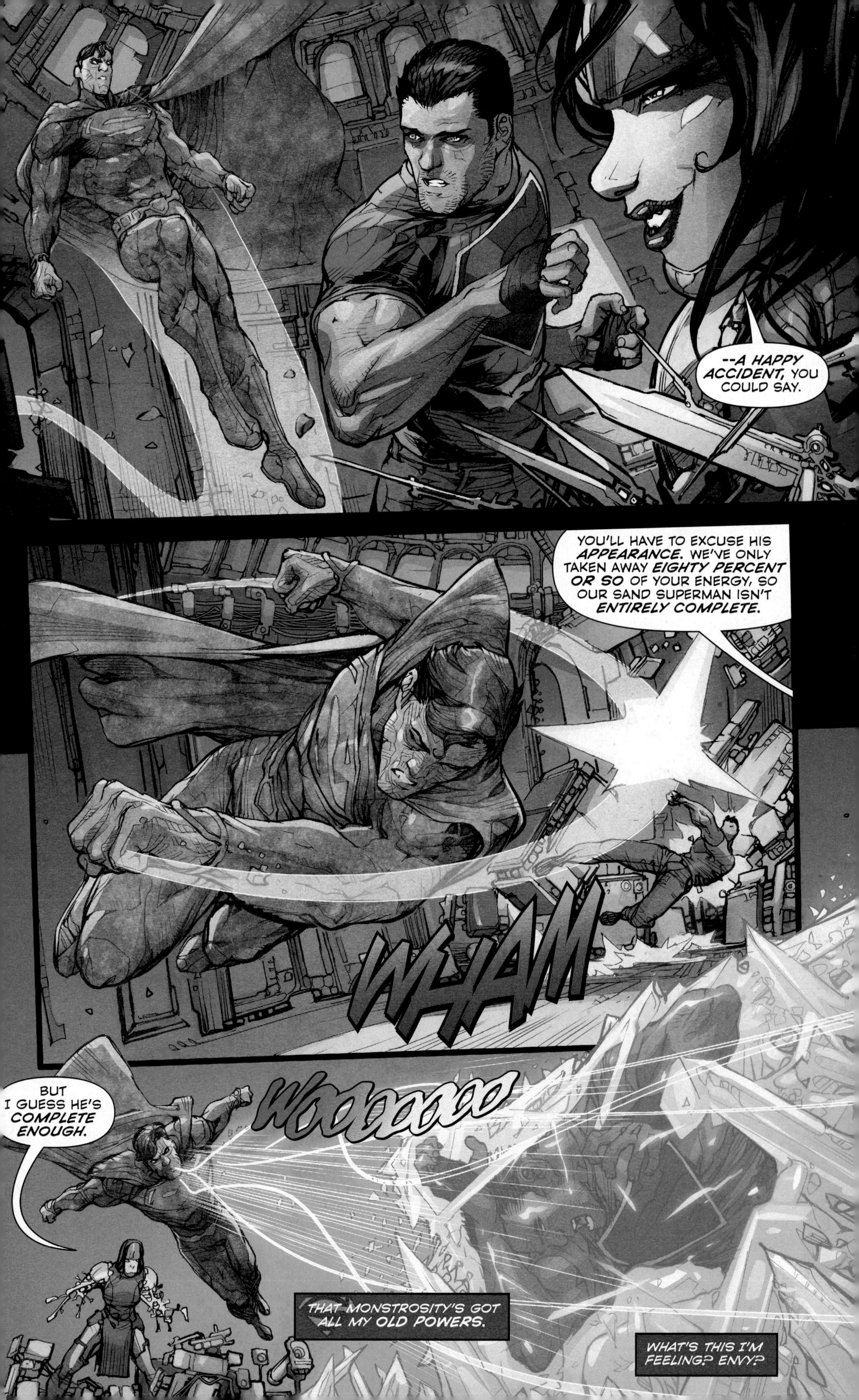
--A HAPPY ACCIDENT, YOU COULD SAY.
YOU'LL HAVE TO EXCUSE HIS APPEARANCE. WE'VE ONLY TAKEN AWAY EIGHTY PERCENT OR SO OF YOUR ENERGY, SO OUR SAND SUPERMAN ISN'T ENTIRELY COMPLETE.
WHAM
BUT I GUESS HE'S COMPLETE ENOUGH.
WOOOOOOO
THAT MONSTROSITY'S GOT ALL MY OLD POWERS.
WHAT'S THIS I'M FEELING? ENVY?

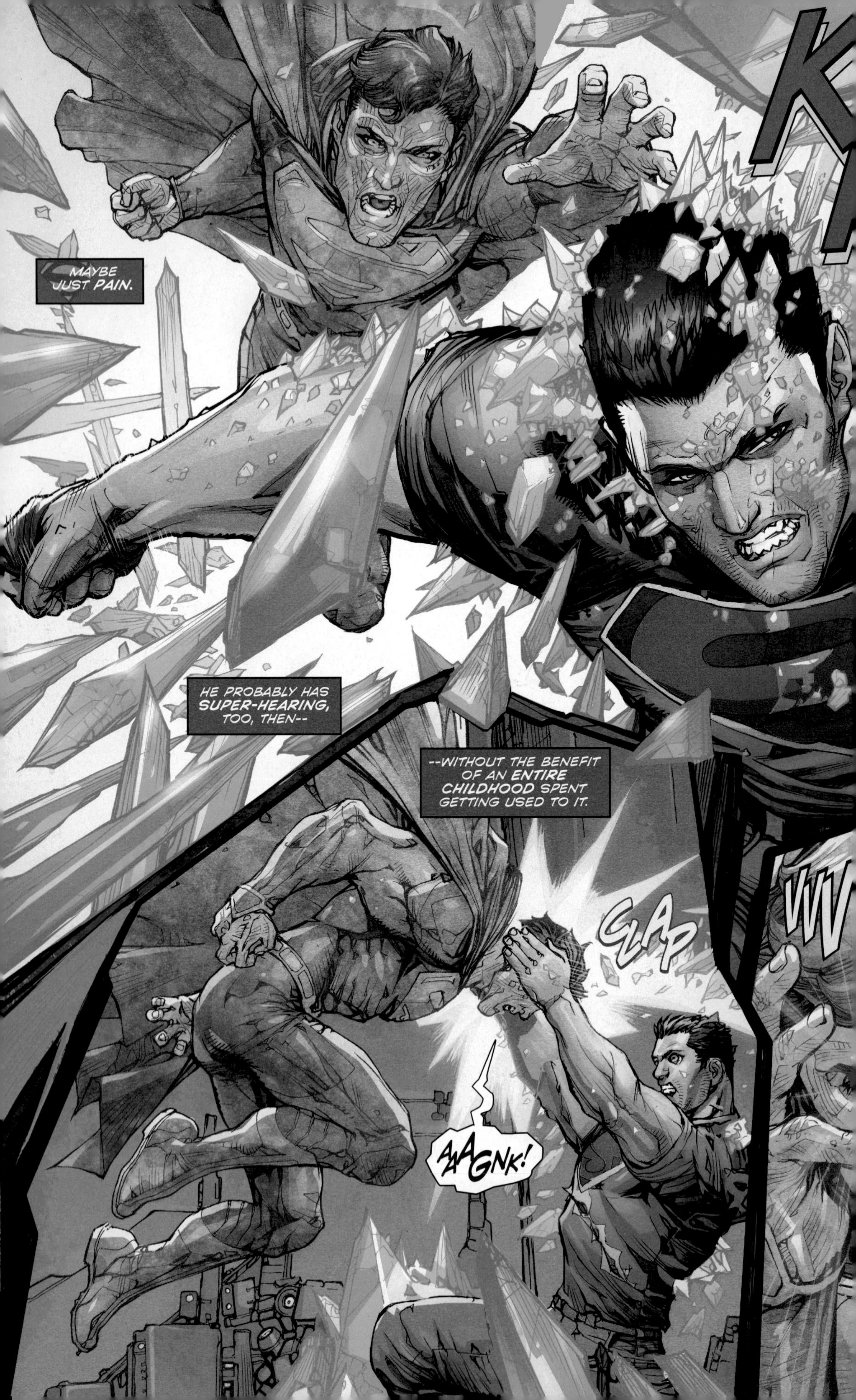
MAYBE JUST PAIN.
HE PROBABLY HAS SUPER-HEARING, TOO, THEN--
--WITHOUT THE BENEFIT OF AN ENTIRE CHILDHOOD SPENT GETTING USED TO IT.
CLAP
AAAGNK!

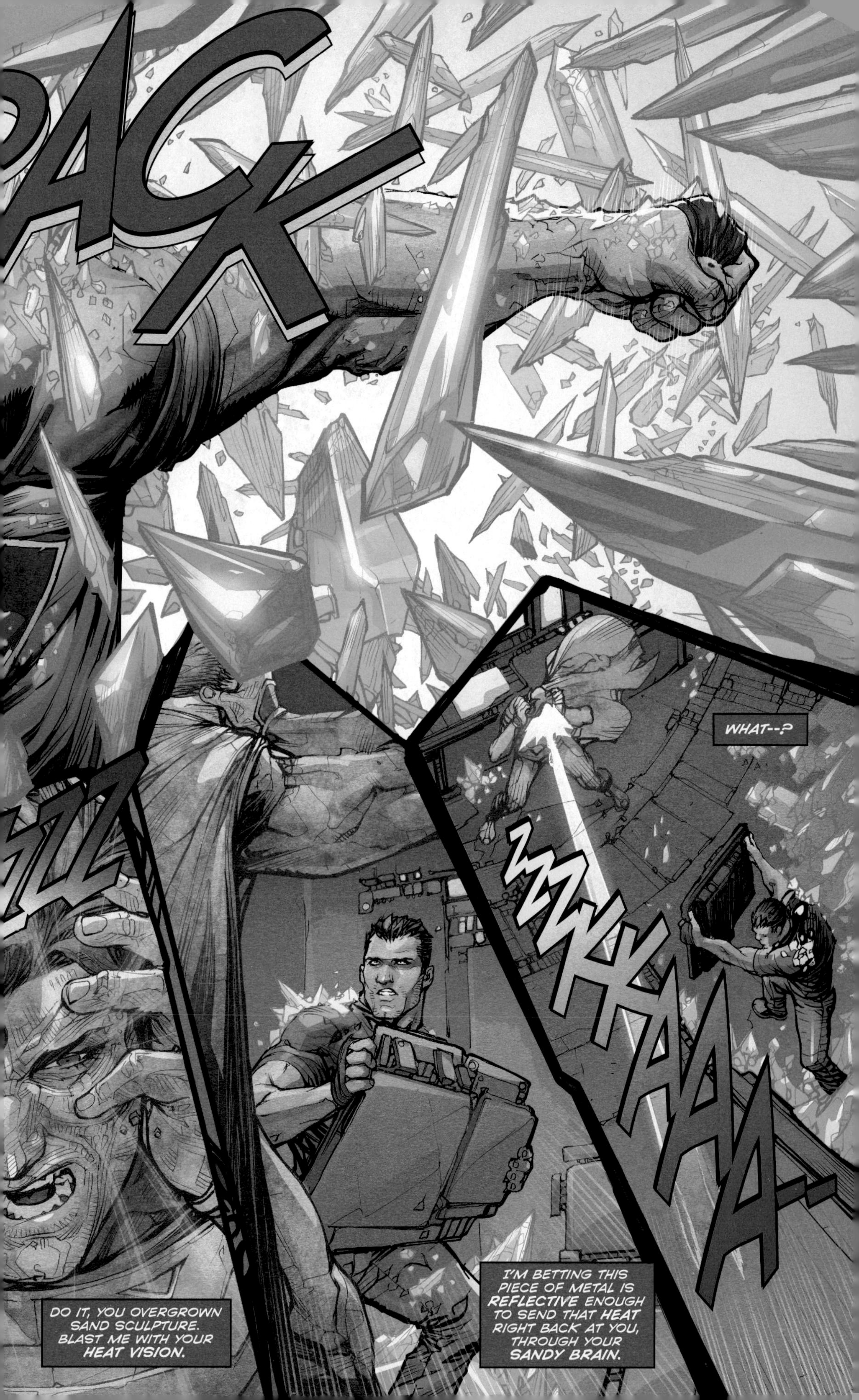
WHAT--?
DO IT, YOU OVERGROWN SAND SCULPTURE. BLAST ME WITH YOUR HEAT VISION.
I'M BETTING THIS PIECE OF METAL IS REFLECTIVE ENOUGH TO SEND THAT HEAT RIGHT BACK AT YOU, THROUGH YOUR SANDY BRAIN.

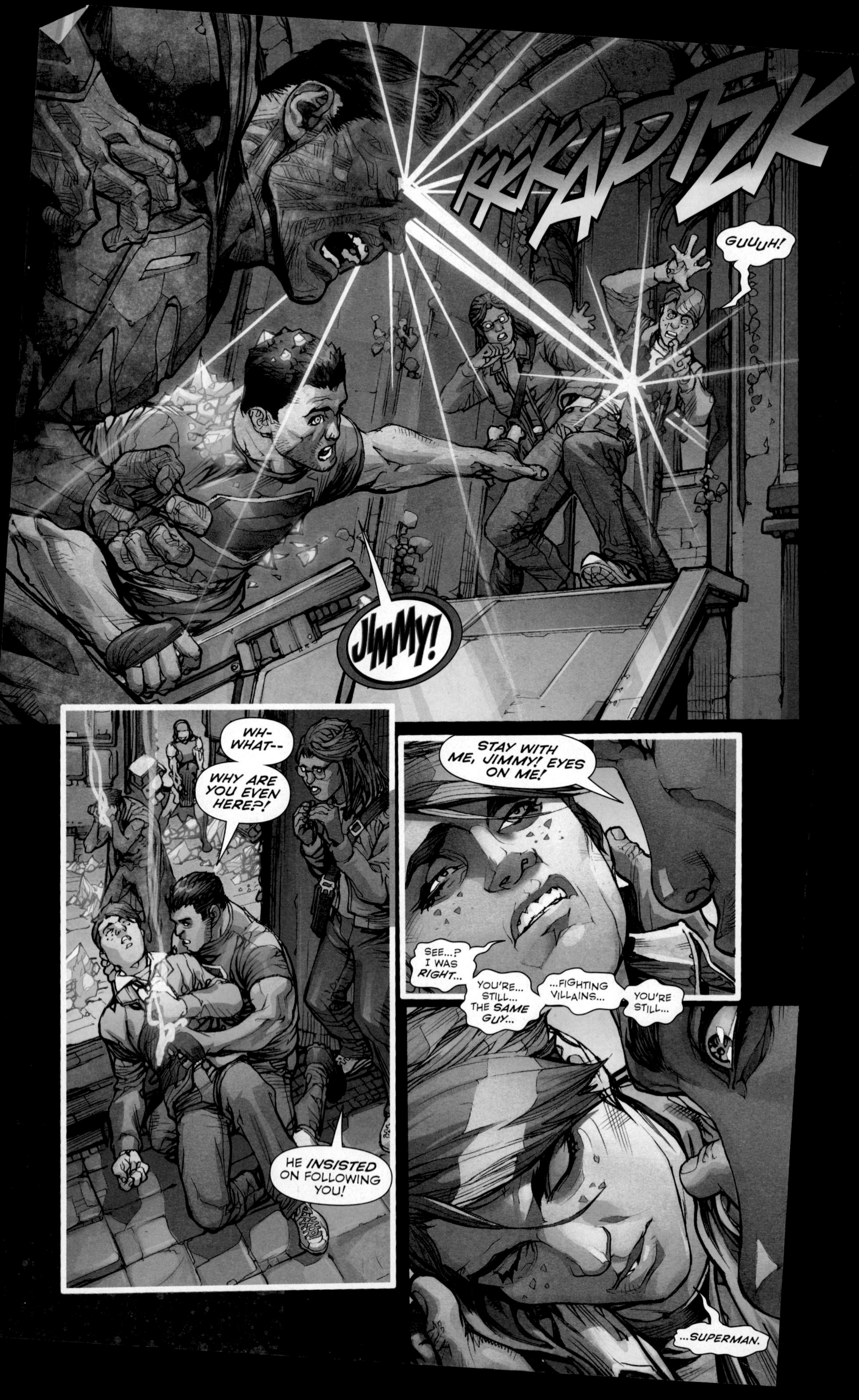
KKKADITZK
GUUUH!
JIMMY!
WH-WHAT--
WHY ARE YOU EVEN HERE?!
HE INSISTED ON FOLLOWING YOU!
STAY WITH ME, JIMMY! EYES ON ME!
SEE...? I WAS RIGHT...
YOU'RE... STILL... THE SAME GUY...
...FIGHTING VILLAINS...
YOU'RE STILL...
...SUPERMAN.

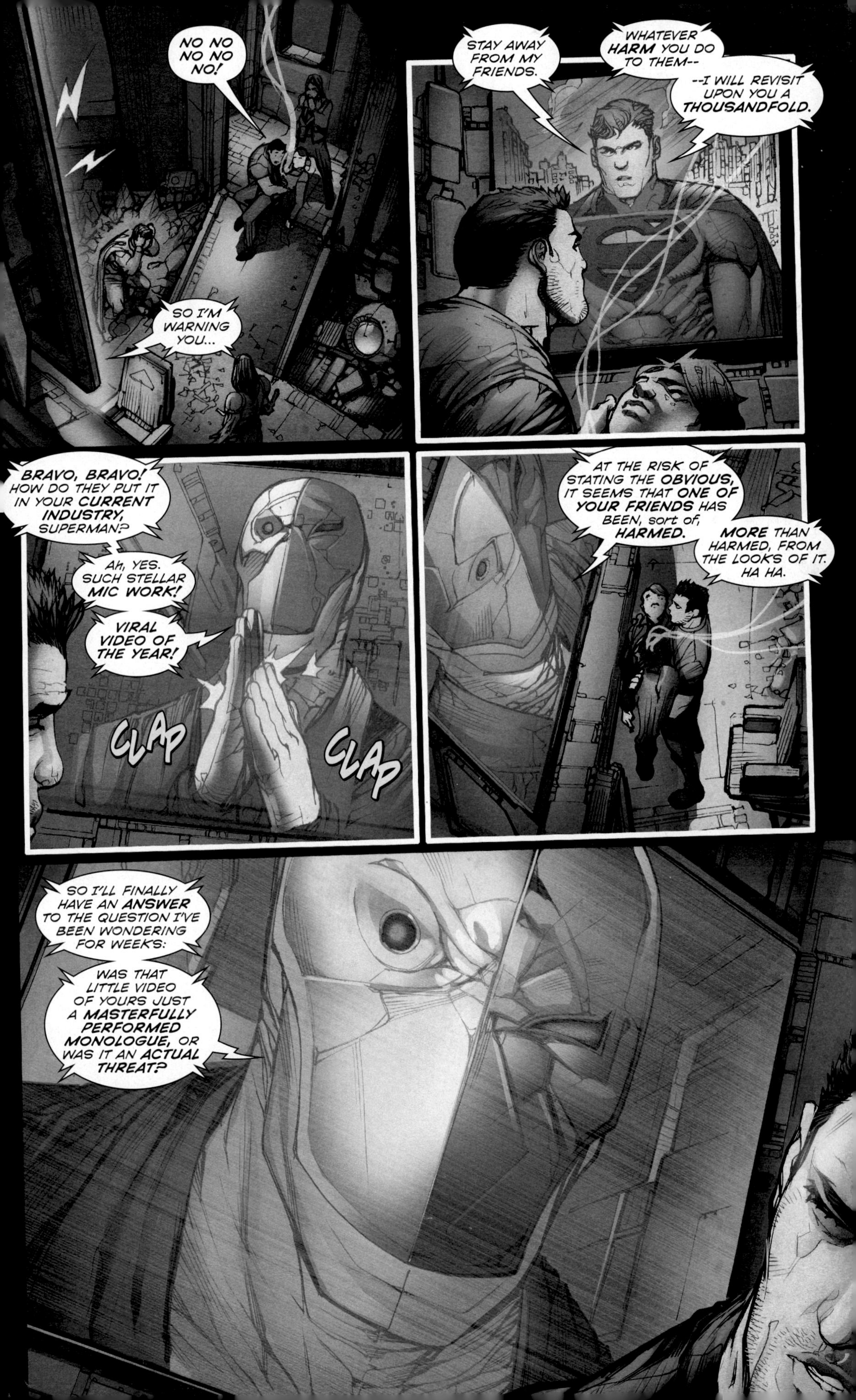
NO NO NO NO NO!
SO I'M WARNING YOU...
STAY AWAY FROM MY FRIENDS.
WHATEVER HARM YOU DO TO THEM--
--I WILL REVISIT UPON YOU A THOUSANDFOLD.
BRAVO, BRAVO! HOW DO THEY PUT IT IN YOUR CURRENT INDUSTRY, SUPERMAN?
Ah, YES. SUCH STELLAR MIC WORK!
VIRAL VIDEO OF THE YEAR!
CLAP
CLAP
AT THE RISK OF STATING THE OBVIOUS, IT SEEMS THAT ONE OF YOUR FRIENDS HAS BEEN, sort of, HARMED.
MORE THAN HARMED, FROM THE LOOKS OF IT. HA HA.
SO I'LL FINALLY HAVE AN ANSWER TO THE QUESTION I'VE BEEN WONDERING FOR WEEKS:
WAS THAT LITTLE VIDEO OF YOURS JUST A MASTERFULLY PERFORMED MONOLOGUE, OR WAS IT AN ACTUAL THREAT?

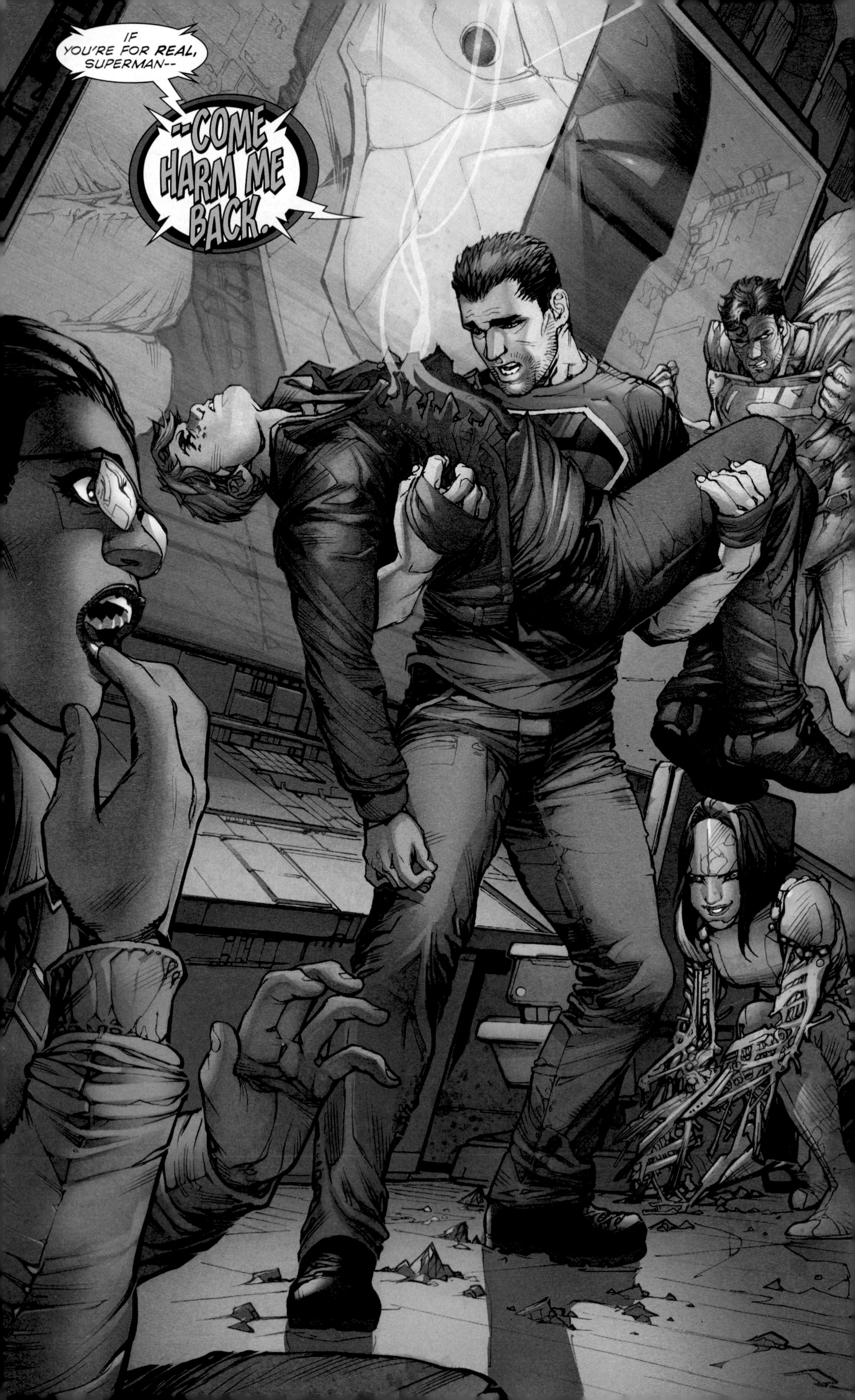
IF YOU'RE FOR REAL, SUPERMAN--
--COME HARM ME BACK.

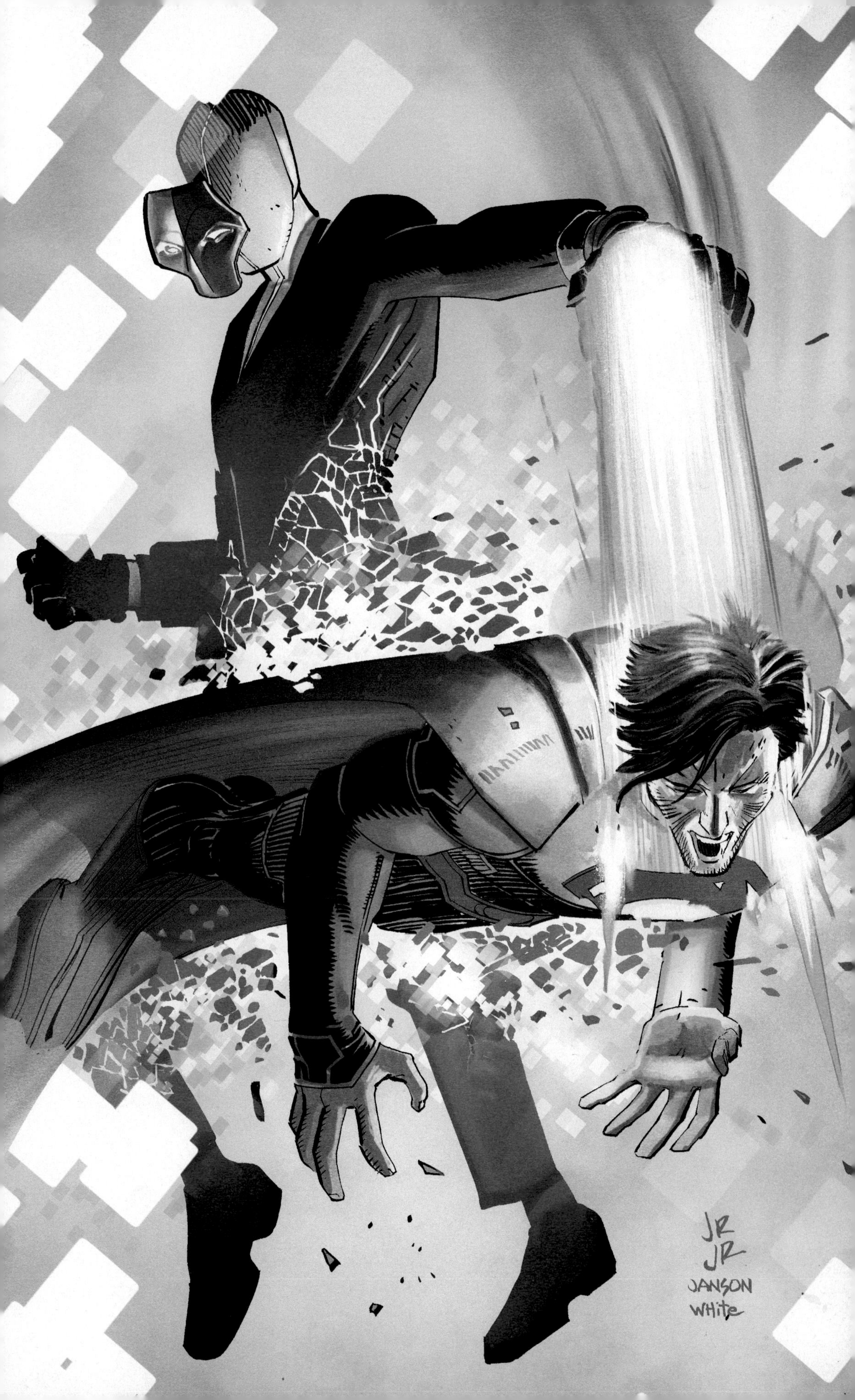
JR JR
JANSON
WHITE

INFILTRATED

GENE LUEN YANG writer HOWARD PORTER, RAYMUND BERMUDEZ, TOM DERENICK artists HI-FI, LEE LOUGHRIDGE colorists ROB LEIGH letterer
JOHN ROMITA JR., KLAUS JANSON, DEAN WHITE cover

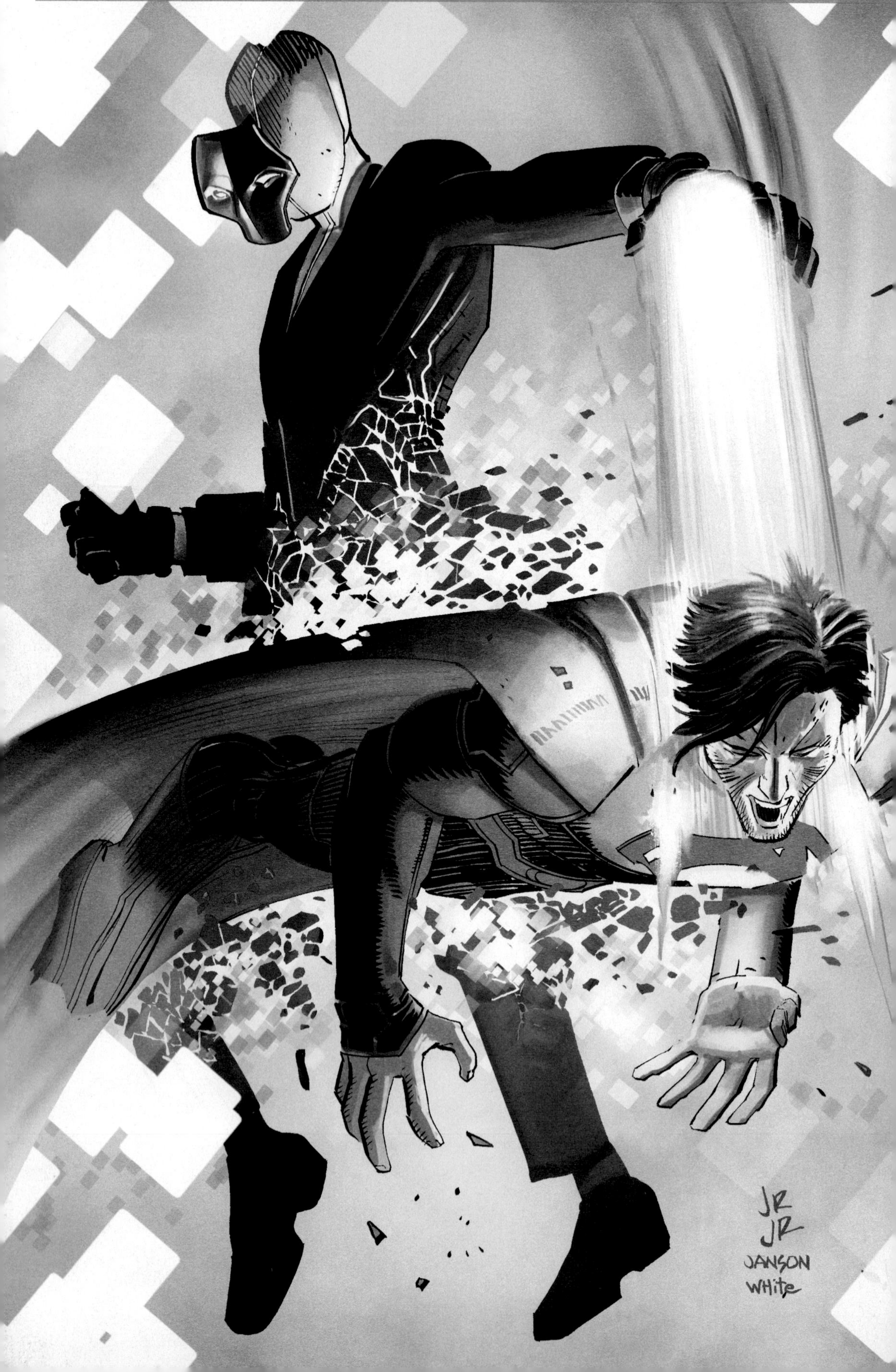
JR JR
JANSON
White

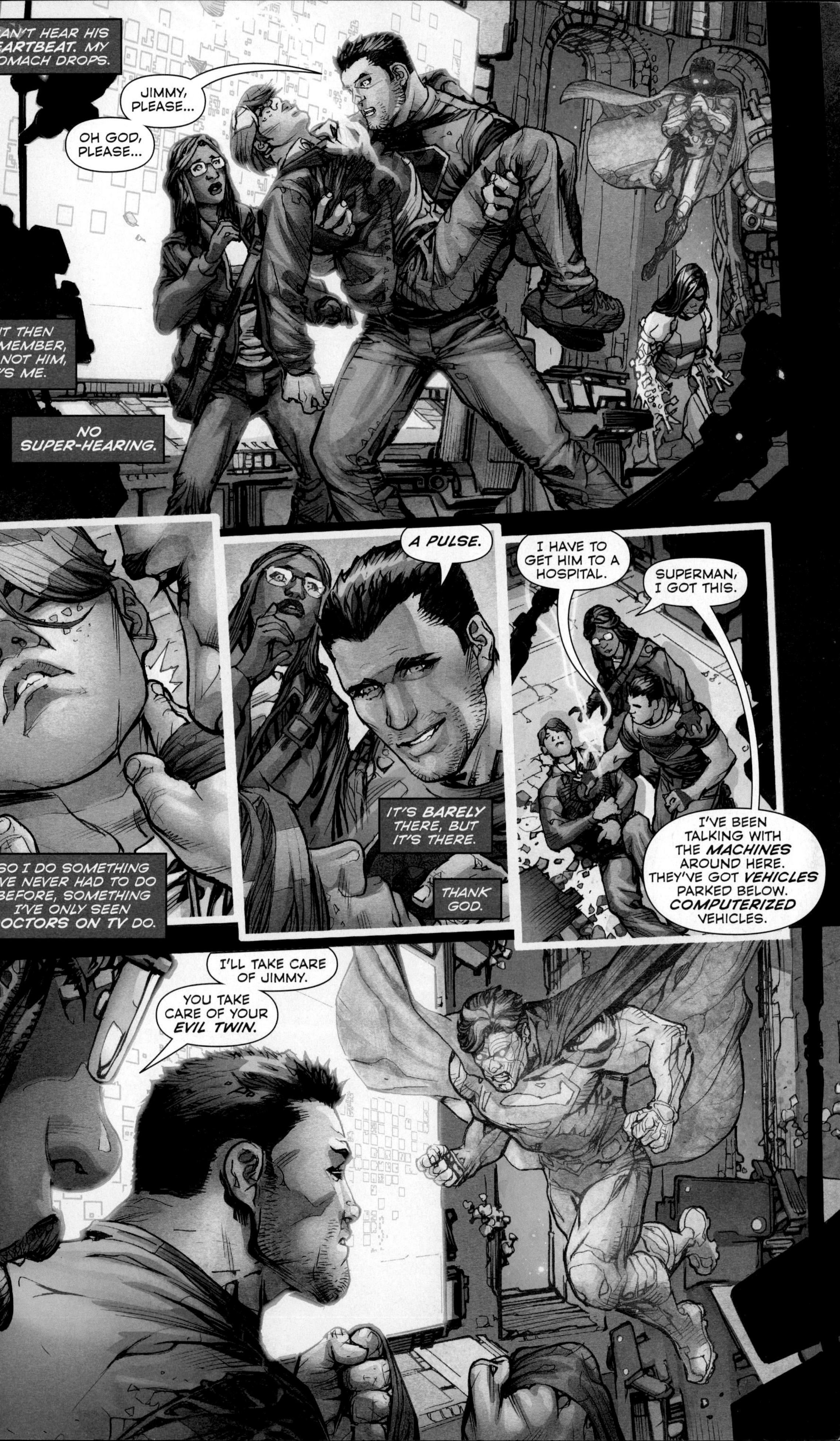

AN'T HEAR HIS EARTBEAT. MY OMACH DROPS.
JIMMY, PLEASE...
OH GOD, PLEASE...
IT THEN MEMBER, NOT HIM, 'S ME.
NO SUPER-HEARING.
SO I DO SOMETHING VE NEVER HAD TO DO BEFORE, SOMETHING I'VE ONLY SEEN OCTORS ON TV DO.
A PULSE.
IT'S BARELY THERE, BUT IT'S THERE.
THANK GOD.
I HAVE TO GET HIM TO A HOSPITAL.
SUPERMAN, I GOT THIS.
I'VE BEEN TALKING WITH THE MACHINES AROUND HERE. THEY'VE GOT VEHICLES PARKED BELOW. COMPUTERIZED VEHICLES.
I'LL TAKE CARE OF JIMMY.
YOU TAKE CARE OF YOUR EVIL TWIN.

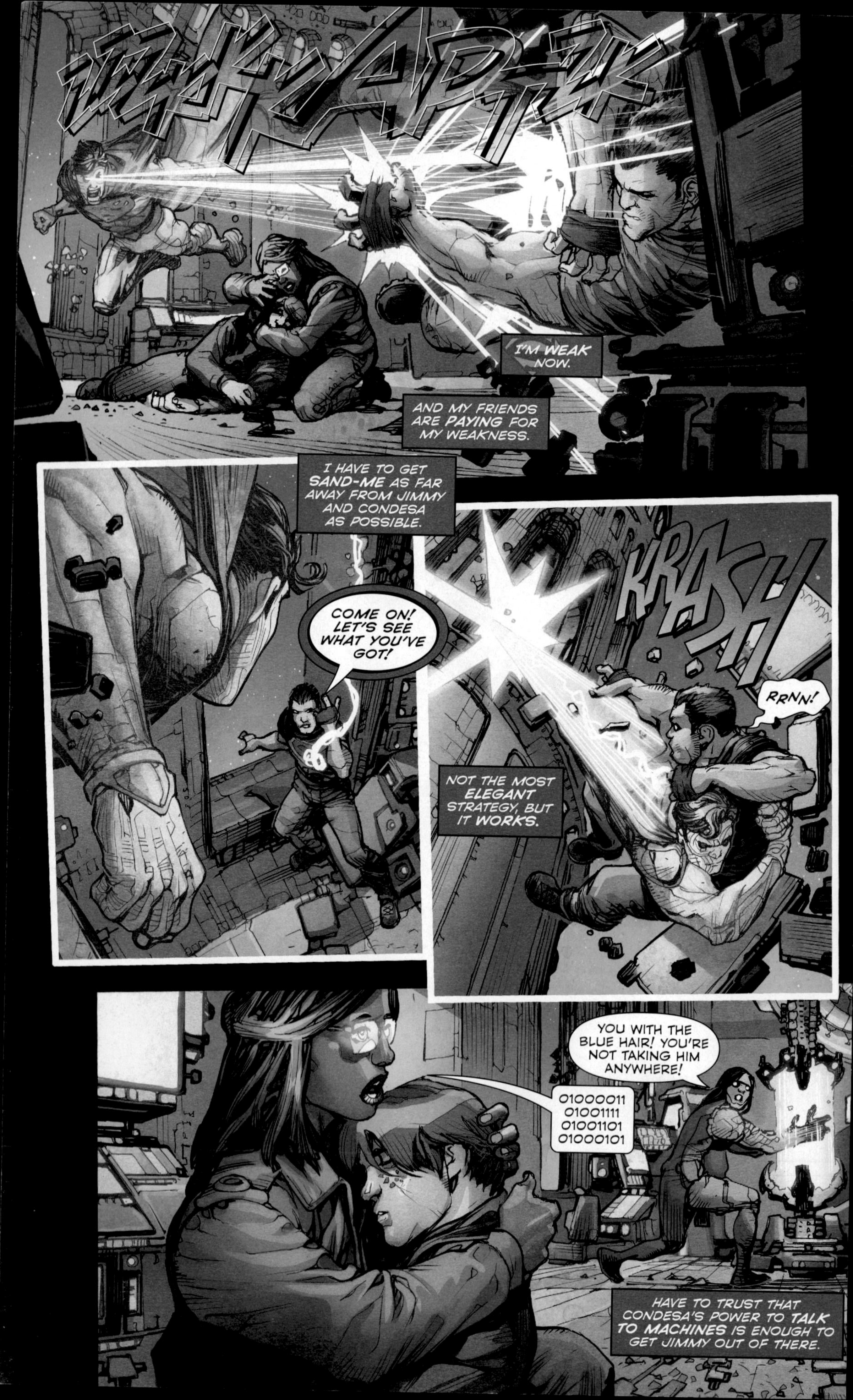

I'M WEAK NOW.
AND MY FRIENDS ARE PAYING FOR MY WEAKNESS.
I HAVE TO GET SAND-ME AS FAR AWAY FROM JIMMY AND CONDESA AS POSSIBLE.
COME ON! LET'S SEE WHAT YOU'VE GOT!
KRASH
RRNN!
NOT THE MOST ELEGANT STRATEGY, BUT IT WORKS.
YOU WITH THE BLUE HAIR! YOU'RE NOT TAKING HIM ANYWHERE!
01000011 01001111 01001101 01000101
HAVE TO TRUST THAT CONDESA'S POWER TO TALK TO MACHINES IS ENOUGH TO GET JIMMY OUT OF THERE.

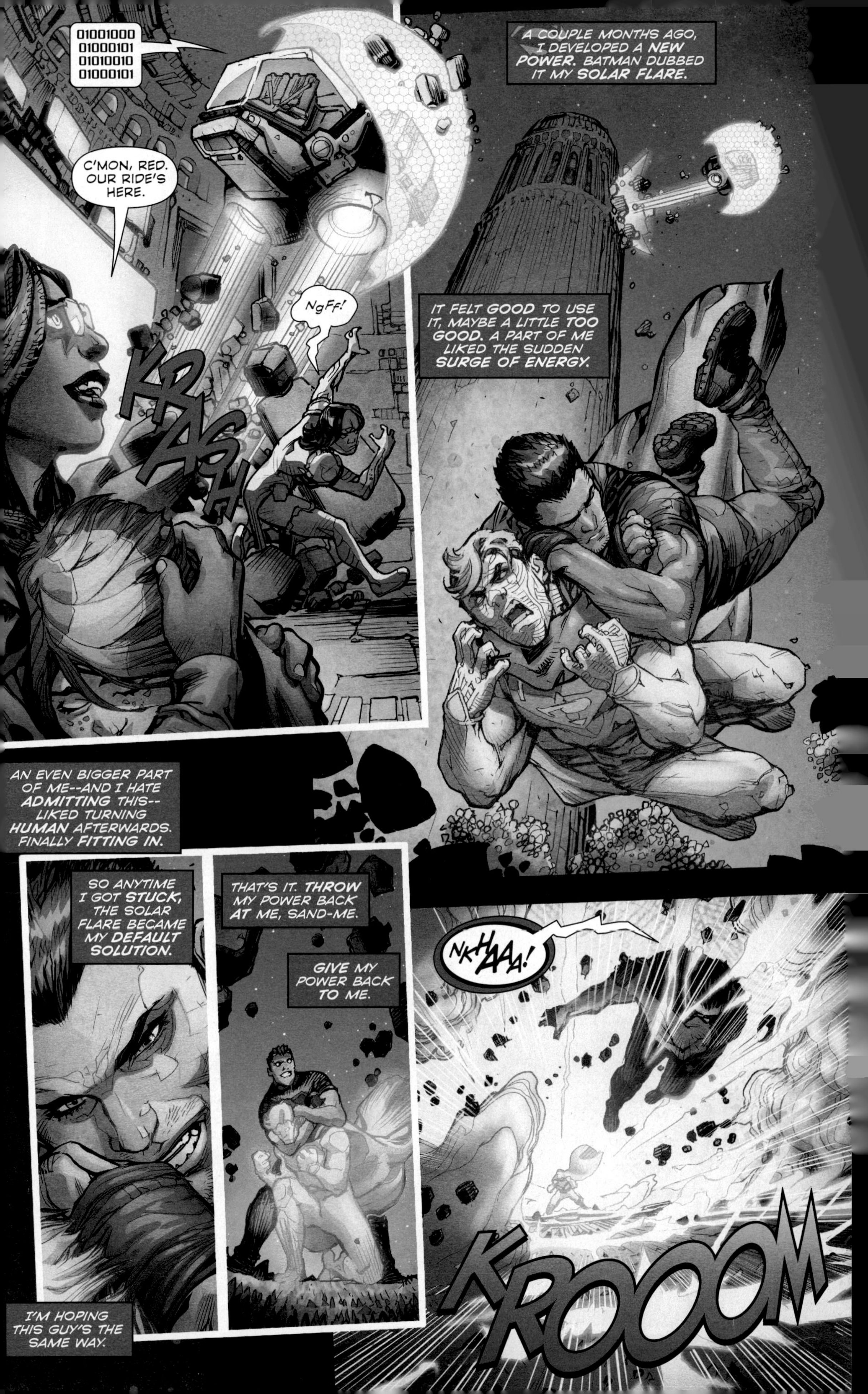
01001000
01000101
01010010
01000101
C'MON, RED. OUR RIDE'S HERE.
NgFf!
KRASH
A COUPLE MONTHS AGO, I DEVELOPED A NEW POWER. BATMAN DUBBED IT MY SOLAR FLARE.
IT FELT GOOD TO USE IT, MAYBE A LITTLE TOO GOOD. A PART OF ME LIKED THE SUDDEN SURGE OF ENERGY.
AN EVEN BIGGER PART OF ME--AND I HATE ADMITTING THIS--LIKED TURNING HUMAN AFTERWARDS. FINALLY FITTING IN.
SO ANYTIME I GOT STUCK, THE SOLAR FLARE BECAME MY DEFAULT SOLUTION.
I'M HOPING THIS GUY'S THE SAME WAY.
THAT'S IT. THROW MY POWER BACK AT ME, SAND-ME.
GIVE MY POWER BACK TO ME.
NKHAAA!
KROOOM

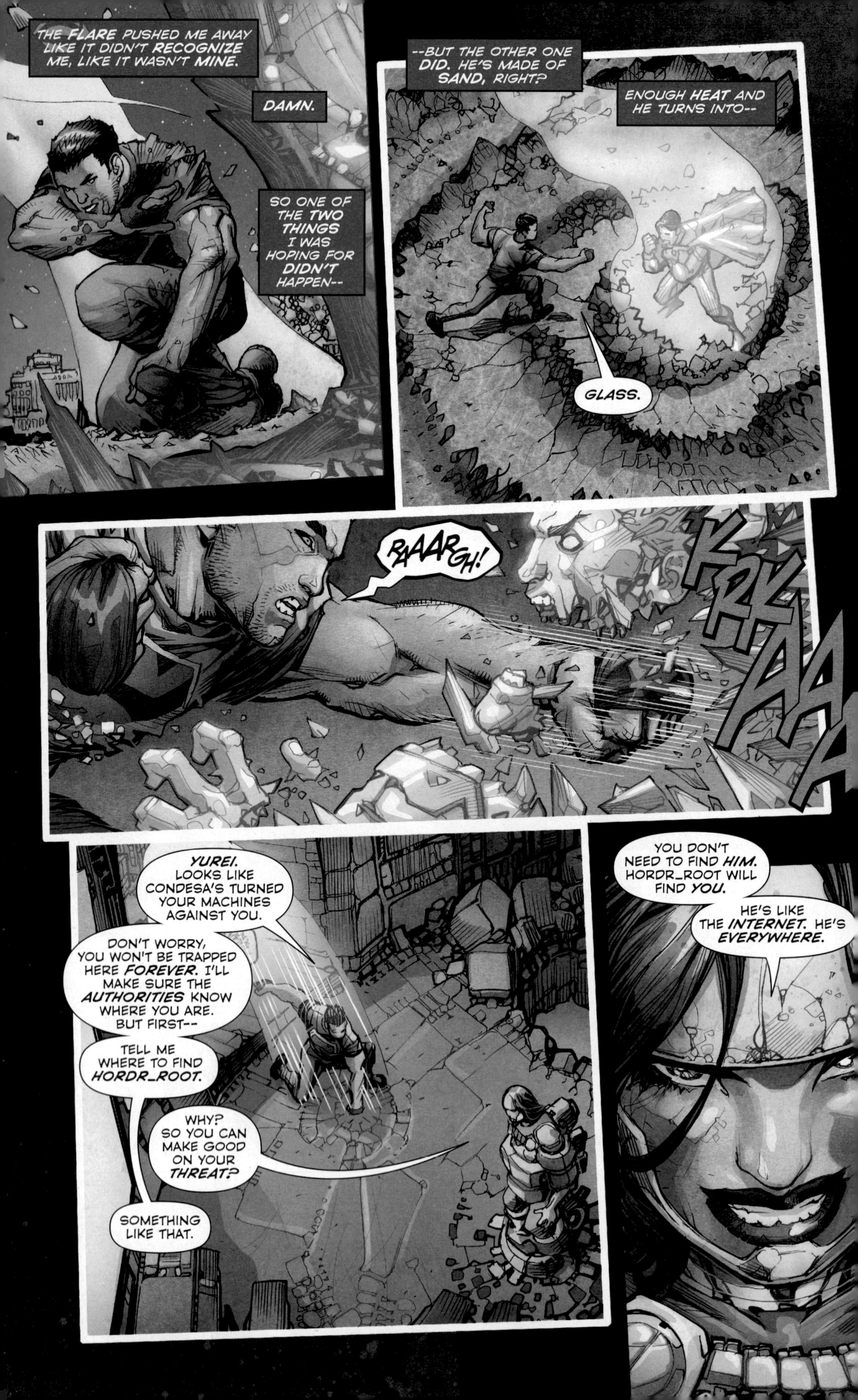
THE FLARE PUSHED ME AWAY LIKE IT DIDN'T RECOGNIZE ME, LIKE IT WASN'T MINE.
DAMN.
SO ONE OF THE TWO THINGS I WAS HOPING FOR DIDN'T HAPPEN--
--BUT THE OTHER ONE DID. HE'S MADE OF SAND, RIGHT?
ENOUGH HEAT AND HE TURNS INTO--
GLASS.
RAAARGH!
KRKAAA
YUREI. LOOKS LIKE CONDESA'S TURNED YOUR MACHINES AGAINST YOU.
DON'T WORRY, YOU WON'T BE TRAPPED HERE FOREVER. I'LL MAKE SURE THE AUTHORITIES KNOW WHERE YOU ARE. BUT FIRST--
TELL ME WHERE TO FIND HORDR_ROOT.
WHY? SO YOU CAN MAKE GOOD ON YOUR THREAT?
SOMETHING LIKE THAT.
YOU DON'T NEED TO FIND HIM. HORDR_ROOT WILL FIND YOU.
HE'S LIKE THE INTERNET. HE'S EVERYWHERE.

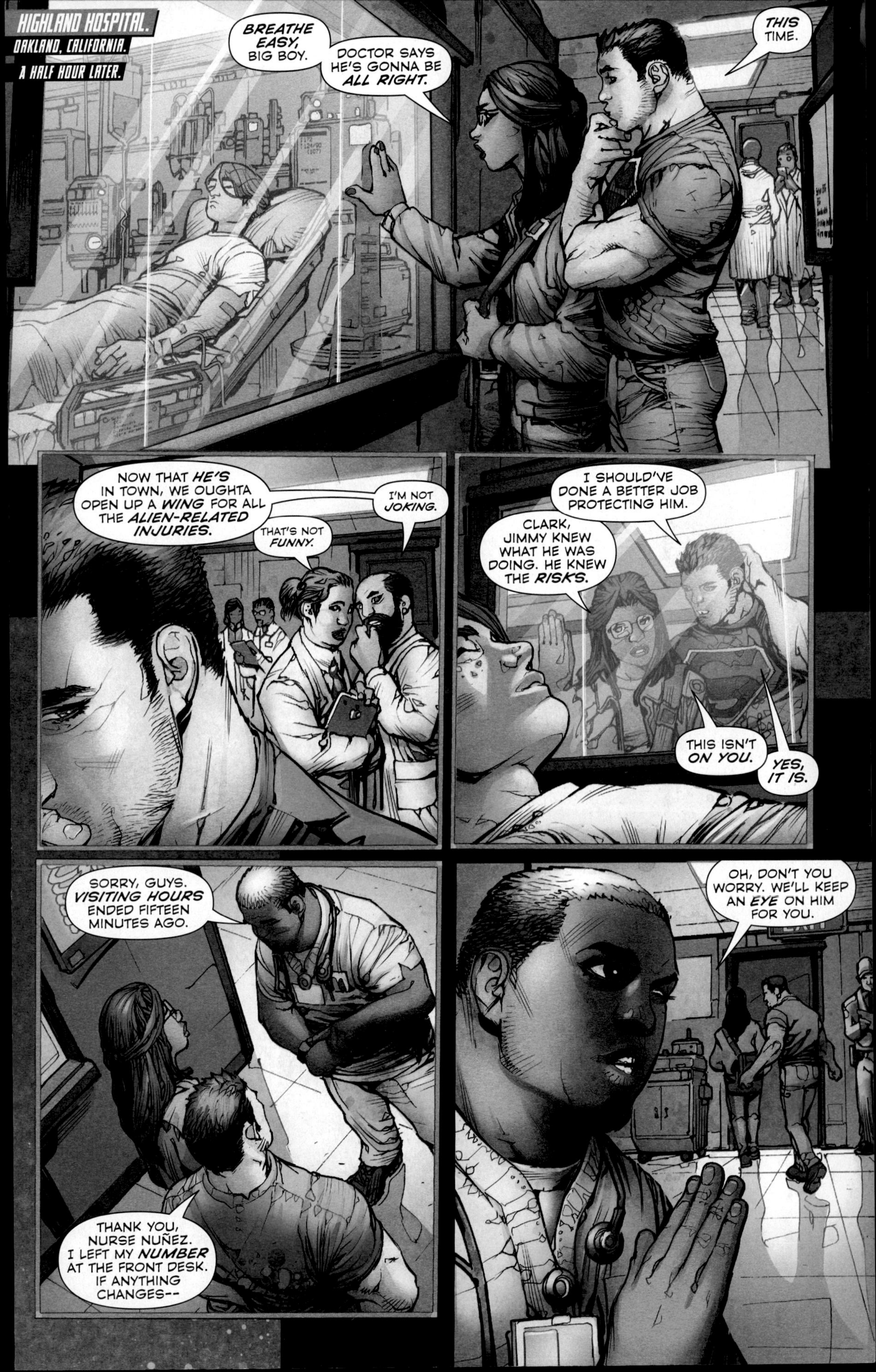
HIGHLAND HOSPITAL.
OAKLAND, CALIFORNIA.
A HALF HOUR LATER.
BREATHE EASY, BIG BOY.
DOCTOR SAYS HE'S GONNA BE ALL RIGHT.
THIS TIME.
NOW THAT HE'S IN TOWN, WE OUGHTA OPEN UP A WING FOR ALL THE ALIEN-RELATED INJURIES.
THAT'S NOT FUNNY.
I'M NOT JOKING.
I SHOULD'VE DONE A BETTER JOB PROTECTING HIM.
CLARK, JIMMY KNEW WHAT HE WAS DOING. HE KNEW THE RISKS.
THIS ISN'T ON YOU.
YES, IT IS.
SORRY, GUYS. VISITING HOURS ENDED FIFTEEN MINUTES AGO.
THANK YOU, NURSE NUÑEZ. I LEFT MY NUMBER AT THE FRONT DESK. IF ANYTHING CHANGES--
OH, DON'T YOU WORRY. WE'LL KEEP AN EYE ON HIM FOR YOU.

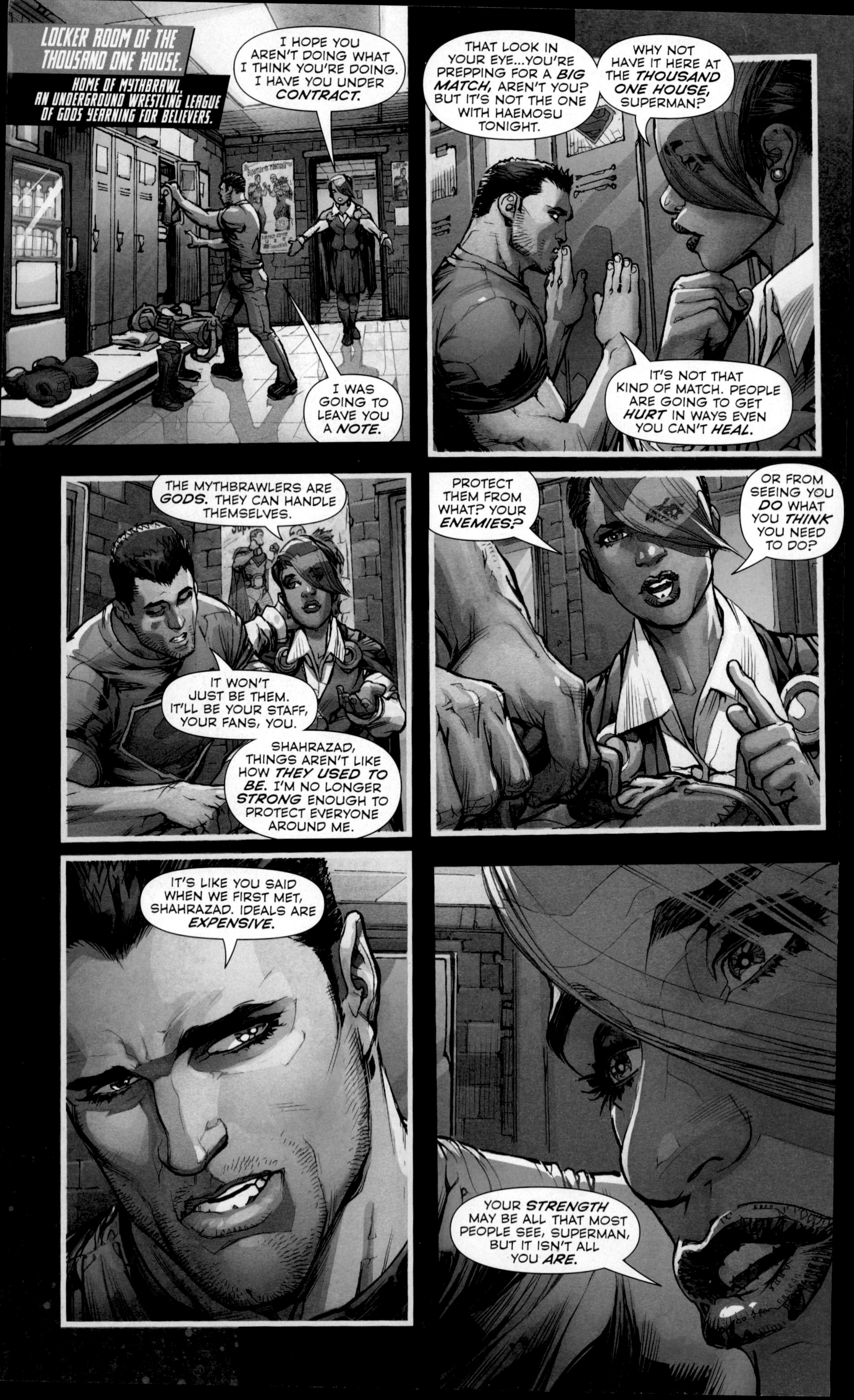

LOCKER ROOM OF THE THOUSAND ONE HOUSE.
HOME OF MYTHBRAWL, AN UNDERGROUND WRESTLING LEAGUE OF GODS YEARNING FOR BELIEVERS.
I HOPE YOU AREN'T DOING WHAT I THINK YOU'RE DOING. I HAVE YOU UNDER CONTRACT.
I WAS GOING TO LEAVE YOU A NOTE.
THAT LOOK IN YOUR EYE...YOU'RE PREPPING FOR A BIG MATCH, AREN'T YOU? BUT IT'S NOT THE ONE WITH HAEMOSU TONIGHT.
WHY NOT HAVE IT HERE AT THE THOUSAND ONE HOUSE, SUPERMAN?
IT'S NOT THAT KIND OF MATCH. PEOPLE ARE GOING TO GET HURT IN WAYS EVEN YOU CAN'T HEAL.
THE MYTHBRAWLERS ARE GODS. THEY CAN HANDLE THEMSELVES.
IT WON'T JUST BE THEM. IT'LL BE YOUR STAFF, YOUR FANS, YOU.
SHAHRAZAD, THINGS AREN'T LIKE HOW THEY USED TO BE. I'M NO LONGER STRONG ENOUGH TO PROTECT EVERYONE AROUND ME.
PROTECT THEM FROM WHAT? YOUR ENEMIES?
OR FROM SEEING YOU DO WHAT YOU THINK YOU NEED TO DO?
IT'S LIKE YOU SAID WHEN WE FIRST MET, SHAHRAZAD. IDEALS ARE EXPENSIVE.
YOUR STRENGTH MAY BE ALL THAT MOST PEOPLE SEE, SUPERMAN, BUT IT ISN'T ALL YOU ARE.

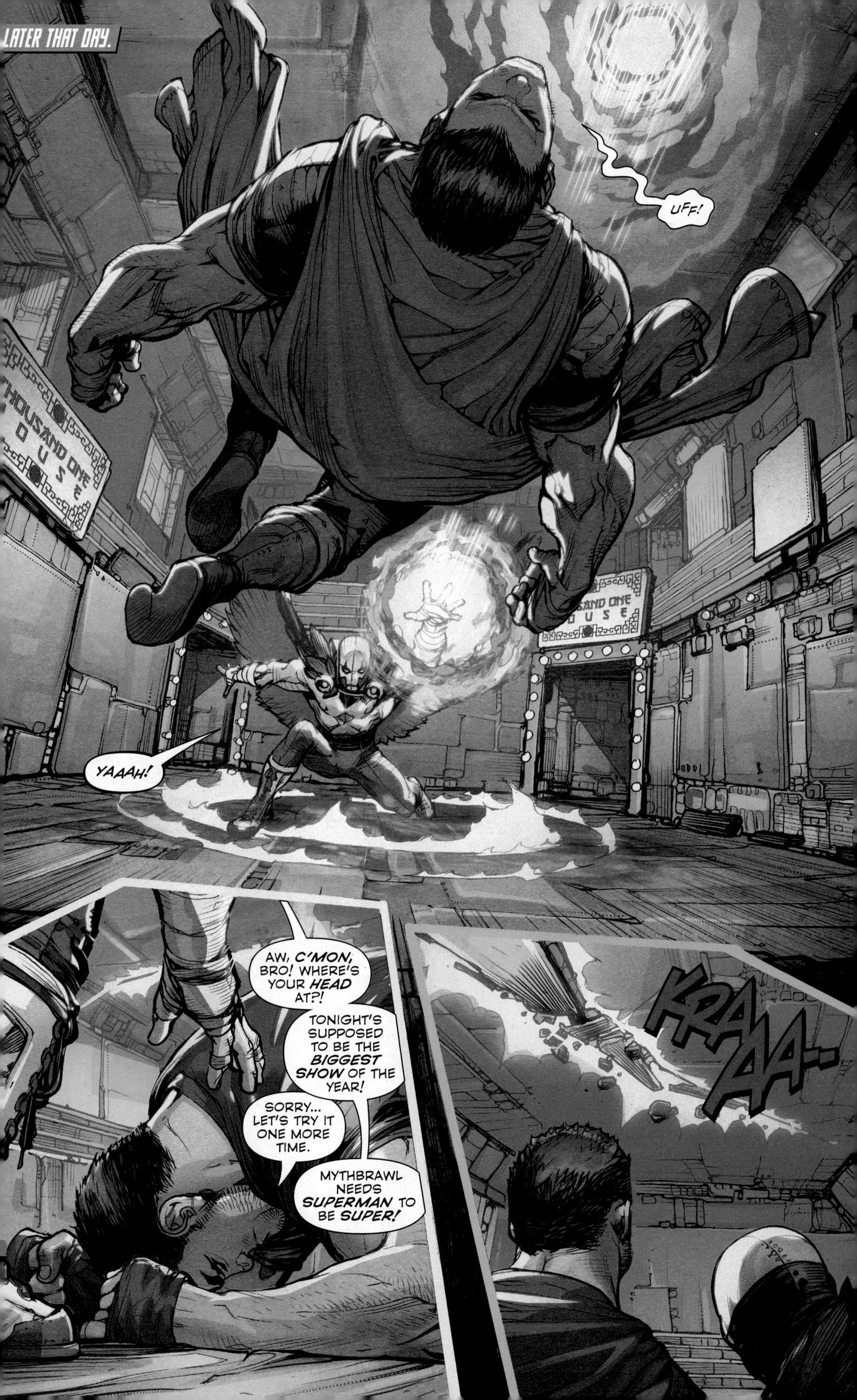
LATER THAT DAY.
UFF!
THOUSAND ONE
O U S E
YAAAH!
AW, C'MON, BRO! WHERE'S YOUR HEAD AT?!
TONIGHT'S SUPPOSED TO BE THE BIGGEST SHOW OF THE YEAR!
SORRY... LET'S TRY IT ONE MORE TIME.
MYTHBRAWL NEEDS SUPERMAN TO BE SUPER!
KRAAAA-

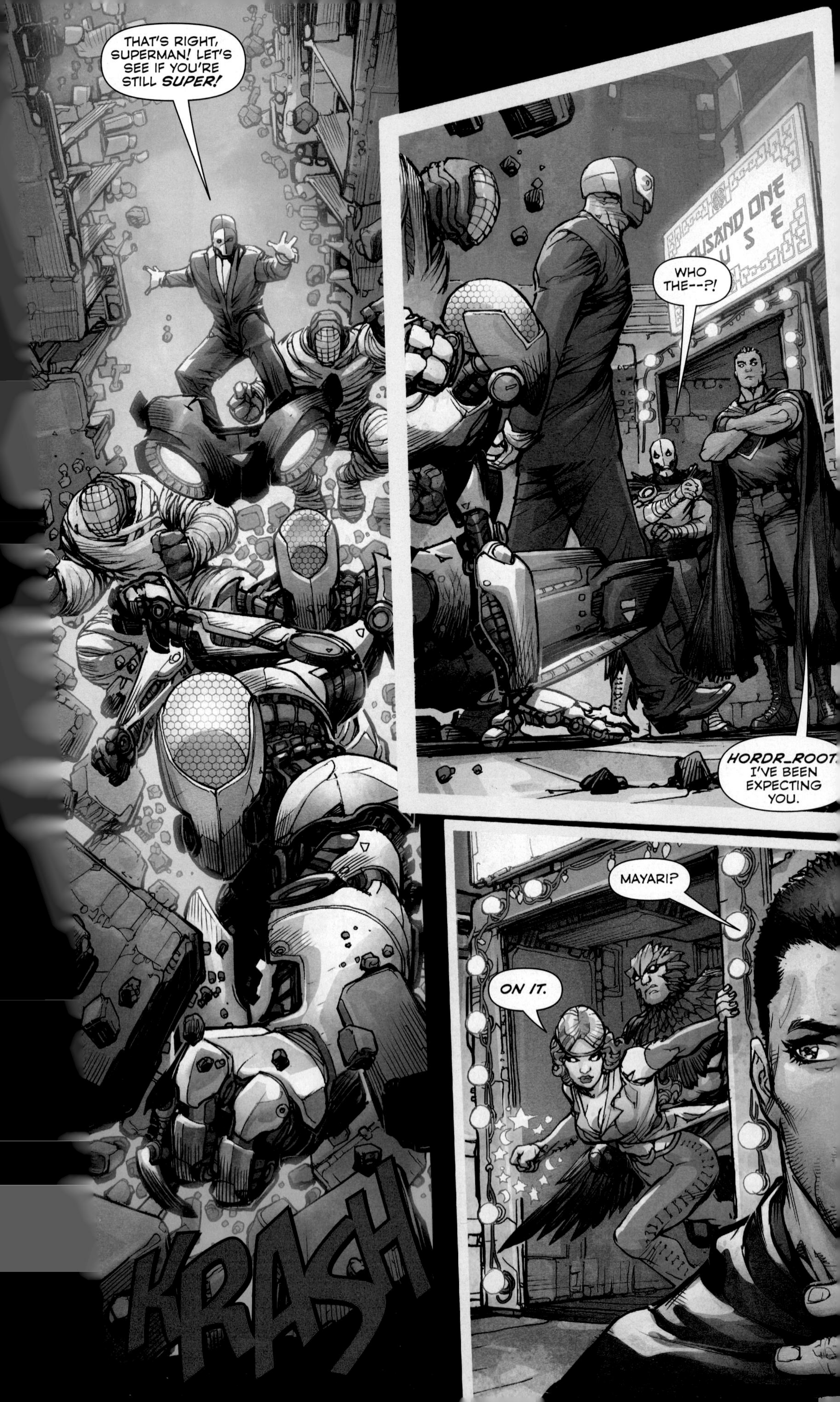
THAT'S RIGHT, SUPERMAN! LET'S SEE IF YOU'RE STILL SUPER!
KRASH
WHO THE--?!
HORDR_ROOT. I'VE BEEN EXPECTING YOU.
MAYARI?
ON IT.

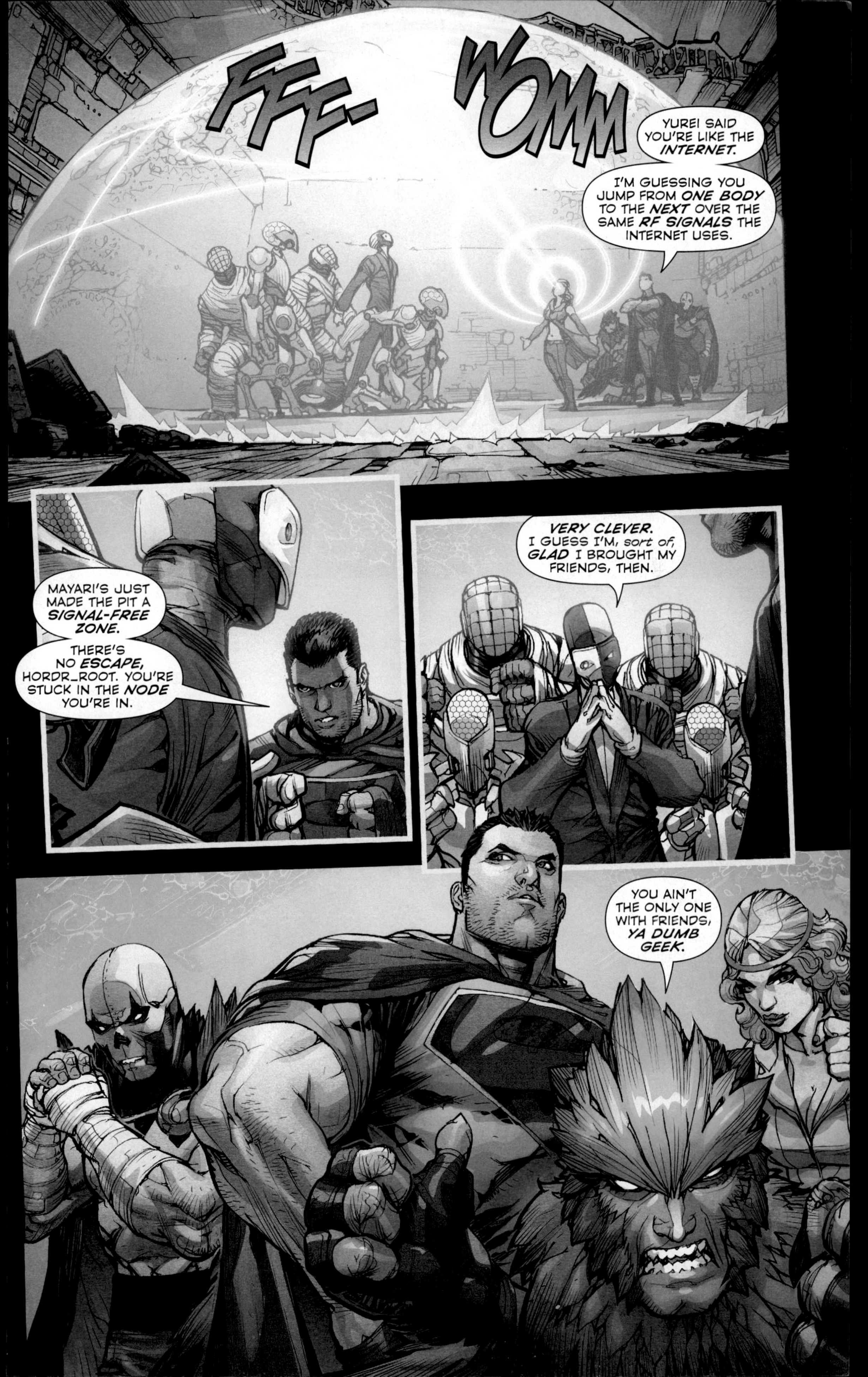

FFF- WOMM
YUREI SAID YOU'RE LIKE THE *INTERNET.*
I'M GUESSING YOU JUMP FROM *ONE BODY* TO THE *NEXT* OVER THE SAME *RF SIGNALS* THE INTERNET USES.
MAYARI'S JUST MADE THE PIT A *SIGNAL-FREE ZONE.*
THERE'S NO *ESCAPE,* HORDR_ROOT. YOU'RE STUCK IN THE *NODE* YOU'RE IN.
VERY CLEVER. I GUESS I'M, *sort of,* *GLAD* I BROUGHT MY FRIENDS, THEN.
YOU AIN'T THE ONLY ONE WITH FRIENDS, *YA DUMB GEEK.*

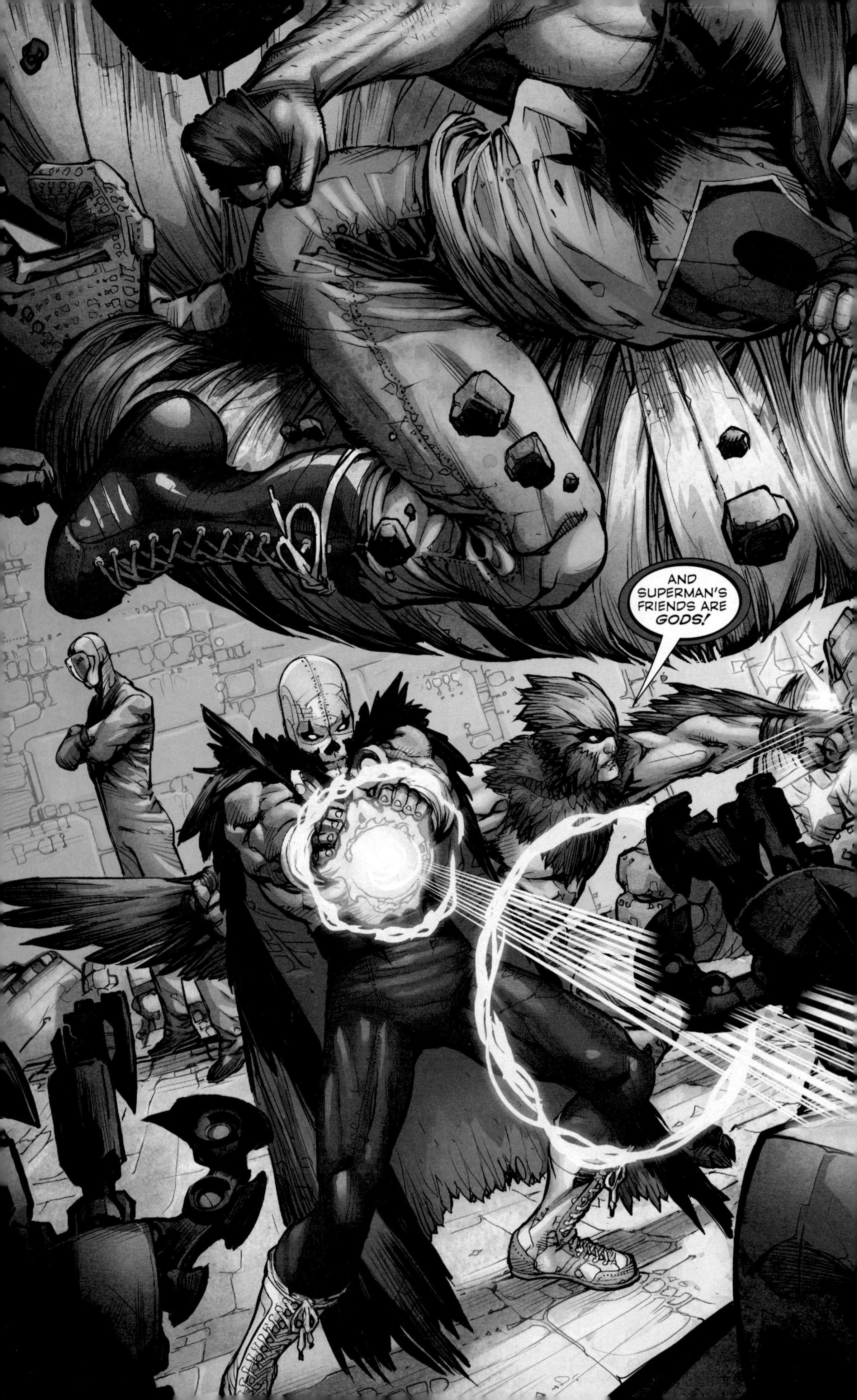
AND SUPERMAN'S FRIENDS ARE *GODS!*

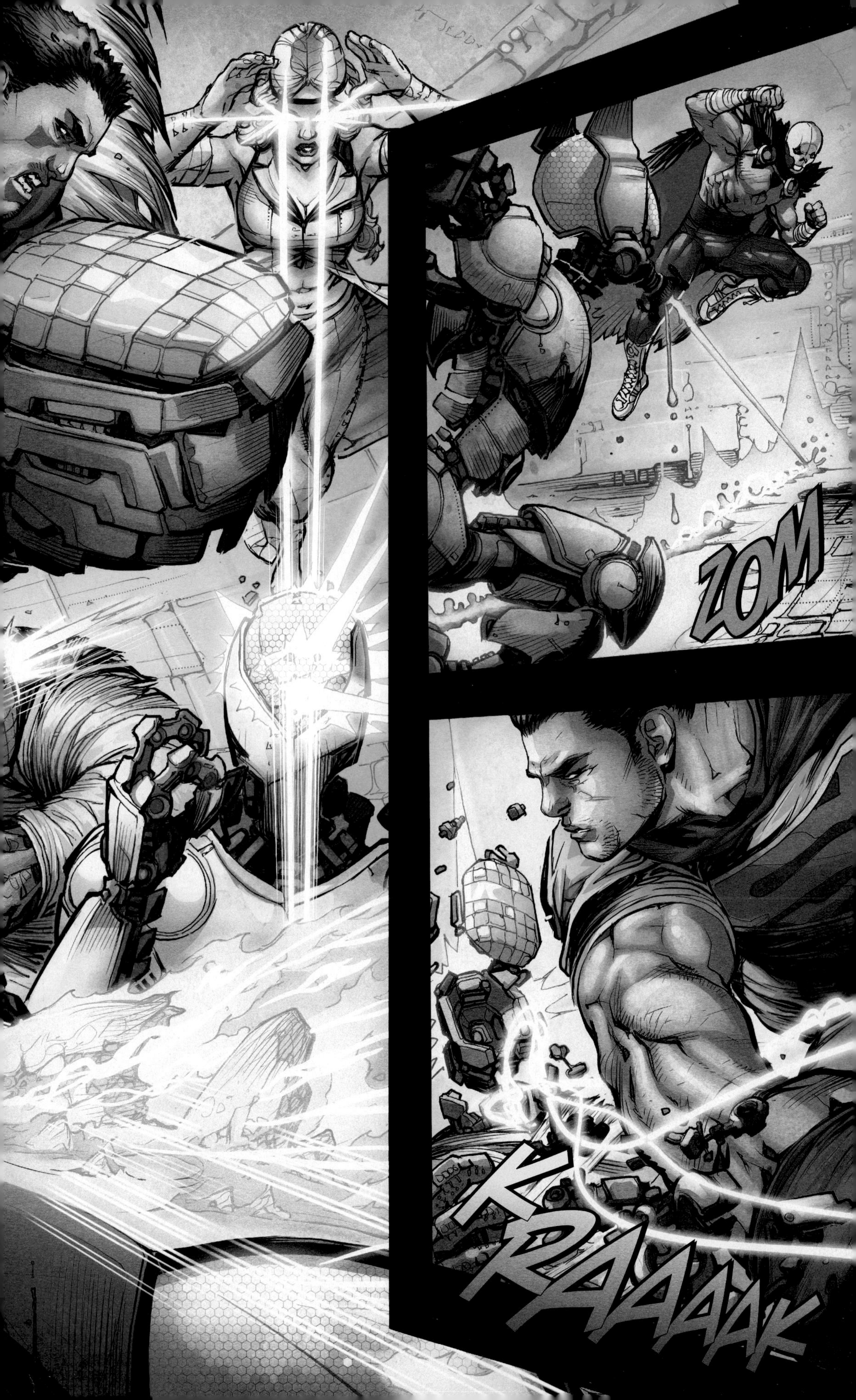
ZOM
KRAAAAK

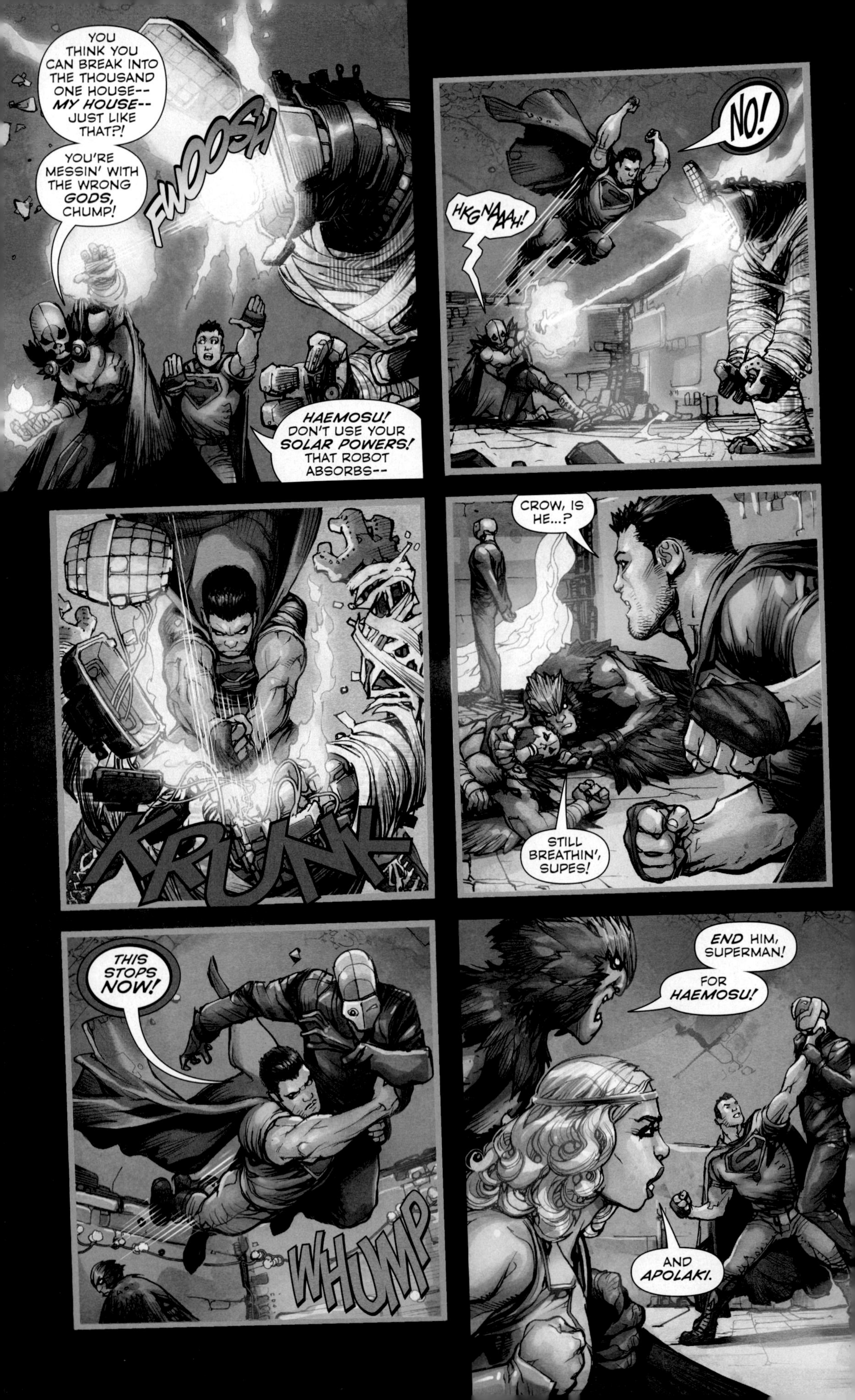

YOU THINK YOU CAN BREAK INTO THE THOUSAND ONE HOUSE-- MY HOUSE-- JUST LIKE THAT?!
YOU'RE MESSIN' WITH THE WRONG GODS, CHUMP!
FWOOSH
HAEMOSU! DON'T USE YOUR SOLAR POWERS! THAT ROBOT ABSORBS--
NO!
HKGNAAAH!
KRUNK
CROW, IS HE...?
STILL BREATHIN', SUPES!
THIS STOPS NOW!
WHUMP
END HIM, SUPERMAN!
FOR HAEMOSU!
AND APOLAKI.

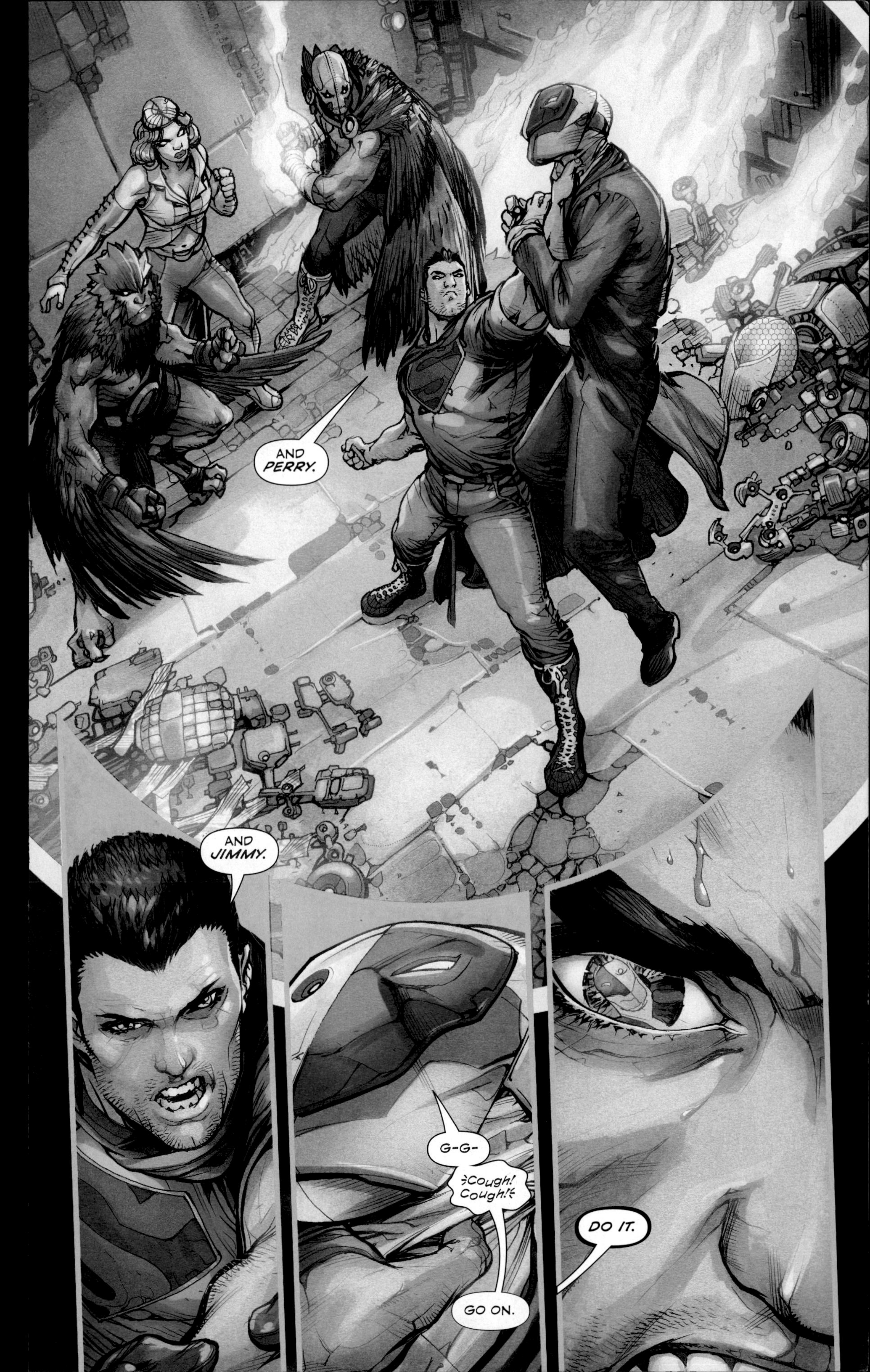
AND PERRY.
AND JIMMY.
G-G-
Cough! Cough!
GO ON.
DO IT.

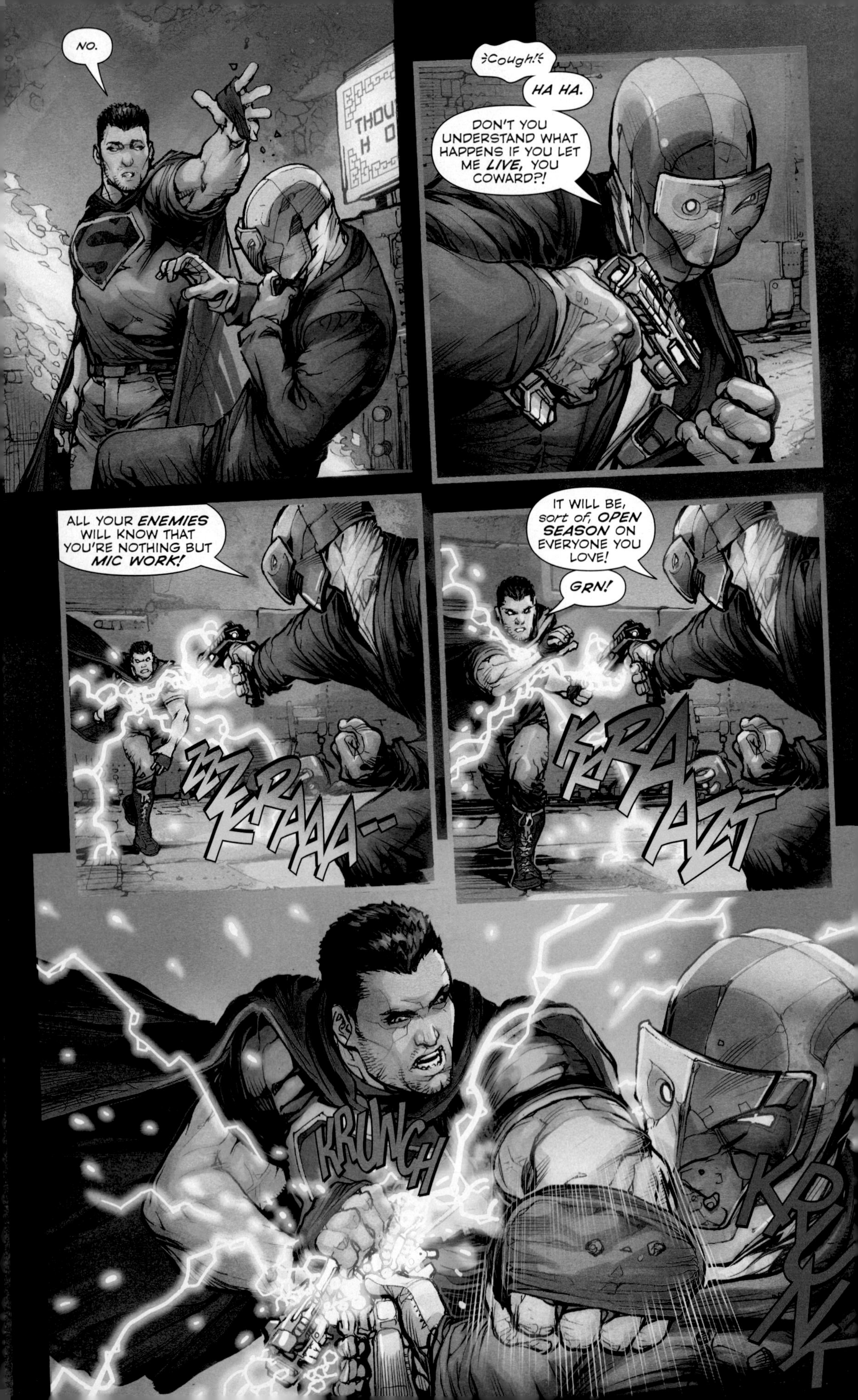
NO.
Cough!
HA HA.
DON'T YOU UNDERSTAND WHAT HAPPENS IF YOU LET ME LIVE, YOU COWARD?!
ALL YOUR ENEMIES WILL KNOW THAT YOU'RE NOTHING BUT MIC WORK!
ZZZKRAAA--
IT WILL BE, sort of, OPEN SEASON ON EVERYONE YOU LOVE!
GRN!
KRAAZT
KRUNCH

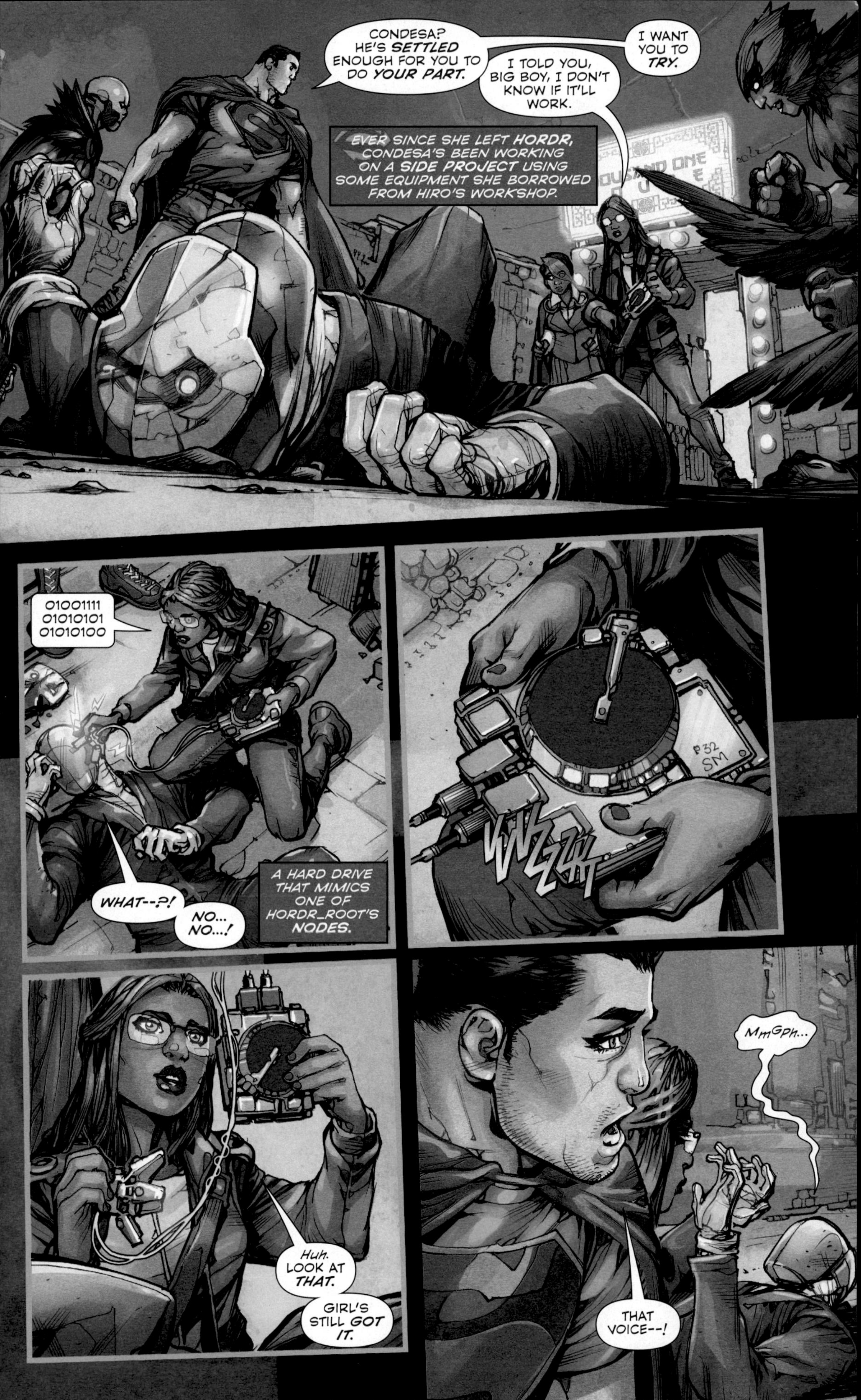
CONDESA? HE'S SETTLED ENOUGH FOR YOU TO DO YOUR PART.
I WANT YOU TO TRY.
I TOLD YOU, BIG BOY, I DON'T KNOW IF IT'LL WORK.
EVER SINCE SHE LEFT HORDR, CONDESA'S BEEN WORKING ON A SIDE PROJECT USING SOME EQUIPMENT SHE BORROWED FROM HIRO'S WORKSHOP.
01001111 01010101 01010100
WHAT--?!
NO... NO...!
A HARD DRIVE THAT MIMICS ONE OF HORDR_ROOT'S NODES.
P32 SM
VVVZZZKT
Huh. LOOK AT THAT.
GIRL'S STILL GOT IT.
MmGph...
THAT VOICE--!

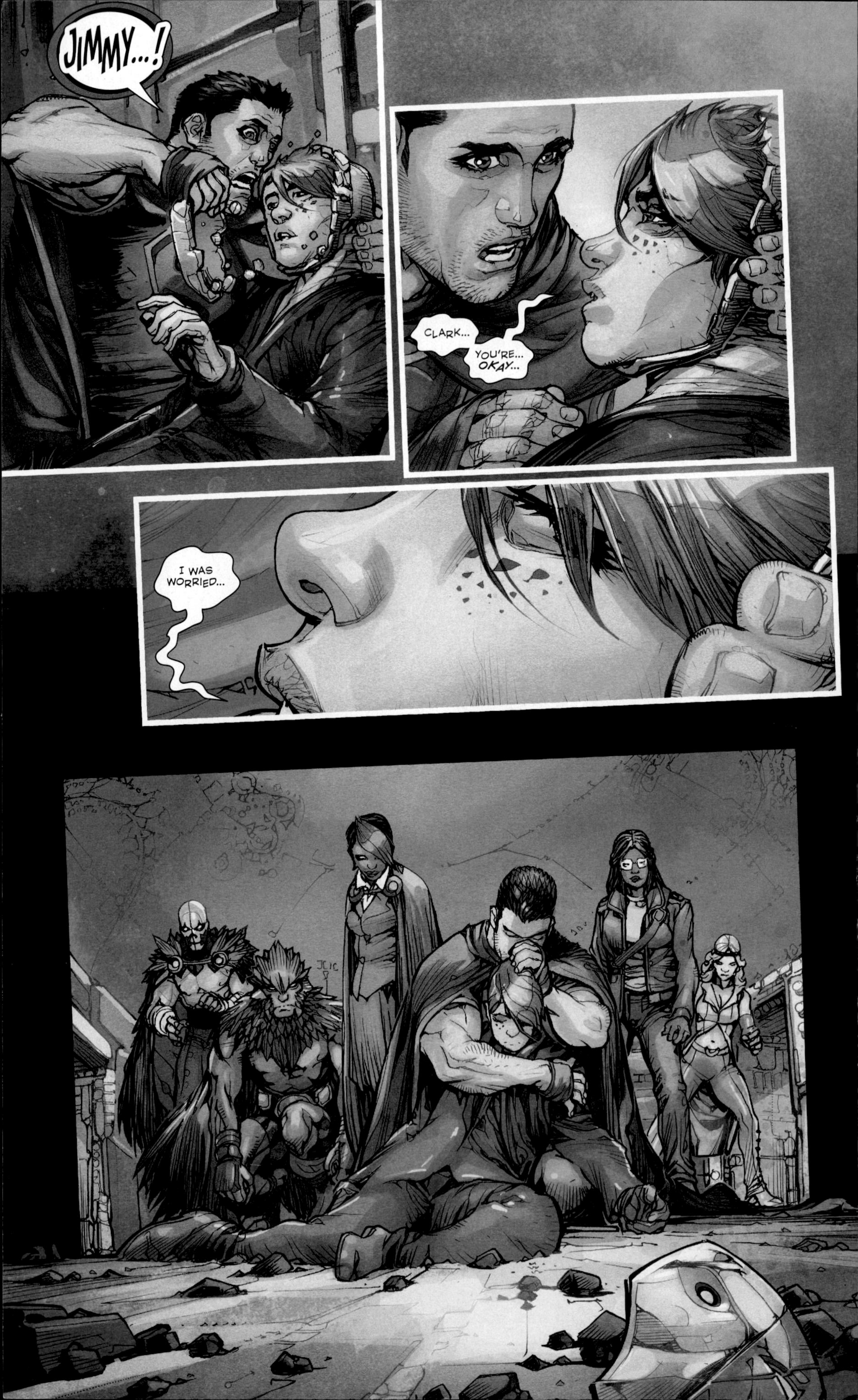
JIMMY...!
CLARK...
YOU'RE... OKAY...
I WAS WORRIED...

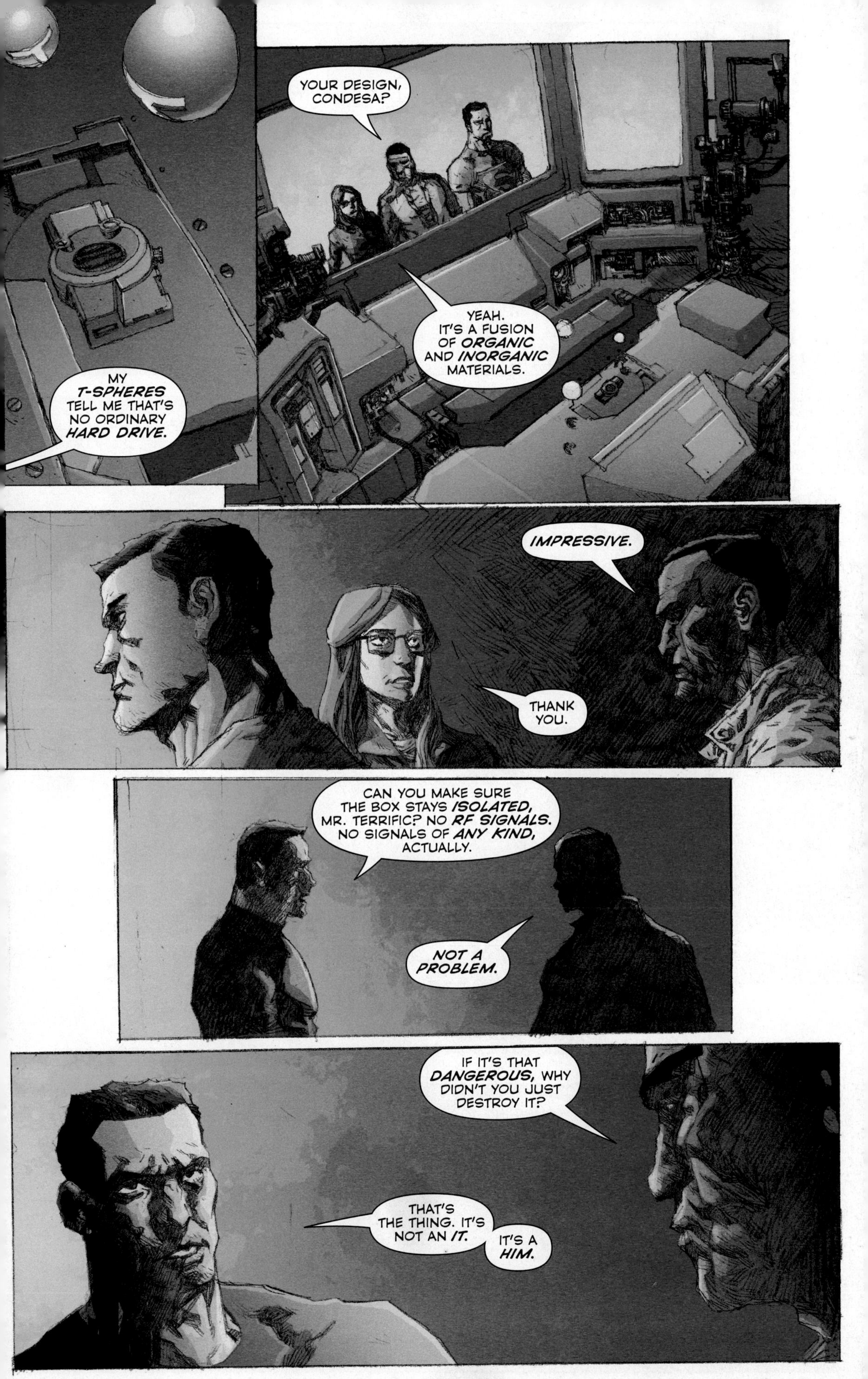
MY T-SPHERES TELL ME THAT'S NO ORDINARY HARD DRIVE.
YOUR DESIGN, CONDESA?
YEAH. IT'S A FUSION OF ORGANIC AND INORGANIC MATERIALS.
IMPRESSIVE.
THANK YOU.
CAN YOU MAKE SURE THE BOX STAYS ISOLATED, MR. TERRIFIC? NO RF SIGNALS. NO SIGNALS OF ANY KIND, ACTUALLY.
NOT A PROBLEM.
IF IT'S THAT DANGEROUS, WHY DIDN'T YOU JUST DESTROY IT?
THAT'S THE THING. IT'S NOT AN IT.
IT'S A HIM.

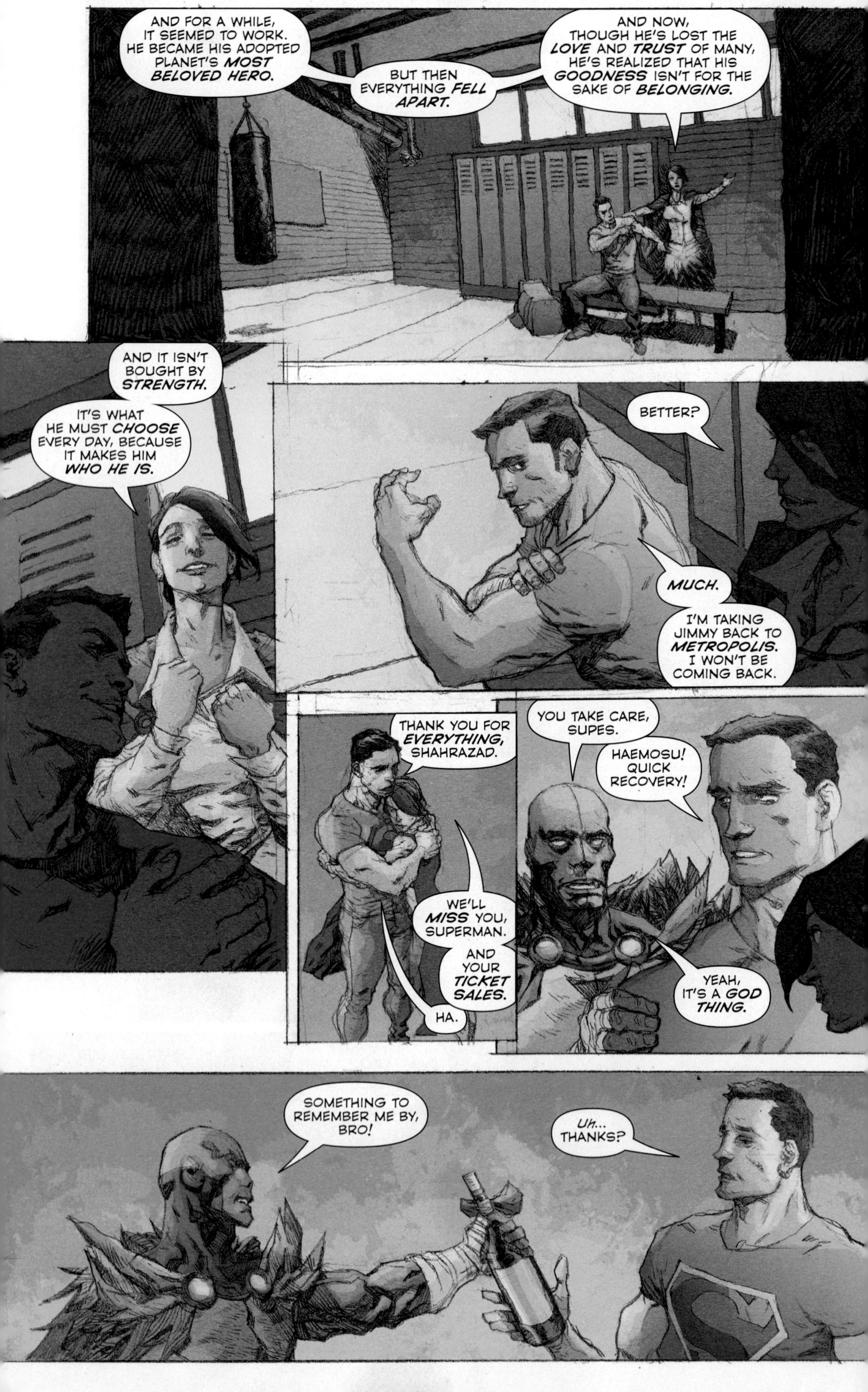
AND FOR A WHILE, IT SEEMED TO WORK. HE BECAME HIS ADOPTED PLANET'S MOST BELOVED HERO.
BUT THEN EVERYTHING FELL APART.
AND NOW, THOUGH HE'S LOST THE LOVE AND TRUST OF MANY, HE'S REALIZED THAT HIS GOODNESS ISN'T FOR THE SAKE OF BELONGING.
AND IT ISN'T BOUGHT BY STRENGTH.
IT'S WHAT HE MUST CHOOSE EVERY DAY, BECAUSE IT MAKES HIM WHO HE IS.
BETTER?
MUCH.
I'M TAKING JIMMY BACK TO METROPOLIS. I WON'T BE COMING BACK.
THANK YOU FOR EVERYTHING, SHAHRAZAD.
WE'LL MISS YOU, SUPERMAN.
AND YOUR TICKET SALES.
HA.
YOU TAKE CARE, SUPES.
HAEMOSU! QUICK RECOVERY!
YEAH, IT'S A GOD THING.
SOMETHING TO REMEMBER ME BY, BRO!
Uh... THANKS?

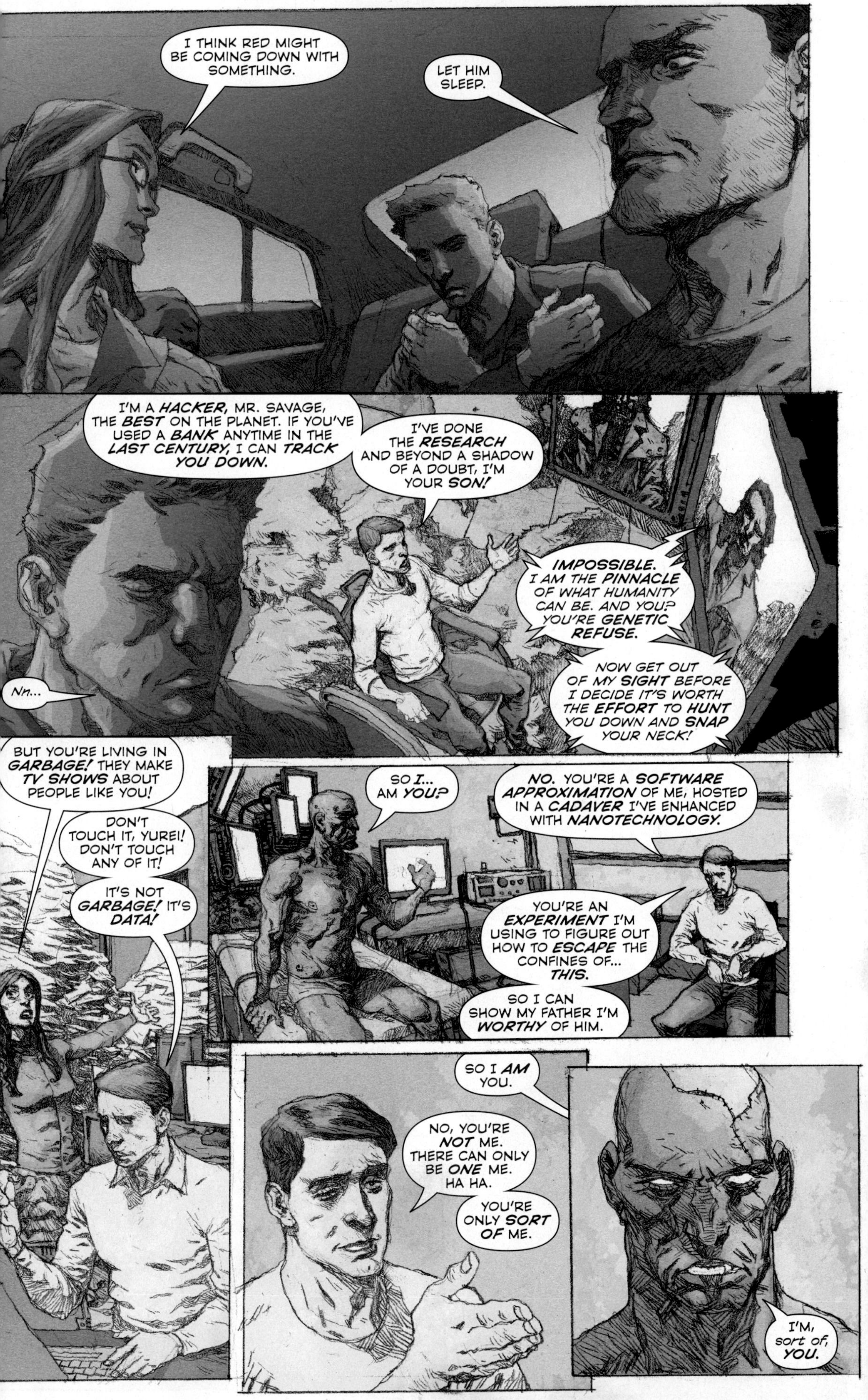

I THINK RED MIGHT BE COMING DOWN WITH SOMETHING.
LET HIM SLEEP.
I'M A HACKER, MR. SAVAGE, THE BEST ON THE PLANET. IF YOU'VE USED A BANK ANYTIME IN THE LAST CENTURY, I CAN TRACK YOU DOWN.
I'VE DONE THE RESEARCH AND BEYOND A SHADOW OF A DOUBT, I'M YOUR SON!
Nn...
IMPOSSIBLE. I AM THE PINNACLE OF WHAT HUMANITY CAN BE. AND YOU? YOU'RE GENETIC REFUSE.
NOW GET OUT OF MY SIGHT BEFORE I DECIDE IT'S WORTH THE EFFORT TO HUNT YOU DOWN AND SNAP YOUR NECK!
BUT YOU'RE LIVING IN GARBAGE! THEY MAKE TV SHOWS ABOUT PEOPLE LIKE YOU!
DON'T TOUCH IT, YUREI! DON'T TOUCH ANY OF IT!
IT'S NOT GARBAGE! IT'S DATA!
SO I... AM YOU?
NO. YOU'RE A SOFTWARE APPROXIMATION OF ME, HOSTED IN A CADAVER I'VE ENHANCED WITH NANOTECHNOLOGY.
YOU'RE AN EXPERIMENT I'M USING TO FIGURE OUT HOW TO ESCAPE THE CONFINES OF... THIS.
SO I CAN SHOW MY FATHER I'M WORTHY OF HIM.
SO I AM YOU.
NO, YOU'RE NOT ME. THERE CAN ONLY BE ONE ME. HA HA.
YOU'RE ONLY SORT OF ME.
I'M, sort of, YOU.

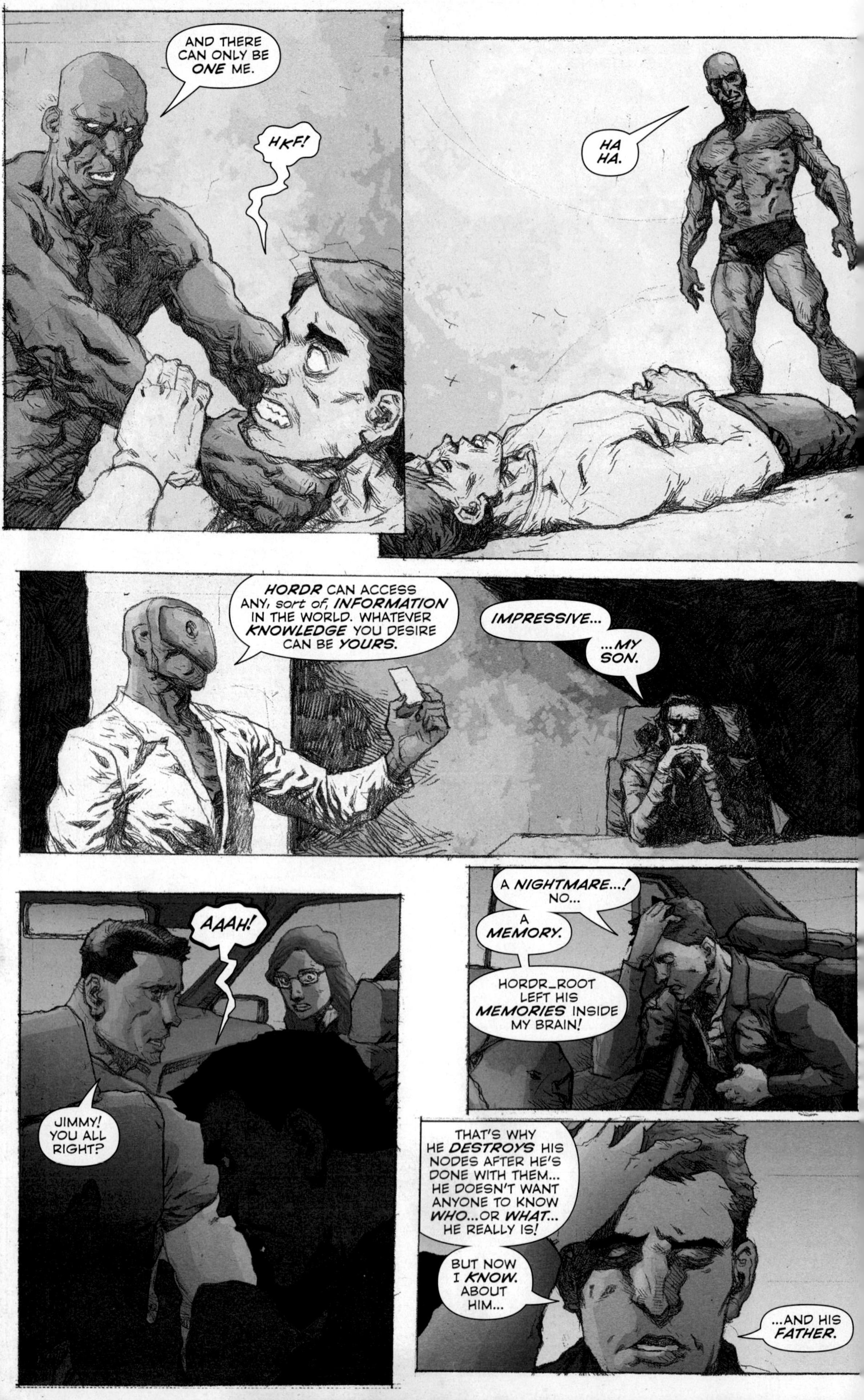
AND THERE CAN ONLY BE ONE ME.
HKF!
HA HA.
HORDR CAN ACCESS ANY, sort of, INFORMATION IN THE WORLD. WHATEVER KNOWLEDGE YOU DESIRE CAN BE YOURS.
IMPRESSIVE...
...MY SON.
AAAH!
JIMMY! YOU ALL RIGHT?
A NIGHTMARE...! NO...
A MEMORY.
HORDR_ROOT LEFT HIS MEMORIES INSIDE MY BRAIN!
THAT'S WHY HE DESTROYS HIS NODES AFTER HE'S DONE WITH THEM... HE DOESN'T WANT ANYONE TO KNOW WHO...OR WHAT... HE REALLY IS!
BUT NOW I KNOW. ABOUT HIM...
...AND HIS FATHER.

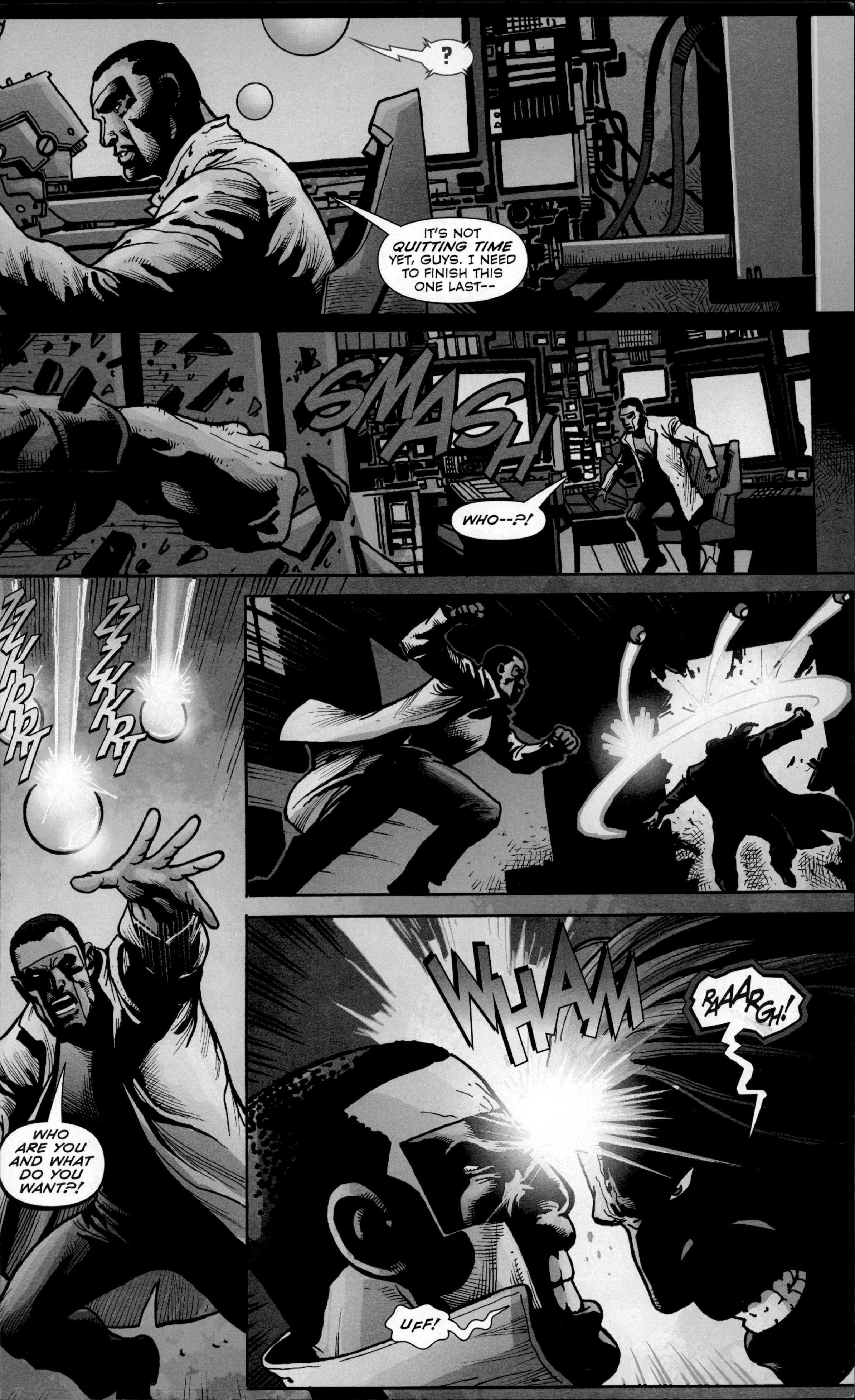
?
IT'S NOT QUITTING TIME YET, GUYS. I NEED TO FINISH THIS ONE LAST--
SMASH
WHO--?!
ZZZKRRT
ZZZKRT
WHO ARE YOU AND WHAT DO YOU WANT?!
WHAM
RAAARGH!
UFF!

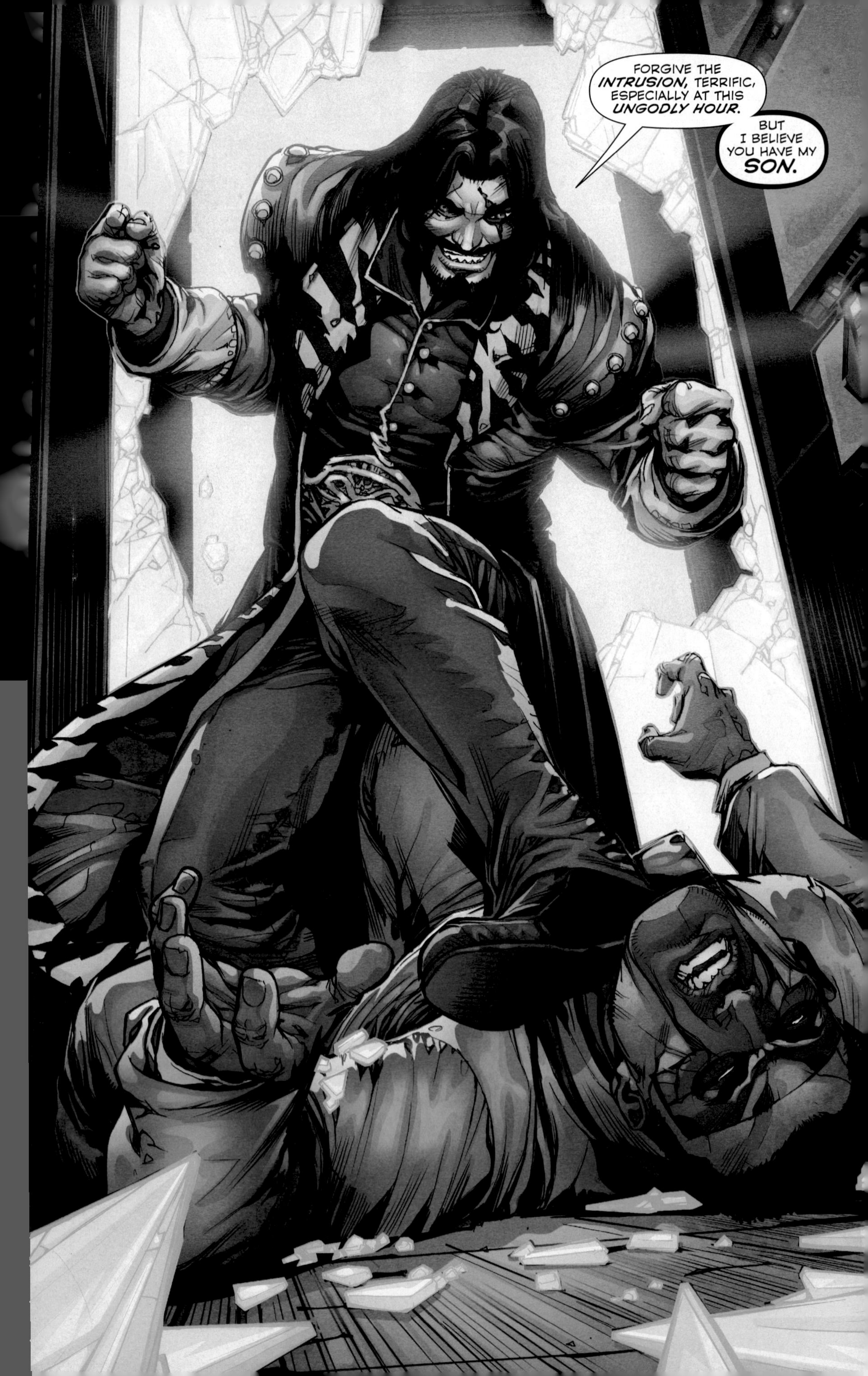
FORGIVE THE INTRUSION, TERRIFIC, ESPECIALLY AT THIS UNGODLY HOUR.
BUT I BELIEVE YOU HAVE MY SON.

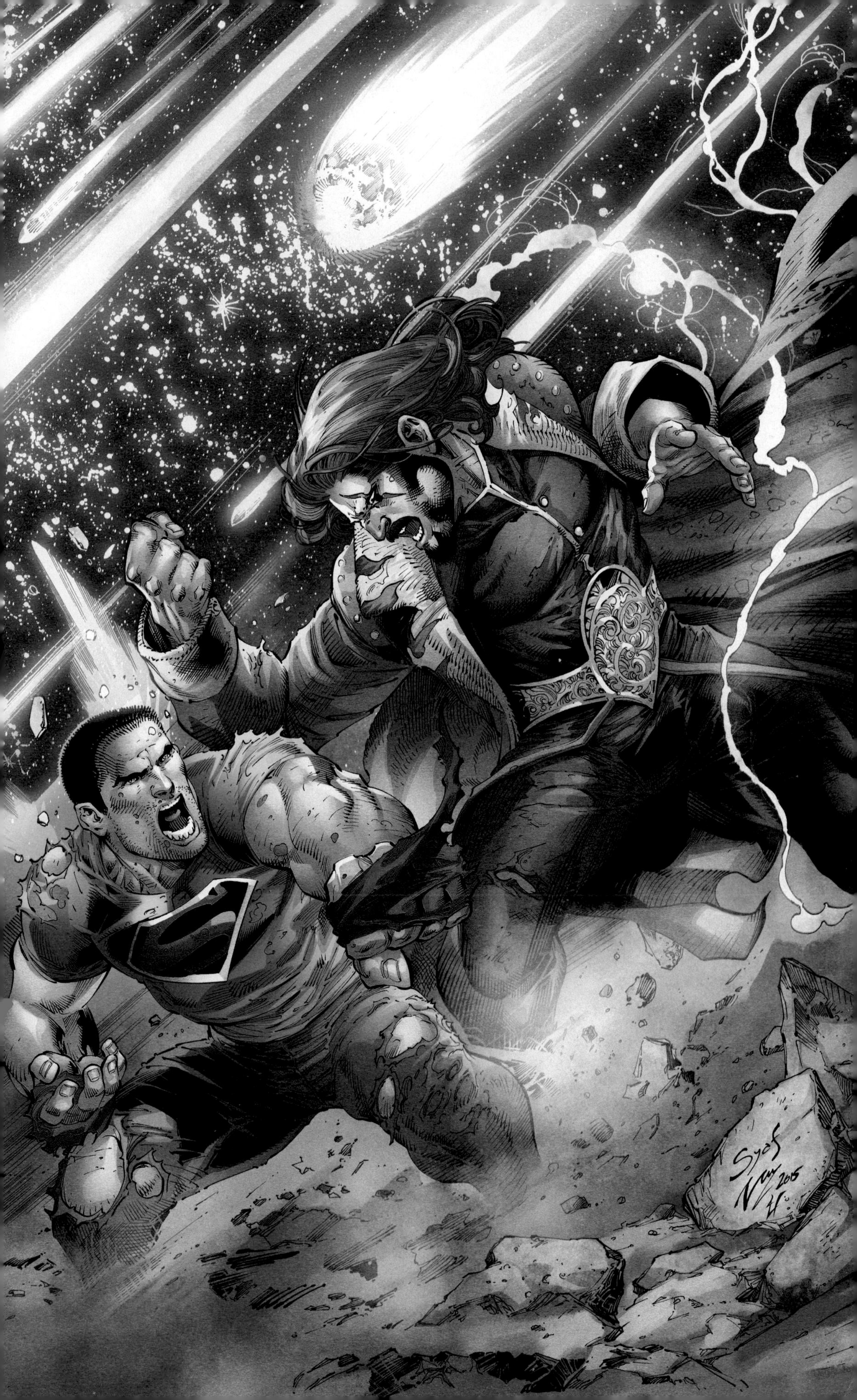

SAVAGE DAWN

GREG PAK, GENE LUEN YANG, PETER J. TOMASI, AARON HUDER writers DAN JURGENS, RAFA SANDOVAL, BEN OLIVER pencillers BILL SIENKIEWICZ, BEN OLIVER inkers TRISH MULVIHILL, LEE LOUGHRIDGE, TOMEU MOREY, BEN OLIVER colorists A LARGER WORLD STUDIOS letterer ARDIAN SYAF, VICENTE CIFUENTES, ULISES ARREOLA cover

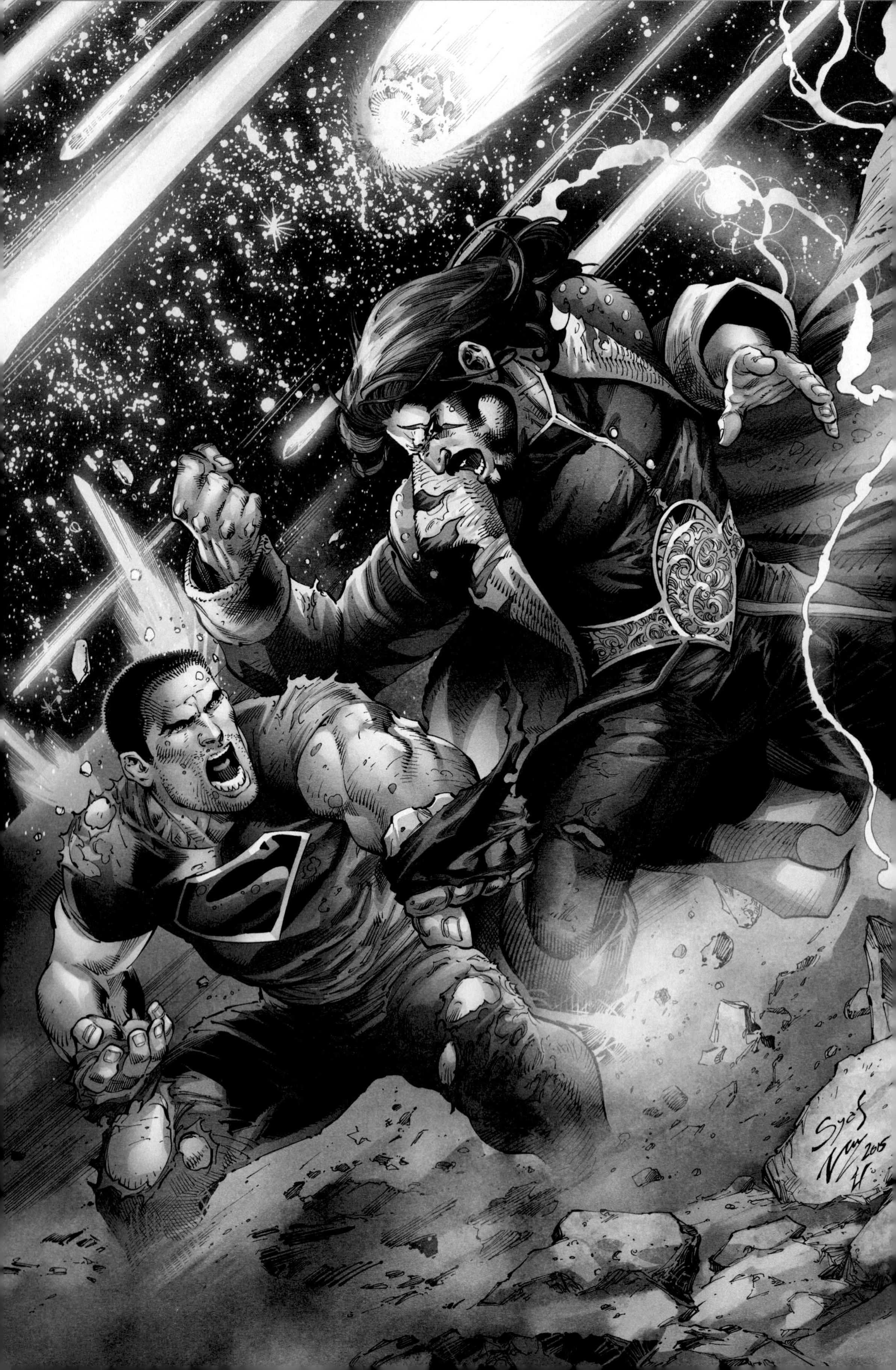

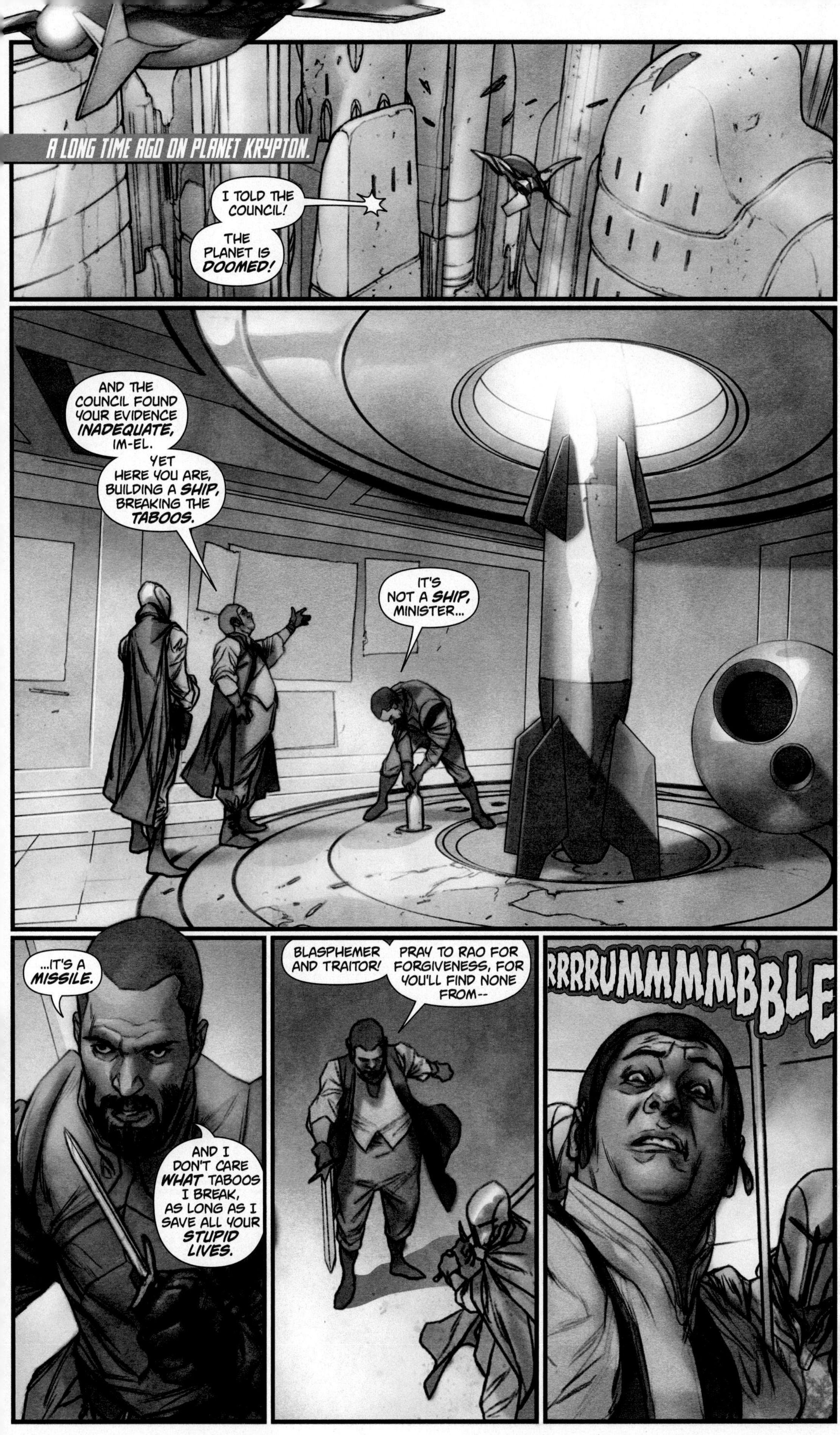
A LONG TIME AGO ON PLANET KRYPTON.
I TOLD THE COUNCIL!
THE PLANET IS DOOMED!
AND THE COUNCIL FOUND YOUR EVIDENCE INADEQUATE, IM-EL.
YET HERE YOU ARE, BUILDING A SHIP, BREAKING THE TABOOS.
IT'S NOT A SHIP, MINISTER...
...IT'S A MISSILE.
AND I DON'T CARE WHAT TABOOS I BREAK, AS LONG AS I SAVE ALL YOUR STUPID LIVES.
BLASPHEMER AND TRAITOR!
PRAY TO RAO FOR FORGIVENESS, FOR YOU'LL FIND NONE FROM--
RRRRUMMMMMBBLE

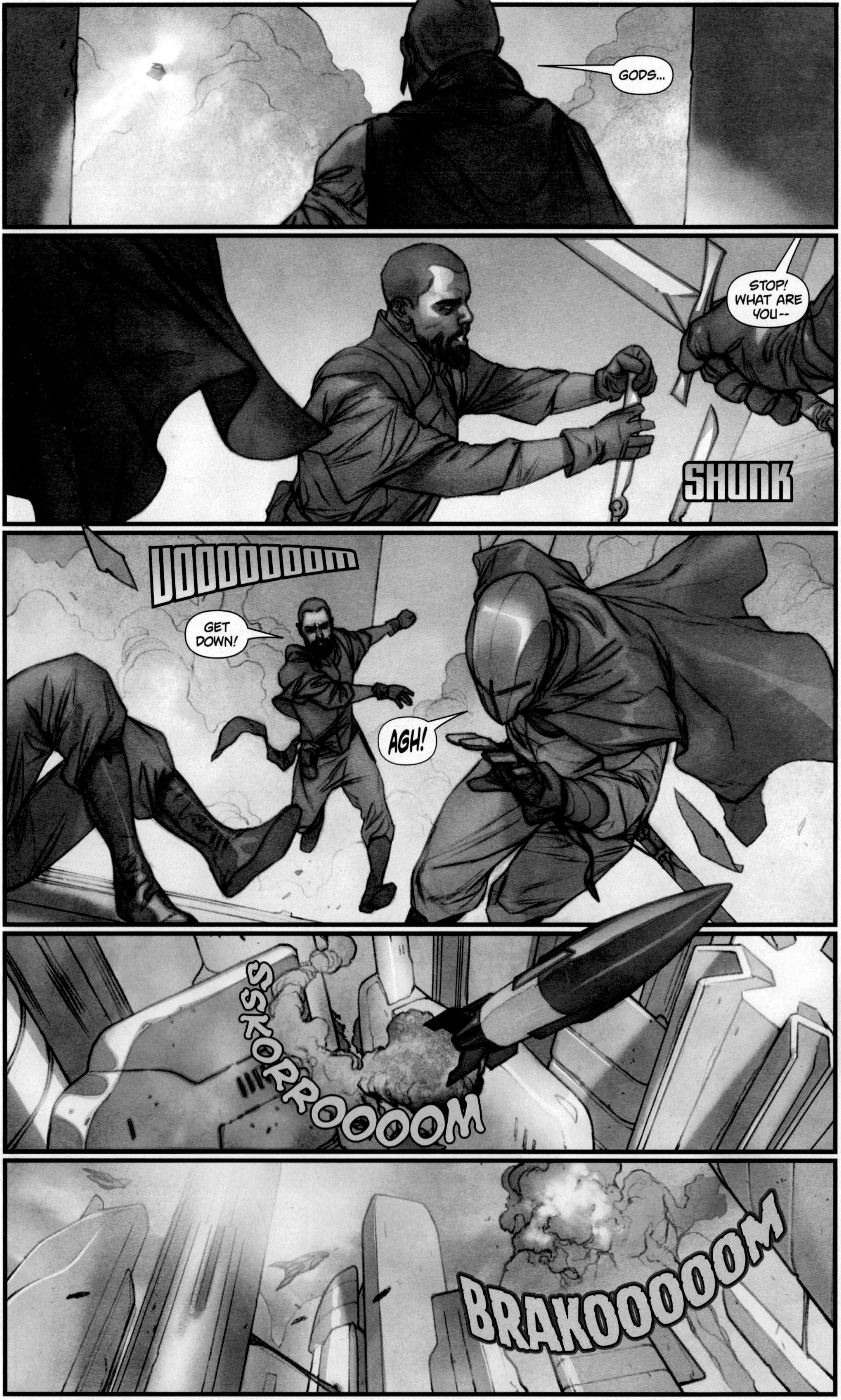
GODS...
STOP! WHAT ARE YOU--
SHUNK
VOOOOOOOOM
GET DOWN!
AGH!
SSKORROOOOM
BRAKOOOOOOM

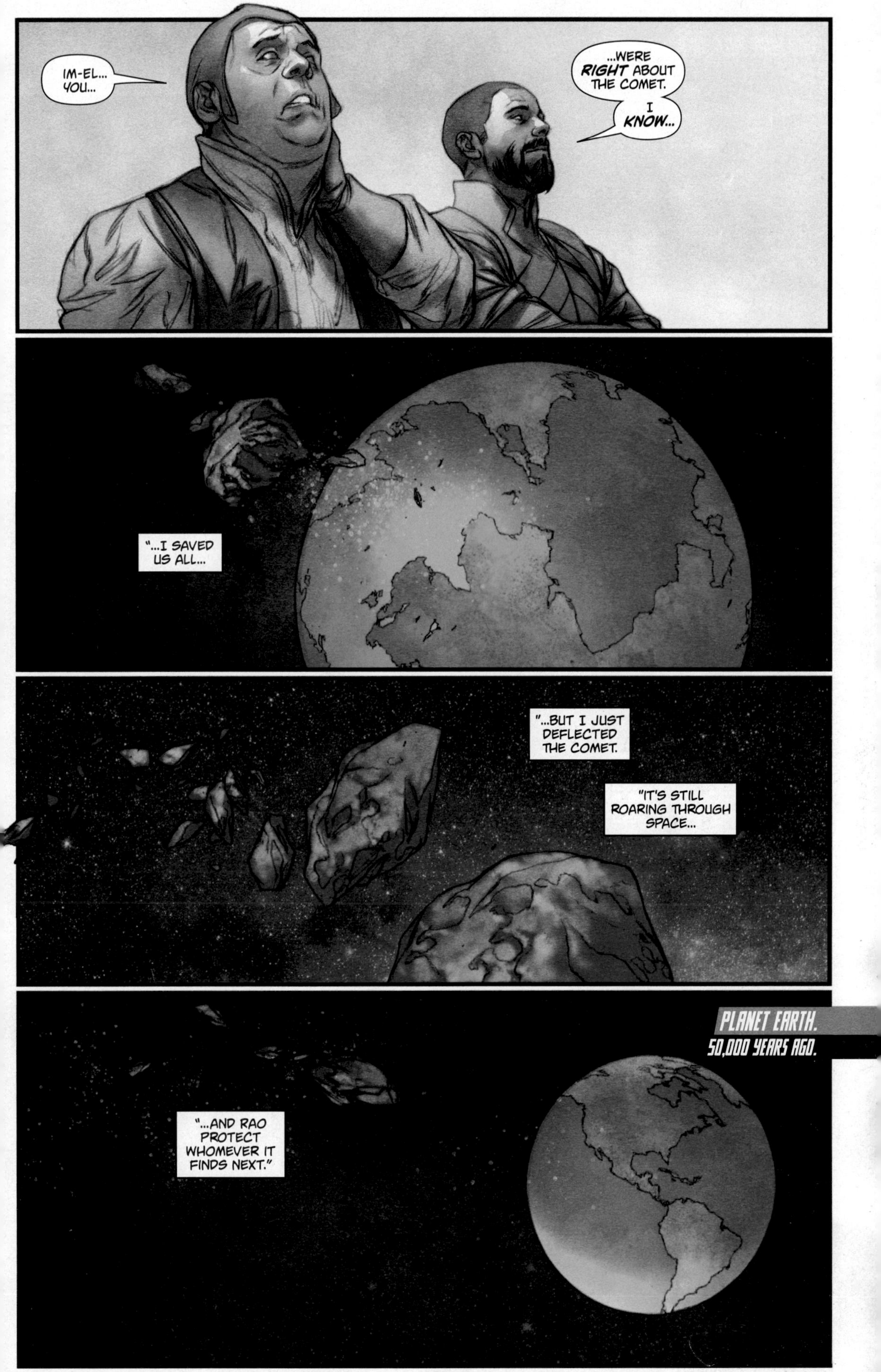
IM-EL... YOU...
...WERE RIGHT ABOUT THE COMET.
I KNOW...
"...I SAVED US ALL...
"...BUT I JUST DEFLECTED THE COMET.
"IT'S STILL ROARING THROUGH SPACE...
PLANET EARTH.
50,000 YEARS AGO.
"...AND RAO PROTECT WHOMEVER IT FINDS NEXT."

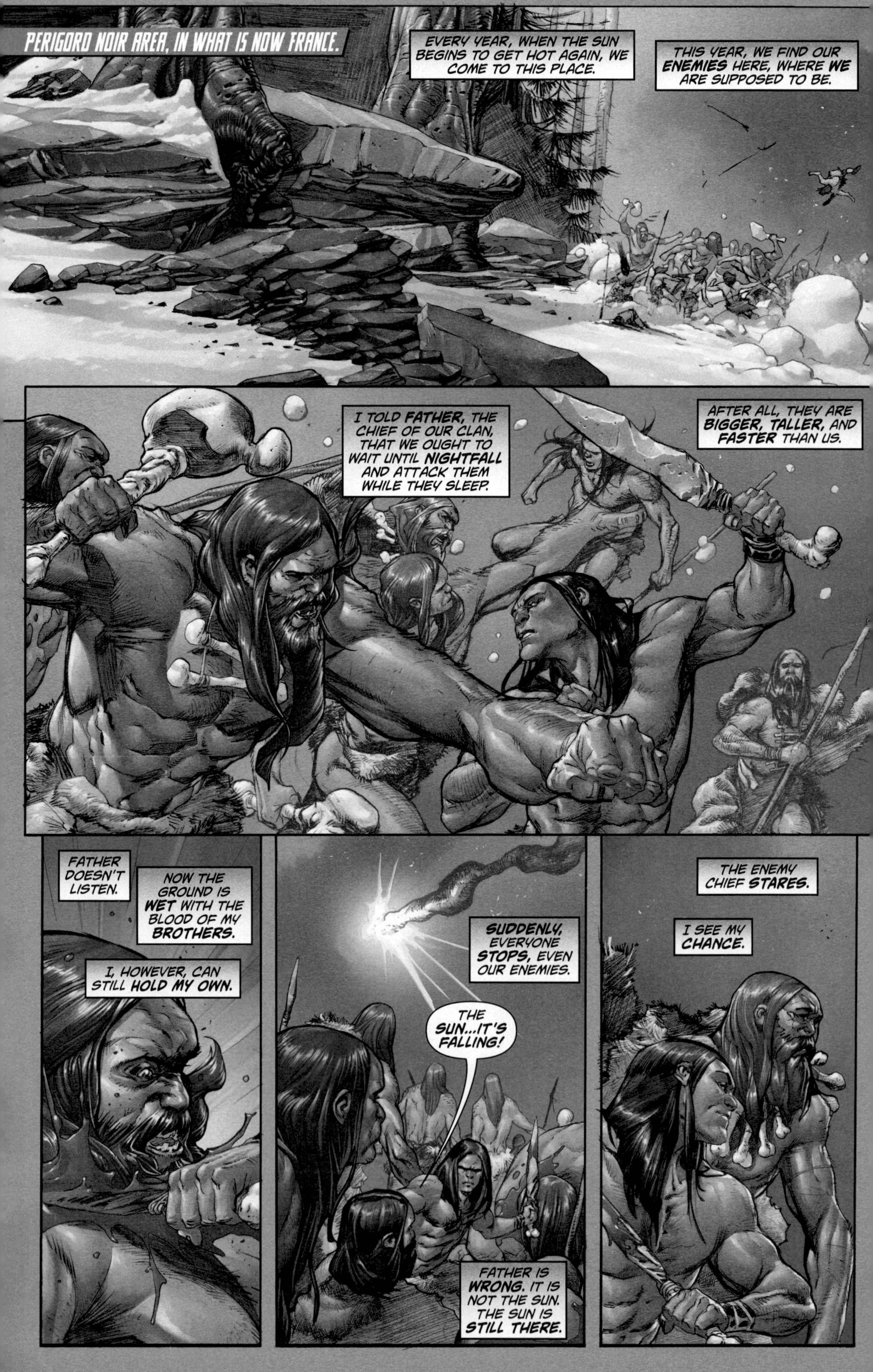
PERIGORD NOIR AREA, IN WHAT IS NOW FRANCE.
EVERY YEAR, WHEN THE SUN BEGINS TO GET HOT AGAIN, WE COME TO THIS PLACE.
THIS YEAR, WE FIND OUR ENEMIES HERE, WHERE WE ARE SUPPOSED TO BE.
I TOLD FATHER, THE CHIEF OF OUR CLAN, THAT WE OUGHT TO WAIT UNTIL NIGHTFALL AND ATTACK THEM WHILE THEY SLEEP.
AFTER ALL, THEY ARE BIGGER, TALLER, AND FASTER THAN US.
FATHER DOESN'T LISTEN.
NOW THE GROUND IS WET WITH THE BLOOD OF MY BROTHERS.
I, HOWEVER, CAN STILL HOLD MY OWN.
SUDDENLY, EVERYONE STOPS, EVEN OUR ENEMIES.
THE SUN...IT'S FALLING!
FATHER IS WRONG. IT IS NOT THE SUN. THE SUN IS STILL THERE.
THE ENEMY CHIEF STARES.
I SEE MY CHANCE.

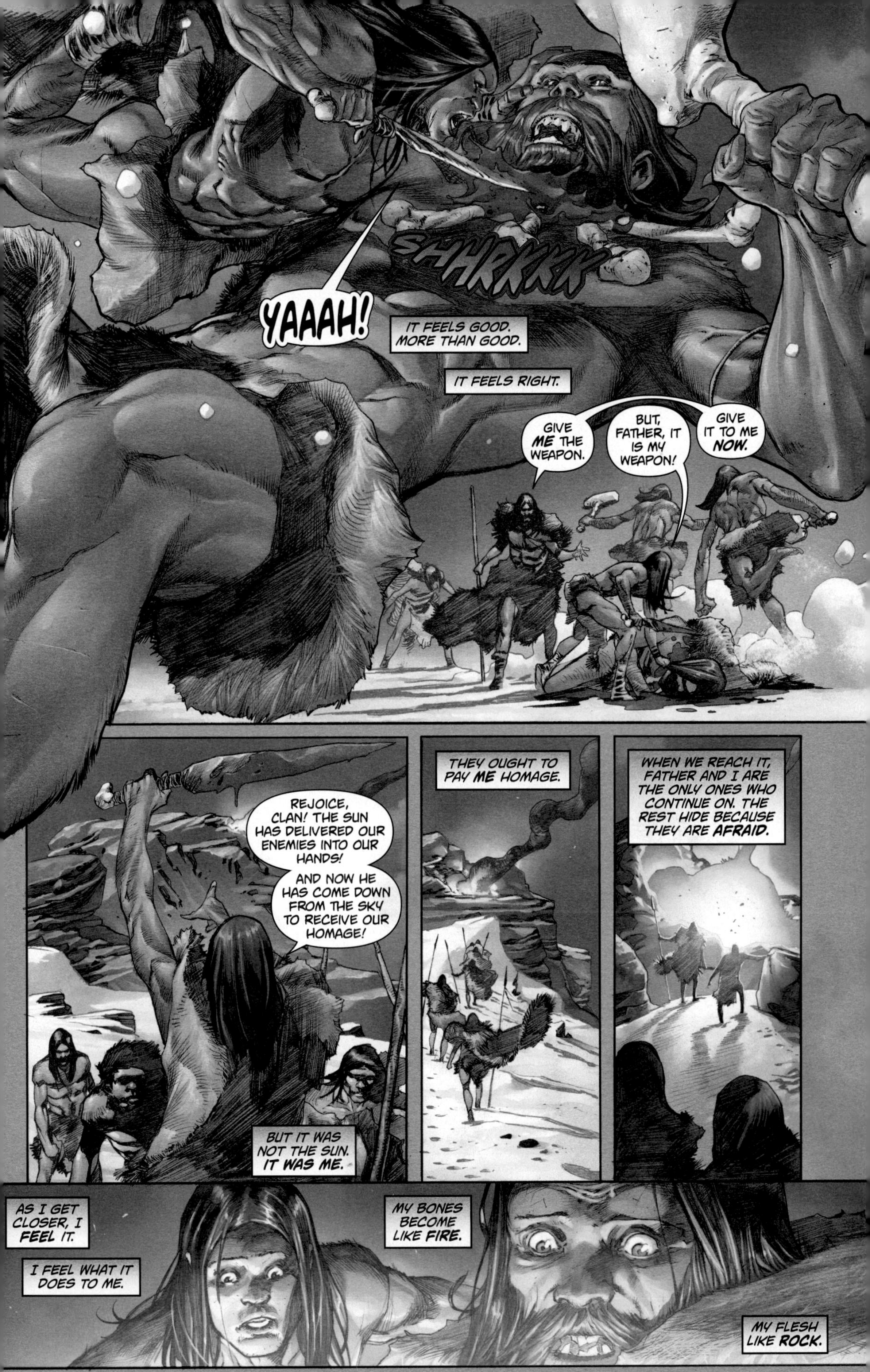
SHHRKKK
YAAAH!
IT FEELS GOOD. MORE THAN GOOD.
IT FEELS RIGHT.
GIVE ME THE WEAPON.
BUT, FATHER, IT IS MY WEAPON!
GIVE IT TO ME NOW.
REJOICE, CLAN! THE SUN HAS DELIVERED OUR ENEMIES INTO OUR HANDS!
AND NOW HE HAS COME DOWN FROM THE SKY TO RECEIVE OUR HOMAGE!
BUT IT WAS NOT THE SUN. IT WAS ME.
THEY OUGHT TO PAY ME HOMAGE.
WHEN WE REACH IT, FATHER AND I ARE THE ONLY ONES WHO CONTINUE ON. THE REST HIDE BECAUSE THEY ARE AFRAID.
AS I GET CLOSER, I FEEL IT.
I FEEL WHAT IT DOES TO ME.
MY BONES BECOME LIKE FIRE.
MY FLESH LIKE ROCK.

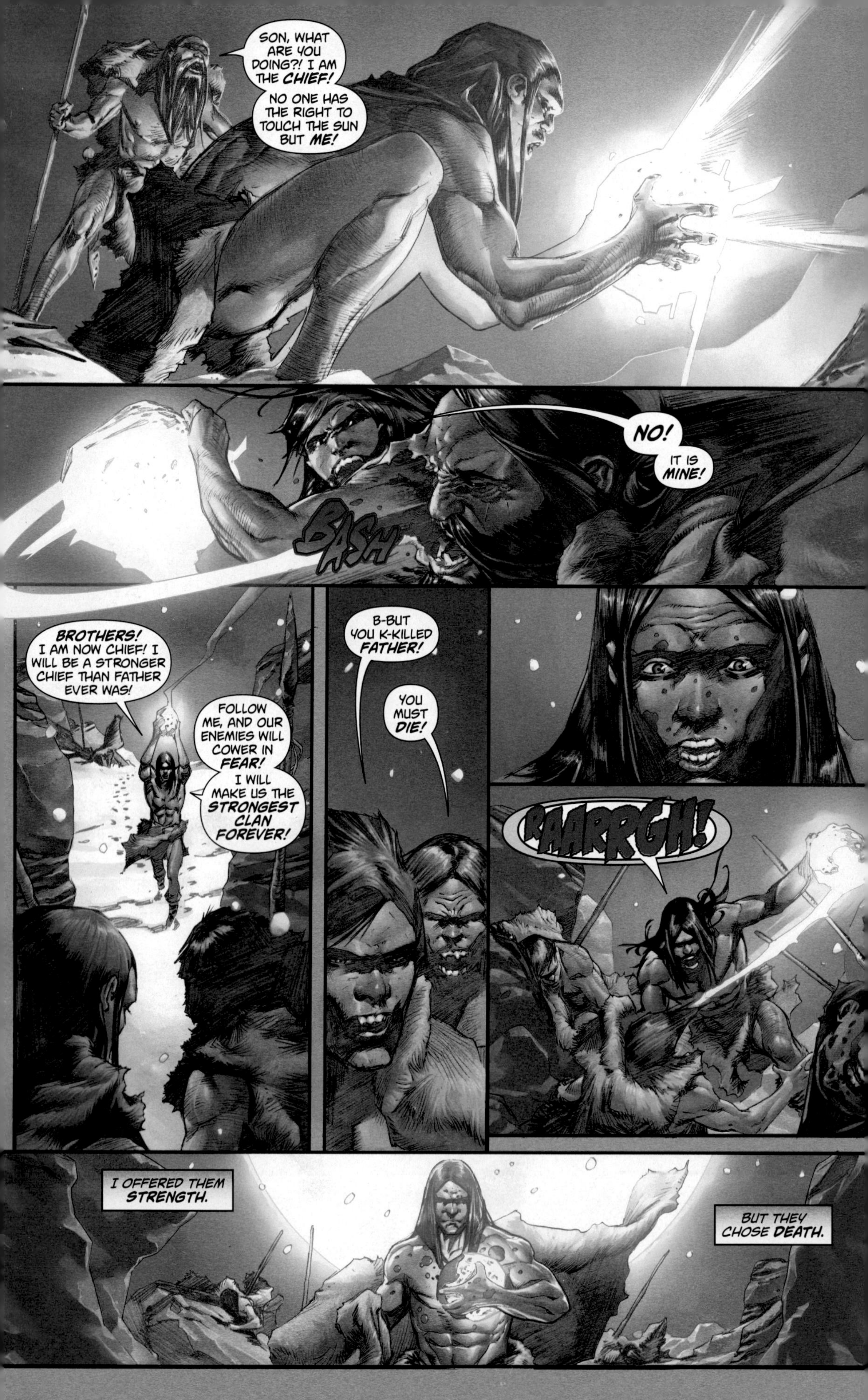
SON, WHAT ARE YOU DOING?! I AM THE CHIEF!
NO ONE HAS THE RIGHT TO TOUCH THE SUN BUT ME!
NO!
IT IS MINE!
BASH
BROTHERS! I AM NOW CHIEF! I WILL BE A STRONGER CHIEF THAN FATHER EVER WAS!
FOLLOW ME, AND OUR ENEMIES WILL COWER IN FEAR!
I WILL MAKE US THE STRONGEST CLAN FOREVER!
B-BUT YOU K-KILLED FATHER!
YOU MUST DIE!
RAARRGH!
I OFFERED THEM STRENGTH.
BUT THEY CHOSE DEATH.

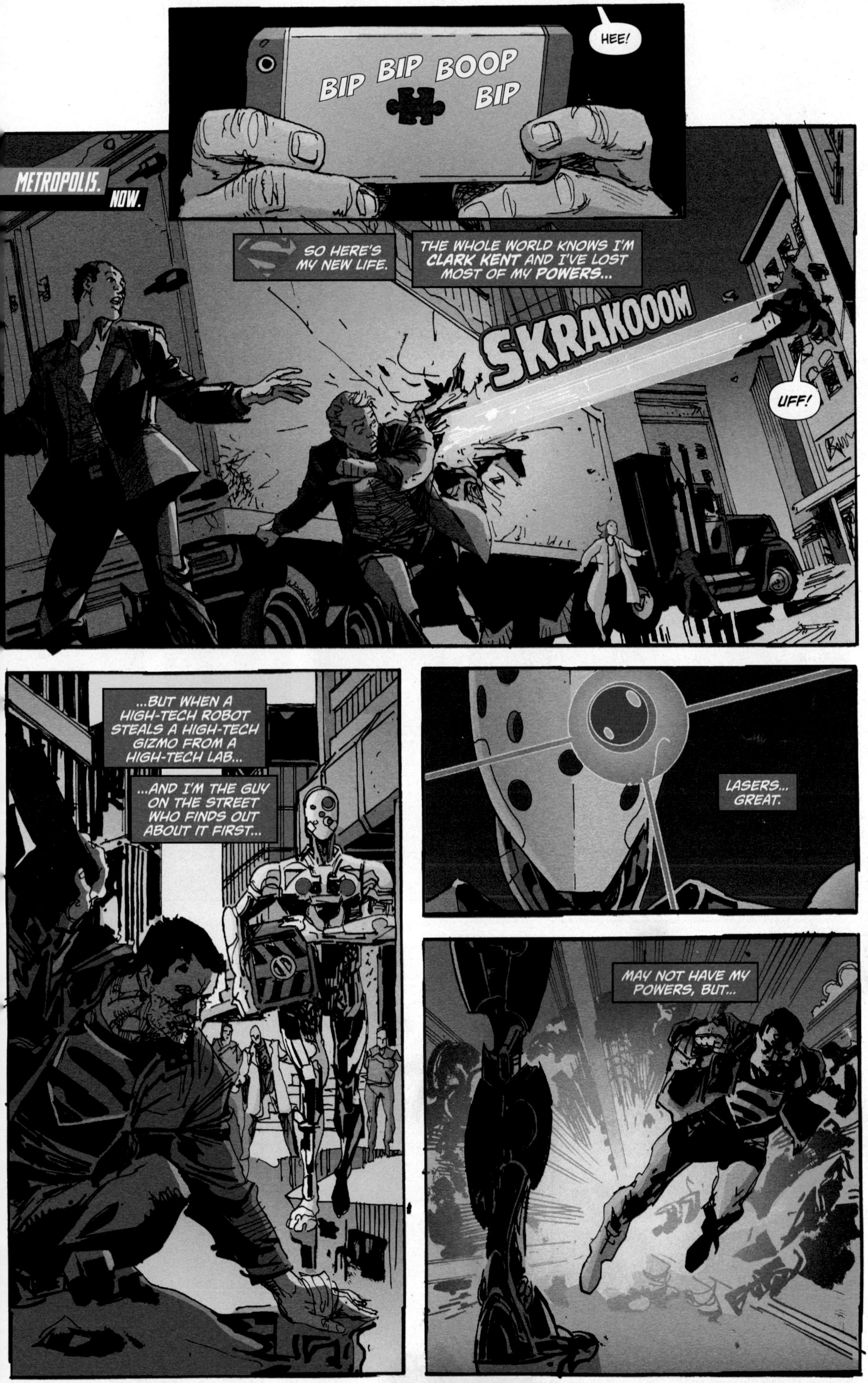
BIP BIP BOOP BIP
HEE!
METROPOLIS. NOW.
SO HERE'S MY NEW LIFE.
THE WHOLE WORLD KNOWS I'M CLARK KENT AND I'VE LOST MOST OF MY POWERS...
SKRAKOOOM
UFF!
...BUT WHEN A HIGH-TECH ROBOT STEALS A HIGH-TECH GIZMO FROM A HIGH-TECH LAB...
...AND I'M THE GUY ON THE STREET WHO FINDS OUT ABOUT IT FIRST...
LASERS... GREAT.
MAY NOT HAVE MY POWERS, BUT...

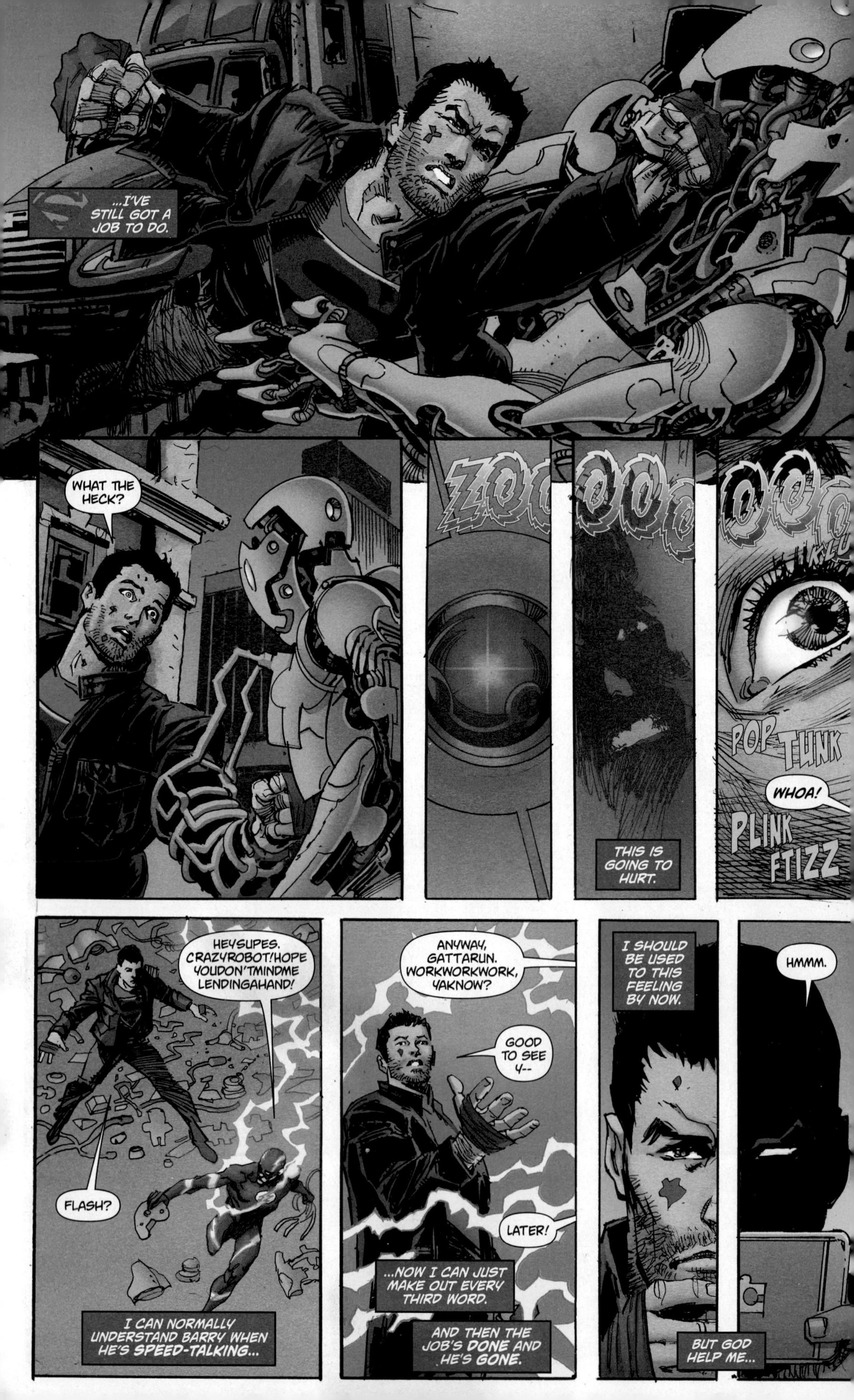

...I'VE STILL GOT A JOB TO DO.
WHAT THE HECK?
ZOOOOOOOO
THIS IS GOING TO HURT.
POP TUNK
WHOA!
PLINK FTIZZ
HEYSUPES. CRAZYROBOT!HOPE YOUDON'TMINDME LENDINGAHAND!
FLASH?
I CAN NORMALLY UNDERSTAND BARRY WHEN HE'S SPEED-TALKING...
ANYWAY, GATTARUN. WORKWORKWORK, YAKNOW?
GOOD TO SEE Y--
LATER!
...NOW I CAN JUST MAKE OUT EVERY THIRD WORD.
AND THEN THE JOB'S DONE AND HE'S GONE.
I SHOULD BE USED TO THIS FEELING BY NOW.
HMMM.
BUT GOD HELP ME...

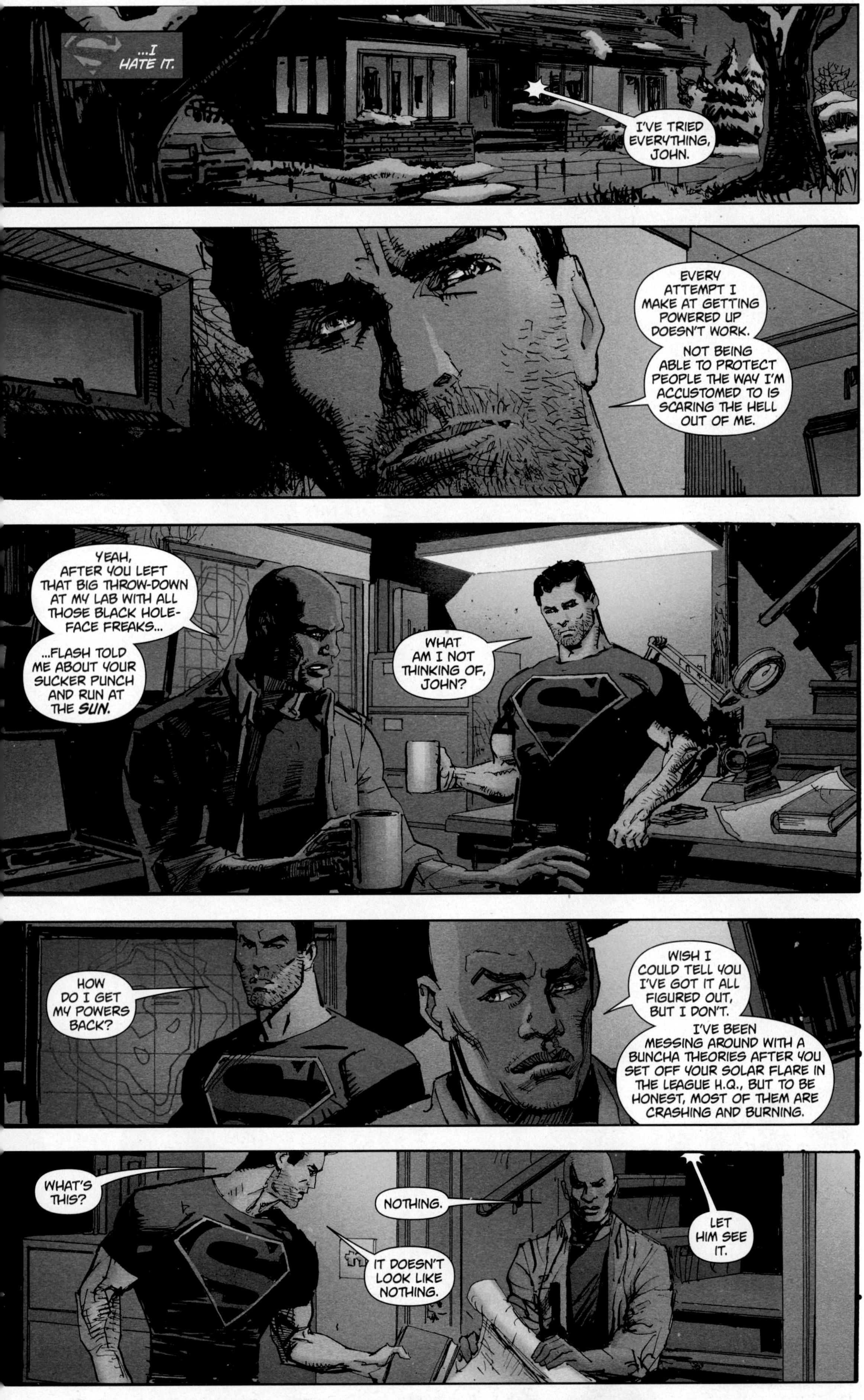
...I HATE IT.
I'VE TRIED EVERYTHING, JOHN.
EVERY ATTEMPT I MAKE AT GETTING POWERED UP DOESN'T WORK.
NOT BEING ABLE TO PROTECT PEOPLE THE WAY I'M ACCUSTOMED TO IS SCARING THE HELL OUT OF ME.
YEAH, AFTER YOU LEFT THAT BIG THROW-DOWN AT MY LAB WITH ALL THOSE BLACK HOLE-FACE FREAKS...
...FLASH TOLD ME ABOUT YOUR SUCKER PUNCH AND RUN AT THE *SUN*.
WHAT AM I NOT THINKING OF, JOHN?
HOW DO I GET MY POWERS BACK?
WISH I COULD TELL YOU I'VE GOT IT ALL FIGURED OUT, BUT I DON'T.
I'VE BEEN MESSING AROUND WITH A BUNCHA THEORIES AFTER YOU SET OFF YOUR SOLAR FLARE IN THE LEAGUE H.Q., BUT TO BE HONEST, MOST OF THEM ARE CRASHING AND BURNING.
WHAT'S THIS?
NOTHING.
IT DOESN'T LOOK LIKE NOTHING.
LET HIM SEE IT.

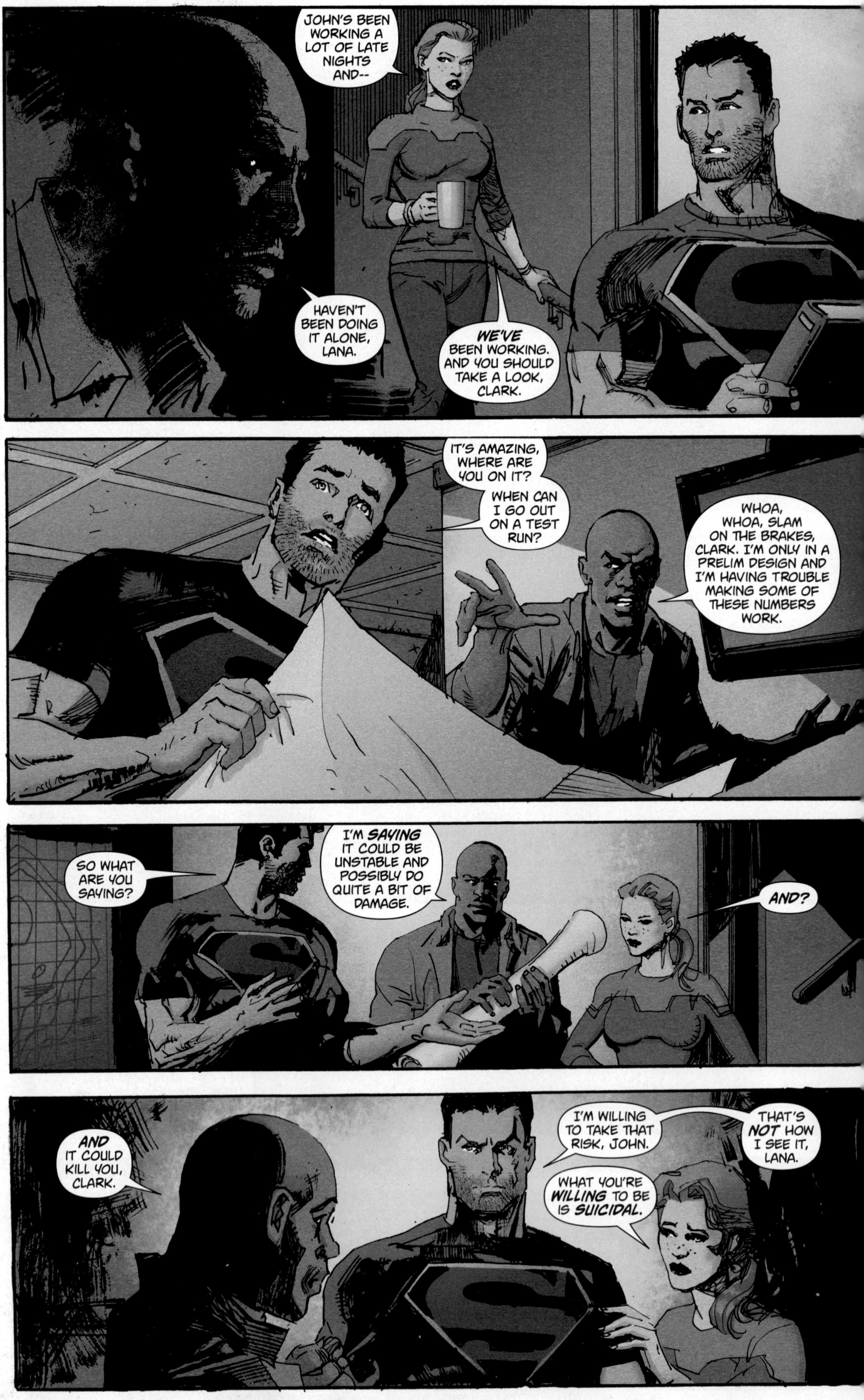
JOHN'S BEEN WORKING A LOT OF LATE NIGHTS AND--
HAVEN'T BEEN DOING IT ALONE, LANA.
WE'VE BEEN WORKING. AND YOU SHOULD TAKE A LOOK, CLARK.
IT'S AMAZING, WHERE ARE YOU ON IT?
WHEN CAN I GO OUT ON A TEST RUN?
WHOA, WHOA, SLAM ON THE BRAKES, CLARK. I'M ONLY IN A PRELIM DESIGN AND I'M HAVING TROUBLE MAKING SOME OF THESE NUMBERS WORK.
SO WHAT ARE YOU SAYING?
I'M SAYING IT COULD BE UNSTABLE AND POSSIBLY DO QUITE A BIT OF DAMAGE.
AND?
AND IT COULD KILL YOU, CLARK.
I'M WILLING TO TAKE THAT RISK, JOHN.
THAT'S NOT HOW I SEE IT, LANA.
WHAT YOU'RE WILLING TO BE IS SUICIDAL.

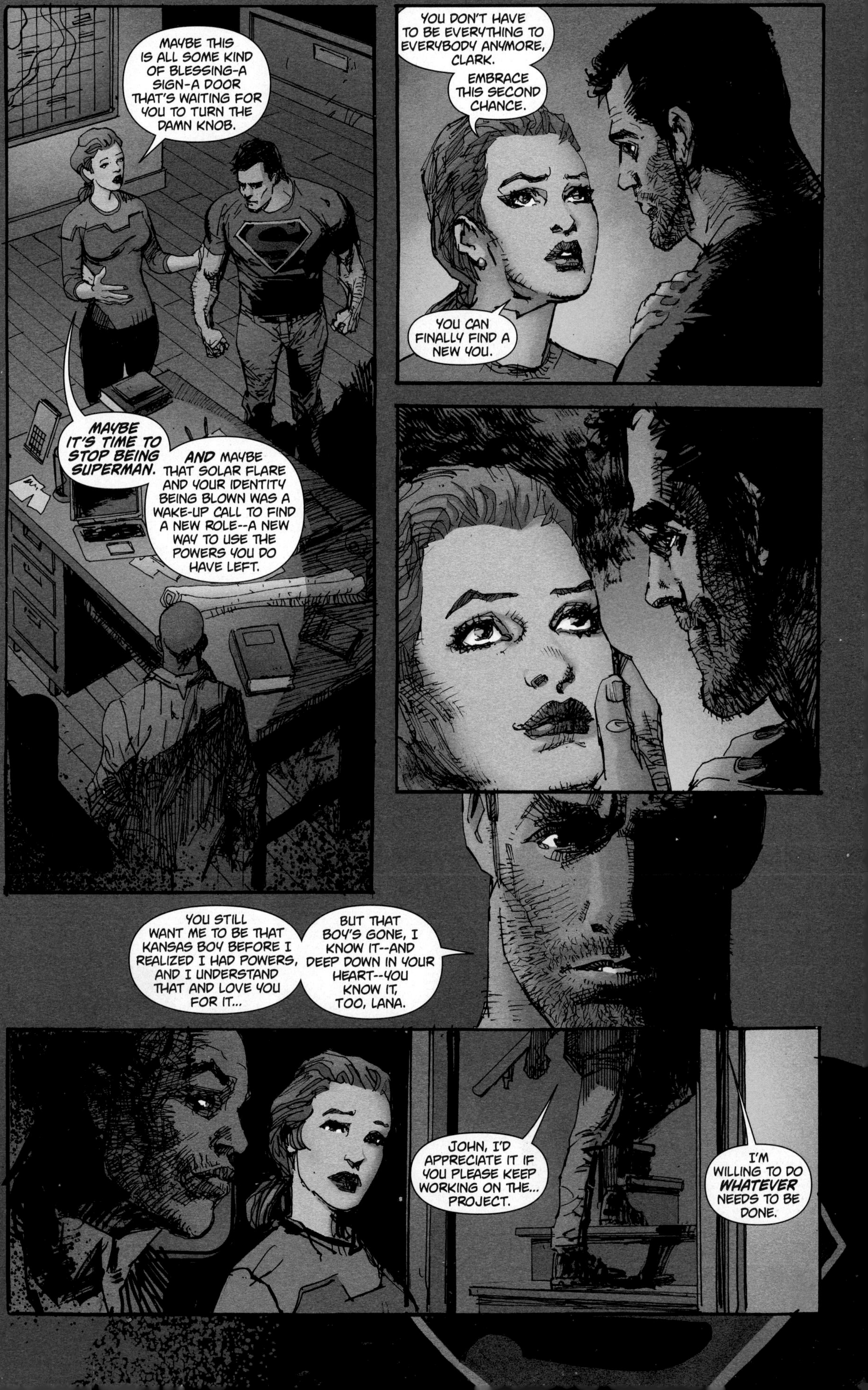
MAYBE THIS IS ALL SOME KIND OF BLESSING-A SIGN-A DOOR THAT'S WAITING FOR YOU TO TURN THE DAMN KNOB.
MAYBE IT'S TIME TO STOP BEING SUPERMAN.
AND MAYBE THAT SOLAR FLARE AND YOUR IDENTITY BEING BLOWN WAS A WAKE-UP CALL TO FIND A NEW ROLE--A NEW WAY TO USE THE POWERS YOU DO HAVE LEFT.
YOU DON'T HAVE TO BE EVERYTHING TO EVERYBODY ANYMORE, CLARK.
EMBRACE THIS SECOND CHANCE.
YOU CAN FINALLY FIND A NEW YOU.
YOU STILL WANT ME TO BE THAT KANSAS BOY BEFORE I REALIZED I HAD POWERS, AND I UNDERSTAND THAT AND LOVE YOU FOR IT...
BUT THAT BOY'S GONE, I KNOW IT--AND DEEP DOWN IN YOUR HEART--YOU KNOW IT, TOO, LANA.
JOHN, I'D APPRECIATE IT IF YOU PLEASE KEEP WORKING ON THE... PROJECT.
I'M WILLING TO DO WHATEVER NEEDS TO BE DONE.

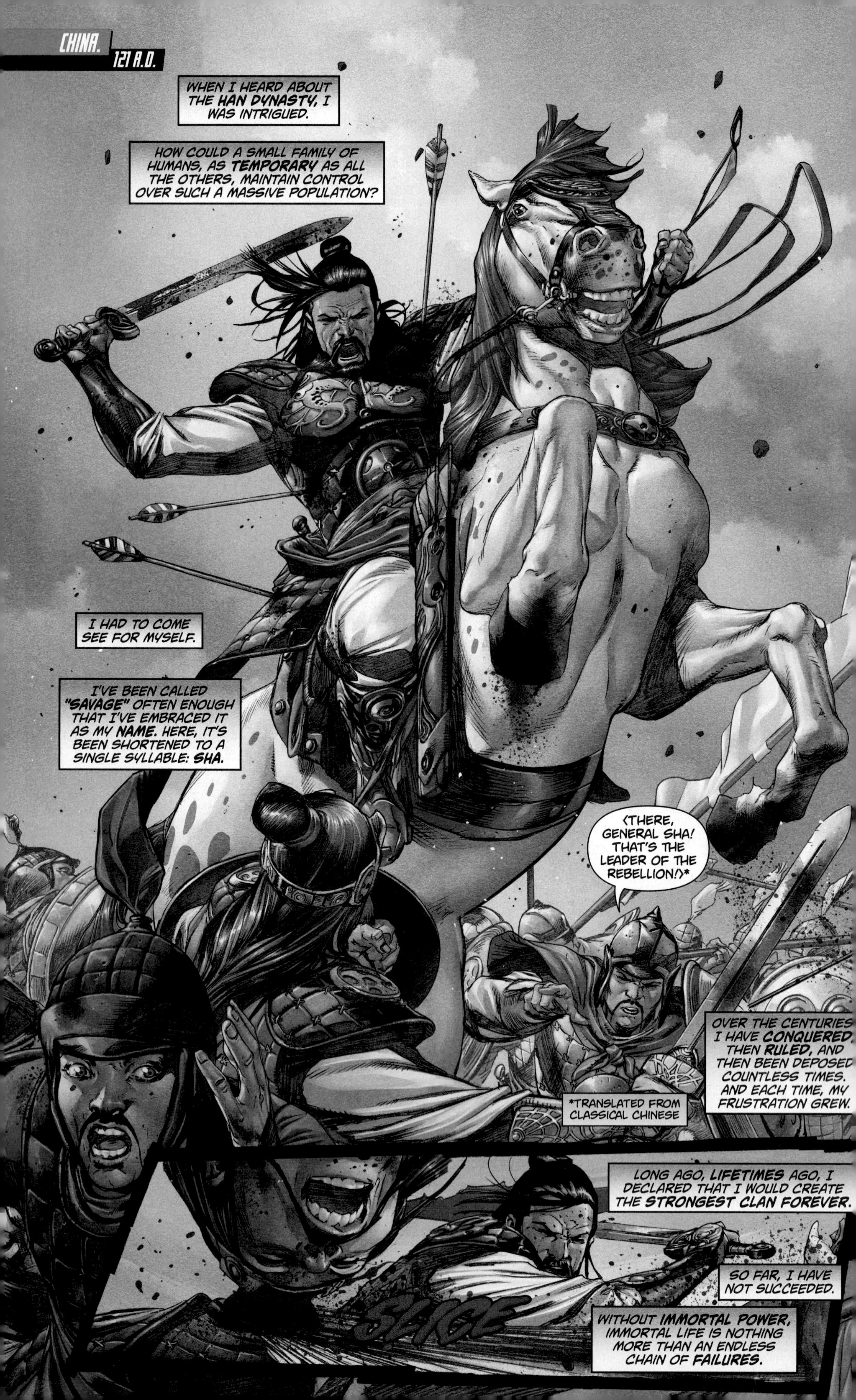
CHINA.
121 A.D.
WHEN I HEARD ABOUT THE HAN DYNASTY, I WAS INTRIGUED.
HOW COULD A SMALL FAMILY OF HUMANS, AS TEMPORARY AS ALL THE OTHERS, MAINTAIN CONTROL OVER SUCH A MASSIVE POPULATION?
I HAD TO COME SEE FOR MYSELF.
I'VE BEEN CALLED "SAVAGE" OFTEN ENOUGH THAT I'VE EMBRACED IT AS MY NAME. HERE, IT'S BEEN SHORTENED TO A SINGLE SYLLABLE: SHA.
⟨THERE, GENERAL SHA! THAT'S THE LEADER OF THE REBELLION!⟩*
OVER THE CENTURIES I HAVE CONQUERED, THEN RULED, AND THEN BEEN DEPOSED COUNTLESS TIMES. AND EACH TIME, MY FRUSTRATION GREW.
*TRANSLATED FROM CLASSICAL CHINESE
LONG AGO, LIFETIMES AGO, I DECLARED THAT I WOULD CREATE THE STRONGEST CLAN FOREVER.
SLICE
SO FAR, I HAVE NOT SUCCEEDED.
WITHOUT IMMORTAL POWER, IMMORTAL LIFE IS NOTHING MORE THAN AN ENDLESS CHAIN OF FAILURES.

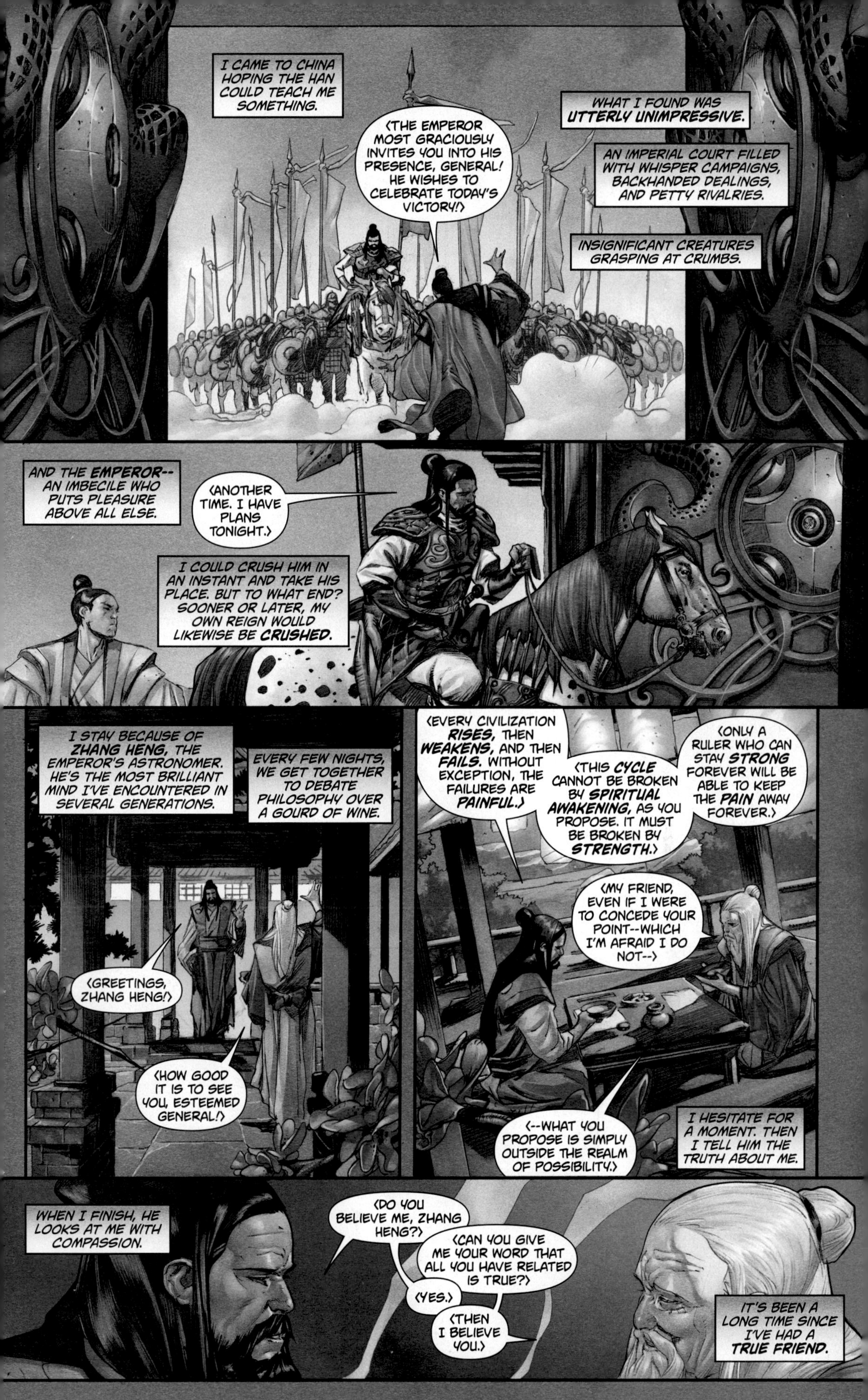

I CAME TO CHINA HOPING THE HAN COULD TEACH ME SOMETHING.
‹THE EMPEROR MOST GRACIOUSLY INVITES YOU INTO HIS PRESENCE, GENERAL! HE WISHES TO CELEBRATE TODAY'S VICTORY!›
WHAT I FOUND WAS **UTTERLY UNIMPRESSIVE.**
AN IMPERIAL COURT FILLED WITH WHISPER CAMPAIGNS, BACKHANDED DEALINGS, AND PETTY RIVALRIES.
INSIGNIFICANT CREATURES GRASPING AT CRUMBS.
AND THE **EMPEROR**--AN IMBECILE WHO PUTS PLEASURE ABOVE ALL ELSE.
‹ANOTHER TIME. I HAVE PLANS TONIGHT.›
I COULD CRUSH HIM IN AN INSTANT AND TAKE HIS PLACE. BUT TO WHAT END? SOONER OR LATER, MY OWN REIGN WOULD LIKEWISE BE **CRUSHED.**
I STAY BECAUSE OF **ZHANG HENG,** THE EMPEROR'S ASTRONOMER. HE'S THE MOST BRILLIANT MIND I'VE ENCOUNTERED IN SEVERAL GENERATIONS.
EVERY FEW NIGHTS, WE GET TOGETHER TO DEBATE PHILOSOPHY OVER A GOURD OF WINE.
‹GREETINGS, ZHANG HENG!›
‹HOW GOOD IT IS TO SEE YOU, ESTEEMED GENERAL!›
‹EVERY CIVILIZATION **RISES,** THEN **WEAKENS,** AND THEN **FAILS.** WITHOUT EXCEPTION, THE FAILURES ARE **PAINFUL.**›
‹THIS **CYCLE** CANNOT BE BROKEN BY **SPIRITUAL AWAKENING,** AS YOU PROPOSE. IT MUST BE BROKEN BY **STRENGTH.**›
‹ONLY A RULER WHO CAN STAY **STRONG** FOREVER WILL BE ABLE TO KEEP THE **PAIN** AWAY FOREVER.›
‹MY FRIEND, EVEN IF I WERE TO CONCEDE YOUR POINT--WHICH I'M AFRAID I DO NOT--›
‹--WHAT YOU PROPOSE IS SIMPLY OUTSIDE THE REALM OF POSSIBILITY.›
I HESITATE FOR A MOMENT. THEN I TELL HIM THE TRUTH ABOUT ME.
WHEN I FINISH, HE LOOKS AT ME WITH COMPASSION.
‹DO YOU BELIEVE ME, ZHANG HENG?›
‹CAN YOU GIVE ME YOUR WORD THAT ALL YOU HAVE RELATED IS TRUE?›
‹YES.›
‹THEN I BELIEVE YOU.›
IT'S BEEN A LONG TIME SINCE I'VE HAD A **TRUE FRIEND.**

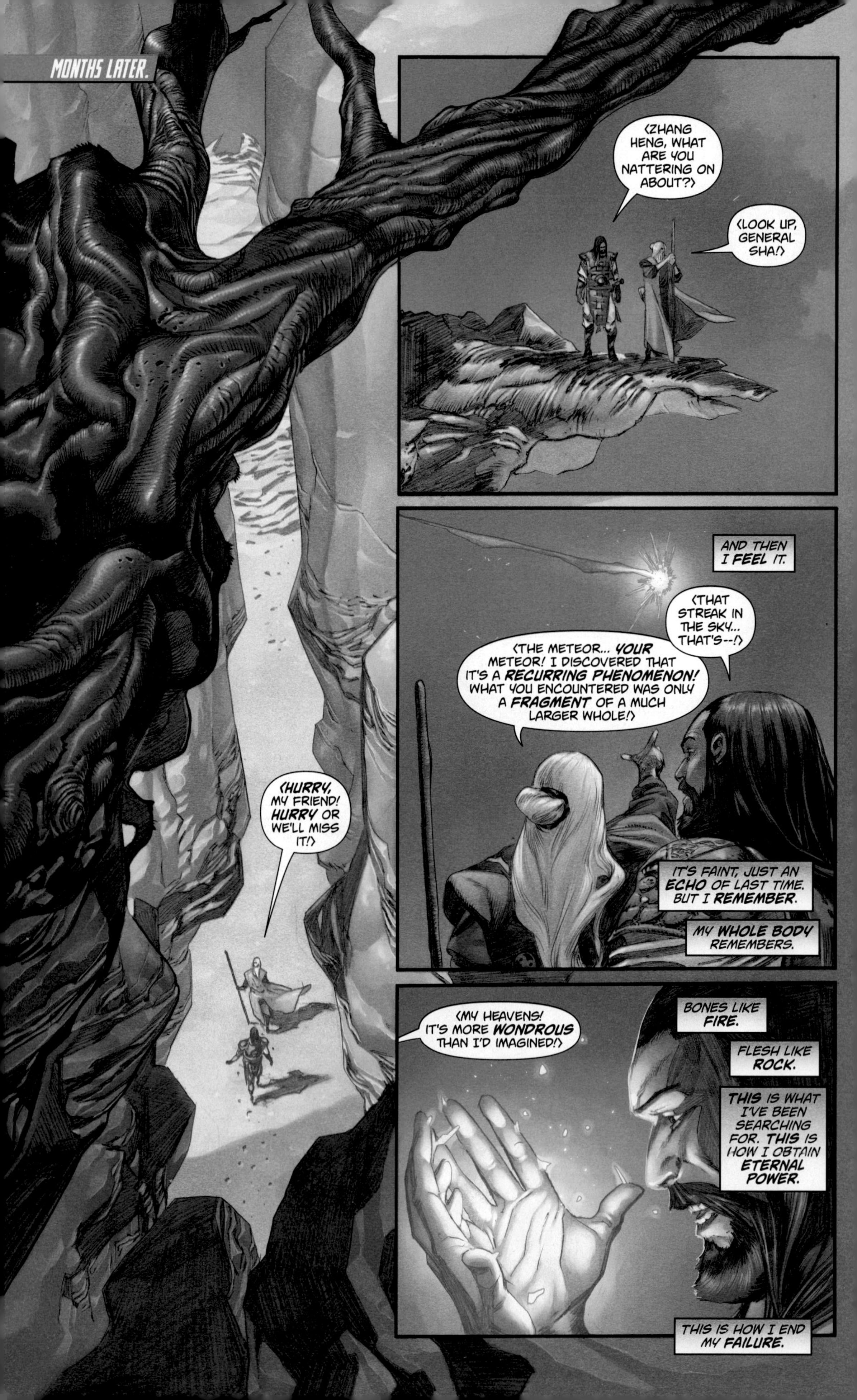
MONTHS LATER.
⟨HURRY, MY FRIEND! HURRY OR WE'LL MISS IT!⟩
⟨ZHANG HENG, WHAT ARE YOU NATTERING ON ABOUT?⟩
⟨LOOK UP, GENERAL SHA!⟩
AND THEN I FEEL IT.
⟨THAT STREAK IN THE SKY... THAT'S--!⟩
⟨THE METEOR... YOUR METEOR! I DISCOVERED THAT IT'S A RECURRING PHENOMENON! WHAT YOU ENCOUNTERED WAS ONLY A FRAGMENT OF A MUCH LARGER WHOLE!⟩
IT'S FAINT, JUST AN ECHO OF LAST TIME. BUT I REMEMBER.
MY WHOLE BODY REMEMBERS.
⟨MY HEAVENS! IT'S MORE WONDROUS THAN I'D IMAGINED!⟩
BONES LIKE FIRE.
FLESH LIKE ROCK.
THIS IS WHAT I'VE BEEN SEARCHING FOR. THIS IS HOW I OBTAIN ETERNAL POWER.
THIS IS HOW I END MY FAILURE.

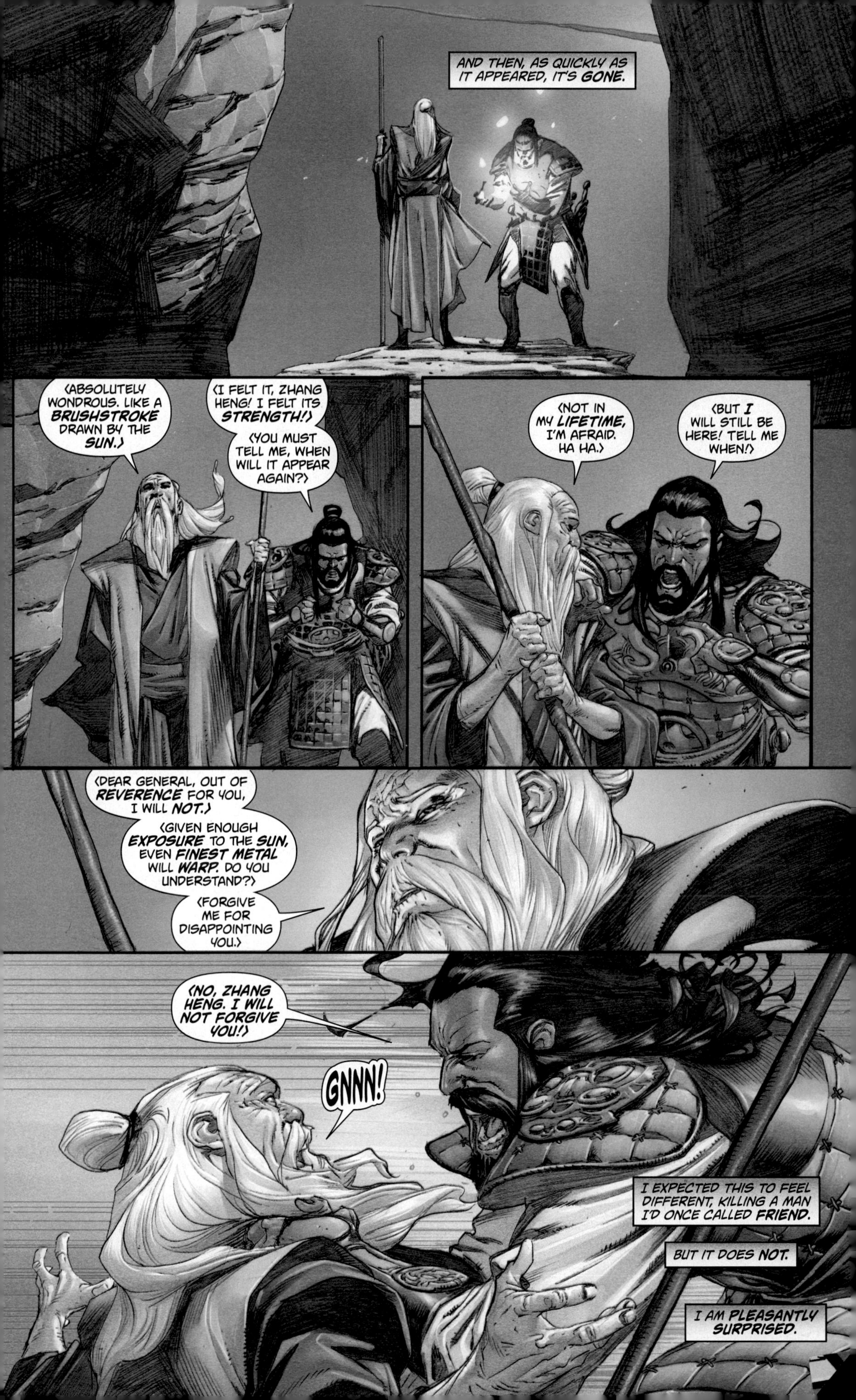
AND THEN, AS QUICKLY AS IT APPEARED, IT'S GONE.
‹ABSOLUTELY WONDROUS. LIKE A BRUSHSTROKE DRAWN BY THE SUN.›
‹I FELT IT, ZHANG HENG! I FELT ITS STRENGTH!›
‹YOU MUST TELL ME, WHEN WILL IT APPEAR AGAIN?›
‹NOT IN MY LIFETIME, I'M AFRAID. HA HA.›
‹BUT I WILL STILL BE HERE! TELL ME WHEN!›
‹DEAR GENERAL, OUT OF REVERENCE FOR YOU, I WILL NOT.›
‹GIVEN ENOUGH EXPOSURE TO THE SUN, EVEN FINEST METAL WILL WARP. DO YOU UNDERSTAND?›
‹FORGIVE ME FOR DISAPPOINTING YOU.›
‹NO, ZHANG HENG. I WILL NOT FORGIVE YOU!›
GNNN!
I EXPECTED THIS TO FEEL DIFFERENT, KILLING A MAN I'D ONCE CALLED FRIEND.
BUT IT DOES NOT.
I AM PLEASANTLY SURPRISED.

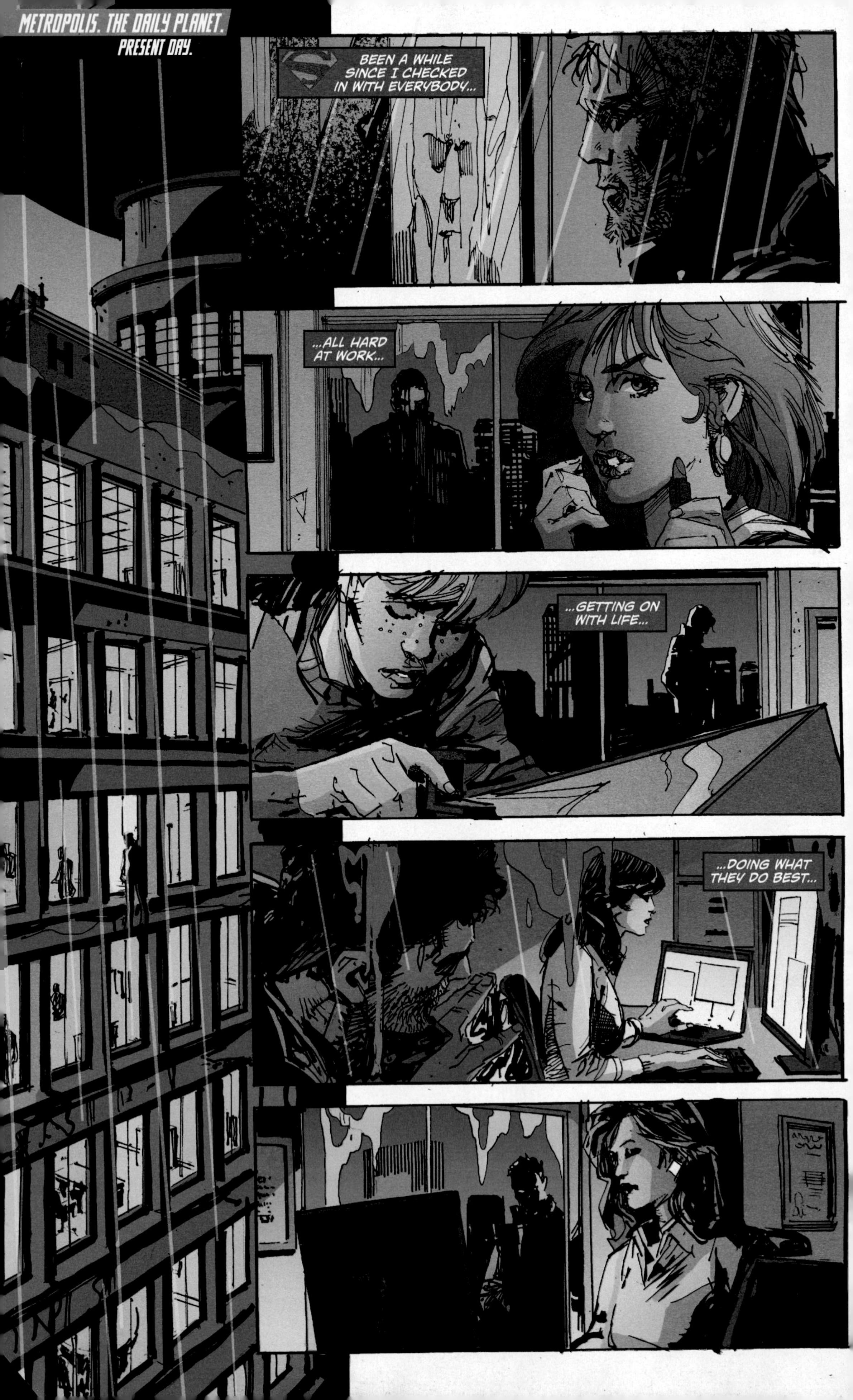
METROPOLIS. THE DAILY PLANET.
PRESENT DAY.
BEEN A WHILE SINCE I CHECKED IN WITH EVERYBODY...
...ALL HARD AT WORK...
...GETTING ON WITH LIFE...
...DOING WHAT THEY DO BEST...

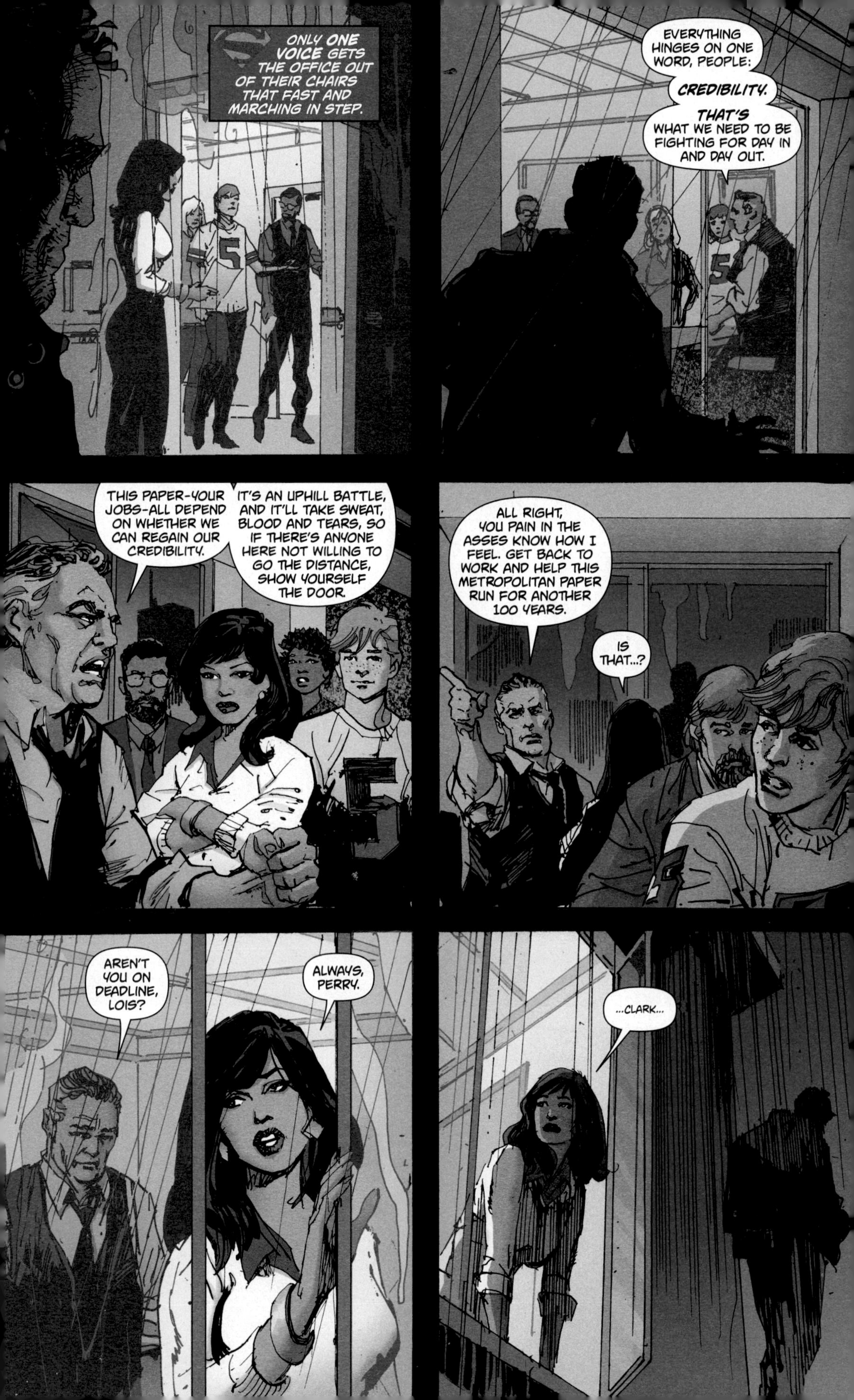
ONLY ONE VOICE GETS THE OFFICE OUT OF THEIR CHAIRS THAT FAST AND MARCHING IN STEP.
EVERYTHING HINGES ON ONE WORD, PEOPLE: CREDIBILITY.
THAT'S WHAT WE NEED TO BE FIGHTING FOR DAY IN AND DAY OUT.
THIS PAPER--YOUR JOBS--ALL DEPEND ON WHETHER WE CAN REGAIN OUR CREDIBILITY.
IT'S AN UPHILL BATTLE, AND IT'LL TAKE SWEAT, BLOOD AND TEARS, SO IF THERE'S ANYONE HERE NOT WILLING TO GO THE DISTANCE, SHOW YOURSELF THE DOOR.
ALL RIGHT, YOU PAIN IN THE ASSES KNOW HOW I FEEL. GET BACK TO WORK AND HELP THIS METROPOLITAN PAPER RUN FOR ANOTHER 100 YEARS.
IS THAT...?
AREN'T YOU ON DEADLINE, LOIS?
ALWAYS, PERRY.
...CLARK...

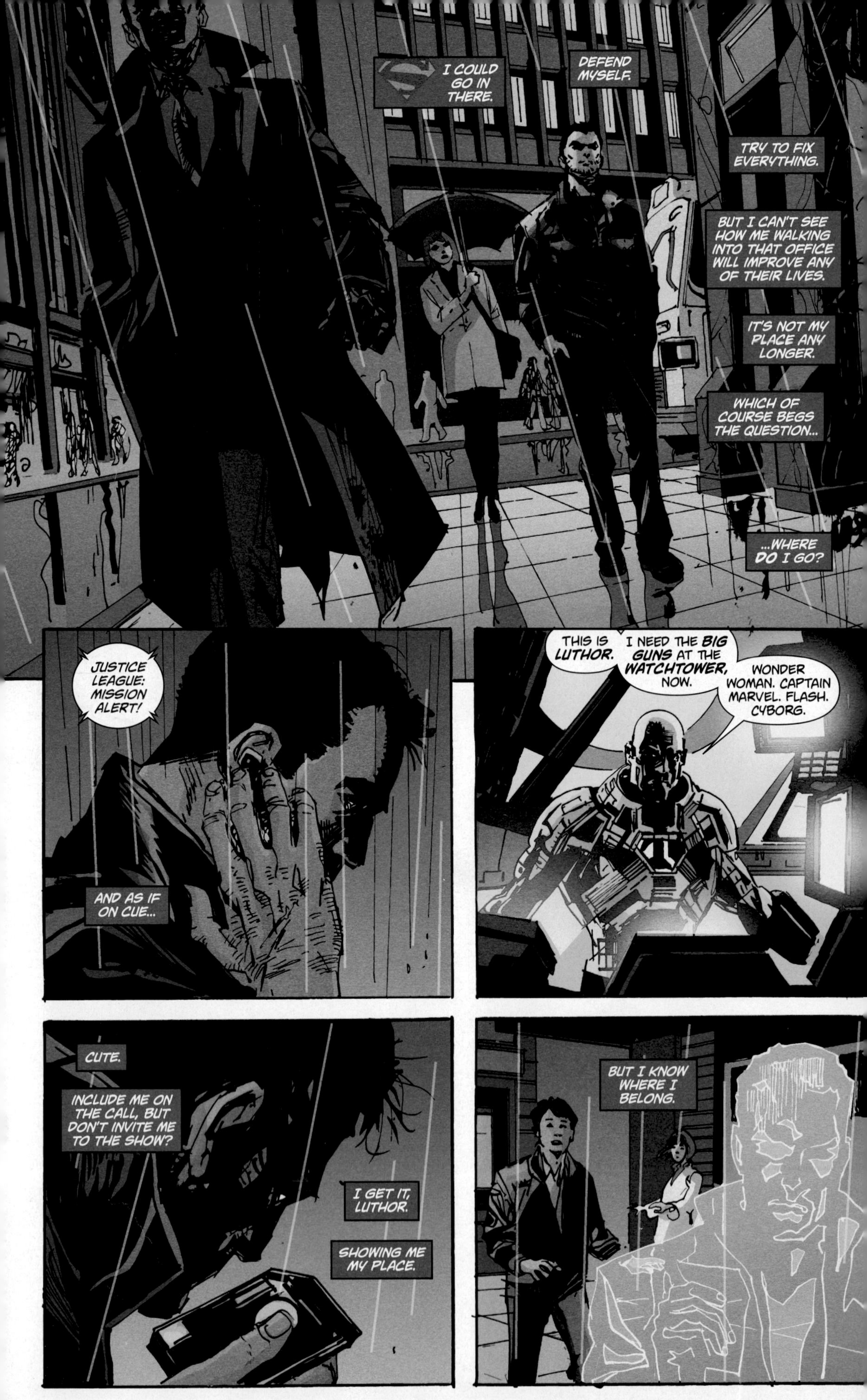
I COULD GO IN THERE.
DEFEND MYSELF.
TRY TO FIX EVERYTHING.
BUT I CAN'T SEE HOW ME WALKING INTO THAT OFFICE WILL IMPROVE ANY OF THEIR LIVES.
IT'S NOT MY PLACE ANY LONGER.
WHICH OF COURSE BEGS THE QUESTION...
...WHERE DO I GO?
JUSTICE LEAGUE: MISSION ALERT!
AND AS IF ON CUE...
THIS IS LUTHOR.
I NEED THE BIG GUNS AT THE WATCHTOWER, NOW.
WONDER WOMAN. CAPTAIN MARVEL. FLASH. CYBORG.
CUTE.
INCLUDE ME ON THE CALL, BUT DON'T INVITE ME TO THE SHOW?
I GET IT, LUTHOR.
SHOWING ME MY PLACE.
BUT I KNOW WHERE I BELONG.

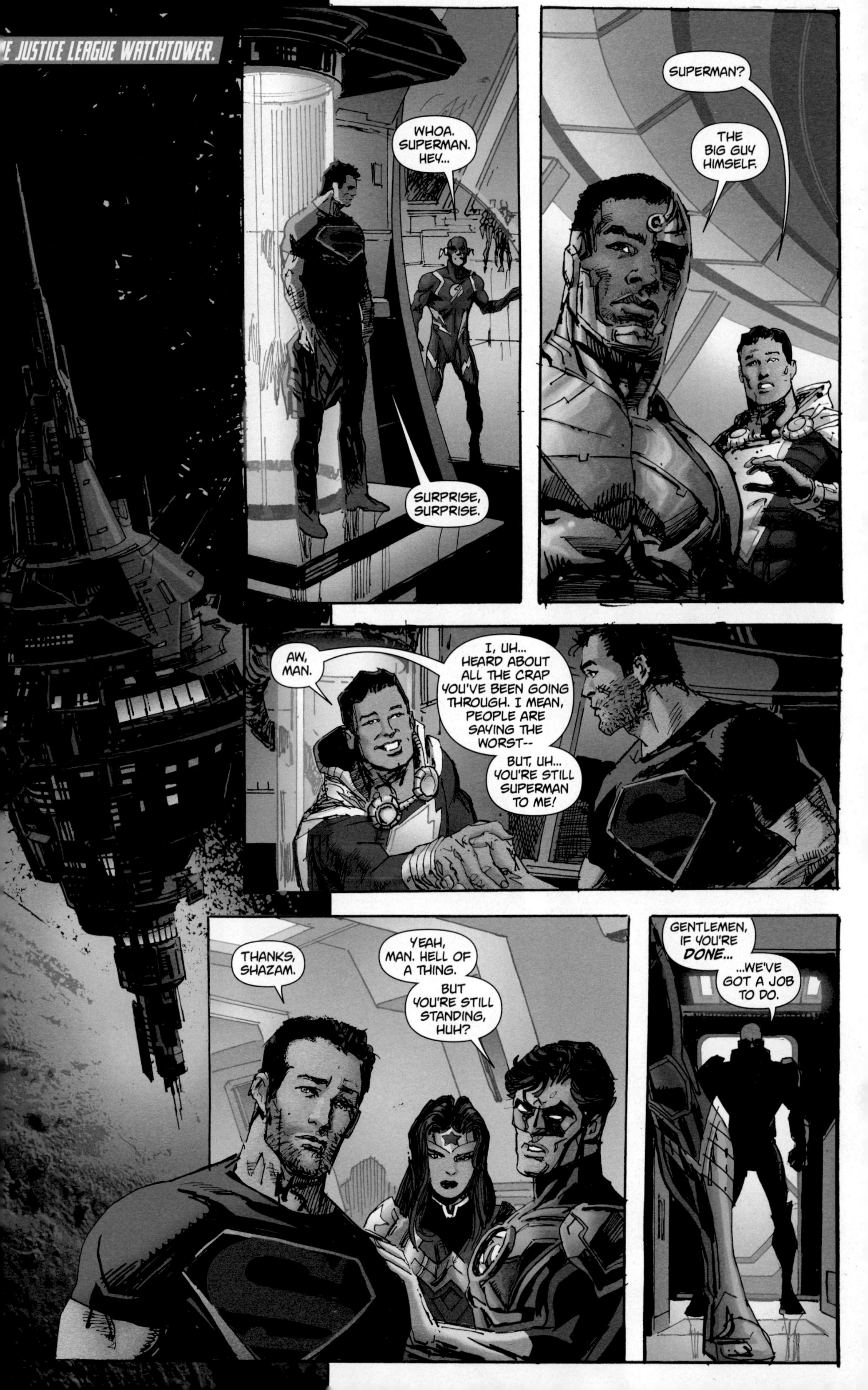
E JUSTICE LEAGUE WATCHTOWER.
WHOA. SUPERMAN. HEY...
SURPRISE, SURPRISE.
SUPERMAN?
THE BIG GUY HIMSELF.
AW, MAN.
I, UH... HEARD ABOUT ALL THE CRAP YOU'VE BEEN GOING THROUGH. I MEAN, PEOPLE ARE SAYING THE WORST--
BUT, UH... YOU'RE STILL SUPERMAN TO ME!
THANKS, SHAZAM.
YEAH, MAN. HELL OF A THING.
BUT YOU'RE STILL STANDING, HUH?
GENTLEMEN, IF YOU'RE DONE...
...WE'VE GOT A JOB TO DO.

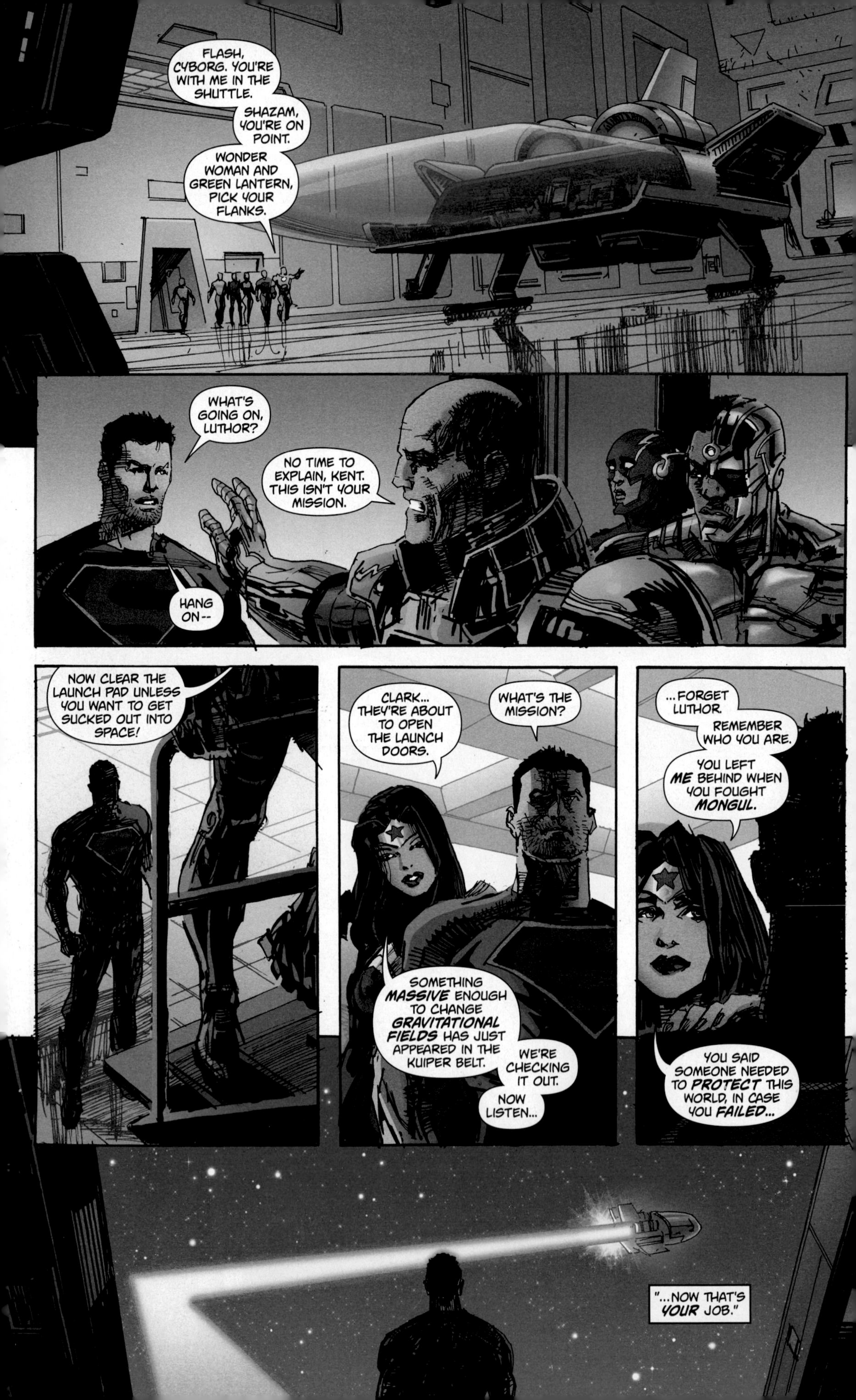
FLASH, CYBORG. YOU'RE WITH ME IN THE SHUTTLE.
SHAZAM, YOU'RE ON POINT.
WONDER WOMAN AND GREEN LANTERN, PICK YOUR FLANKS.
WHAT'S GOING ON, LUTHOR?
NO TIME TO EXPLAIN, KENT. THIS ISN'T YOUR MISSION.
HANG ON--
NOW CLEAR THE LAUNCH PAD UNLESS YOU WANT TO GET SUCKED OUT INTO SPACE!
CLARK... THEY'RE ABOUT TO OPEN THE LAUNCH DOORS.
WHAT'S THE MISSION?
SOMETHING MASSIVE ENOUGH TO CHANGE GRAVITATIONAL FIELDS HAS JUST APPEARED IN THE KUIPER BELT.
WE'RE CHECKING IT OUT.
NOW LISTEN...
...FORGET LUTHOR.
REMEMBER WHO YOU ARE.
YOU LEFT ME BEHIND WHEN YOU FOUGHT MONGUL.
YOU SAID SOMEONE NEEDED TO PROTECT THIS WORLD, IN CASE YOU FAILED...
"...NOW THAT'S YOUR JOB."

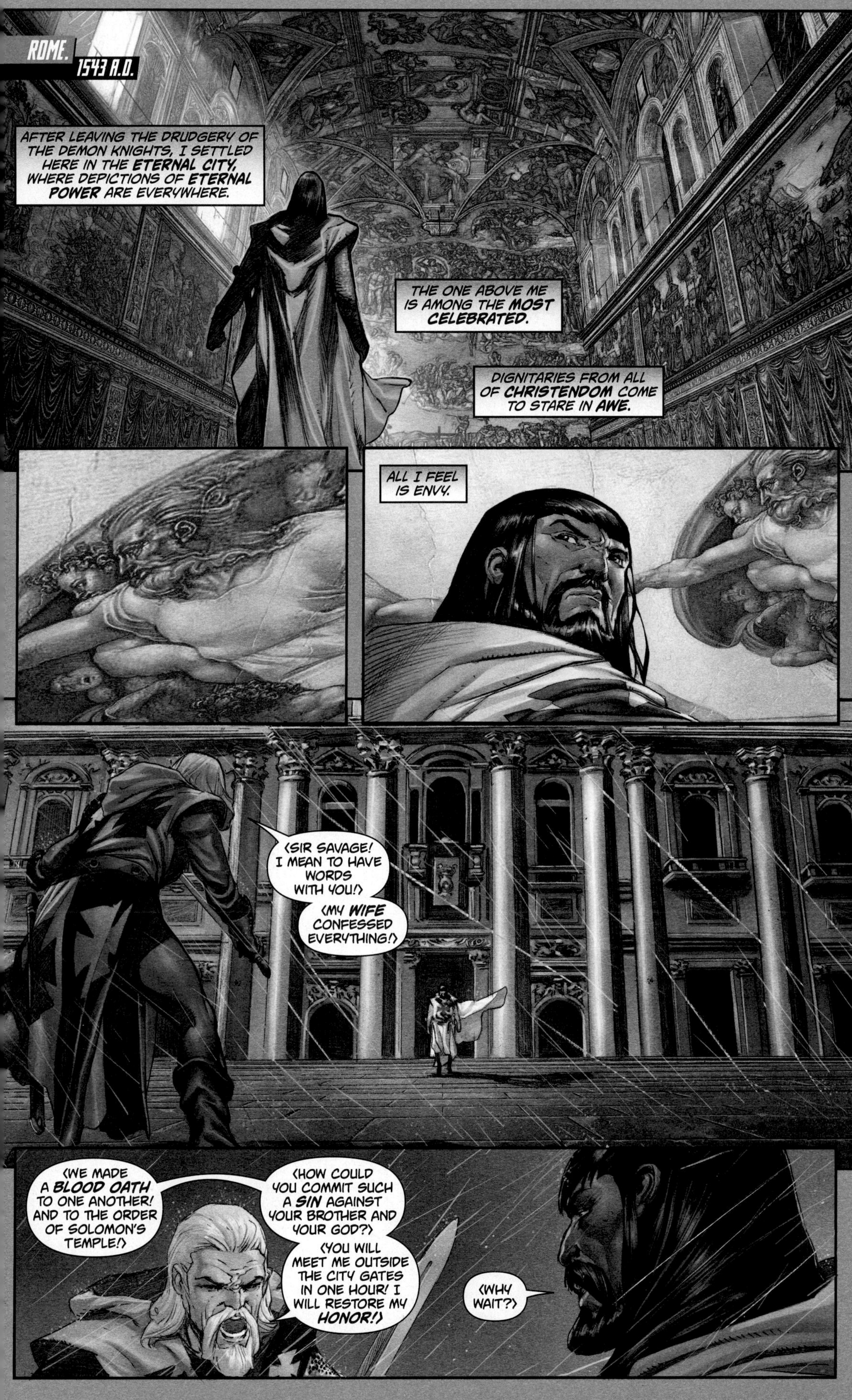
ROME.
1543 A.D.
AFTER LEAVING THE DRUDGERY OF THE DEMON KNIGHTS, I SETTLED HERE IN THE ETERNAL CITY, WHERE DEPICTIONS OF ETERNAL POWER ARE EVERYWHERE.
THE ONE ABOVE ME IS AMONG THE MOST CELEBRATED.
DIGNITARIES FROM ALL OF CHRISTENDOM COME TO STARE IN AWE.
ALL I FEEL IS ENVY.
‹SIR SAVAGE! I MEAN TO HAVE WORDS WITH YOU!›
‹MY WIFE CONFESSED EVERYTHING!›
‹WE MADE A BLOOD OATH TO ONE ANOTHER! AND TO THE ORDER OF SOLOMON'S TEMPLE!›
‹HOW COULD YOU COMMIT SUCH A SIN AGAINST YOUR BROTHER AND YOUR GOD?›
‹YOU WILL MEET ME OUTSIDE THE CITY GATES IN ONE HOUR! I WILL RESTORE MY HONOR!›
‹WHY WAIT?›

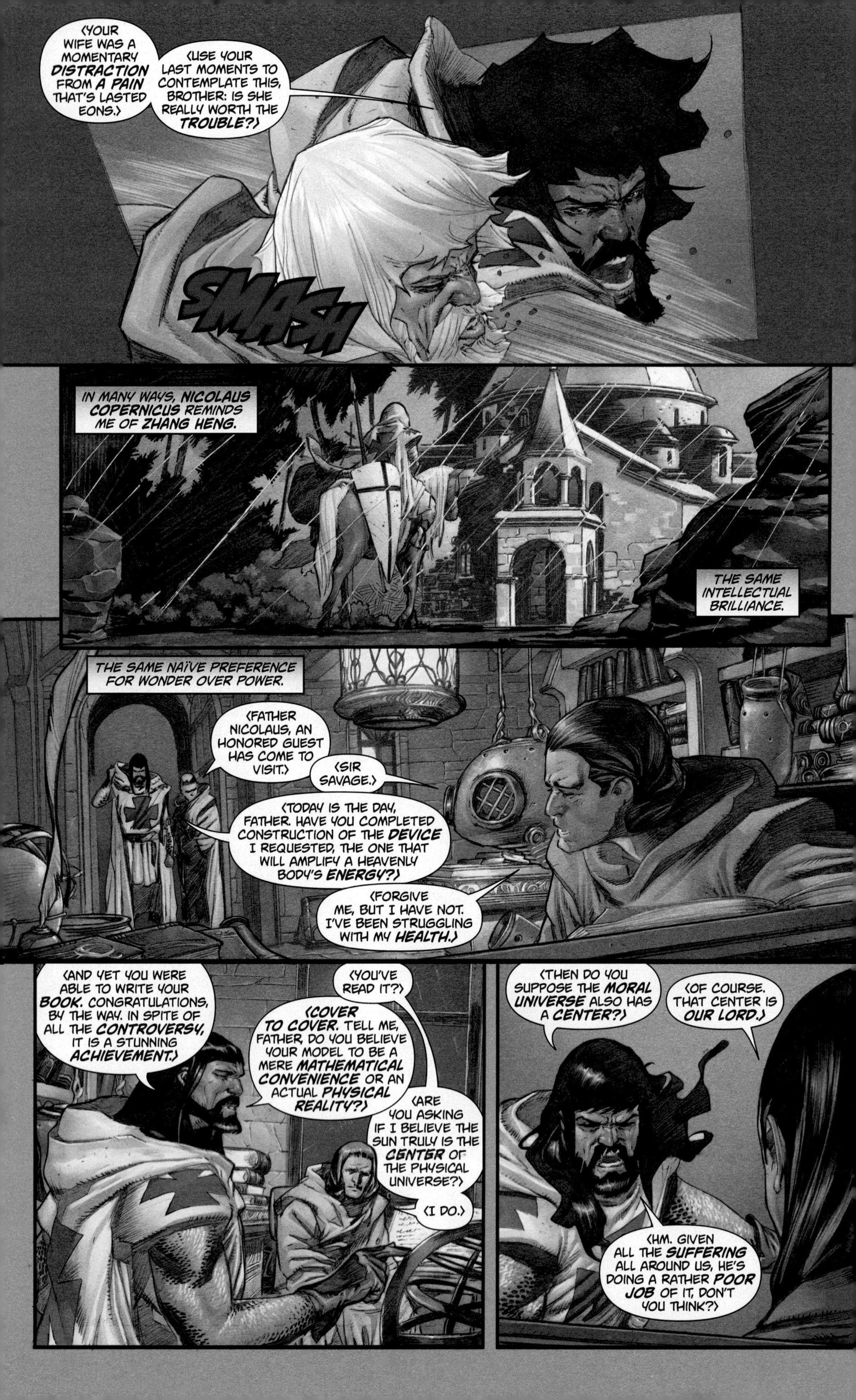
‹YOUR WIFE WAS A MOMENTARY DISTRACTION FROM A PAIN THAT'S LASTED EONS.›
‹USE YOUR LAST MOMENTS TO CONTEMPLATE THIS, BROTHER: IS SHE REALLY WORTH THE TROUBLE?›
SMASH
IN MANY WAYS, NICOLAUS COPERNICUS REMINDS ME OF ZHANG HENG.
THE SAME INTELLECTUAL BRILLIANCE.
THE SAME NAÏVE PREFERENCE FOR WONDER OVER POWER.
‹FATHER NICOLAUS, AN HONORED GUEST HAS COME TO VISIT.›
‹SIR SAVAGE.›
‹TODAY IS THE DAY, FATHER. HAVE YOU COMPLETED CONSTRUCTION OF THE DEVICE I REQUESTED, THE ONE THAT WILL AMPLIFY A HEAVENLY BODY'S ENERGY?›
‹FORGIVE ME, BUT I HAVE NOT. I'VE BEEN STRUGGLING WITH MY HEALTH.›
‹AND YET YOU WERE ABLE TO WRITE YOUR BOOK. CONGRATULATIONS, BY THE WAY. IN SPITE OF ALL THE CONTROVERSY, IT IS A STUNNING ACHIEVEMENT.›
‹YOU'VE READ IT?›
‹COVER TO COVER. TELL ME, FATHER, DO YOU BELIEVE YOUR MODEL TO BE A MERE MATHEMATICAL CONVENIENCE OR AN ACTUAL PHYSICAL REALITY?›
‹ARE YOU ASKING IF I BELIEVE THE SUN TRULY IS THE CENTER OF THE PHYSICAL UNIVERSE?›
‹I DO.›
‹THEN DO YOU SUPPOSE THE MORAL UNIVERSE ALSO HAS A CENTER?›
‹OF COURSE. THAT CENTER IS OUR LORD.›
‹HM. GIVEN ALL THE SUFFERING ALL AROUND US, HE'S DOING A RATHER POOR JOB OF IT, DON'T YOU THINK?›

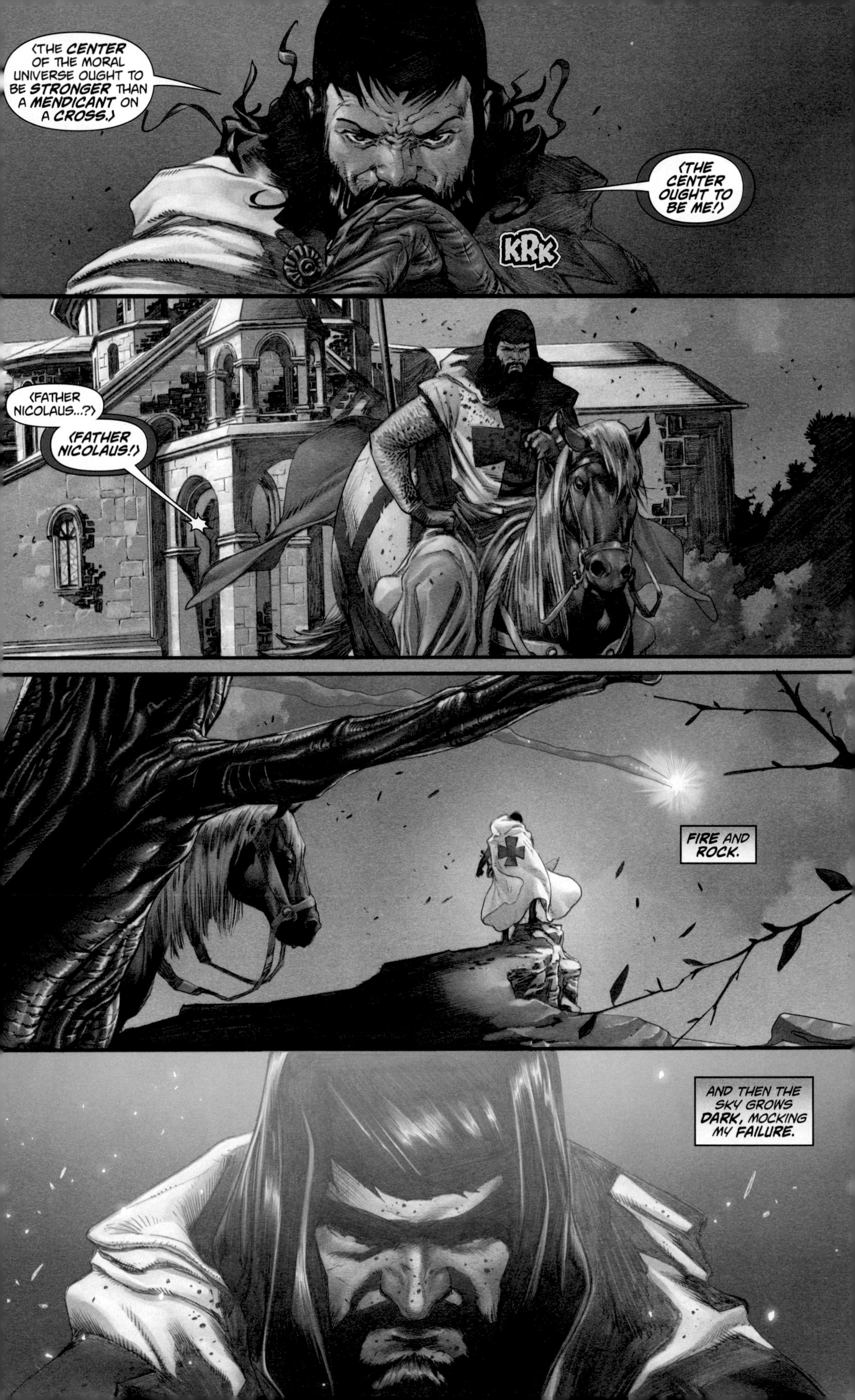
‹THE CENTER OF THE MORAL UNIVERSE OUGHT TO BE STRONGER THAN A MENDICANT ON A CROSS.›
‹THE CENTER OUGHT TO BE ME!›
KRK
‹FATHER NICOLAUS...?›
‹FATHER NICOLAUS!›
FIRE AND ROCK.
AND THEN THE SKY GROWS DARK, MOCKING MY FAILURE.

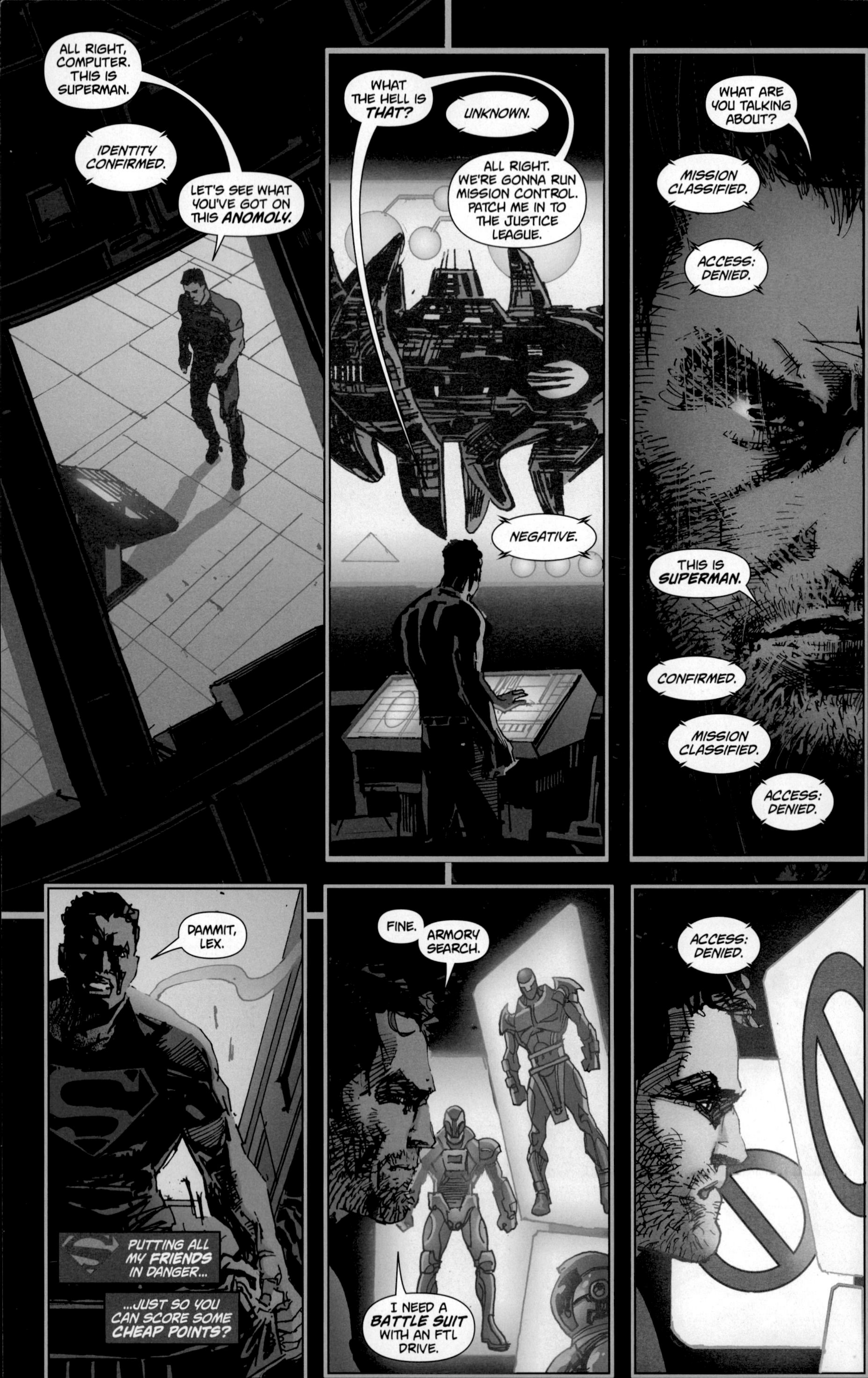
ALL RIGHT, COMPUTER. THIS IS SUPERMAN.
IDENTITY CONFIRMED.
LET'S SEE WHAT YOU'VE GOT ON THIS ANOMOLY.
WHAT THE HELL IS THAT?
UNKNOWN.
ALL RIGHT. WE'RE GONNA RUN MISSION CONTROL. PATCH ME IN TO THE JUSTICE LEAGUE.
NEGATIVE.
WHAT ARE YOU TALKING ABOUT?
MISSION CLASSIFIED.
ACCESS: DENIED.
THIS IS SUPERMAN.
CONFIRMED.
MISSION CLASSIFIED.
ACCESS: DENIED.
DAMMIT, LEX.
PUTTING ALL MY FRIENDS IN DANGER...
...JUST SO YOU CAN SCORE SOME CHEAP POINTS?
FINE.
ARMORY SEARCH.
I NEED A BATTLE SUIT WITH AN FTL DRIVE.
ACCESS: DENIED.

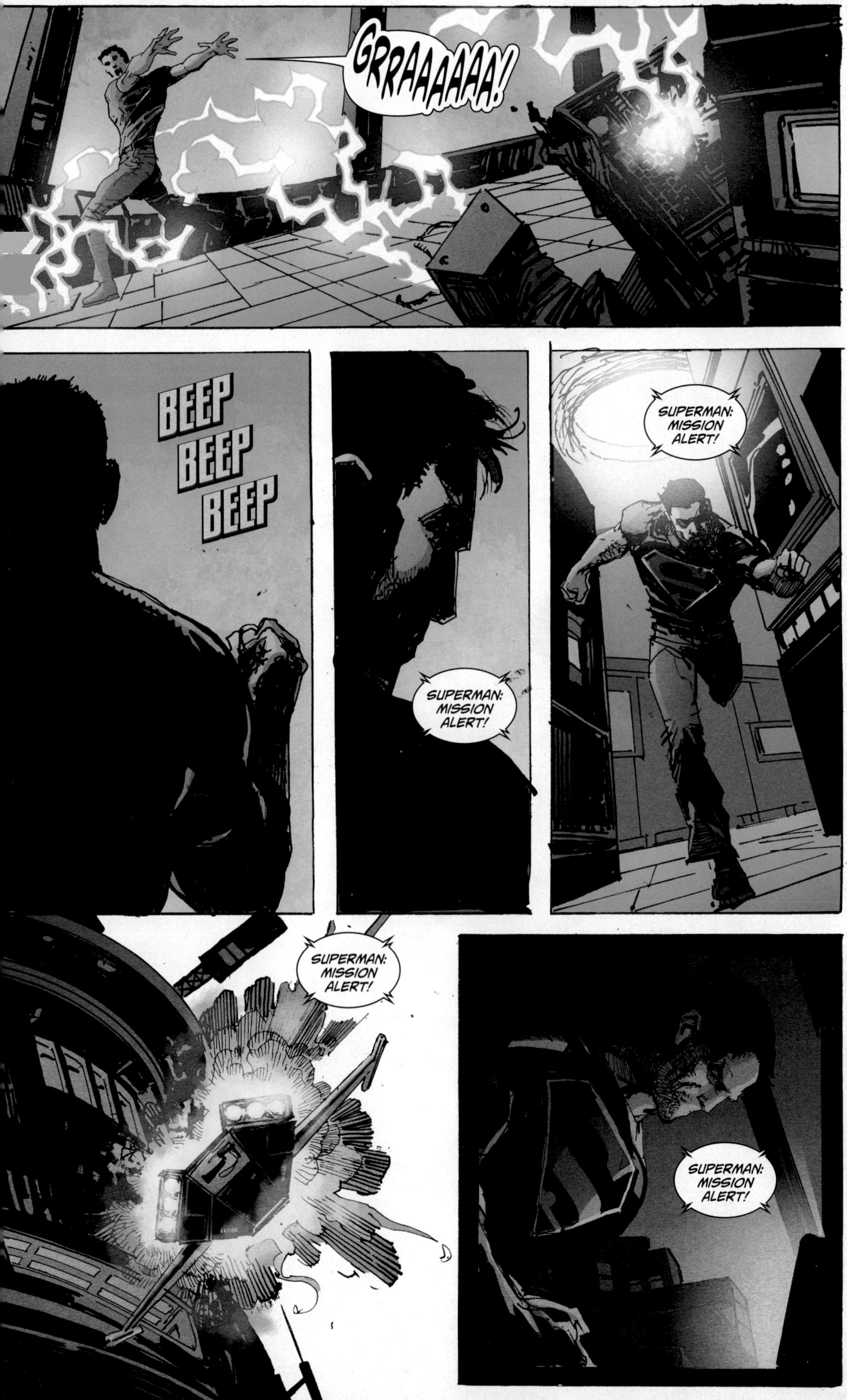
GRRAAAAAA!
BEEP
BEEP
BEEP
SUPERMAN: MISSION ALERT!
SUPERMAN: MISSION ALERT!
SUPERMAN: MISSION ALERT!
SUPERMAN: MISSION ALERT!

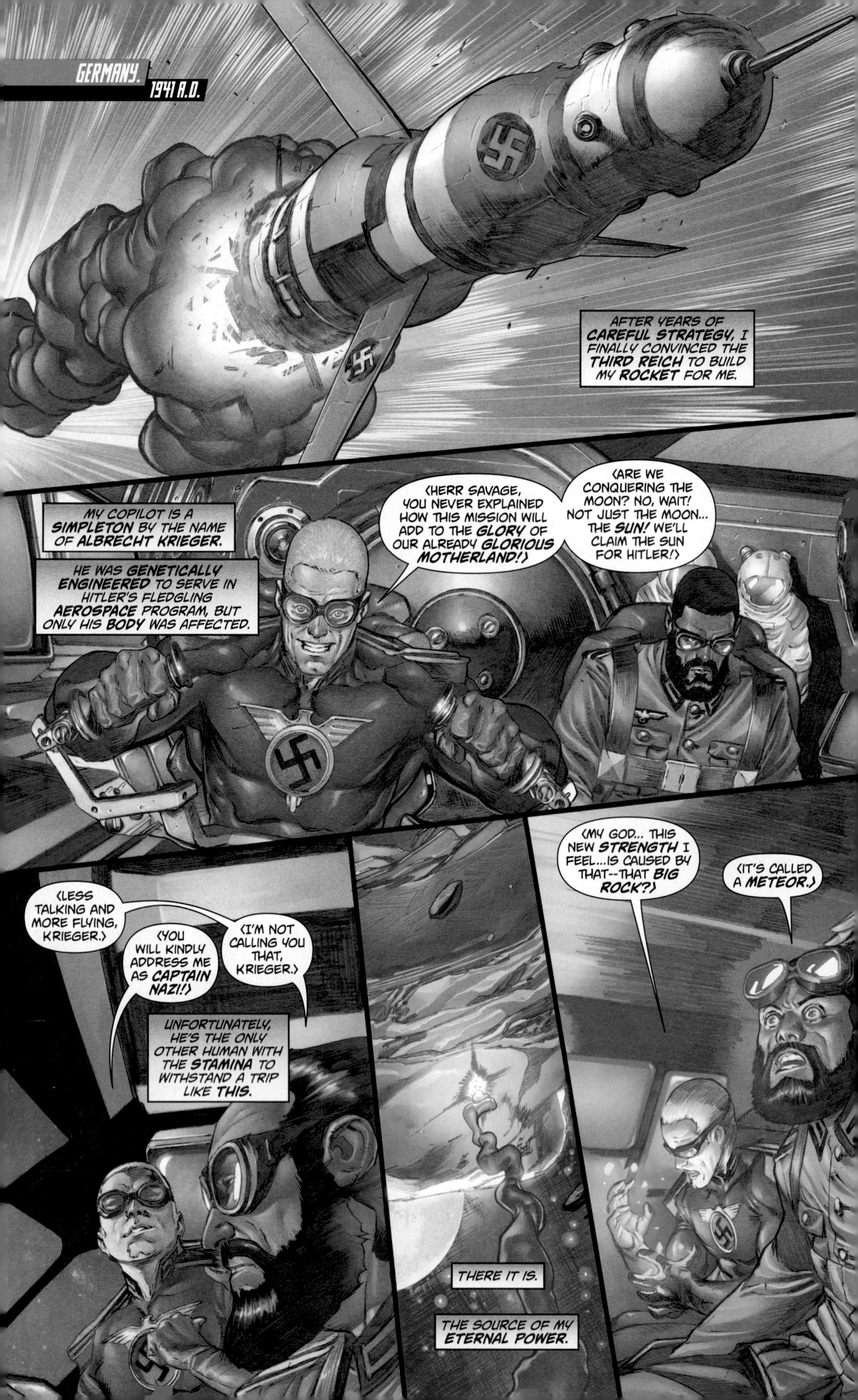
GERMANY.
1941 A.D.
AFTER YEARS OF CAREFUL STRATEGY, I FINALLY CONVINCED THE THIRD REICH TO BUILD MY ROCKET FOR ME.
MY COPILOT IS A SIMPLETON BY THE NAME OF ALBRECHT KRIEGER.
HE WAS GENETICALLY ENGINEERED TO SERVE IN HITLER'S FLEDGLING AEROSPACE PROGRAM, BUT ONLY HIS BODY WAS AFFECTED.
‹HERR SAVAGE, YOU NEVER EXPLAINED HOW THIS MISSION WILL ADD TO THE GLORY OF OUR ALREADY GLORIOUS MOTHERLAND!›
‹ARE WE CONQUERING THE MOON? NO, WAIT! NOT JUST THE MOON... THE SUN! WE'LL CLAIM THE SUN FOR HITLER!›
‹LESS TALKING AND MORE FLYING, KRIEGER.›
‹YOU WILL KINDLY ADDRESS ME AS CAPTAIN NAZI!›
‹I'M NOT CALLING YOU THAT, KRIEGER.›
UNFORTUNATELY, HE'S THE ONLY OTHER HUMAN WITH THE STAMINA TO WITHSTAND A TRIP LIKE THIS.
THERE IT IS.
THE SOURCE OF MY ETERNAL POWER.
‹MY GOD... THIS NEW STRENGTH I FEEL...IS CAUSED BY THAT--THAT BIG ROCK?›
‹IT'S CALLED A METEOR.›

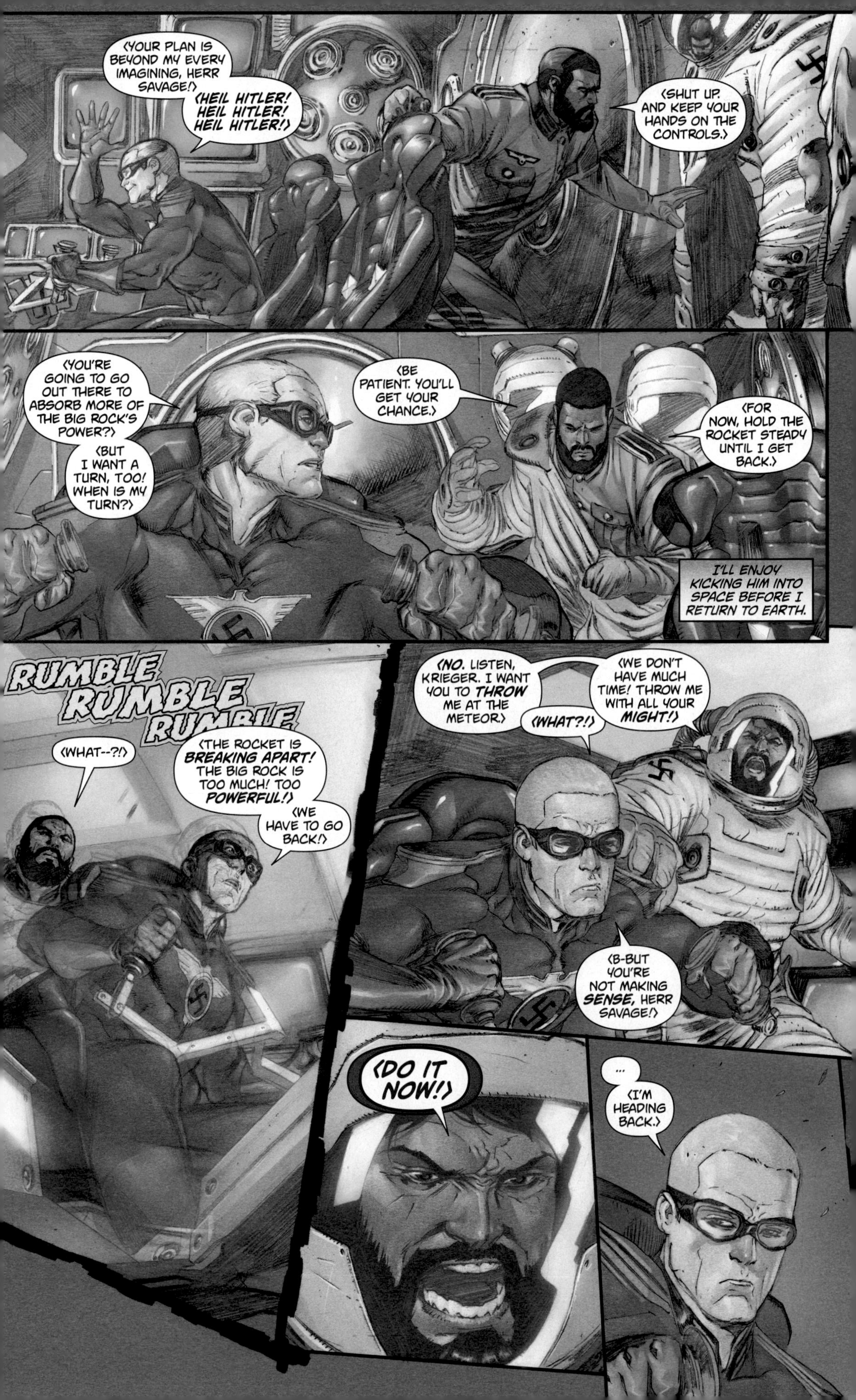

‹YOUR PLAN IS BEYOND MY EVERY IMAGINING, HERR SAVAGE!›
‹HEIL HITLER! HEIL HITLER! HEIL HITLER!›
‹SHUT UP. AND KEEP YOUR HANDS ON THE CONTROLS.›
‹YOU'RE GOING TO GO OUT THERE TO ABSORB MORE OF THE BIG ROCK'S POWER?›
‹BUT I WANT A TURN, TOO! WHEN IS MY TURN?›
‹BE PATIENT. YOU'LL GET YOUR CHANCE.›
‹FOR NOW, HOLD THE ROCKET STEADY UNTIL I GET BACK.›
I'LL ENJOY KICKING HIM INTO SPACE BEFORE I RETURN TO EARTH.
RUMBLE RUMBLE RUMBLE
‹WHAT--?!›
‹THE ROCKET IS BREAKING APART! THE BIG ROCK IS TOO MUCH! TOO POWERFUL!›
‹WE HAVE TO GO BACK!›
‹NO. LISTEN, KRIEGER. I WANT YOU TO THROW ME AT THE METEOR.›
‹WHAT?!›
‹WE DON'T HAVE MUCH TIME! THROW ME WITH ALL YOUR MIGHT!›
‹B-BUT YOU'RE NOT MAKING SENSE, HERR SAVAGE!›
‹DO IT NOW!›
...
‹I'M HEADING BACK.›

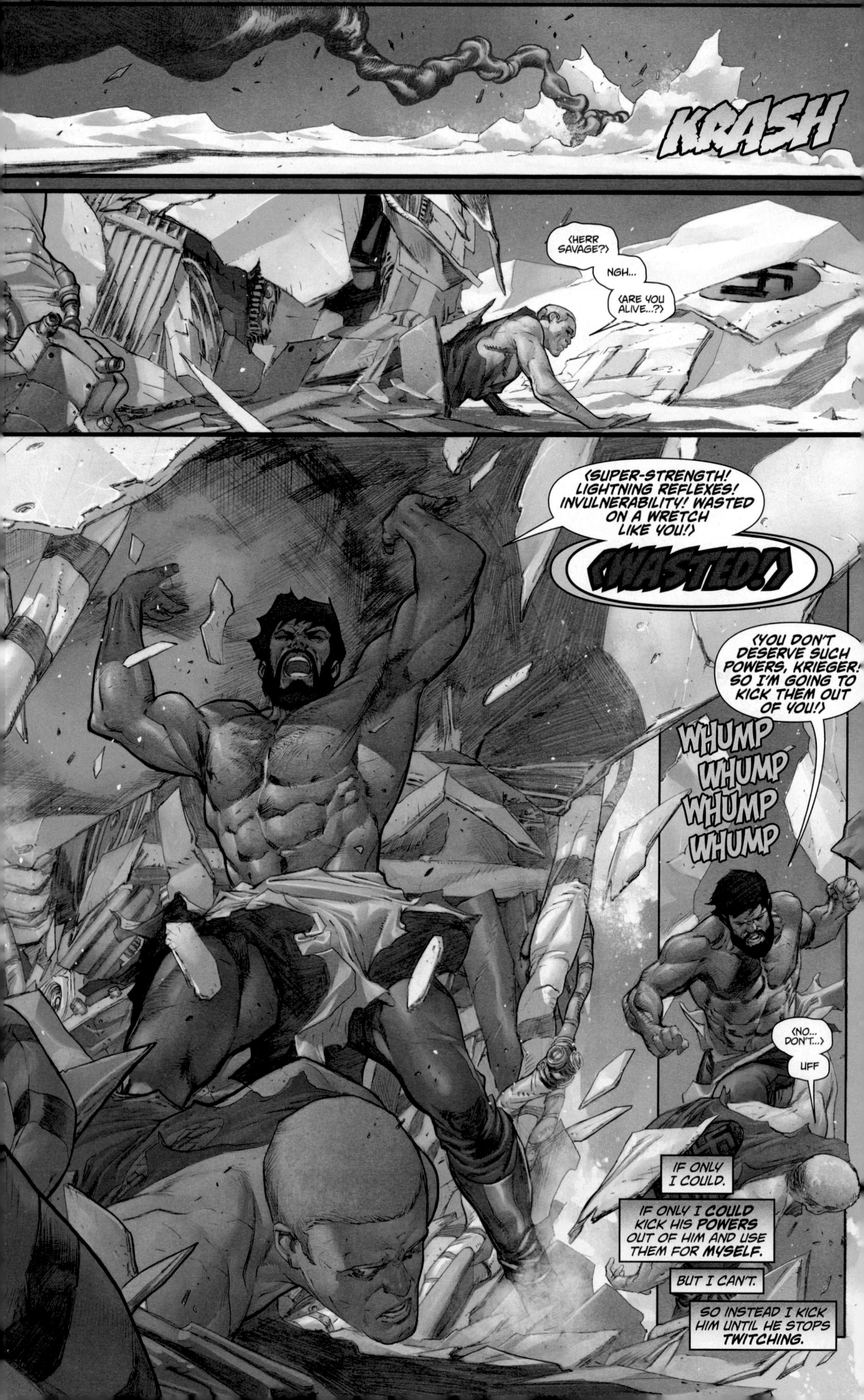
KRASH
⟨HERR SAVAGE?⟩
NGH...
⟨ARE YOU ALIVE...?⟩
⟨SUPER-STRENGTH! LIGHTNING REFLEXES! INVULNERABILITY! WASTED ON A WRETCH LIKE YOU!⟩
⟨WASTED!⟩
⟨YOU DON'T DESERVE SUCH POWERS, KRIEGER! SO I'M GOING TO KICK THEM OUT OF YOU!⟩
WHUMP
WHUMP
WHUMP
WHUMP
⟨NO... DON'T...⟩
UFF
IF ONLY I COULD.
IF ONLY I **COULD** KICK HIS **POWERS** OUT OF HIM AND USE THEM FOR **MYSELF**.
BUT I CAN'T.
SO INSTEAD I KICK HIM UNTIL HE STOPS **TWITCHING**.

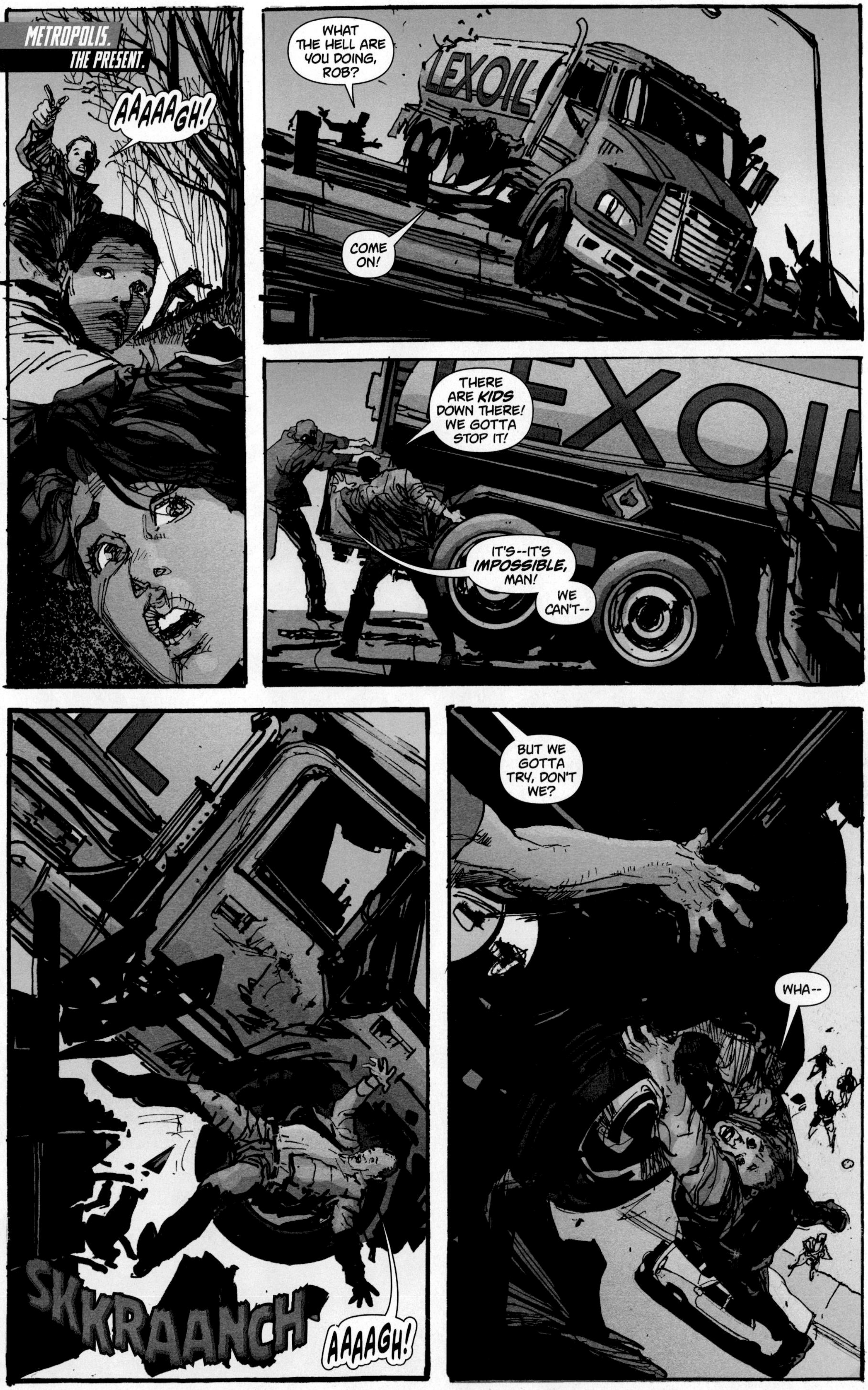
METROPOLIS. THE PRESENT.
AAAAAGH!
WHAT THE HELL ARE YOU DOING, ROB?
LEXOIL
COME ON!
THERE ARE KIDS DOWN THERE! WE GOTTA STOP IT!
IT'S--IT'S IMPOSSIBLE, MAN!
WE CAN'T--
SKKRAANCH
AAAAGH!
BUT WE GOTTA TRY, DON'T WE?
WHA--

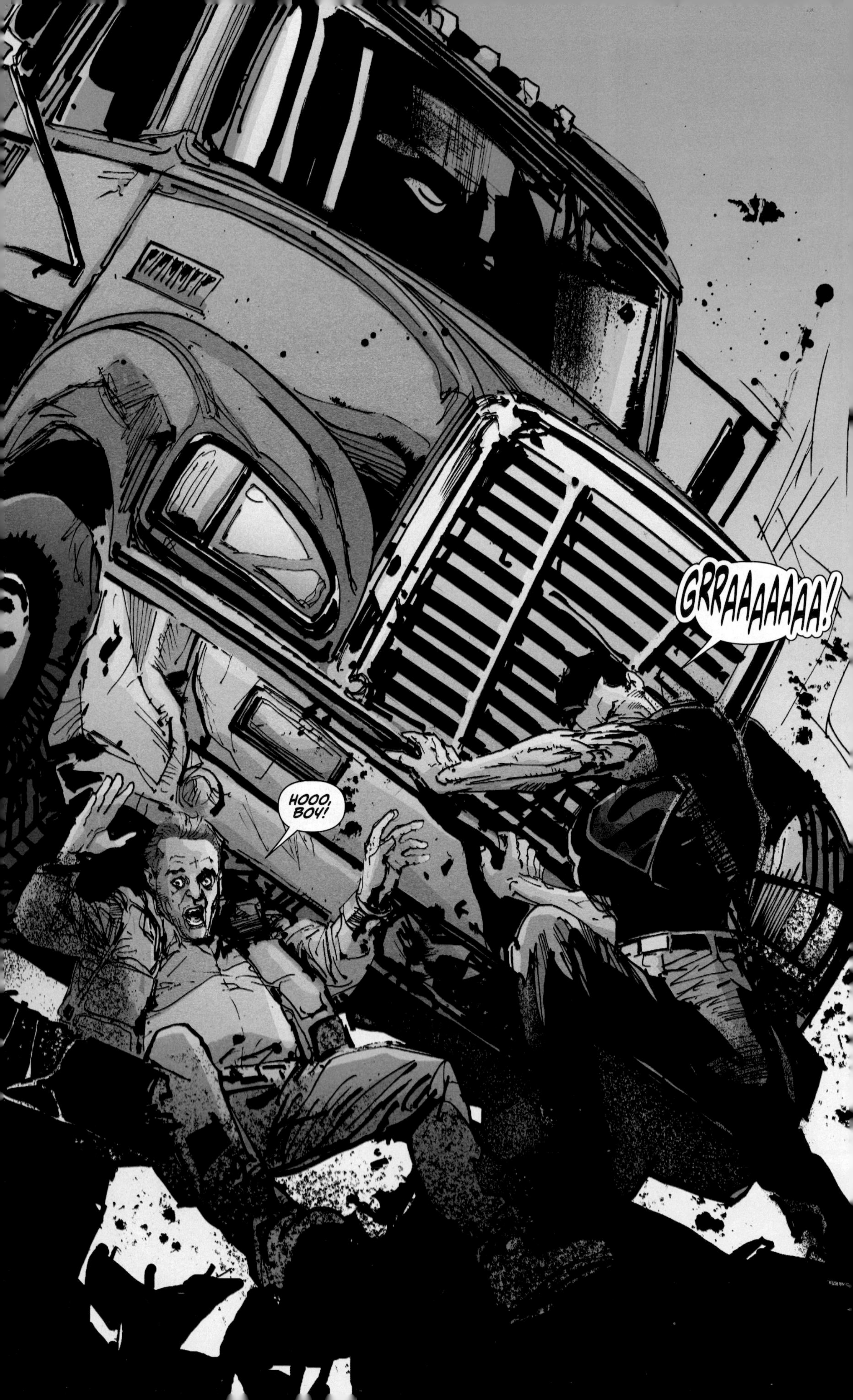
GRRAAAAAAA!
HOOO, BOY!

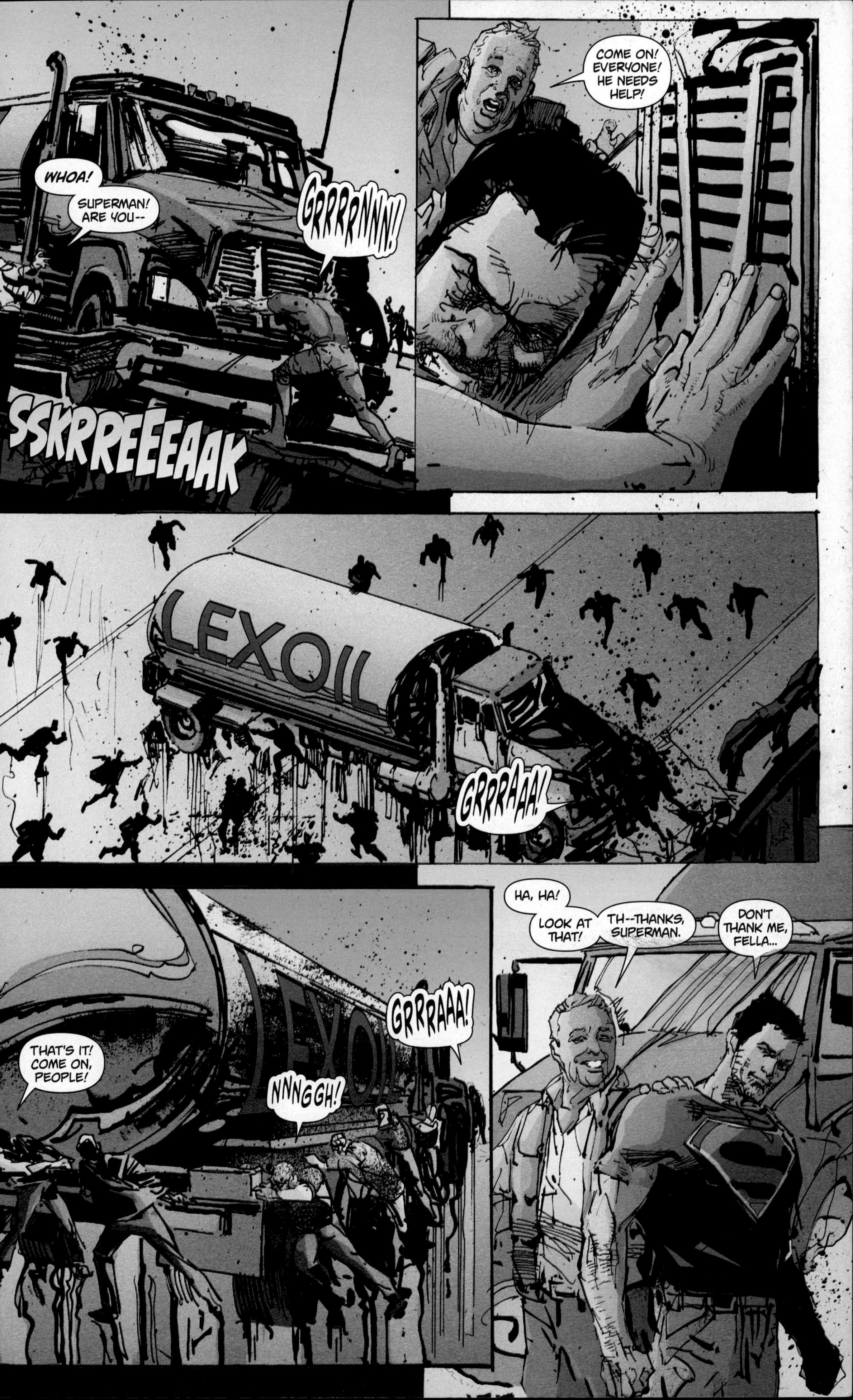
WHOA!
SUPERMAN! ARE YOU--
GRRRRNNN!
SSKRREEEAAK
COME ON! EVERYONE! HE NEEDS HELP!
LEXOIL
GRRRAAA!
LEXOIL
THAT'S IT! COME ON, PEOPLE!
GRRRAAA!
NNNGGH!
HA, HA!
LOOK AT THAT!
TH--THANKS, SUPERMAN.
DON'T THANK ME, FELLA...

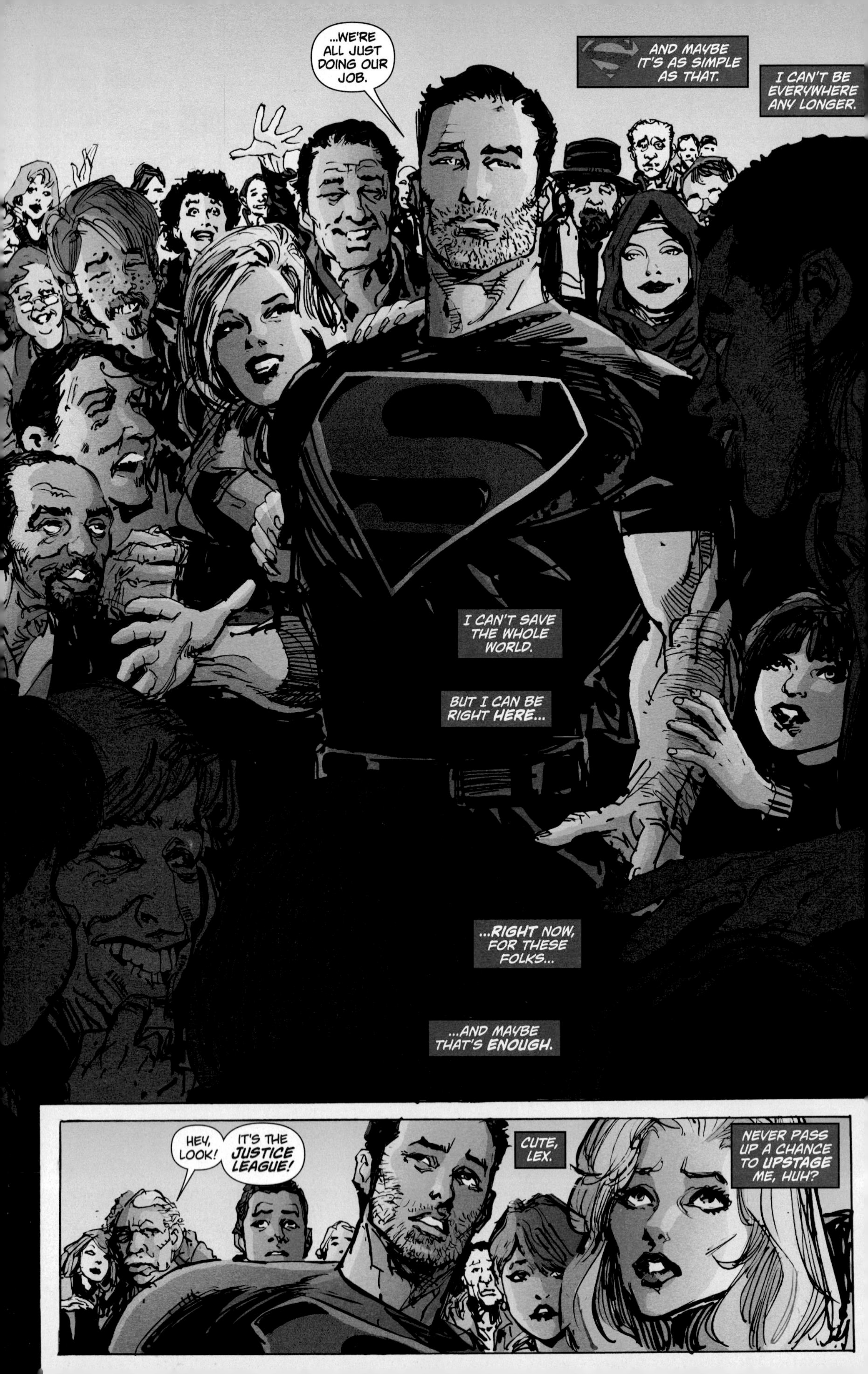
...WE'RE ALL JUST DOING OUR JOB.
AND MAYBE IT'S AS SIMPLE AS THAT.
I CAN'T BE EVERYWHERE ANY LONGER.
I CAN'T SAVE THE WHOLE WORLD.
BUT I CAN BE RIGHT HERE...
...RIGHT NOW, FOR THESE FOLKS...
...AND MAYBE THAT'S ENOUGH.
HEY, LOOK!
IT'S THE JUSTICE LEAGUE!
CUTE, LEX.
NEVER PASS UP A CHANCE TO UPSTAGE ME, HUH?

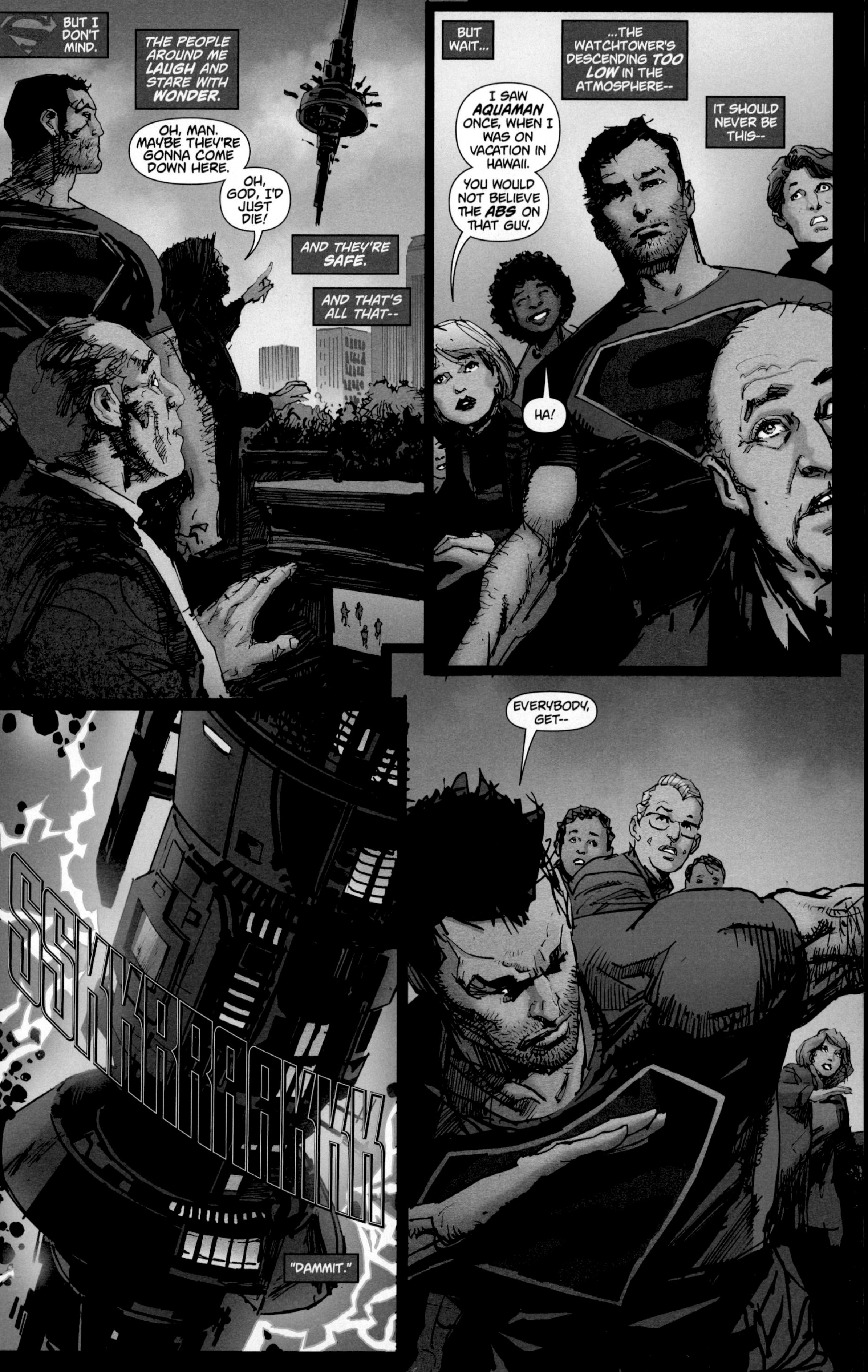
BUT I DON'T MIND.
THE PEOPLE AROUND ME LAUGH AND STARE WITH WONDER.
OH, MAN. MAYBE THEY'RE GONNA COME DOWN HERE.
OH, GOD, I'D JUST DIE!
AND THEY'RE SAFE.
AND THAT'S ALL THAT--
BUT WAIT...
...THE WATCHTOWER'S DESCENDING TOO LOW IN THE ATMOSPHERE--
IT SHOULD NEVER BE THIS--
I SAW AQUAMAN ONCE, WHEN I WAS ON VACATION IN HAWAII.
YOU WOULD NOT BELIEVE THE ABS ON THAT GUY.
HA!
SSKKRRAAKKKK
"DAMMIT."
EVERYBODY, GET--

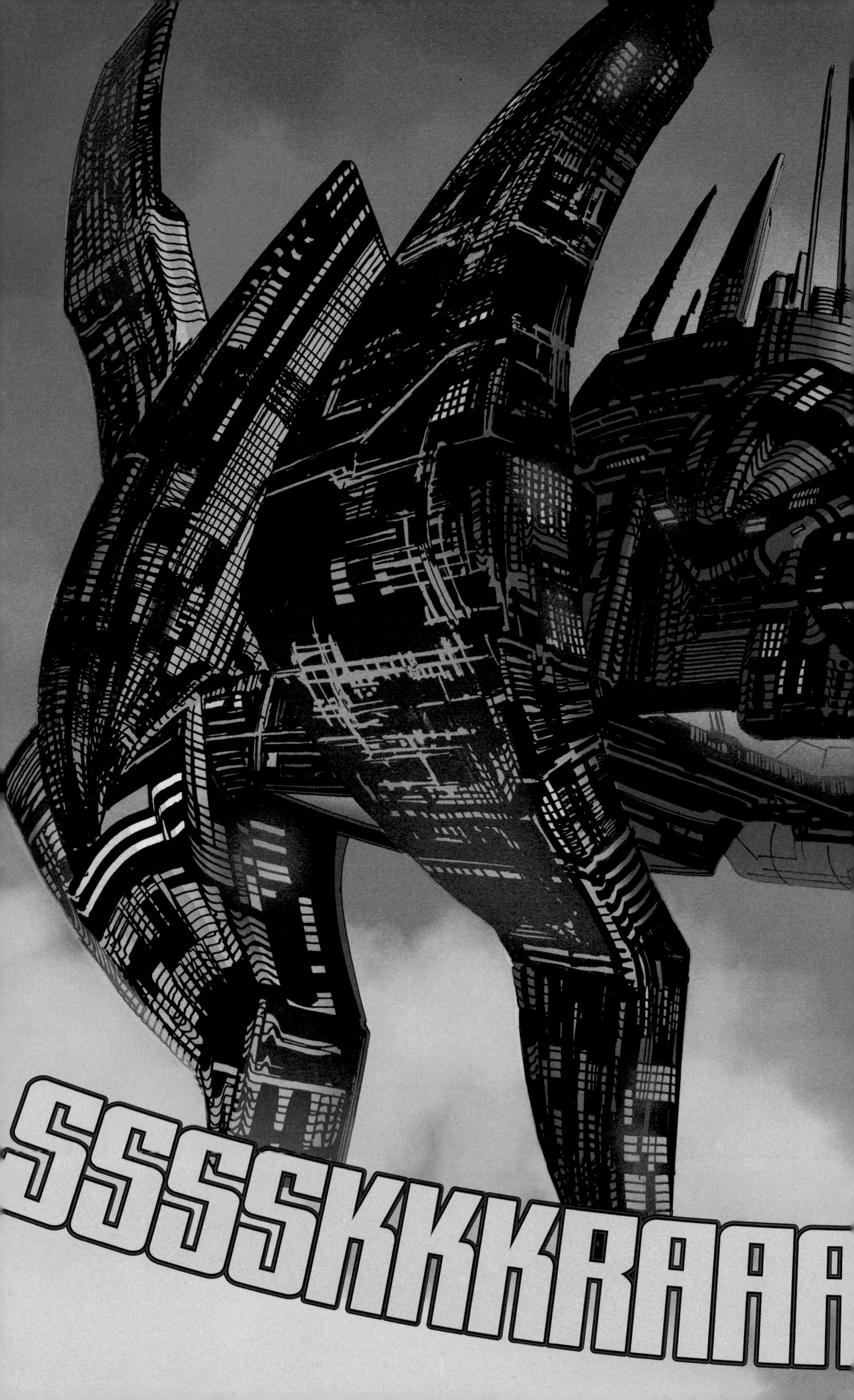
SSSSKKKRAAA

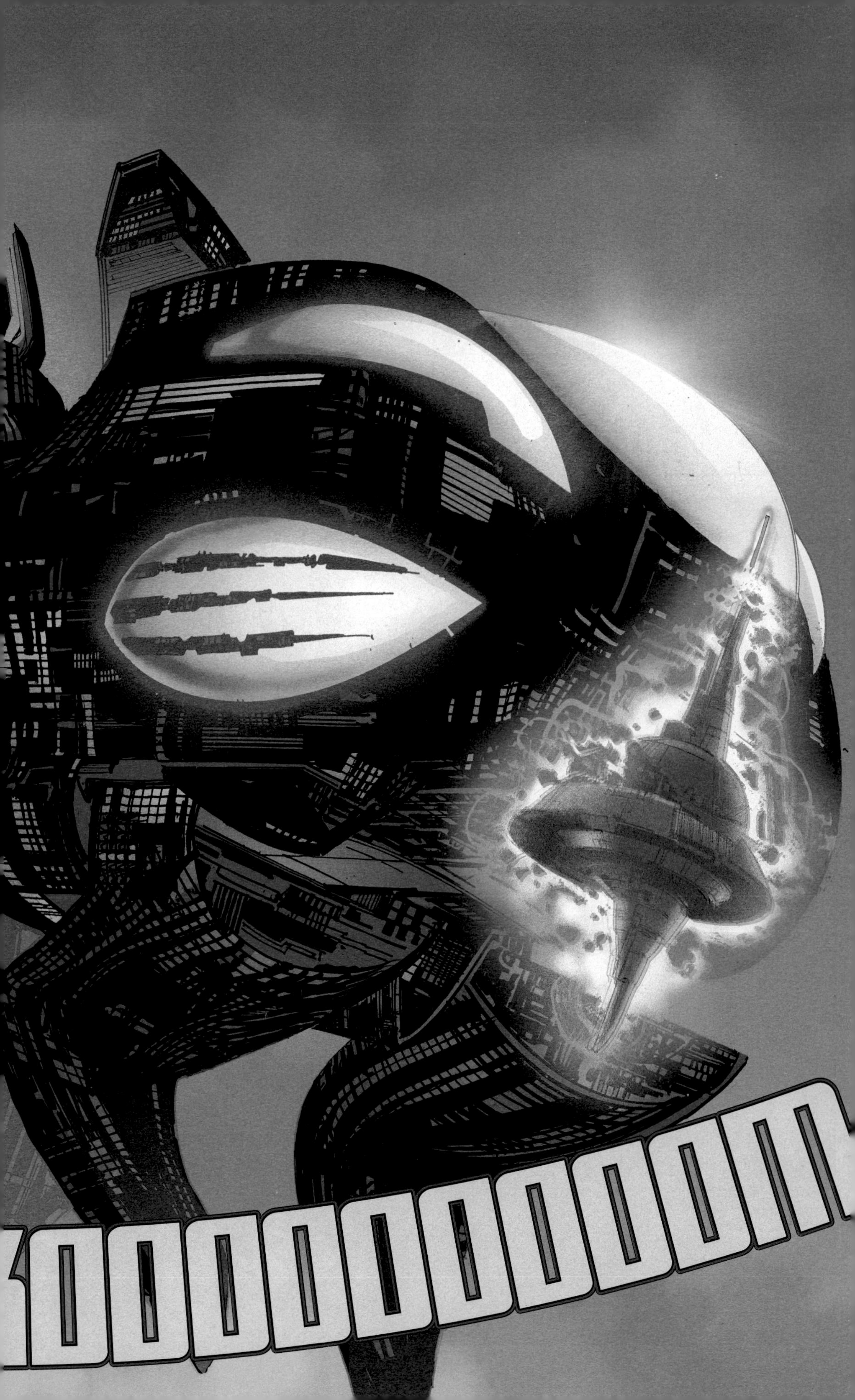
OOOOOOOOOM

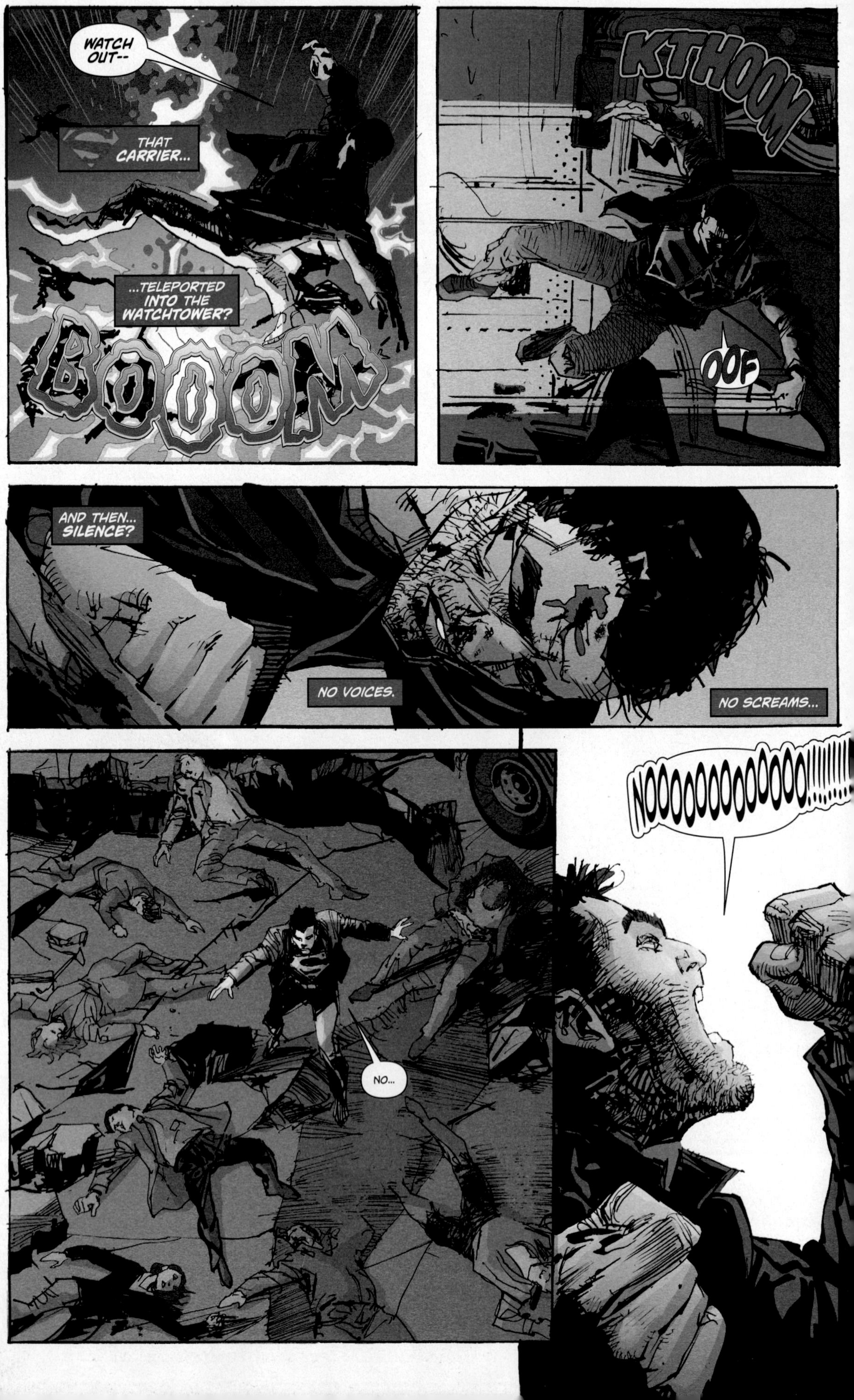
WATCH OUT--
THAT CARRIER...
...TELEPORTED INTO THE WATCHTOWER?
BOOOM
KTHOOM
OOF
AND THEN... SILENCE?
NO VOICES.
NO SCREAMS...
NO...
NOOOOOOOOOOOO!!!!!!!

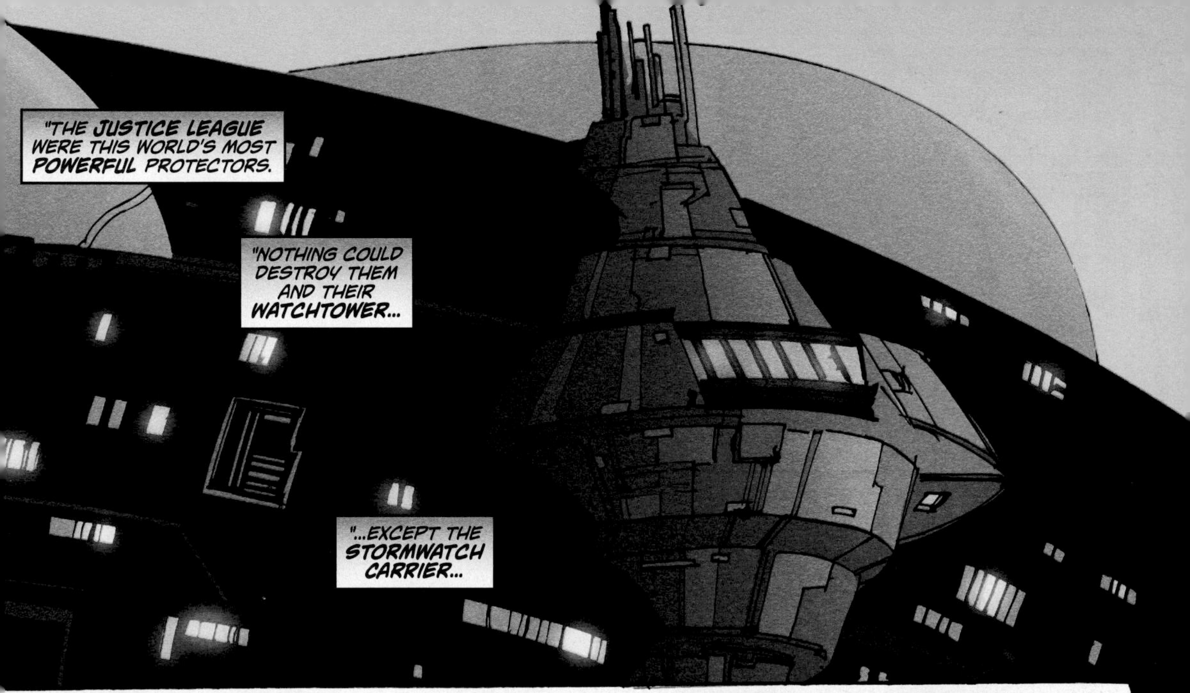
"THE JUSTICE LEAGUE WERE THIS WORLD'S MOST POWERFUL PROTECTORS.
"NOTHING COULD DESTROY THEM AND THEIR WATCHTOWER...
"...EXCEPT THE STORMWATCH CARRIER...

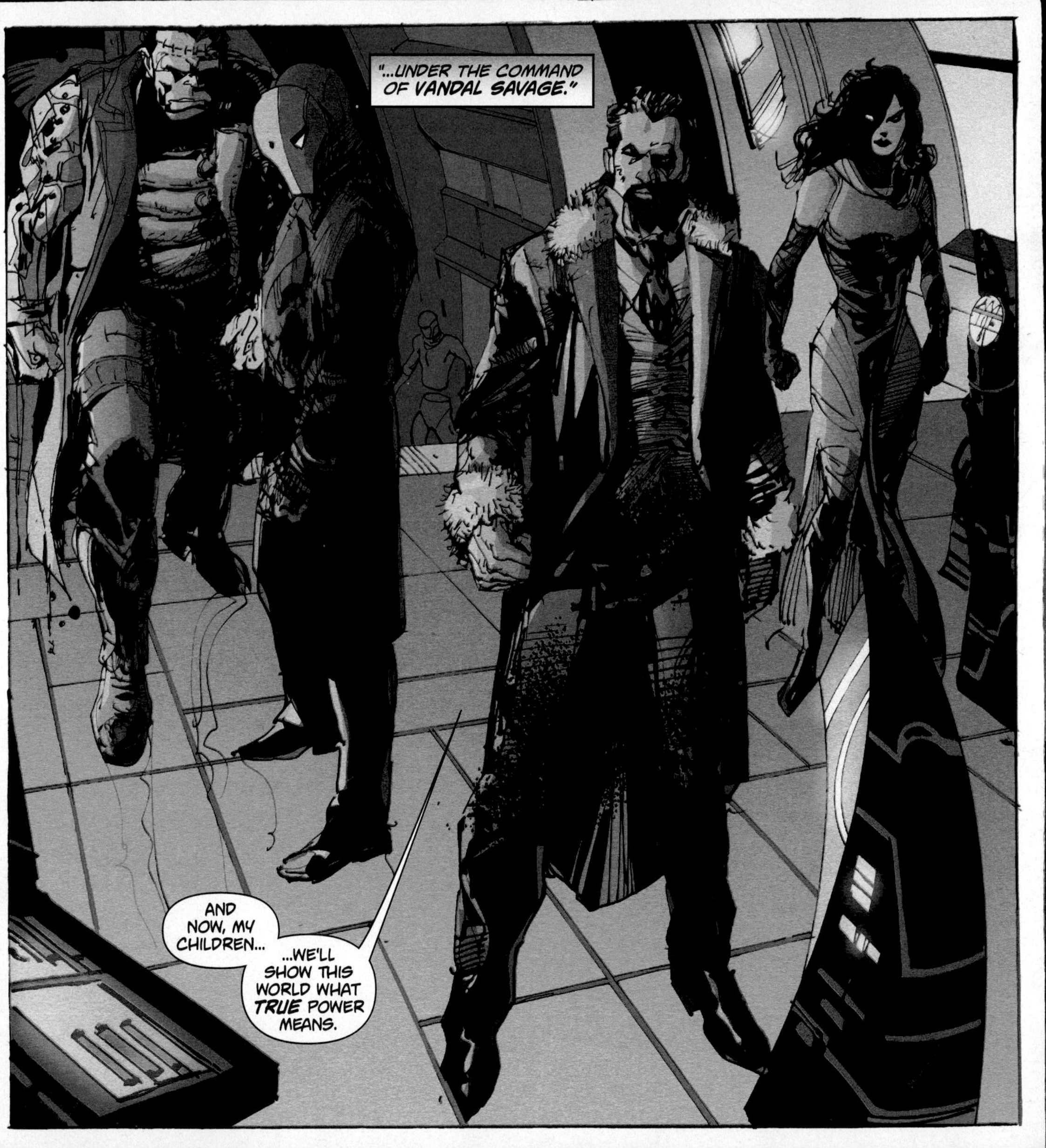
"...UNDER THE COMMAND OF VANDAL SAVAGE."
AND NOW, MY CHILDREN...
...WE'LL SHOW THIS WORLD WHAT TRUE POWER MEANS.

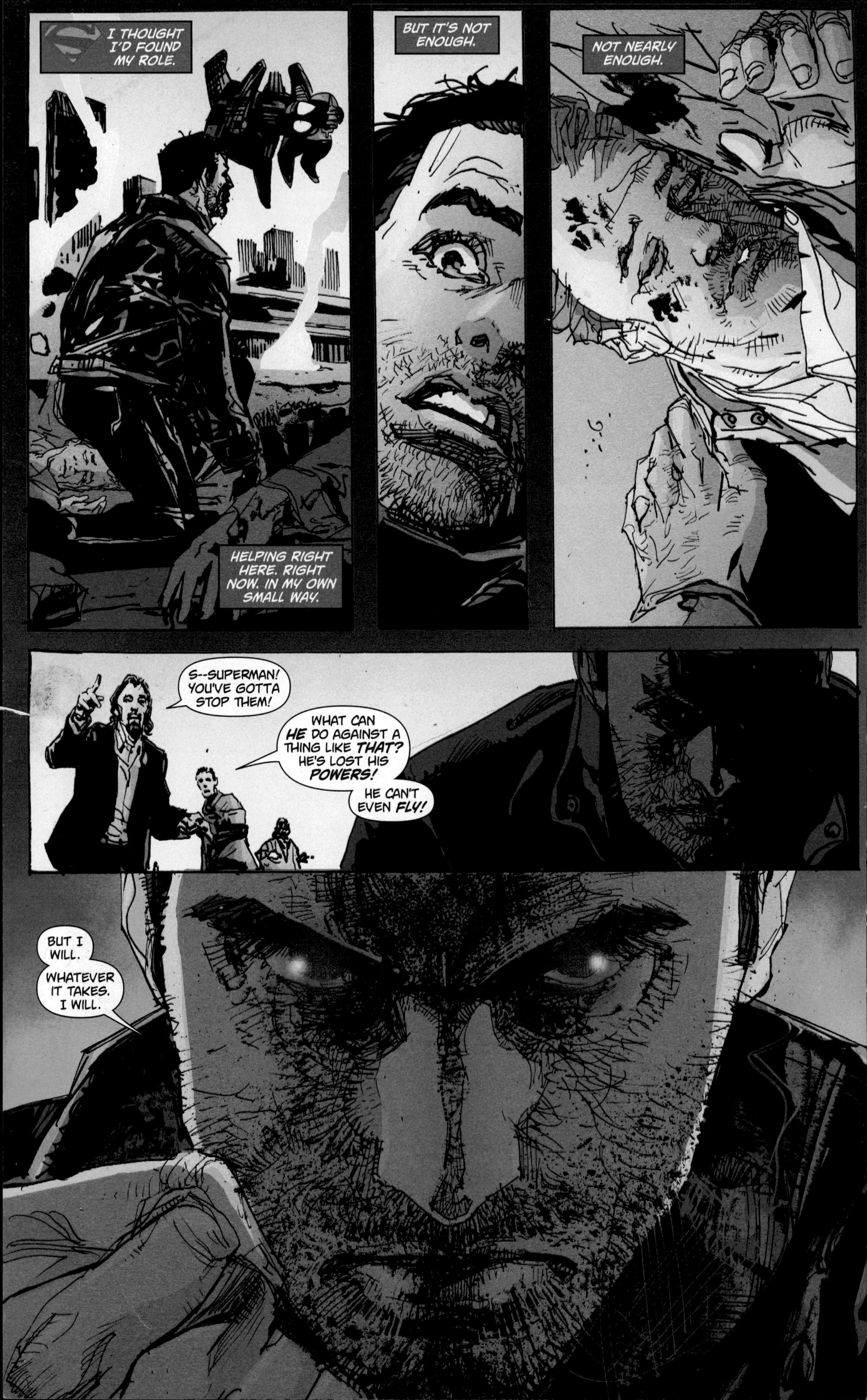
I THOUGHT I'D FOUND MY ROLE.
HELPING RIGHT HERE. RIGHT NOW. IN MY OWN SMALL WAY.
BUT IT'S NOT ENOUGH.
NOT NEARLY ENOUGH.
S--SUPERMAN! YOU'VE GOTTA STOP THEM!
WHAT CAN HE DO AGAINST A THING LIKE THAT? HE'S LOST HIS POWERS!
HE CAN'T EVEN FLY!
BUT I WILL.
WHATEVER IT TAKES. I WILL.

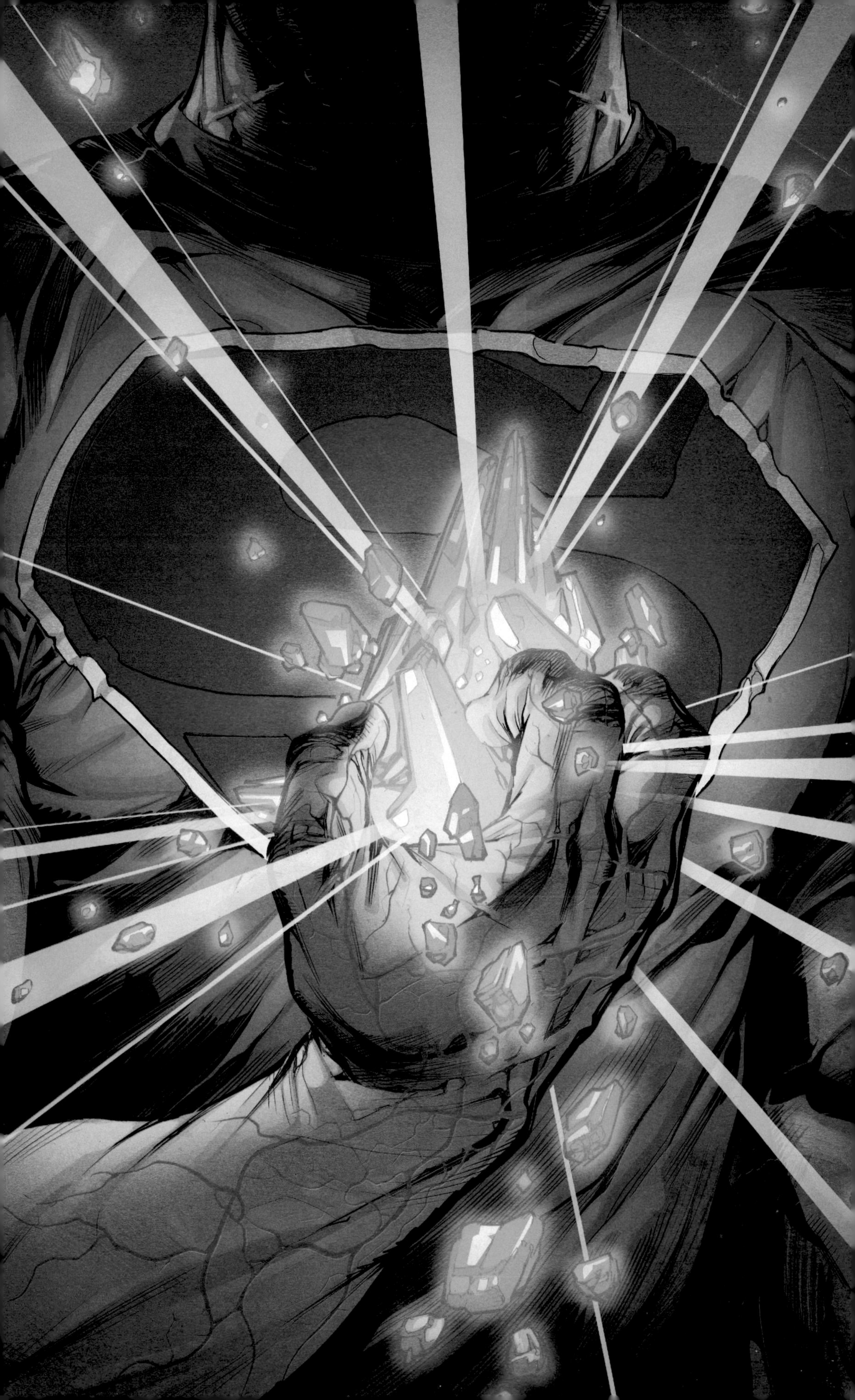

TREATMENT

GENE LUEN YANG writer   HOWARD PORTER, ARDIAN SYAF pencillers   HOWARD PORTER, DON HO, JEROME K. MOORE inkers   HI-FI colorist   ROB LEIGH letterer
HOWARD PORTER, HI-FI cover

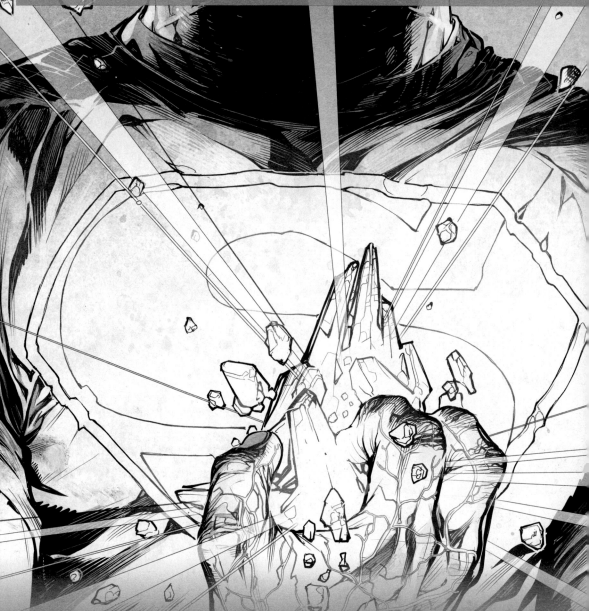

Previously, in SUPERMAN: SAVAGE DAWN ...

Having successfully merged the Justice League Watchtower with the Stormwatch Carrier, Vandal Savage and his army have defeated the Justice League. As Savage siphons the imprisoned League members' powers for his own use, a desperate Superman, aided by Steel and members of the Justice League United, temporarily finds renewed strength through charging his cells inside Metallo's original Kryptonite-powered armor. The move almost proves fatal – after freeing Wonder Woman, the Man of Steel lays motionless while Savage's forces capture the remaining Leaguers and power up his spacecraft for the next step of the immortal's grand design.

Diana, fearing the man she loves has breathed his last, brings Superman to the Greek Gods in the hopes they will bestow the Gift of Healing. After putting Superman's spiritual form through an emotionally grueling series of tests to determine his worthiness, they agree to heal him – and in doing so, make him completely and fully mortal...

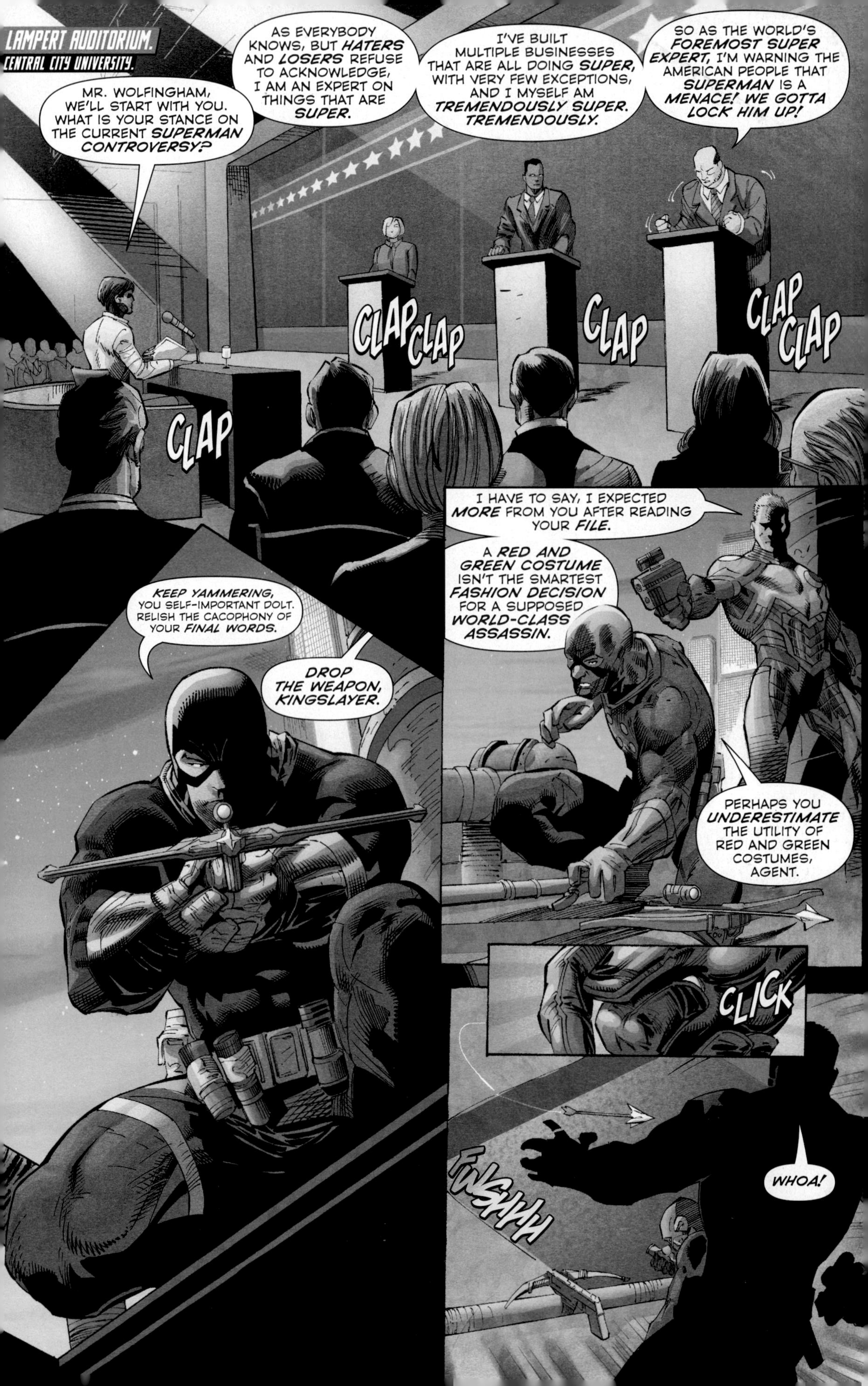
LAMPERT AUDITORIUM.
CENTRAL CITY UNIVERSITY.
MR. WOLFINGHAM, WE'LL START WITH YOU. WHAT IS YOUR STANCE ON THE CURRENT SUPERMAN CONTROVERSY?
AS EVERYBODY KNOWS, BUT HATERS AND LOSERS REFUSE TO ACKNOWLEDGE, I AM AN EXPERT ON THINGS THAT ARE SUPER.
I'VE BUILT MULTIPLE BUSINESSES THAT ARE ALL DOING SUPER, WITH VERY FEW EXCEPTIONS, AND I MYSELF AM TREMENDOUSLY SUPER. TREMENDOUSLY.
SO AS THE WORLD'S FOREMOST SUPER EXPERT, I'M WARNING THE AMERICAN PEOPLE THAT SUPERMAN IS A MENACE! WE GOTTA LOCK HIM UP!
CLAP CLAP
CLAP
CLAP CLAP
CLAP
KEEP YAMMERING, YOU SELF-IMPORTANT DOLT. RELISH THE CACOPHONY OF YOUR FINAL WORDS.
DROP THE WEAPON, KINGSLAYER.
I HAVE TO SAY, I EXPECTED MORE FROM YOU AFTER READING YOUR FILE.
A RED AND GREEN COSTUME ISN'T THE SMARTEST FASHION DECISION FOR A SUPPOSED WORLD-CLASS ASSASSIN.
PERHAPS YOU UNDERESTIMATE THE UTILITY OF RED AND GREEN COSTUMES, AGENT.
CLICK
FWSHHH
WHOA!

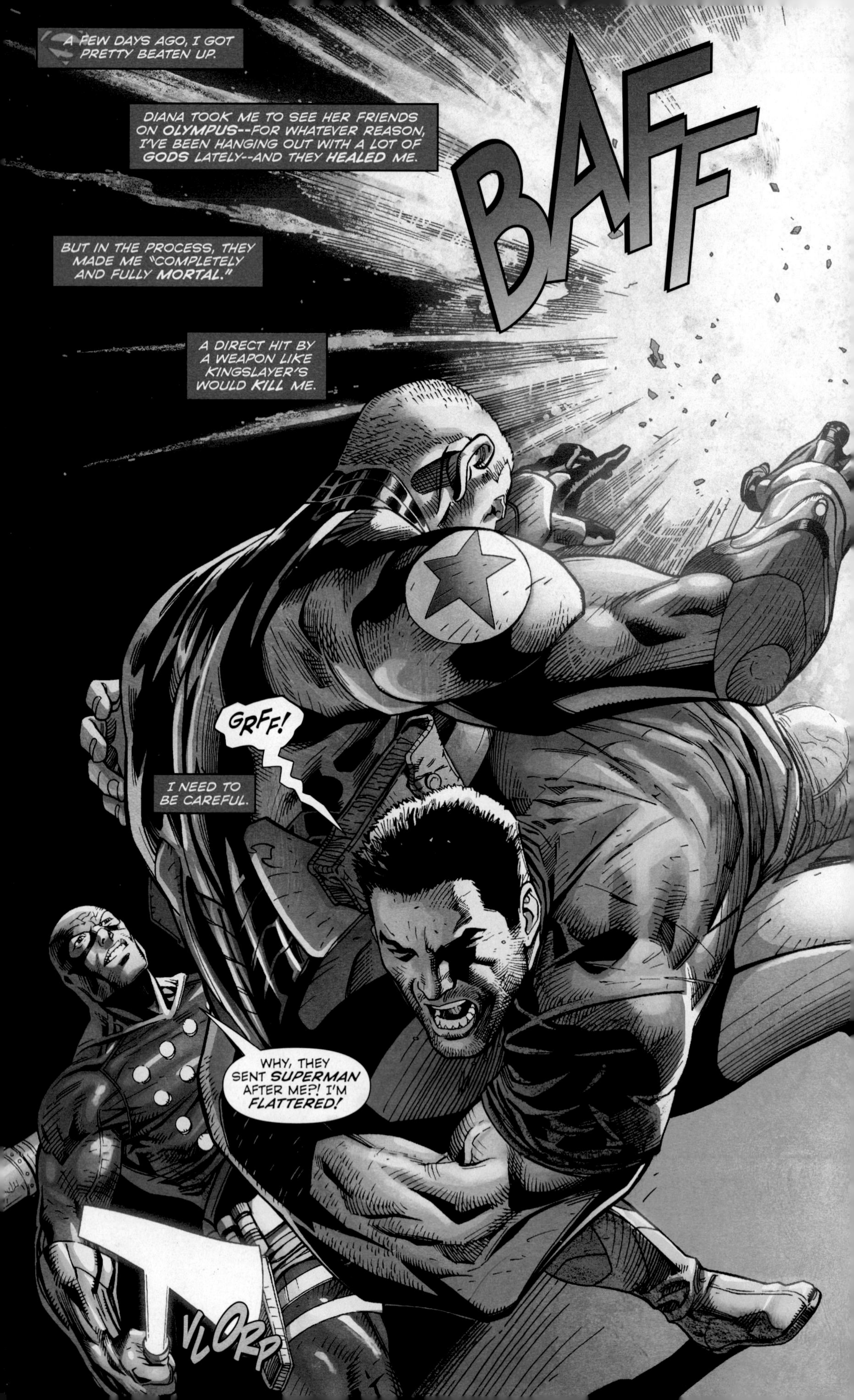
A FEW DAYS AGO, I GOT PRETTY BEATEN UP.
DIANA TOOK ME TO SEE HER FRIENDS ON OLYMPUS--FOR WHATEVER REASON, I'VE BEEN HANGING OUT WITH A LOT OF GODS LATELY--AND THEY HEALED ME.
BAFF
BUT IN THE PROCESS, THEY MADE ME "COMPLETELY AND FULLY MORTAL."
A DIRECT HIT BY A WEAPON LIKE KINGSLAYER'S WOULD KILL ME.
GRFF!
I NEED TO BE CAREFUL.
WHY, THEY SENT SUPERMAN AFTER ME?! I'M FLATTERED!
VLORP

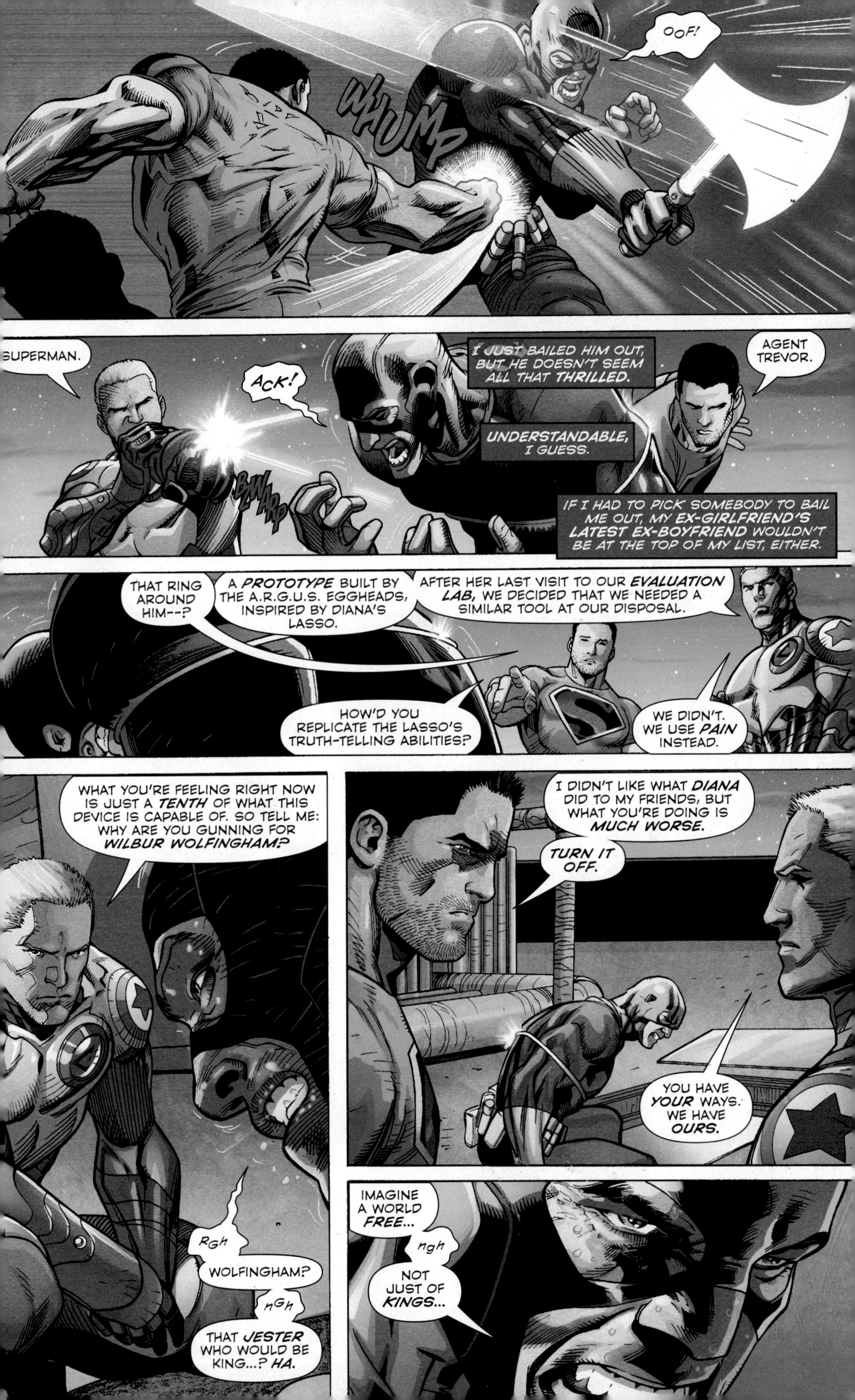
OOF!
WHUMP
SUPERMAN.
ACK!
BWARP
I JUST BAILED HIM OUT, BUT HE DOESN'T SEEM ALL THAT THRILLED.
UNDERSTANDABLE, I GUESS.
AGENT TREVOR.
IF I HAD TO PICK SOMEBODY TO BAIL ME OUT, MY EX-GIRLFRIEND'S LATEST EX-BOYFRIEND WOULDN'T BE AT THE TOP OF MY LIST, EITHER.
THAT RING AROUND HIM--?
A PROTOTYPE BUILT BY THE A.R.G.U.S. EGGHEADS, INSPIRED BY DIANA'S LASSO.
AFTER HER LAST VISIT TO OUR EVALUATION LAB, WE DECIDED THAT WE NEEDED A SIMILAR TOOL AT OUR DISPOSAL.
HOW'D YOU REPLICATE THE LASSO'S TRUTH-TELLING ABILITIES?
WE DIDN'T. WE USE PAIN INSTEAD.
WHAT YOU'RE FEELING RIGHT NOW IS JUST A TENTH OF WHAT THIS DEVICE IS CAPABLE OF. SO TELL ME: WHY ARE YOU GUNNING FOR WILBUR WOLFINGHAM?
RGH
WOLFINGHAM?
NGH
THAT JESTER WHO WOULD BE KING...? HA.
I DIDN'T LIKE WHAT DIANA DID TO MY FRIENDS, BUT WHAT YOU'RE DOING IS MUCH WORSE.
TURN IT OFF.
YOU HAVE YOUR WAYS. WE HAVE OURS.
IMAGINE A WORLD FREE...
NGH
NOT JUST OF KINGS...

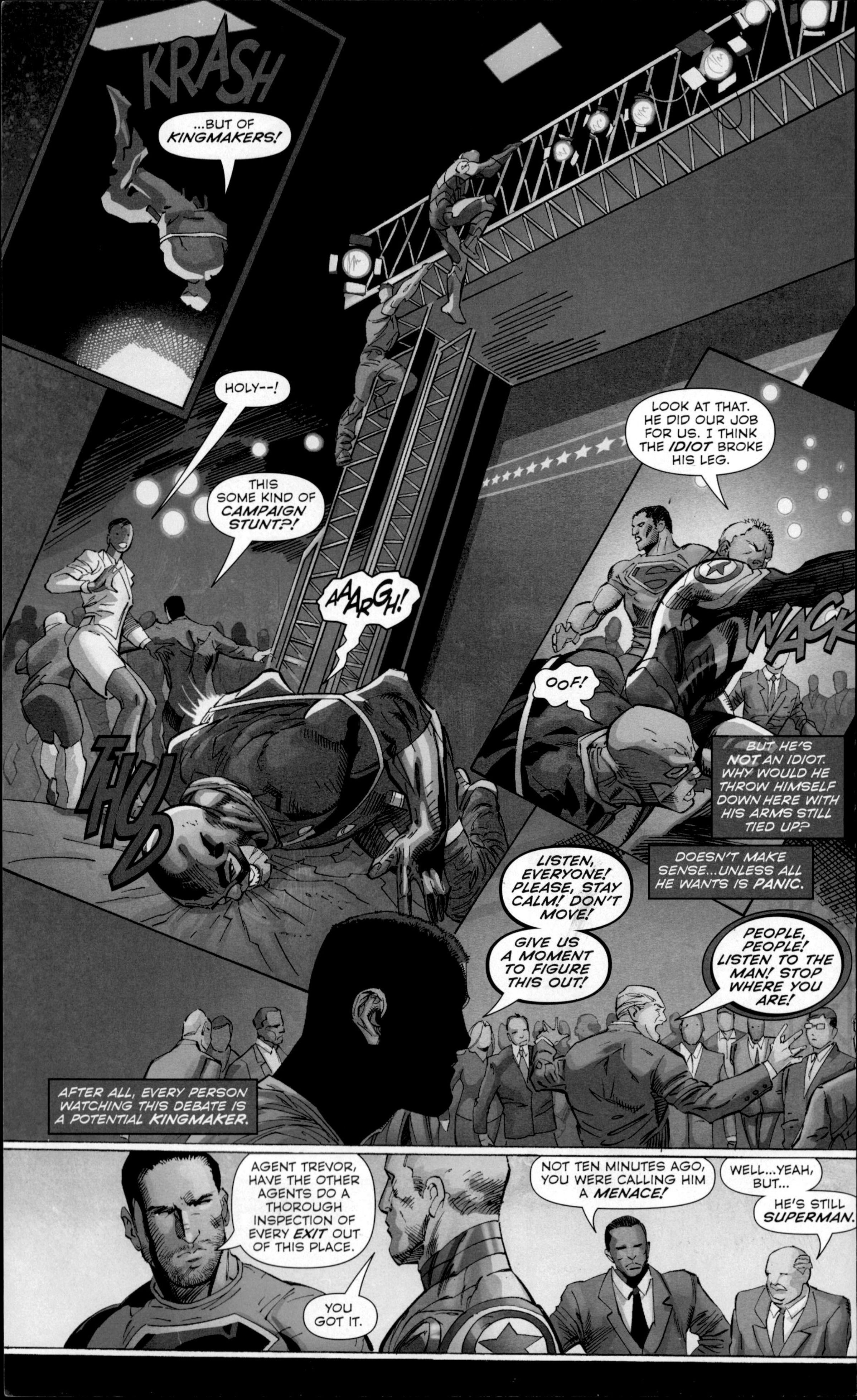
KRASH
...BUT OF KINGMAKERS!
HOLY--!
THIS SOME KIND OF CAMPAIGN STUNT?!
AAARGH!
THUD
LOOK AT THAT. HE DID OUR JOB FOR US. I THINK THE IDIOT BROKE HIS LEG.
WACK
OOF!
BUT HE'S NOT AN IDIOT. WHY WOULD HE THROW HIMSELF DOWN HERE WITH HIS ARMS STILL TIED UP?
DOESN'T MAKE SENSE...UNLESS ALL HE WANTS IS PANIC.
LISTEN, EVERYONE! PLEASE, STAY CALM! DON'T MOVE!
GIVE US A MOMENT TO FIGURE THIS OUT!
PEOPLE, PEOPLE! LISTEN TO THE MAN! STOP WHERE YOU ARE!
AFTER ALL, EVERY PERSON WATCHING THIS DEBATE IS A POTENTIAL KINGMAKER.
AGENT TREVOR, HAVE THE OTHER AGENTS DO A THOROUGH INSPECTION OF EVERY EXIT OUT OF THIS PLACE.
YOU GOT IT.
NOT TEN MINUTES AGO, YOU WERE CALLING HIM A MENACE!
WELL...YEAH, BUT...
HE'S STILL SUPERMAN.

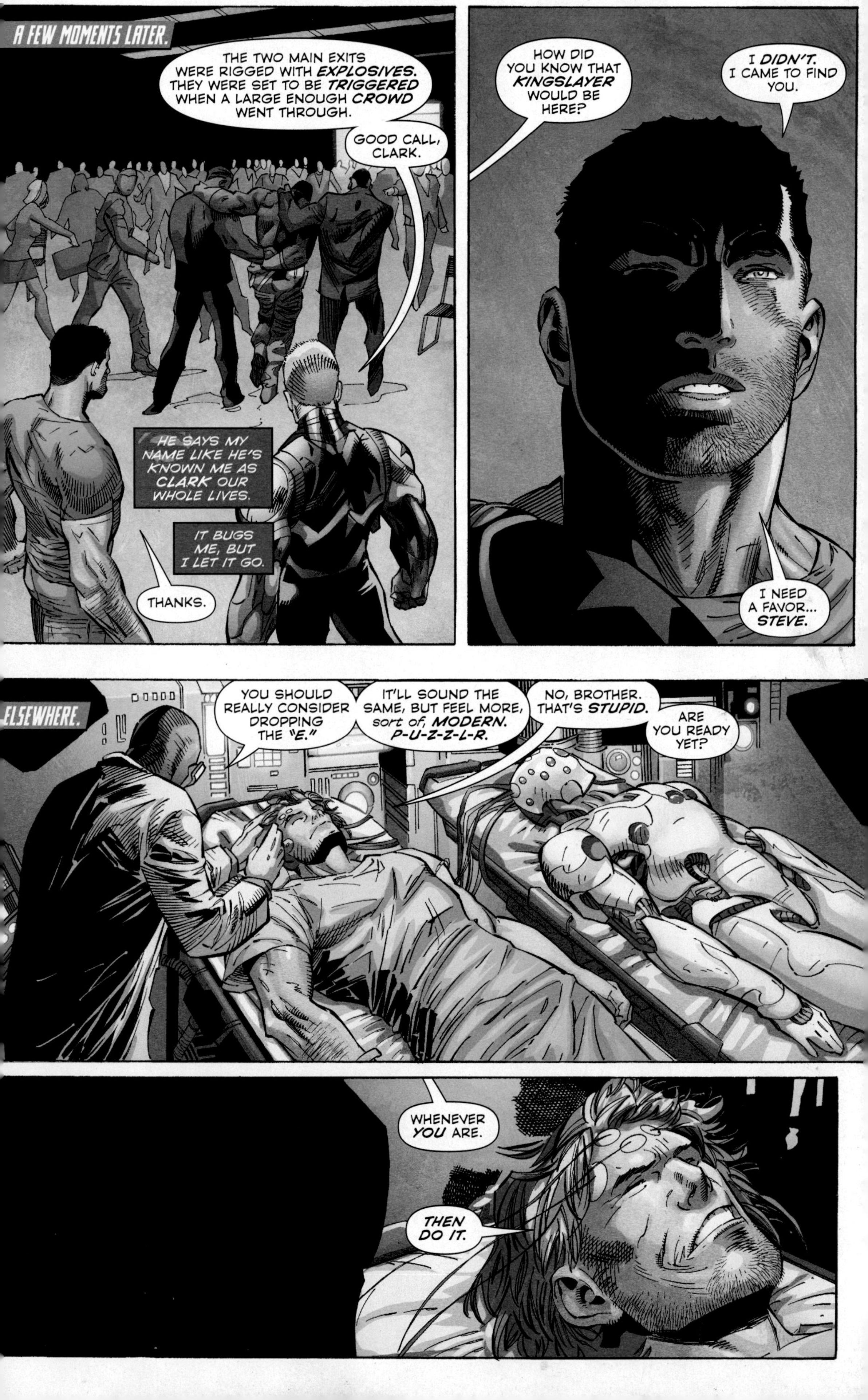
A FEW MOMENTS LATER.
THE TWO MAIN EXITS WERE RIGGED WITH EXPLOSIVES. THEY WERE SET TO BE TRIGGERED WHEN A LARGE ENOUGH CROWD WENT THROUGH.
GOOD CALL, CLARK.
HE SAYS MY NAME LIKE HE'S KNOWN ME AS CLARK OUR WHOLE LIVES.
IT BUGS ME, BUT I LET IT GO.
THANKS.
HOW DID YOU KNOW THAT KINGSLAYER WOULD BE HERE?
I DIDN'T. I CAME TO FIND YOU.
I NEED A FAVOR... STEVE.
ELSEWHERE.
YOU SHOULD REALLY CONSIDER DROPPING THE "E."
IT'LL SOUND THE SAME, BUT FEEL MORE, sort of, MODERN. P-U-Z-Z-L-R.
NO, BROTHER. THAT'S STUPID.
ARE YOU READY YET?
WHENEVER YOU ARE.
THEN DO IT.

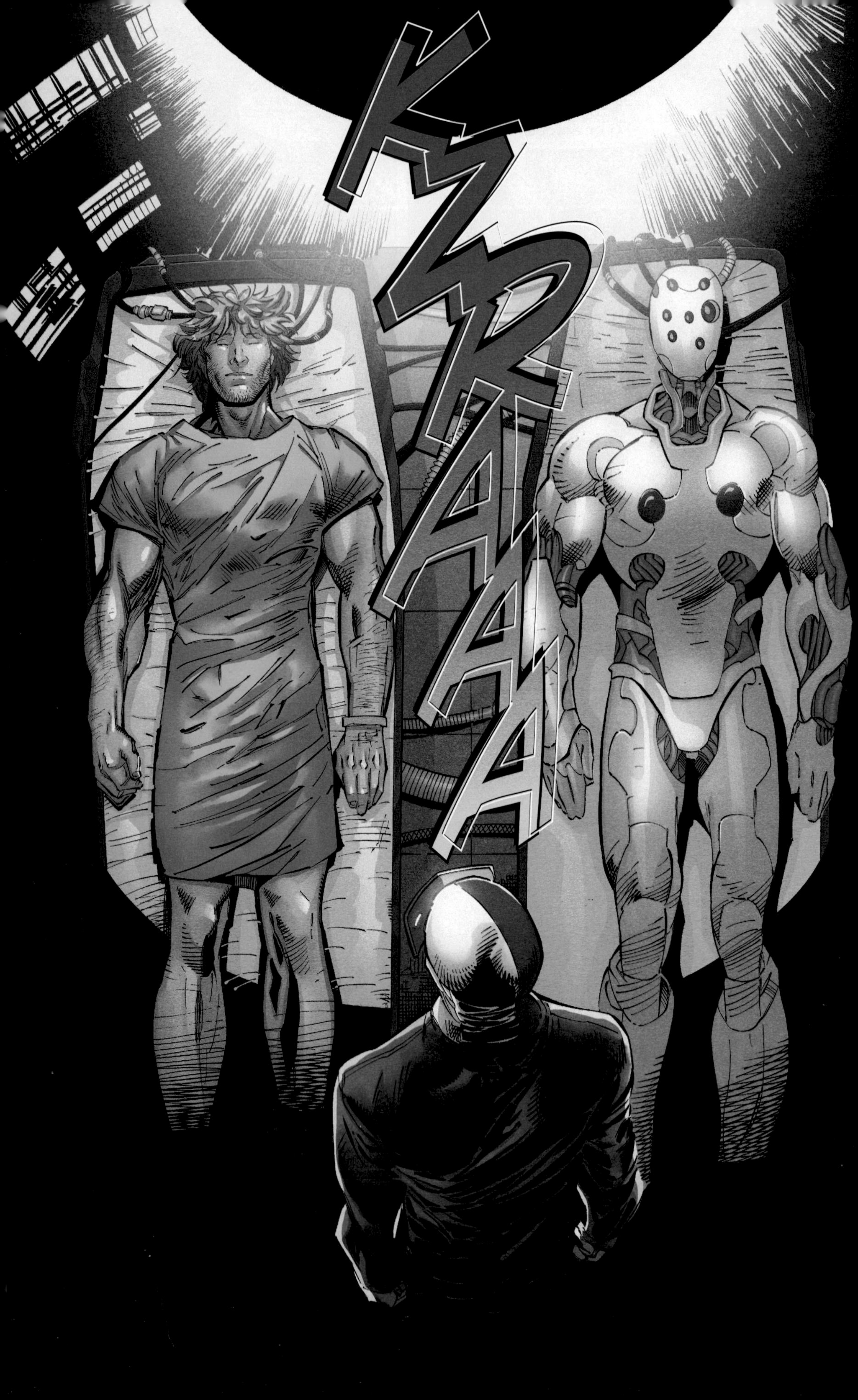
KZRAAAAA

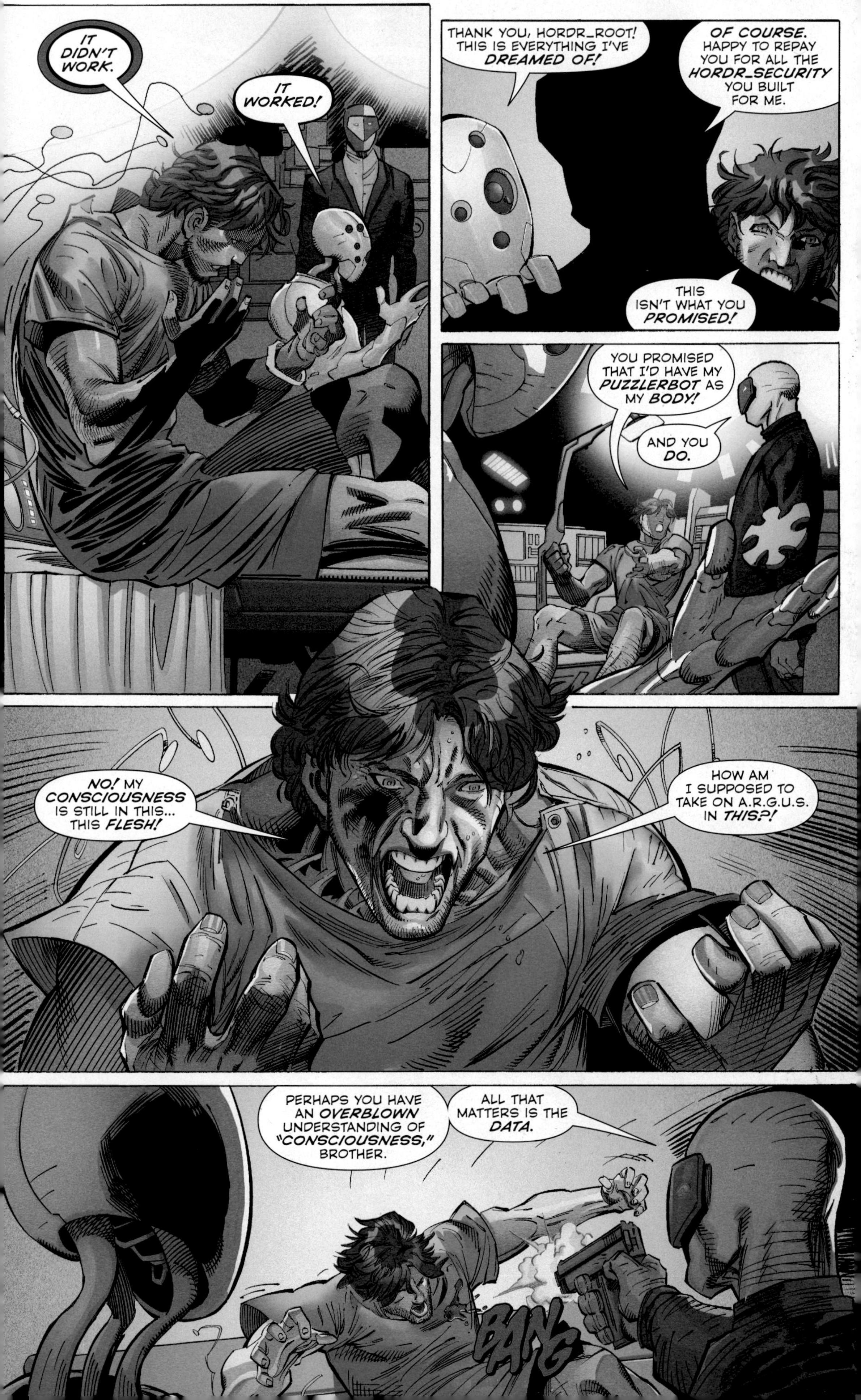
IT DIDN'T WORK.
IT WORKED!
THANK YOU, HORDR_ROOT! THIS IS EVERYTHING I'VE DREAMED OF!
OF COURSE. HAPPY TO REPAY YOU FOR ALL THE HORDR_SECURITY YOU BUILT FOR ME.
THIS ISN'T WHAT YOU PROMISED!
YOU PROMISED THAT I'D HAVE MY PUZZLERBOT AS MY BODY!
AND YOU DO.
NO! MY CONSCIOUSNESS IS STILL IN THIS... THIS FLESH!
HOW AM I SUPPOSED TO TAKE ON A.R.G.U.S. IN THIS?!
PERHAPS YOU HAVE AN OVERBLOWN UNDERSTANDING OF "CONSCIOUSNESS," BROTHER.
ALL THAT MATTERS IS THE DATA.
BANG

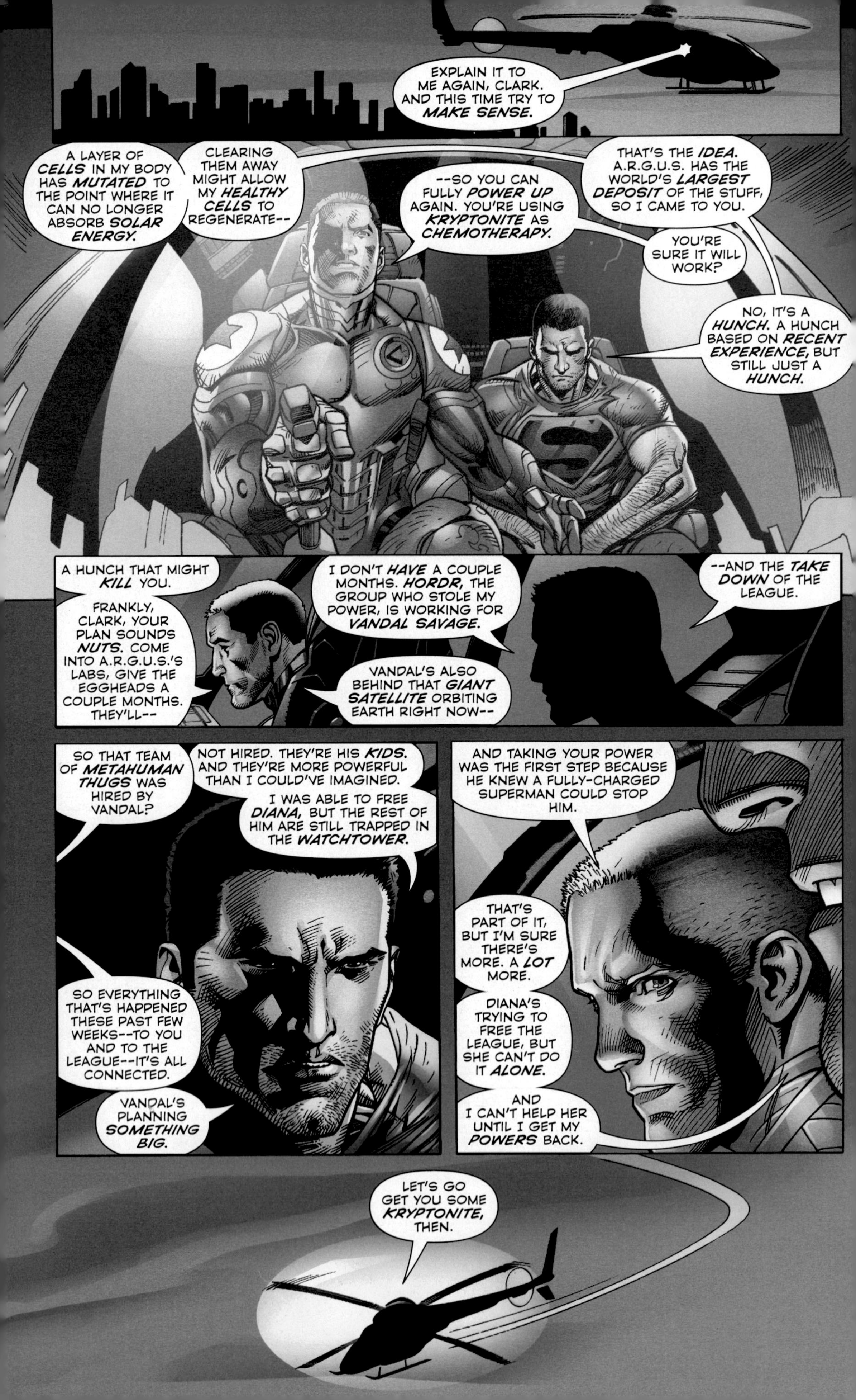
EXPLAIN IT TO ME AGAIN, CLARK. AND THIS TIME TRY TO MAKE SENSE.
A LAYER OF CELLS IN MY BODY HAS MUTATED TO THE POINT WHERE IT CAN NO LONGER ABSORB SOLAR ENERGY.
CLEARING THEM AWAY MIGHT ALLOW MY HEALTHY CELLS TO REGENERATE--
--SO YOU CAN FULLY POWER UP AGAIN. YOU'RE USING KRYPTONITE AS CHEMOTHERAPY.
THAT'S THE IDEA. A.R.G.U.S. HAS THE WORLD'S LARGEST DEPOSIT OF THE STUFF, SO I CAME TO YOU.
YOU'RE SURE IT WILL WORK?
NO, IT'S A HUNCH. A HUNCH BASED ON RECENT EXPERIENCE, BUT STILL JUST A HUNCH.
A HUNCH THAT MIGHT KILL YOU.
FRANKLY, CLARK, YOUR PLAN SOUNDS NUTS. COME INTO A.R.G.U.S.'S LABS, GIVE THE EGGHEADS A COUPLE MONTHS. THEY'LL--
I DON'T HAVE A COUPLE MONTHS. HORDR, THE GROUP WHO STOLE MY POWER, IS WORKING FOR VANDAL SAVAGE.
VANDAL'S ALSO BEHIND THAT GIANT SATELLITE ORBITING EARTH RIGHT NOW--
--AND THE TAKE DOWN OF THE LEAGUE.
SO THAT TEAM OF METAHUMAN THUGS WAS HIRED BY VANDAL?
NOT HIRED. THEY'RE HIS KIDS. AND THEY'RE MORE POWERFUL THAN I COULD'VE IMAGINED.
I WAS ABLE TO FREE DIANA, BUT THE REST OF HIM ARE STILL TRAPPED IN THE WATCHTOWER.
SO EVERYTHING THAT'S HAPPENED THESE PAST FEW WEEKS--TO YOU AND TO THE LEAGUE--IT'S ALL CONNECTED.
VANDAL'S PLANNING SOMETHING BIG.
AND TAKING YOUR POWER WAS THE FIRST STEP BECAUSE HE KNEW A FULLY-CHARGED SUPERMAN COULD STOP HIM.
THAT'S PART OF IT, BUT I'M SURE THERE'S MORE. A LOT MORE.
DIANA'S TRYING TO FREE THE LEAGUE, BUT SHE CAN'T DO IT ALONE.
AND I CAN'T HELP HER UNTIL I GET MY POWERS BACK.
LET'S GO GET YOU SOME KRYPTONITE, THEN.

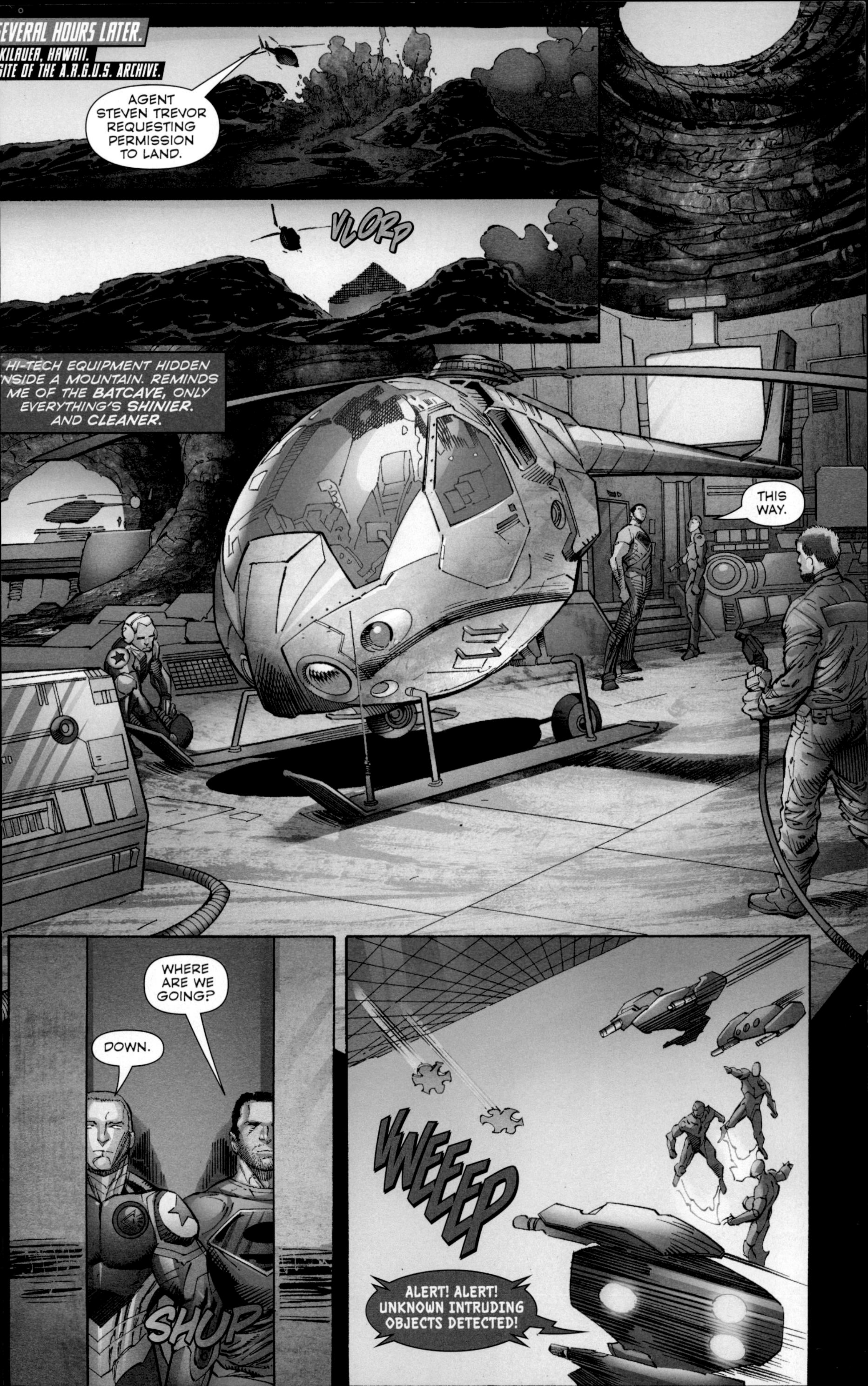

SEVERAL HOURS LATER.
KILAUEA, HAWAII.
SITE OF THE A.R.G.U.S. ARCHIVE.
AGENT STEVEN TREVOR REQUESTING PERMISSION TO LAND.
VLORP
HI-TECH EQUIPMENT HIDDEN INSIDE A MOUNTAIN. REMINDS ME OF THE BATCAVE, ONLY EVERYTHING'S SHINIER. AND CLEANER.
THIS WAY.
WHERE ARE WE GOING?
DOWN.
SHUP
VWEEEP
ALERT! ALERT! UNKNOWN INTRUDING OBJECTS DETECTED!

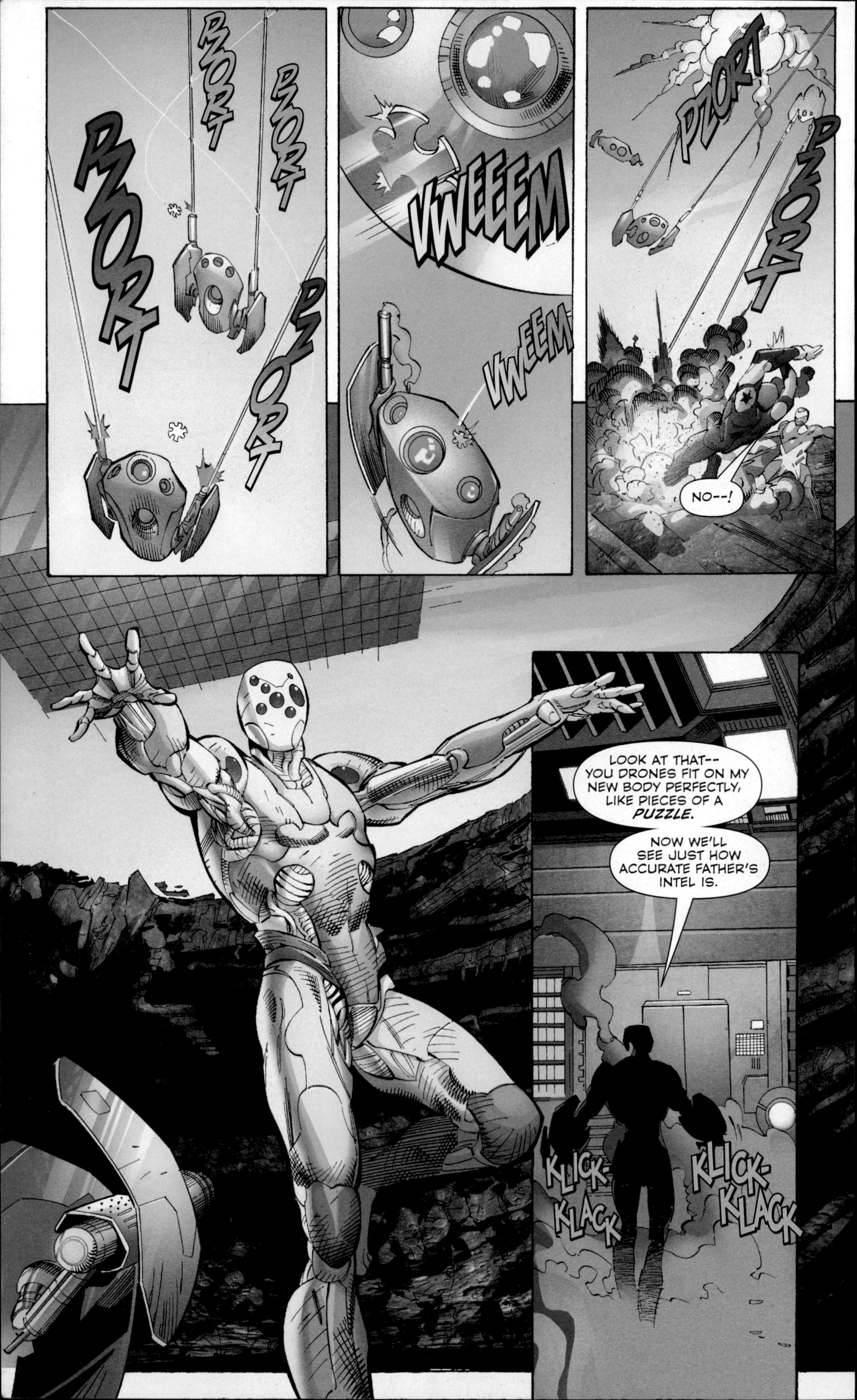
PZORT
PZORT
PZORT
PZORT
VWEEEM
VWEEM
PZORT
PZORT
NO--!
LOOK AT THAT-- YOU DRONES FIT ON MY NEW BODY PERFECTLY, LIKE PIECES OF A *PUZZLE*.
NOW WE'LL SEE JUST HOW ACCURATE FATHER'S INTEL IS.
KLICK-KLACK
KLICK-KLACK

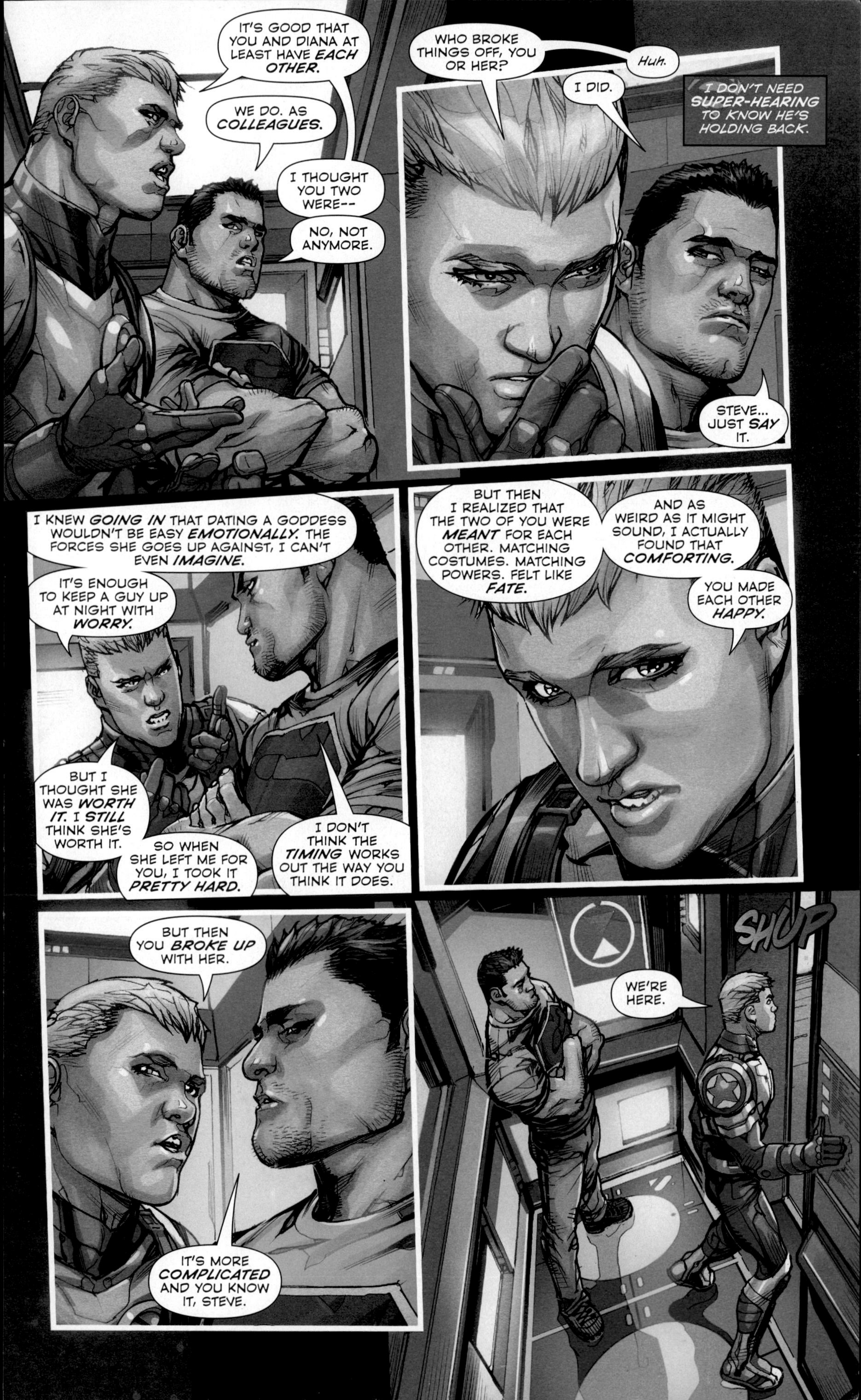
IT'S GOOD THAT YOU AND DIANA AT LEAST HAVE EACH OTHER.
WE DO. AS COLLEAGUES.
I THOUGHT YOU TWO WERE--
NO, NOT ANYMORE.
WHO BROKE THINGS OFF, YOU OR HER?
I DID.
Huh.
I DON'T NEED SUPER-HEARING TO KNOW HE'S HOLDING BACK.
STEVE... JUST SAY IT.
I KNEW GOING IN THAT DATING A GODDESS WOULDN'T BE EASY EMOTIONALLY. THE FORCES SHE GOES UP AGAINST, I CAN'T EVEN IMAGINE.
IT'S ENOUGH TO KEEP A GUY UP AT NIGHT WITH WORRY.
BUT I THOUGHT SHE WAS WORTH IT. I STILL THINK SHE'S WORTH IT.
SO WHEN SHE LEFT ME FOR YOU, I TOOK IT PRETTY HARD.
I DON'T THINK THE TIMING WORKS OUT THE WAY YOU THINK IT DOES.
BUT THEN I REALIZED THAT THE TWO OF YOU WERE MEANT FOR EACH OTHER. MATCHING COSTUMES. MATCHING POWERS. FELT LIKE FATE.
AND AS WEIRD AS IT MIGHT SOUND, I ACTUALLY FOUND THAT COMFORTING.
YOU MADE EACH OTHER HAPPY.
BUT THEN YOU BROKE UP WITH HER.
IT'S MORE COMPLICATED AND YOU KNOW IT, STEVE.
SHUP
WE'RE HERE.

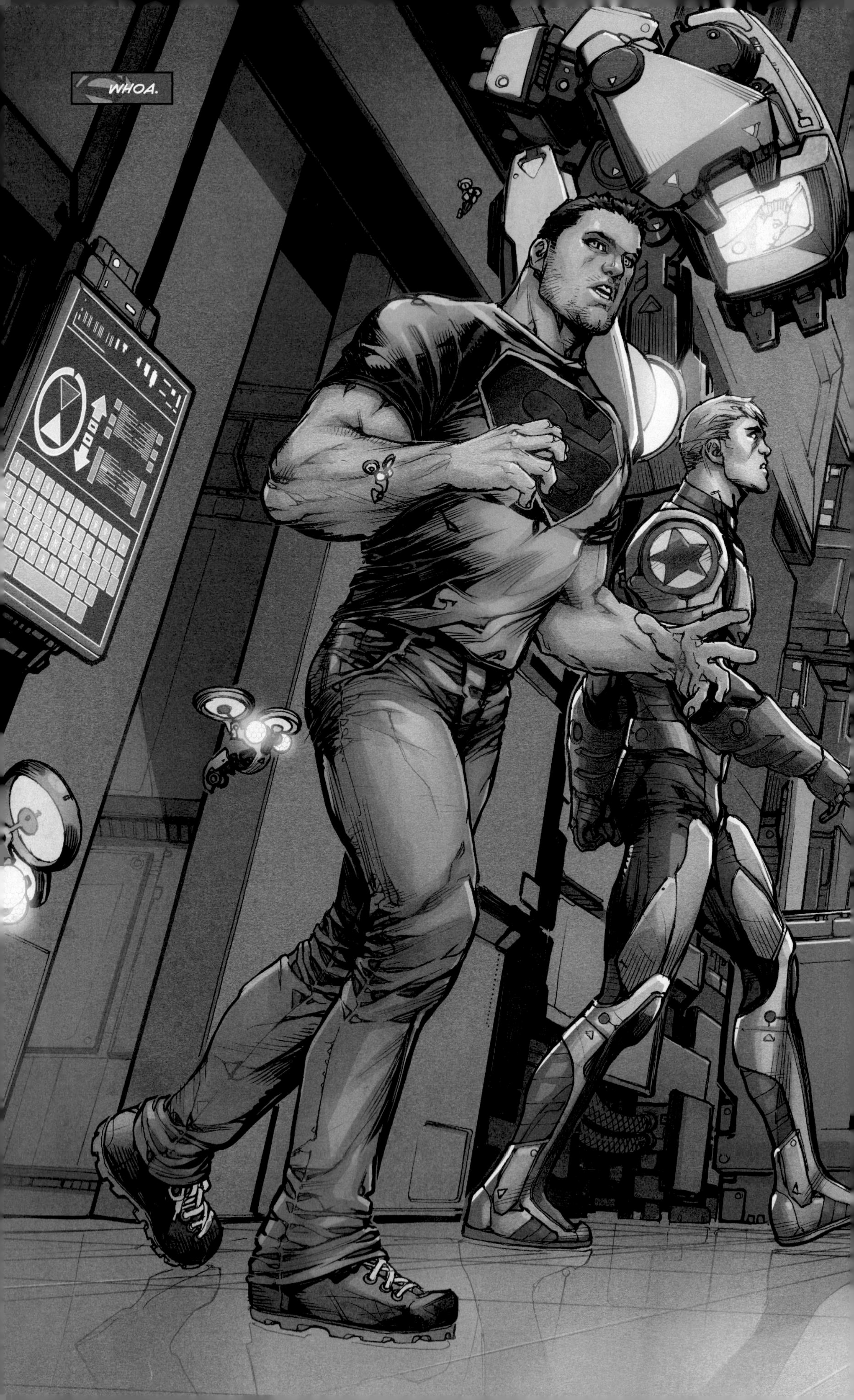
WHOA.

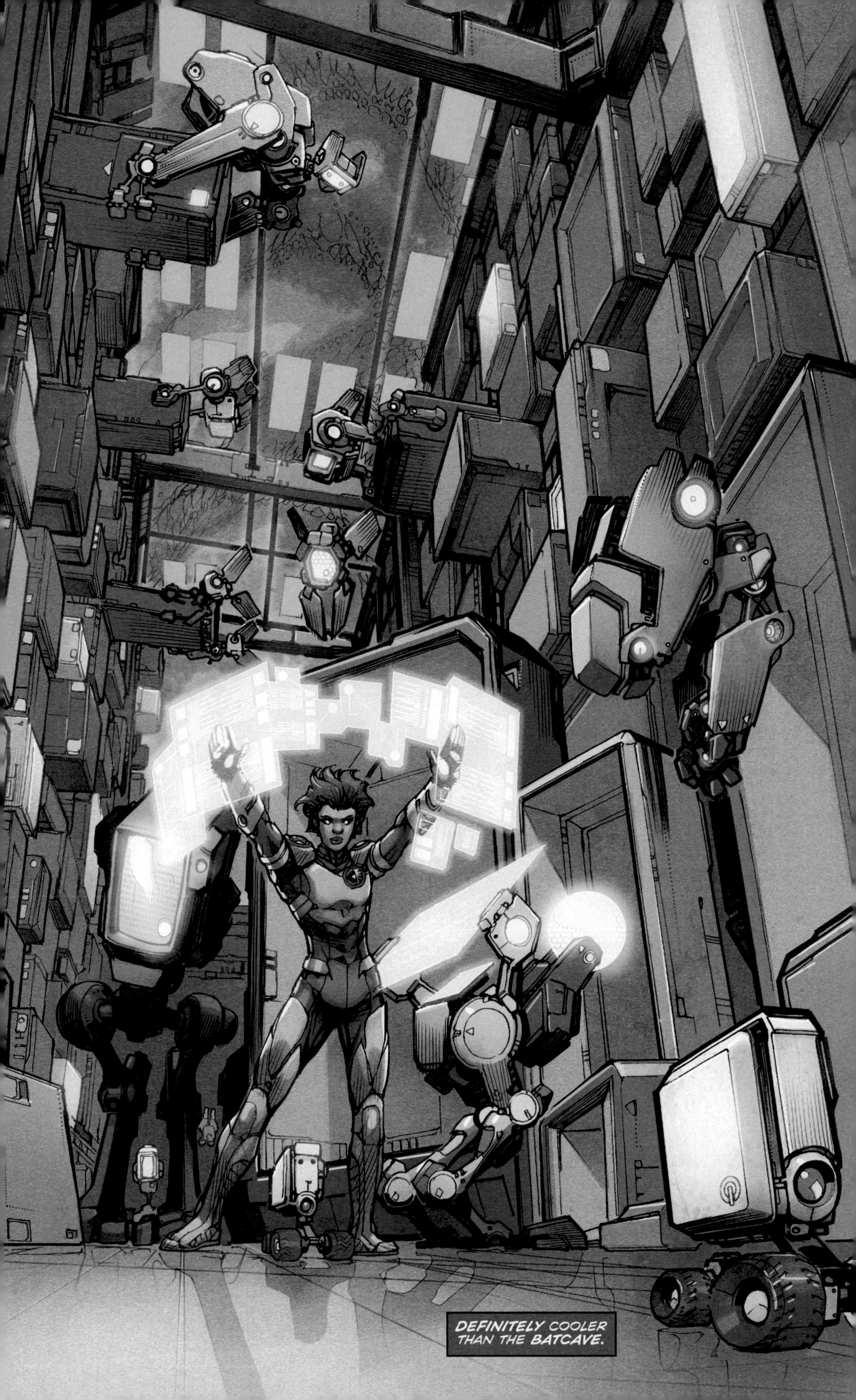
DEFINITELY COOLER THAN THE BATCAVE.

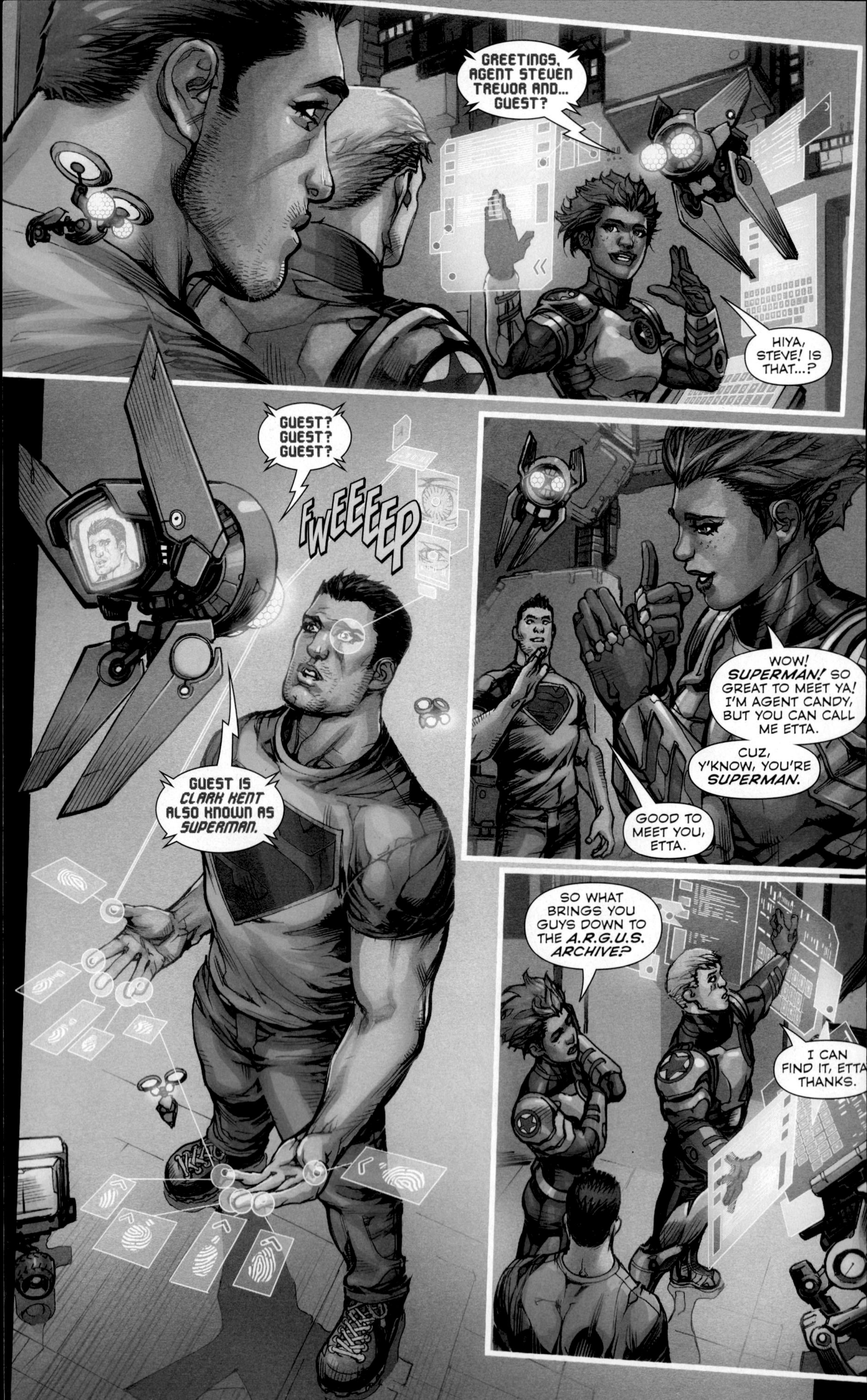
GREETINGS, AGENT STEVEN TREVOR AND... GUEST?
HIYA, STEVE! IS THAT...?
GUEST? GUEST? GUEST?
FWEEEEEP
GUEST IS CLARK KENT ALSO KNOWN AS SUPERMAN.
WOW! SUPERMAN! SO GREAT TO MEET YA! I'M AGENT CANDY, BUT YOU CAN CALL ME ETTA.
CUZ, Y'KNOW, YOU'RE SUPERMAN.
GOOD TO MEET YOU, ETTA.
SO WHAT BRINGS YOU GUYS DOWN TO THE A.R.G.U.S. ARCHIVE?
I CAN FIND IT, ETTA. THANKS.

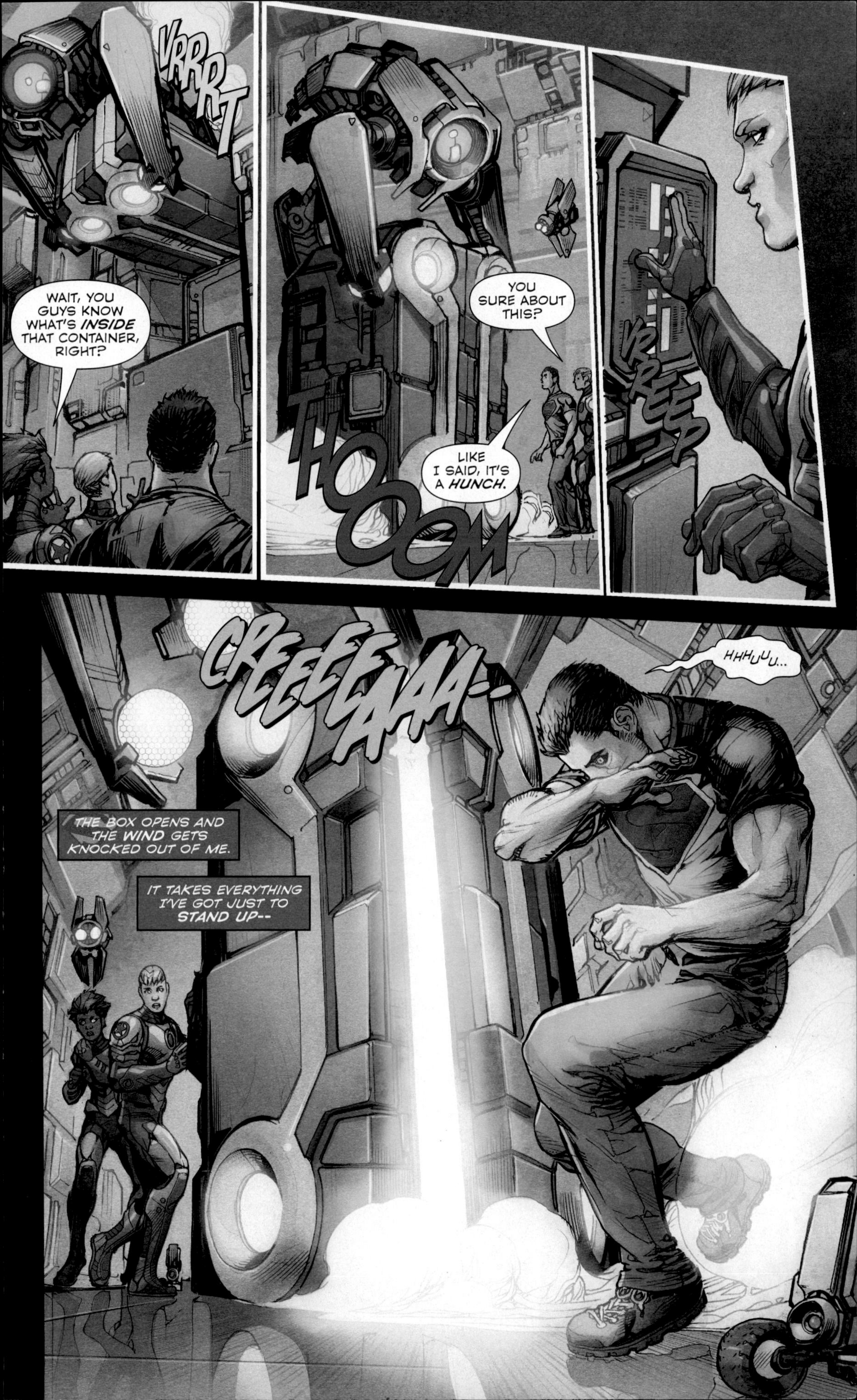
VRRRRT
WAIT, YOU GUYS KNOW WHAT'S *INSIDE* THAT CONTAINER, RIGHT?
YOU SURE ABOUT THIS?
LIKE I SAID, IT'S A *HUNCH.*
THOOOOM
VREEEP
CREEEEAAAA--
HHHUUU...
THE BOX OPENS AND THE **WIND** GETS KNOCKED OUT OF ME.
IT TAKES EVERYTHING I'VE GOT JUST TO **STAND UP--**

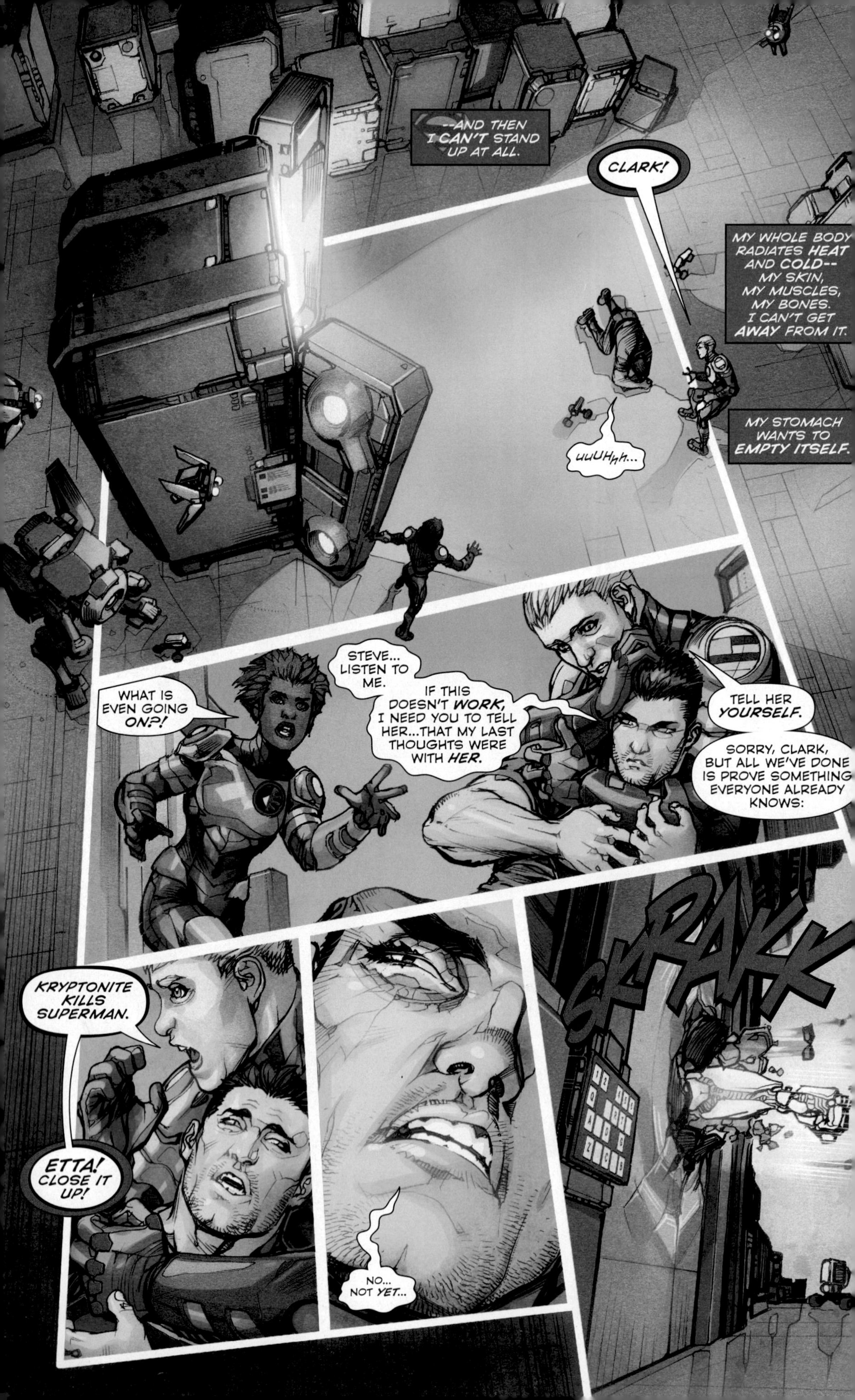
--AND THEN I CAN'T STAND UP AT ALL.
CLARK!
MY WHOLE BODY RADIATES HEAT AND COLD-- MY SKIN, MY MUSCLES, MY BONES. I CAN'T GET AWAY FROM IT.
MY STOMACH WANTS TO EMPTY ITSELF.
uuUHhh...
WHAT IS EVEN GOING ON?!
STEVE... LISTEN TO ME.
IF THIS DOESN'T WORK, I NEED YOU TO TELL HER...THAT MY LAST THOUGHTS WERE WITH HER.
TELL HER YOURSELF.
SORRY, CLARK, BUT ALL WE'VE DONE IS PROVE SOMETHING EVERYONE ALREADY KNOWS:
KRYPTONITE KILLS SUPERMAN.
ETTA! CLOSE IT UP!
NO... NOT YET...
SKRAKK

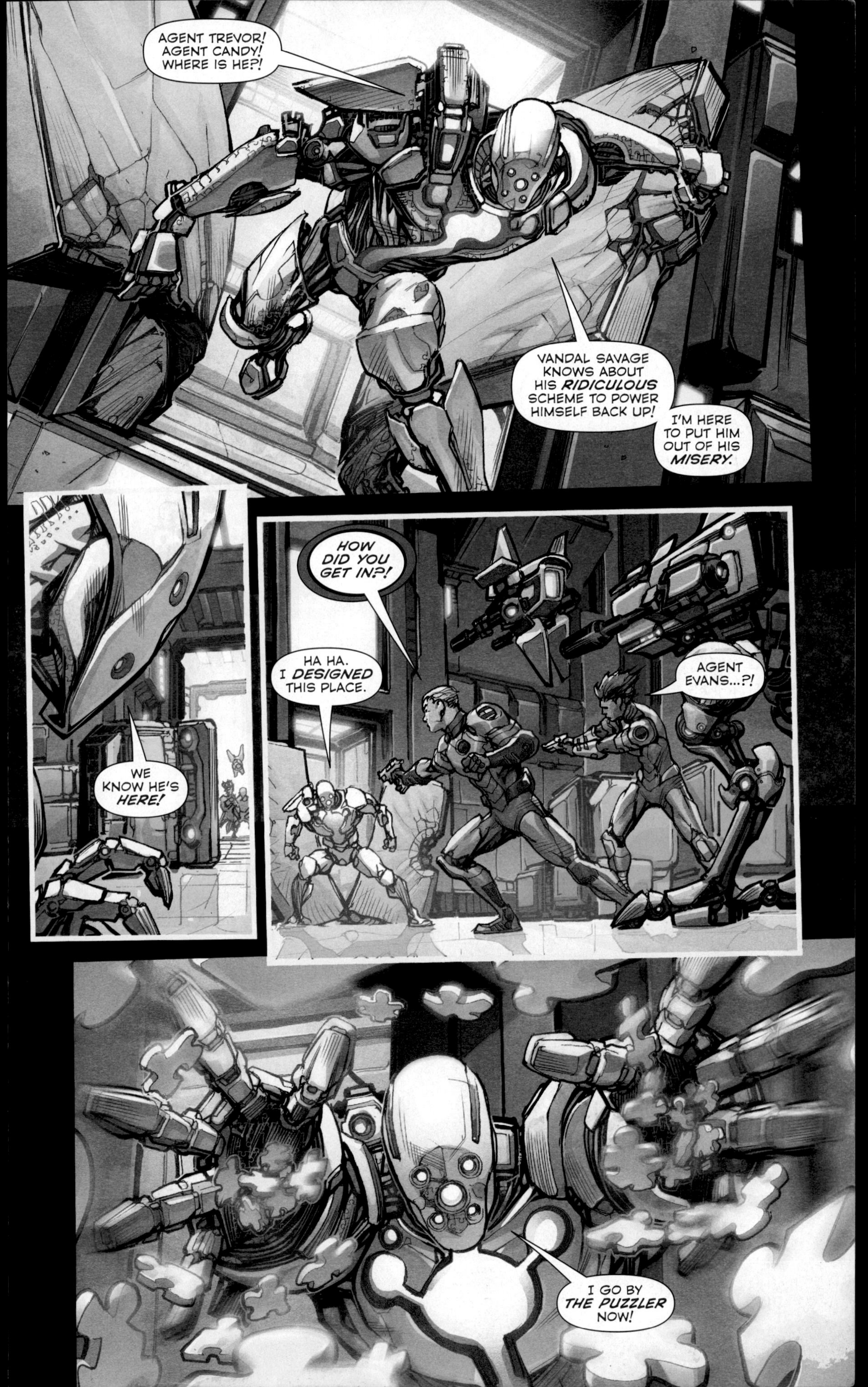
AGENT TREVOR! AGENT CANDY! WHERE IS HE?!
VANDAL SAVAGE KNOWS ABOUT HIS RIDICULOUS SCHEME TO POWER HIMSELF BACK UP!
I'M HERE TO PUT HIM OUT OF HIS MISERY.
WE KNOW HE'S HERE!
HOW DID YOU GET IN?!
HA HA. I DESIGNED THIS PLACE.
AGENT EVANS...?!
I GO BY THE PUZZLER NOW!

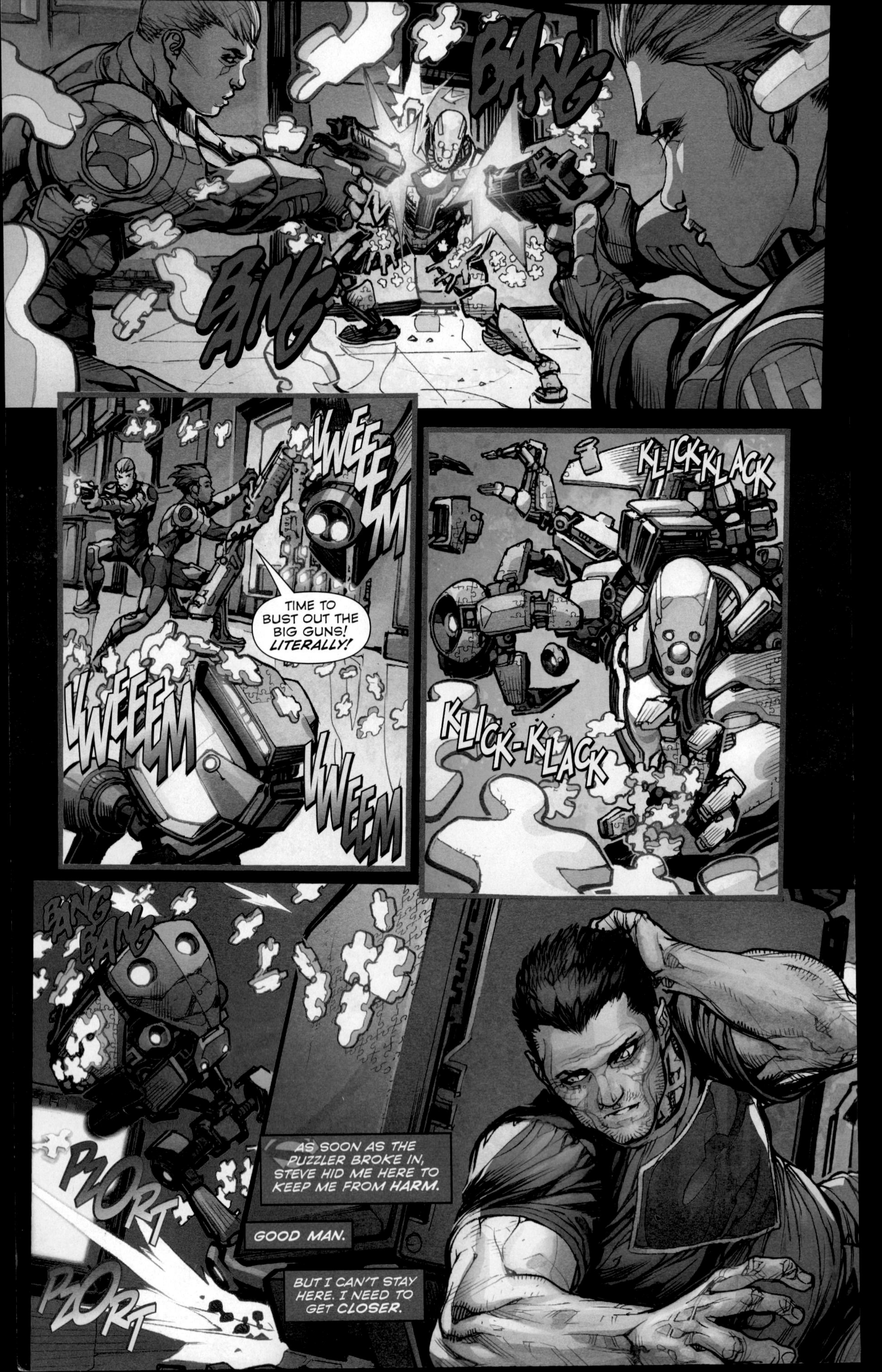

BANG
BANG
VWEEEM
TIME TO BUST OUT THE BIG GUNS! LITERALLY!
VWEEEM
VWEEM
KLICK-KLACK
KLICK-KLACK
BANG BANG
PLORT
PLORT
AS SOON AS THE PUZZLER BROKE IN, STEVE HID ME HERE TO KEEP ME FROM HARM.
GOOD MAN.
BUT I CAN'T STAY HERE. I NEED TO GET CLOSER.

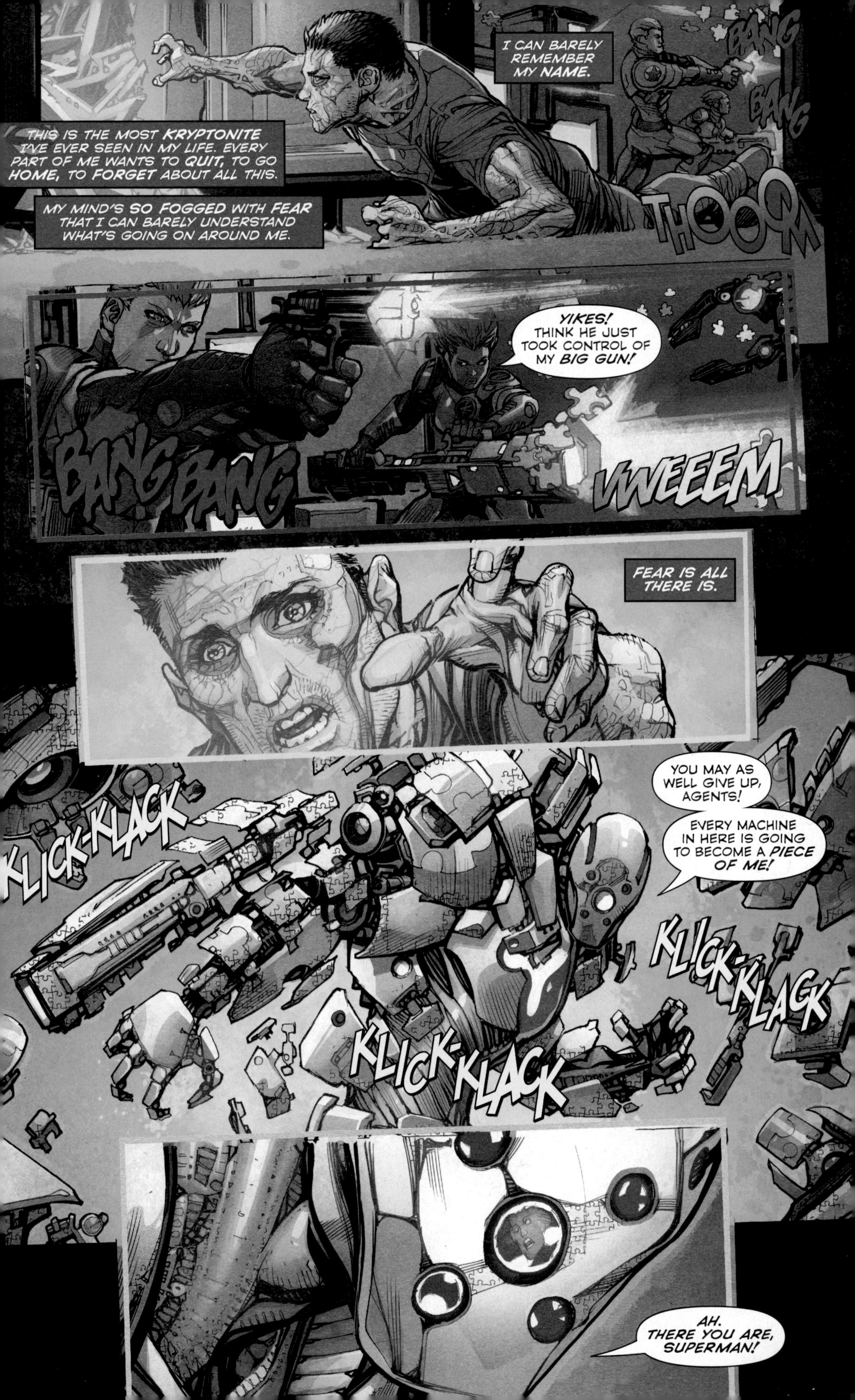
I CAN BARELY REMEMBER MY NAME.
BANG
BANG
THIS IS THE MOST KRYPTONITE I'VE EVER SEEN IN MY LIFE. EVERY PART OF ME WANTS TO QUIT, TO GO HOME, TO FORGET ABOUT ALL THIS.
MY MIND'S SO FOGGED WITH FEAR THAT I CAN BARELY UNDERSTAND WHAT'S GOING ON AROUND ME.
THOOOM
YIKES! THINK HE JUST TOOK CONTROL OF MY BIG GUN!
BANG BANG
VWEEEM
FEAR IS ALL THERE IS.
KLICK-KLACK
YOU MAY AS WELL GIVE UP, AGENTS!
EVERY MACHINE IN HERE IS GOING TO BECOME A PIECE OF ME!
KLICK-KLACK
KLICK-KLACK
AH. THERE YOU ARE, SUPERMAN!

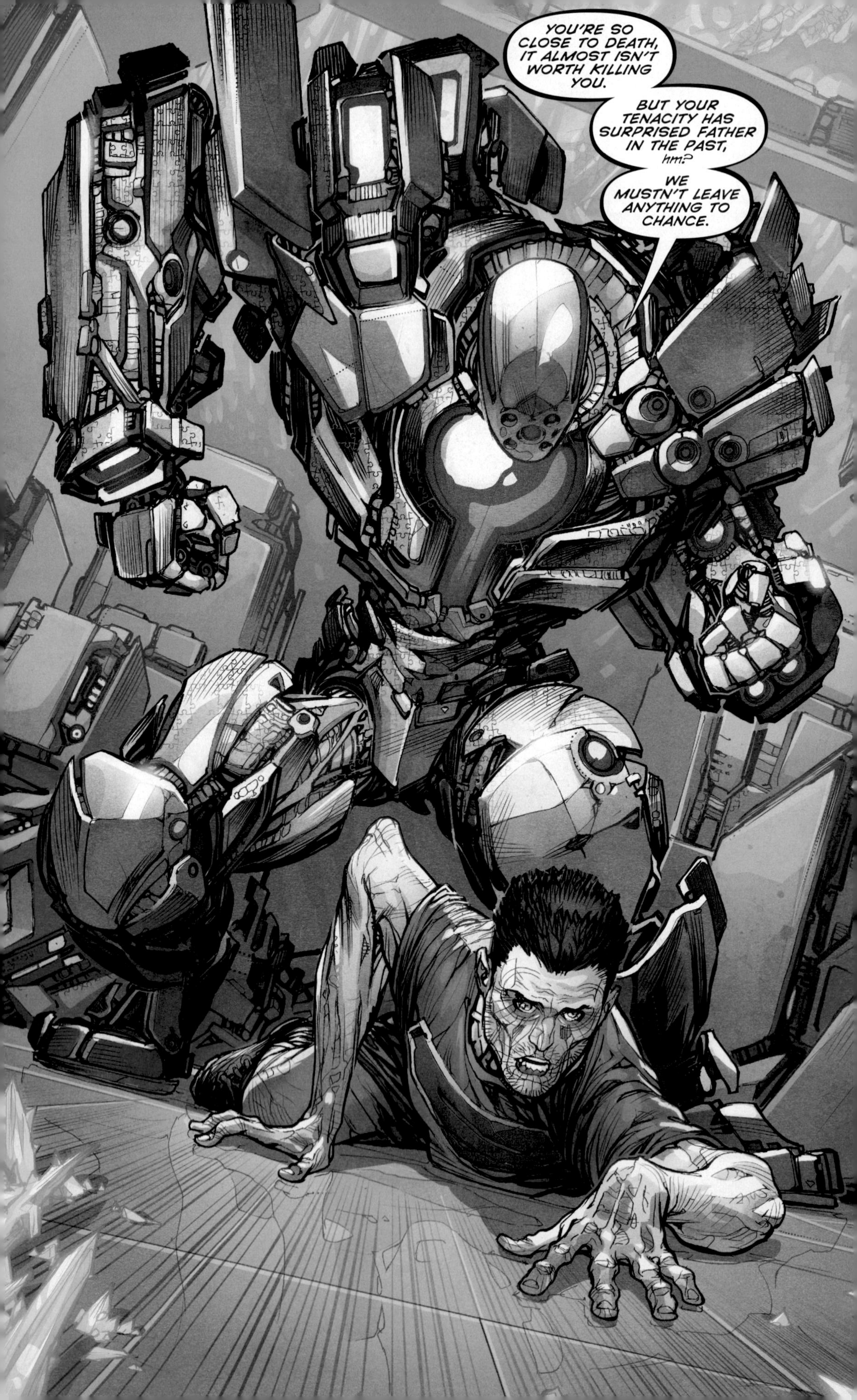
YOU'RE SO CLOSE TO DEATH, IT ALMOST ISN'T WORTH KILLING YOU.
BUT YOUR TENACITY HAS SURPRISED FATHER IN THE PAST, hm?
WE MUSTN'T LEAVE ANYTHING TO CHANCE.

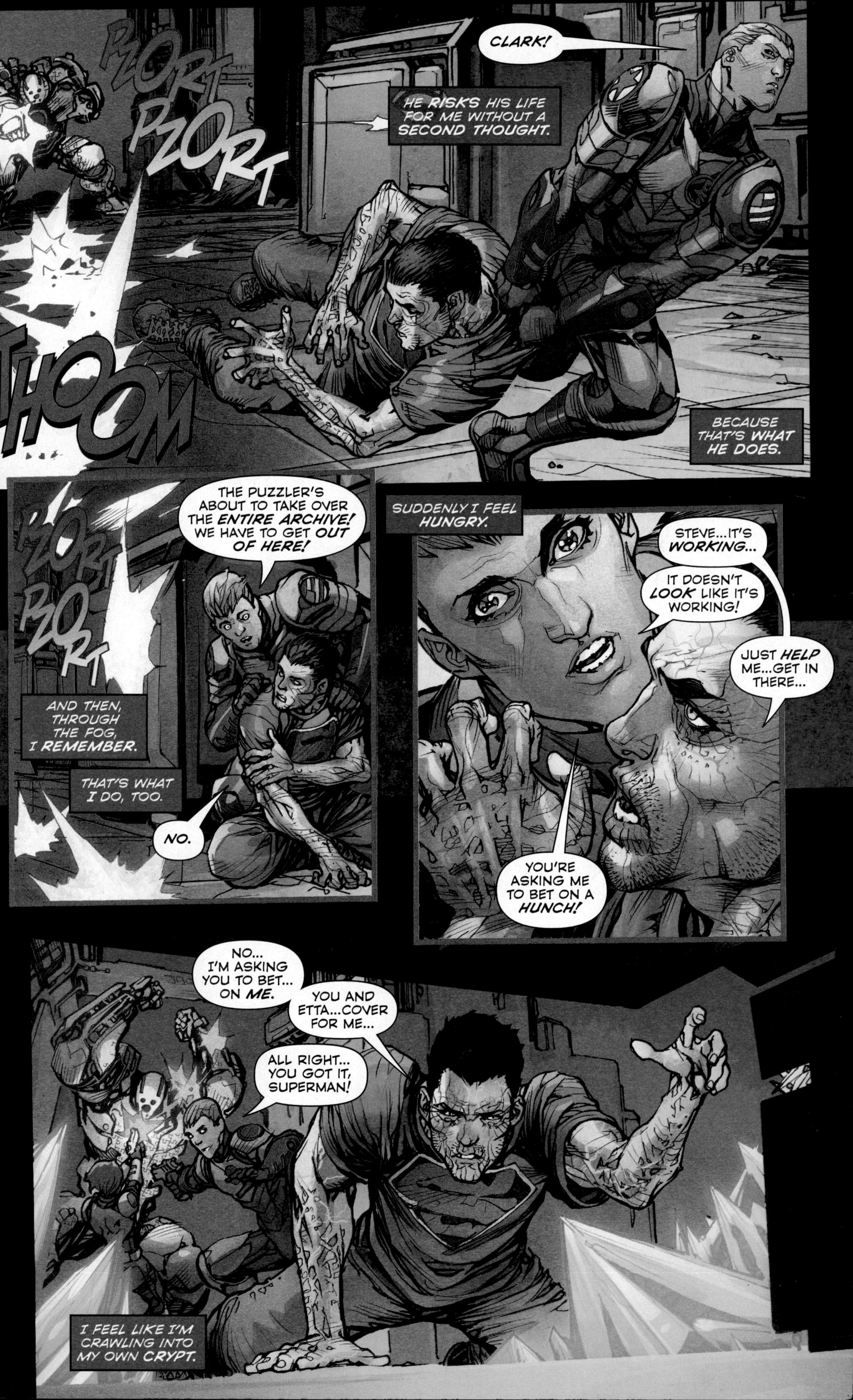
PZORT PZORT
CLARK!
HE RISKS HIS LIFE FOR ME WITHOUT A SECOND THOUGHT.
THOOM
BECAUSE THAT'S WHAT HE DOES.
PZORT PZORT
THE PUZZLER'S ABOUT TO TAKE OVER THE ENTIRE ARCHIVE! WE HAVE TO GET OUT OF HERE!
AND THEN, THROUGH THE FOG, I REMEMBER.
THAT'S WHAT I DO, TOO.
NO.
SUDDENLY I FEEL HUNGRY.
STEVE...IT'S WORKING...
IT DOESN'T LOOK LIKE IT'S WORKING!
JUST HELP ME...GET IN THERE...
YOU'RE ASKING ME TO BET ON A HUNCH!
NO... I'M ASKING YOU TO BET... ON ME.
YOU AND ETTA...COVER FOR ME...
ALL RIGHT... YOU GOT IT, SUPERMAN!
I FEEL LIKE I'M CRAWLING INTO MY OWN CRYPT.

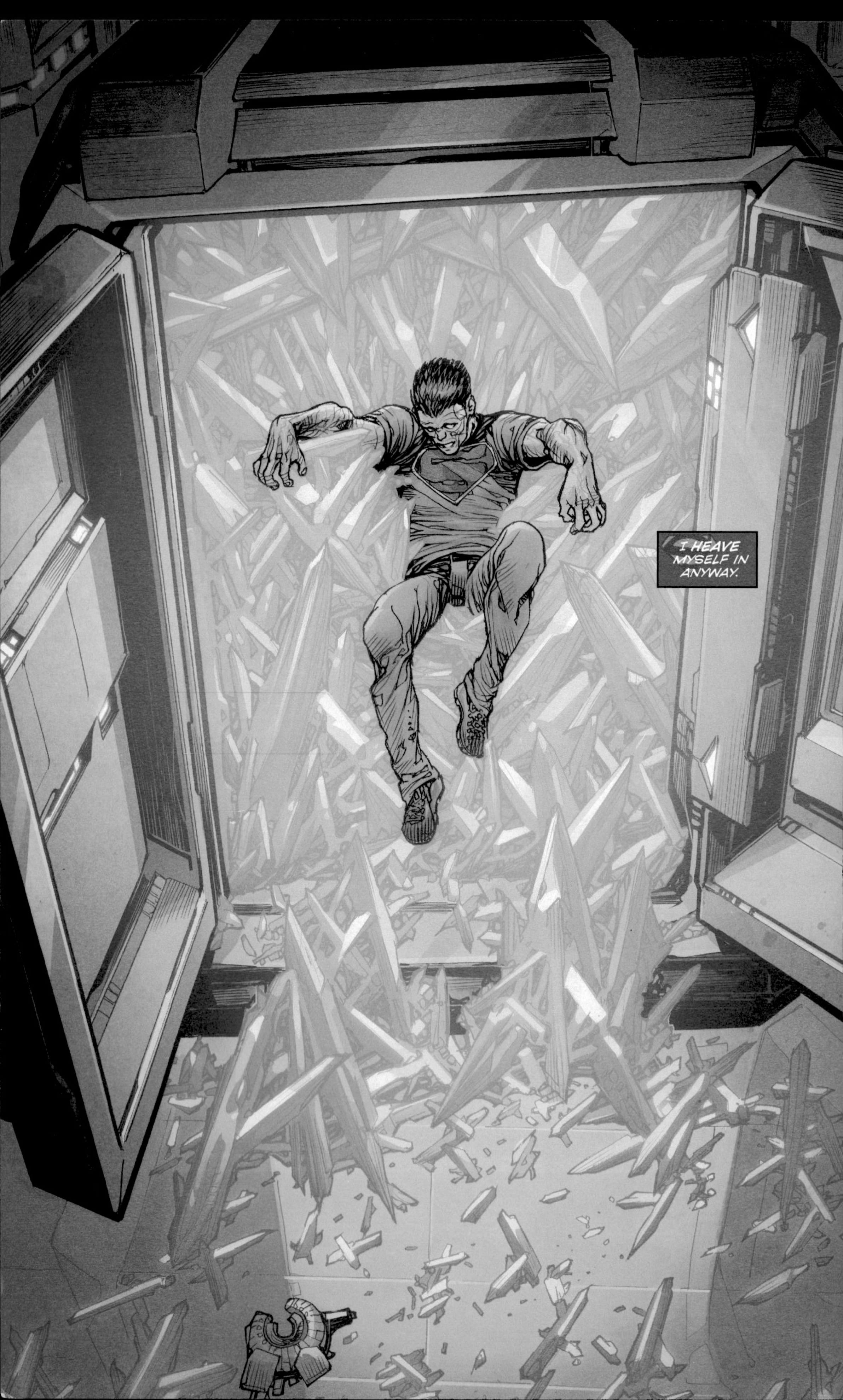
I HEAVE MYSELF IN ANYWAY.

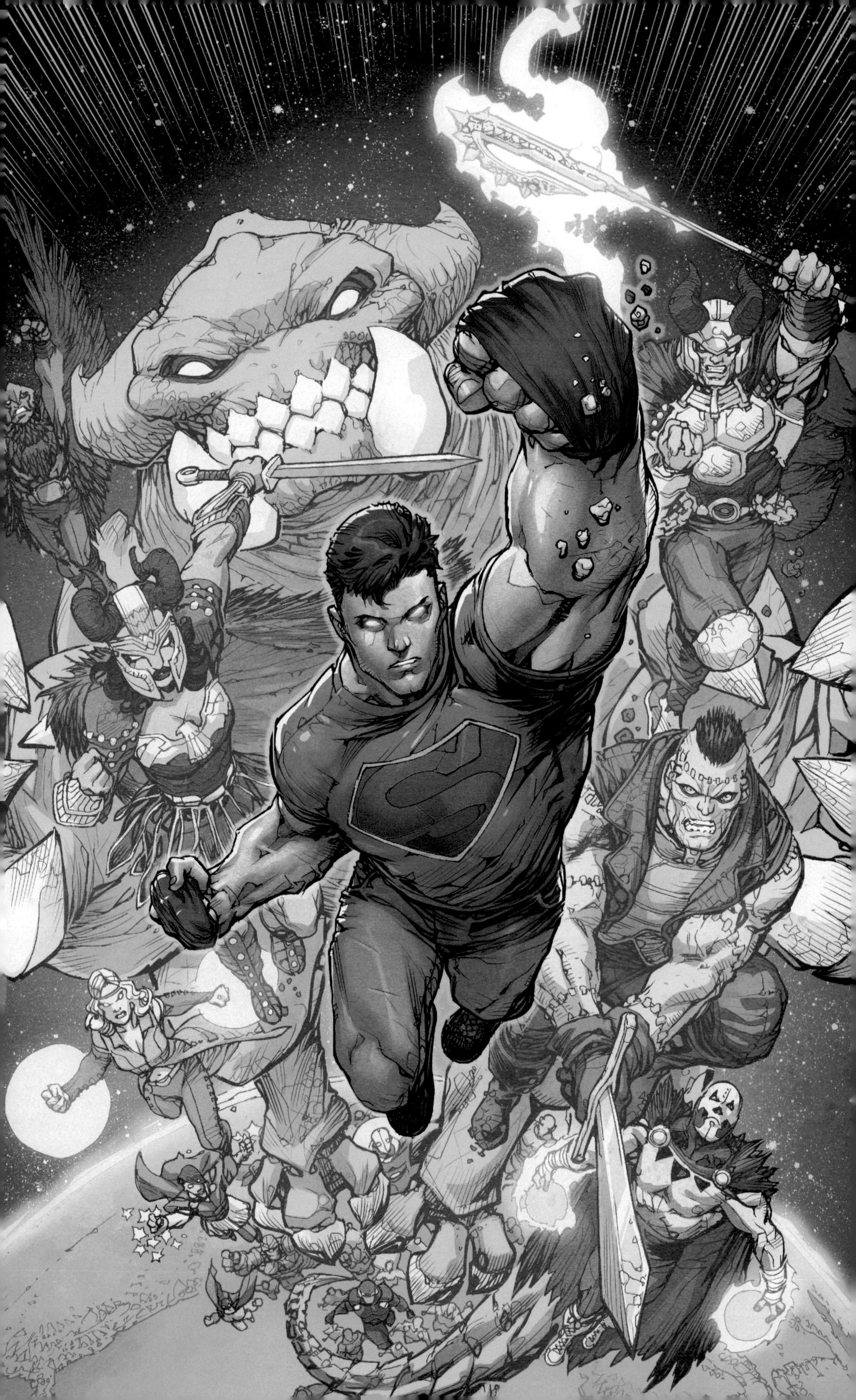

SACRIFICE

GENE LUEN YANG writer JACK HERBERT artist HI-FI, BLOND colorists STEVE WANDS letterer HOWARD PORTER, HI-FI cover

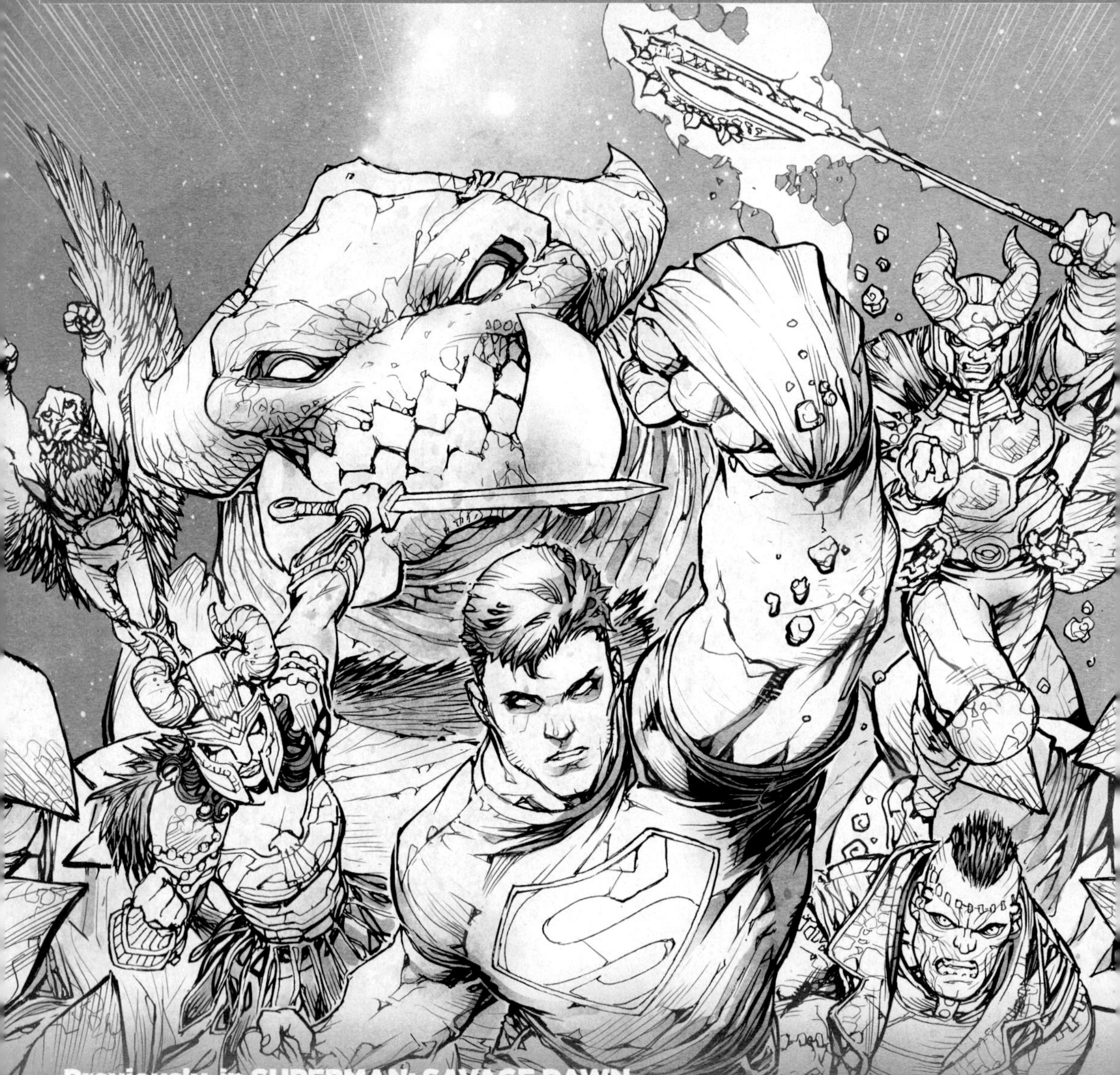

Previously, in SUPERMAN: SAVAGE DAWN ...

Heaving himself into a chamber of Kryptonite within the A.R.G.U.S. Archives, Superman's dangerous gamble pays off – sort of. The Kryptonite, while killing off his healthy cells, re-powers the Man of Steel in unpredictable ways and enables him to defeat the Puzzlerbot attacking A.R.G.U.S.

Joining Wonder Woman for a dual assault against Vandal Savage, Superman is instead distracted by the first of Savage's Black Mist-saturated "offspring": a young boy-turned-maddened behemoth called Salvaxe. The diversion proves costly, allowing Savage to realign Jupiter's moons and merge the Man of Steel's Fortress of Solitude with the already-fused Justice League Watchtower and Stormwatch Carrier.

As Wonder Woman rejoins Superman to aid him against more of Savage's super-powered progeny, the three structures, completely aligned and charged at maximum strength, create a tractor beam strong enough to draw toward Earth the comet that first granted Savage his immortality. The effort also nearly brings the bonded base down on Metropolis, until Superman makes a supreme effort to push it just outside the city – and unfortunately, right on top of him...

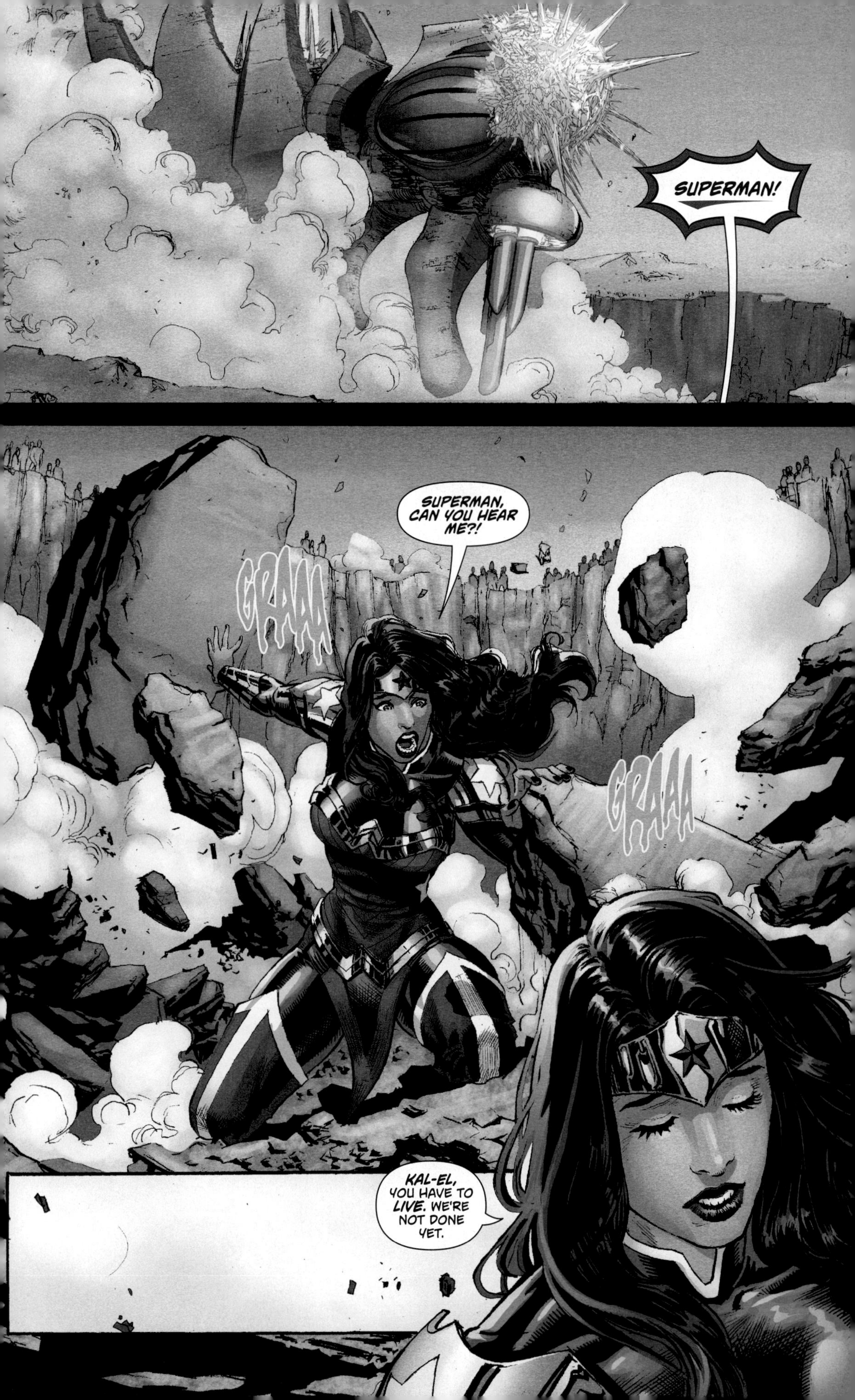
SUPERMAN!
SUPERMAN, CAN YOU HEAR ME?!
GRAAA
GRAAA
KAL-EL, YOU HAVE TO LIVE. WE'RE NOT DONE YET.

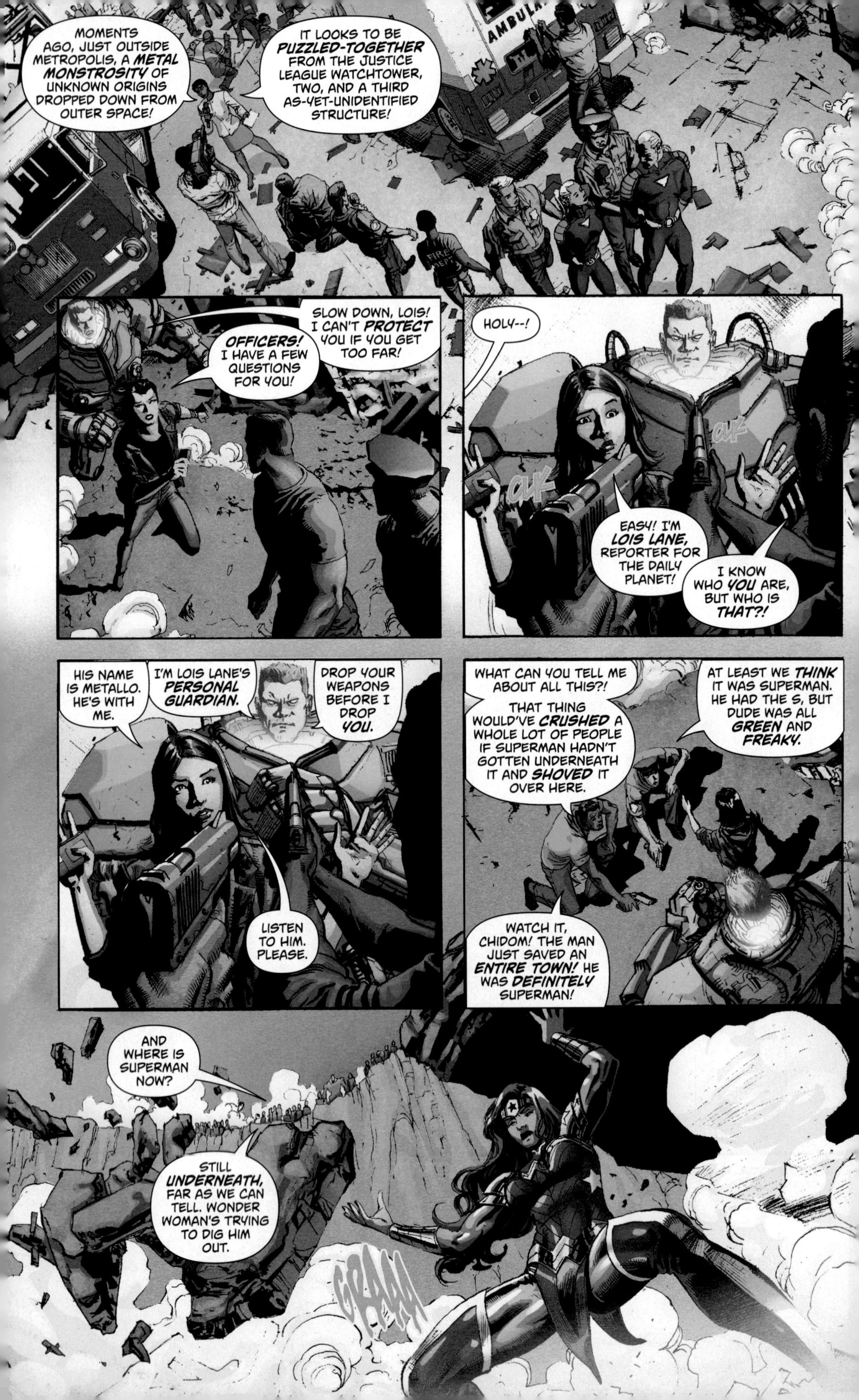
MOMENTS AGO, JUST OUTSIDE METROPOLIS, A METAL MONSTROSITY OF UNKNOWN ORIGINS DROPPED DOWN FROM OUTER SPACE!
IT LOOKS TO BE PUZZLED-TOGETHER FROM THE JUSTICE LEAGUE WATCHTOWER, TWO, AND A THIRD AS-YET-UNIDENTIFIED STRUCTURE!
AMBULA
FIRE DEPT
SLOW DOWN, LOIS! I CAN'T PROTECT YOU IF YOU GET TOO FAR!
OFFICERS! I HAVE A FEW QUESTIONS FOR YOU!
HOLY--!
CLIK
CLIK
EASY! I'M LOIS LANE, REPORTER FOR THE DAILY PLANET!
I KNOW WHO YOU ARE, BUT WHO IS THAT?!
HIS NAME IS METALLO. HE'S WITH ME.
I'M LOIS LANE'S PERSONAL GUARDIAN.
DROP YOUR WEAPONS BEFORE I DROP YOU.
LISTEN TO HIM. PLEASE.
WHAT CAN YOU TELL ME ABOUT ALL THIS?!
THAT THING WOULD'VE CRUSHED A WHOLE LOT OF PEOPLE IF SUPERMAN HADN'T GOTTEN UNDERNEATH IT AND SHOVED IT OVER HERE.
AT LEAST WE THINK IT WAS SUPERMAN. HE HAD THE S, BUT DUDE WAS ALL GREEN AND FREAKY.
WATCH IT, CHIDOM! THE MAN JUST SAVED AN ENTIRE TOWN! HE WAS DEFINITELY SUPERMAN!
AND WHERE IS SUPERMAN NOW?
STILL UNDERNEATH, FAR AS WE CAN TELL. WONDER WOMAN'S TRYING TO DIG HIM OUT.
GRAAA

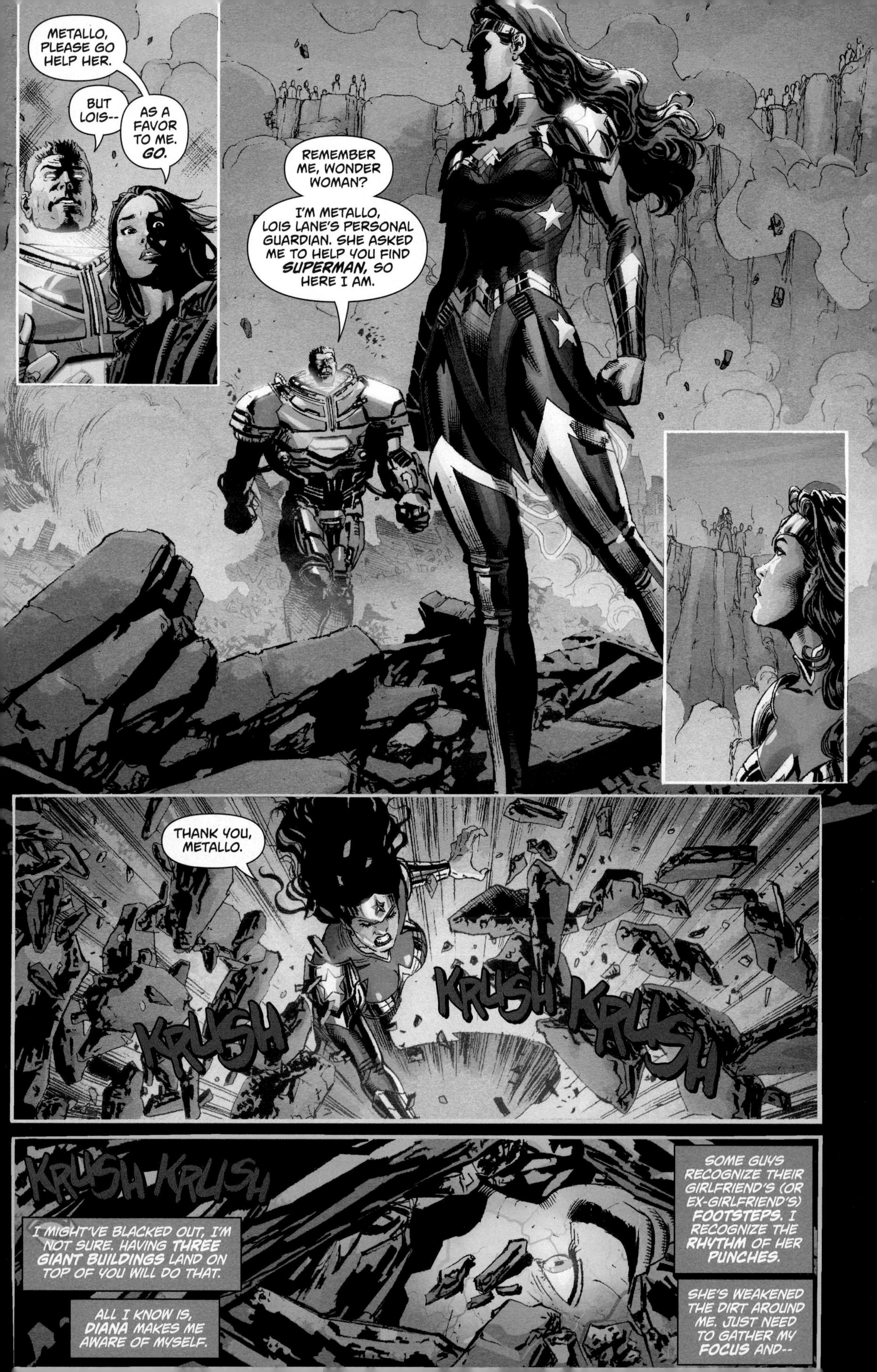
METALLO, PLEASE GO HELP HER.
BUT LOIS--
AS A FAVOR TO ME. **GO.**
REMEMBER ME, WONDER WOMAN?
I'M METALLO, LOIS LANE'S PERSONAL GUARDIAN. SHE ASKED ME TO HELP YOU FIND **SUPERMAN,** SO HERE I AM.
THANK YOU, METALLO.
KRUSH
KRUSH KRUSH
KRUSH KRUSH
I MIGHT'VE BLACKED OUT, I'M NOT SURE. HAVING **THREE GIANT BUILDINGS** LAND ON TOP OF YOU WILL DO THAT.
ALL I KNOW IS, **DIANA** MAKES ME AWARE OF MYSELF.
SOME GUYS RECOGNIZE THEIR GIRLFRIEND'S (OR EX-GIRLFRIEND'S) **FOOTSTEPS.** I RECOGNIZE THE **RHYTHM** OF HER **PUNCHES.**
SHE'S WEAKENED THE DIRT AROUND ME. JUST NEED TO GATHER MY **FOCUS** AND--

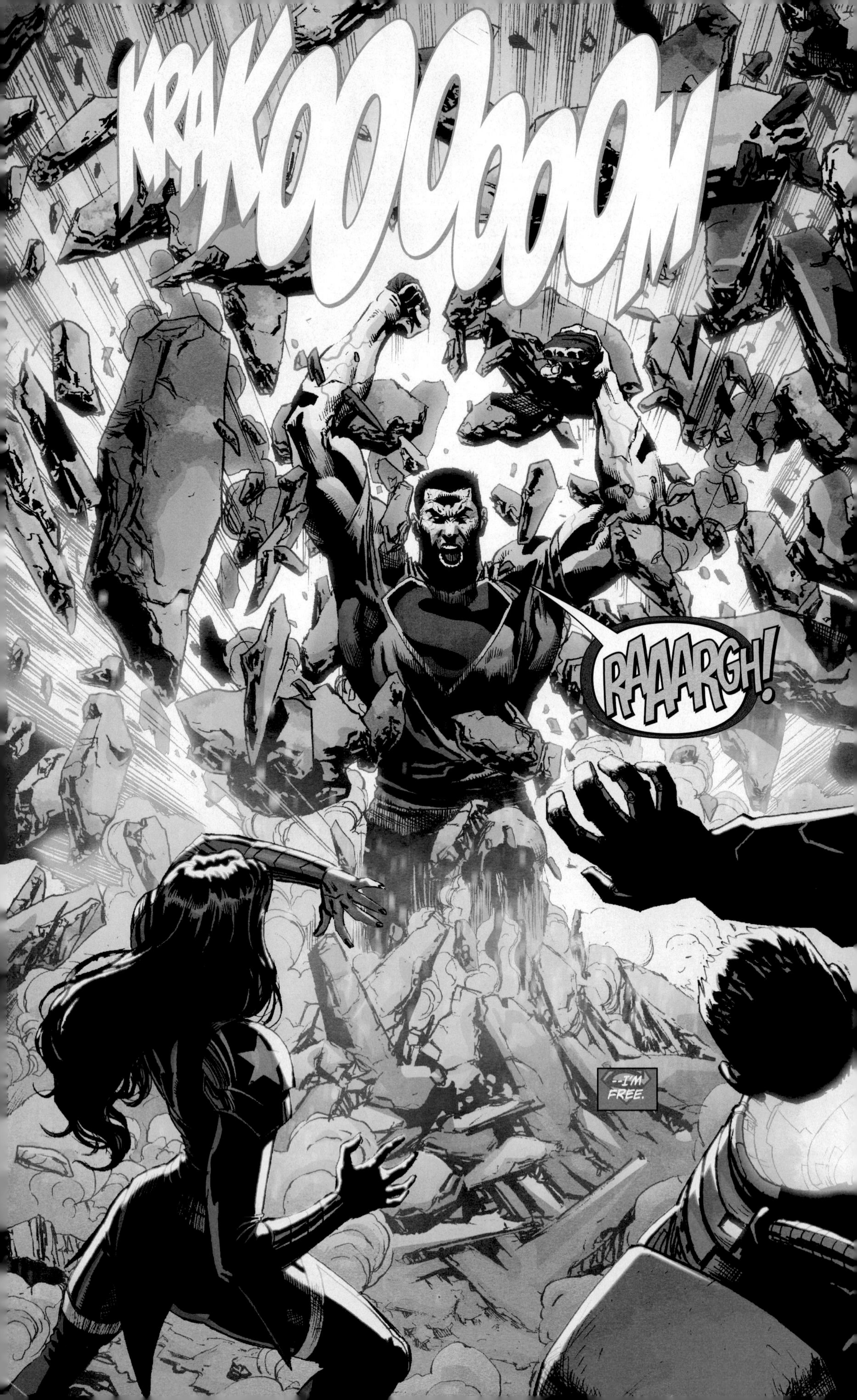
KRAKOOOOOOM
RAAARGH!
--I'M FREE.

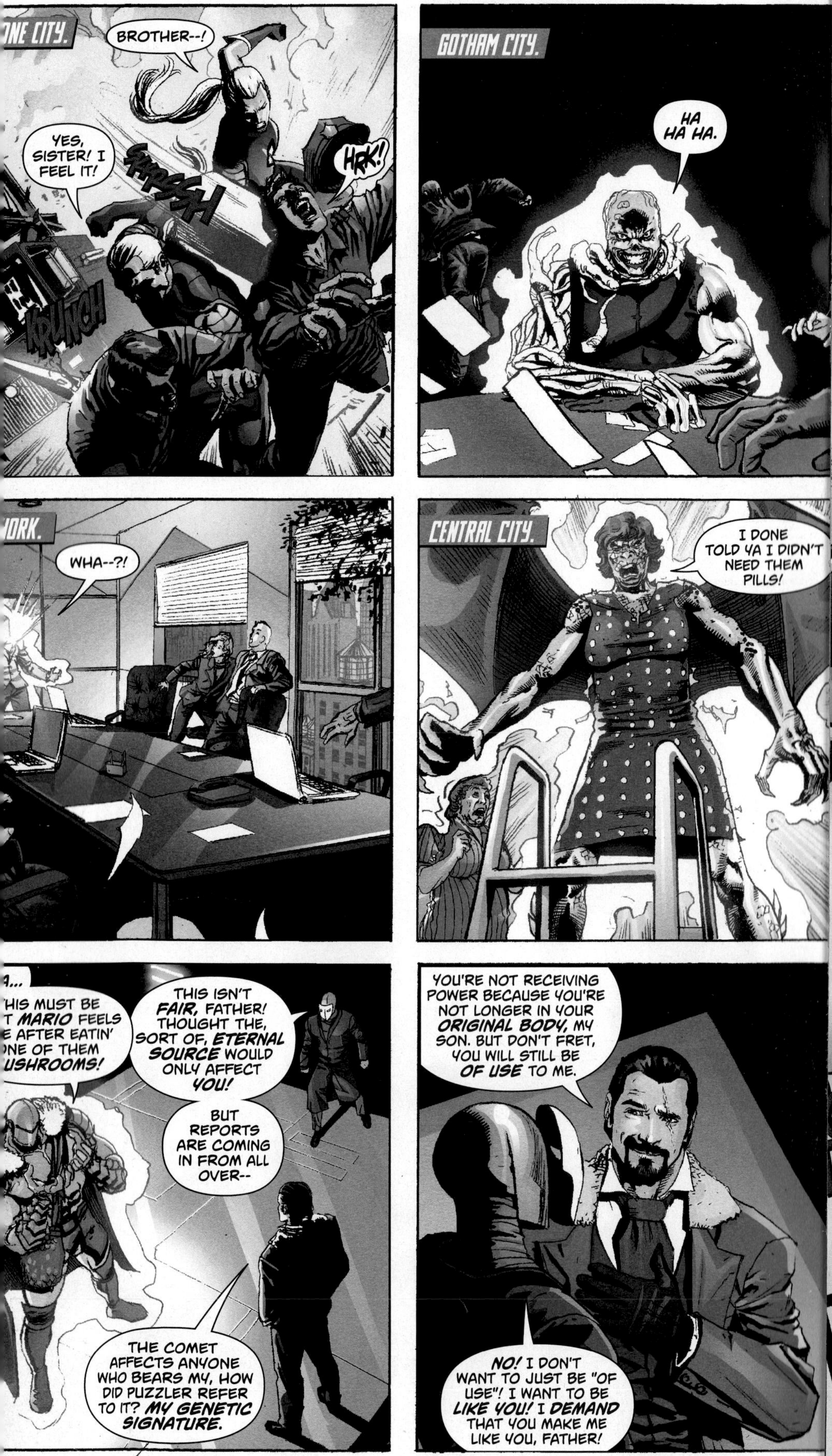

ONE CITY.
BROTHER--!
YES, SISTER! I FEEL IT!
HRK!
KRUNCH
GOTHAM CITY.
HA HA HA.
ORK.
WHA--?!
CENTRAL CITY.
I DONE TOLD YA I DIDN'T NEED THEM PILLS!
THIS MUST BE
T MARIO FEELS
E AFTER EATIN'
ONE OF THEM
USHROOMS!
THIS ISN'T FAIR, FATHER! THOUGHT THE, SORT OF, ETERNAL SOURCE WOULD ONLY AFFECT YOU!
BUT REPORTS ARE COMING IN FROM ALL OVER--
THE COMET AFFECTS ANYONE WHO BEARS MY, HOW DID PUZZLER REFER TO IT? MY GENETIC SIGNATURE.
YOU'RE NOT RECEIVING POWER BECAUSE YOU'RE NOT LONGER IN YOUR ORIGINAL BODY, MY SON. BUT DON'T FRET, YOU WILL STILL BE OF USE TO ME.
NO! I DON'T WANT TO JUST BE "OF USE"! I WANT TO BE LIKE YOU! I DEMAND THAT YOU MAKE ME LIKE YOU, FATHER!

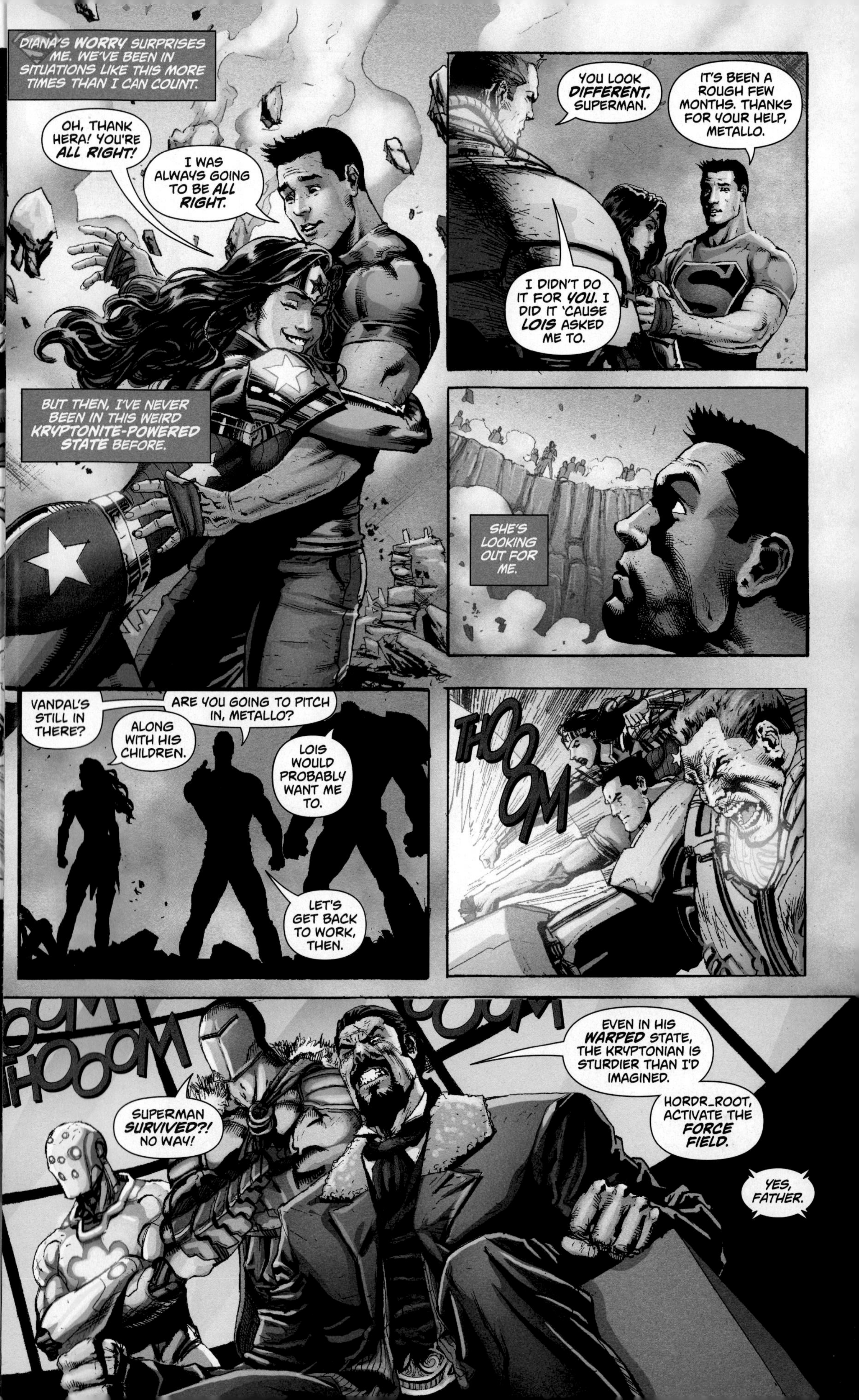

DIANA'S WORRY SURPRISES ME. WE'VE BEEN IN SITUATIONS LIKE THIS MORE TIMES THAN I CAN COUNT.
OH, THANK HERA! YOU'RE ALL RIGHT!
I WAS ALWAYS GOING TO BE ALL RIGHT.
BUT THEN, I'VE NEVER BEEN IN THIS WEIRD KRYPTONITE-POWERED STATE BEFORE.
YOU LOOK DIFFERENT, SUPERMAN.
IT'S BEEN A ROUGH FEW MONTHS. THANKS FOR YOUR HELP, METALLO.
I DIDN'T DO IT FOR YOU. I DID IT 'CAUSE LOIS ASKED ME TO.
SHE'S LOOKING OUT FOR ME.
VANDAL'S STILL IN THERE?
ARE YOU GOING TO PITCH IN, METALLO?
ALONG WITH HIS CHILDREN.
LOIS WOULD PROBABLY WANT ME TO.
LET'S GET BACK TO WORK, THEN.
THOOOM
THOOOM
EVEN IN HIS WARPED STATE, THE KRYPTONIAN IS STURDIER THAN I'D IMAGINED.
SUPERMAN SURVIVED?! NO WAY!
HORDR_ROOT, ACTIVATE THE FORCE FIELD.
YES, FATHER.

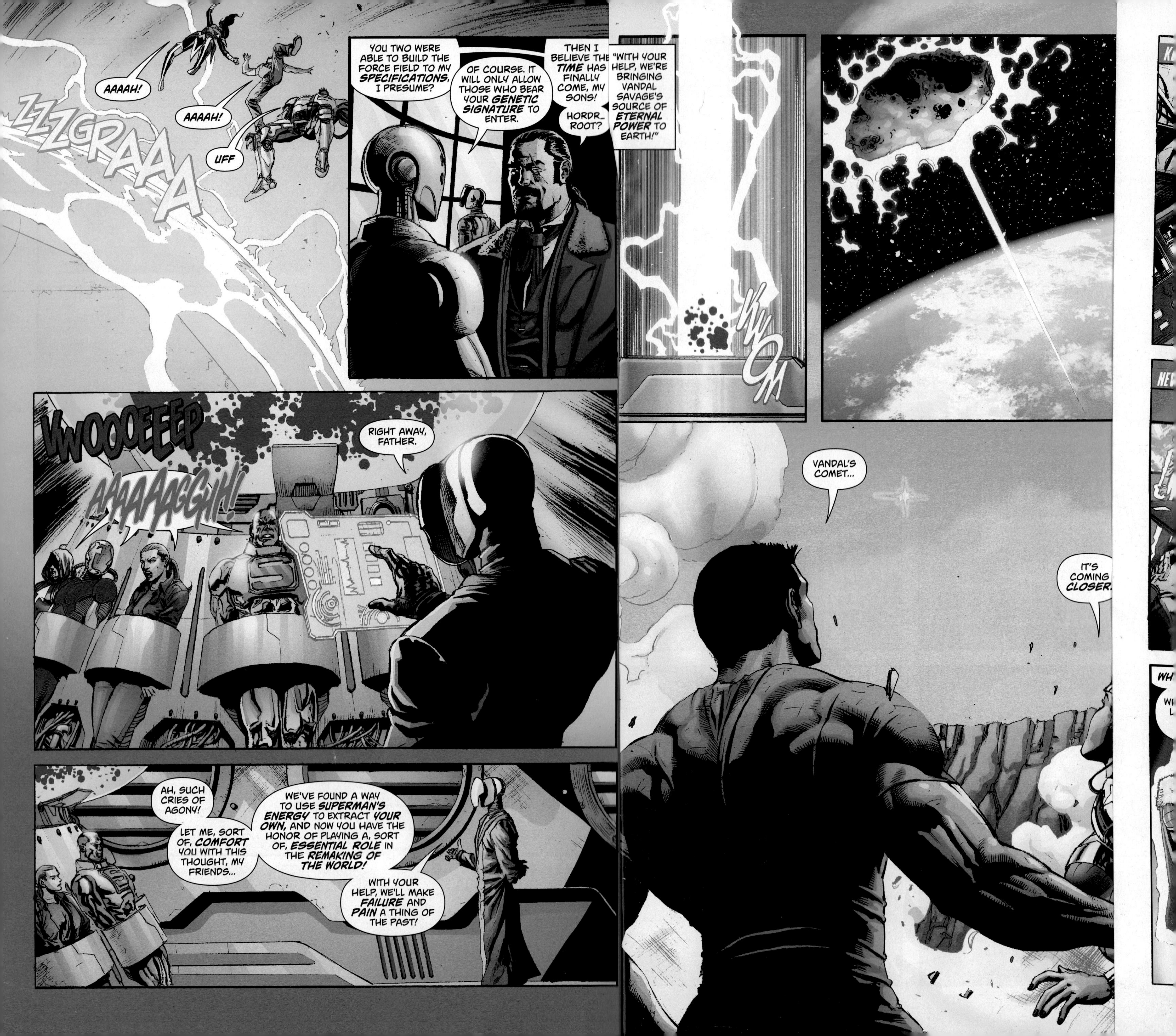
ZZZGRAAAA
AAAAH!
AAAAH!
UFF
YOU TWO WERE ABLE TO BUILD THE FORCE FIELD TO MY SPECIFICATIONS, I PRESUME?
OF COURSE. IT WILL ONLY ALLOW THOSE WHO BEAR YOUR GENETIC SIGNATURE TO ENTER.
THEN I BELIEVE THE TIME HAS FINALLY COME, MY SONS!
HORDR_ROOT?
RIGHT AWAY, FATHER.
VWOOOEEEP
AAAAAAGGHH!
AH, SUCH CRIES OF AGONY!
LET ME, SORT OF, COMFORT YOU WITH THIS THOUGHT, MY FRIENDS...
WE'VE FOUND A WAY TO USE SUPERMAN'S ENERGY TO EXTRACT YOUR OWN, AND NOW YOU HAVE THE HONOR OF PLAYING A, SORT OF, ESSENTIAL ROLE IN THE REMAKING OF THE WORLD!
WITH YOUR HELP, WE'LL MAKE FAILURE AND PAIN A THING OF THE PAST!
"WITH YOUR HELP, WE'RE BRINGING VANDAL SAVAGE'S SOURCE OF ETERNAL POWER TO EARTH!"
WWOM
VANDAL'S COMET...
IT'S COMING CLOSER.

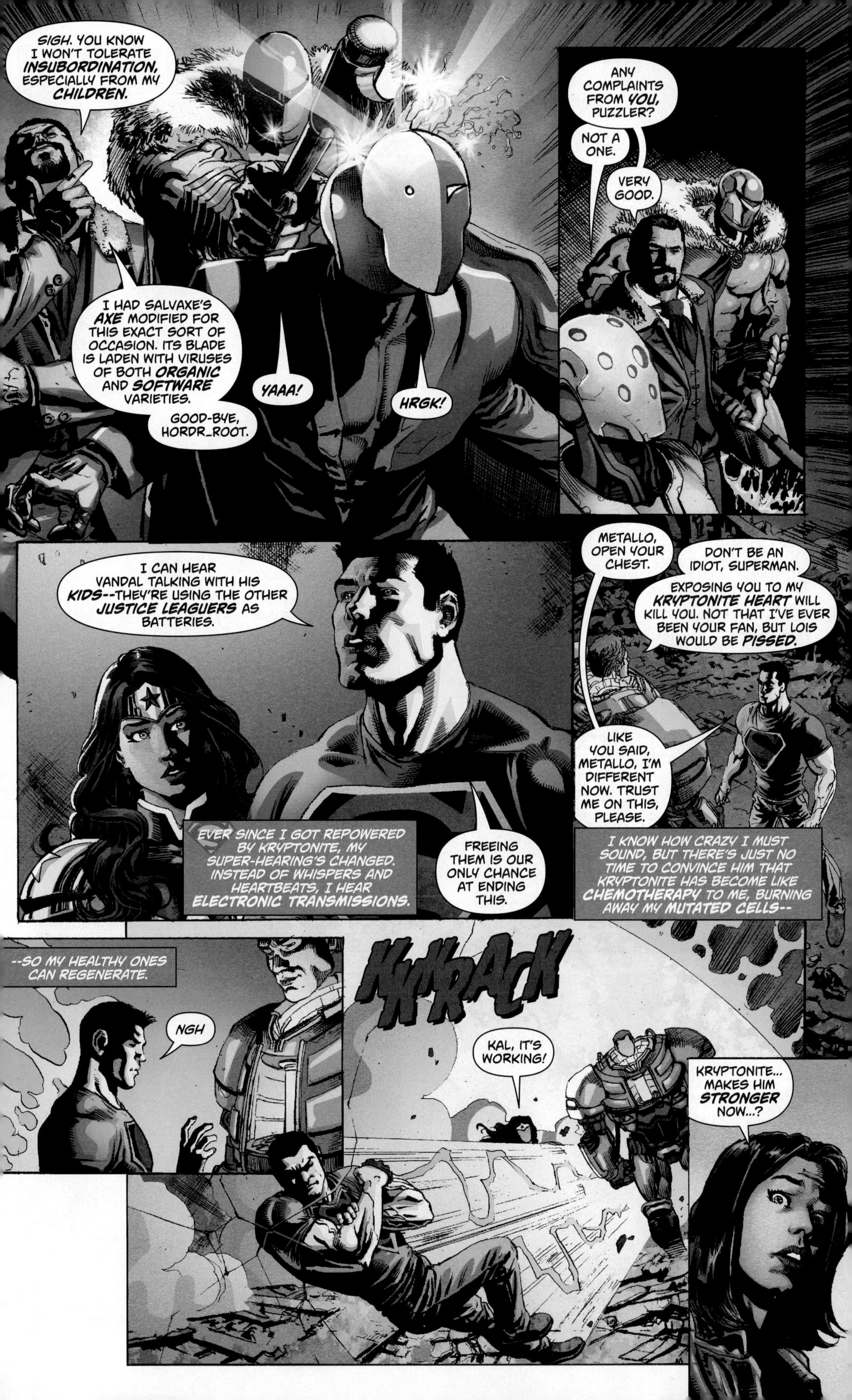

SIGH. YOU KNOW I WON'T TOLERATE INSUBORDINATION, ESPECIALLY FROM MY CHILDREN.
I HAD SALVAXE'S AXE MODIFIED FOR THIS EXACT SORT OF OCCASION. ITS BLADE IS LADEN WITH VIRUSES OF BOTH ORGANIC AND SOFTWARE VARIETIES.
GOOD-BYE, HORDR_ROOT.
YAAA!
HRGK!
ANY COMPLAINTS FROM YOU, PUZZLER?
NOT A ONE.
VERY GOOD.
I CAN HEAR VANDAL TALKING WITH HIS KIDS--THEY'RE USING THE OTHER JUSTICE LEAGUERS AS BATTERIES.
EVER SINCE I GOT REPOWERED BY KRYPTONITE, MY SUPER-HEARING'S CHANGED. INSTEAD OF WHISPERS AND HEARTBEATS, I HEAR ELECTRONIC TRANSMISSIONS.
FREEING THEM IS OUR ONLY CHANCE AT ENDING THIS.
METALLO, OPEN YOUR CHEST.
DON'T BE AN IDIOT, SUPERMAN.
EXPOSING YOU TO MY KRYPTONITE HEART WILL KILL YOU. NOT THAT I'VE EVER BEEN YOUR FAN, BUT LOIS WOULD BE PISSED.
LIKE YOU SAID, METALLO, I'M DIFFERENT NOW. TRUST ME ON THIS, PLEASE.
I KNOW HOW CRAZY I MUST SOUND, BUT THERE'S JUST NO TIME TO CONVINCE HIM THAT KRYPTONITE HAS BECOME LIKE CHEMOTHERAPY TO ME, BURNING AWAY MY MUTATED CELLS--
--SO MY HEALTHY ONES CAN REGENERATE.
NGH
KKKRACK
KAL, IT'S WORKING!
KRYPTONITE... MAKES HIM STRONGER NOW...?

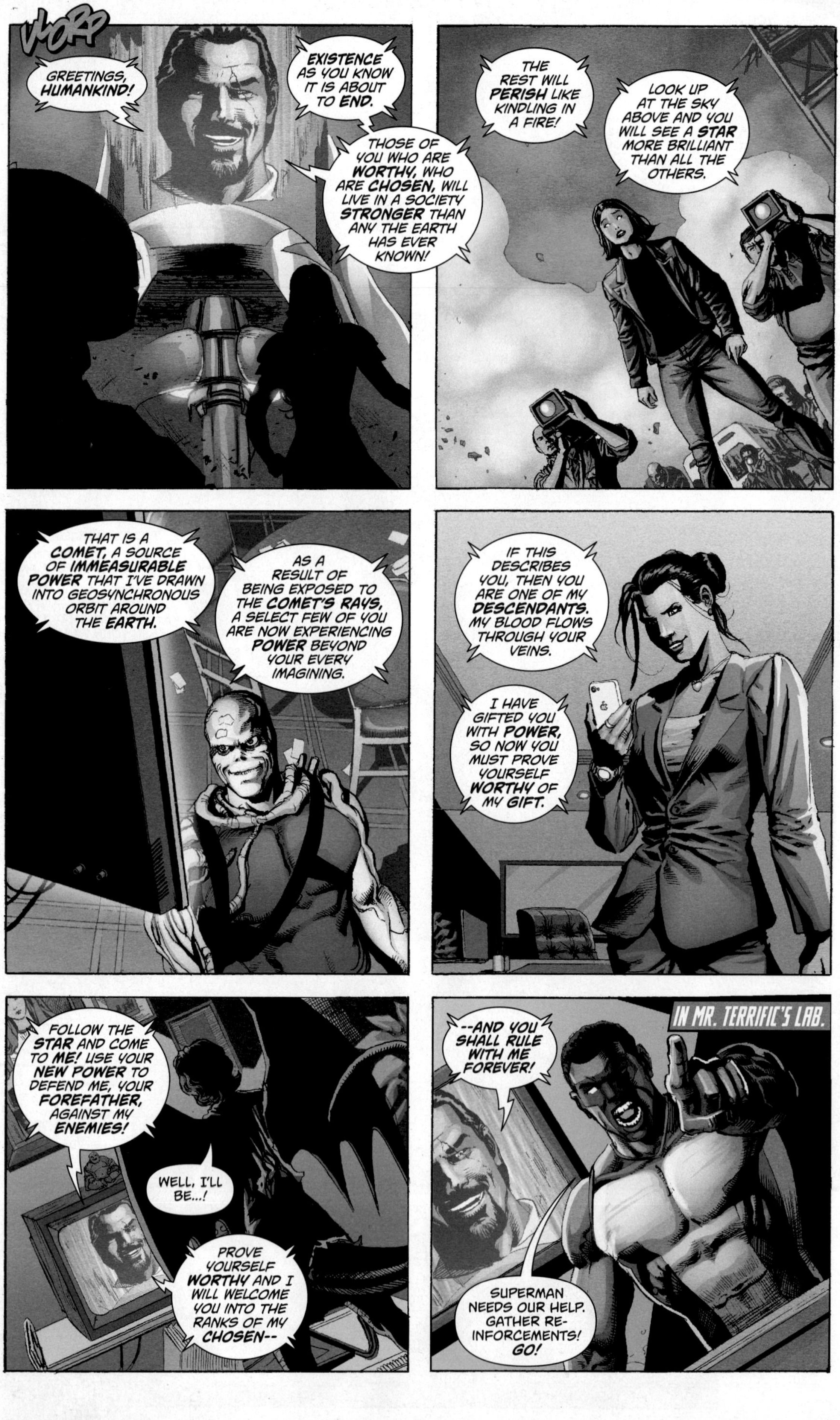
VWORP
GREETINGS, HUMANKIND!
EXISTENCE AS YOU KNOW IT IS ABOUT TO END.
THOSE OF YOU WHO ARE WORTHY, WHO ARE CHOSEN, WILL LIVE IN A SOCIETY STRONGER THAN ANY THE EARTH HAS EVER KNOWN!
THE REST WILL PERISH LIKE KINDLING IN A FIRE!
LOOK UP AT THE SKY ABOVE AND YOU WILL SEE A STAR MORE BRILLIANT THAN ALL THE OTHERS.
THAT IS A COMET, A SOURCE OF IMMEASURABLE POWER THAT I'VE DRAWN INTO GEOSYNCHRONOUS ORBIT AROUND THE EARTH.
AS A RESULT OF BEING EXPOSED TO THE COMET'S RAYS, A SELECT FEW OF YOU ARE NOW EXPERIENCING POWER BEYOND YOUR EVERY IMAGINING.
IF THIS DESCRIBES YOU, THEN YOU ARE ONE OF MY DESCENDANTS. MY BLOOD FLOWS THROUGH YOUR VEINS.
I HAVE GIFTED YOU WITH POWER, SO NOW YOU MUST PROVE YOURSELF WORTHY OF MY GIFT.
FOLLOW THE STAR AND COME TO ME! USE YOUR NEW POWER TO DEFEND ME, YOUR FOREFATHER, AGAINST MY ENEMIES!
WELL, I'LL BE...!
PROVE YOURSELF WORTHY AND I WILL WELCOME YOU INTO THE RANKS OF MY CHOSEN--
IN MR. TERRIFIC'S LAB.
--AND YOU SHALL RULE WITH ME FOREVER!
SUPERMAN NEEDS OUR HELP. GATHER RE-INFORCEMENTS! GO!

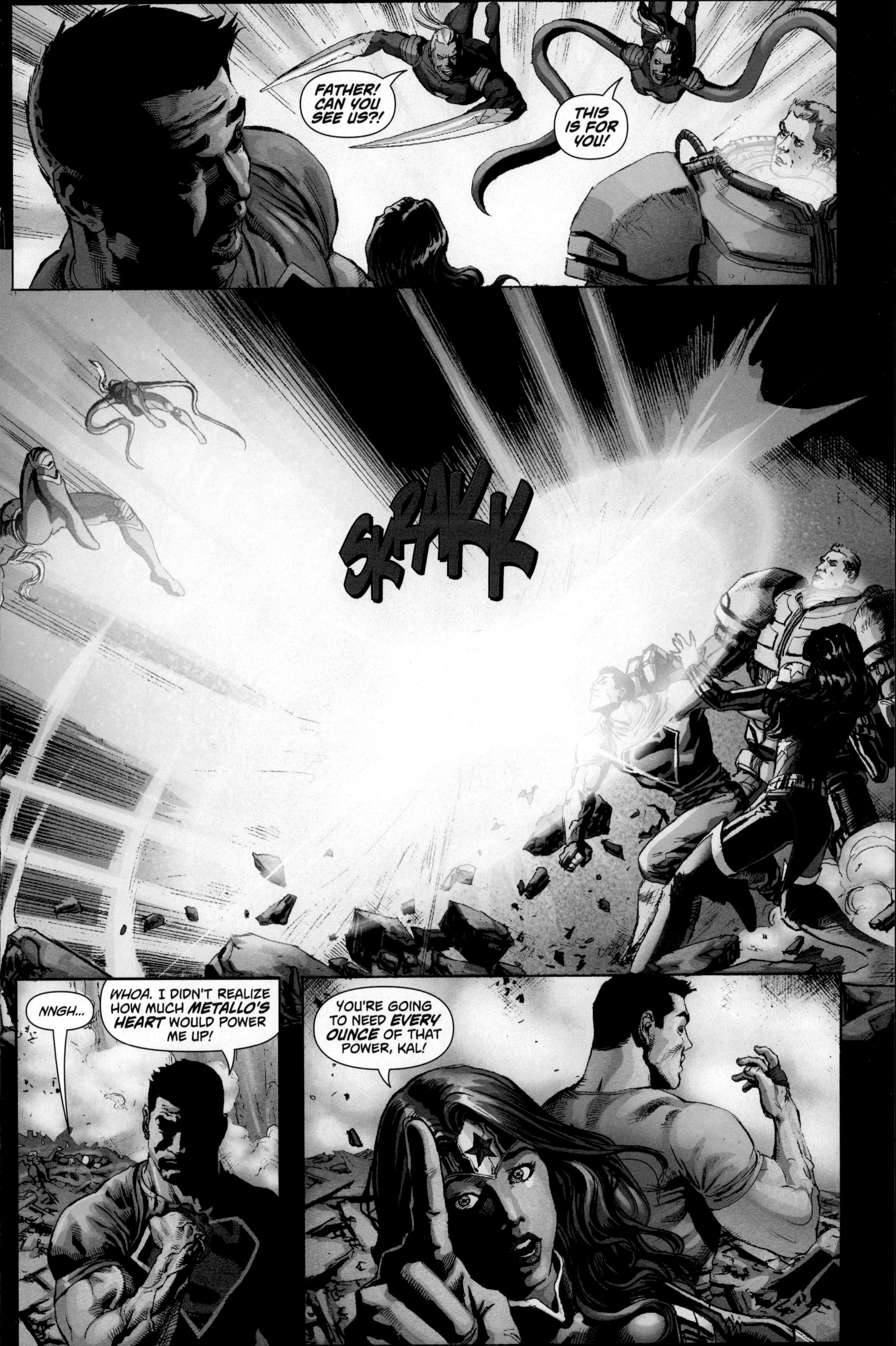

FATHER! CAN YOU SEE US?!
THIS IS FOR YOU!
SKRAKK
NNGH...
WHOA. I DIDN'T REALIZE HOW MUCH METALLO'S HEART WOULD POWER ME UP!
YOU'RE GOING TO NEED EVERY OUNCE OF THAT POWER, KAL!

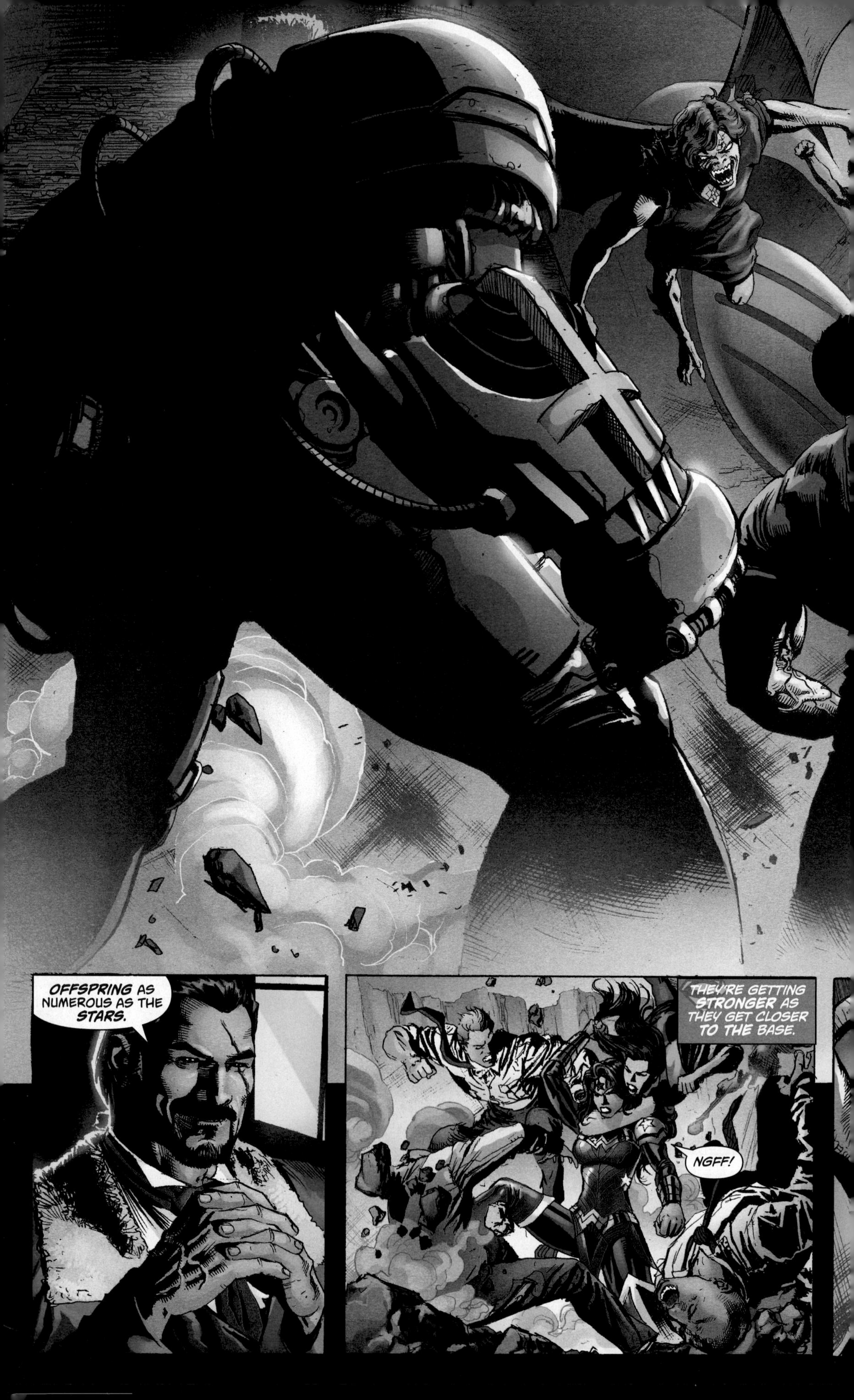
OFFSPRING AS NUMEROUS AS THE STARS.
THEY'RE GETTING STRONGER AS THEY GET CLOSER TO THE BASE.
NGFF!

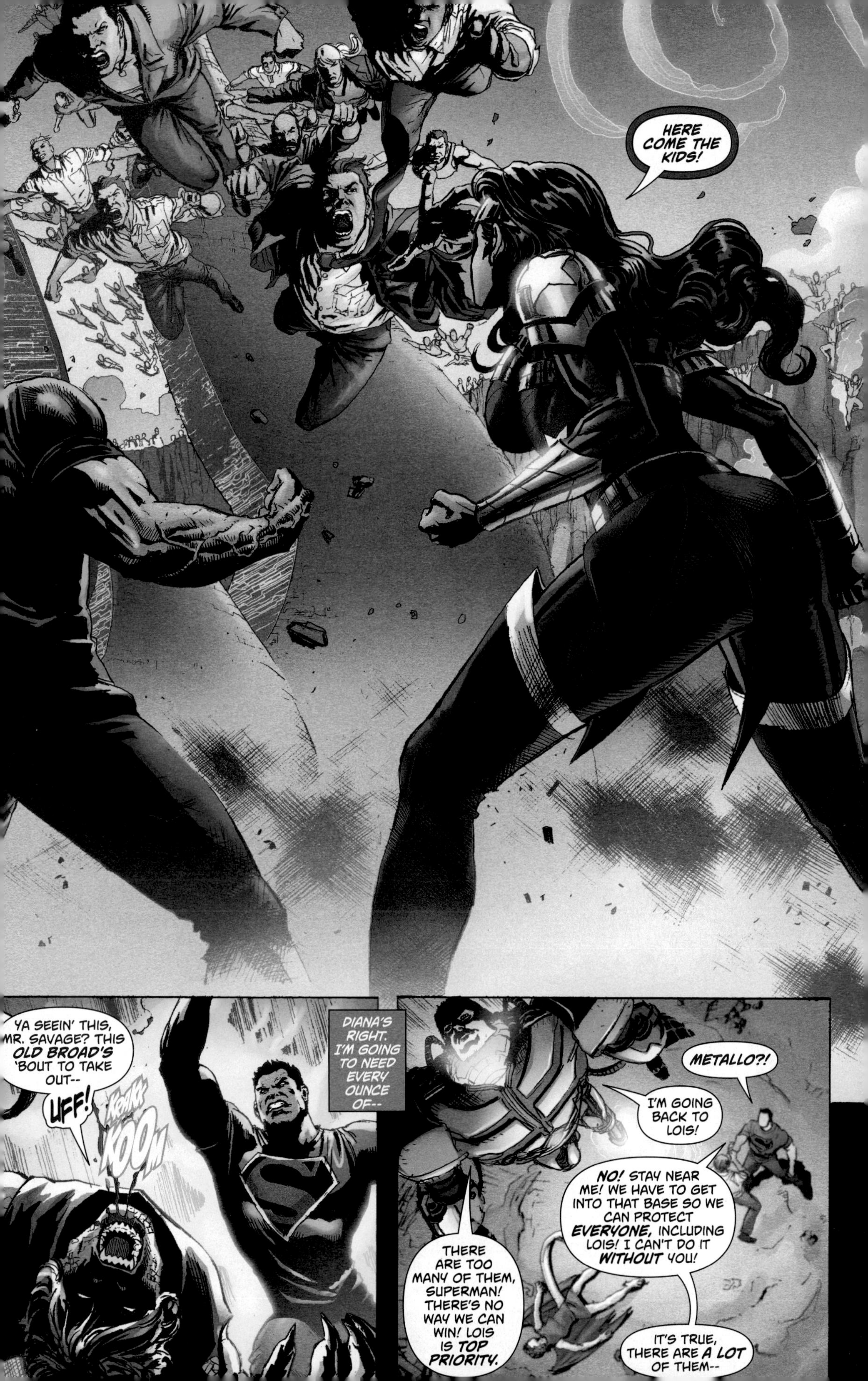
HERE COME THE KIDS!
YA SEEIN' THIS, MR. SAVAGE? THIS OLD BROAD'S 'BOUT TO TAKE OUT--
UFF!
KRAKK KOOM
DIANA'S RIGHT. I'M GOING TO NEED EVERY OUNCE OF--
METALLO?!
I'M GOING BACK TO LOIS!
NO! STAY NEAR ME! WE HAVE TO GET INTO THAT BASE SO WE CAN PROTECT EVERYONE, INCLUDING LOIS! I CAN'T DO IT WITHOUT YOU!
THERE ARE TOO MANY OF THEM, SUPERMAN! THERE'S NO WAY WE CAN WIN! LOIS IS TOP PRIORITY.
IT'S TRUE, THERE ARE A LOT OF THEM--

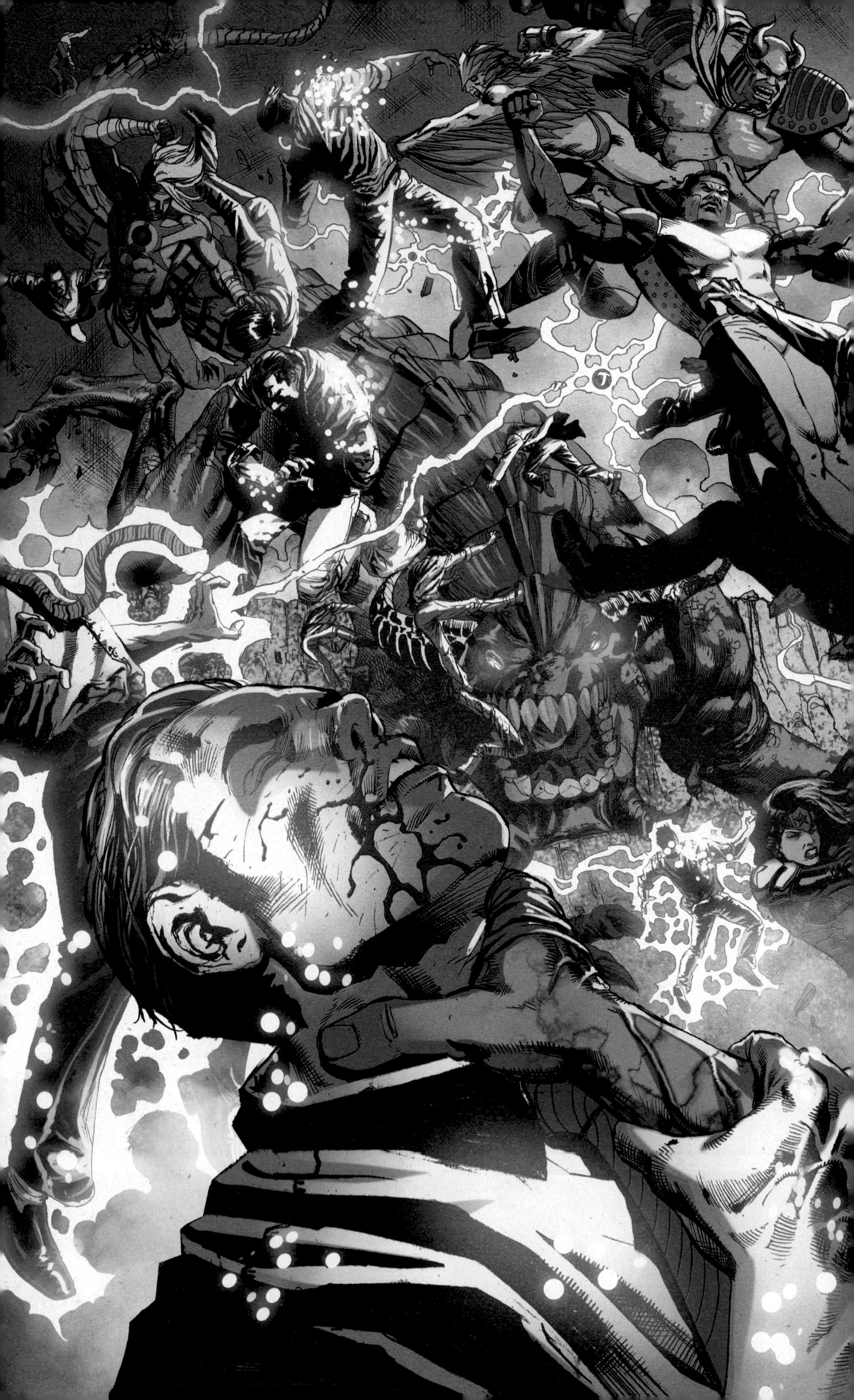

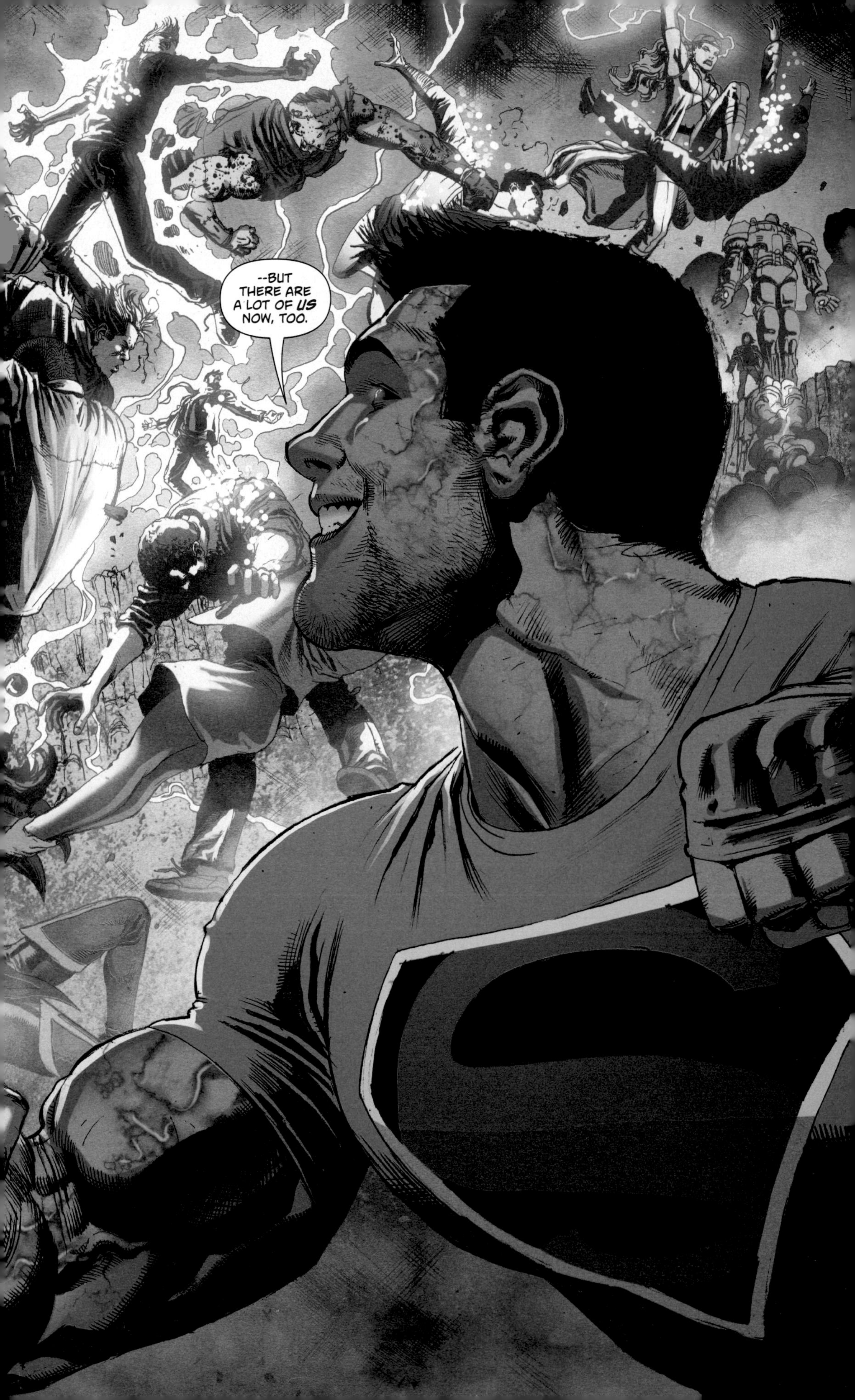
--BUT THERE ARE A LOT OF US NOW, TOO.

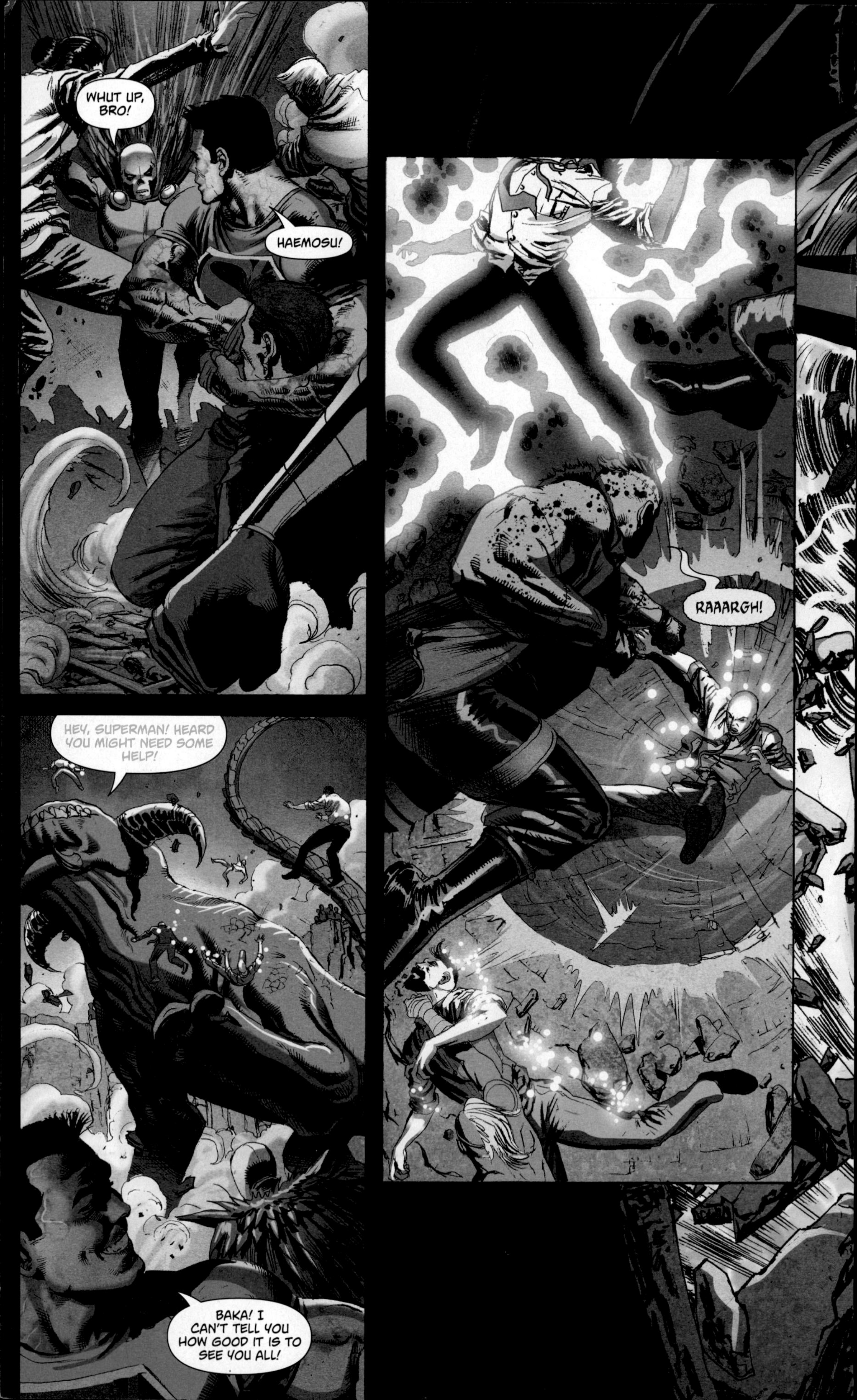
WHUT UP, BRO!
HAEMOSU!
HEY, SUPERMAN! HEARD YOU MIGHT NEED SOME HELP!
BAKA! I CAN'T TELL YOU HOW GOOD IT IS TO SEE YOU ALL!
RAAARGH!

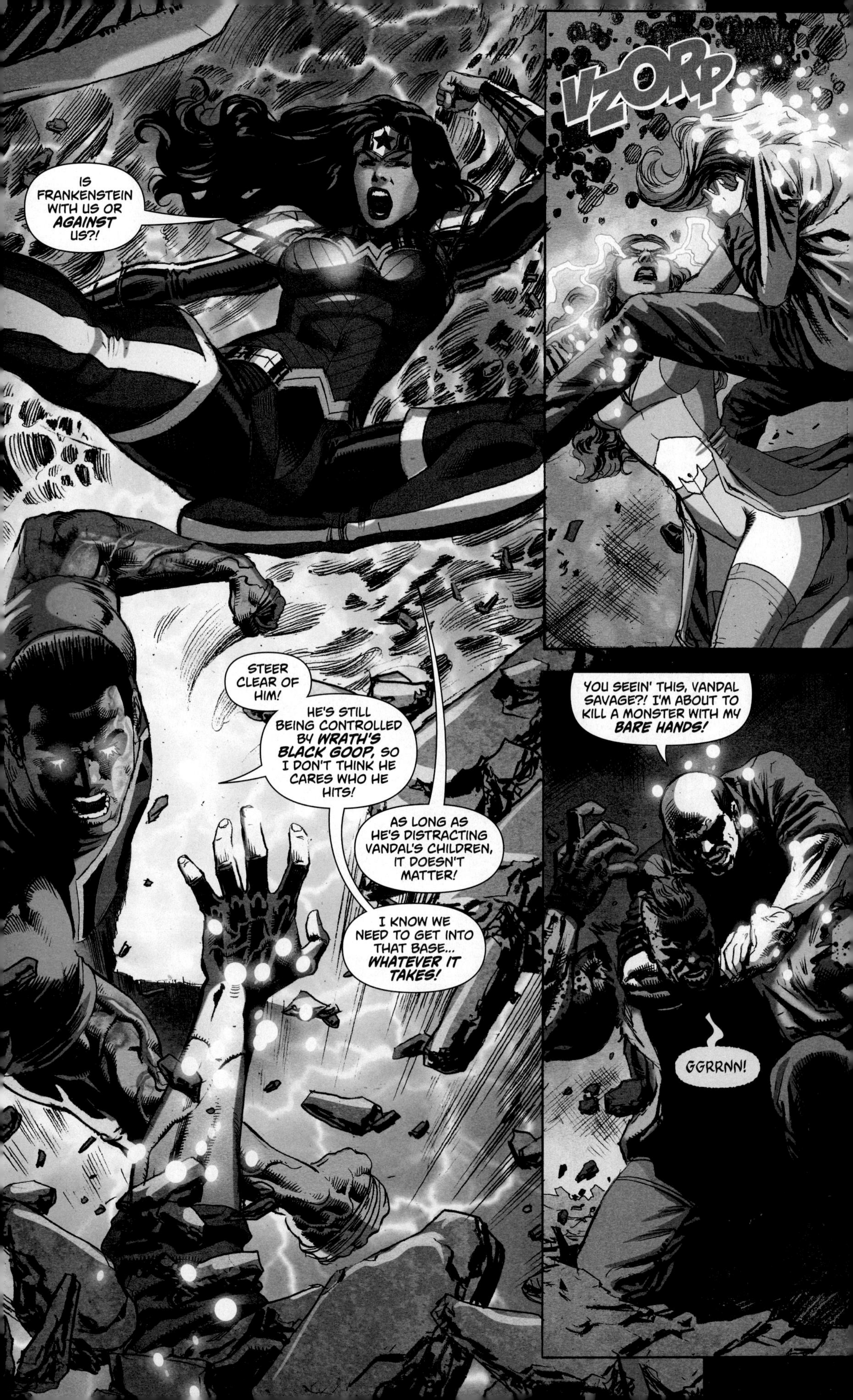
IS FRANKENSTEIN WITH US OR AGAINST US?!
VZORP
STEER CLEAR OF HIM!
HE'S STILL BEING CONTROLLED BY WRATH'S BLACK GOOP, SO I DON'T THINK HE CARES WHO HE HITS!
AS LONG AS HE'S DISTRACTING VANDAL'S CHILDREN, IT DOESN'T MATTER!
I KNOW WE NEED TO GET INTO THAT BASE... WHATEVER IT TAKES!
YOU SEEIN' THIS, VANDAL SAVAGE?! I'M ABOUT TO KILL A MONSTER WITH MY BARE HANDS!
GGRRNN!

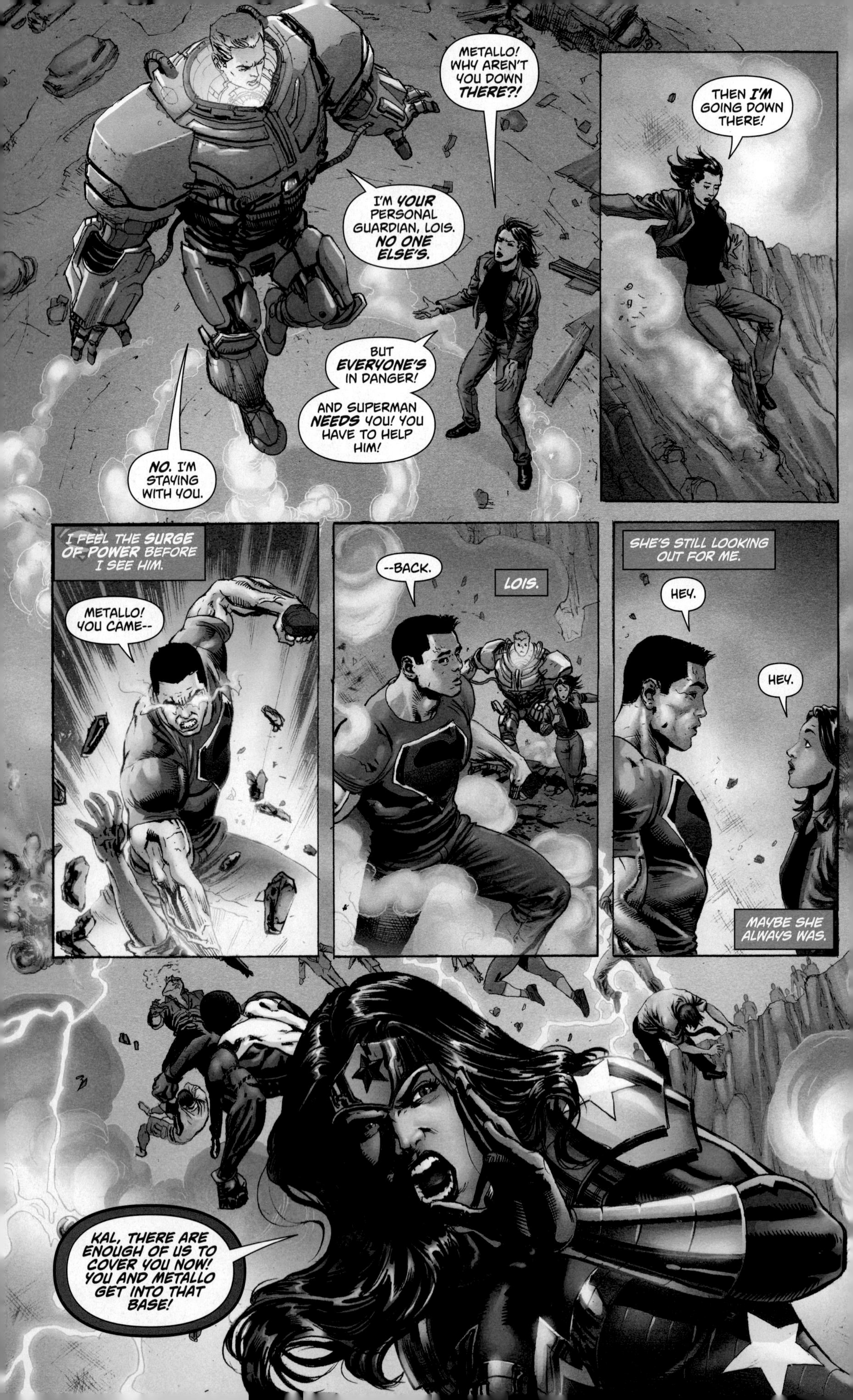
METALLO! WHY AREN'T YOU DOWN THERE?!
I'M YOUR PERSONAL GUARDIAN, LOIS. NO ONE ELSE'S.
BUT EVERYONE'S IN DANGER!
AND SUPERMAN NEEDS YOU! YOU HAVE TO HELP HIM!
NO. I'M STAYING WITH YOU.
THEN I'M GOING DOWN THERE!
I FEEL THE SURGE OF POWER BEFORE I SEE HIM.
METALLO! YOU CAME--
--BACK.
LOIS.
SHE'S STILL LOOKING OUT FOR ME.
HEY.
HEY.
MAYBE SHE ALWAYS WAS.
KAL, THERE ARE ENOUGH OF US TO COVER YOU NOW! YOU AND METALLO GET INTO THAT BASE!

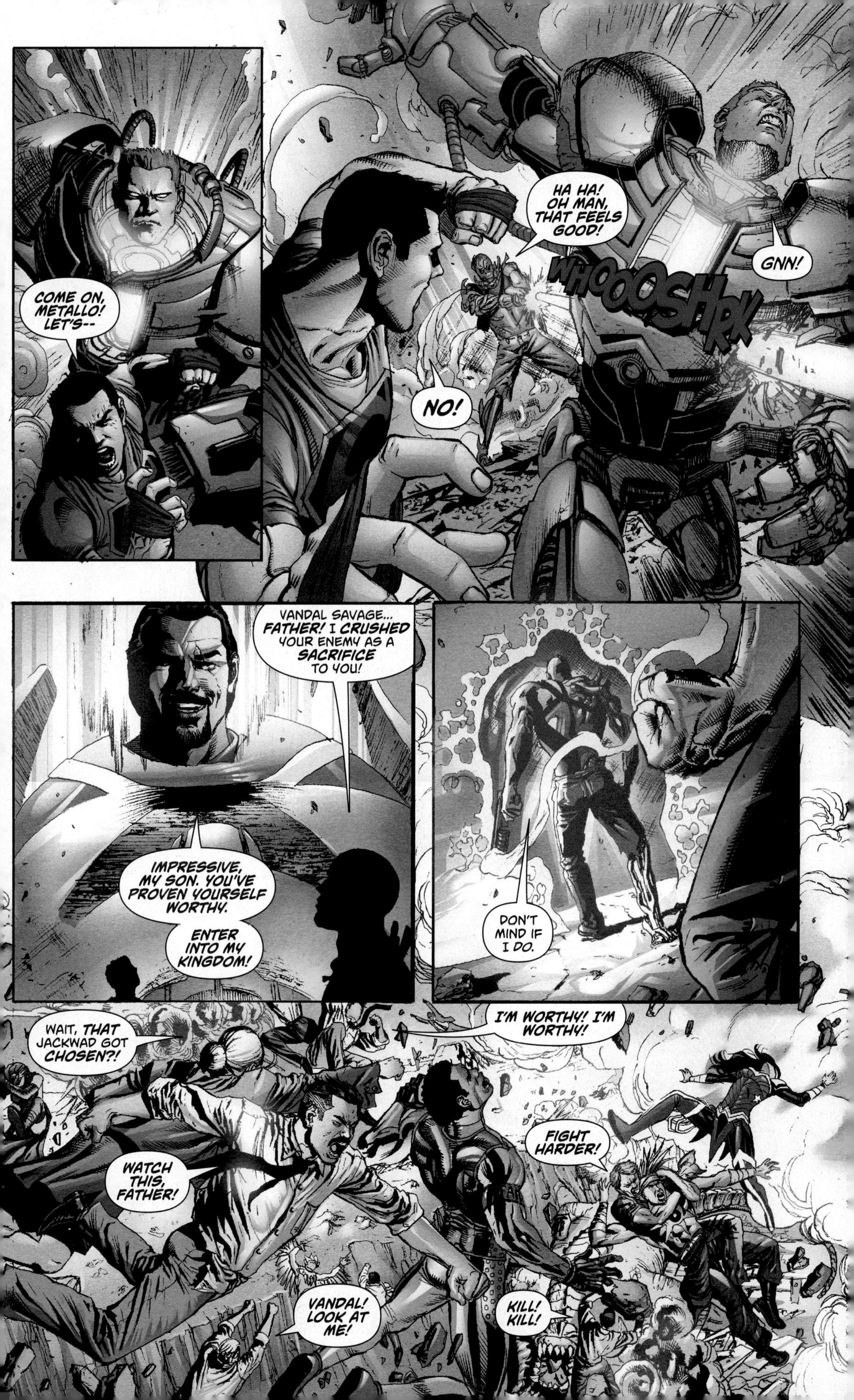
COME ON, METALLO! LET'S--
HA HA! OH MAN, THAT FEELS GOOD!
WHOOOOSHRK
GNN!
NO!
VANDAL SAVAGE... FATHER! I CRUSHED YOUR ENEMY AS A SACRIFICE TO YOU!
IMPRESSIVE, MY SON. YOU'VE PROVEN YOURSELF WORTHY.
ENTER INTO MY KINGDOM!
DON'T MIND IF I DO.
WAIT, THAT JACKWAD GOT CHOSEN?!
I'M WORTHY! I'M WORTHY!
FIGHT HARDER!
WATCH THIS, FATHER!
VANDAL! LOOK AT ME!
KILL! KILL!

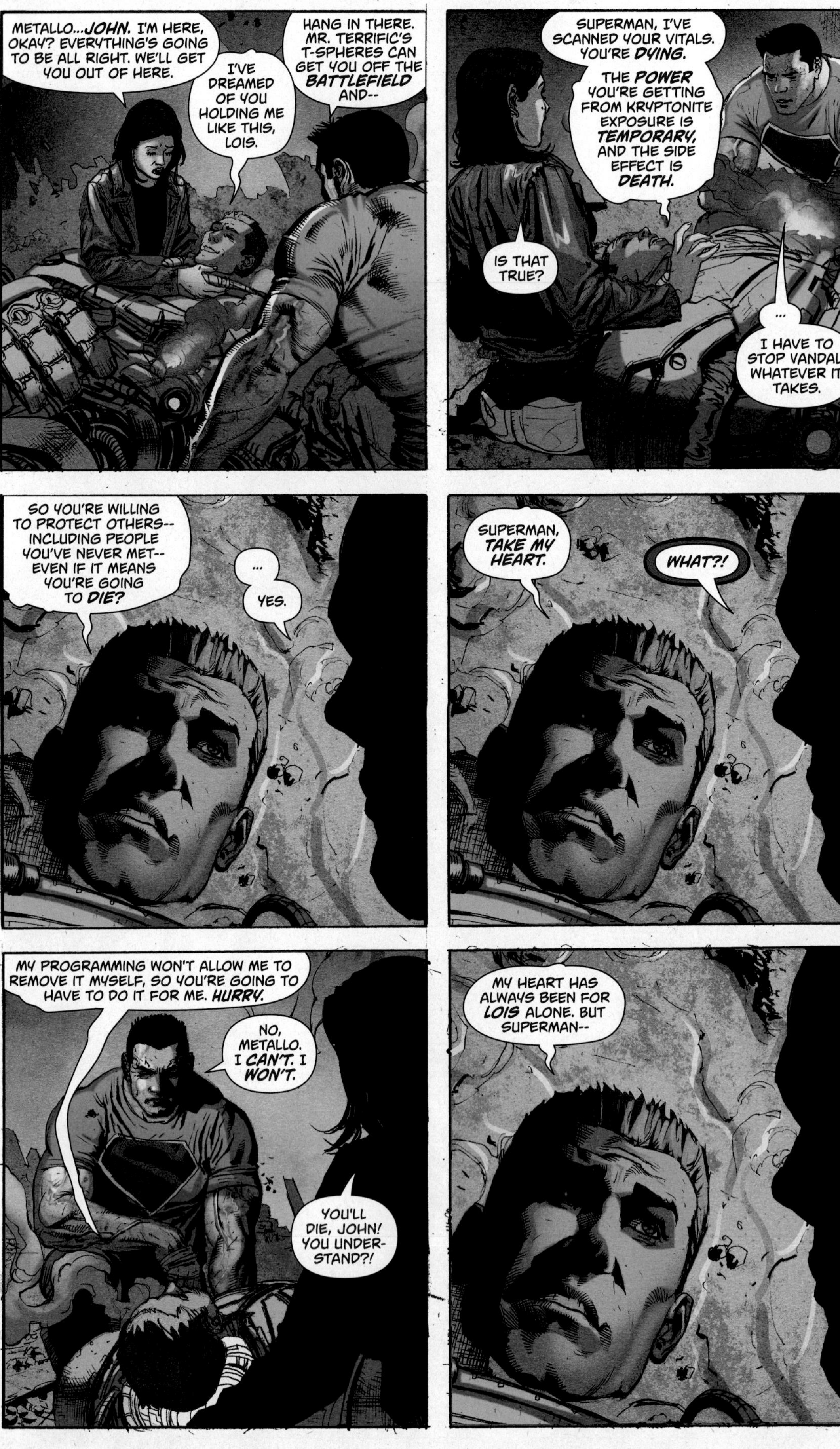
METALLO...JOHN. I'M HERE, OKAY? EVERYTHING'S GOING TO BE ALL RIGHT. WE'LL GET YOU OUT OF HERE.
I'VE DREAMED OF YOU HOLDING ME LIKE THIS, LOIS.
HANG IN THERE. MR. TERRIFIC'S T-SPHERES CAN GET YOU OFF THE BATTLEFIELD AND--
SUPERMAN, I'VE SCANNED YOUR VITALS. YOU'RE DYING.
THE POWER YOU'RE GETTING FROM KRYPTONITE EXPOSURE IS TEMPORARY, AND THE SIDE EFFECT IS DEATH.
IS THAT TRUE?
...
I HAVE TO STOP VANDAL. WHATEVER IT TAKES.
SO YOU'RE WILLING TO PROTECT OTHERS-- INCLUDING PEOPLE YOU'VE NEVER MET-- EVEN IF IT MEANS YOU'RE GOING TO DIE?
...
YES.
SUPERMAN, TAKE MY HEART.
WHAT?!
MY PROGRAMMING WON'T ALLOW ME TO REMOVE IT MYSELF, SO YOU'RE GOING TO HAVE TO DO IT FOR ME. HURRY.
NO, METALLO. I CAN'T. I WON'T.
YOU'LL DIE, JOHN! YOU UNDERSTAND?!
MY HEART HAS ALWAYS BEEN FOR LOIS ALONE. BUT SUPERMAN--

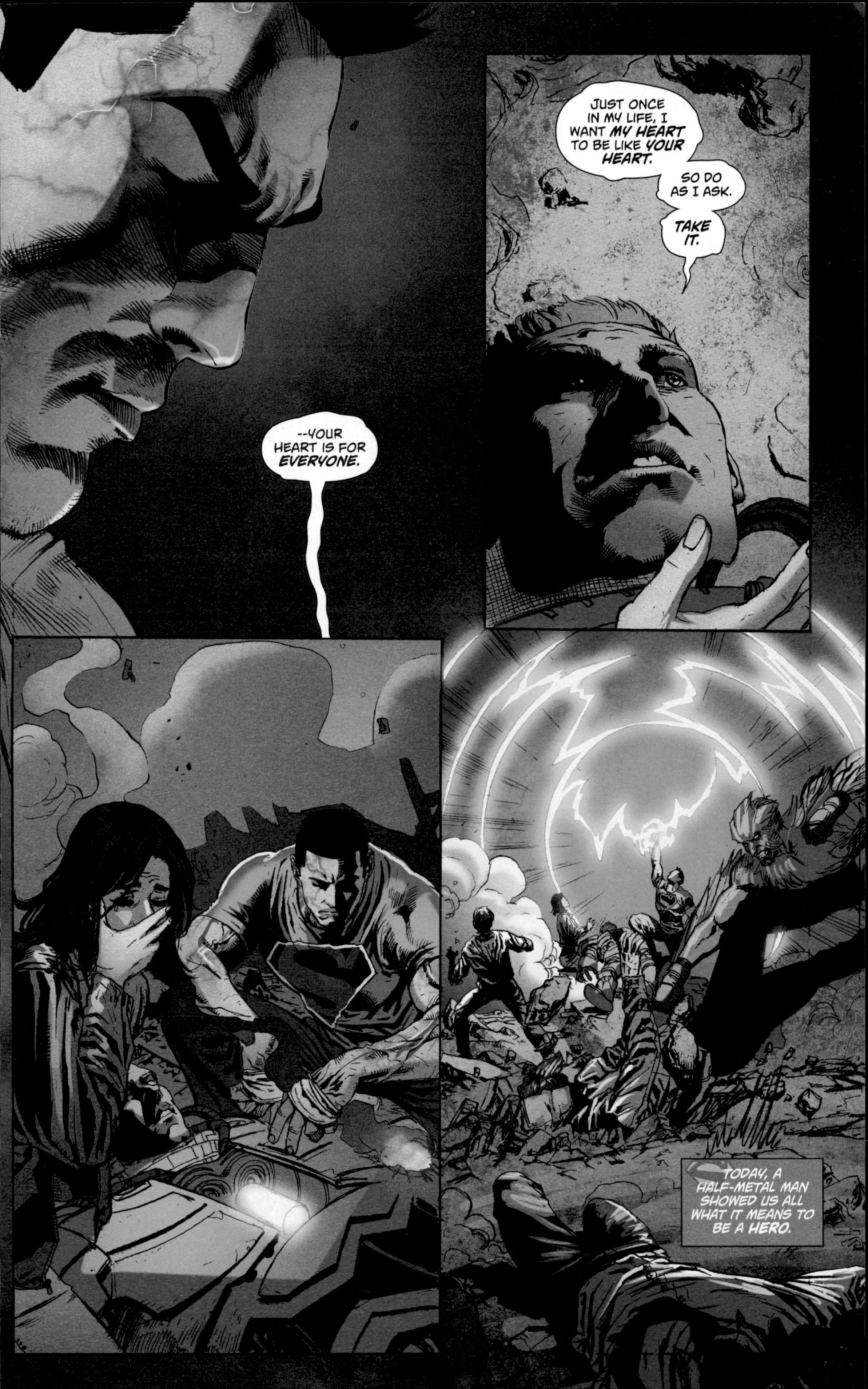
--YOUR HEART IS FOR EVERYONE.
JUST ONCE IN MY LIFE, I WANT MY HEART TO BE LIKE YOUR HEART.
SO DO AS I ASK.
TAKE IT.
TODAY, A HALF-METAL MAN SHOWED US ALL WHAT IT MEANS TO BE A HERO.

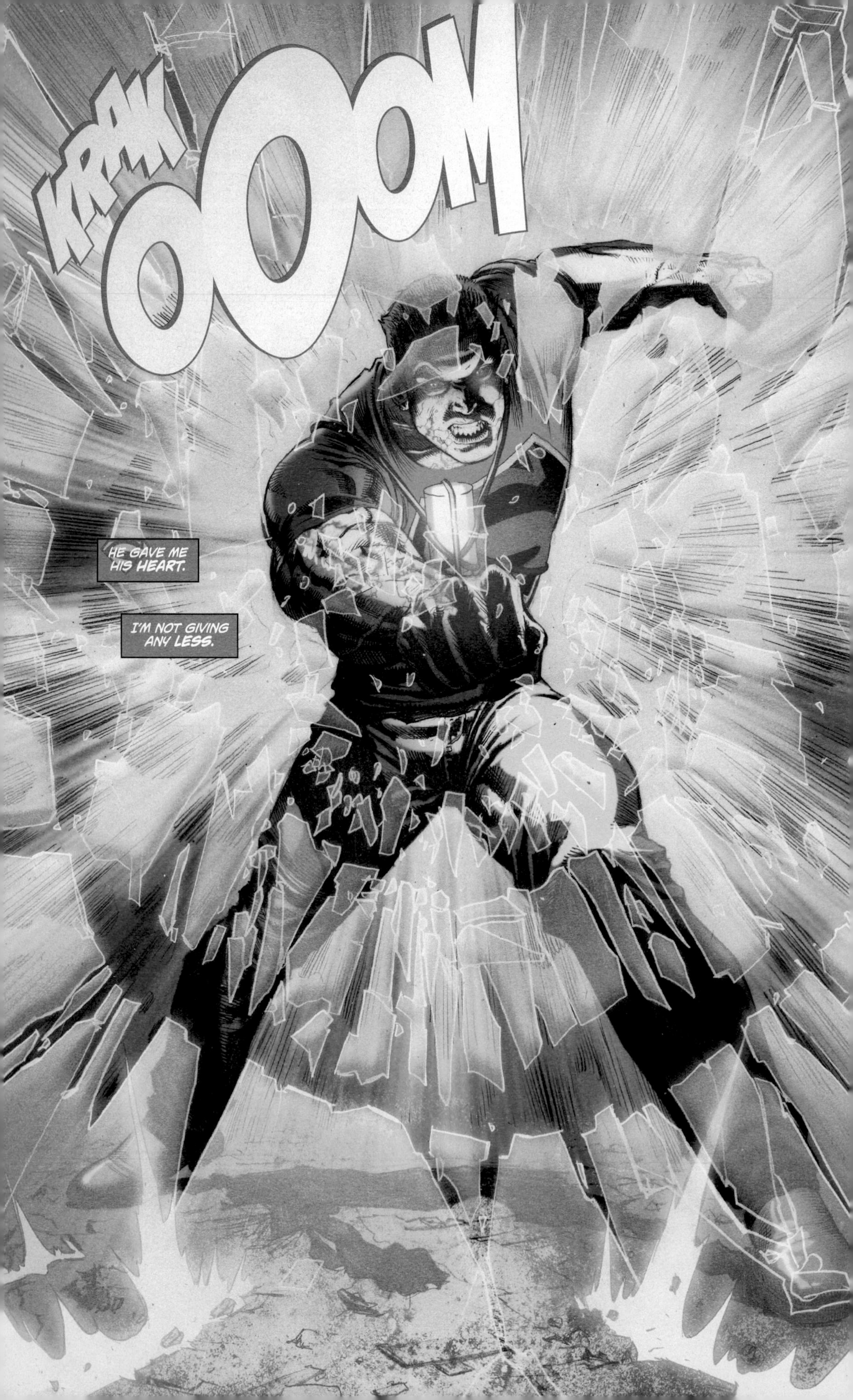
KRAKOOOM
HE GAVE ME HIS HEART.
I'M NOT GIVING ANY LESS.

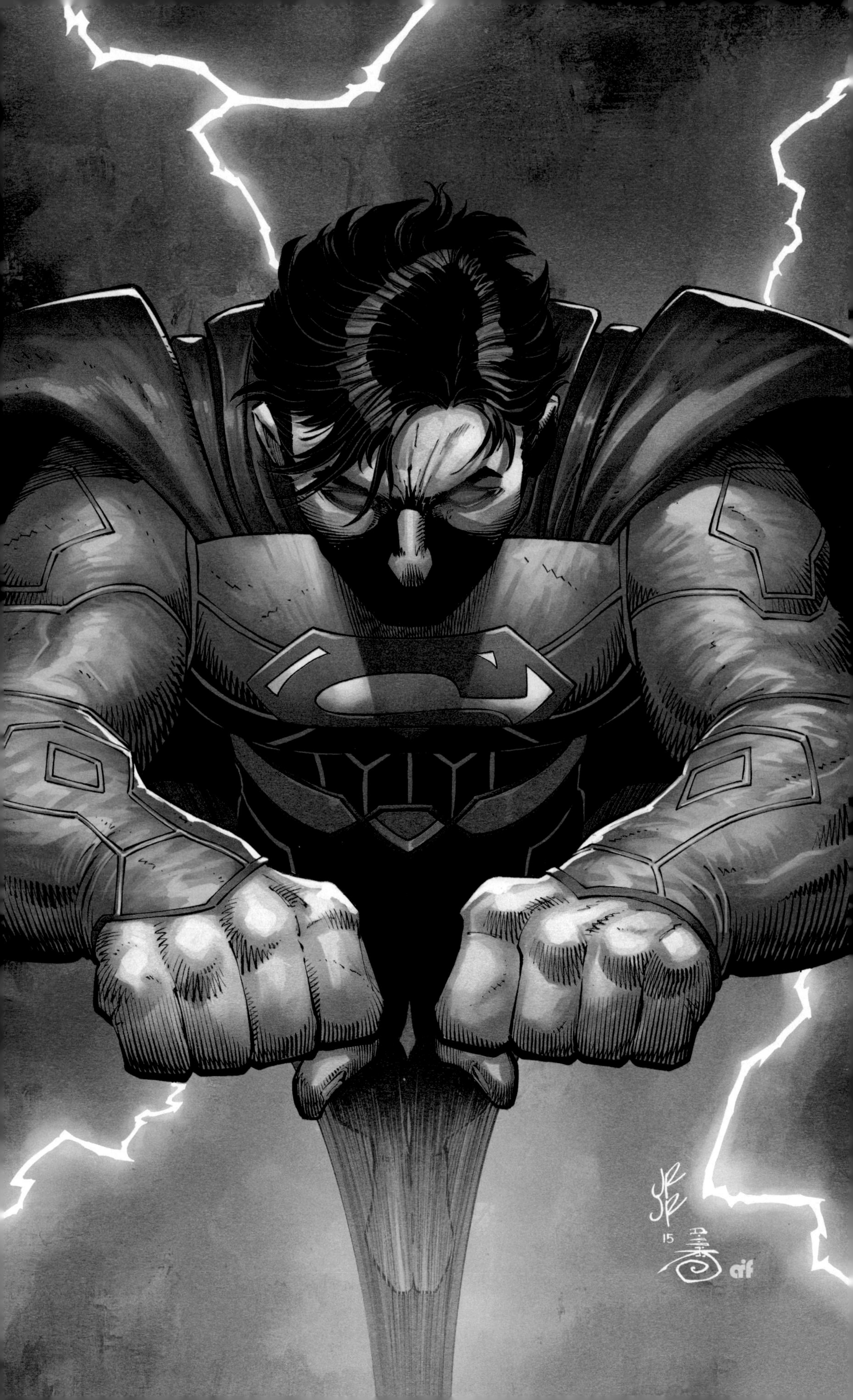

WHAT COULD HAVE BEEN, WHAT CAN STILL BE, AND WHAT IS

GENE LUEN YANG writer HOWARD PORTER, ARDIAN SYAF, PATRICK ZIRCHER, JON BOGDANOVE artists HI-FI colorist ROB LEIGH letterer HOWARD PORTER, HI-FI cover

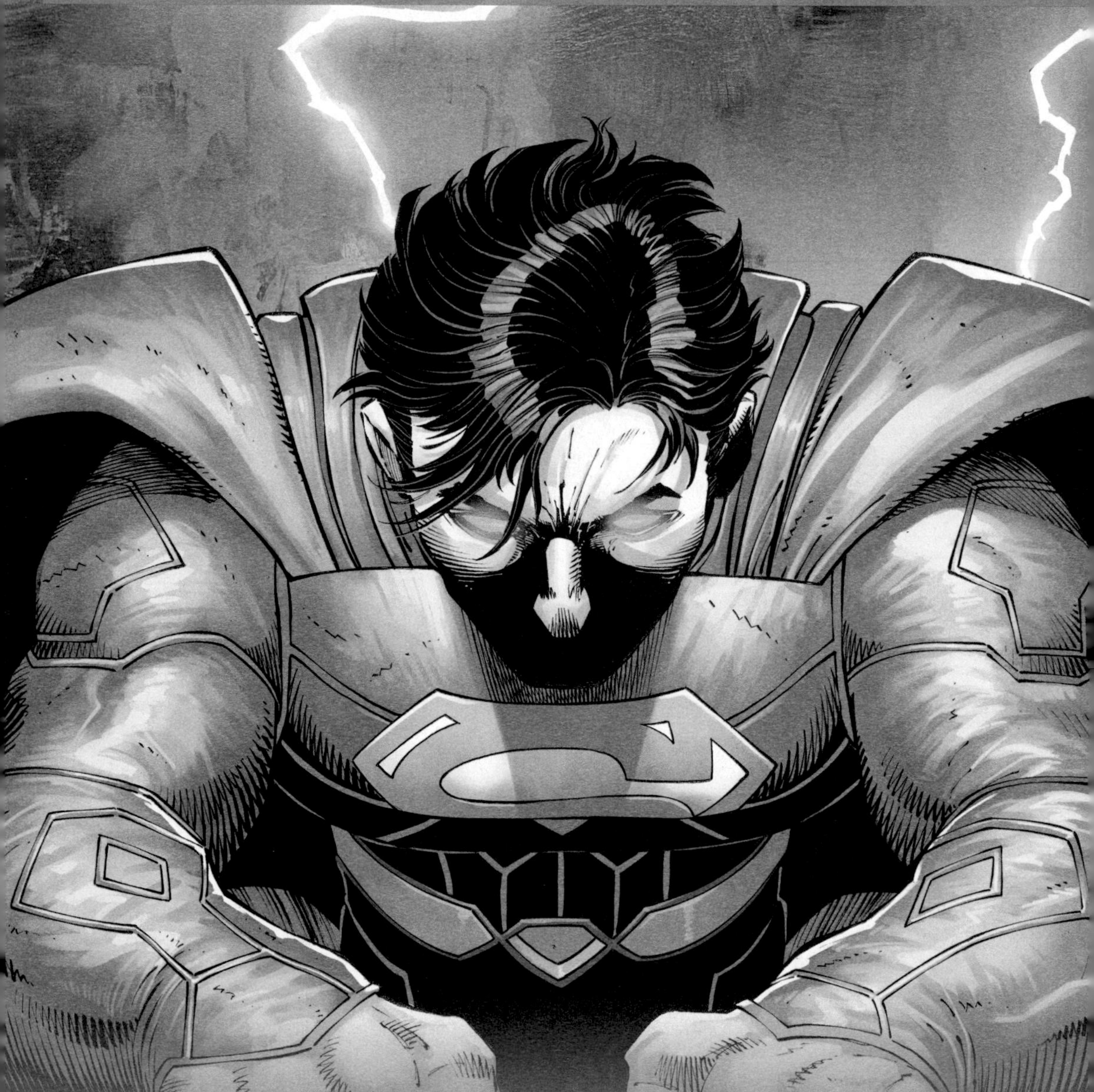

Previously, in SUPERMAN: SAVAGE DAWN ...

As the comet draws closer to Earth, the rise of the House of Savage appears inevitable. Yet Superman keeps fighting, strengthened by the Kryptonite heart given to him by Metallo in his final moments, plus the rallying support of his friends and heroic allies. After rescuing the Justice League from their imprisonment in the Watchtower, he tries to stop Vandal Savage from shuttling his children toward the approaching comet. But the immortal tyrant fires off a kill shot of toxins that sends Superman plummeting from the sky, toward his Fortress and what looks like certain demise.

Miraculously, the Fortress recognizes Superman's recharged DNA and regenerates his cells, bringing the Man of Steel back to full power. And just in time – further motivated by seeing his spawn ablaze with energy from the comet, Savage propels himself closer to the astronomical object to claim his eternal power. His progeny's bodies, however, can't contain the massive energy for long, and they literally burn themselves up while battling Wonder Woman and the Justice League. Superman, meanwhile, gives chase to the architect that's destroyed nearly every aspect of his life – and is now dangerously close to achieving unspeakable might...

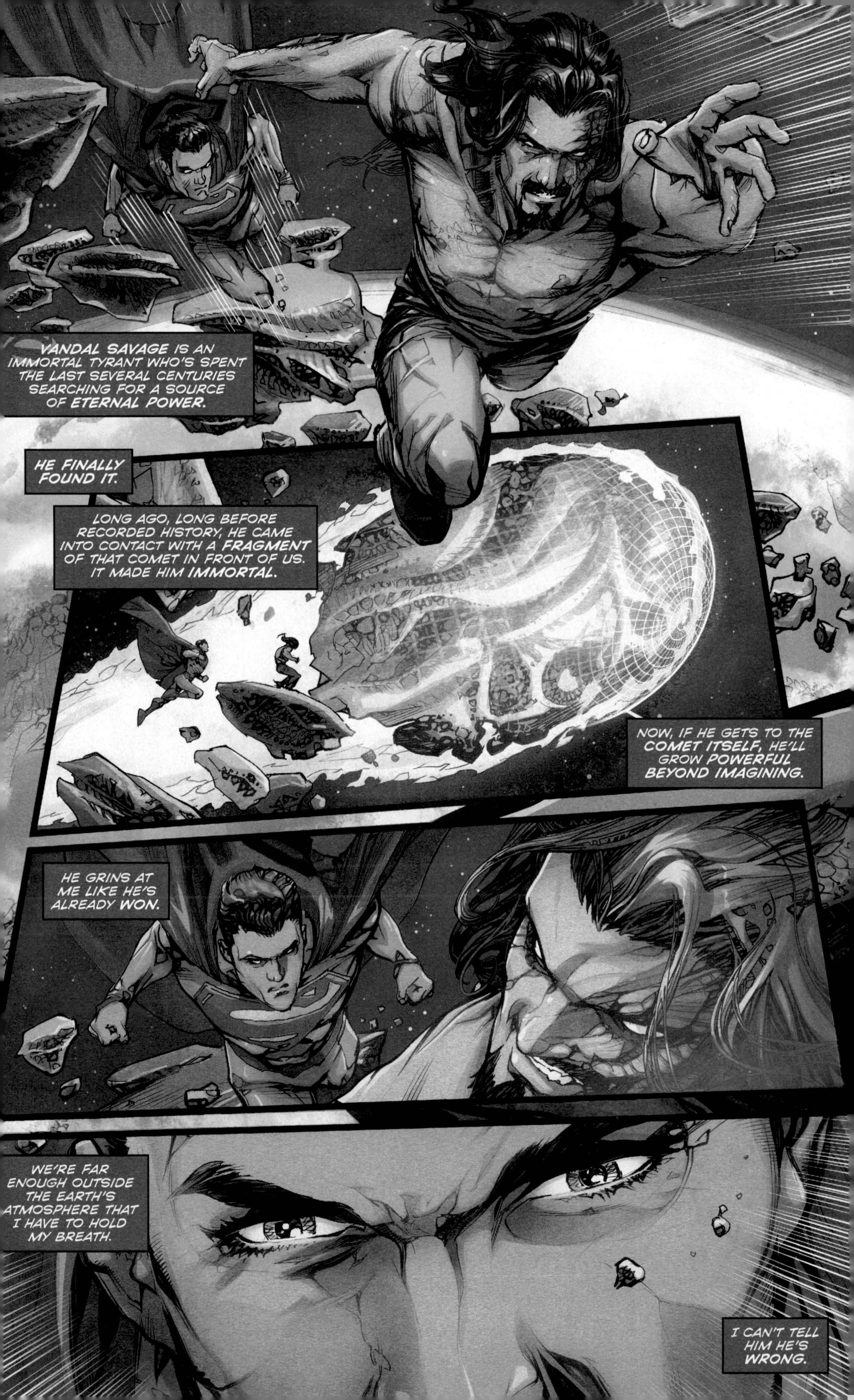
VANDAL SAVAGE IS AN IMMORTAL TYRANT WHO'S SPENT THE LAST SEVERAL CENTURIES SEARCHING FOR A SOURCE OF ETERNAL POWER.
HE FINALLY FOUND IT.
LONG AGO, LONG BEFORE RECORDED HISTORY, HE CAME INTO CONTACT WITH A FRAGMENT OF THAT COMET IN FRONT OF US. IT MADE HIM IMMORTAL.
NOW, IF HE GETS TO THE COMET ITSELF, HE'LL GROW POWERFUL BEYOND IMAGINING.
HE GRINS AT ME LIKE HE'S ALREADY WON.
WE'RE FAR ENOUGH OUTSIDE THE EARTH'S ATMOSPHERE THAT I HAVE TO HOLD MY BREATH.
I CAN'T TELL HIM HE'S WRONG.

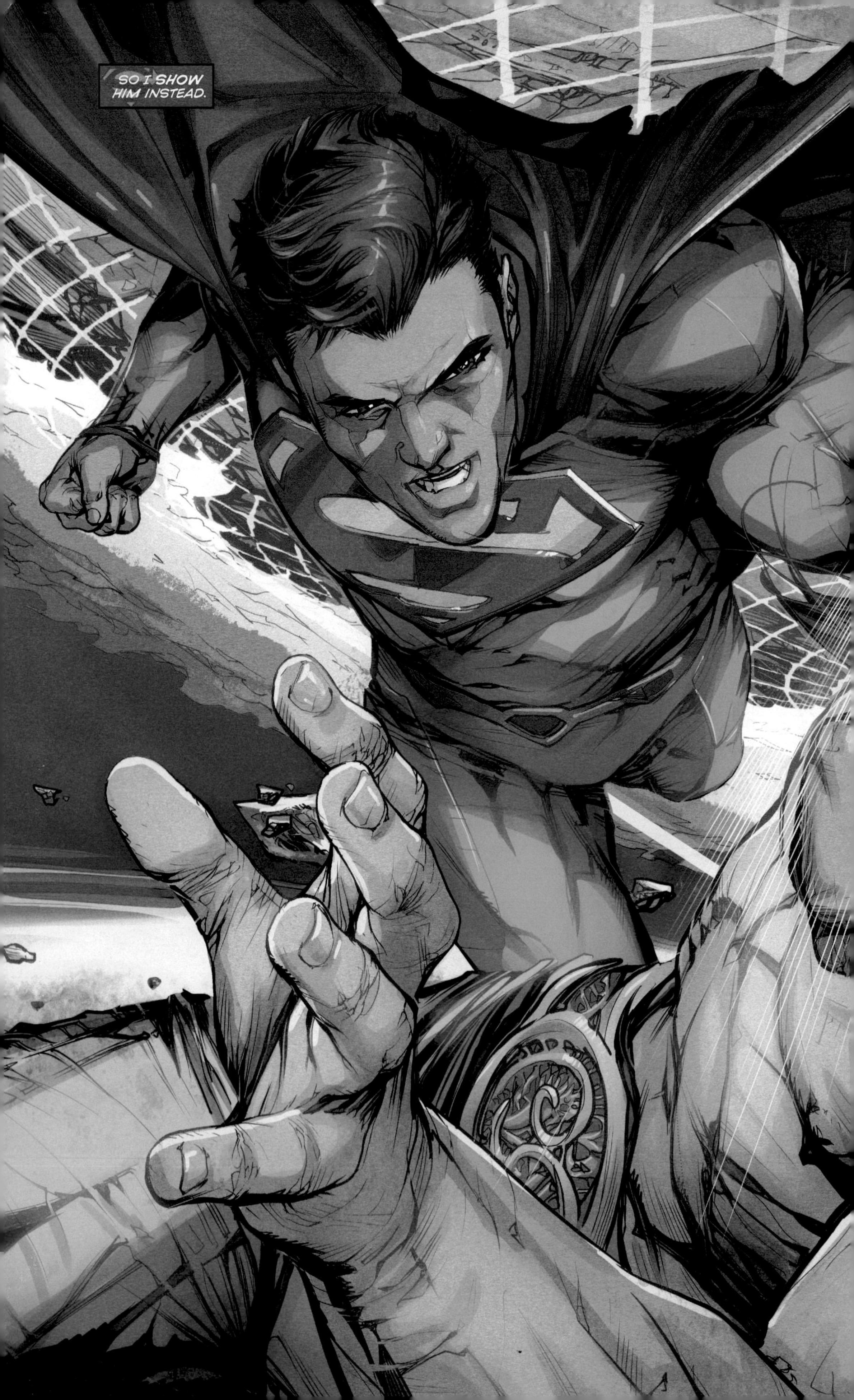
SO I SHOW HIM INSTEAD.

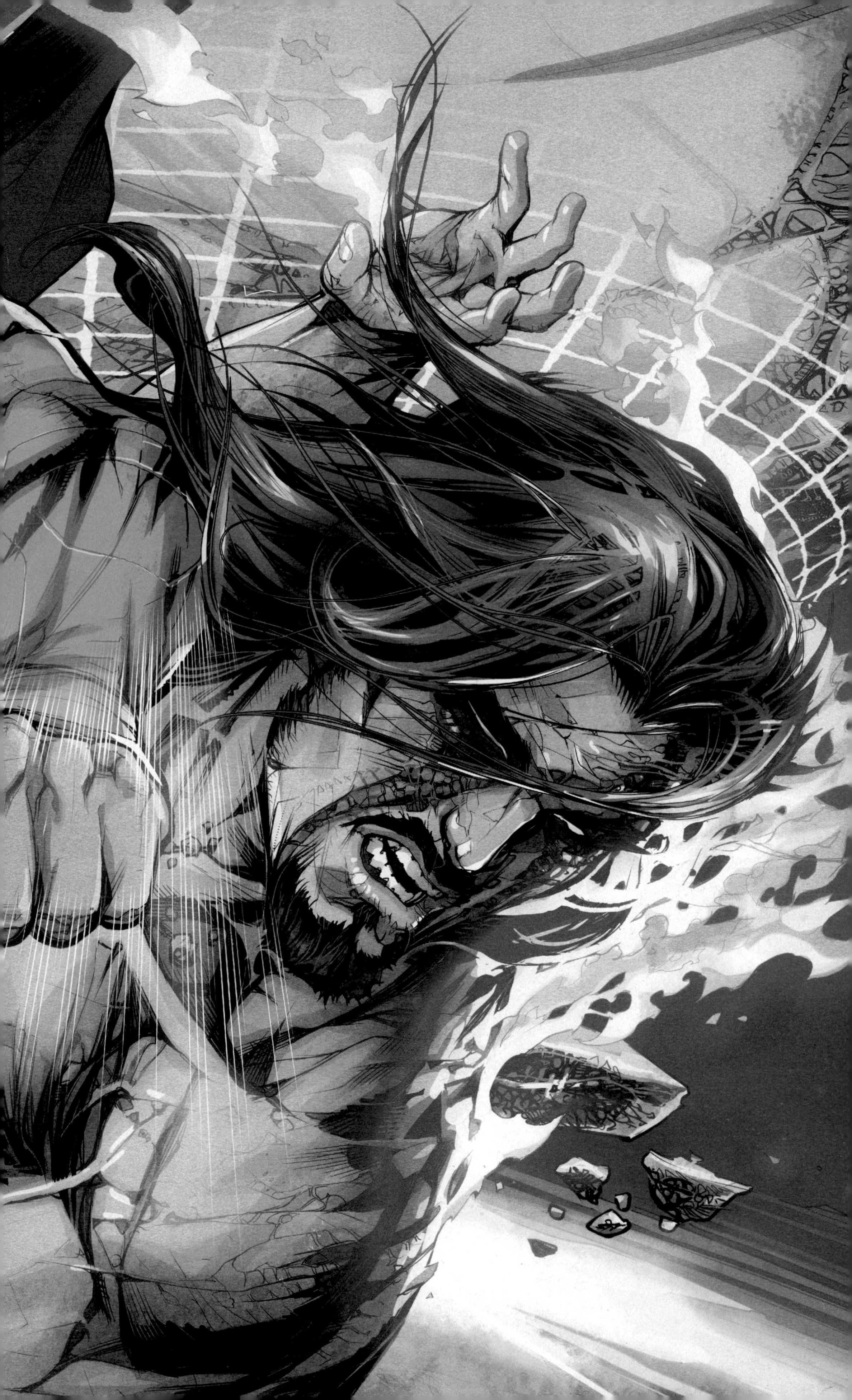

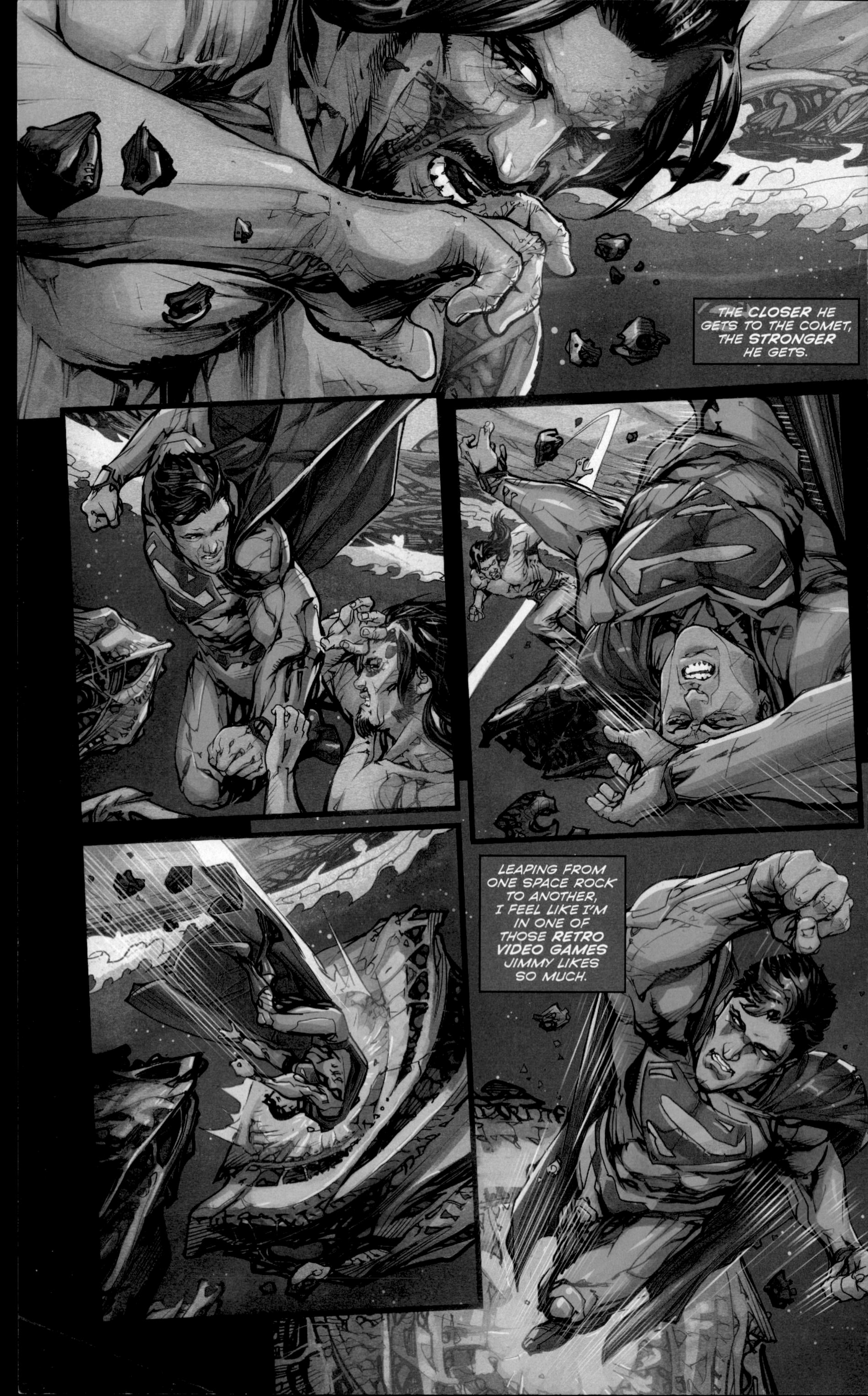
THE CLOSER HE GETS TO THE COMET, THE STRONGER HE GETS.
LEAPING FROM ONE SPACE ROCK TO ANOTHER, I FEEL LIKE I'M IN ONE OF THOSE RETRO VIDEO GAMES JIMMY LIKES SO MUCH.

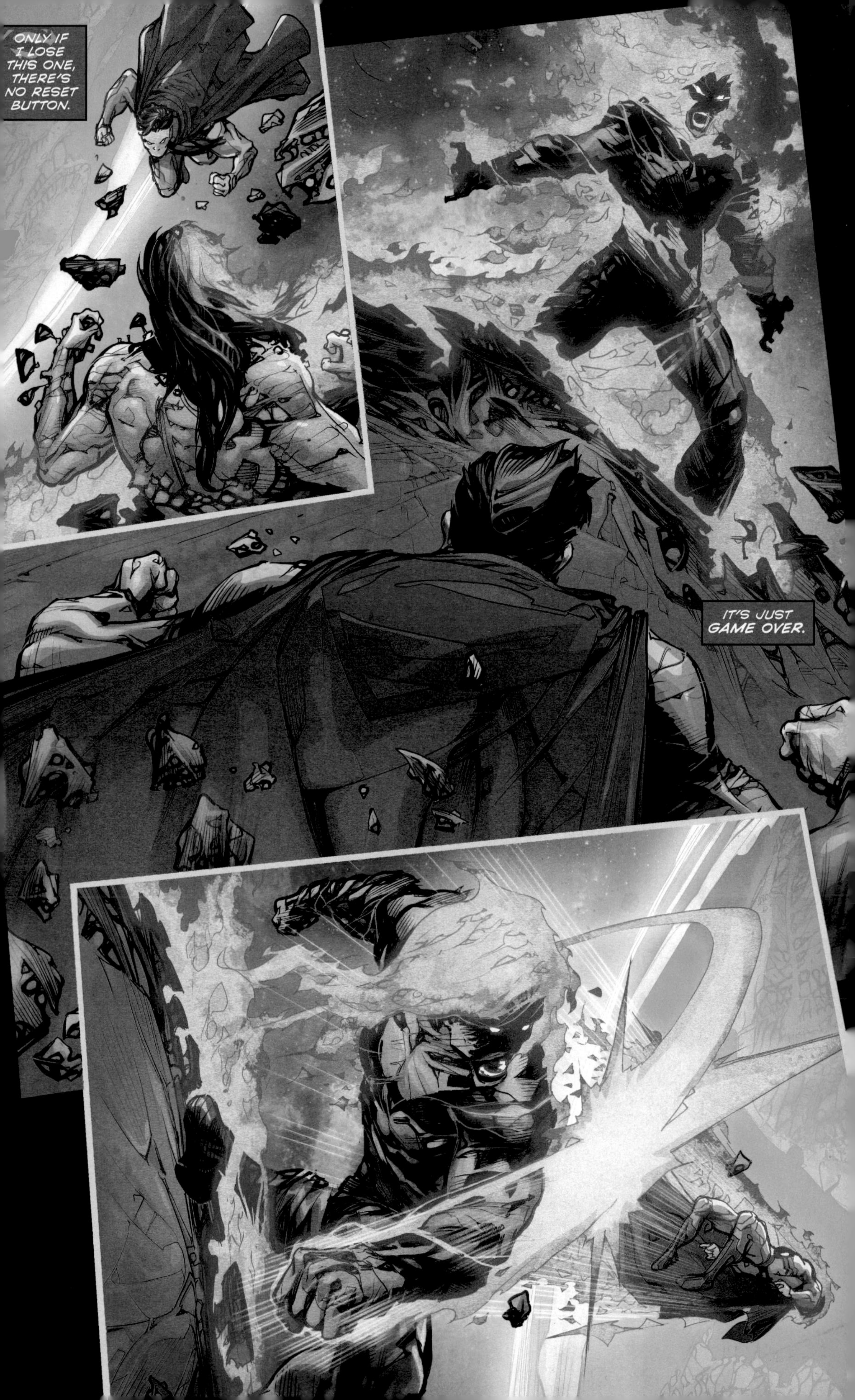
ONLY IF I LOSE THIS ONE, THERE'S NO RESET BUTTON.
IT'S JUST GAME OVER.

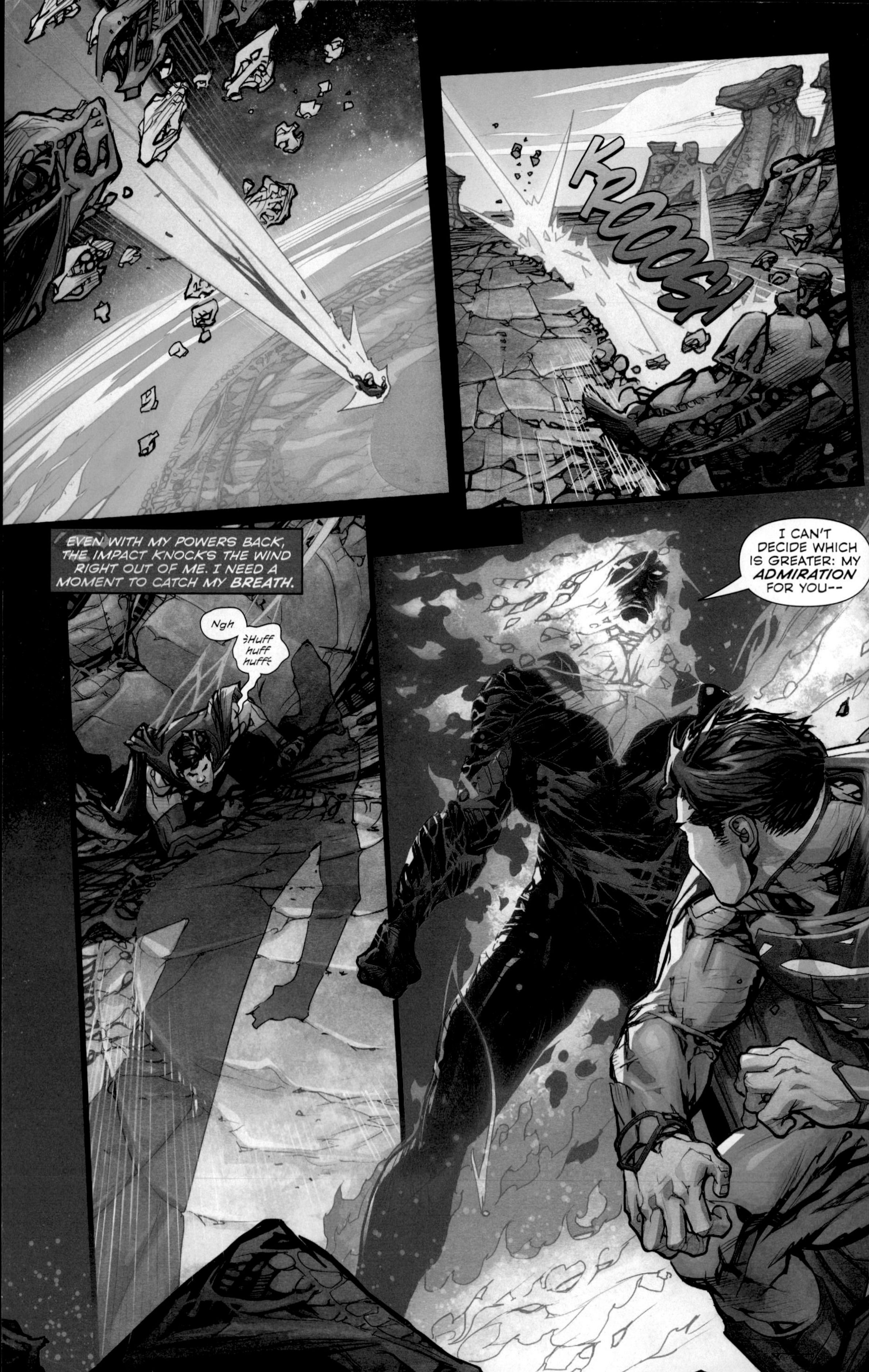
KROOOSH
EVEN WITH MY POWERS BACK, THE IMPACT KNOCKS THE WIND RIGHT OUT OF ME. I NEED A MOMENT TO CATCH MY BREATH.
Ngh
Huff huff huff
I CAN'T DECIDE WHICH IS GREATER: MY ADMIRATION FOR YOU--

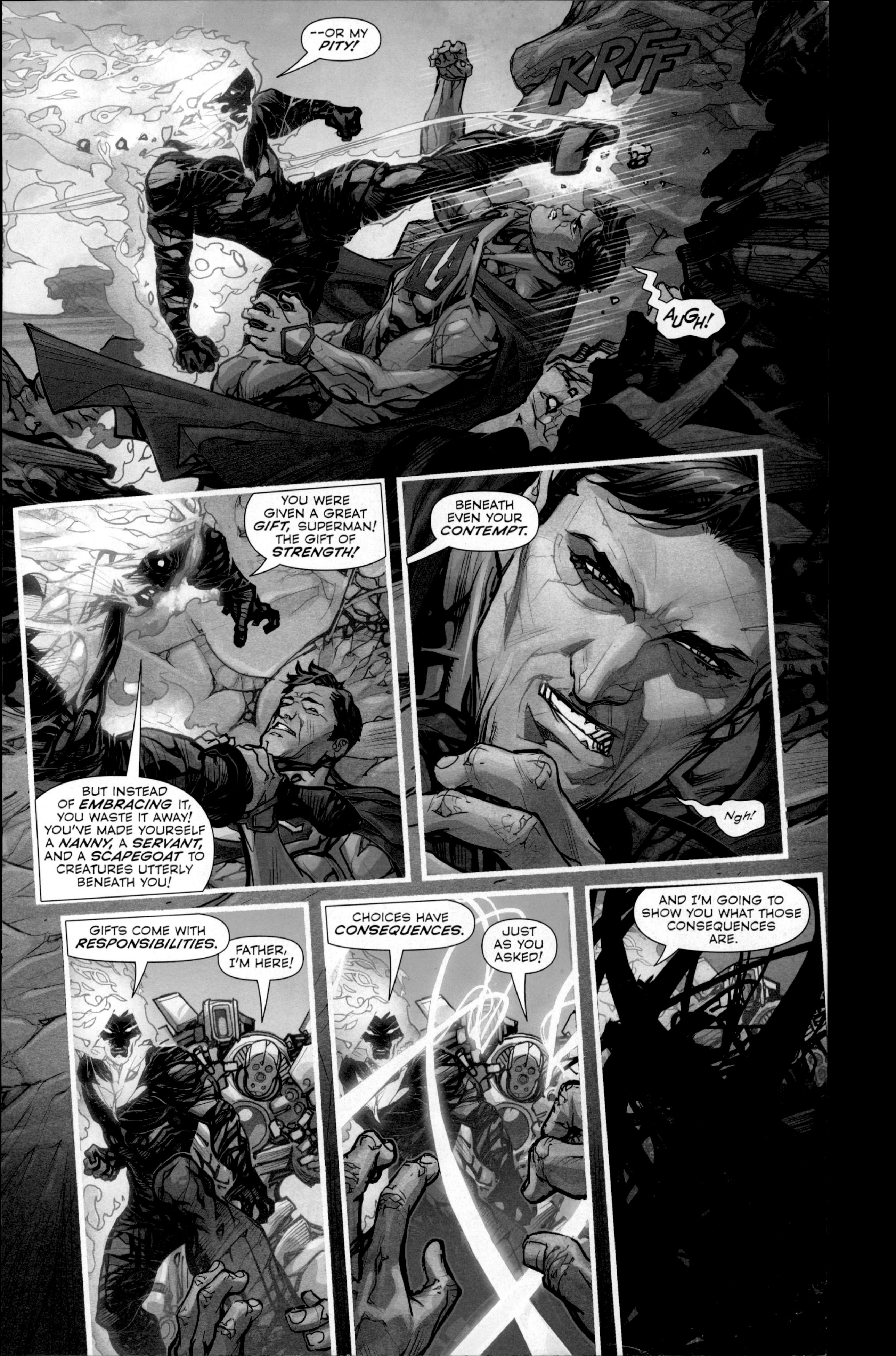
--OR MY PITY!
KRFF
AUGH!
YOU WERE GIVEN A GREAT GIFT, SUPERMAN! THE GIFT OF STRENGTH!
BUT INSTEAD OF EMBRACING IT, YOU WASTE IT AWAY! YOU'VE MADE YOURSELF A NANNY, A SERVANT, AND A SCAPEGOAT TO CREATURES UTTERLY BENEATH YOU!
BENEATH EVEN YOUR CONTEMPT.
Ngh!
GIFTS COME WITH RESPONSIBILITIES.
FATHER, I'M HERE!
CHOICES HAVE CONSEQUENCES.
JUST AS YOU ASKED!
AND I'M GOING TO SHOW YOU WHAT THOSE CONSEQUENCES ARE.

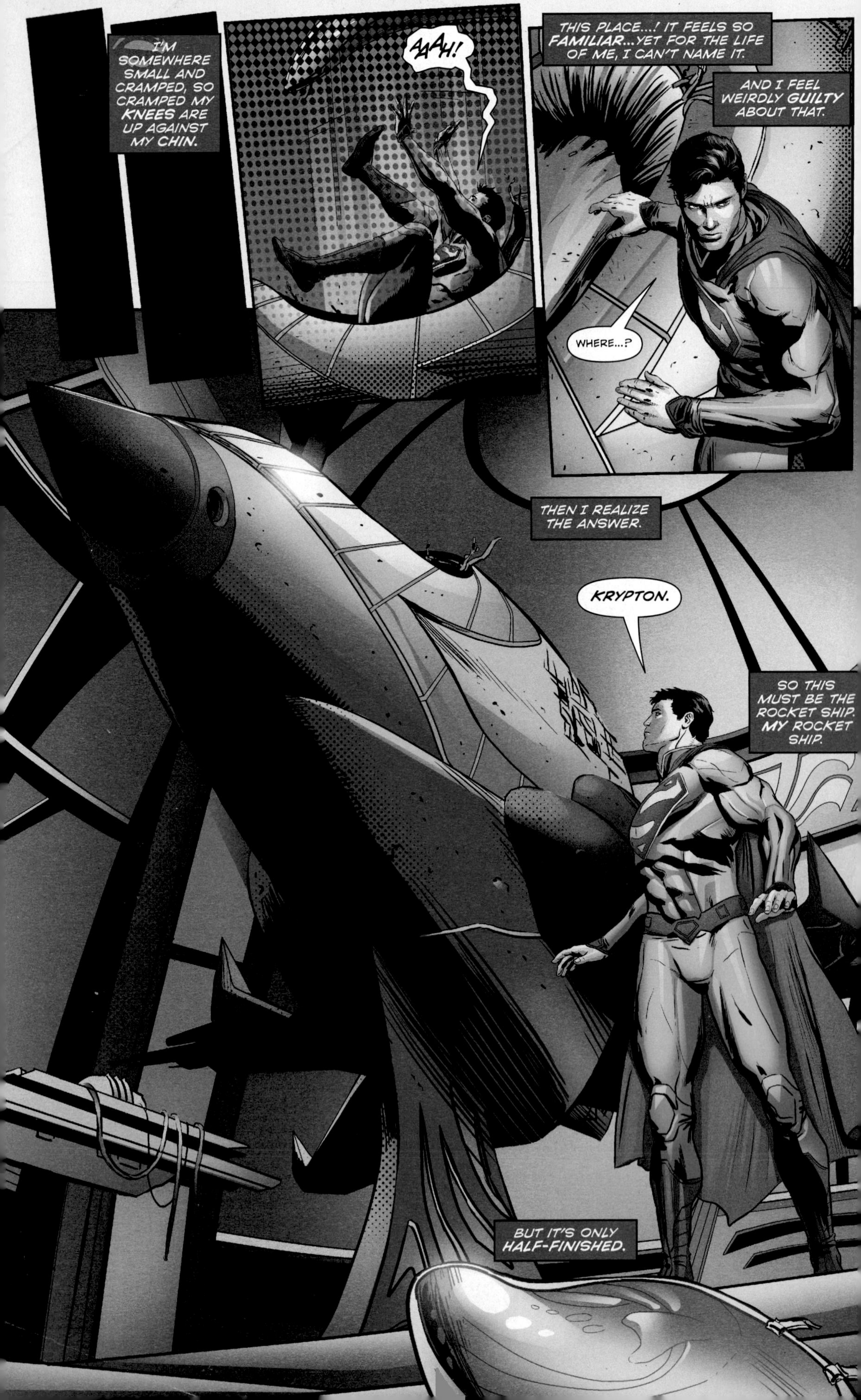
I'M SOMEWHERE SMALL AND CRAMPED, SO CRAMPED MY KNEES ARE UP AGAINST MY CHIN.
AAAH!
THIS PLACE...! IT FEELS SO FAMILIAR...YET FOR THE LIFE OF ME, I CAN'T NAME IT.
AND I FEEL WEIRDLY GUILTY ABOUT THAT.
WHERE...?
THEN I REALIZE THE ANSWER.
KRYPTON.
SO THIS MUST BE THE ROCKET SHIP. MY ROCKET SHIP.
BUT IT'S ONLY HALF-FINISHED.

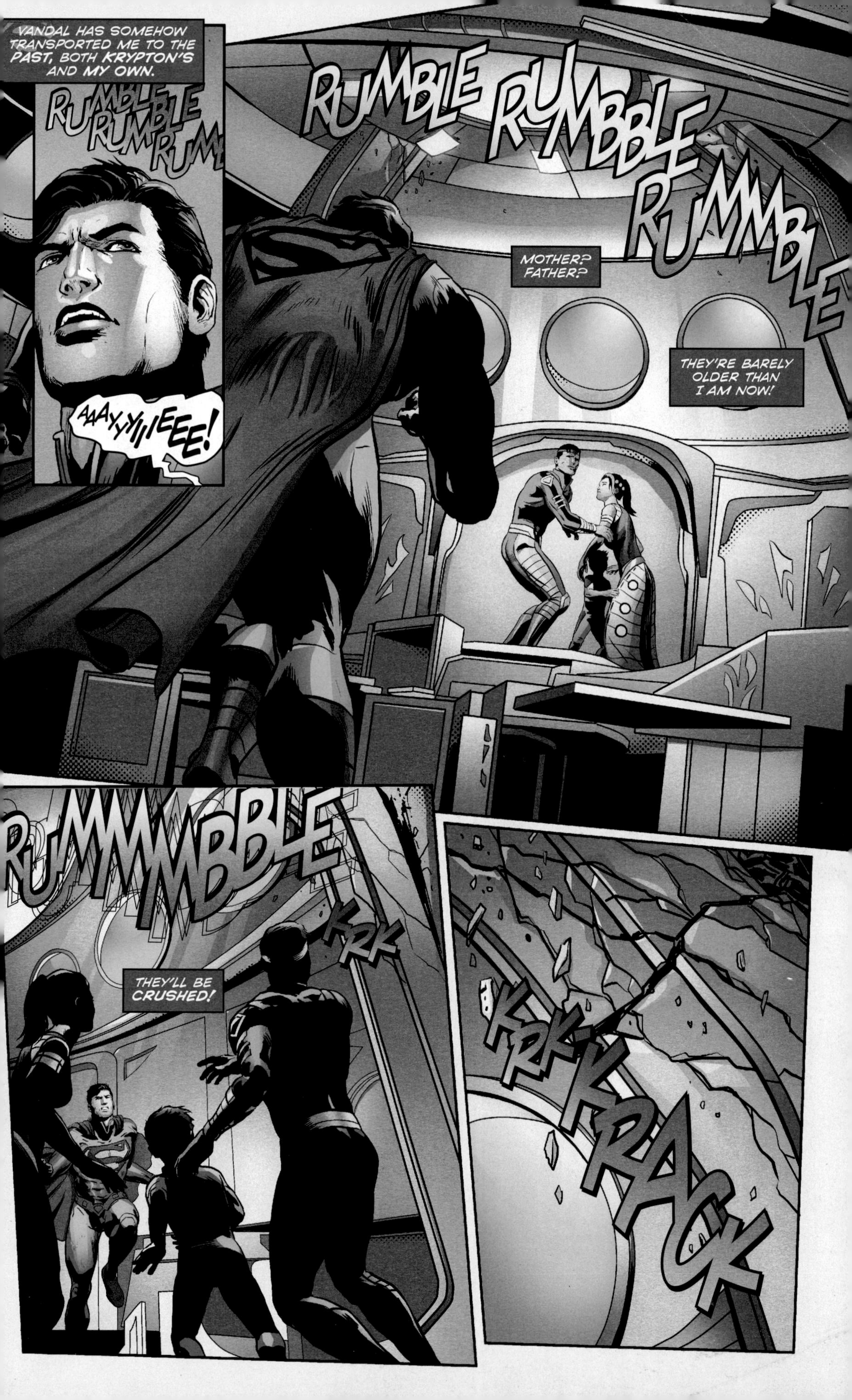
VANDAL HAS SOMEHOW TRANSPORTED ME TO THE PAST, BOTH KRYPTON'S AND MY OWN.
RUMBLE RUMBLE RUMBLE RUMBLE
AAAYYYIIIIEEE!
RUMBLE RUMBBLE RUMMBLE
MOTHER? FATHER?
THEY'RE BARELY OLDER THAN I AM NOW!
RUMMMBBLE
KRK
THEY'LL BE CRUSHED!
KRK-KRACK

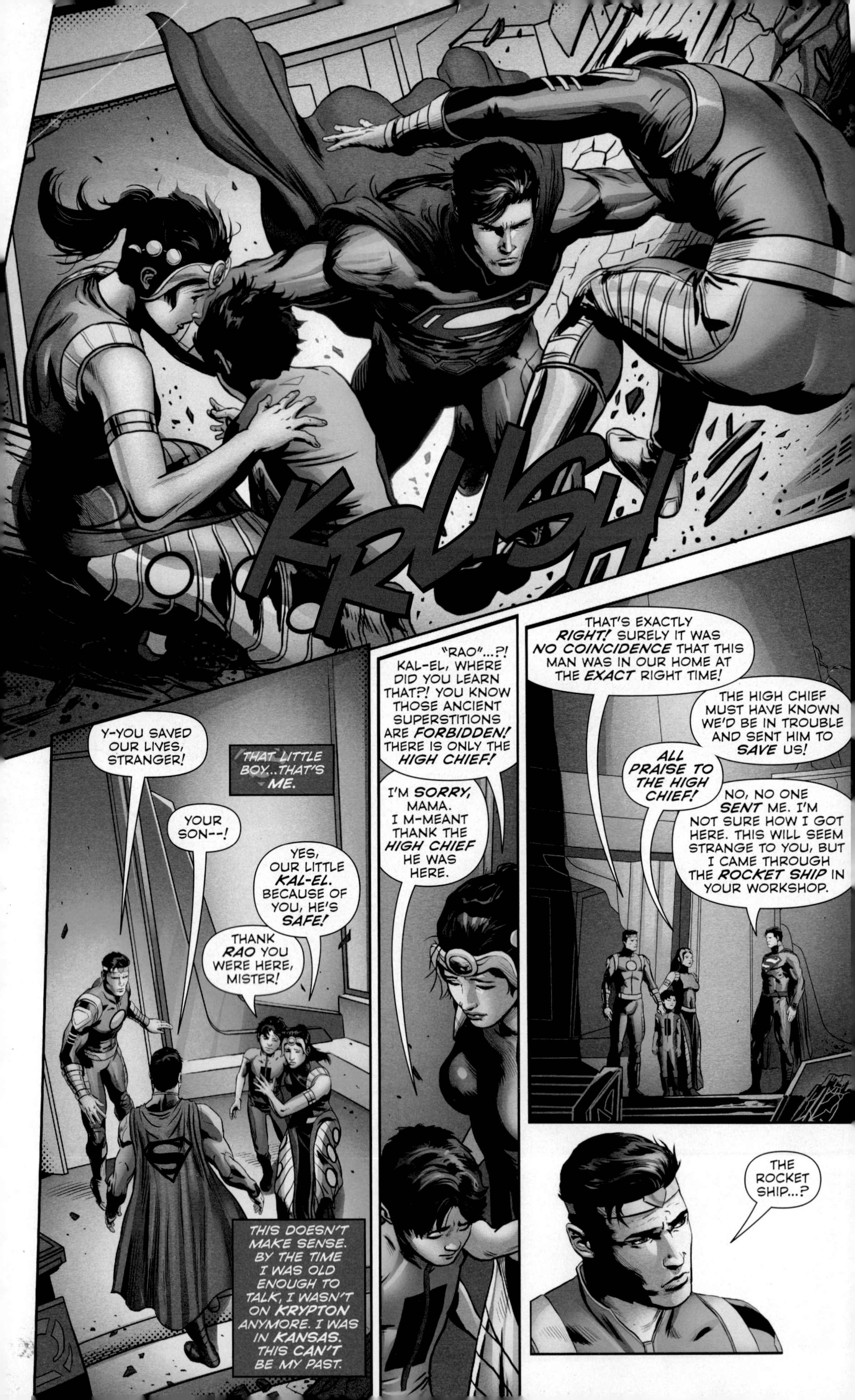
KRUSH
Y-YOU SAVED OUR LIVES, STRANGER!
THAT LITTLE BOY...THAT'S ME.
YOUR SON--!
YES, OUR LITTLE KAL-EL. BECAUSE OF YOU, HE'S SAFE!
THANK RAO YOU WERE HERE, MISTER!
THIS DOESN'T MAKE SENSE. BY THE TIME I WAS OLD ENOUGH TO TALK, I WASN'T ON KRYPTON ANYMORE. I WAS IN KANSAS. THIS CAN'T BE MY PAST.
"RAO"...?! KAL-EL, WHERE DID YOU LEARN THAT?! YOU KNOW THOSE ANCIENT SUPERSTITIONS ARE FORBIDDEN! THERE IS ONLY THE HIGH CHIEF!
I'M SORRY, MAMA. I M-MEANT THANK THE HIGH CHIEF HE WAS HERE.
THAT'S EXACTLY RIGHT! SURELY IT WAS NO COINCIDENCE THAT THIS MAN WAS IN OUR HOME AT THE EXACT RIGHT TIME!
THE HIGH CHIEF MUST HAVE KNOWN WE'D BE IN TROUBLE AND SENT HIM TO SAVE US!
ALL PRAISE TO THE HIGH CHIEF!
NO, NO ONE SENT ME. I'M NOT SURE HOW I GOT HERE. THIS WILL SEEM STRANGE TO YOU, BUT I CAME THROUGH THE ROCKET SHIP IN YOUR WORKSHOP.
THE ROCKET SHIP...?

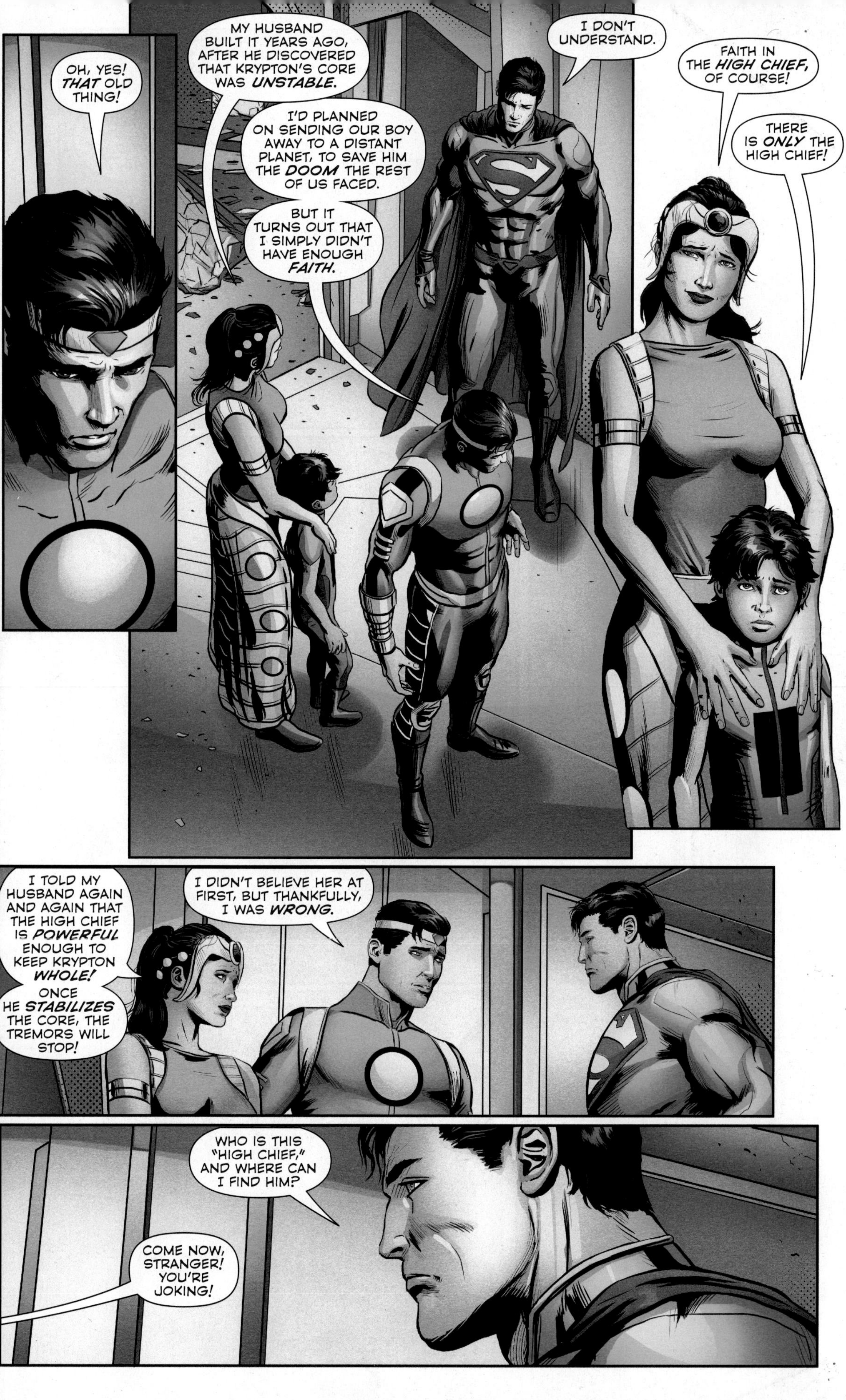

OH, YES! *THAT* OLD THING!
MY HUSBAND BUILT IT YEARS AGO, AFTER HE DISCOVERED THAT KRYPTON'S CORE WAS *UNSTABLE*.
I'D PLANNED ON SENDING OUR BOY AWAY TO A DISTANT PLANET, TO SAVE HIM THE *DOOM* THE REST OF US FACED.
BUT IT TURNS OUT THAT I SIMPLY DIDN'T HAVE ENOUGH *FAITH*.
I DON'T UNDERSTAND.
FAITH IN THE *HIGH CHIEF*, OF COURSE!
THERE IS *ONLY* THE HIGH CHIEF!
I TOLD MY HUSBAND AGAIN AND AGAIN THAT THE HIGH CHIEF IS *POWERFUL* ENOUGH TO KEEP KRYPTON *WHOLE!*
ONCE HE *STABILIZES* THE CORE, THE TREMORS WILL STOP!
I DIDN'T BELIEVE HER AT FIRST, BUT THANKFULLY, I WAS *WRONG*.
WHO IS THIS "HIGH CHIEF," AND WHERE CAN I FIND HIM?
COME NOW, STRANGER! YOU'RE JOKING!

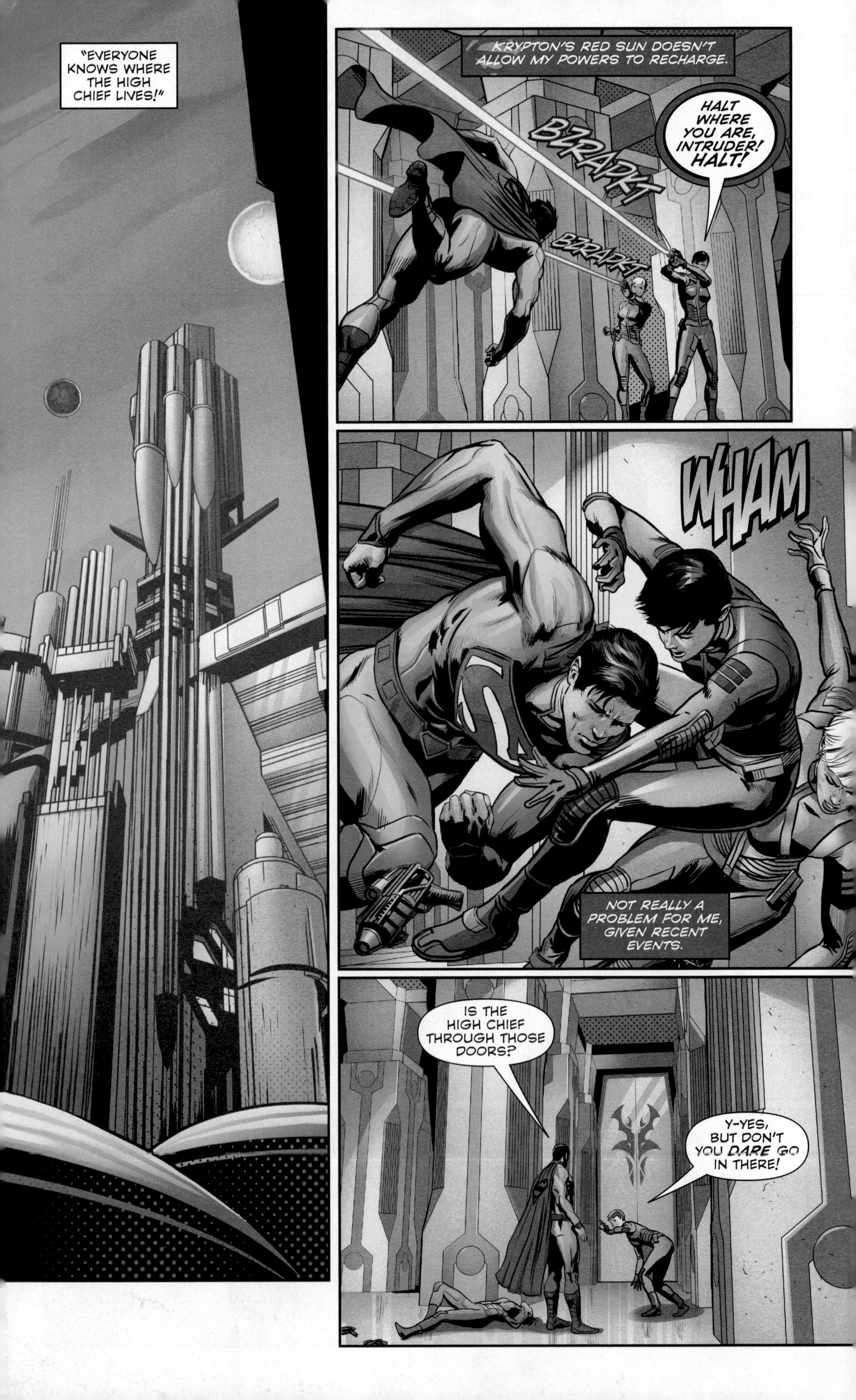
"EVERYONE KNOWS WHERE THE HIGH CHIEF LIVES!"
KRYPTON'S RED SUN DOESN'T ALLOW MY POWERS TO RECHARGE.
HALT WHERE YOU ARE, INTRUDER! HALT!
BZRAPKT
BZRAPKT
WHAM
NOT REALLY A PROBLEM FOR ME, GIVEN RECENT EVENTS.
IS THE HIGH CHIEF THROUGH THOSE DOORS?
Y-YES, BUT DON'T YOU DARE GO IN THERE!

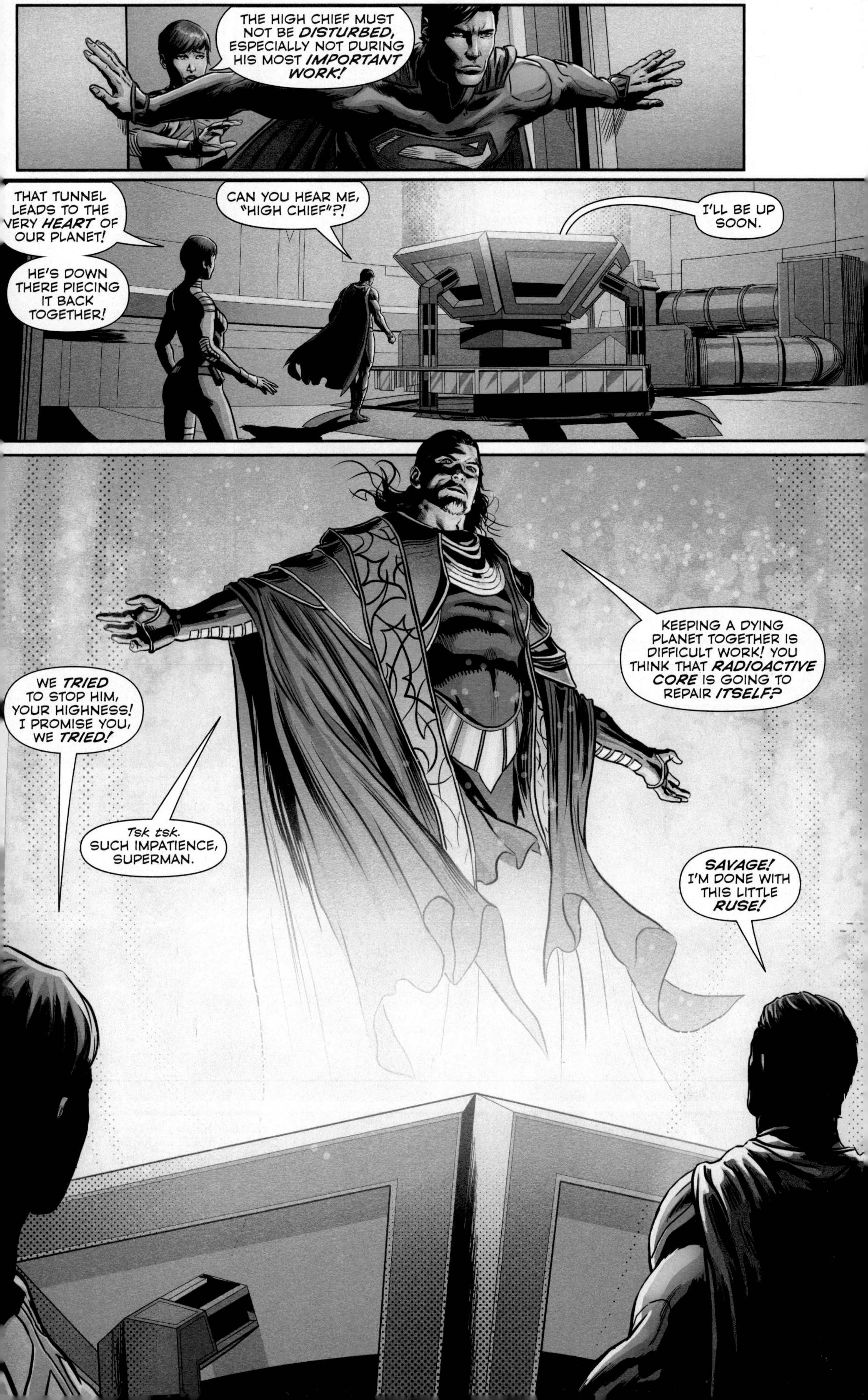
THE HIGH CHIEF MUST NOT BE *DISTURBED*, ESPECIALLY NOT DURING HIS MOST *IMPORTANT WORK!*
THAT TUNNEL LEADS TO THE VERY *HEART* OF OUR PLANET!
HE'S DOWN THERE PIECING IT BACK TOGETHER!
CAN YOU HEAR ME, "HIGH CHIEF"?!
I'LL BE UP SOON.
KEEPING A DYING PLANET TOGETHER IS DIFFICULT WORK! YOU THINK THAT *RADIOACTIVE CORE* IS GOING TO REPAIR *ITSELF?*
WE *TRIED* TO STOP HIM, YOUR HIGHNESS! I PROMISE YOU, WE *TRIED!*
Tsk tsk. SUCH IMPATIENCE, SUPERMAN.
SAVAGE! I'M DONE WITH THIS LITTLE *RUSE!*

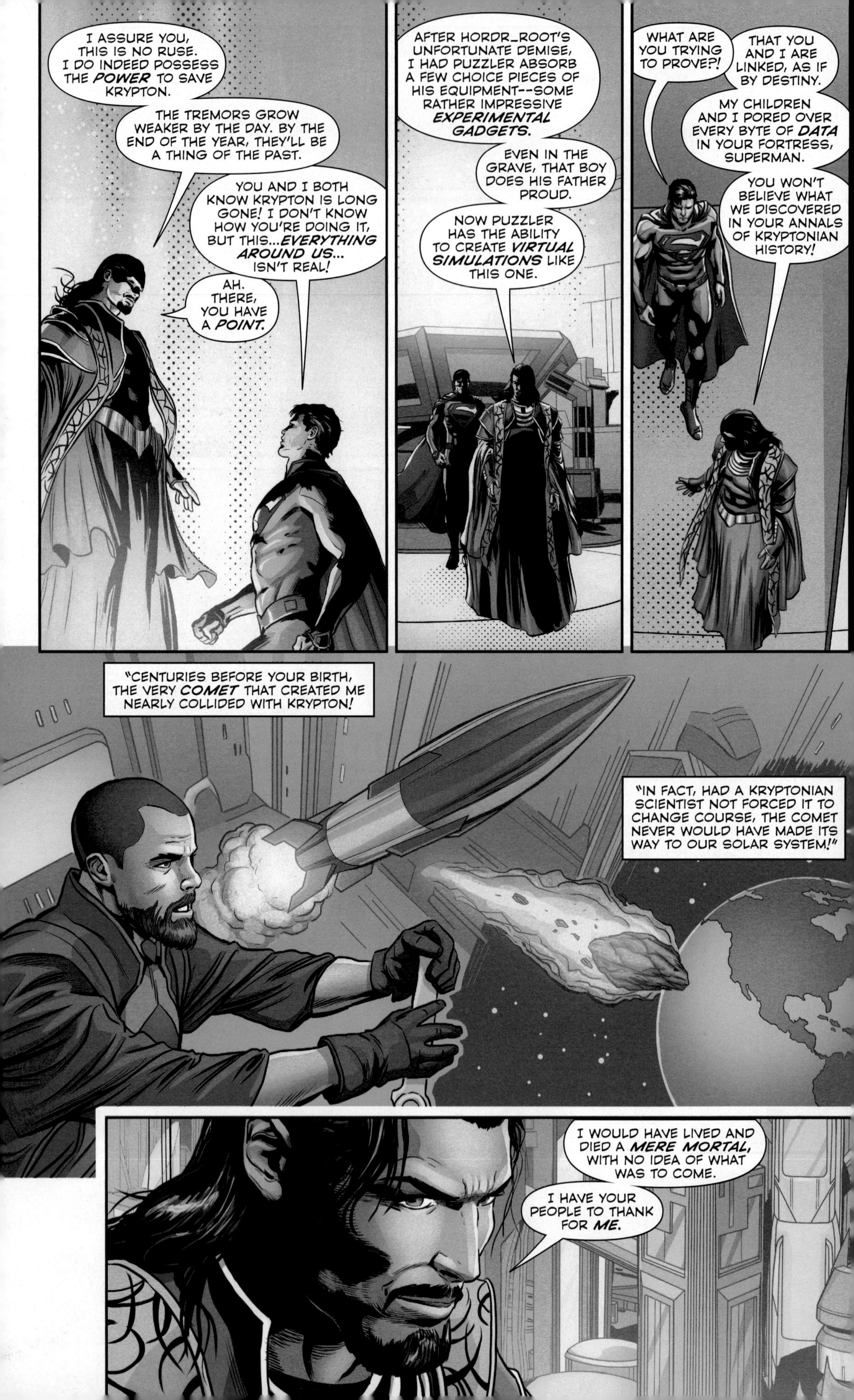
I ASSURE YOU, THIS IS NO RUSE. I DO INDEED POSSESS THE POWER TO SAVE KRYPTON.
THE TREMORS GROW WEAKER BY THE DAY. BY THE END OF THE YEAR, THEY'LL BE A THING OF THE PAST.
YOU AND I BOTH KNOW KRYPTON IS LONG GONE! I DON'T KNOW HOW YOU'RE DOING IT, BUT THIS...EVERYTHING AROUND US... ISN'T REAL!
AH. THERE, YOU HAVE A POINT.
AFTER HORDR_ROOT'S UNFORTUNATE DEMISE, I HAD PUZZLER ABSORB A FEW CHOICE PIECES OF HIS EQUIPMENT--SOME RATHER IMPRESSIVE EXPERIMENTAL GADGETS.
EVEN IN THE GRAVE, THAT BOY DOES HIS FATHER PROUD.
NOW PUZZLER HAS THE ABILITY TO CREATE VIRTUAL SIMULATIONS LIKE THIS ONE.
WHAT ARE YOU TRYING TO PROVE?!
THAT YOU AND I ARE LINKED, AS IF BY DESTINY.
MY CHILDREN AND I PORED OVER EVERY BYTE OF DATA IN YOUR FORTRESS, SUPERMAN.
YOU WON'T BELIEVE WHAT WE DISCOVERED IN YOUR ANNALS OF KRYPTONIAN HISTORY!
"CENTURIES BEFORE YOUR BIRTH, THE VERY COMET THAT CREATED ME NEARLY COLLIDED WITH KRYPTON!
"IN FACT, HAD A KRYPTONIAN SCIENTIST NOT FORCED IT TO CHANGE COURSE, THE COMET NEVER WOULD HAVE MADE ITS WAY TO OUR SOLAR SYSTEM!"
I WOULD HAVE LIVED AND DIED A MERE MORTAL, WITH NO IDEA OF WHAT WAS TO COME.
I HAVE YOUR PEOPLE TO THANK FOR ME.

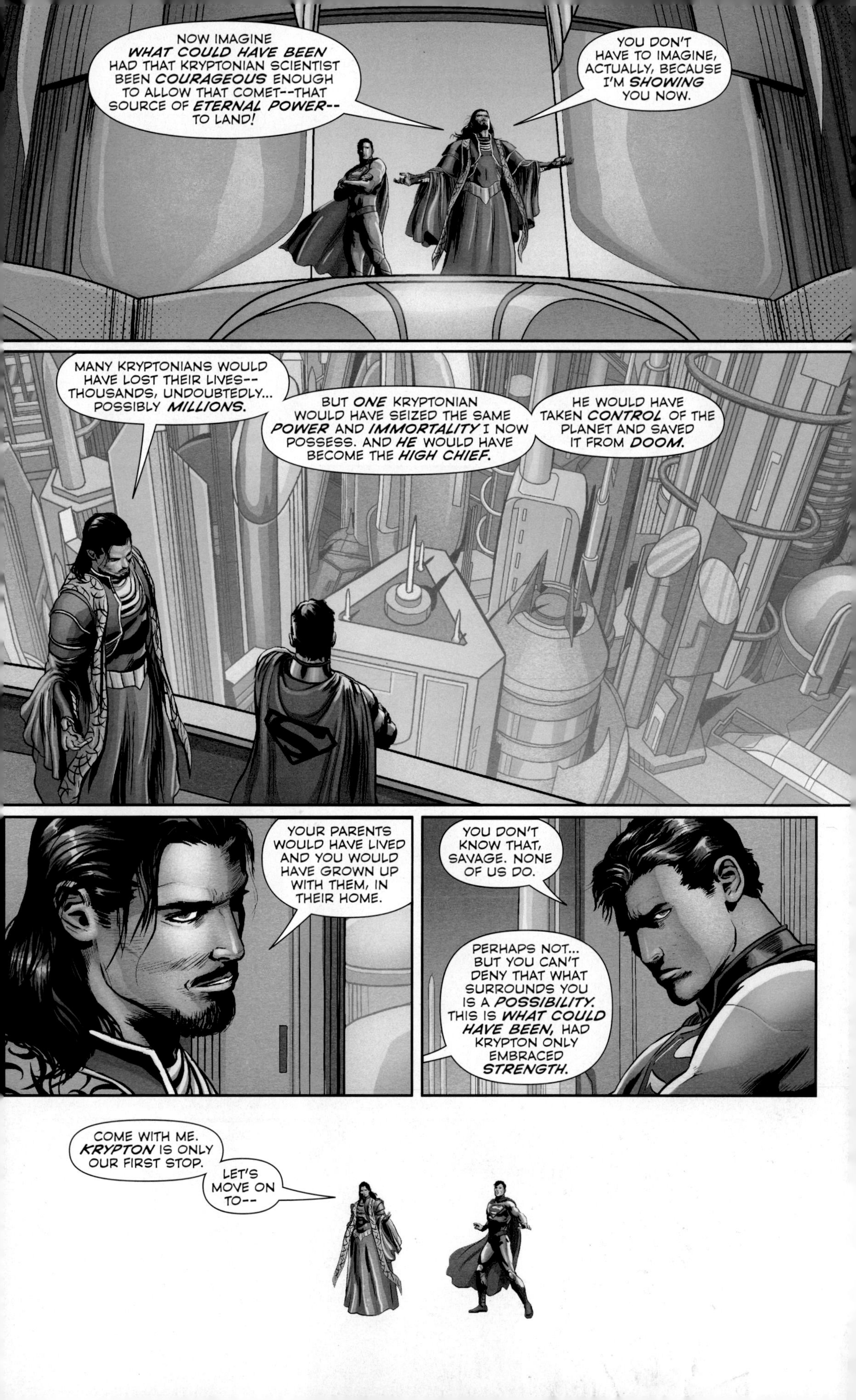
NOW IMAGINE WHAT COULD HAVE BEEN HAD THAT KRYPTONIAN SCIENTIST BEEN COURAGEOUS ENOUGH TO ALLOW THAT COMET--THAT SOURCE OF ETERNAL POWER-- TO LAND!
YOU DON'T HAVE TO IMAGINE, ACTUALLY, BECAUSE I'M SHOWING YOU NOW.
MANY KRYPTONIANS WOULD HAVE LOST THEIR LIVES-- THOUSANDS, UNDOUBTEDLY... POSSIBLY MILLIONS.
BUT ONE KRYPTONIAN WOULD HAVE SEIZED THE SAME POWER AND IMMORTALITY I NOW POSSESS. AND HE WOULD HAVE BECOME THE HIGH CHIEF.
HE WOULD HAVE TAKEN CONTROL OF THE PLANET AND SAVED IT FROM DOOM.
YOUR PARENTS WOULD HAVE LIVED AND YOU WOULD HAVE GROWN UP WITH THEM, IN THEIR HOME.
YOU DON'T KNOW THAT, SAVAGE. NONE OF US DO.
PERHAPS NOT... BUT YOU CAN'T DENY THAT WHAT SURROUNDS YOU IS A POSSIBILITY. THIS IS WHAT COULD HAVE BEEN, HAD KRYPTON ONLY EMBRACED STRENGTH.
COME WITH ME. KRYPTON IS ONLY OUR FIRST STOP.
LET'S MOVE ON TO--

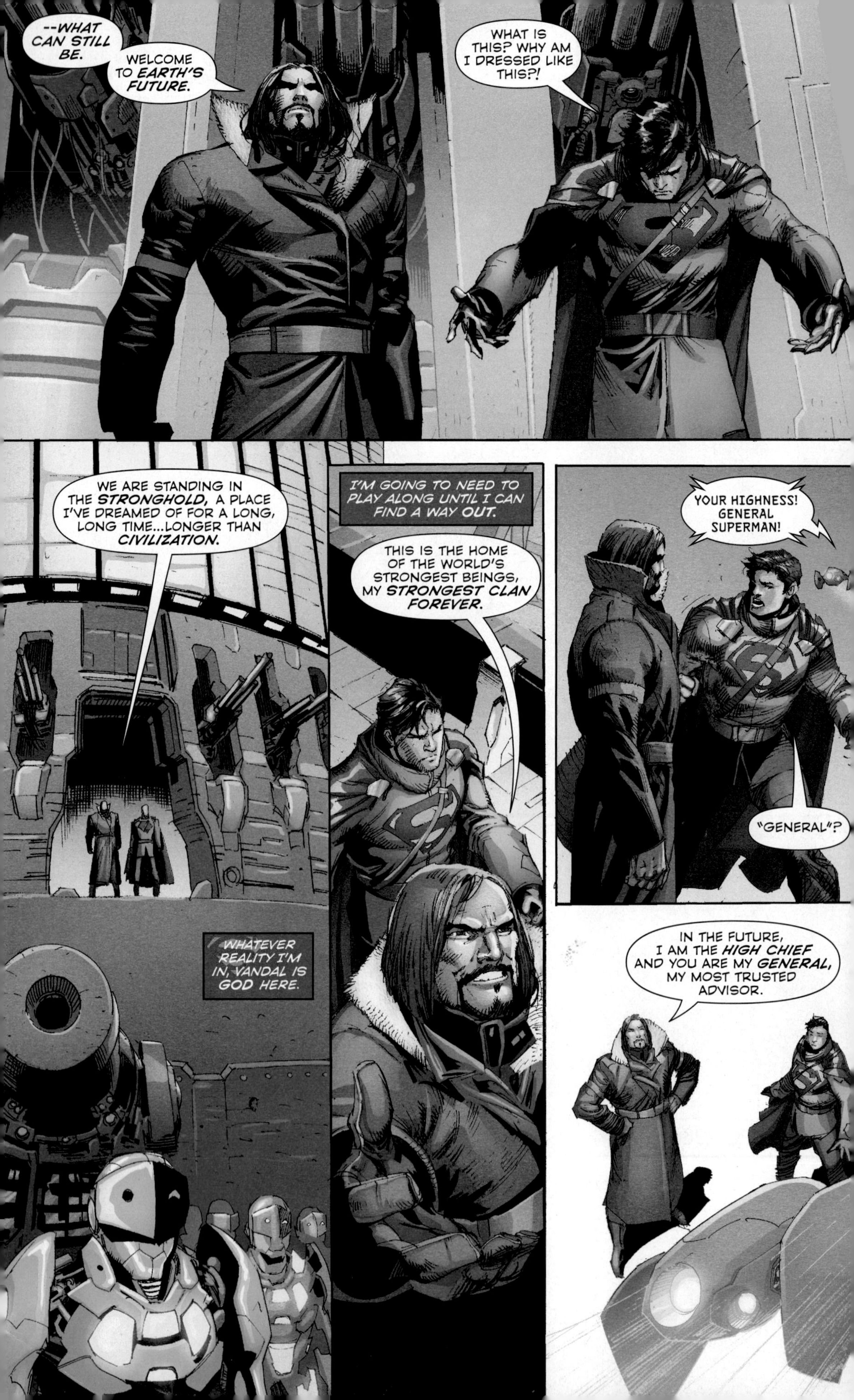
--WHAT CAN STILL BE.
WELCOME TO EARTH'S FUTURE.
WHAT IS THIS? WHY AM I DRESSED LIKE THIS?!
WE ARE STANDING IN THE STRONGHOLD, A PLACE I'VE DREAMED OF FOR A LONG, LONG TIME...LONGER THAN CIVILIZATION.
I'M GOING TO NEED TO PLAY ALONG UNTIL I CAN FIND A WAY OUT.
THIS IS THE HOME OF THE WORLD'S STRONGEST BEINGS, MY STRONGEST CLAN FOREVER.
YOUR HIGHNESS! GENERAL SUPERMAN!
"GENERAL"?
WHATEVER REALITY I'M IN, VANDAL IS GOD HERE.
IN THE FUTURE, I AM THE HIGH CHIEF AND YOU ARE MY GENERAL, MY MOST TRUSTED ADVISOR.

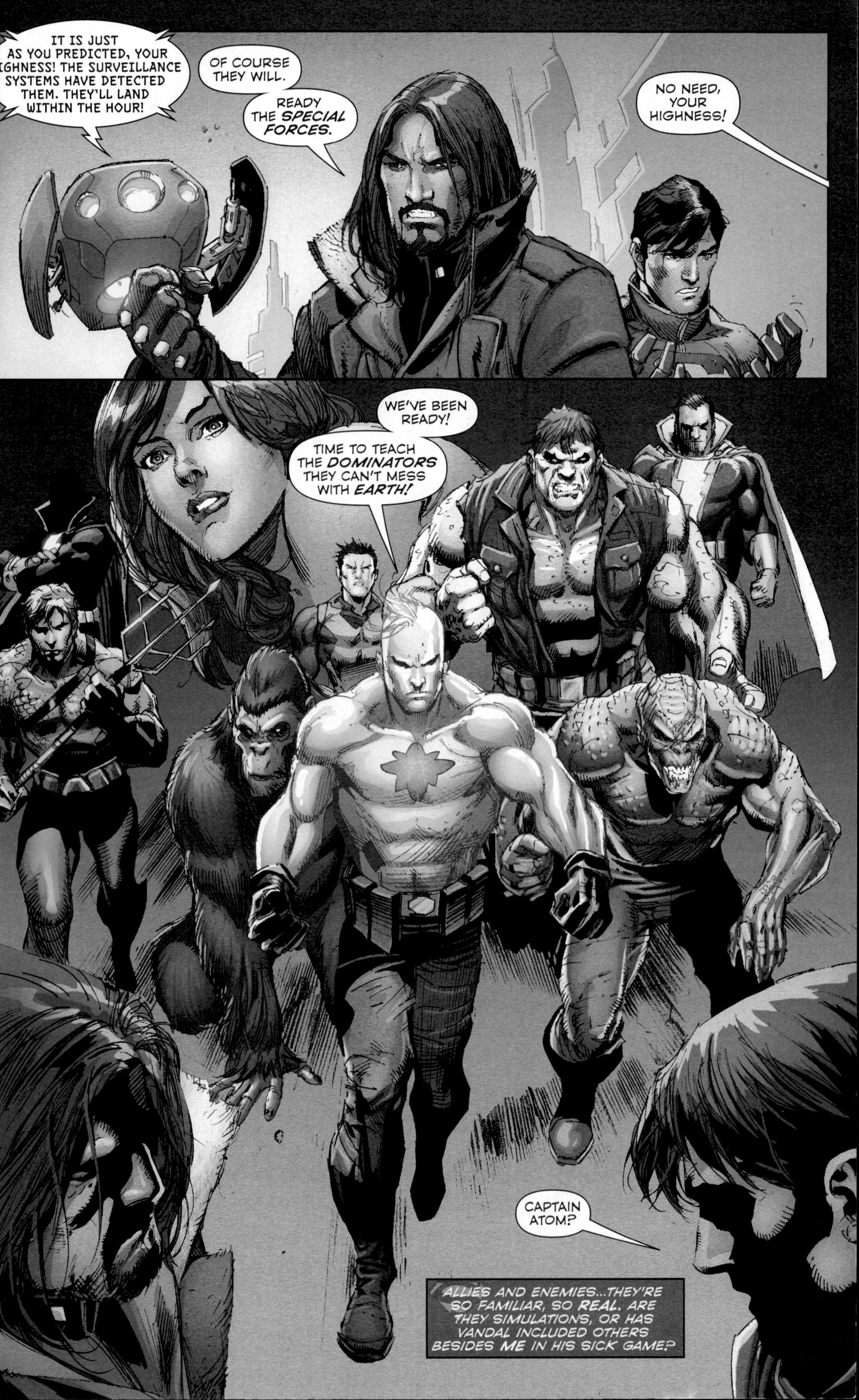
IT IS JUST AS YOU PREDICTED, YOUR HIGHNESS! THE SURVEILLANCE SYSTEMS HAVE DETECTED THEM. THEY'LL LAND WITHIN THE HOUR!
OF COURSE THEY WILL.
READY THE *SPECIAL FORCES.*
NO NEED, YOUR HIGHNESS!
WE'VE BEEN READY!
TIME TO TEACH THE *DOMINATORS* THEY CAN'T MESS WITH *EARTH!*
CAPTAIN ATOM?
*ALLIES AND ENEMIES...THEY'RE SO FAMILIAR, SO **REAL**. ARE THEY SIMULATIONS, OR HAS VANDAL INCLUDED OTHERS BESIDES **ME** IN HIS SICK GAME?*

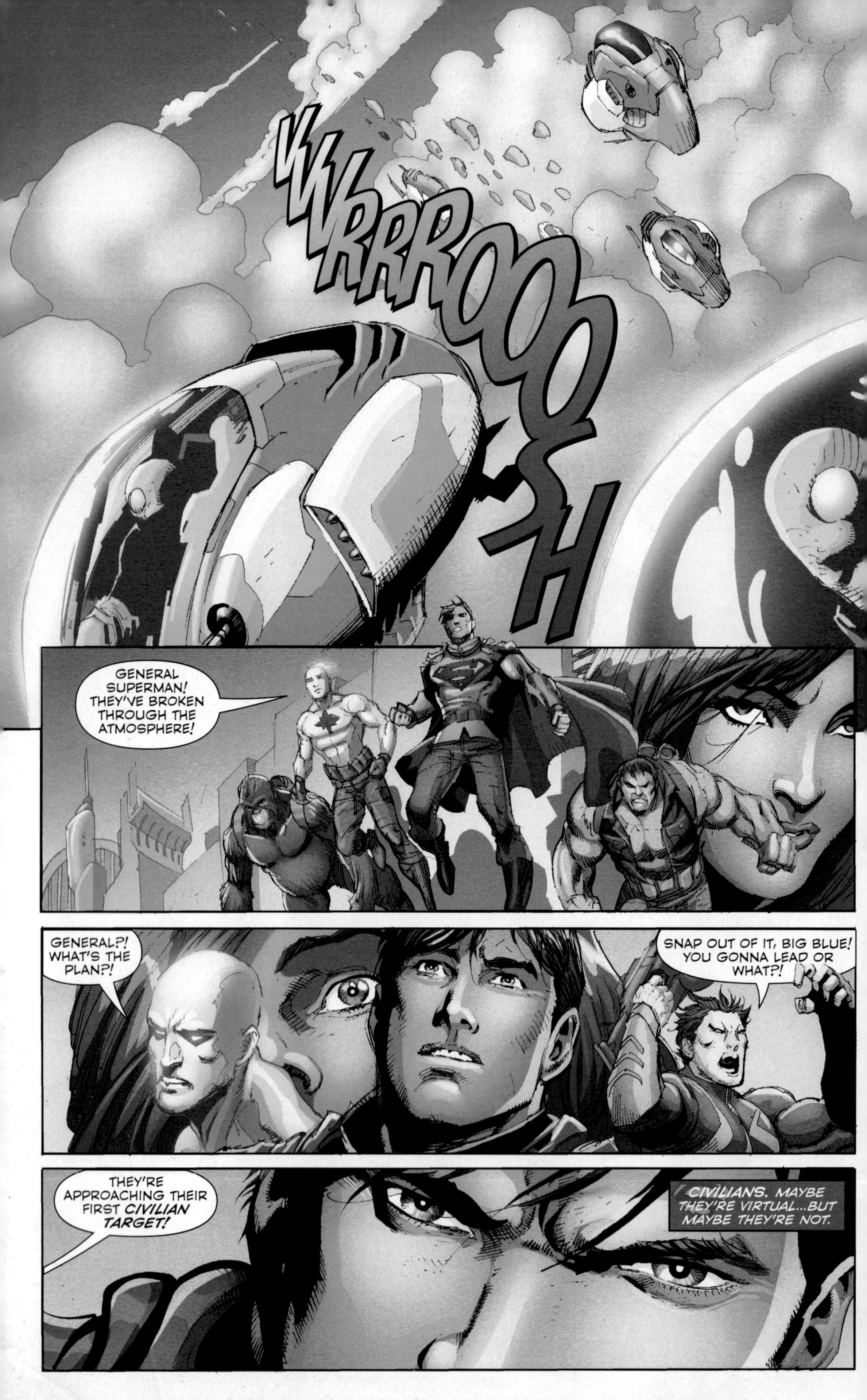
VVVRRROOOOSH
GENERAL SUPERMAN! THEY'VE BROKEN THROUGH THE ATMOSPHERE!
GENERAL?! WHAT'S THE PLAN?!
SNAP OUT OF IT, BIG BLUE! YOU GONNA LEAD OR WHAT?!
THEY'RE APPROACHING THEIR FIRST CIVILIAN TARGET!
CIVILIANS. MAYBE THEY'RE VIRTUAL...BUT MAYBE THEY'RE NOT.

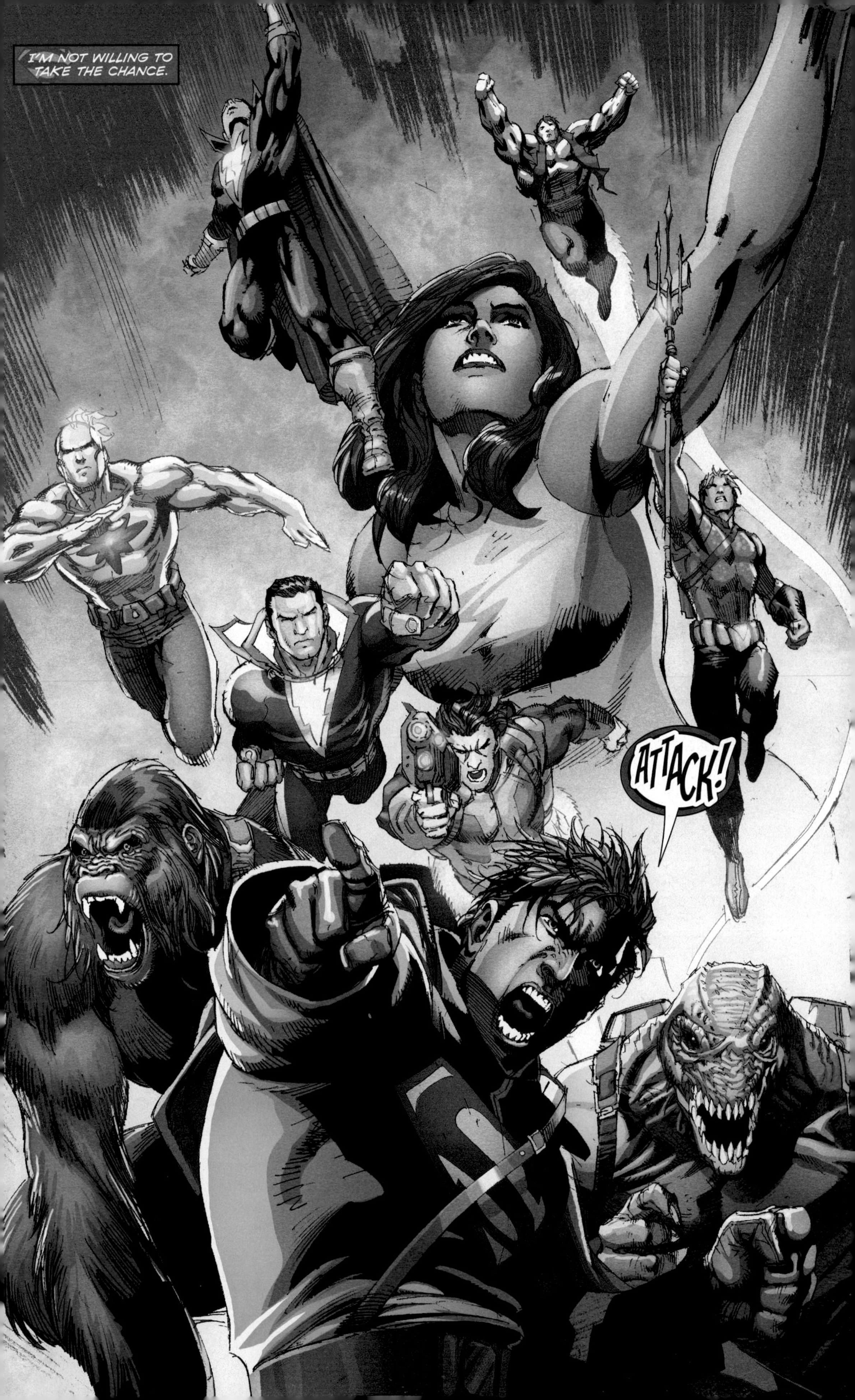
I'M NOT WILLING TO TAKE THE CHANCE.
ATTACK!

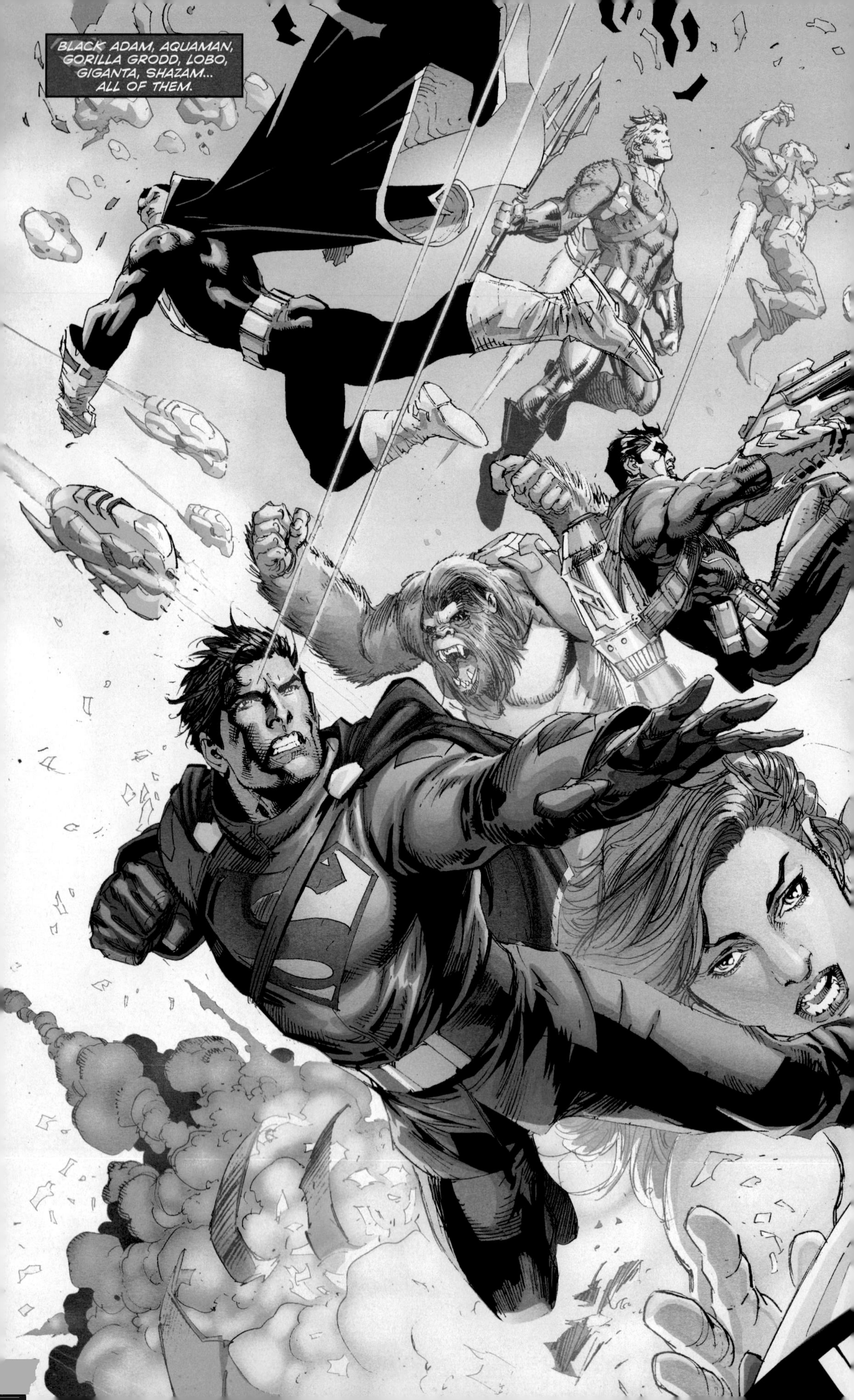
BLACK ADAM, AQUAMAN, GORILLA GRODD, LOBO, GIGANTA, SHAZAM... ALL OF THEM.

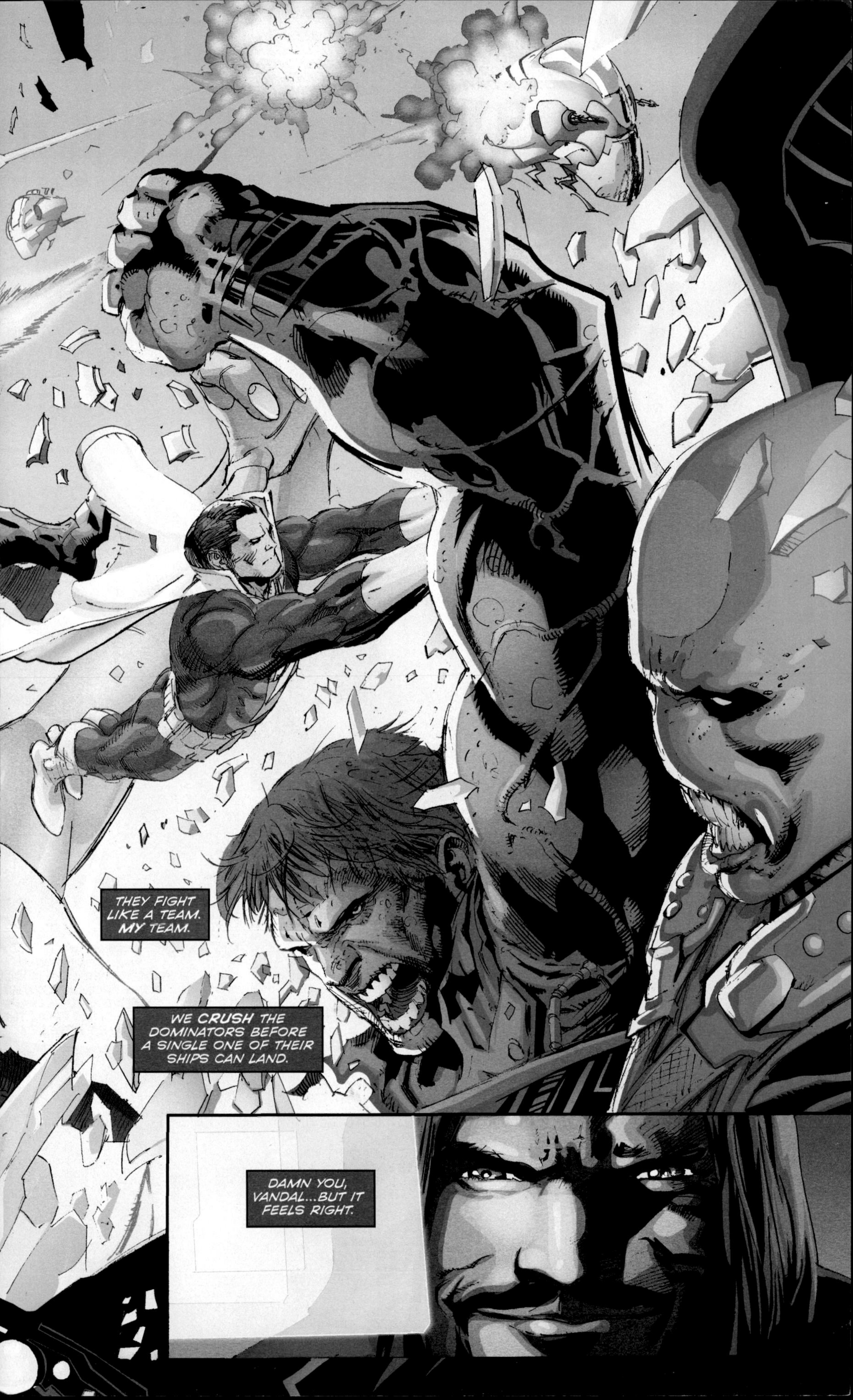
THEY FIGHT LIKE A TEAM. MY TEAM.
WE CRUSH THE DOMINATORS BEFORE A SINGLE ONE OF THEIR SHIPS CAN LAND.
DAMN YOU, VANDAL...BUT IT FEELS RIGHT.

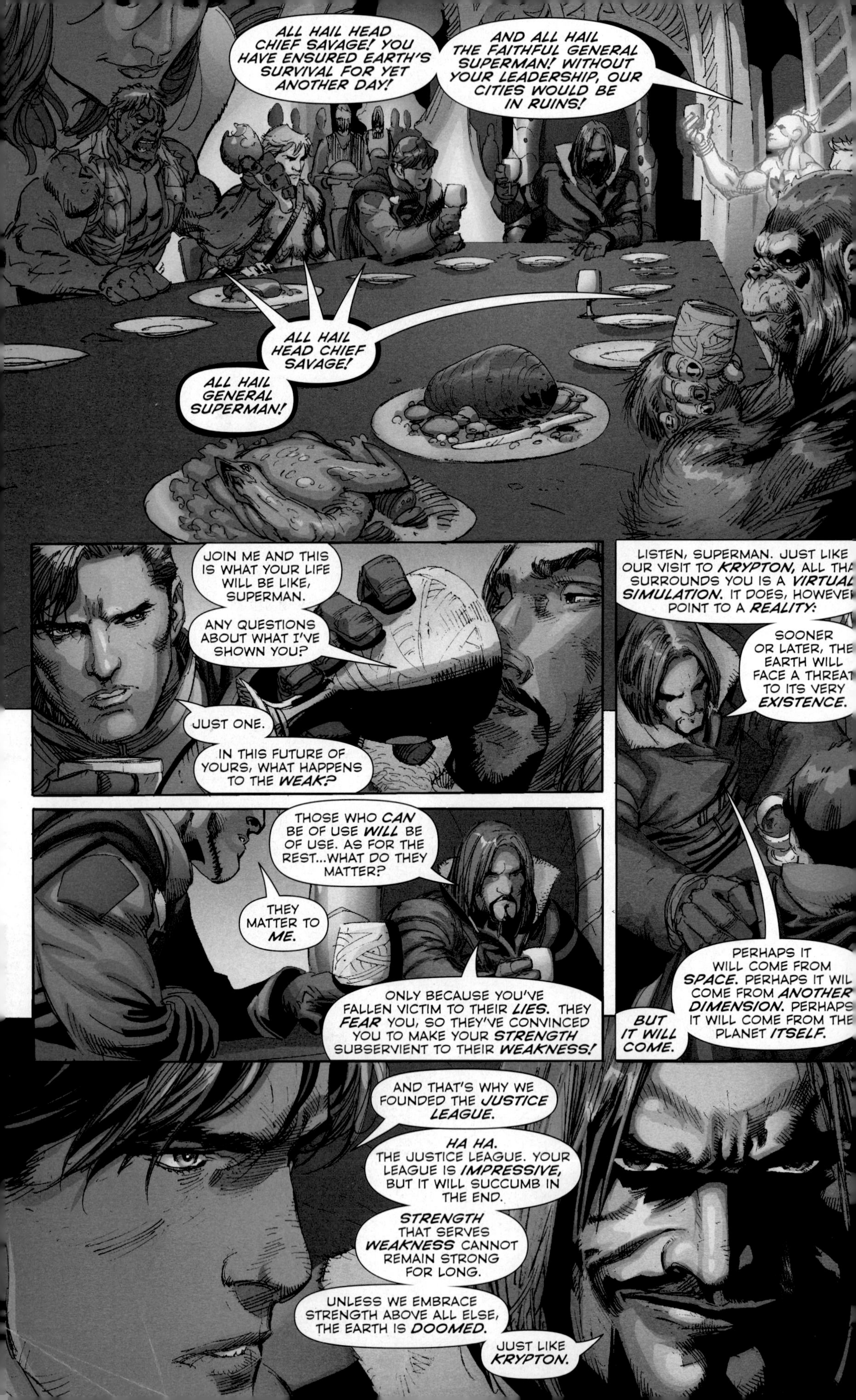
ALL HAIL HEAD CHIEF SAVAGE! YOU HAVE ENSURED EARTH'S SURVIVAL FOR YET ANOTHER DAY!
AND ALL HAIL THE FAITHFUL GENERAL SUPERMAN! WITHOUT YOUR LEADERSHIP, OUR CITIES WOULD BE IN RUINS!
ALL HAIL HEAD CHIEF SAVAGE!
ALL HAIL GENERAL SUPERMAN!
JOIN ME AND THIS IS WHAT YOUR LIFE WILL BE LIKE, SUPERMAN.
ANY QUESTIONS ABOUT WHAT I'VE SHOWN YOU?
JUST ONE.
IN THIS FUTURE OF YOURS, WHAT HAPPENS TO THE WEAK?
THOSE WHO CAN BE OF USE WILL BE OF USE. AS FOR THE REST...WHAT DO THEY MATTER?
THEY MATTER TO ME.
ONLY BECAUSE YOU'VE FALLEN VICTIM TO THEIR LIES. THEY FEAR YOU, SO THEY'VE CONVINCED YOU TO MAKE YOUR STRENGTH SUBSERVIENT TO THEIR WEAKNESS!
LISTEN, SUPERMAN. JUST LIKE OUR VISIT TO KRYPTON, ALL THA SURROUNDS YOU IS A VIRTUAL SIMULATION. IT DOES, HOWEVER POINT TO A REALITY:
SOONER OR LATER, THE EARTH WILL FACE A THREAT TO ITS VERY EXISTENCE.
PERHAPS IT WILL COME FROM SPACE. PERHAPS IT WIL COME FROM ANOTHER DIMENSION. PERHAPS IT WILL COME FROM THE PLANET ITSELF.
BUT IT WILL COME.
AND THAT'S WHY WE FOUNDED THE JUSTICE LEAGUE.
HA HA. THE JUSTICE LEAGUE. YOUR LEAGUE IS IMPRESSIVE, BUT IT WILL SUCCUMB IN THE END.
STRENGTH THAT SERVES WEAKNESS CANNOT REMAIN STRONG FOR LONG.
UNLESS WE EMBRACE STRENGTH ABOVE ALL ELSE, THE EARTH IS DOOMED.
JUST LIKE KRYPTON.

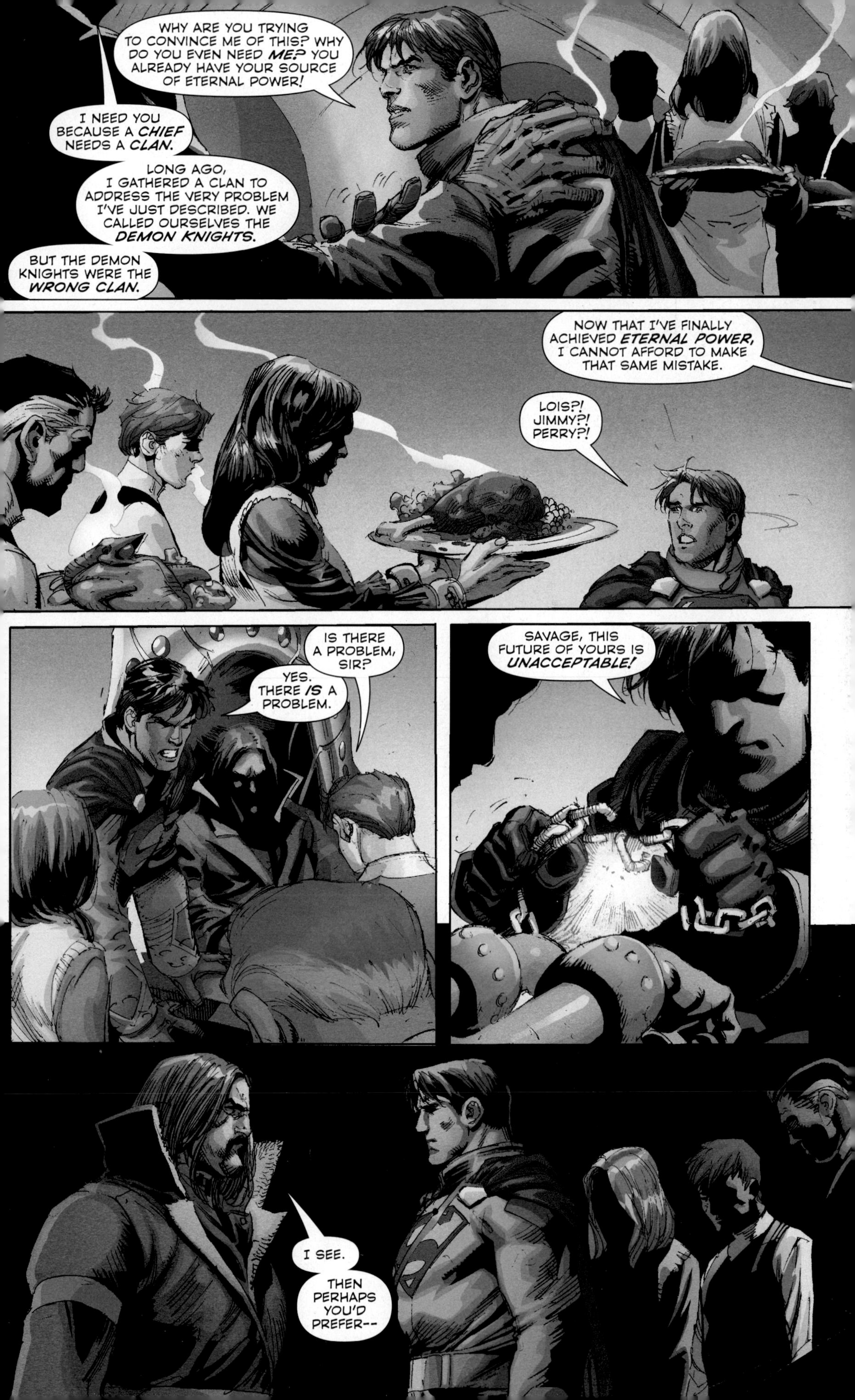
WHY ARE YOU TRYING TO CONVINCE ME OF THIS? WHY DO YOU EVEN NEED ME? YOU ALREADY HAVE YOUR SOURCE OF ETERNAL POWER!
I NEED YOU BECAUSE A CHIEF NEEDS A CLAN.
LONG AGO, I GATHERED A CLAN TO ADDRESS THE VERY PROBLEM I'VE JUST DESCRIBED. WE CALLED OURSELVES THE DEMON KNIGHTS.
BUT THE DEMON KNIGHTS WERE THE WRONG CLAN.
NOW THAT I'VE FINALLY ACHIEVED ETERNAL POWER, I CANNOT AFFORD TO MAKE THAT SAME MISTAKE.
LOIS?! JIMMY?! PERRY?!
IS THERE A PROBLEM, SIR?
YES. THERE IS A PROBLEM.
SAVAGE, THIS FUTURE OF YOURS IS UNACCEPTABLE!
I SEE.
THEN PERHAPS YOU'D PREFER--

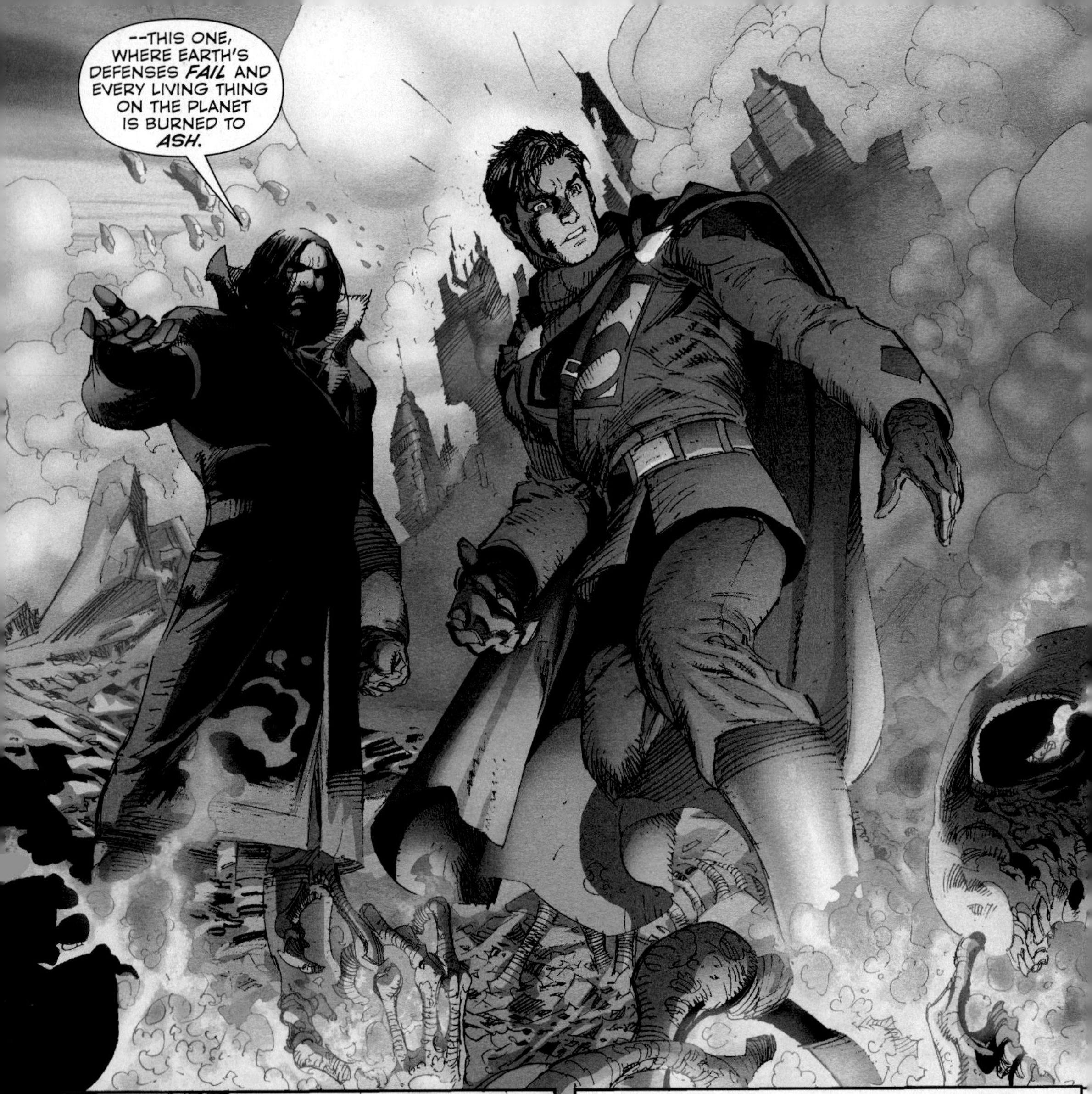
--THIS ONE, WHERE EARTH'S DEFENSES FAIL AND EVERY LIVING THING ON THE PLANET IS BURNED TO ASH.

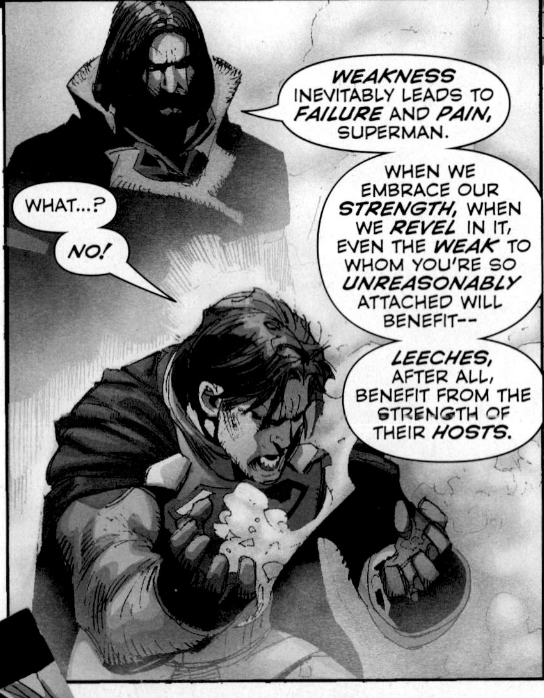
WEAKNESS INEVITABLY LEADS TO FAILURE AND PAIN, SUPERMAN.
WHAT...?
NO!
WHEN WE EMBRACE OUR STRENGTH, WHEN WE REVEL IN IT, EVEN THE WEAK TO WHOM YOU'RE SO UNREASONABLY ATTACHED WILL BENEFIT--
LEECHES, AFTER ALL, BENEFIT FROM THE STRENGTH OF THEIR HOSTS.

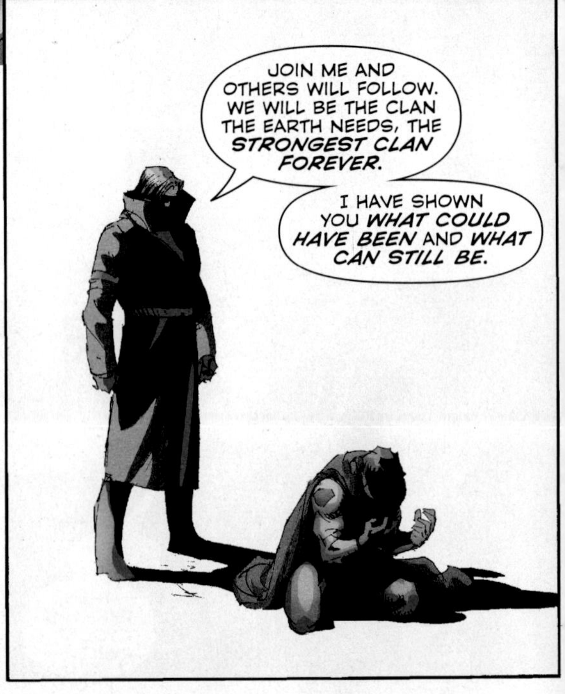
JOIN ME AND OTHERS WILL FOLLOW. WE WILL BE THE CLAN THE EARTH NEEDS, THE STRONGEST CLAN FOREVER.
I HAVE SHOWN YOU WHAT COULD HAVE BEEN AND WHAT CAN STILL BE.

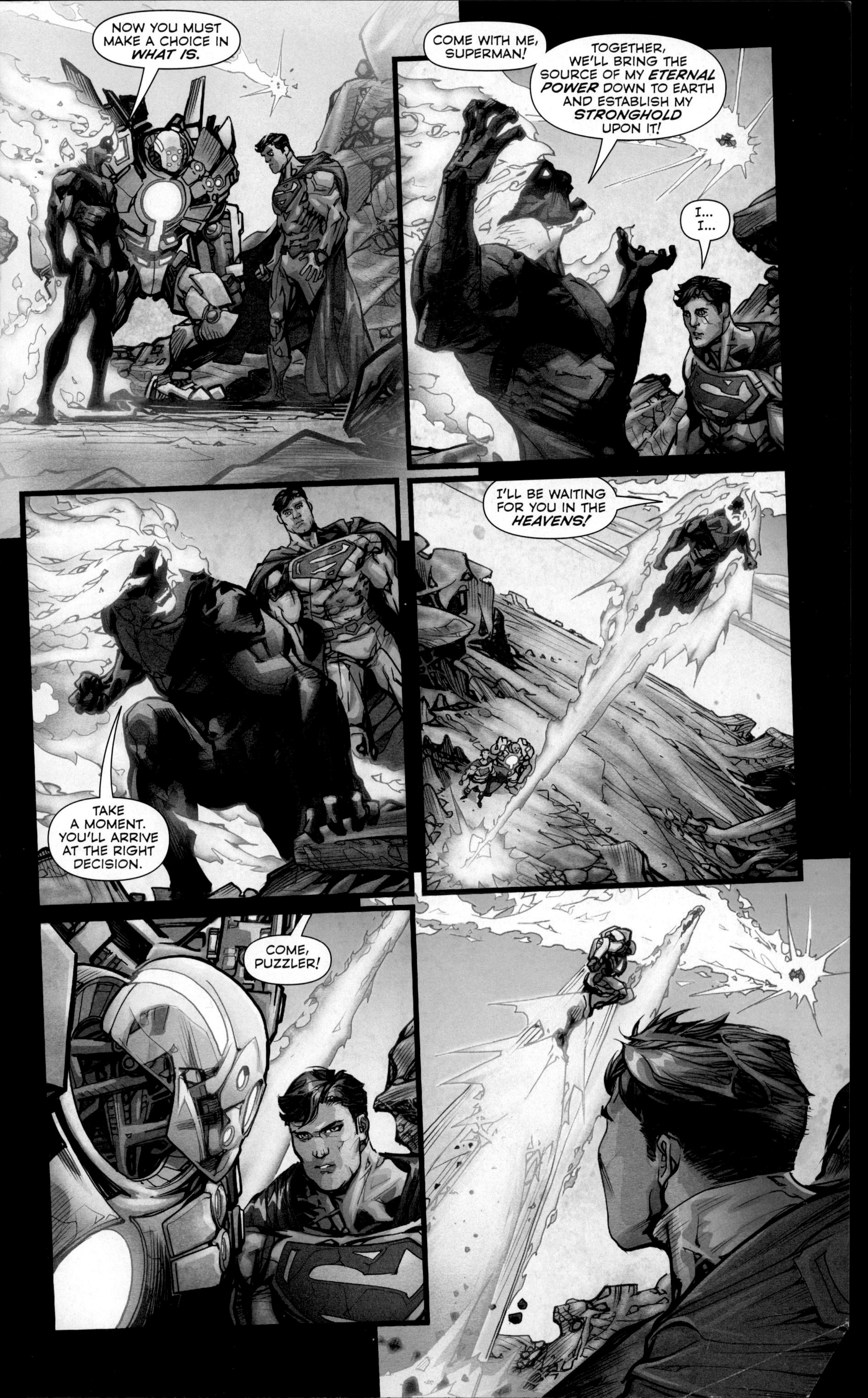
NOW YOU MUST MAKE A CHOICE IN *WHAT IS.*
COME WITH ME, SUPERMAN!
TOGETHER, WE'LL BRING THE SOURCE OF MY *ETERNAL POWER* DOWN TO EARTH AND ESTABLISH MY *STRONGHOLD* UPON IT!
I... I...
TAKE A MOMENT. YOU'LL ARRIVE AT THE RIGHT DECISION.
I'LL BE WAITING FOR YOU IN THE *HEAVENS!*
COME, PUZZLER!

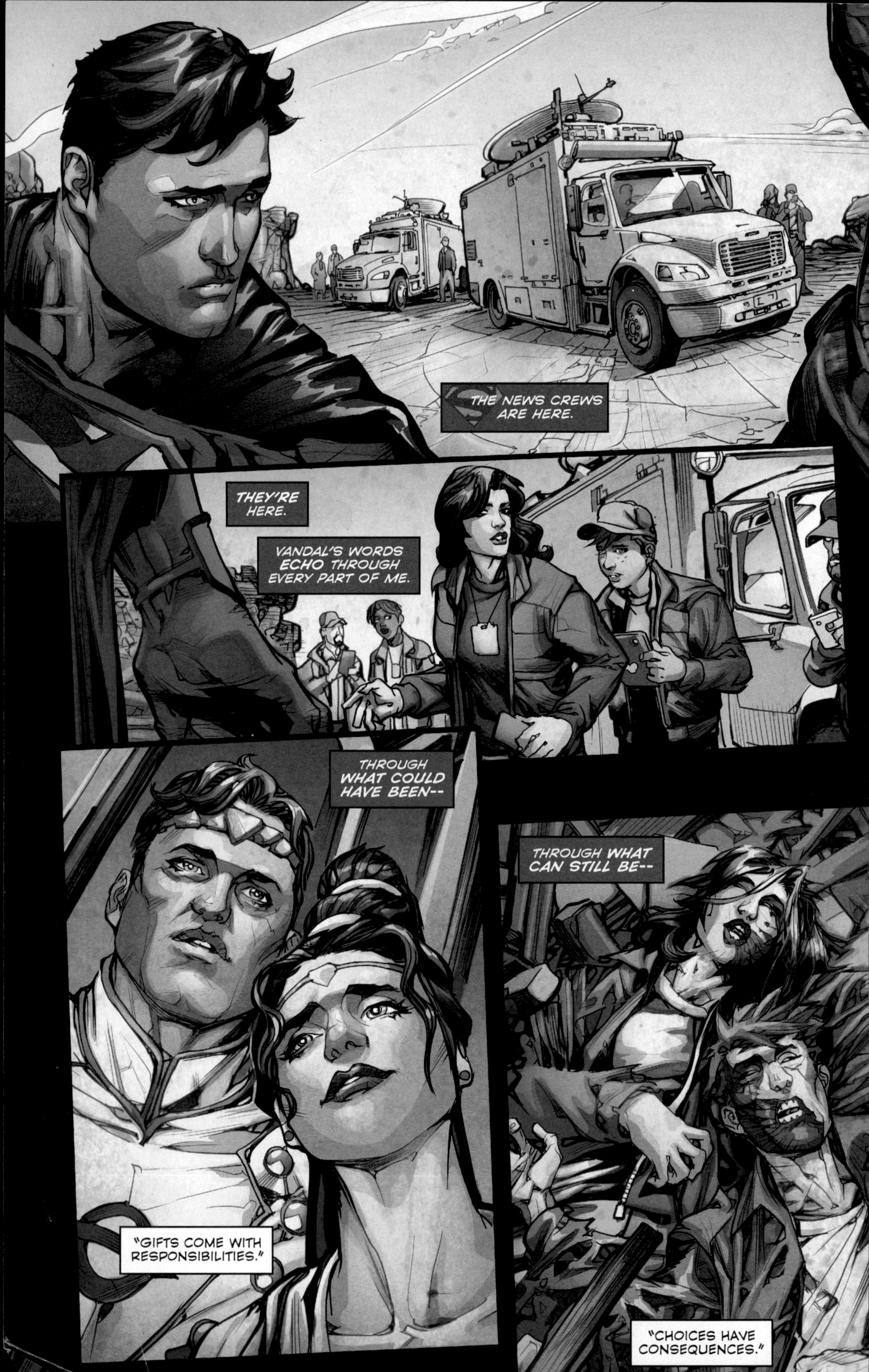
THE NEWS CREWS ARE HERE.
THEY'RE HERE.
VANDAL'S WORDS ECHO THROUGH EVERY PART OF ME.
THROUGH WHAT COULD HAVE BEEN--
"GIFTS COME WITH RESPONSIBILITIES."
THROUGH WHAT CAN STILL BE--
"CHOICES HAVE CONSEQUENCES."

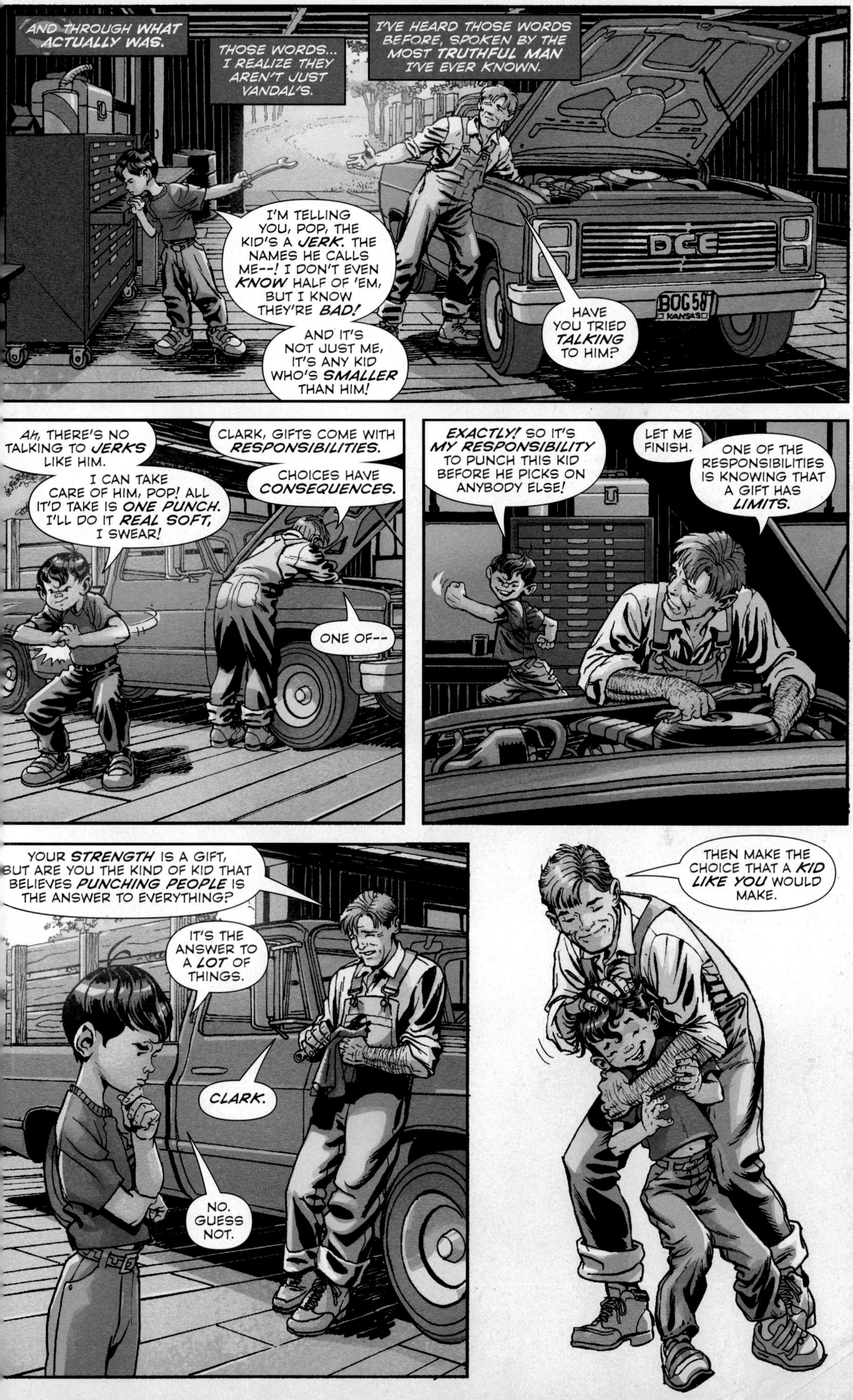
AND THROUGH WHAT ACTUALLY WAS.
THOSE WORDS... I REALIZE THEY AREN'T JUST VANDAL'S.
I'VE HEARD THOSE WORDS BEFORE, SPOKEN BY THE MOST TRUTHFUL MAN I'VE EVER KNOWN.
I'M TELLING YOU, POP, THE KID'S A JERK. THE NAMES HE CALLS ME--! I DON'T EVEN KNOW HALF OF 'EM, BUT I KNOW THEY'RE BAD!
AND IT'S NOT JUST ME, IT'S ANY KID WHO'S SMALLER THAN HIM!
HAVE YOU TRIED TALKING TO HIM?
DCE
BOG 58
KANSAS
Ah, THERE'S NO TALKING TO JERKS LIKE HIM.
CLARK, GIFTS COME WITH RESPONSIBILITIES.
I CAN TAKE CARE OF HIM, POP! ALL IT'D TAKE IS ONE PUNCH. I'LL DO IT REAL SOFT, I SWEAR!
CHOICES HAVE CONSEQUENCES.
ONE OF--
EXACTLY! SO IT'S MY RESPONSIBILITY TO PUNCH THIS KID BEFORE HE PICKS ON ANYBODY ELSE!
LET ME FINISH.
ONE OF THE RESPONSIBILITIES IS KNOWING THAT A GIFT HAS LIMITS.
YOUR STRENGTH IS A GIFT, BUT ARE YOU THE KIND OF KID THAT BELIEVES PUNCHING PEOPLE IS THE ANSWER TO EVERYTHING?
IT'S THE ANSWER TO A LOT OF THINGS.
CLARK.
NO. GUESS NOT.
THEN MAKE THE CHOICE THAT A KID LIKE YOU WOULD MAKE.

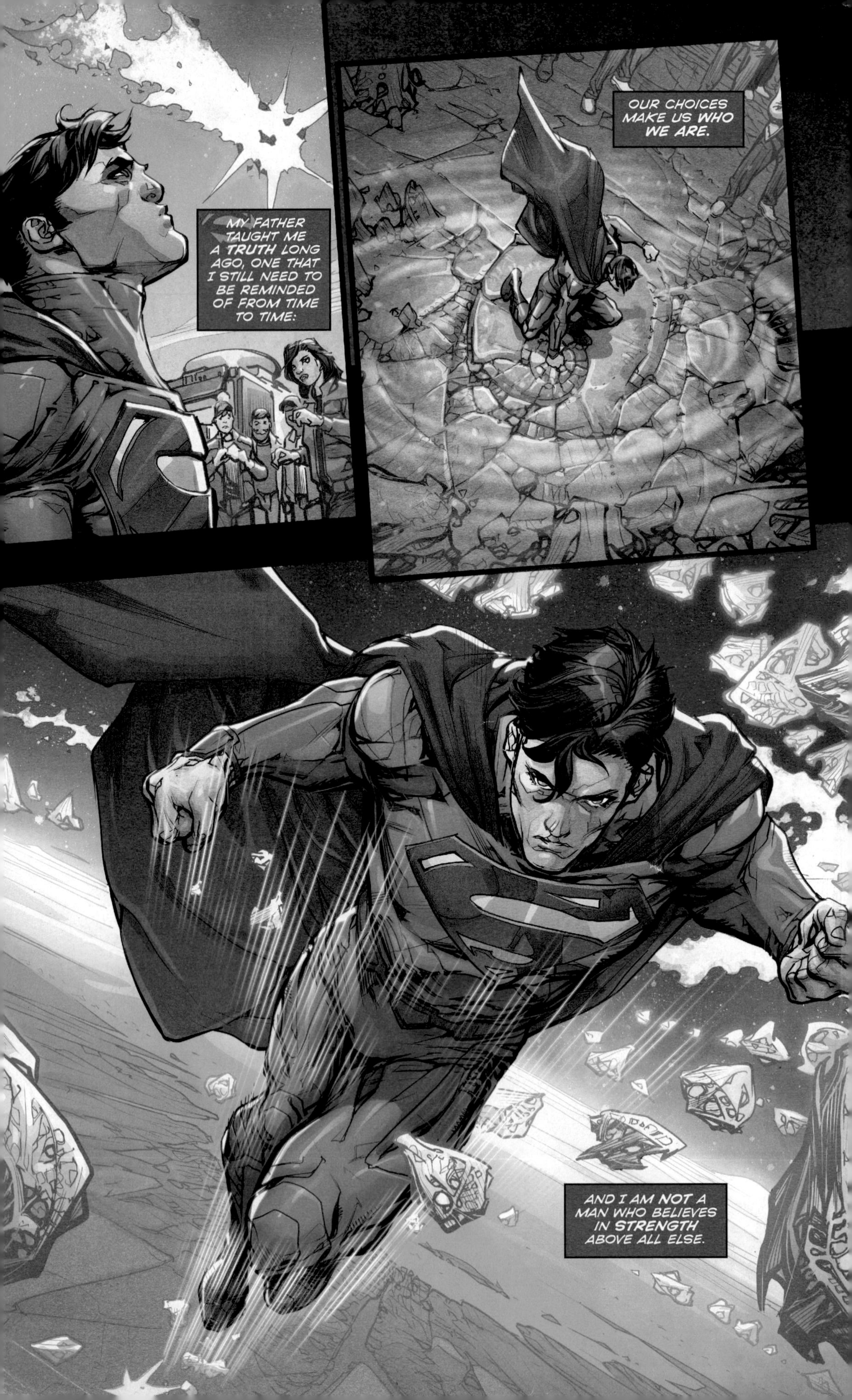
MY FATHER TAUGHT ME A TRUTH LONG AGO, ONE THAT I STILL NEED TO BE REMINDED OF FROM TIME TO TIME:
OUR CHOICES MAKE US WHO WE ARE.
AND I AM NOT A MAN WHO BELIEVES IN STRENGTH ABOVE ALL ELSE.

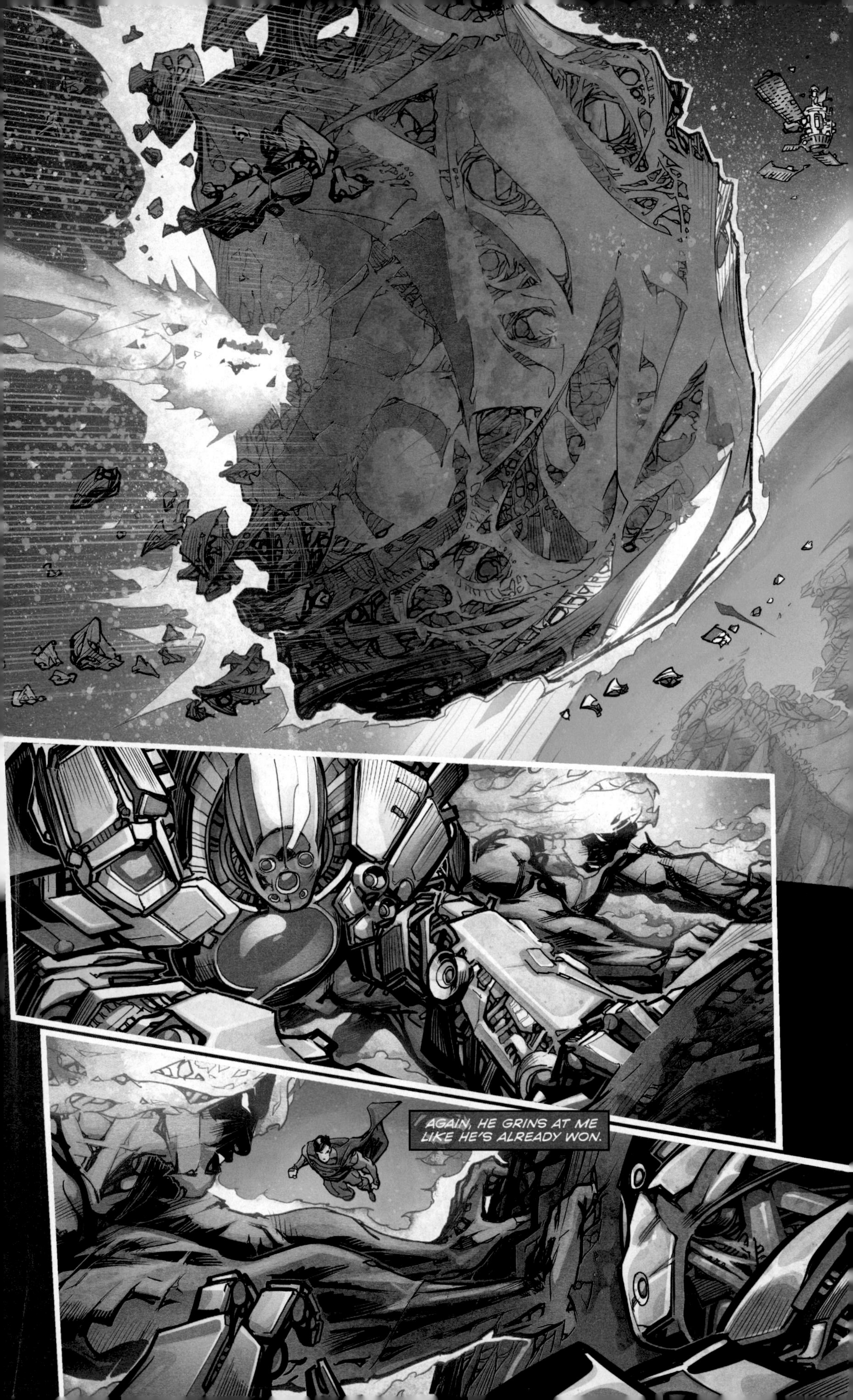
AGAIN, HE GRINS AT ME LIKE HE'S ALREADY WON.

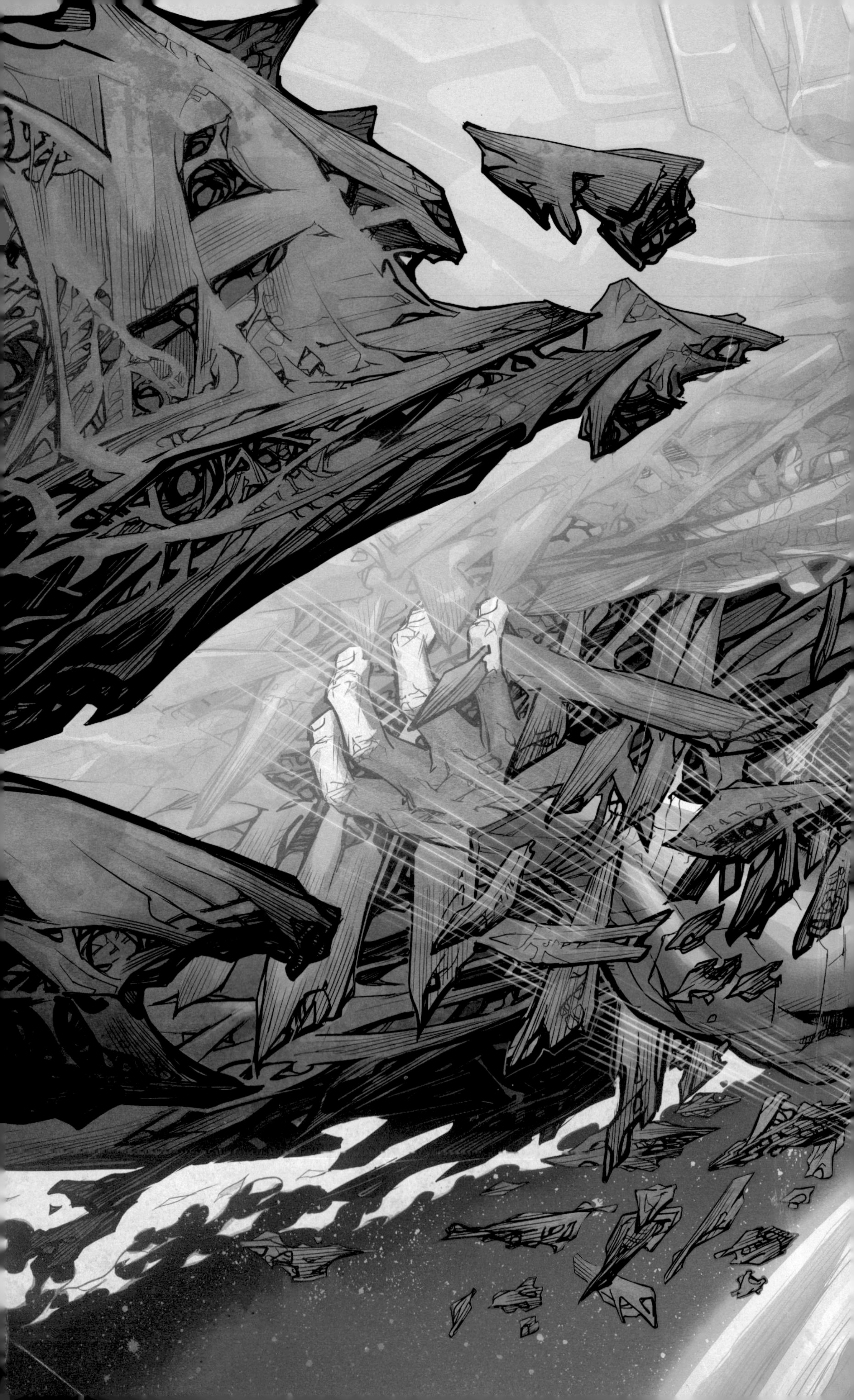

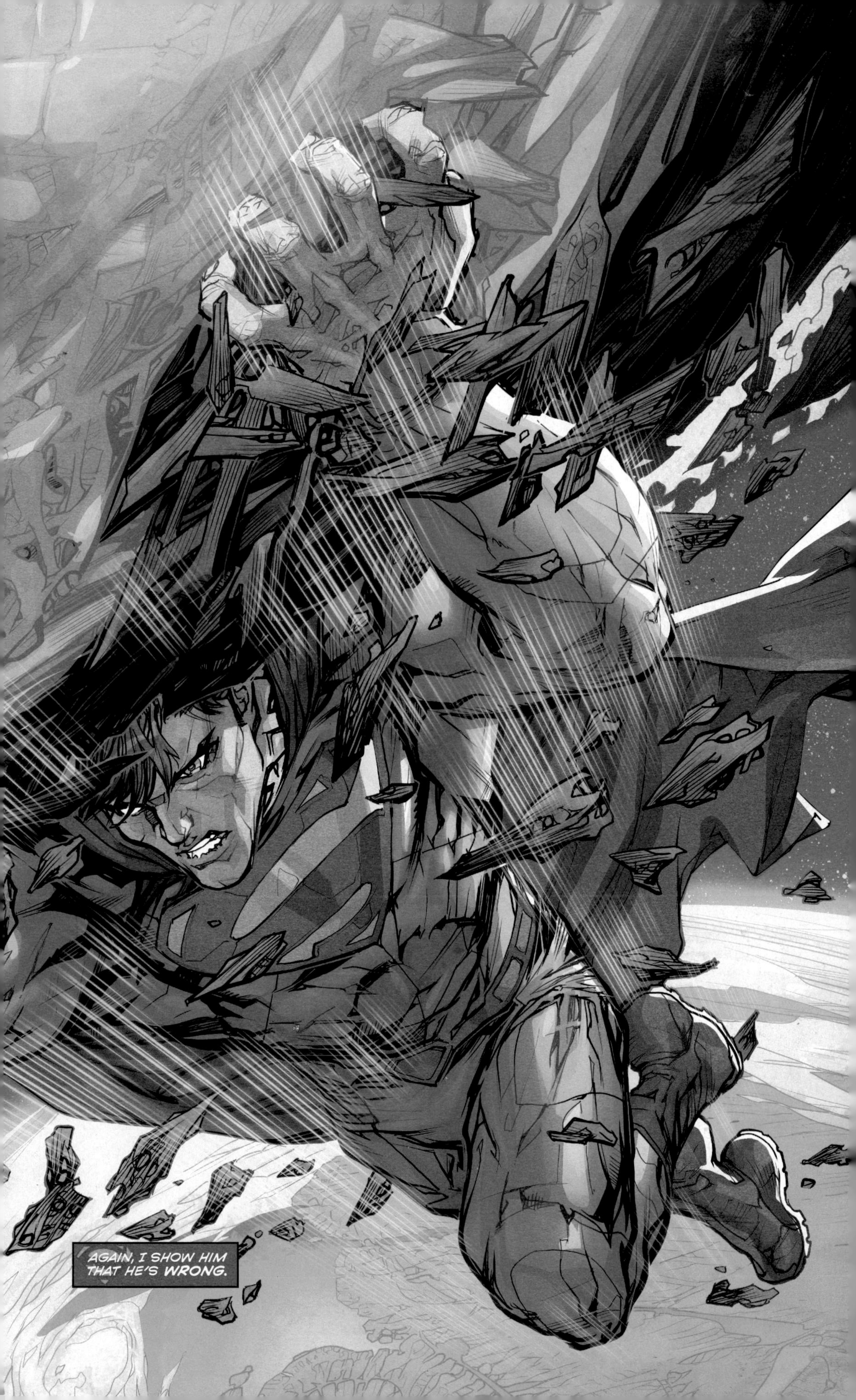
AGAIN, I SHOW HIM THAT HE'S WRONG.

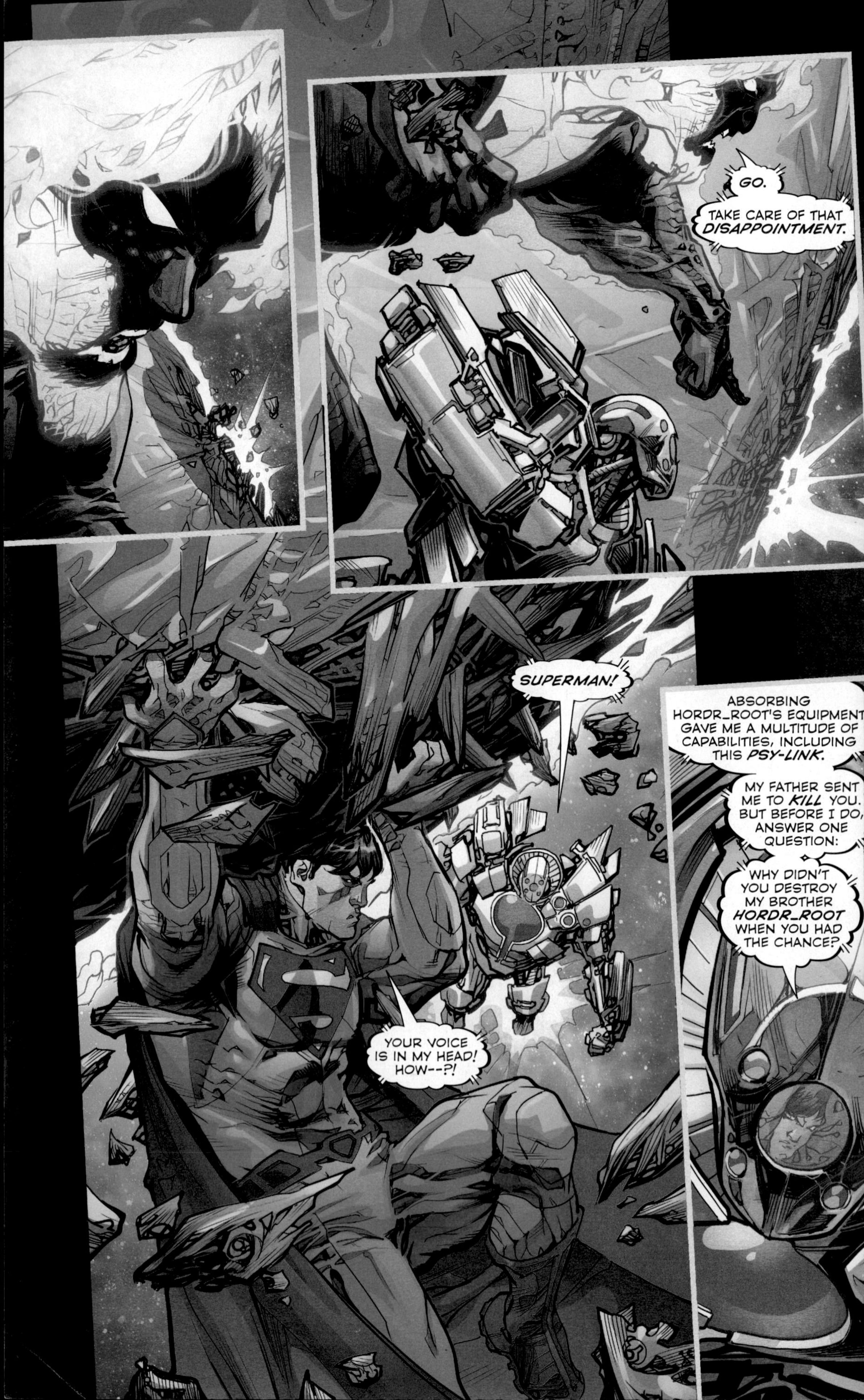
GO.
TAKE CARE OF THAT DISAPPOINTMENT.
SUPERMAN!
ABSORBING HORDR_ROOT'S EQUIPMENT GAVE ME A MULTITUDE OF CAPABILITIES, INCLUDING THIS PSY-LINK.
MY FATHER SENT ME TO KILL YOU. BUT BEFORE I DO, ANSWER ONE QUESTION:
WHY DIDN'T YOU DESTROY MY BROTHER HORDR_ROOT WHEN YOU HAD THE CHANCE?
YOUR VOICE IS IN MY HEAD! HOW--?!

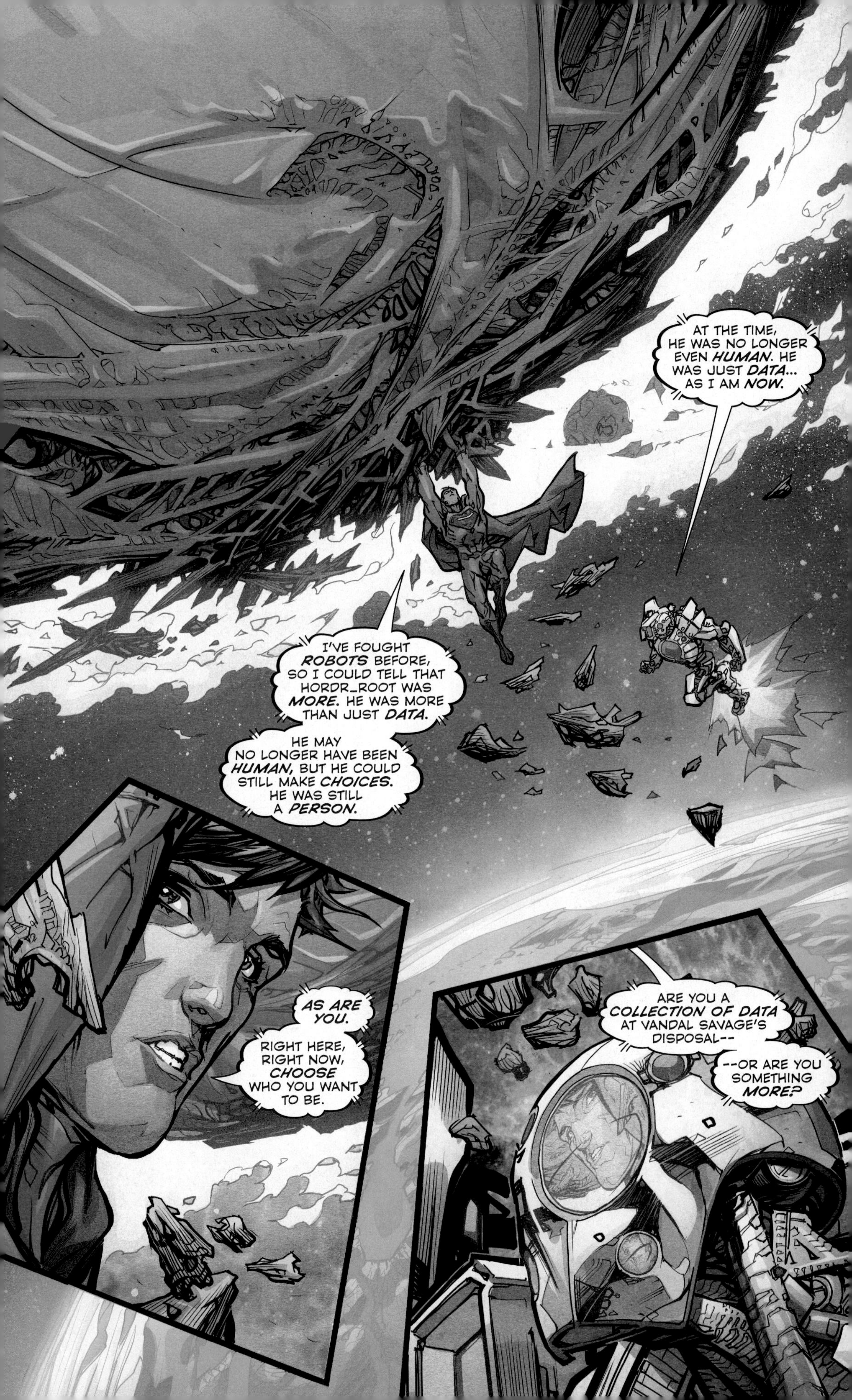

AT THE TIME, HE WAS NO LONGER EVEN HUMAN. HE WAS JUST DATA... AS I AM NOW.
I'VE FOUGHT ROBOTS BEFORE, SO I COULD TELL THAT HORDR_ROOT WAS MORE. HE WAS MORE THAN JUST DATA.
HE MAY NO LONGER HAVE BEEN HUMAN, BUT HE COULD STILL MAKE CHOICES. HE WAS STILL A PERSON.
AS ARE YOU.
RIGHT HERE, RIGHT NOW, CHOOSE WHO YOU WANT TO BE.
ARE YOU A COLLECTION OF DATA AT VANDAL SAVAGE'S DISPOSAL--
--OR ARE YOU SOMETHING MORE?

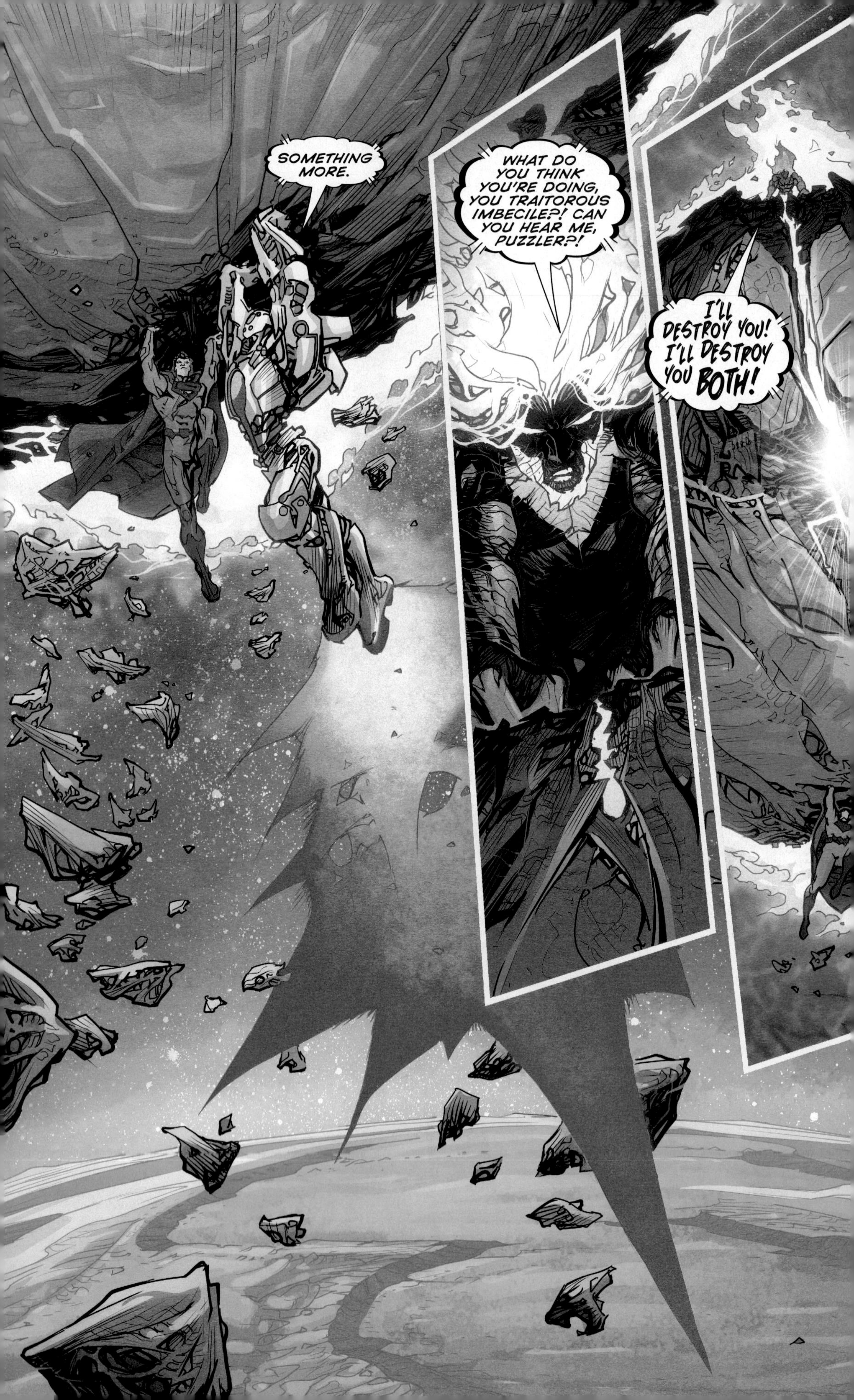
SOMETHING MORE.
WHAT DO YOU THINK YOU'RE DOING, YOU TRAITOROUS IMBECILE?! CAN YOU HEAR ME, PUZZLER?!
I'LL DESTROY YOU! I'LL DESTROY YOU BOTH!

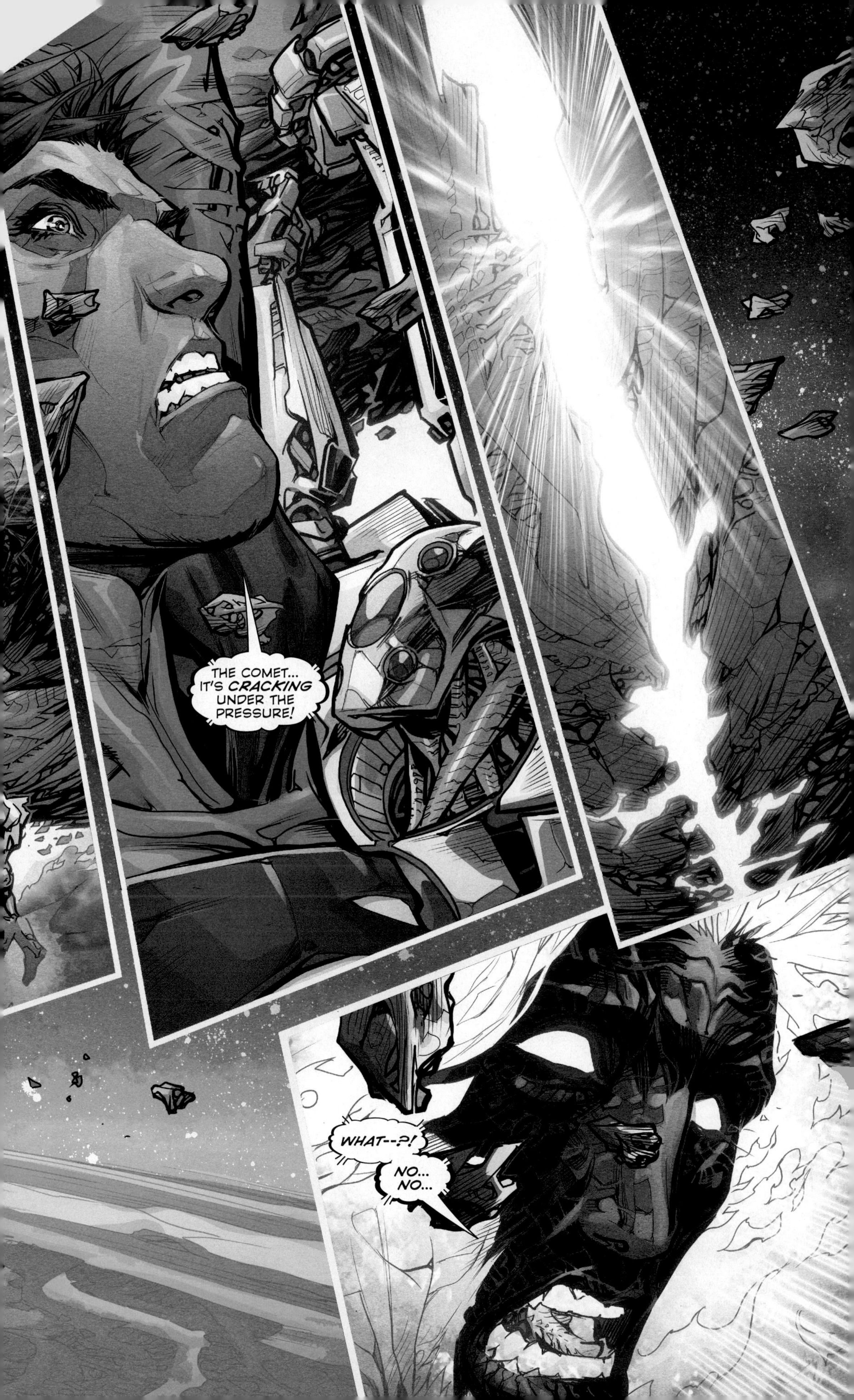
THE COMET... IT'S CRACKING UNDER THE PRESSURE!
WHAT--?!
NO... NO...

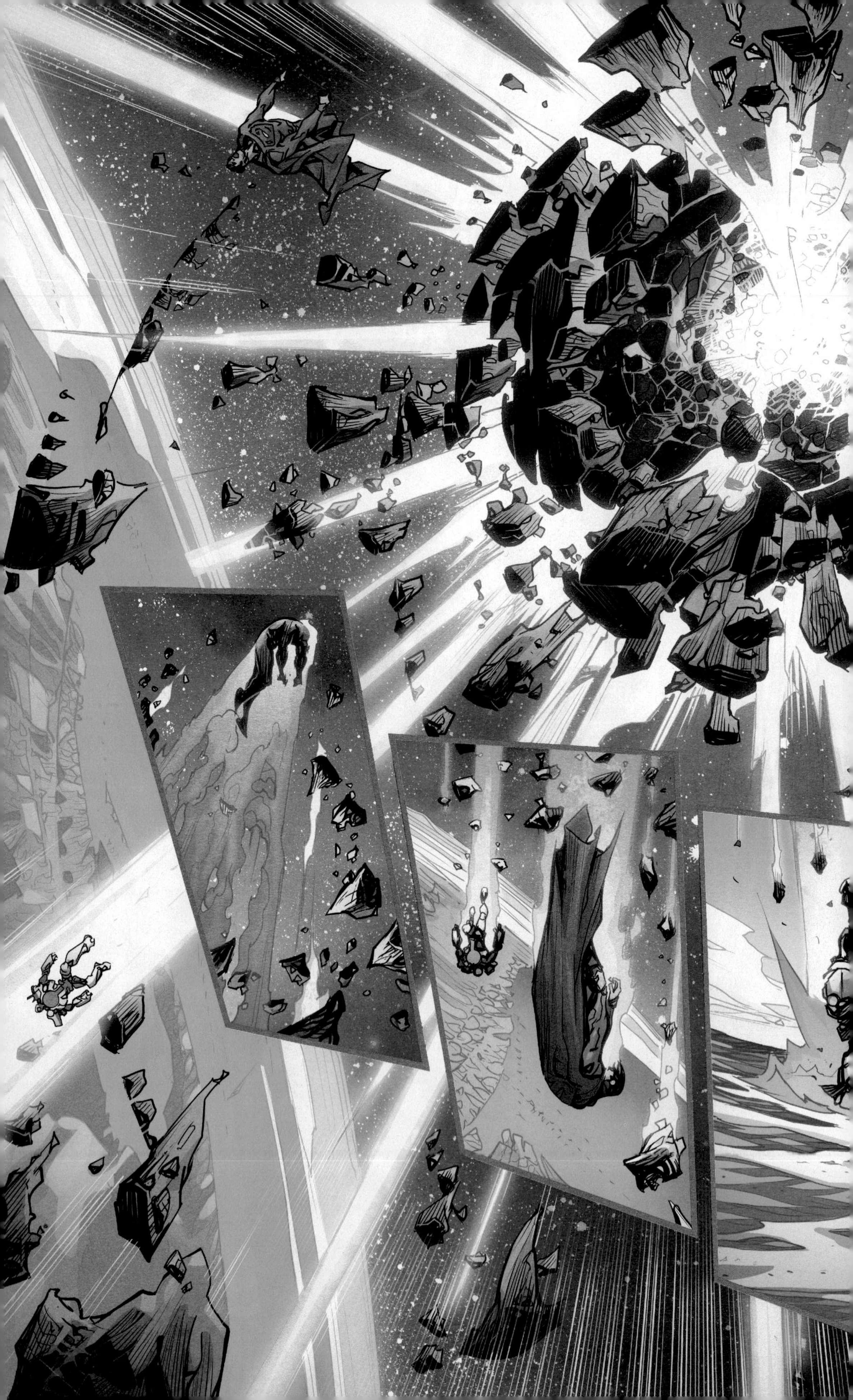

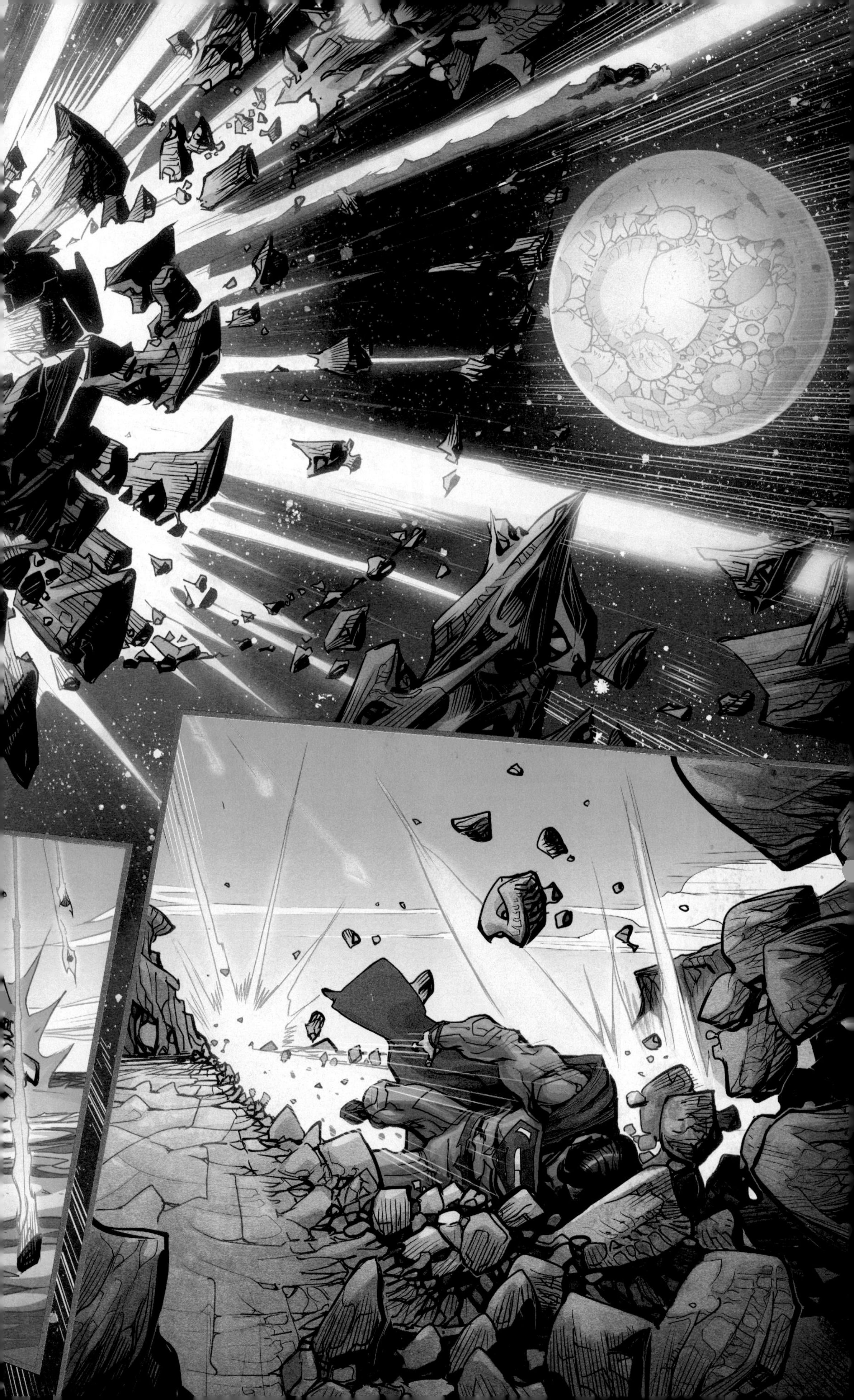

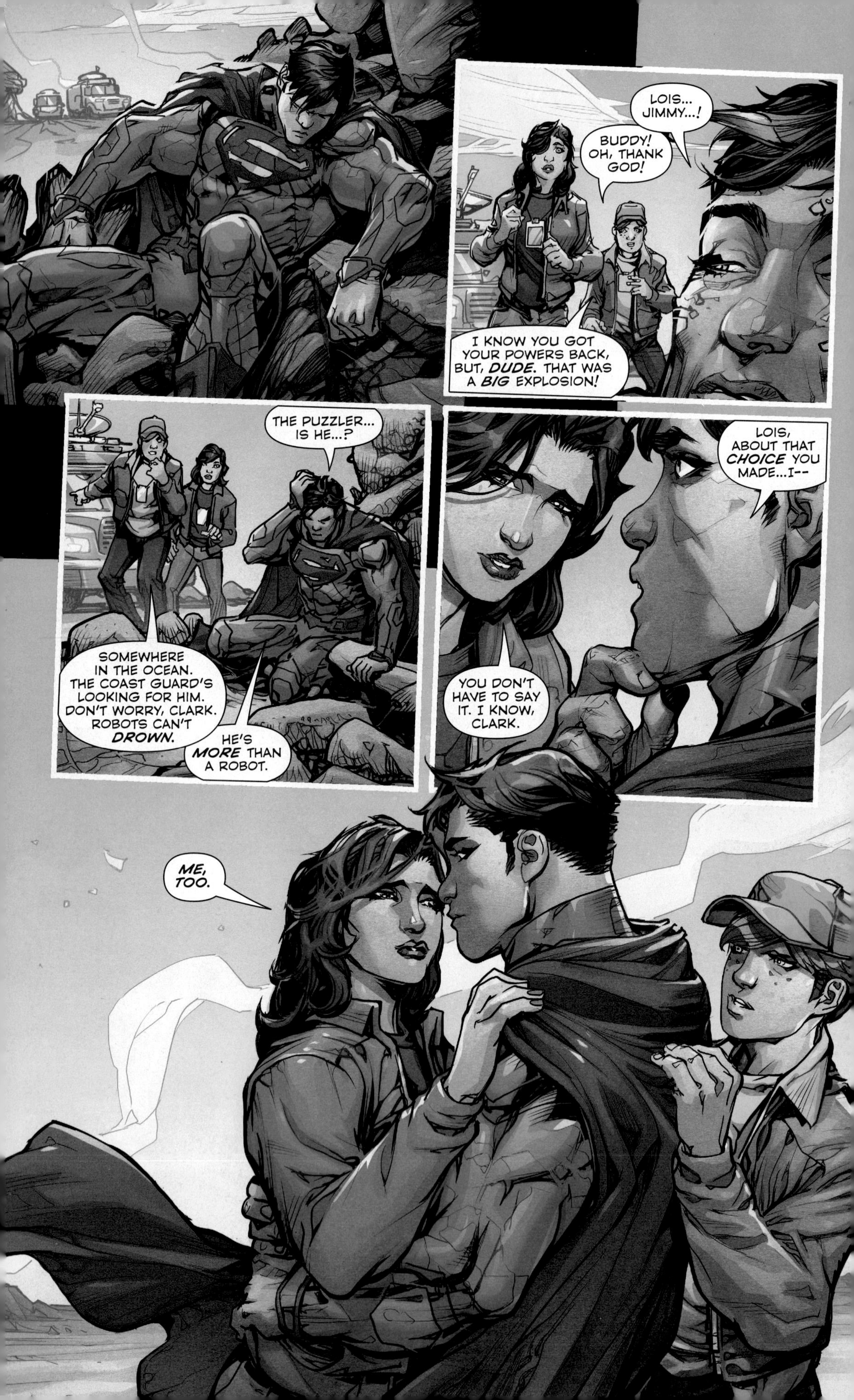
LOIS... JIMMY...!
BUDDY! OH, THANK GOD!
I KNOW YOU GOT YOUR POWERS BACK, BUT, DUDE. THAT WAS A BIG EXPLOSION!
THE PUZZLER... IS HE...?
SOMEWHERE IN THE OCEAN. THE COAST GUARD'S LOOKING FOR HIM. DON'T WORRY, CLARK. ROBOTS CAN'T DROWN.
HE'S MORE THAN A ROBOT.
LOIS, ABOUT THAT CHOICE YOU MADE...I--
YOU DON'T HAVE TO SAY IT. I KNOW, CLARK.
ME, TOO.

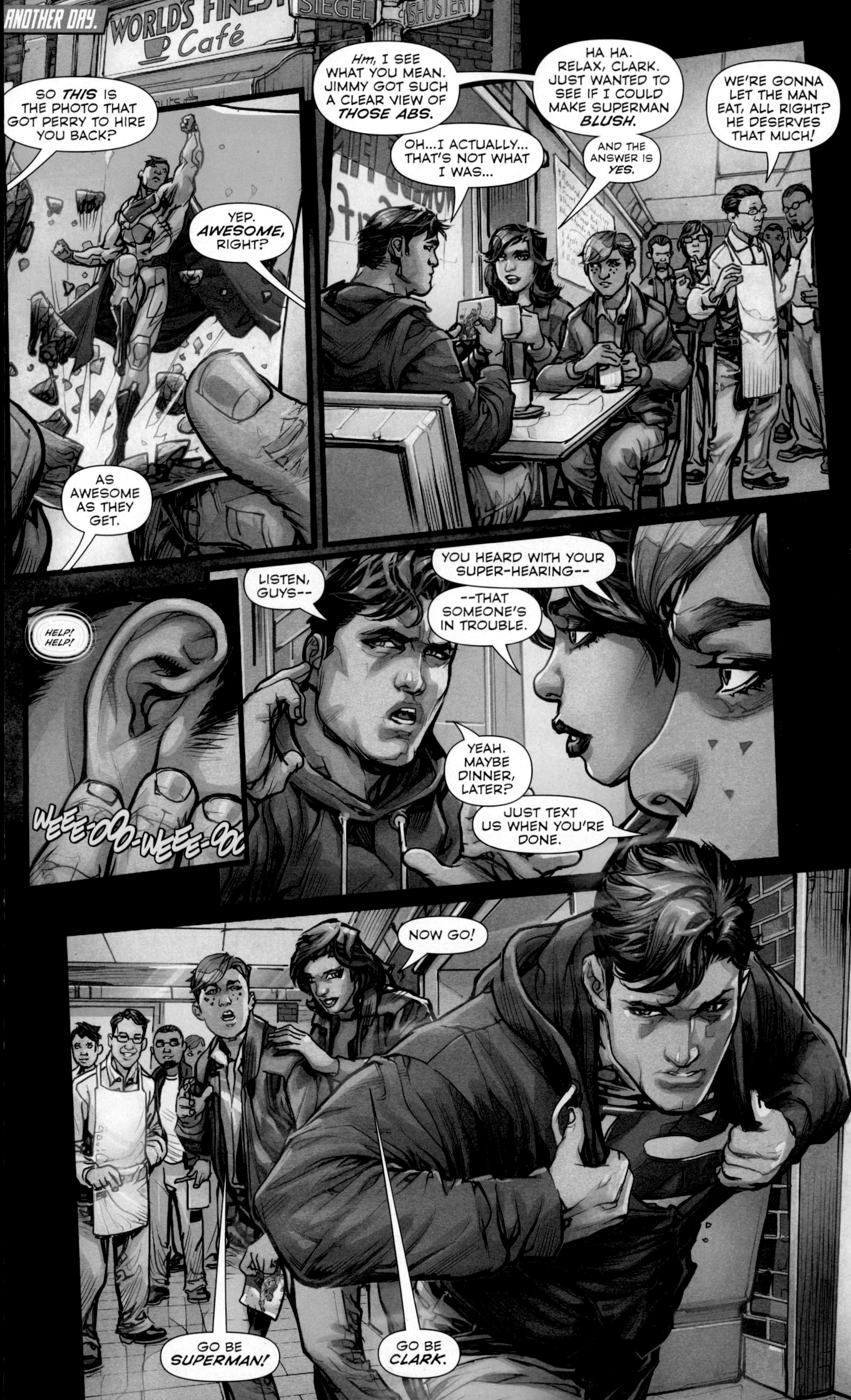
ANOTHER DAY.
WORLD'S FINEST Café
SIEGEL
SHUSTER
SO THIS IS THE PHOTO THAT GOT PERRY TO HIRE YOU BACK?
YEP. AWESOME, RIGHT?
AS AWESOME AS THEY GET.
Hm, I SEE WHAT YOU MEAN. JIMMY GOT SUCH A CLEAR VIEW OF THOSE ABS.
OH...I ACTUALLY... THAT'S NOT WHAT I WAS...
HA HA. RELAX, CLARK. JUST WANTED TO SEE IF I COULD MAKE SUPERMAN BLUSH.
AND THE ANSWER IS YES.
WE'RE GONNA LET THE MAN EAT, ALL RIGHT? HE DESERVES THAT MUCH!
HELP! HELP!
WEEE-OOO-WEEE-OOO
LISTEN, GUYS--
YOU HEARD WITH YOUR SUPER-HEARING--
--THAT SOMEONE'S IN TROUBLE.
YEAH. MAYBE DINNER, LATER?
JUST TEXT US WHEN YOU'RE DONE.
NOW GO!
GO BE SUPERMAN!
GO BE CLARK.

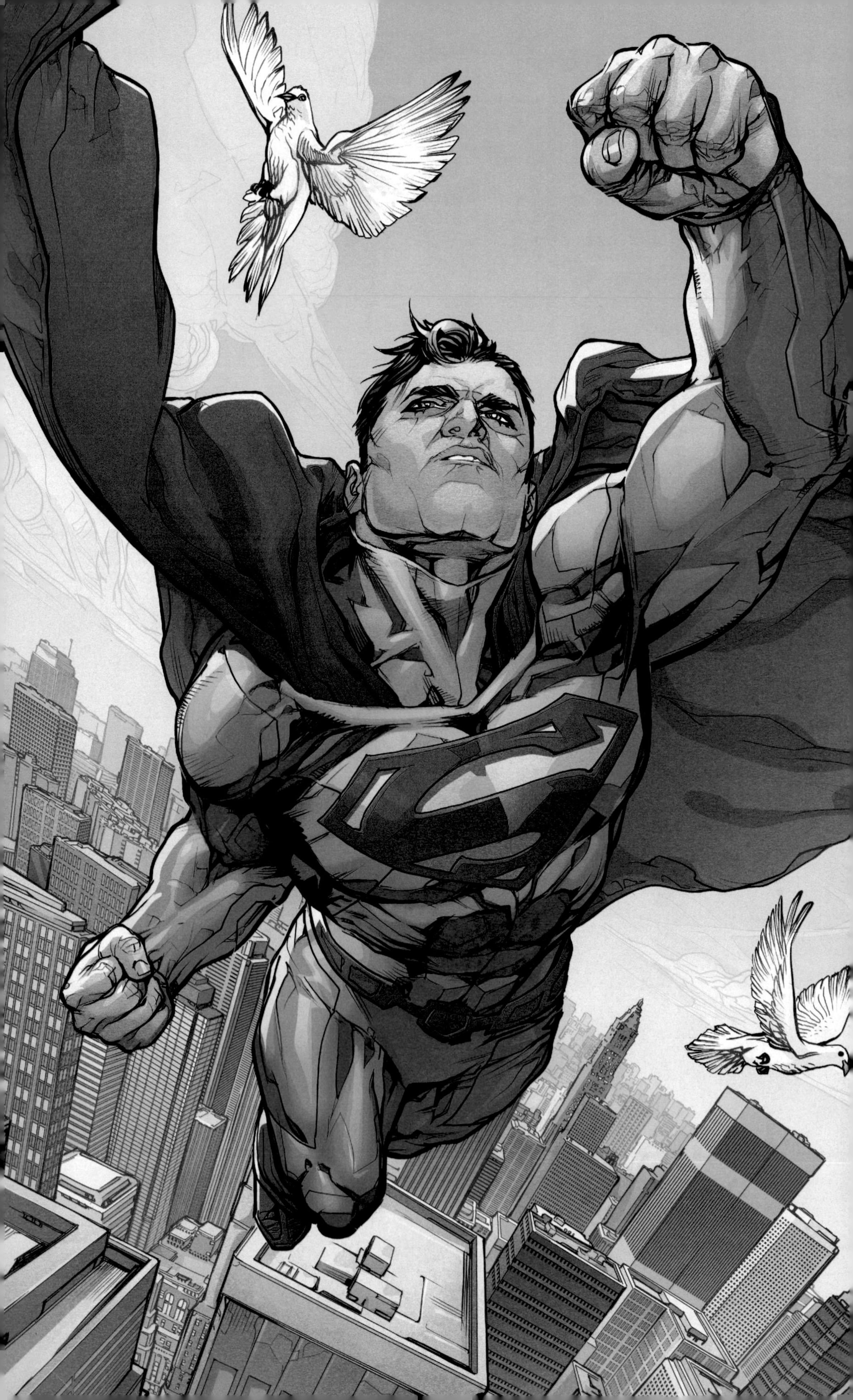

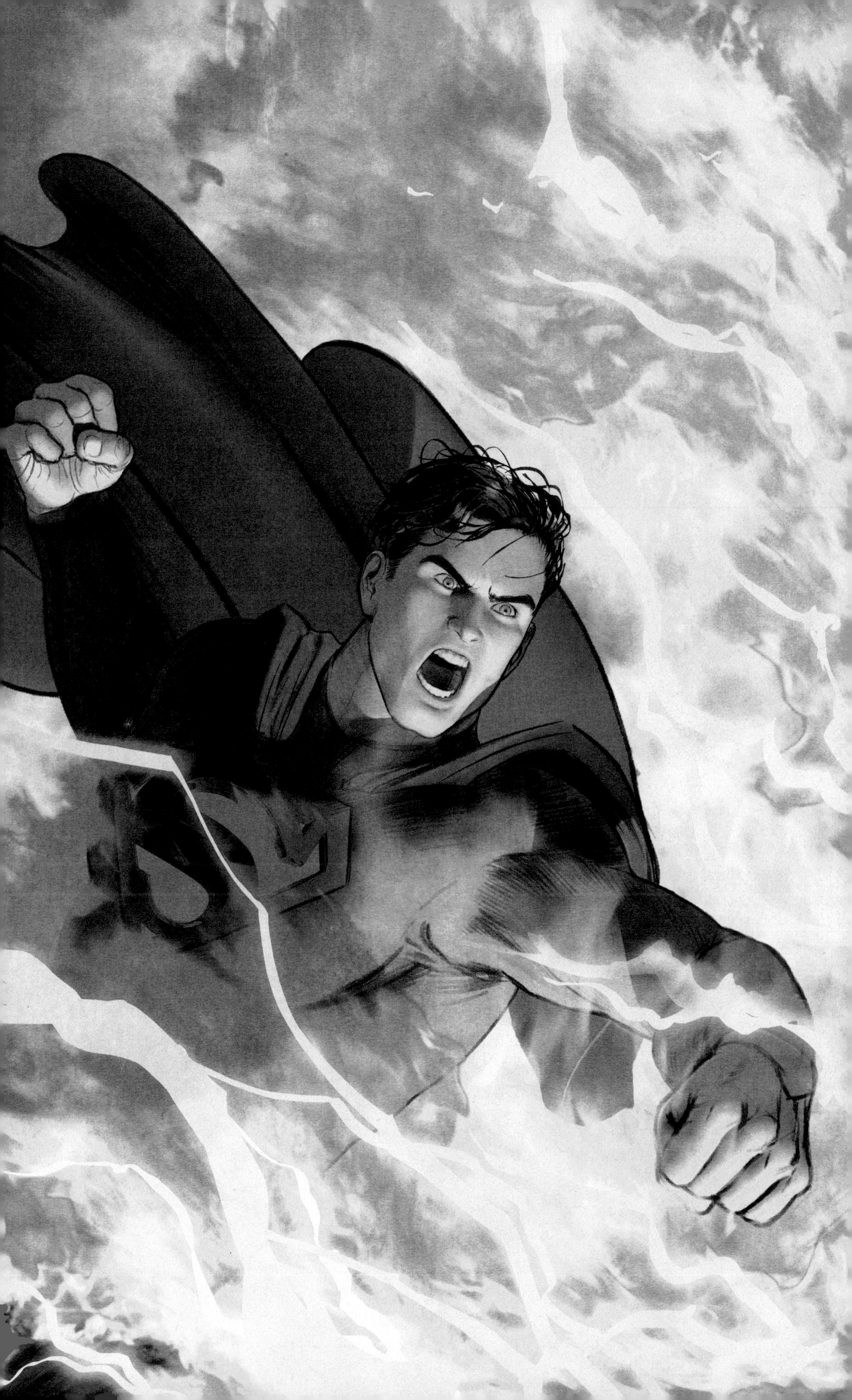

THE FINAL DAYS OF SUPERMAN PART 1: THIS MORTAL COIL

PETER J. TOMASI writer **MIKEL JANÍN** artist **MIKEL JANÍN** colorist **ROB LEIGH** letterer **MIKEL JANÍN** cover

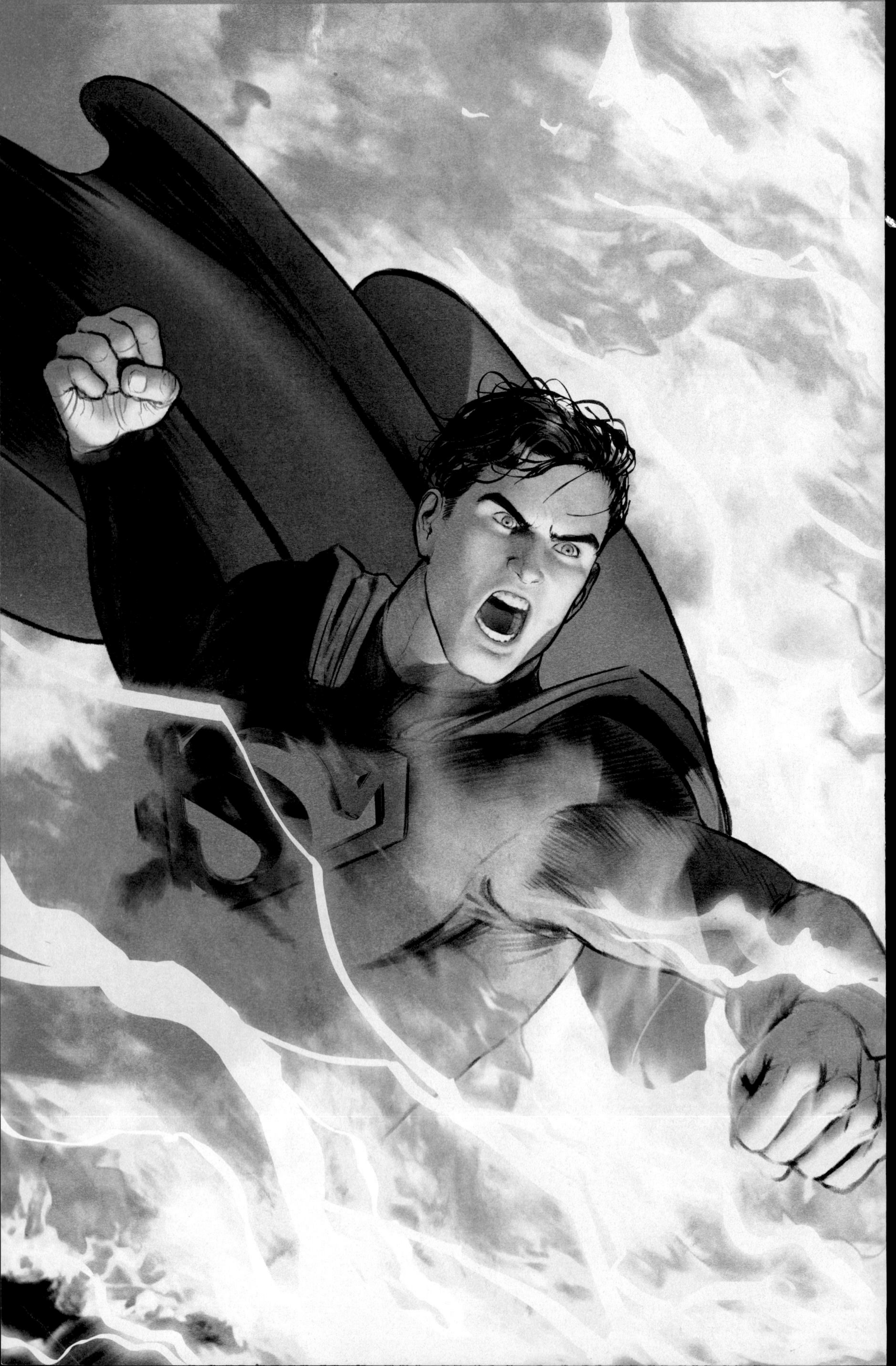

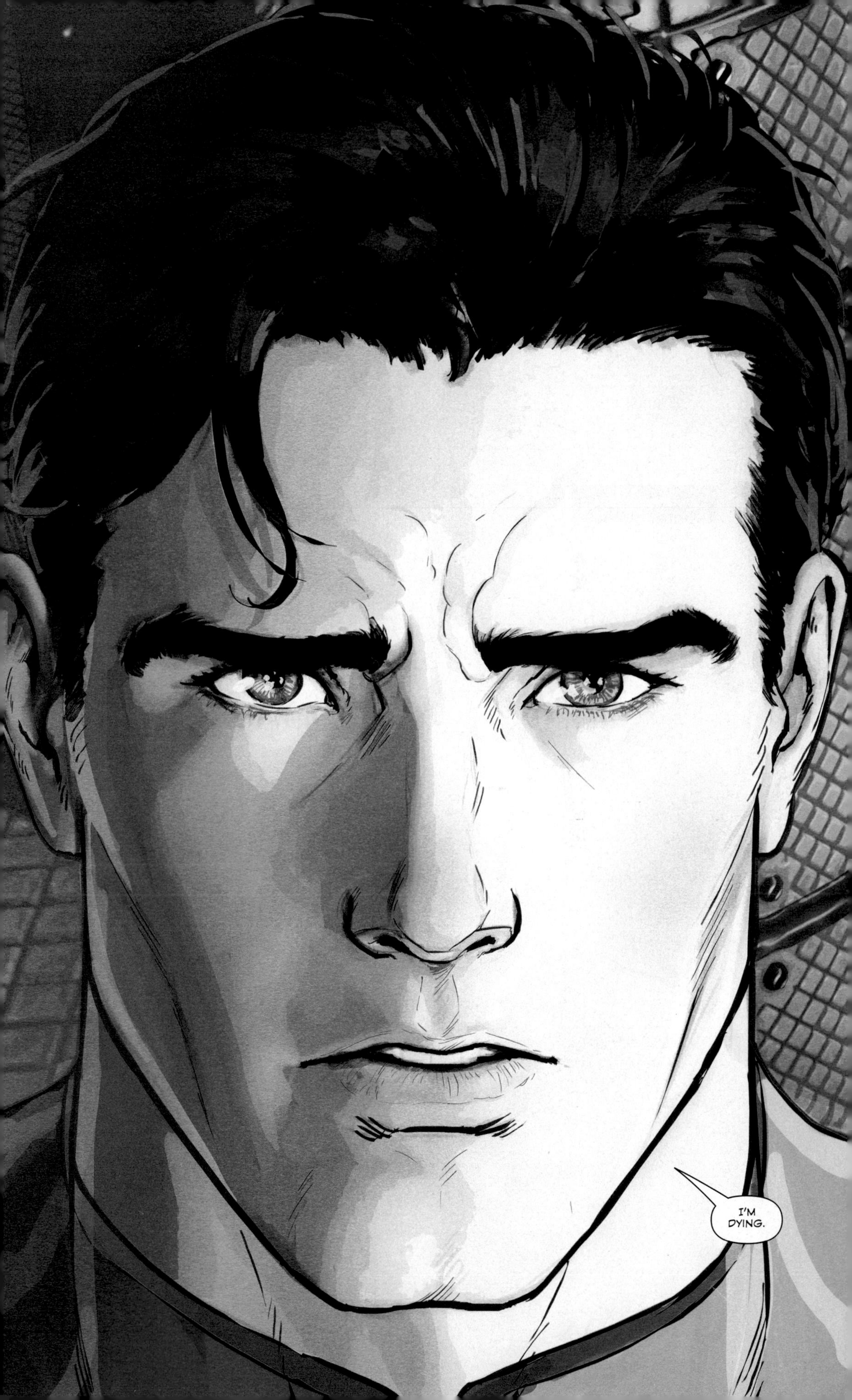
I'M DYING.

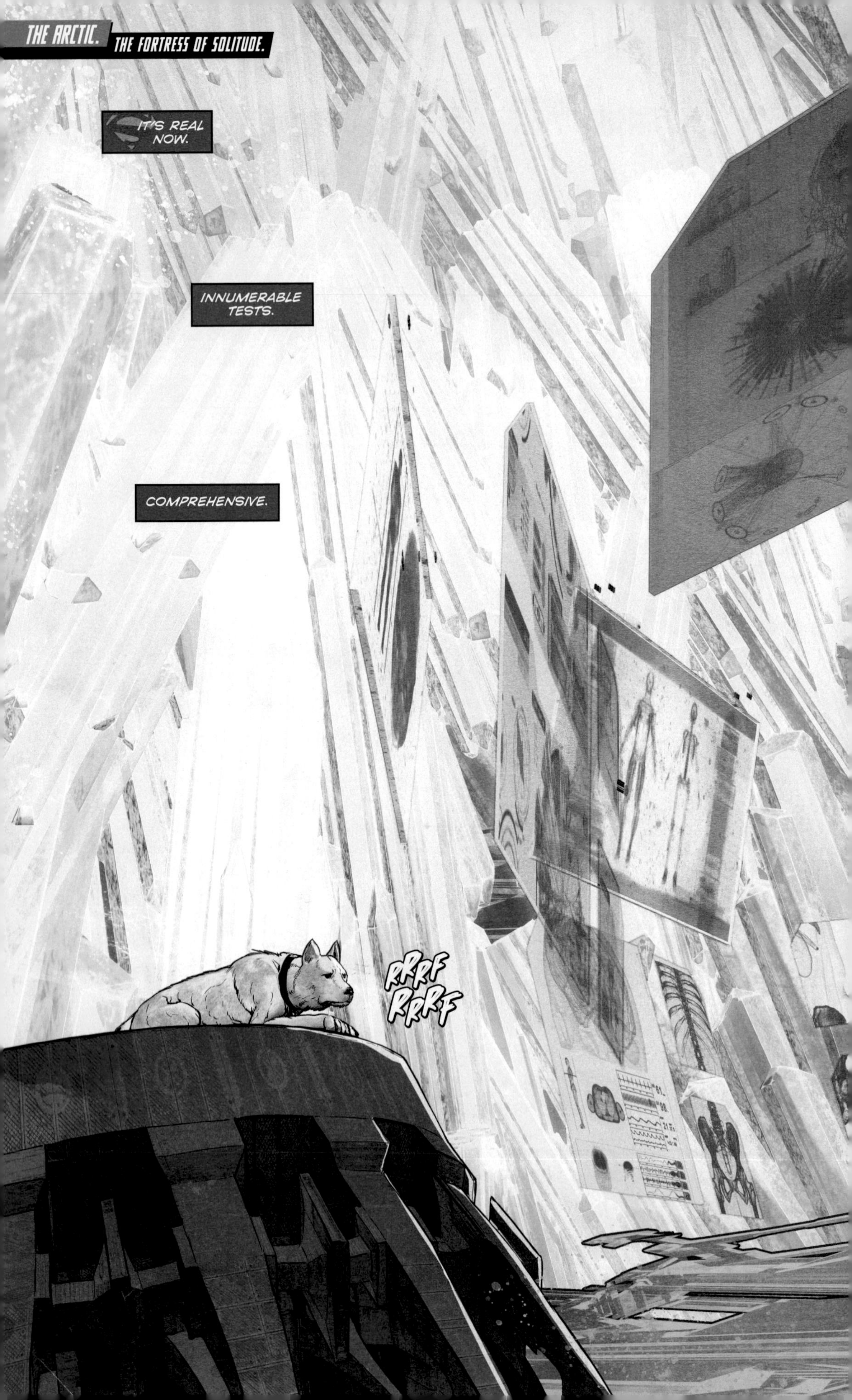
THE ARCTIC.
THE FORTRESS OF SOLITUDE.
IT'S REAL NOW.
INNUMERABLE TESTS.
COMPREHENSIVE.
RRRF RRRF

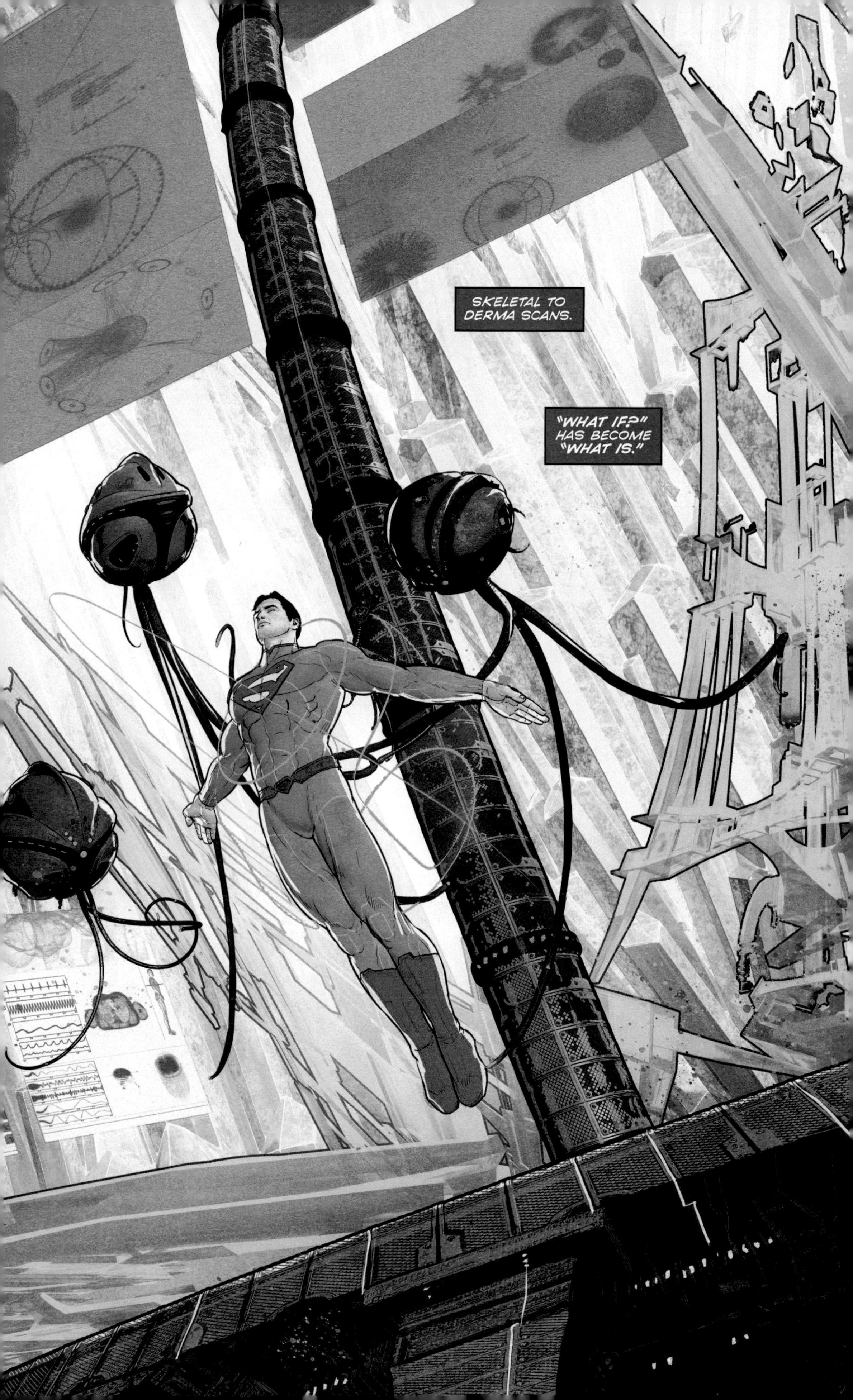
SKELETAL TO DERMA SCANS.
"WHAT IF?" HAS BECOME "WHAT IS."

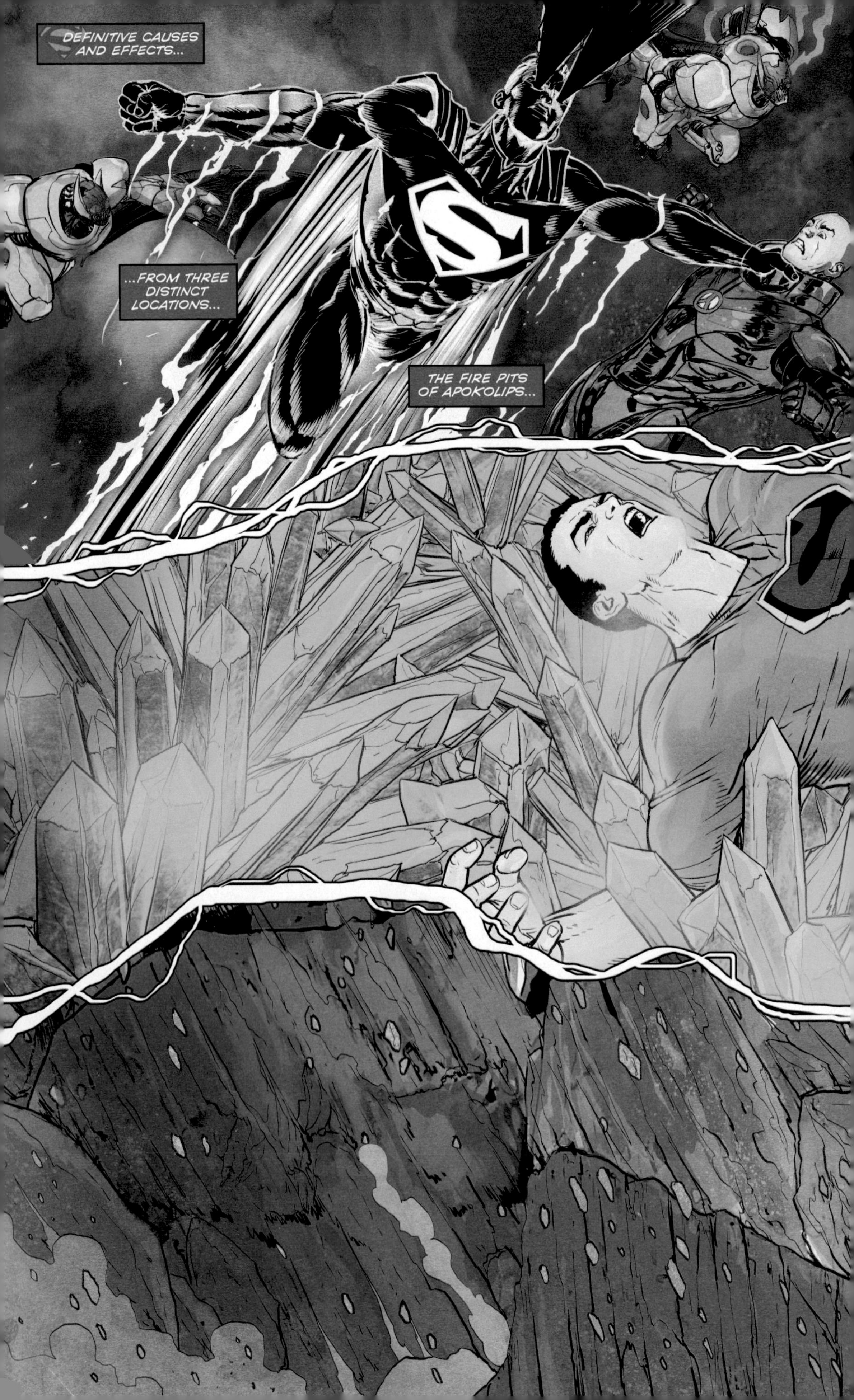
DEFINITIVE CAUSES AND EFFECTS...
...FROM THREE DISTINCT LOCATIONS...
THE FIRE PITS OF APOKOLIPS...

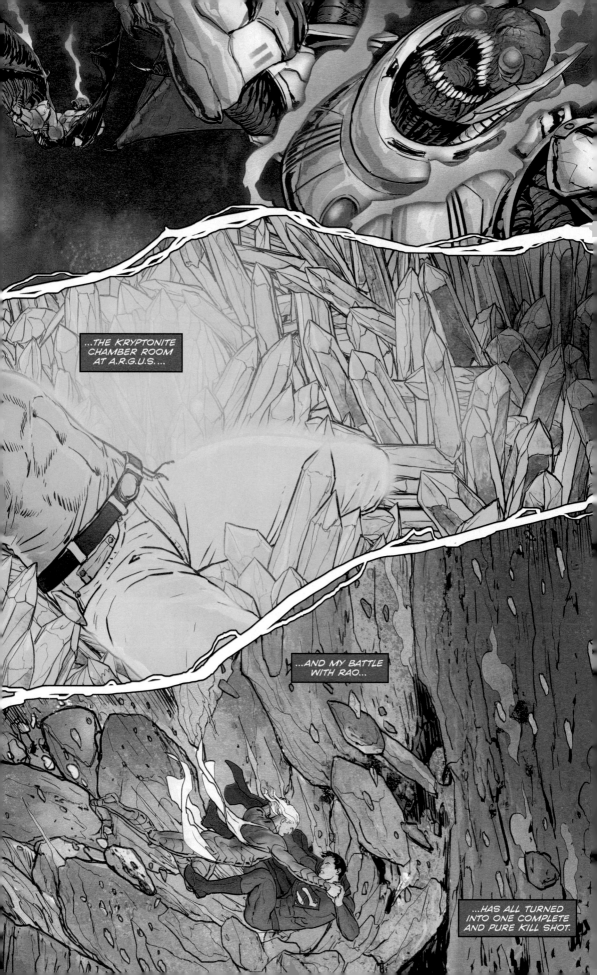

...THE KRYPTONITE CHAMBER ROOM AT A.R.G.U.S....

...AND MY BATTLE WITH RAO...

...HAS ALL TURNED INTO ONE COMPLETE AND PURE KILL SHOT.

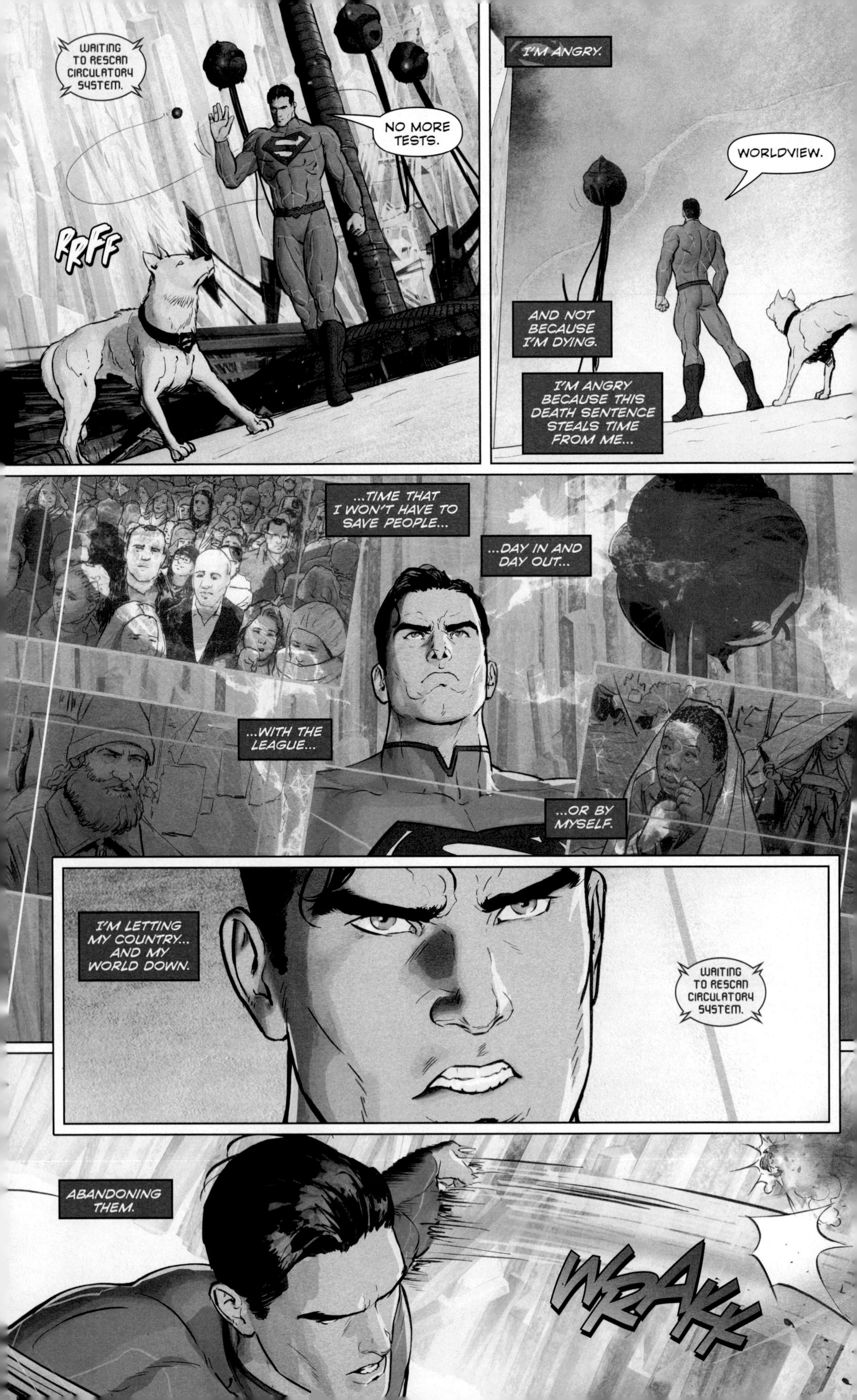
WAITING TO RESCAN CIRCULATORY SYSTEM.
NO MORE TESTS.
RRFF
I'M ANGRY.
WORLDVIEW.
AND NOT BECAUSE I'M DYING.
I'M ANGRY BECAUSE THIS DEATH SENTENCE STEALS TIME FROM ME...
...TIME THAT I WON'T HAVE TO SAVE PEOPLE...
...DAY IN AND DAY OUT...
...WITH THE LEAGUE...
...OR BY MYSELF.
I'M LETTING MY COUNTRY... AND MY WORLD DOWN.
WAITING TO RESCAN CIRCULATORY SYSTEM.
ABANDONING THEM.
WRAKK

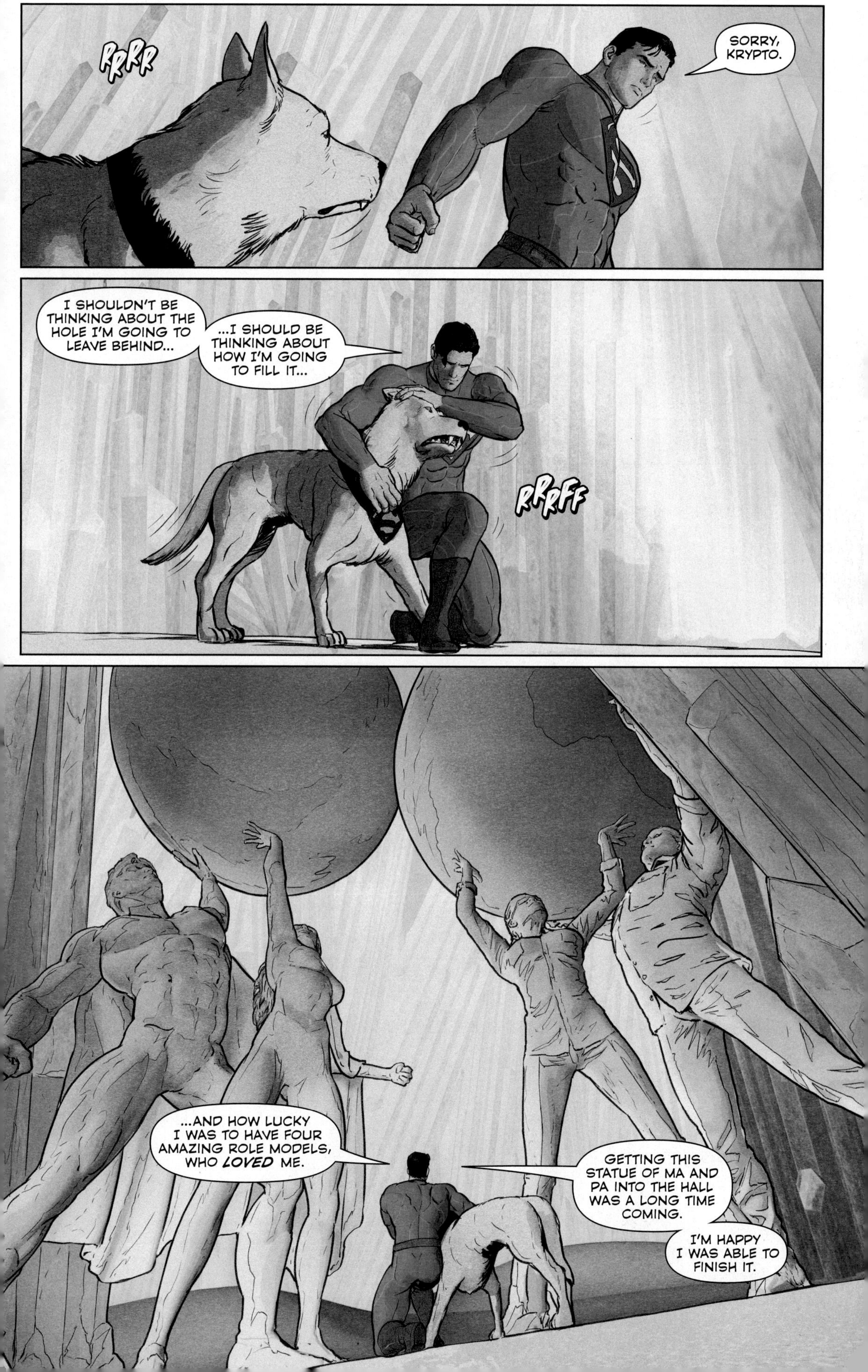
RRRR
SORRY, KRYPTO.
I SHOULDN'T BE THINKING ABOUT THE HOLE I'M GOING TO LEAVE BEHIND...
...I SHOULD BE THINKING ABOUT HOW I'M GOING TO FILL IT...
RRRFF
...AND HOW LUCKY I WAS TO HAVE FOUR AMAZING ROLE MODELS, WHO *LOVED* ME.
GETTING THIS STATUE OF MA AND PA INTO THE HALL WAS A LONG TIME COMING.
I'M HAPPY I WAS ABLE TO FINISH IT.

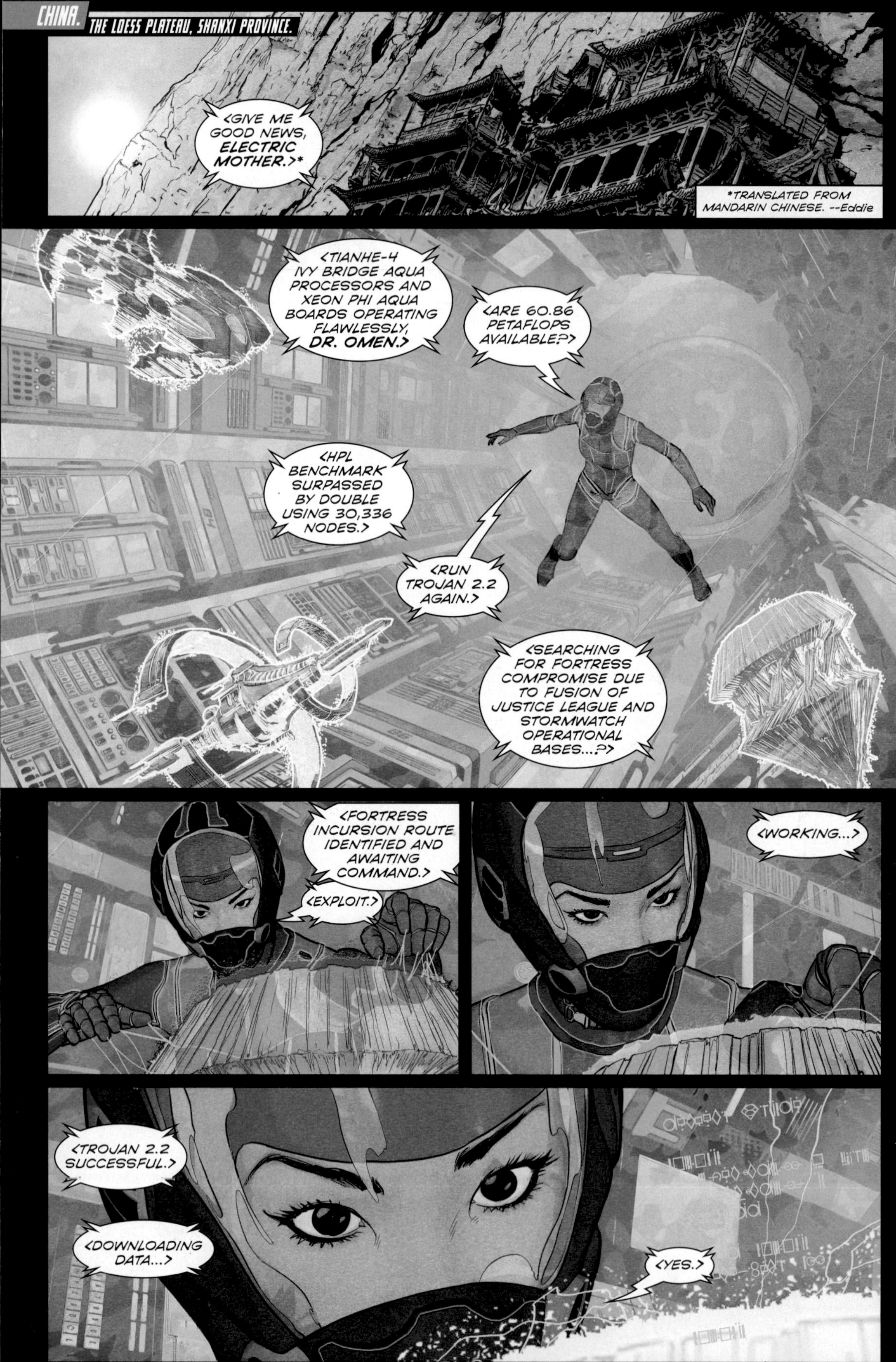
CHINA.
THE LOESS PLATEAU, SHANXI PROVINCE.
<GIVE ME GOOD NEWS, ELECTRIC MOTHER.>*
*TRANSLATED FROM MANDARIN CHINESE. --Eddie
<TIANHE-4 IVY BRIDGE AQUA PROCESSORS AND XEON PHI AQUA BOARDS OPERATING FLAWLESSLY, DR. OMEN.>
<ARE 60.86 PETAFLOPS AVAILABLE?>
<HPL BENCHMARK SURPASSED BY DOUBLE USING 30,336 NODES.>
<RUN TROJAN 2.2 AGAIN.>
<SEARCHING FOR FORTRESS COMPROMISE DUE TO FUSION OF JUSTICE LEAGUE AND STORMWATCH OPERATIONAL BASES...?>
<FORTRESS INCURSION ROUTE IDENTIFIED AND AWAITING COMMAND.>
<EXPLOIT.>
<WORKING...>
<TROJAN 2.2 SUCCESSFUL.>
<DOWNLOADING DATA...>
<YES.>

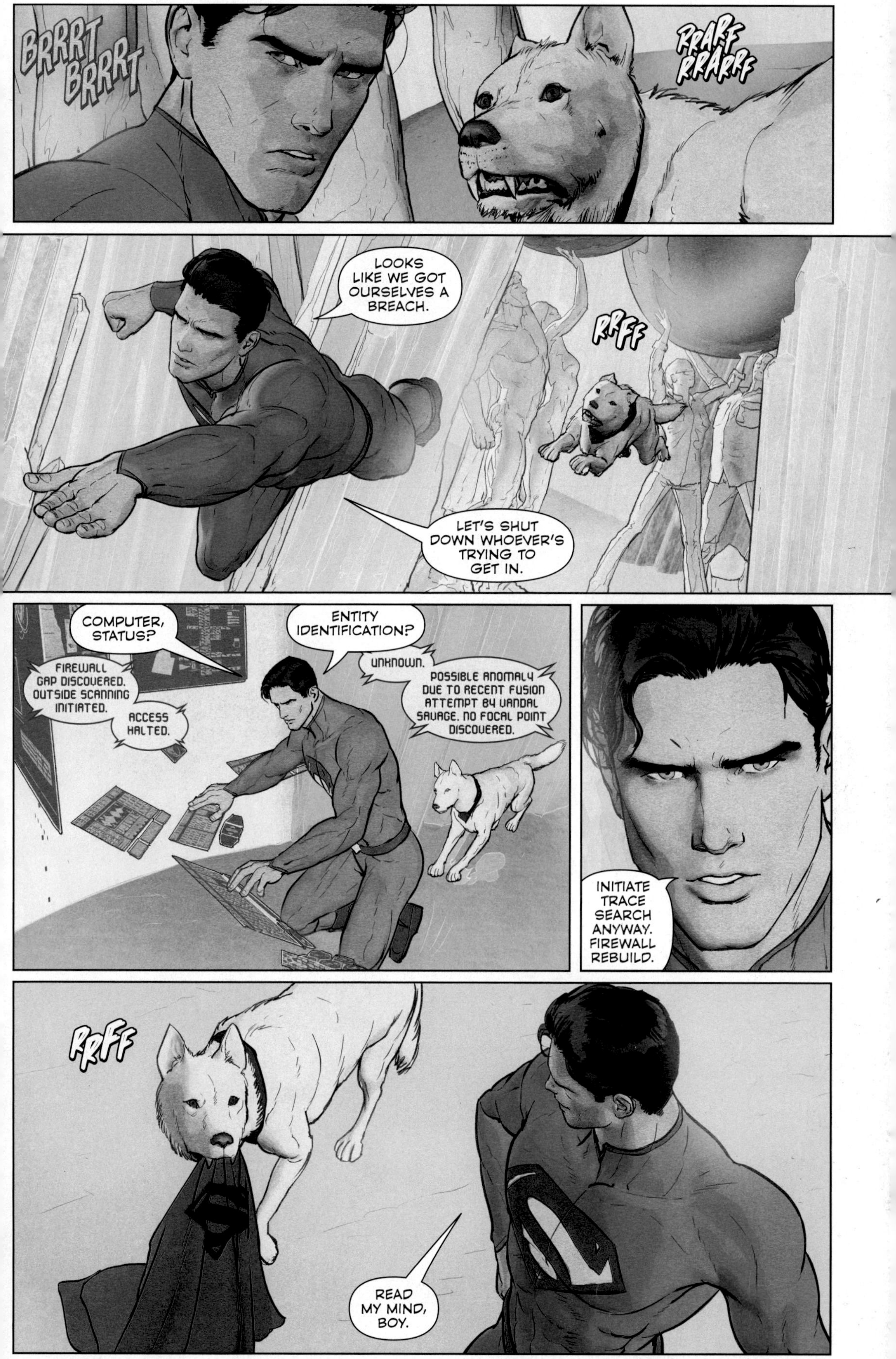
BRRRT BRRRT
RRARF RRARF
LOOKS LIKE WE GOT OURSELVES A BREACH.
RRFF
LET'S SHUT DOWN WHOEVER'S TRYING TO GET IN.
COMPUTER, STATUS?
FIREWALL GAP DISCOVERED. OUTSIDE SCANNING INITIATED.
ACCESS HALTED.
ENTITY IDENTIFICATION?
UNKNOWN.
POSSIBLE ANOMALY DUE TO RECENT FUSION ATTEMPT BY VANDAL SAVAGE. NO FOCAL POINT DISCOVERED.
INITIATE TRACE SEARCH ANYWAY. FIREWALL REBUILD.
RRFF
READ MY MIND, BOY.

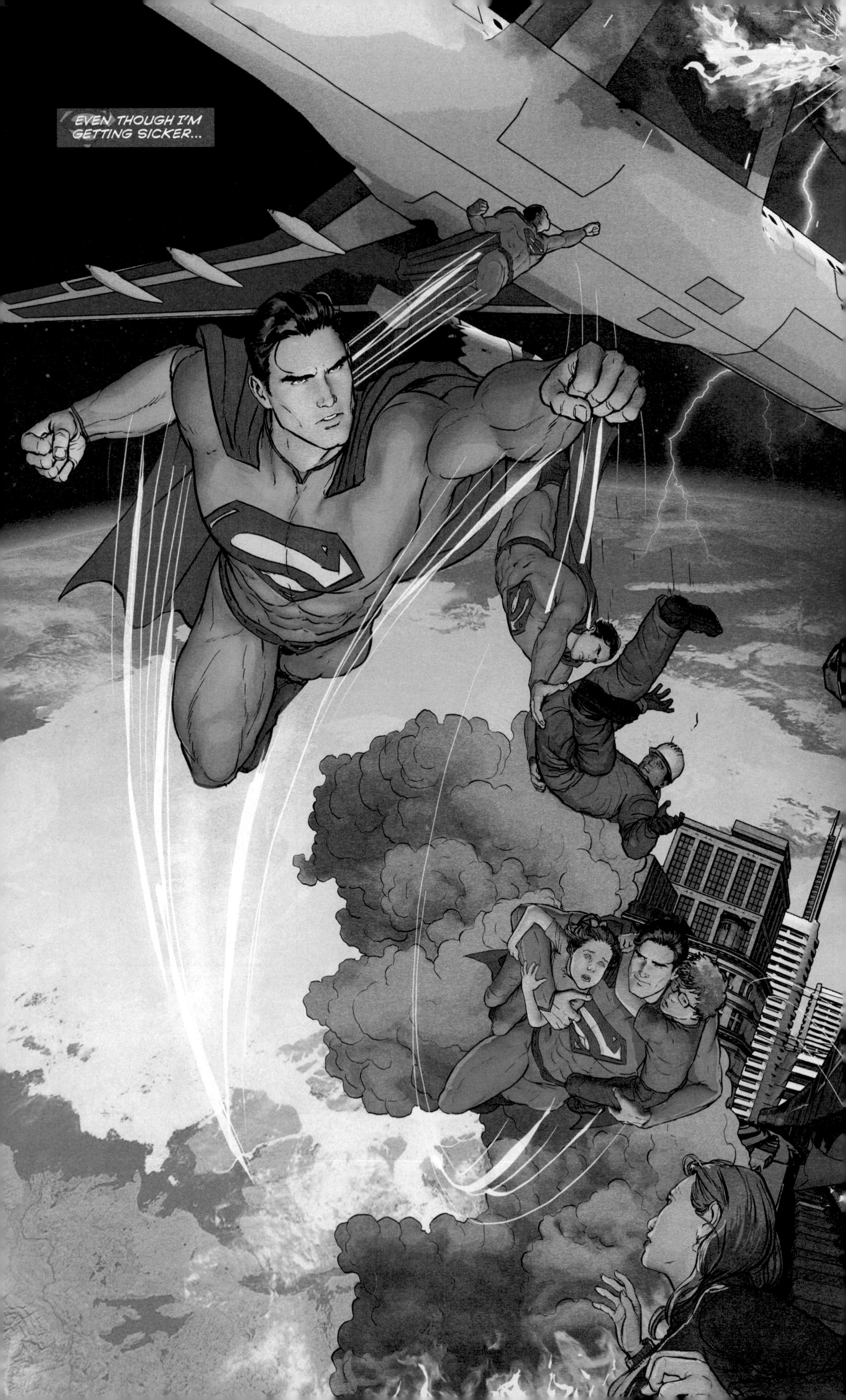
EVEN THOUGH I'M GETTING SICKER...

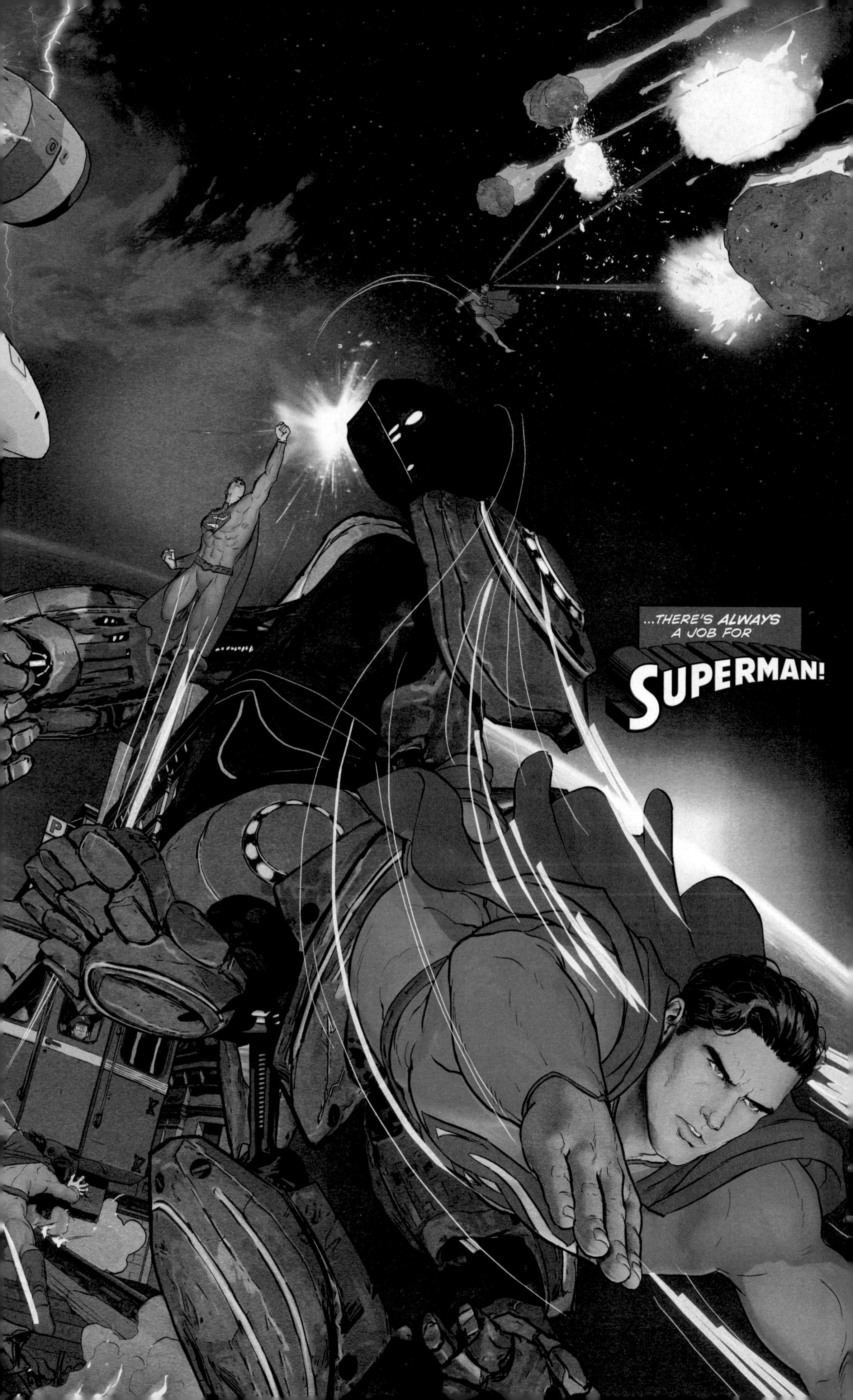
...THERE'S ALWAYS A JOB FOR
SUPERMAN!

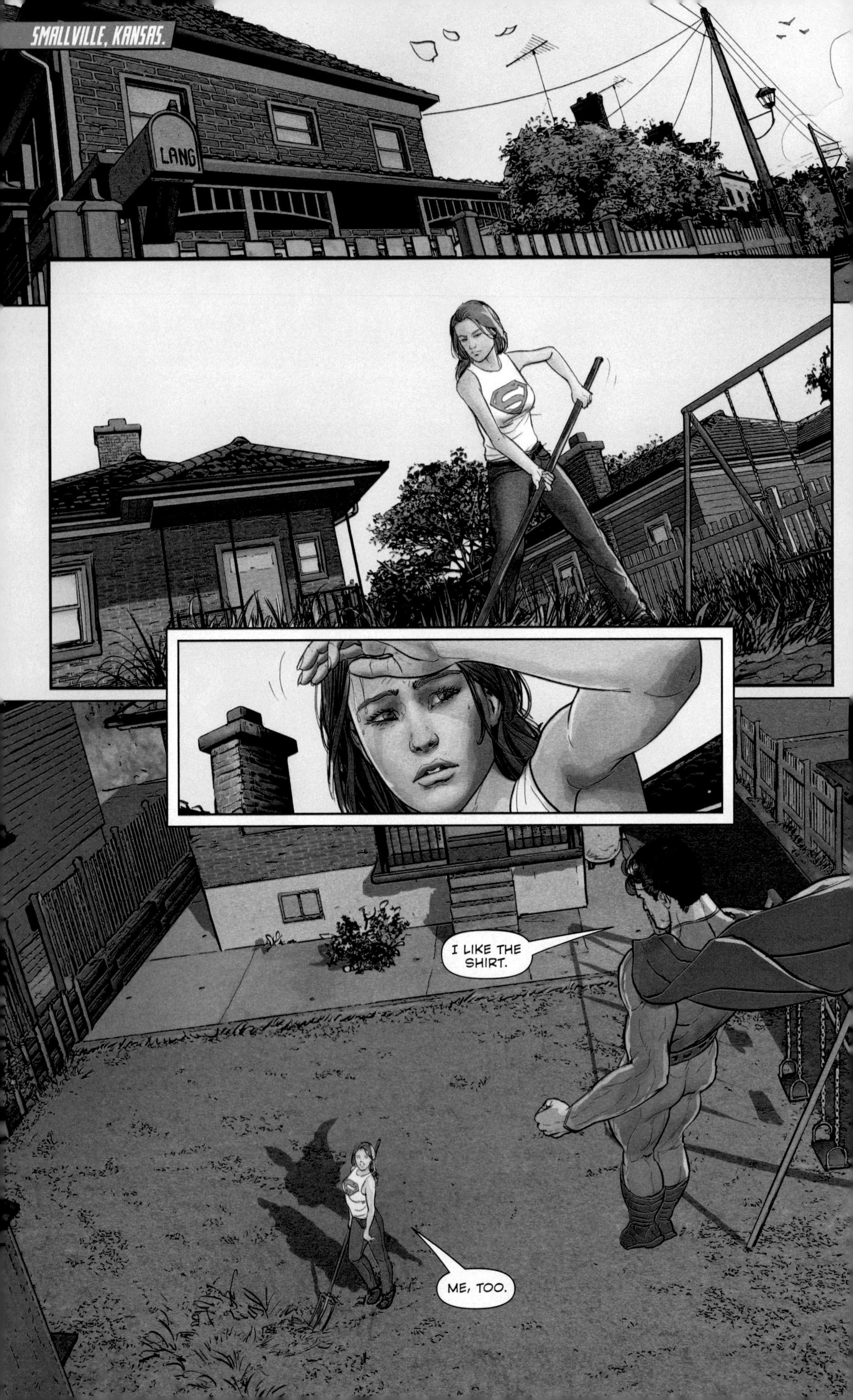
SMALLVILLE, KANSAS.
LANG
I LIKE THE SHIRT.
ME, TOO.

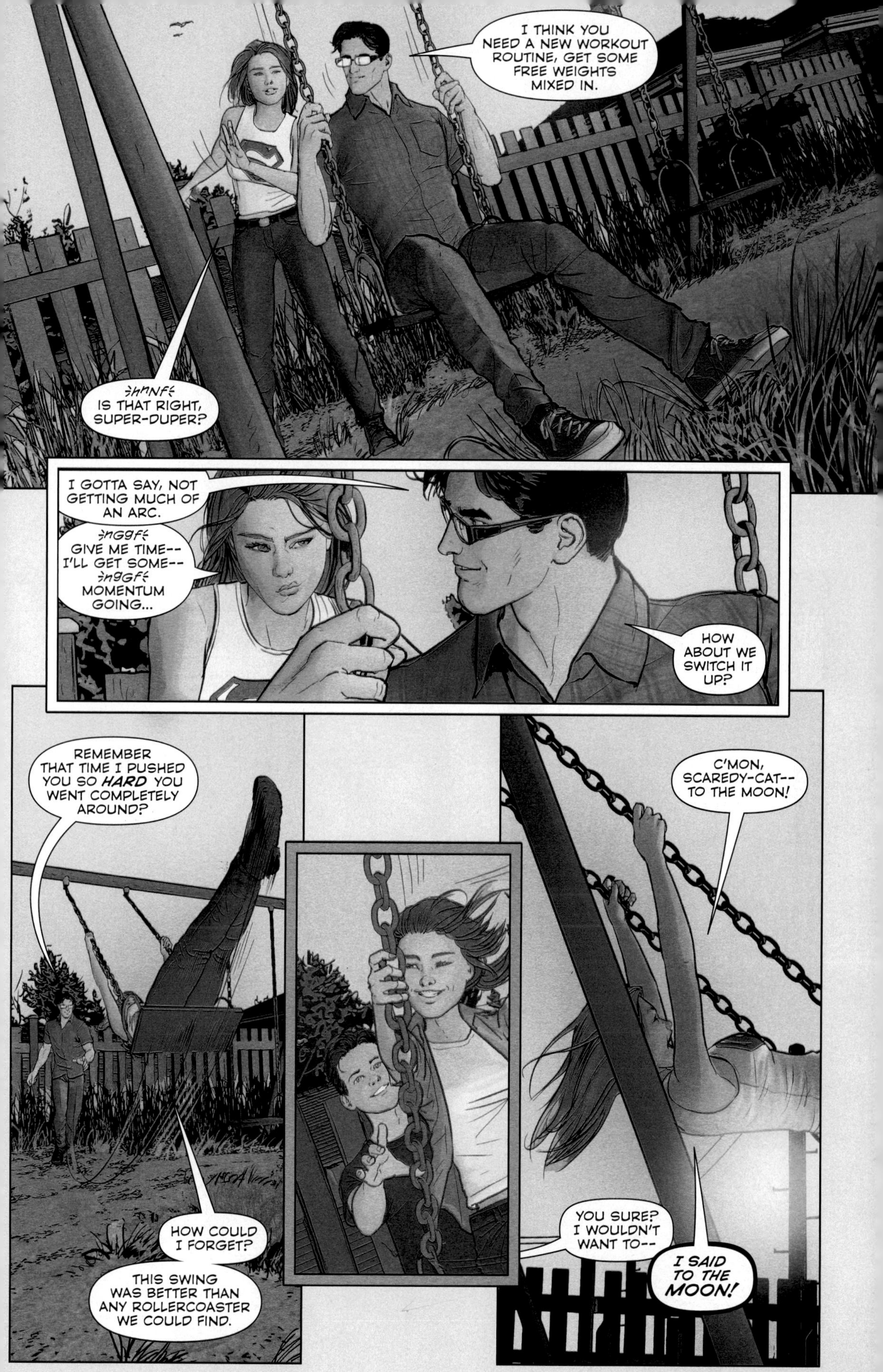
I THINK YOU NEED A NEW WORKOUT ROUTINE, GET SOME FREE WEIGHTS MIXED IN.
HNNF IS THAT RIGHT, SUPER-DUPER?
I GOTTA SAY, NOT GETTING MUCH OF AN ARC.
NGGF GIVE ME TIME-- I'LL GET SOME-- *NGGF* MOMENTUM GOING...
HOW ABOUT WE SWITCH IT UP?
REMEMBER THAT TIME I PUSHED YOU SO HARD YOU WENT COMPLETELY AROUND?
HOW COULD I FORGET?
THIS SWING WAS BETTER THAN ANY ROLLERCOASTER WE COULD FIND.
C'MON, SCAREDY-CAT-- TO THE MOON!
YOU SURE? I WOULDN'T WANT TO--
I SAID TO THE MOON!

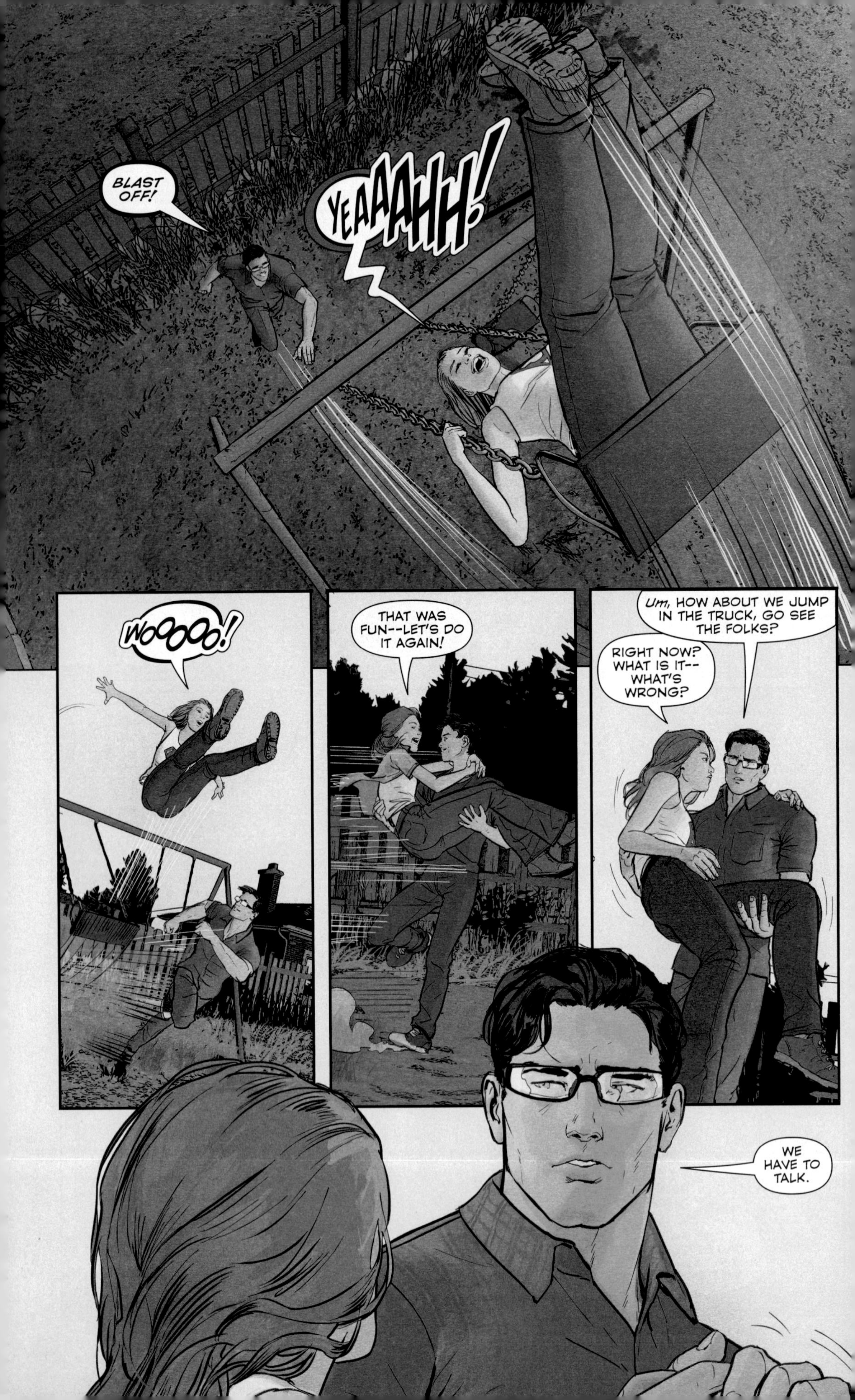
BLAST OFF!
YEAAAHH!
WOOOOO!
THAT WAS FUN--LET'S DO IT AGAIN!
Um, HOW ABOUT WE JUMP IN THE TRUCK, GO SEE THE FOLKS?
RIGHT NOW? WHAT IS IT-- WHAT'S WRONG?
WE HAVE TO TALK.

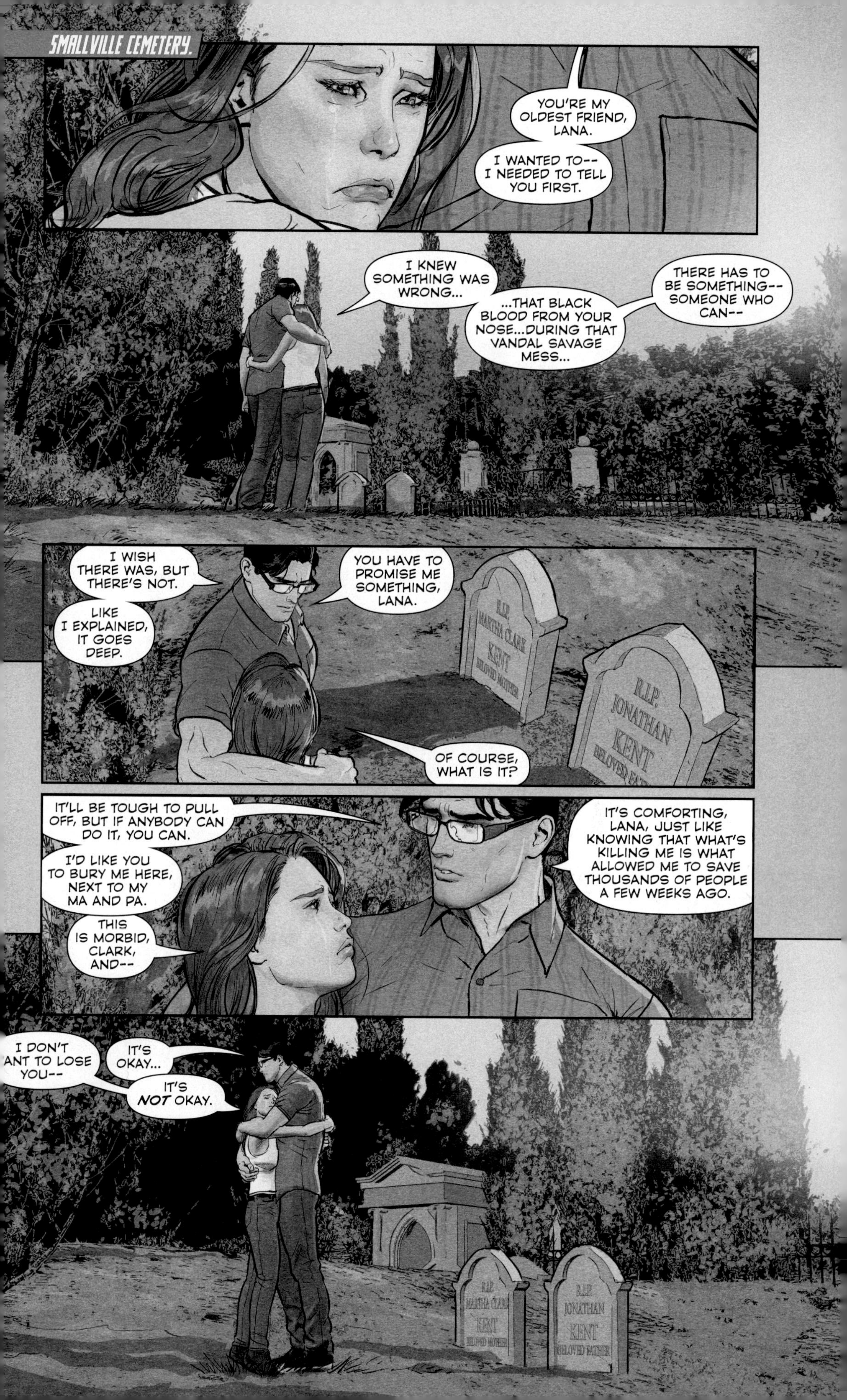
SMALLVILLE CEMETERY.
YOU'RE MY OLDEST FRIEND, LANA.
I WANTED TO-- I NEEDED TO TELL YOU FIRST.
I KNEW SOMETHING WAS WRONG...
...THAT BLACK BLOOD FROM YOUR NOSE...DURING THAT VANDAL SAVAGE MESS...
THERE HAS TO BE SOMETHING-- SOMEONE WHO CAN--
I WISH THERE WAS, BUT THERE'S NOT.
LIKE I EXPLAINED, IT GOES DEEP.
YOU HAVE TO PROMISE ME SOMETHING, LANA.
R.I.P. MARTHA CLARK KENT BELOVED MOTHER
R.I.P. JONATHAN KENT
OF COURSE, WHAT IS IT?
I'D LIKE YOU TO BURY ME HERE, NEXT TO MY MA AND PA.
THIS IS MORBID, CLARK, AND--
IT'S COMFORTING, LANA, JUST LIKE KNOWING THAT WHAT'S KILLING ME IS WHAT ALLOWED ME TO SAVE THOUSANDS OF PEOPLE A FEW WEEKS AGO.
IT'LL BE TOUGH TO PULL OFF, BUT IF ANYBODY CAN DO IT, YOU CAN.
I DON'T ANT TO LOSE YOU--
IT'S OKAY...
IT'S *NOT* OKAY.

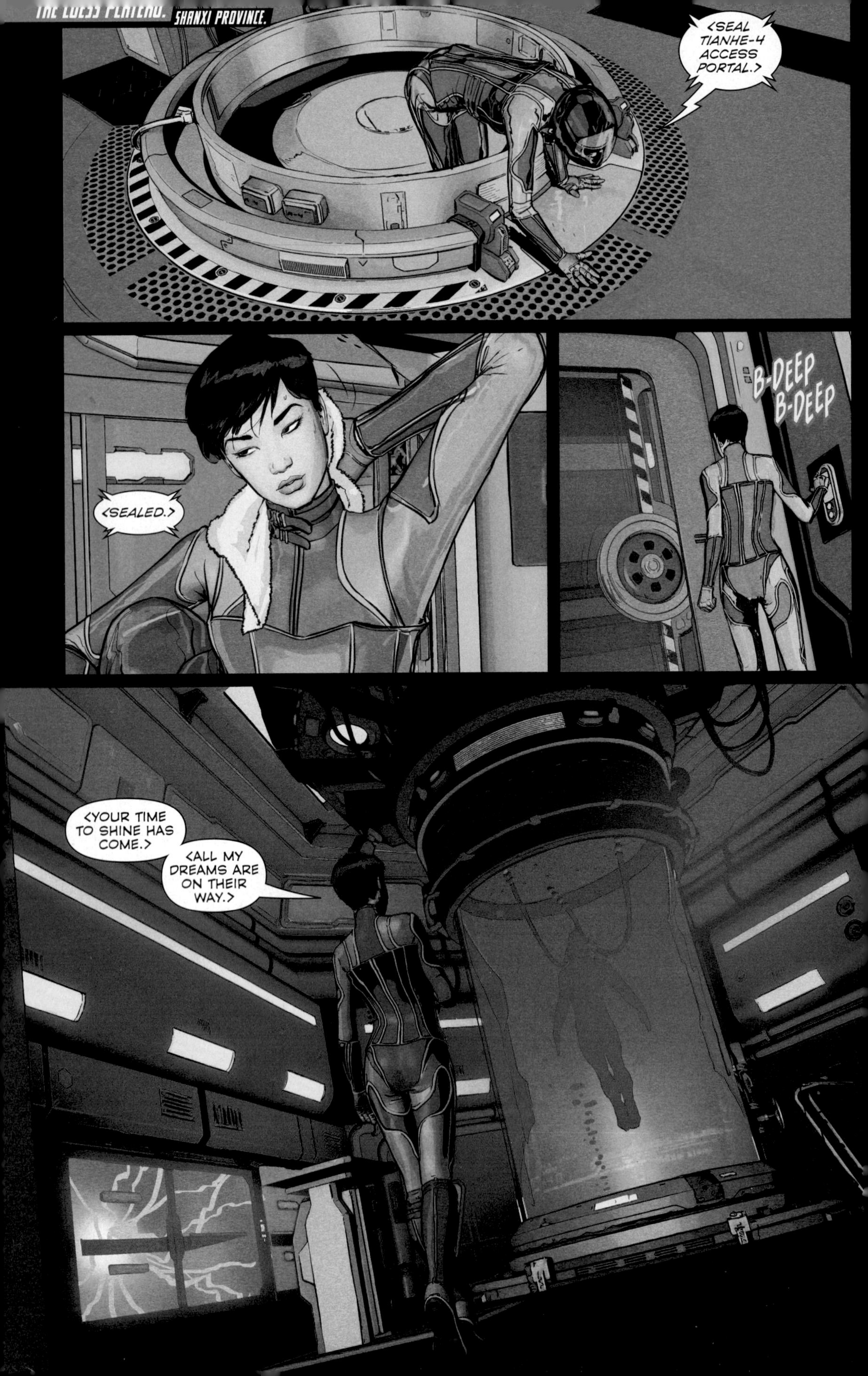
SHANXI PROVINCE.
<SEAL TIANHE-4 ACCESS PORTAL.>
<SEALED.>
B-DEEP B-DEEP
<YOUR TIME TO SHINE HAS COME.>
<ALL MY DREAMS ARE ON THEIR WAY.>

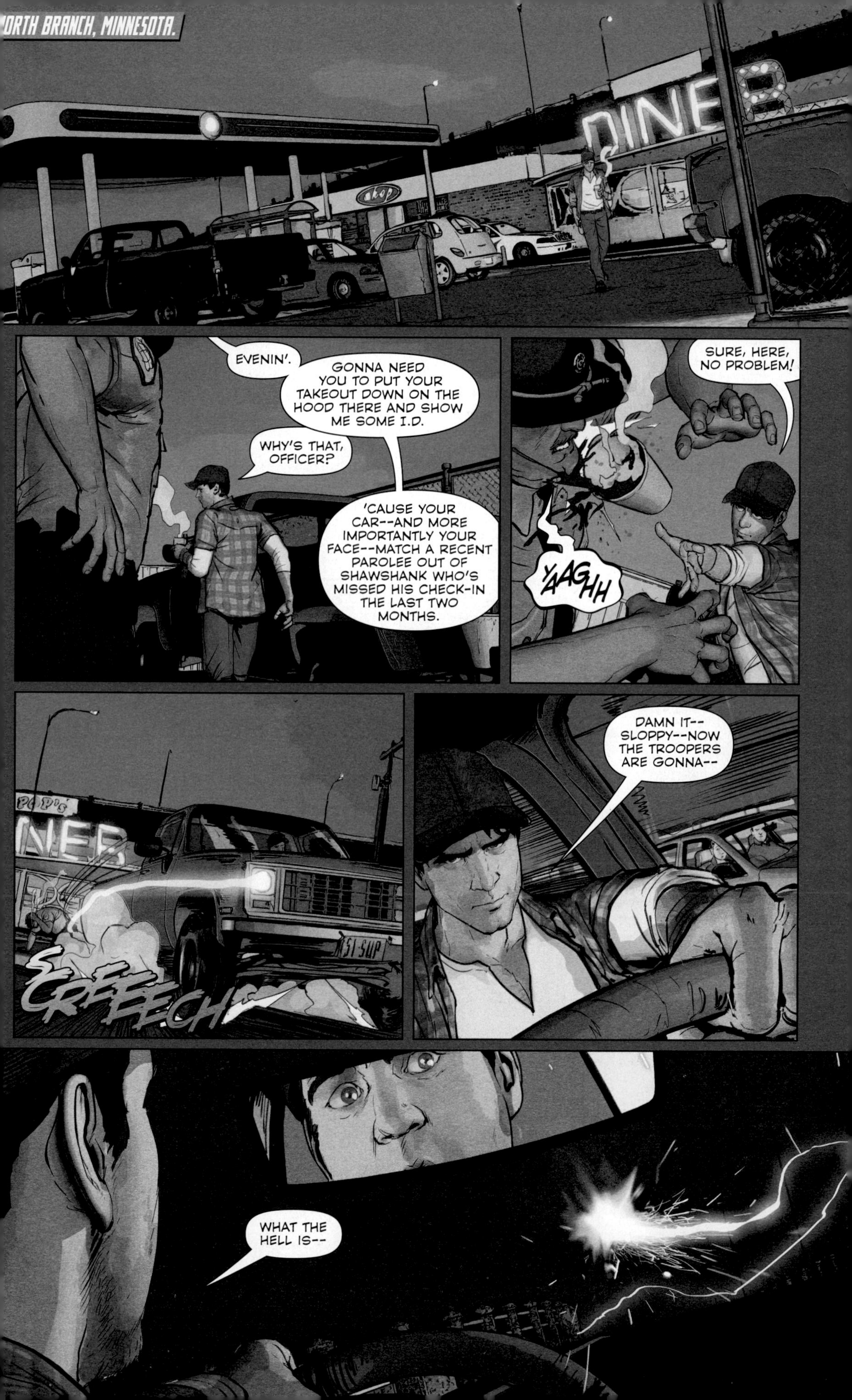

ORTH BRANCH, MINNESOTA.
EVENIN'.
GONNA NEED YOU TO PUT YOUR TAKEOUT DOWN ON THE HOOD THERE AND SHOW ME SOME I.D.
WHY'S THAT, OFFICER?
'CAUSE YOUR CAR--AND MORE IMPORTANTLY YOUR FACE--MATCH A RECENT PAROLEE OUT OF SHAWSHANK WHO'S MISSED HIS CHECK-IN THE LAST TWO MONTHS.
SURE, HERE, NO PROBLEM!
YAAGHH
EEEECH
DAMN IT--SLOPPY--NOW THE TROOPERS ARE GONNA--
WHAT THE HELL IS--

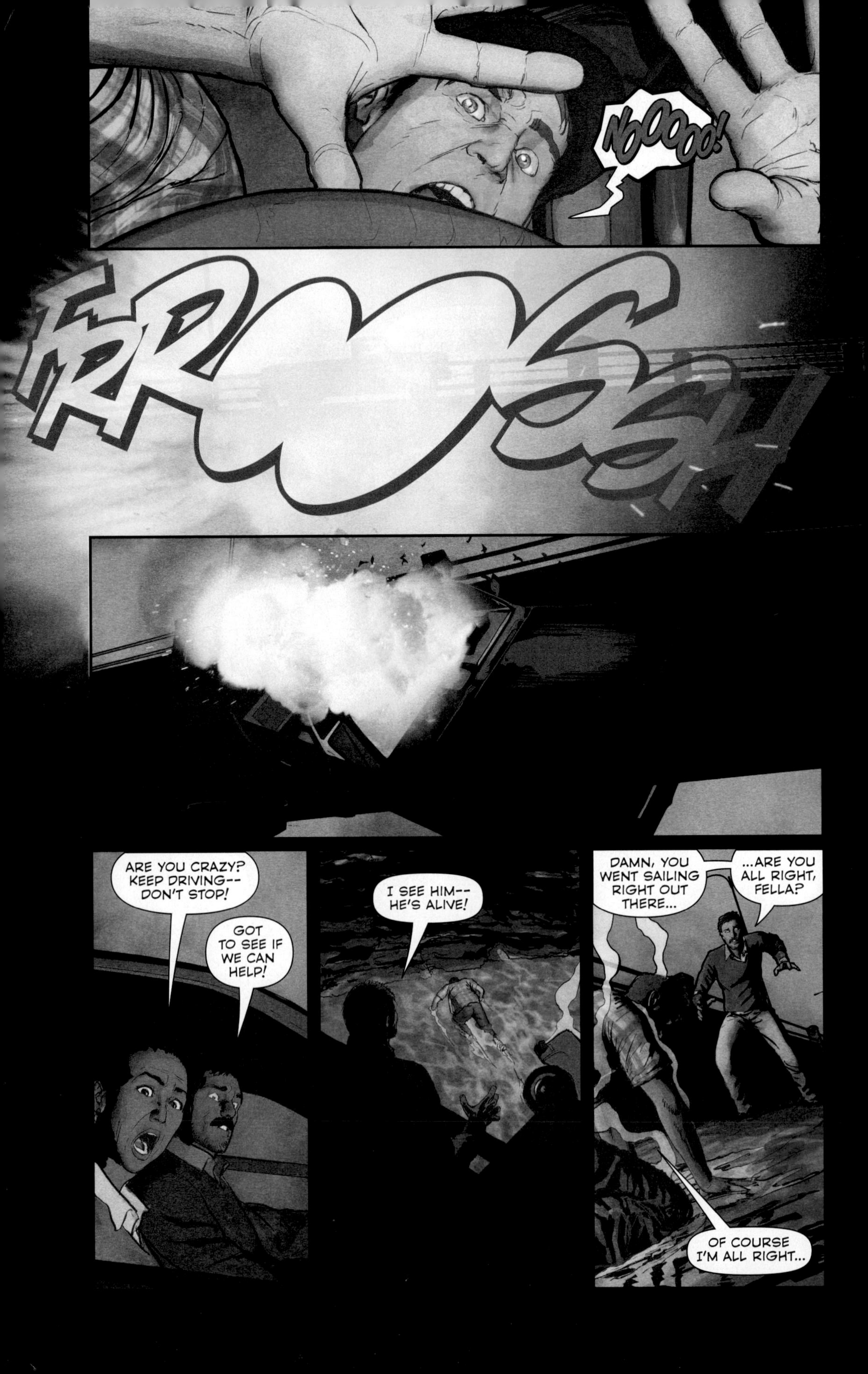
NOOOOO!
FROOSH
ARE YOU CRAZY? KEEP DRIVING--DON'T STOP!
GOT TO SEE IF WE CAN HELP!
I SEE HIM--HE'S ALIVE!
DAMN, YOU WENT SAILING RIGHT OUT THERE...
...ARE YOU ALL RIGHT, FELLA?
OF COURSE I'M ALL RIGHT...

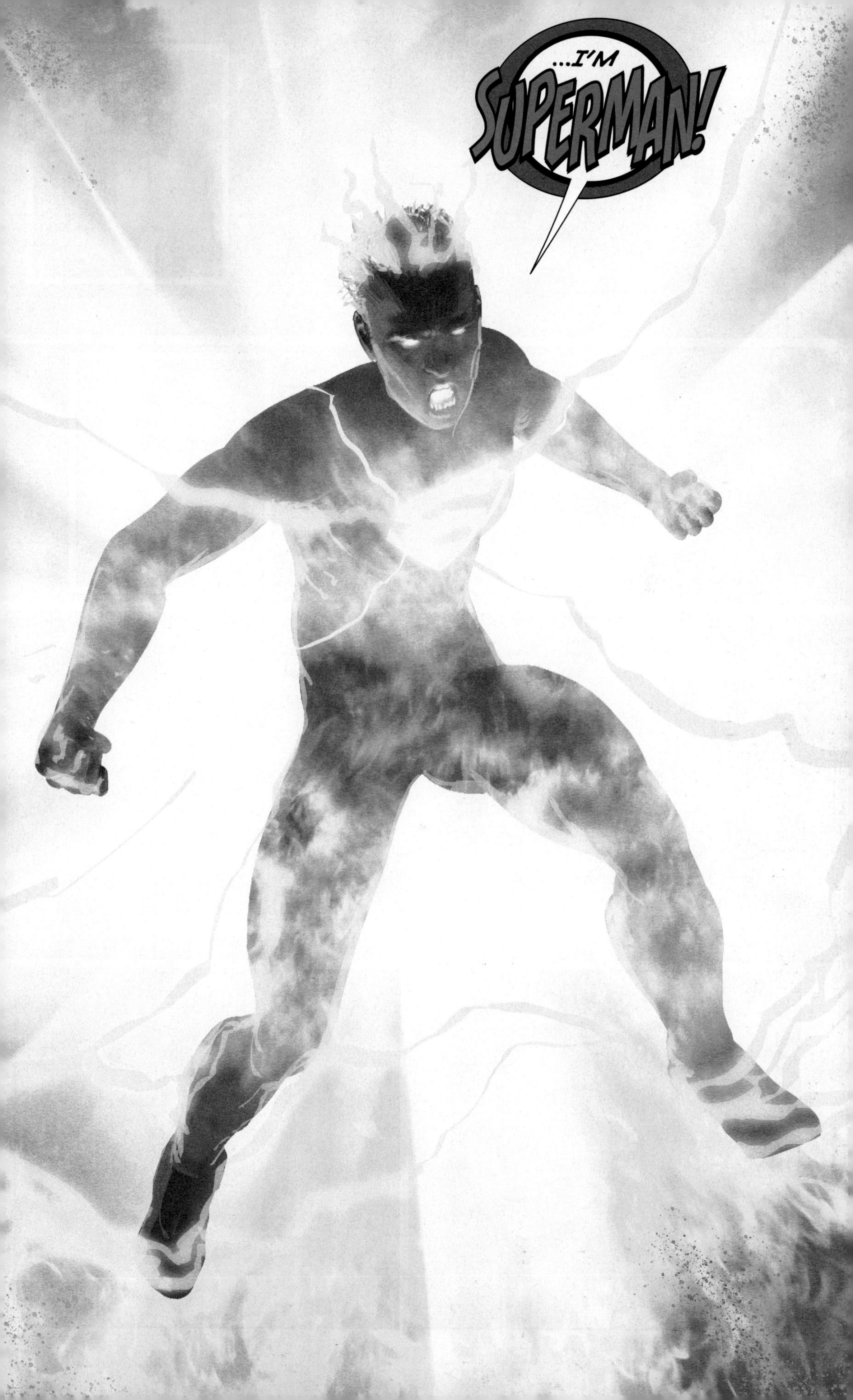
...I'M SUPERMAN!

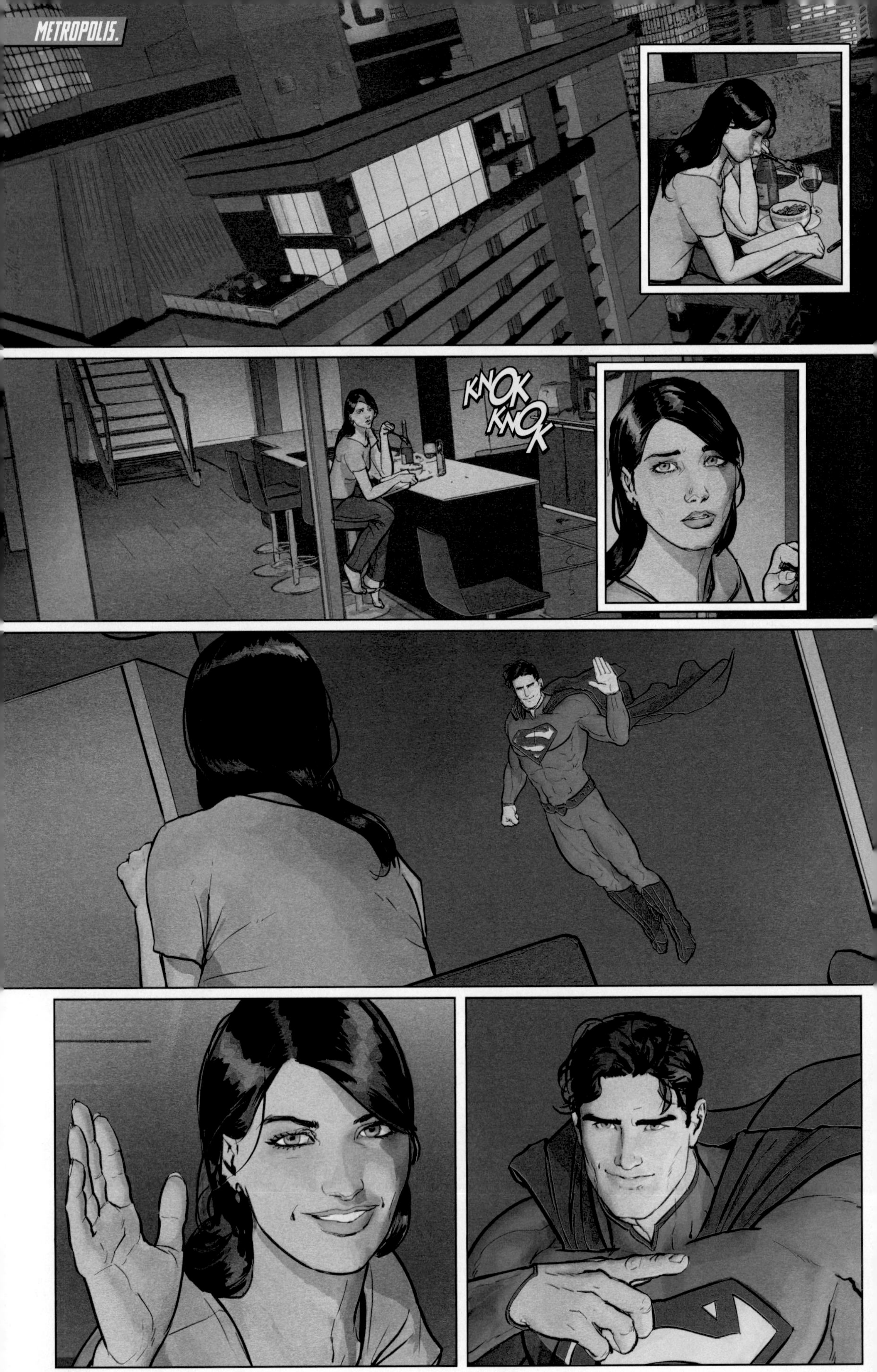
METROPOLIS.
KNOK KNOK

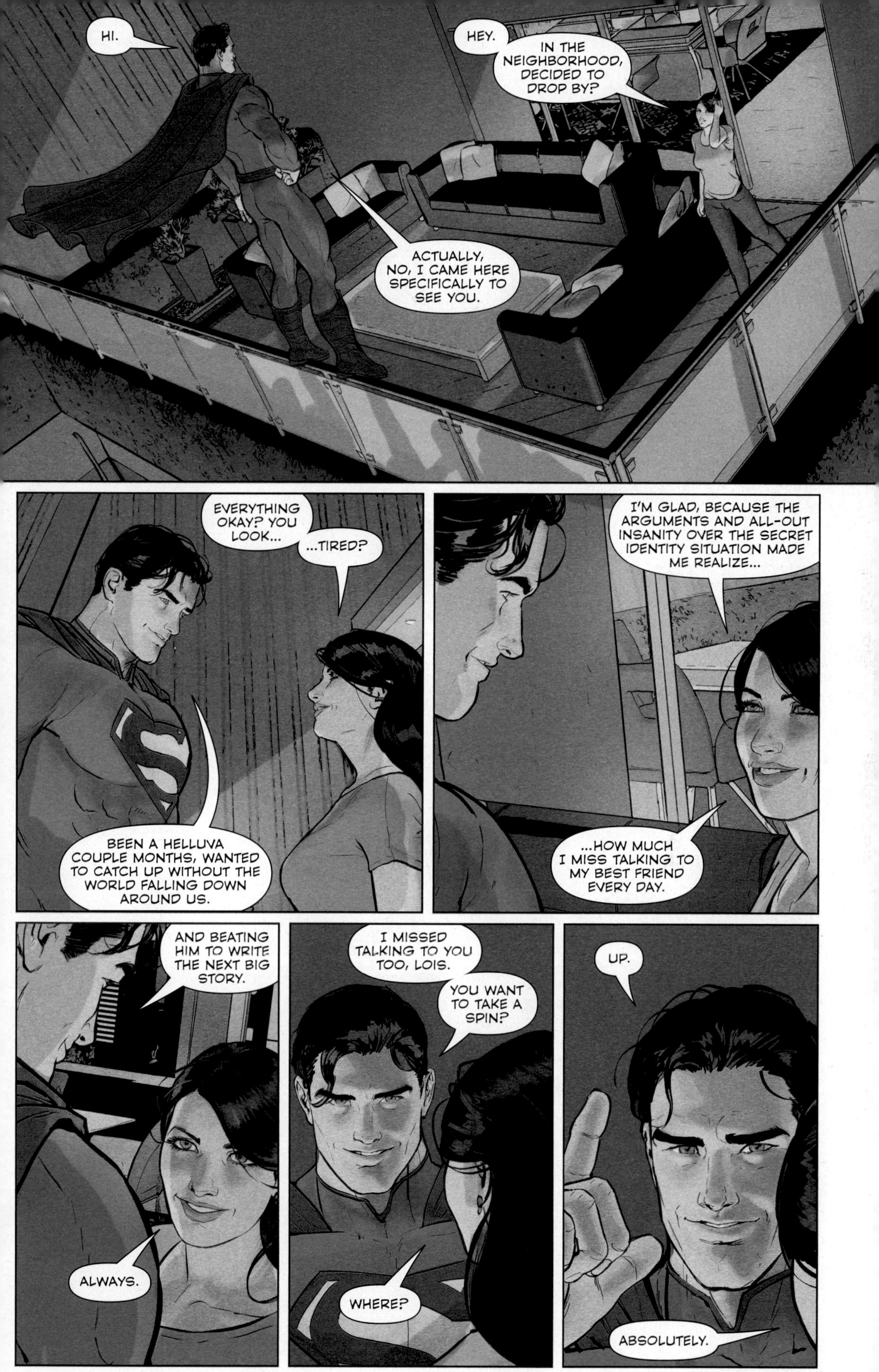
HI.
HEY.
IN THE NEIGHBORHOOD, DECIDED TO DROP BY?
ACTUALLY, NO, I CAME HERE SPECIFICALLY TO SEE YOU.
EVERYTHING OKAY? YOU LOOK...
...TIRED?
BEEN A HELLUVA COUPLE MONTHS, WANTED TO CATCH UP WITHOUT THE WORLD FALLING DOWN AROUND US.
I'M GLAD, BECAUSE THE ARGUMENTS AND ALL-OUT INSANITY OVER THE SECRET IDENTITY SITUATION MADE ME REALIZE...
...HOW MUCH I MISS TALKING TO MY BEST FRIEND EVERY DAY.
AND BEATING HIM TO WRITE THE NEXT BIG STORY.
ALWAYS.
I MISSED TALKING TO YOU TOO, LOIS.
YOU WANT TO TAKE A SPIN?
WHERE?
UP.
ABSOLUTELY.

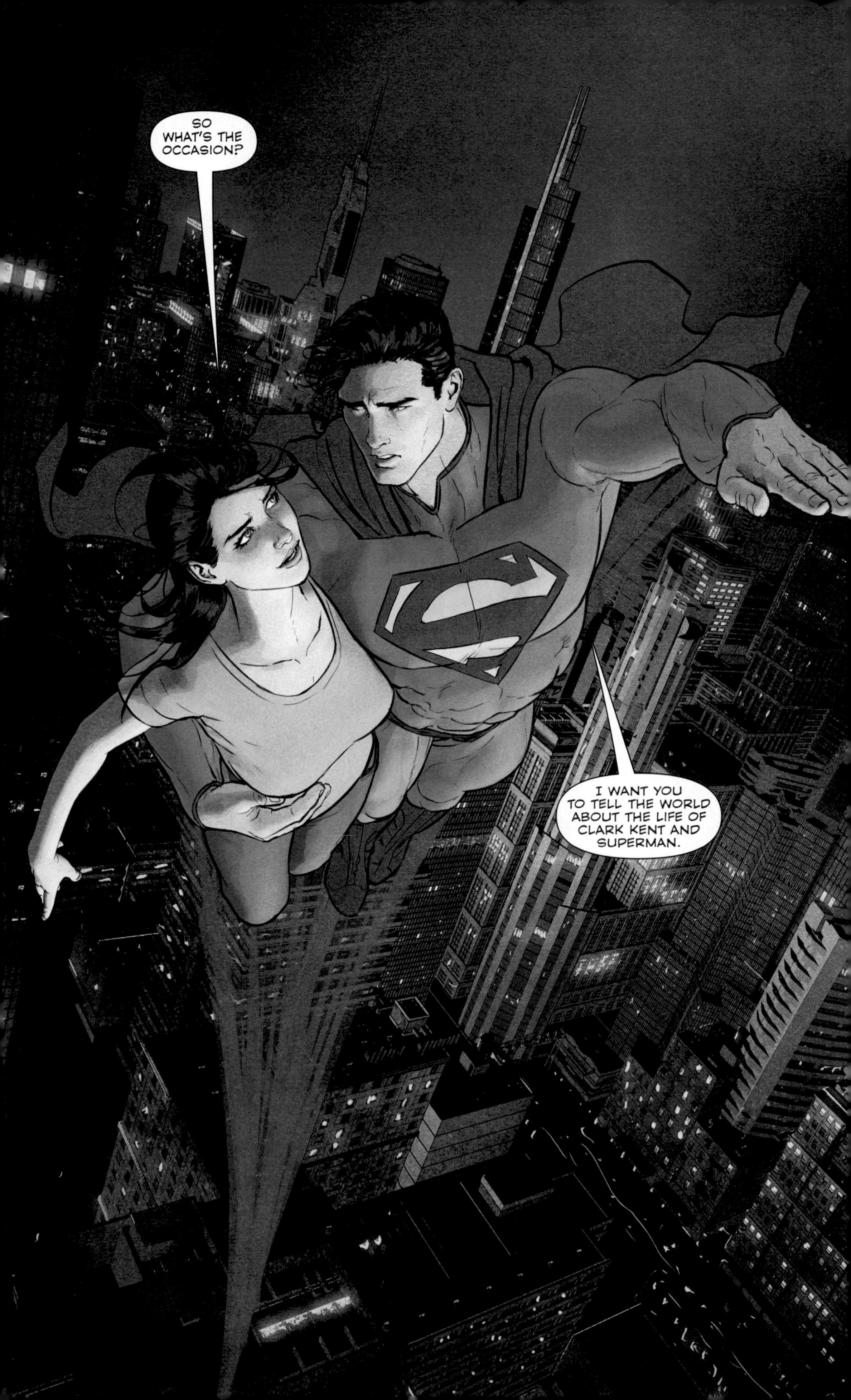
SO WHAT'S THE OCCASION?
I WANT YOU TO TELL THE WORLD ABOUT THE LIFE OF CLARK KENT AND SUPERMAN.

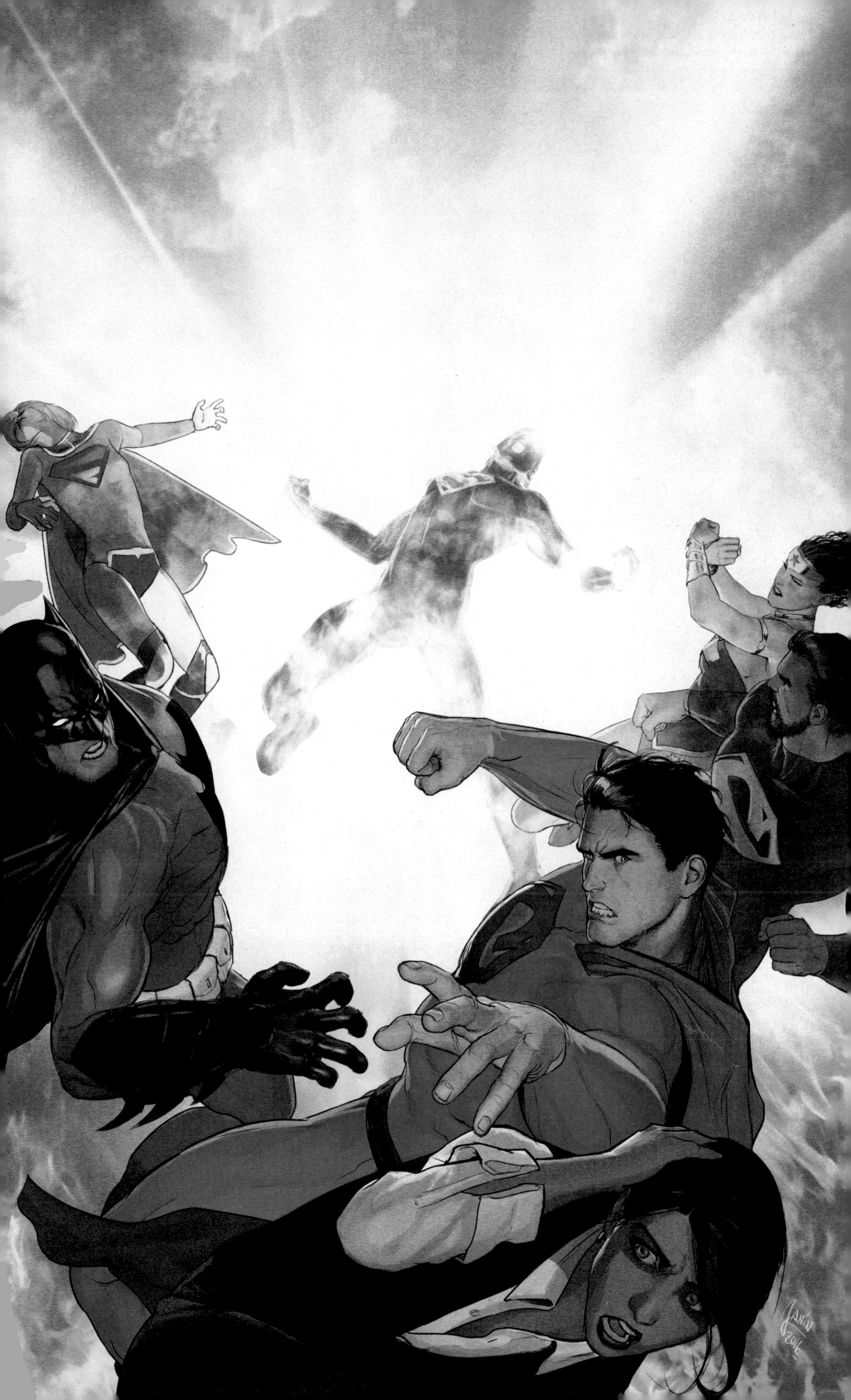
JANÍN
2016

THE FINAL DAYS OF SUPERMAN PART 8: DO OR DIE

PETER J. TOMASI writer **MIKEL JANIN, MIGUEL SEPULVEDA** artist **MIKEL JANIN, JEROMY COX** colorist **ROB LEIGH** letterer **MIKEL JANIN** cover

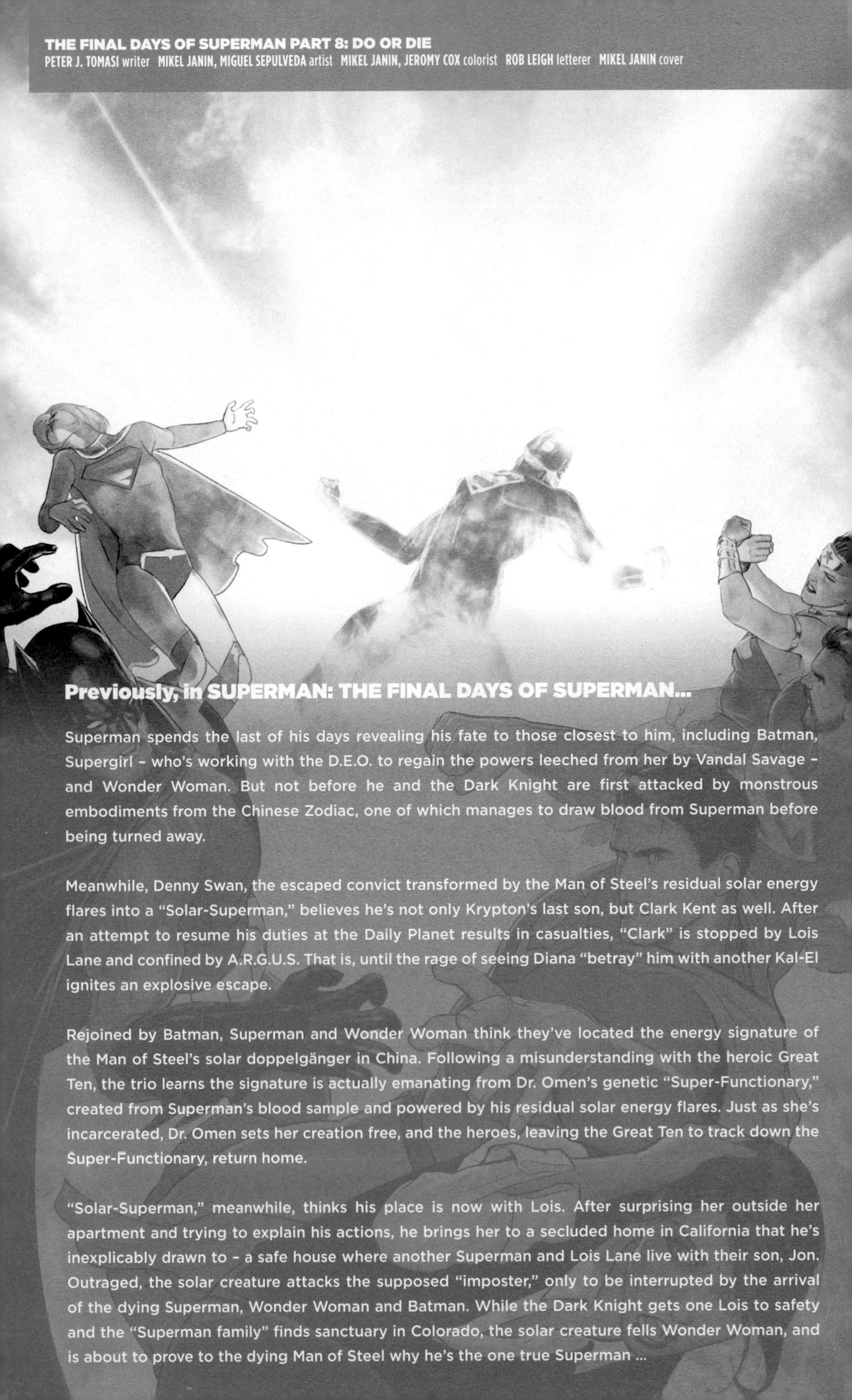

Previously, in SUPERMAN: THE FINAL DAYS OF SUPERMAN...

Superman spends the last of his days revealing his fate to those closest to him, including Batman, Supergirl – who's working with the D.E.O. to regain the powers leeched from her by Vandal Savage – and Wonder Woman. But not before he and the Dark Knight are first attacked by monstrous embodiments from the Chinese Zodiac, one of which manages to draw blood from Superman before being turned away.

Meanwhile, Denny Swan, the escaped convict transformed by the Man of Steel's residual solar energy flares into a "Solar-Superman," believes he's not only Krypton's last son, but Clark Kent as well. After an attempt to resume his duties at the Daily Planet results in casualties, "Clark" is stopped by Lois Lane and confined by A.R.G.U.S. That is, until the rage of seeing Diana "betray" him with another Kal-El ignites an explosive escape.

Rejoined by Batman, Superman and Wonder Woman think they've located the energy signature of the Man of Steel's solar doppelgänger in China. Following a misunderstanding with the heroic Great Ten, the trio learns the signature is actually emanating from Dr. Omen's genetic "Super-Functionary," created from Superman's blood sample and powered by his residual solar energy flares. Just as she's incarcerated, Dr. Omen sets her creation free, and the heroes, leaving the Great Ten to track down the Super-Functionary, return home.

"Solar-Superman," meanwhile, thinks his place is now with Lois. After surprising her outside her apartment and trying to explain his actions, he brings her to a secluded home in California that he's inexplicably drawn to – a safe house where another Superman and Lois Lane live with their son, Jon. Outraged, the solar creature attacks the supposed "imposter," only to be interrupted by the arrival of the dying Superman, Wonder Woman and Batman. While the Dark Knight gets one Lois to safety and the "Superman family" finds sanctuary in Colorado, the solar creature fells Wonder Woman, and is about to prove to the dying Man of Steel why he's the one true Superman ...

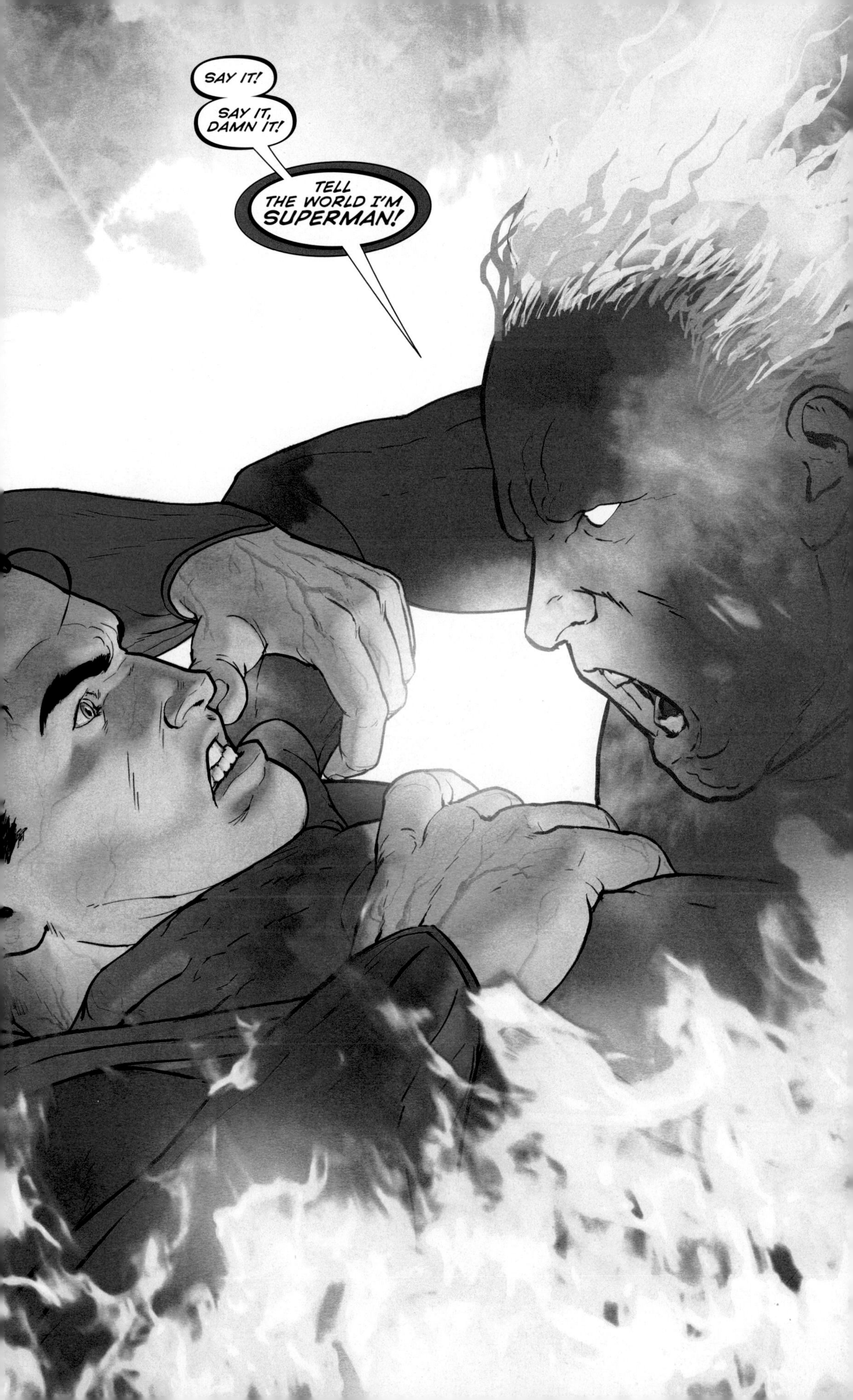
SAY IT!
SAY IT, DAMN IT!
TELL THE WORLD I'M SUPERMAN!

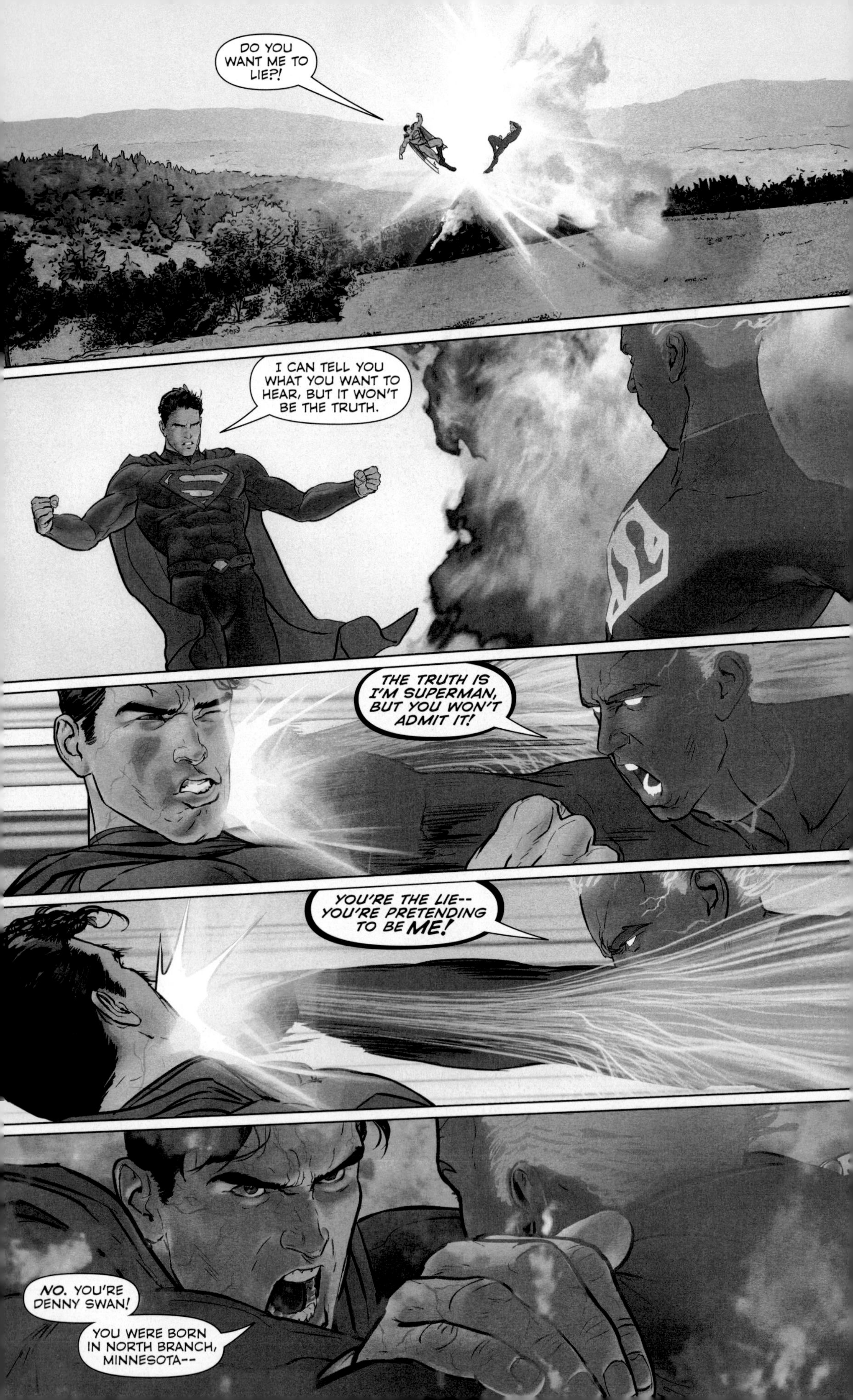
DO YOU WANT ME TO LIE?!
I CAN TELL YOU WHAT YOU WANT TO HEAR, BUT IT WON'T BE THE TRUTH.
THE TRUTH IS I'M SUPERMAN, BUT YOU WON'T ADMIT IT!
YOU'RE THE LIE-- YOU'RE PRETENDING TO BE ME!
NO. YOU'RE DENNY SWAN!
YOU WERE BORN IN NORTH BRANCH, MINNESOTA--

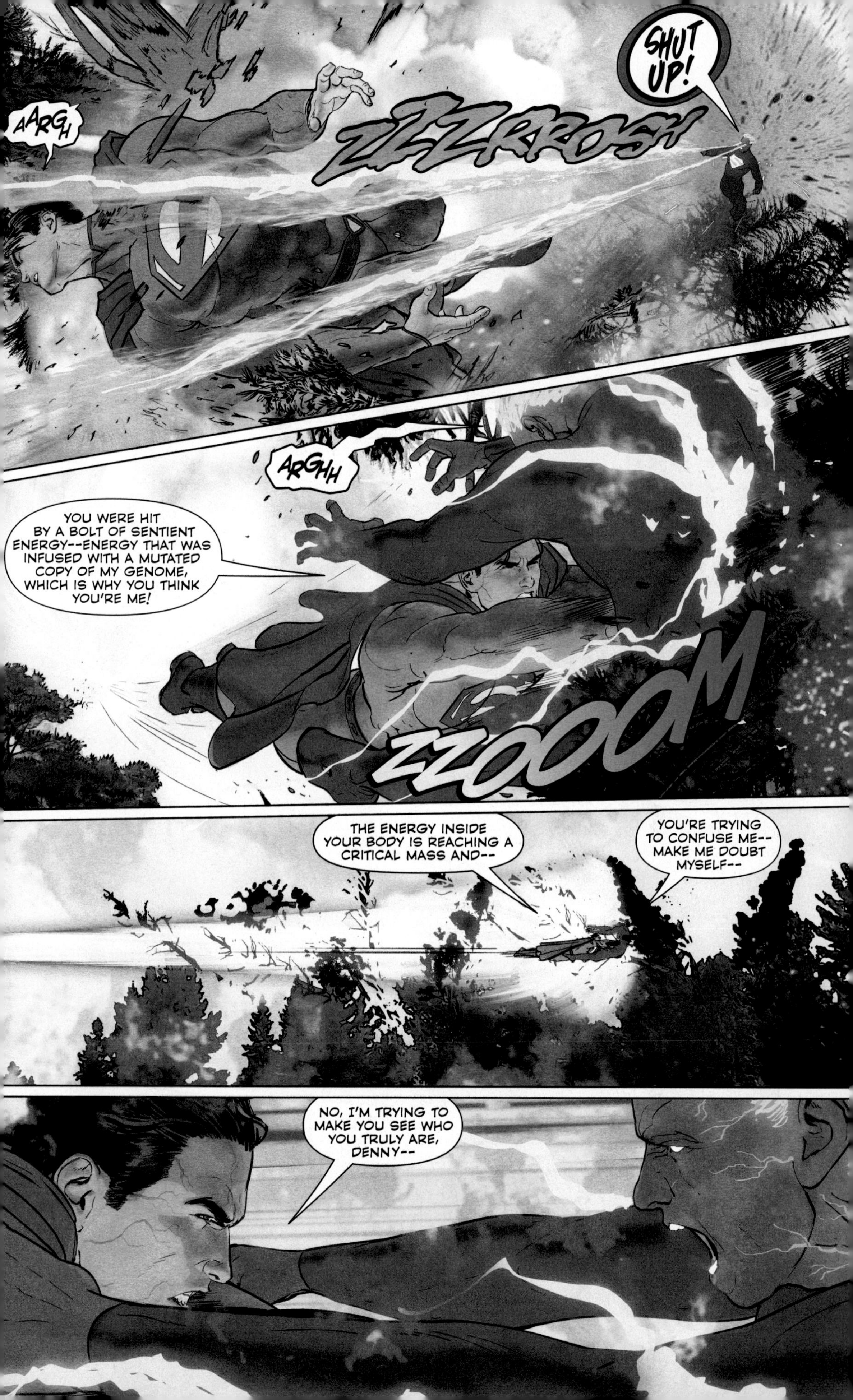

AARGH
SHUT UP!
ZIZZRROSH
ARGHH
YOU WERE HIT BY A BOLT OF SENTIENT ENERGY--ENERGY THAT WAS INFUSED WITH A MUTATED COPY OF MY GENOME, WHICH IS WHY YOU THINK YOU'RE ME!
ZZOOOM
THE ENERGY INSIDE YOUR BODY IS REACHING A CRITICAL MASS AND--
YOU'RE TRYING TO CONFUSE ME--MAKE ME DOUBT MYSELF--
NO, I'M TRYING TO MAKE YOU SEE WHO YOU TRULY ARE, DENNY--

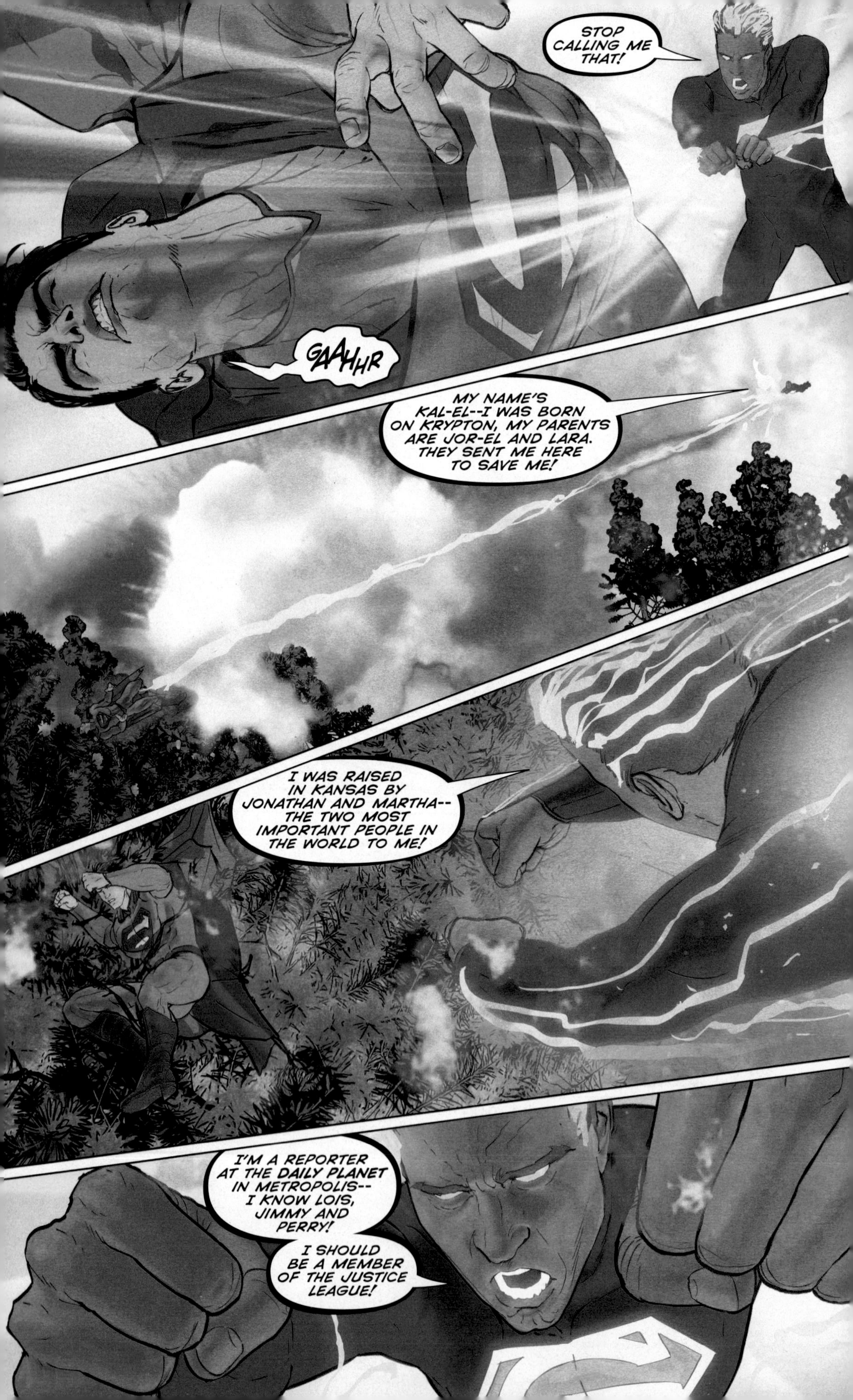
STOP CALLING ME THAT!
GAAHHR
MY NAME'S KAL-EL--I WAS BORN ON KRYPTON, MY PARENTS ARE JOR-EL AND LARA. THEY SENT ME HERE TO SAVE ME!
I WAS RAISED IN KANSAS BY JONATHAN AND MARTHA-- THE TWO MOST IMPORTANT PEOPLE IN THE WORLD TO ME!
I'M A REPORTER AT THE DAILY PLANET IN METROPOLIS-- I KNOW LOIS, JIMMY AND PERRY!
I SHOULD BE A MEMBER OF THE JUSTICE LEAGUE!

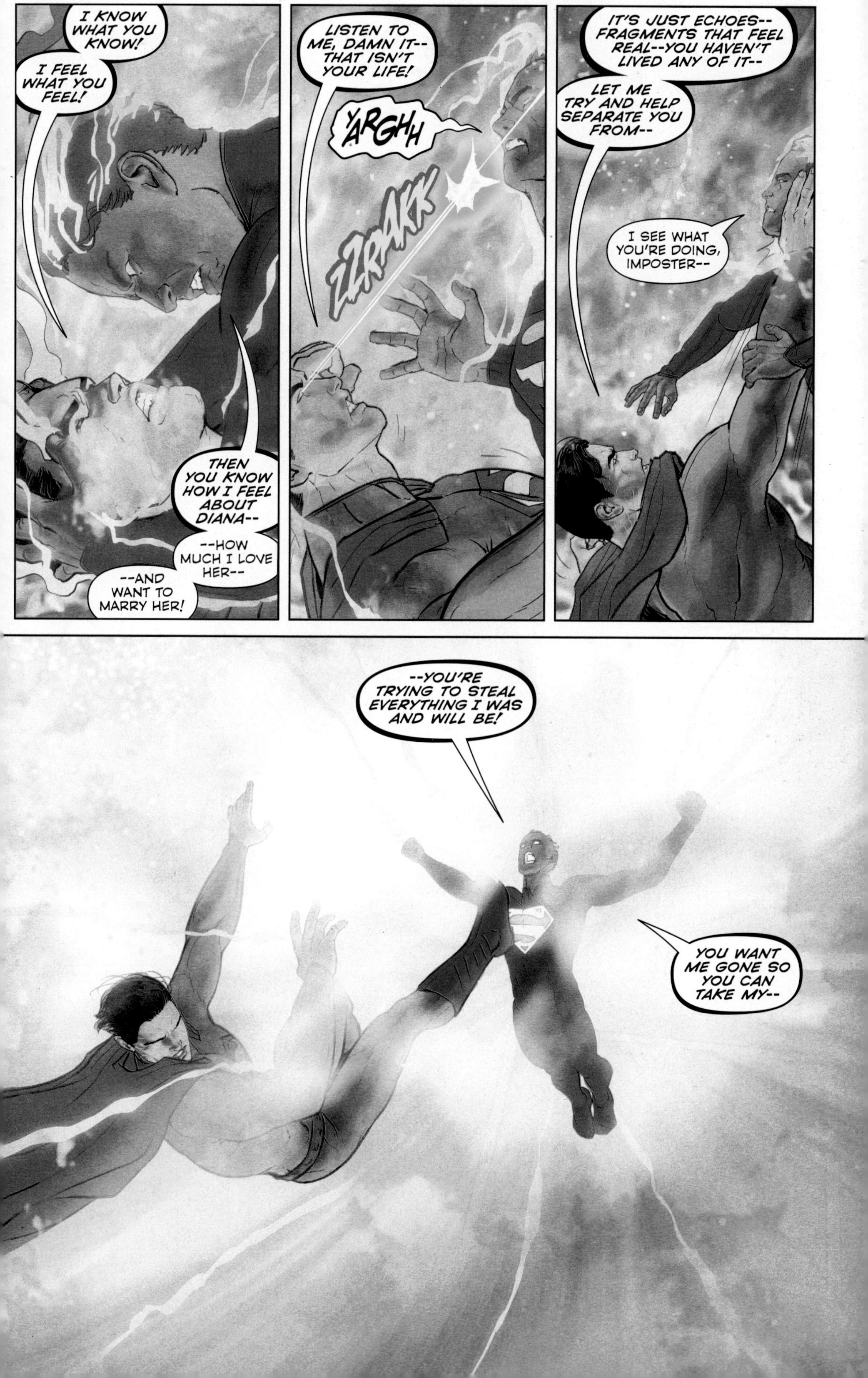
I KNOW WHAT YOU KNOW!
I FEEL WHAT YOU FEEL!
THEN YOU KNOW HOW I FEEL ABOUT DIANA--
--HOW MUCH I LOVE HER--
--AND WANT TO MARRY HER!
LISTEN TO ME, DAMN IT-- THAT ISN'T YOUR LIFE!
YARGHH
ZZRAKK
IT'S JUST ECHOES-- FRAGMENTS THAT FEEL REAL--YOU HAVEN'T LIVED ANY OF IT--
LET ME TRY AND HELP SEPARATE YOU FROM--
I SEE WHAT YOU'RE DOING, IMPOSTER--
--YOU'RE TRYING TO STEAL EVERYTHING I WAS AND WILL BE!
YOU WANT ME GONE SO YOU CAN TAKE MY--

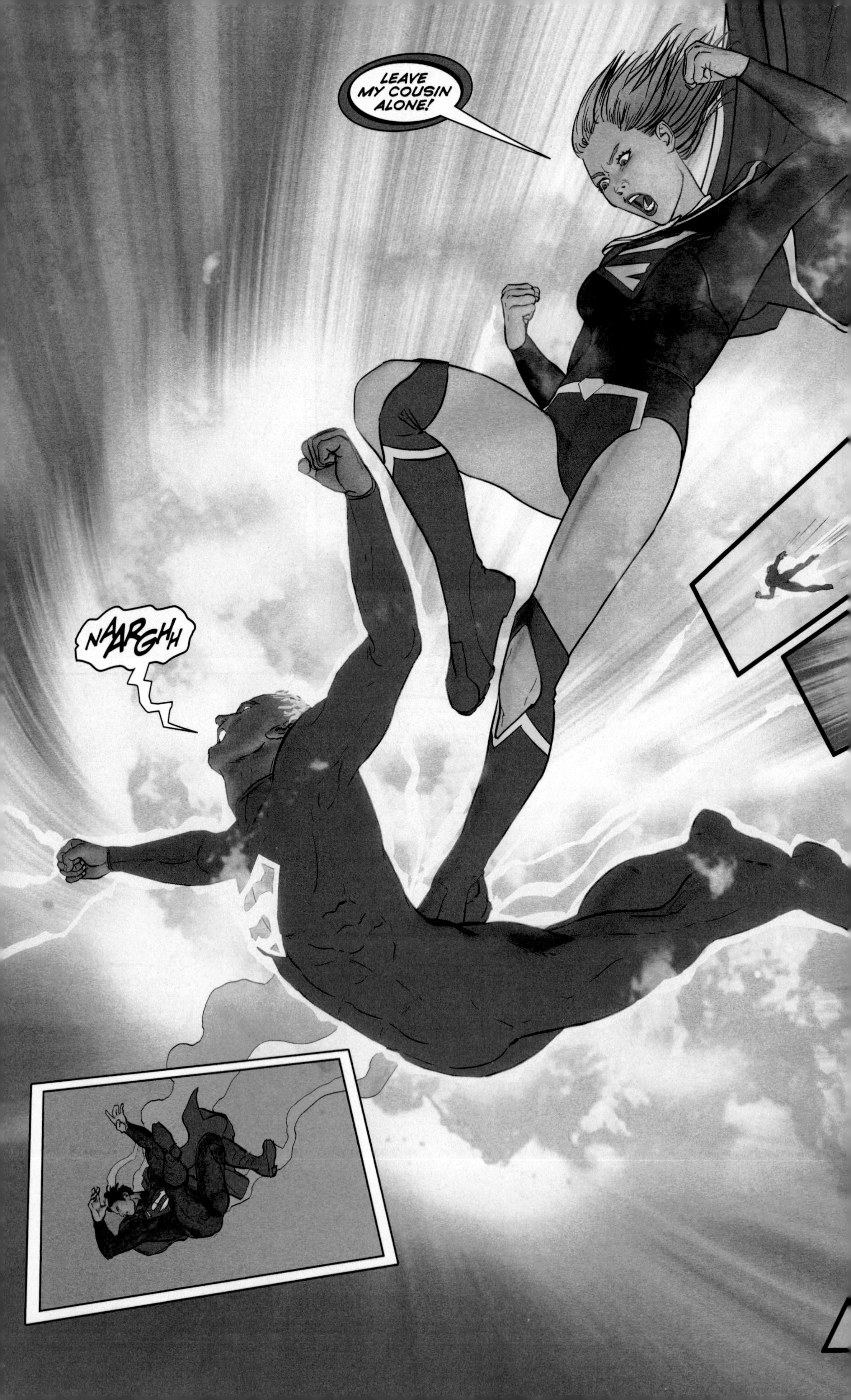
LEAVE MY COUSIN ALONE!
NAARGHH

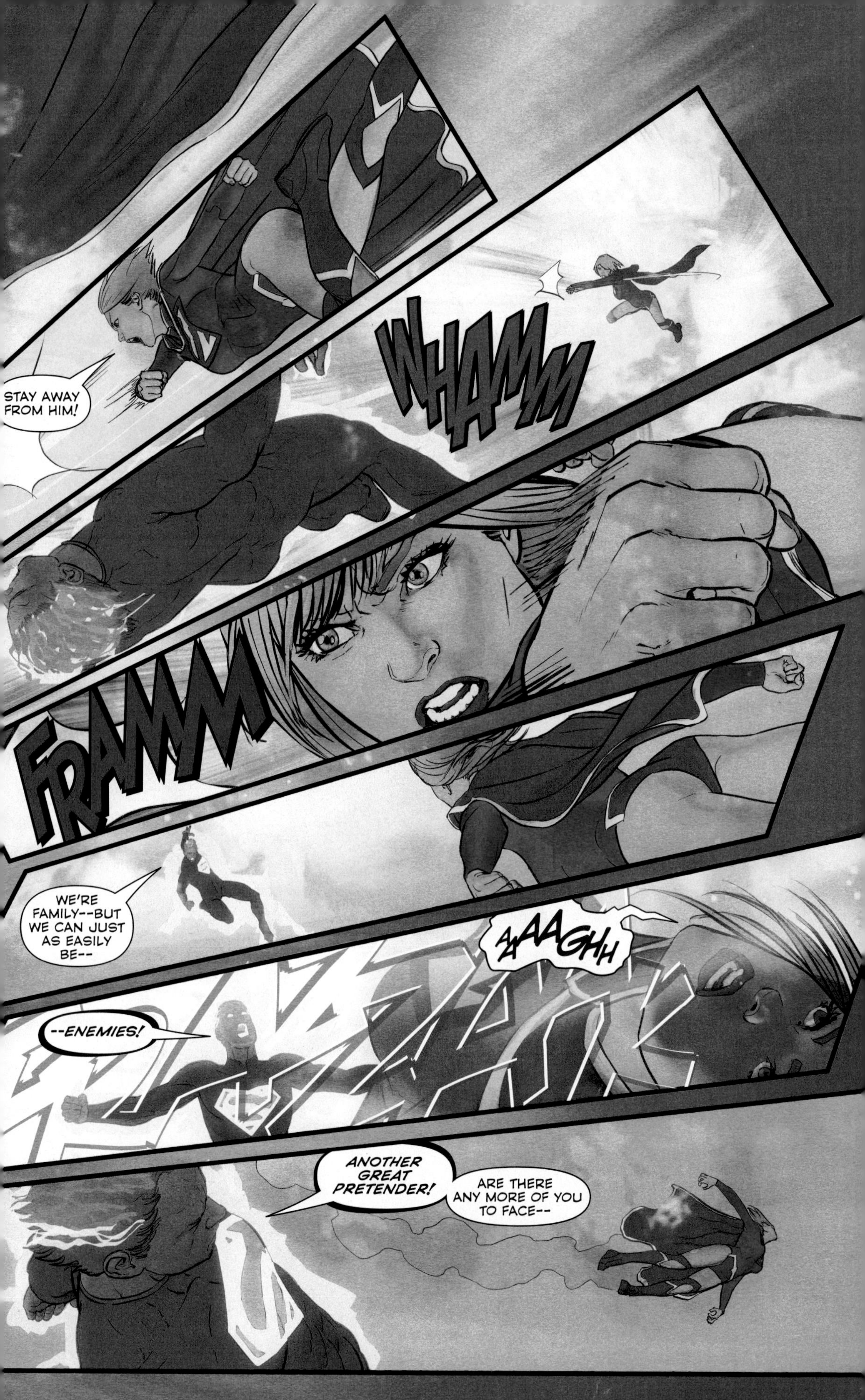
STAY AWAY FROM HIM!
WHAMMM
FRAMMM
WE'RE FAMILY--BUT WE CAN JUST AS EASILY BE--
AAAAGHH
--ENEMIES!
ANOTHER GREAT PRETENDER!
ARE THERE ANY MORE OF YOU TO FACE--

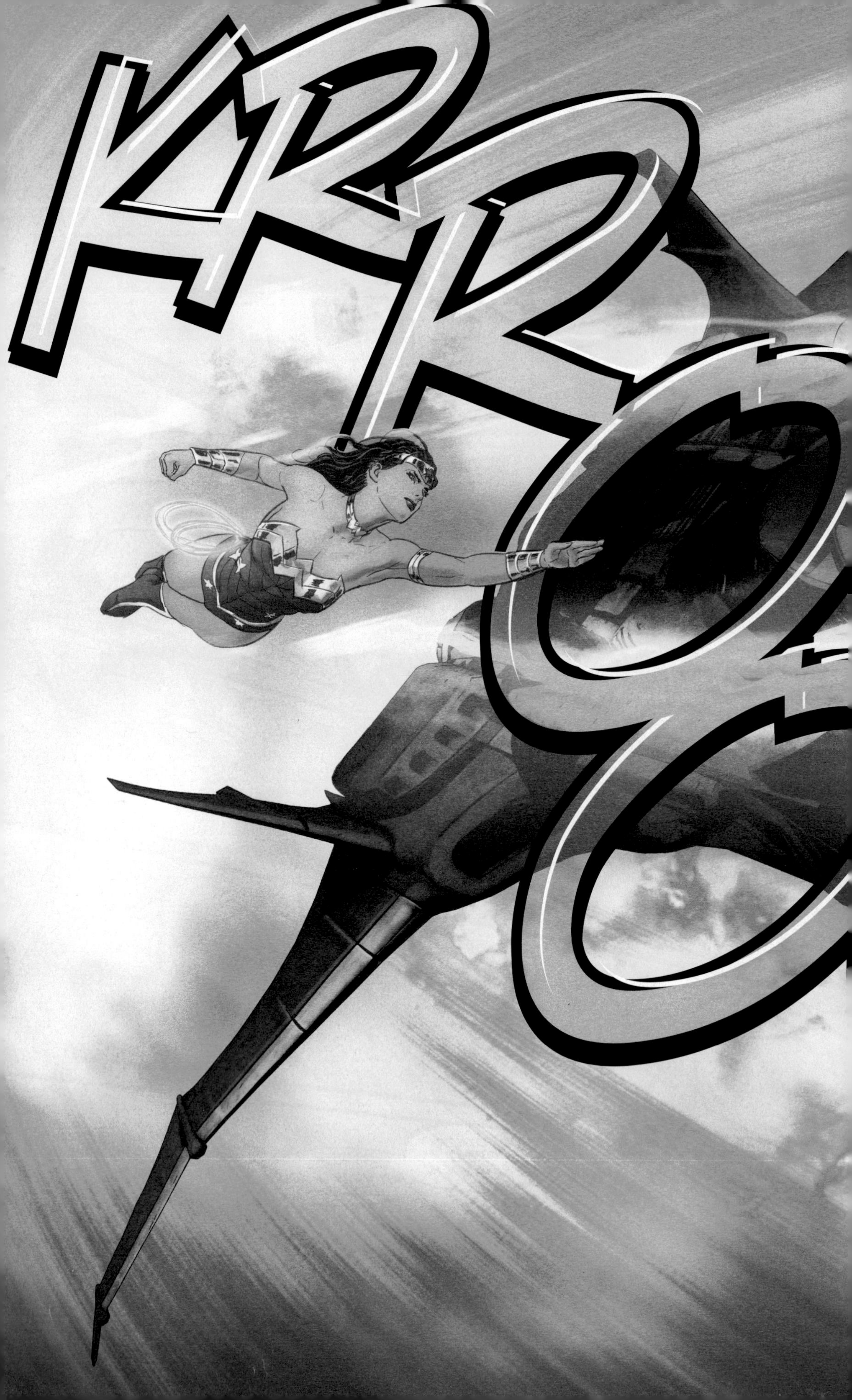
KRROOO

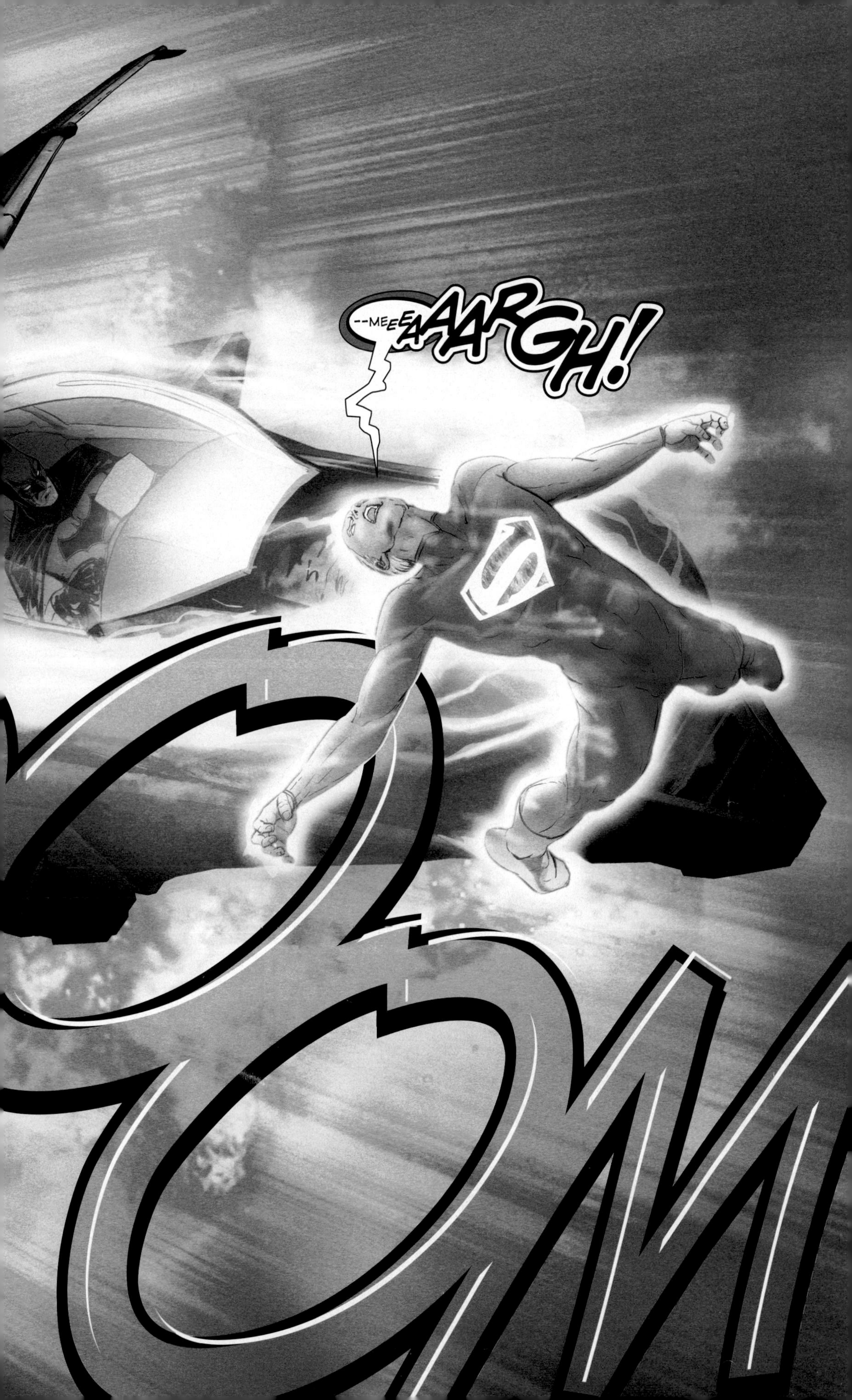
--MEEEAAAARGH!

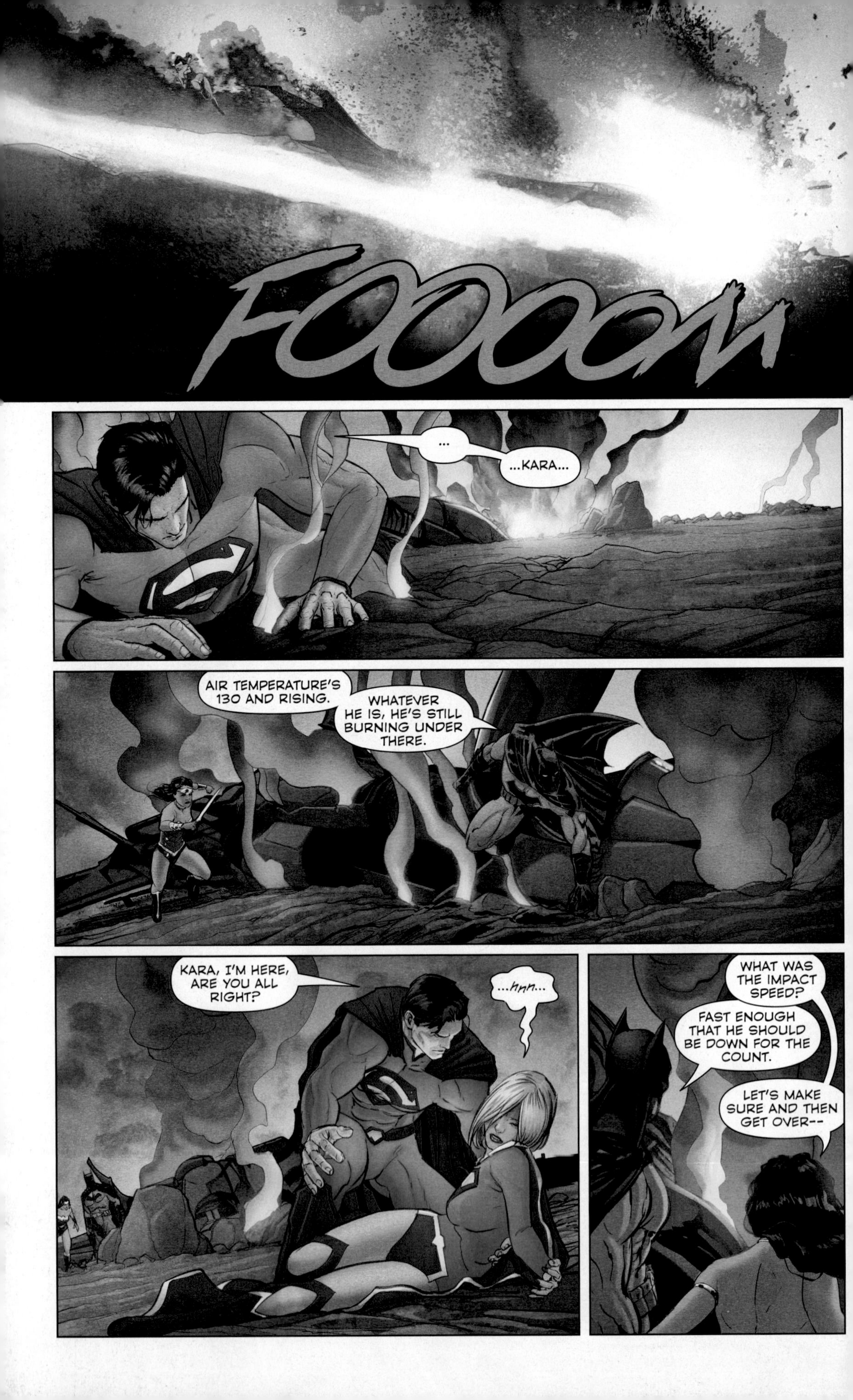
FOOOOM
...
...KARA...
AIR TEMPERATURE'S 130 AND RISING.
WHATEVER HE IS, HE'S STILL BURNING UNDER THERE.
KARA, I'M HERE, ARE YOU ALL RIGHT?
...hnn...
WHAT WAS THE IMPACT SPEED?
FAST ENOUGH THAT HE SHOULD BE DOWN FOR THE COUNT.
LET'S MAKE SURE AND THEN GET OVER--

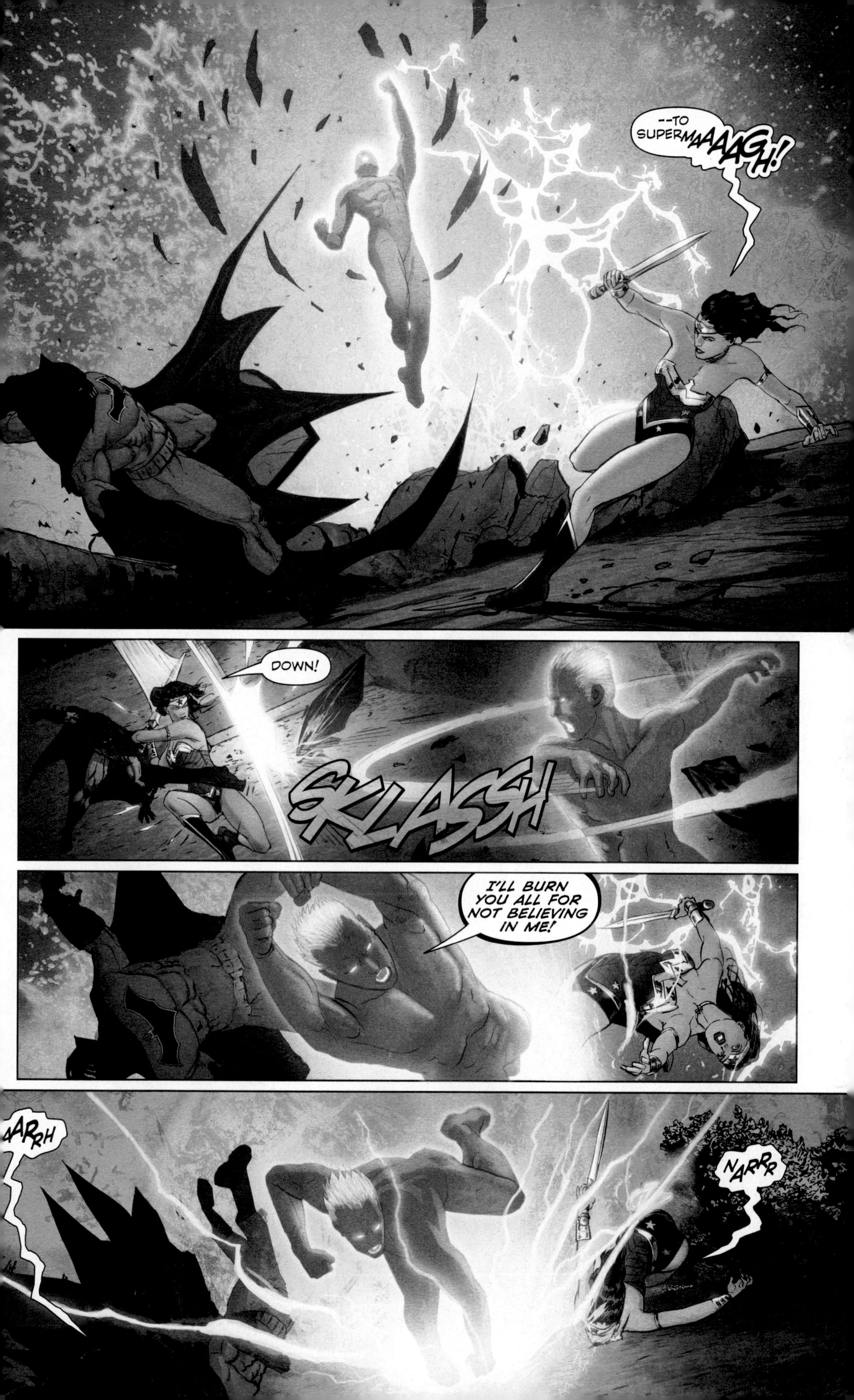
--TO SUPERMAAAAGH!
DOWN!
SKLASSH
I'LL BURN YOU ALL FOR NOT BELIEVING IN ME!
AARRH
NARRR

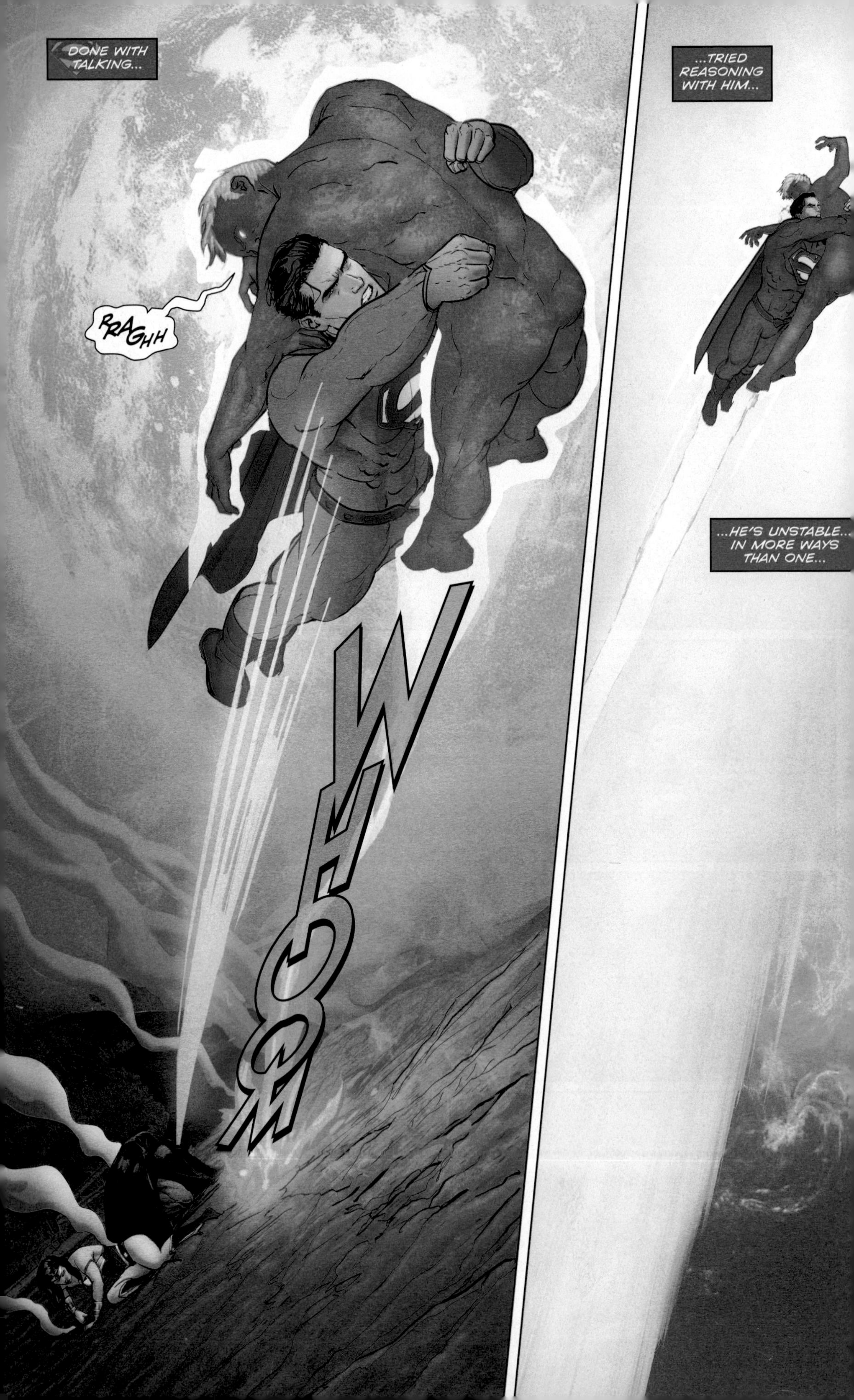
DONE WITH TALKING...
RRAGHH
WHOOM
...TRIED REASONING WITH HIM...
...HE'S UNSTABLE... IN MORE WAYS THAN ONE...

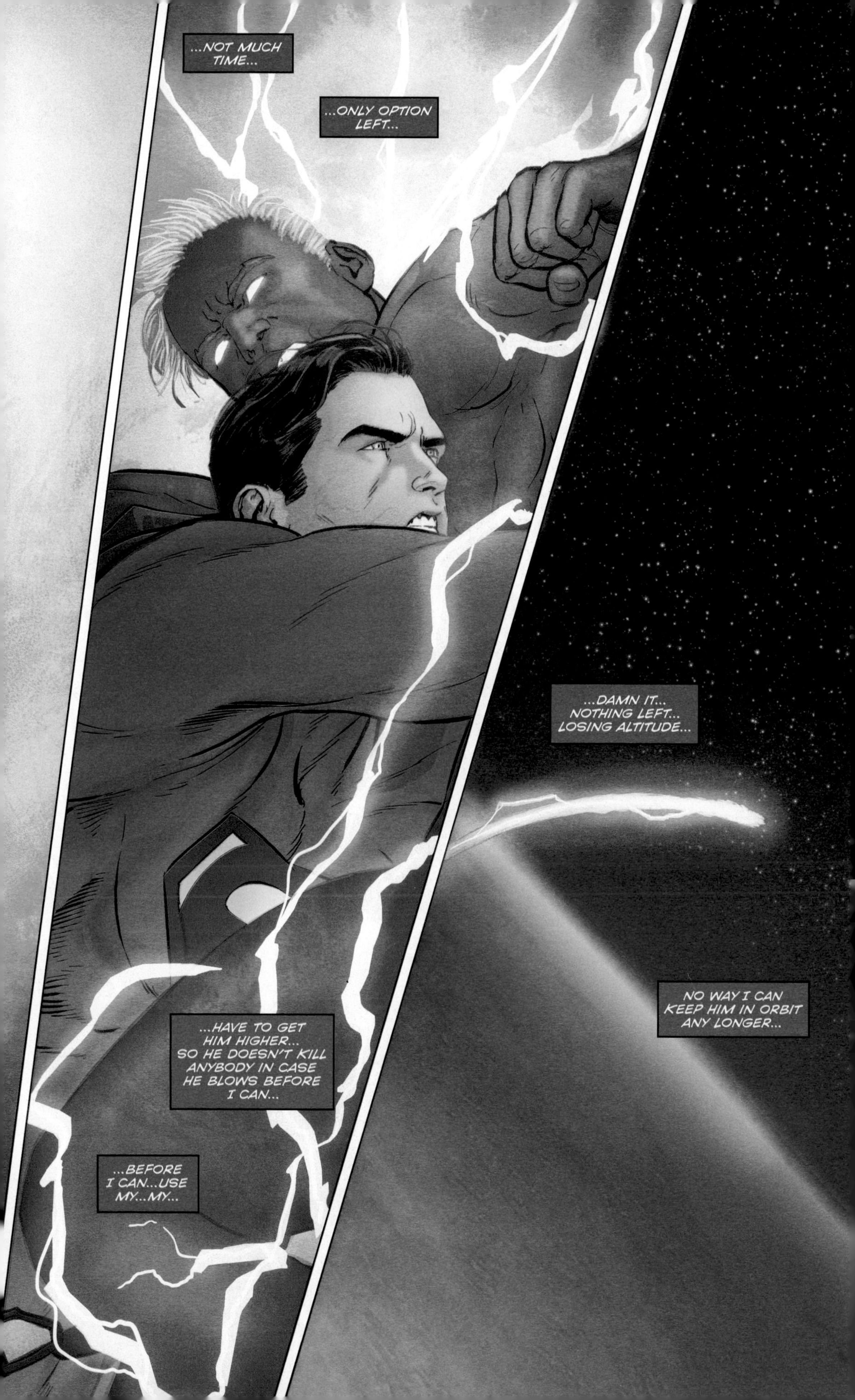
...NOT MUCH TIME...
...ONLY OPTION LEFT...
...HAVE TO GET HIM HIGHER... SO HE DOESN'T KILL ANYBODY IN CASE HE BLOWS BEFORE I CAN...
...BEFORE I CAN...USE MY...MY...
...DAMN IT... NOTHING LEFT... LOSING ALTITUDE...
NO WAY I CAN KEEP HIM IN ORBIT ANY LONGER...

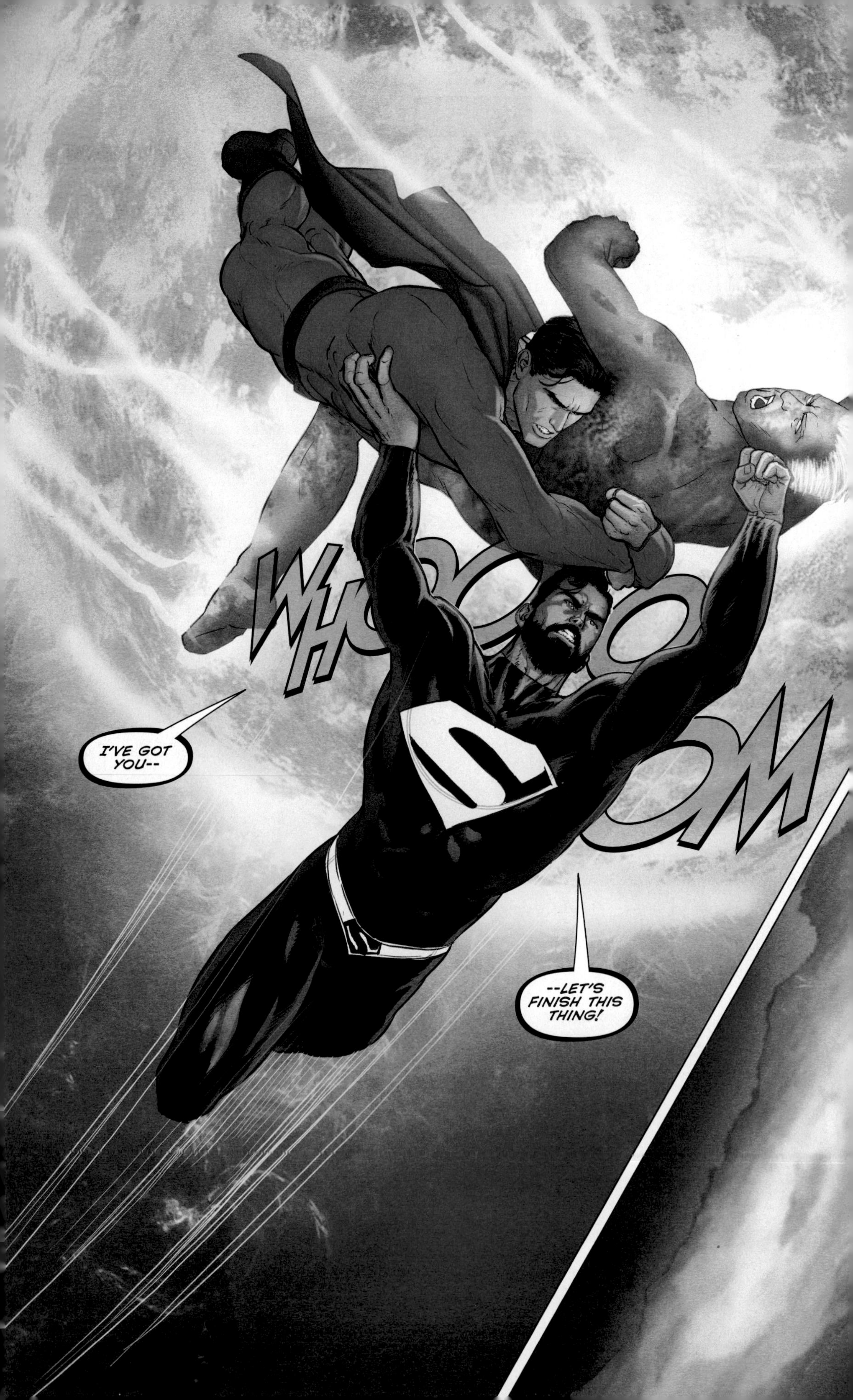
WHOOOOOM
I'VE GOT YOU--
--LET'S FINISH THIS THING!

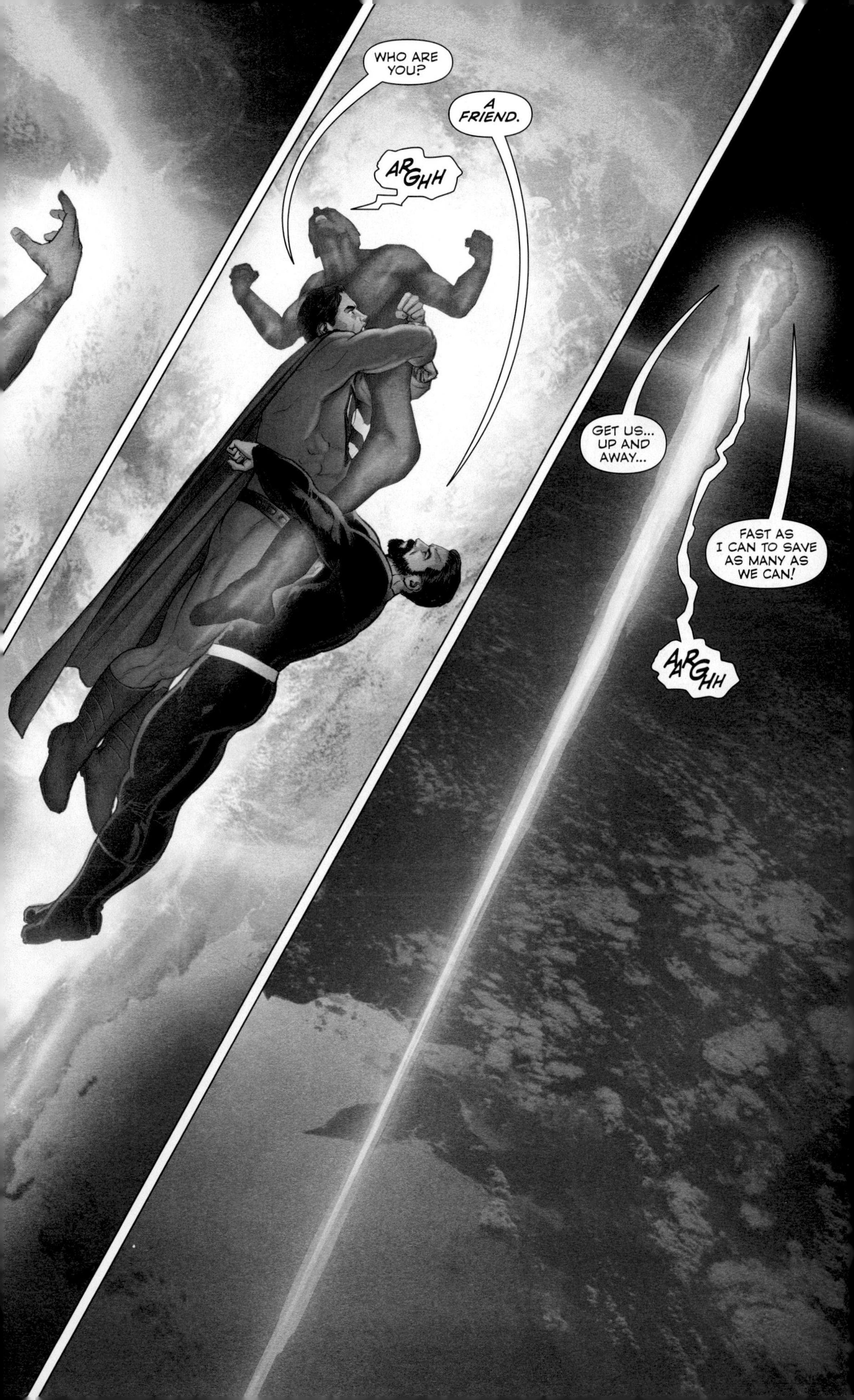
WHO ARE YOU?
A FRIEND.
ARGHH
GET US... UP AND AWAY...
FAST AS I CAN TO SAVE AS MANY AS WE CAN!
AARGHH

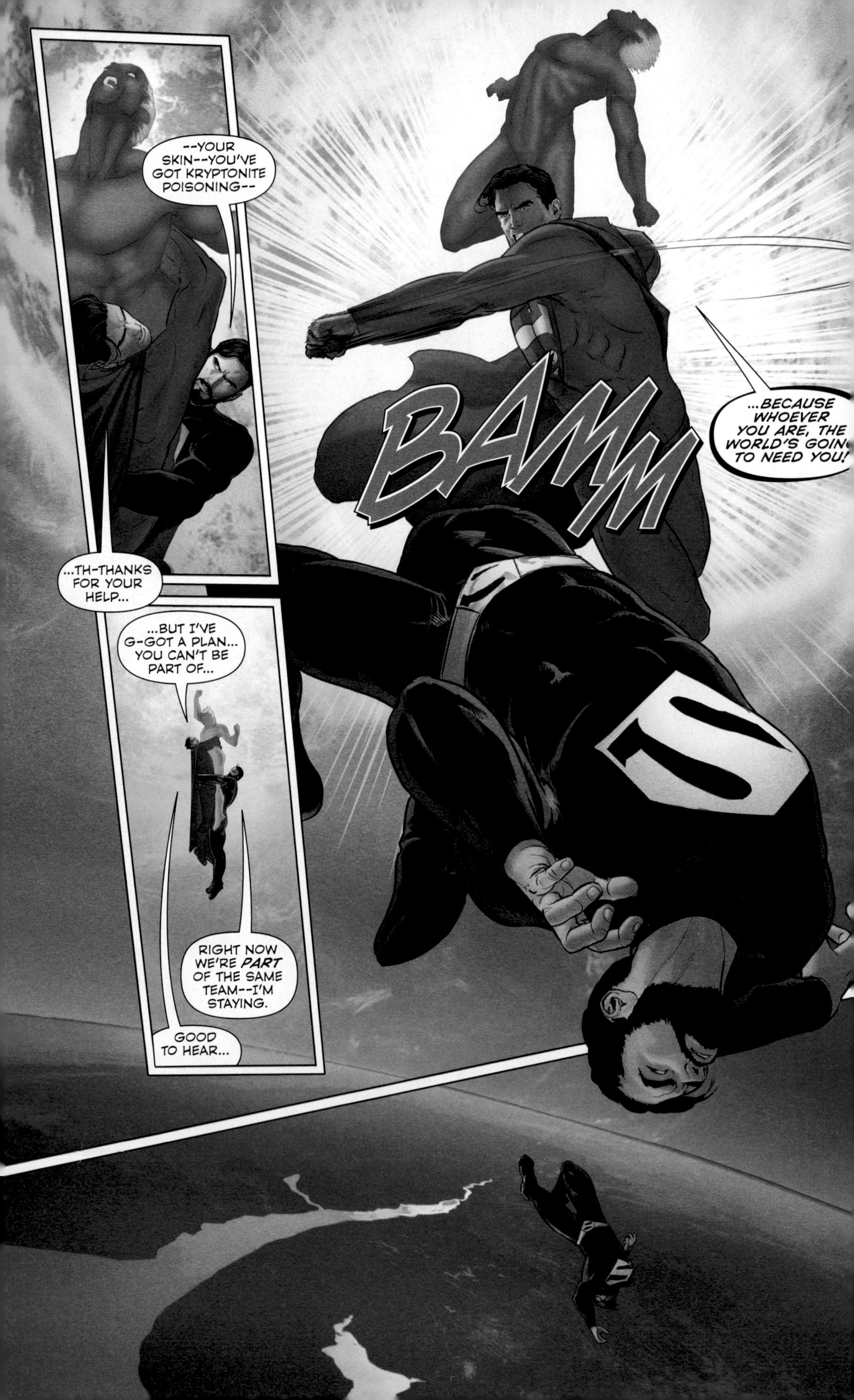
--YOUR SKIN--YOU'VE GOT KRYPTONITE POISONING--
...TH-THANKS FOR YOUR HELP...
...BUT I'VE G-GOT A PLAN... YOU CAN'T BE PART OF...
RIGHT NOW WE'RE *PART* OF THE SAME TEAM--I'M STAYING.
GOOD TO HEAR...
...BECAUSE WHOEVER YOU ARE, THE WORLD'S GOING TO NEED YOU!
BAMM

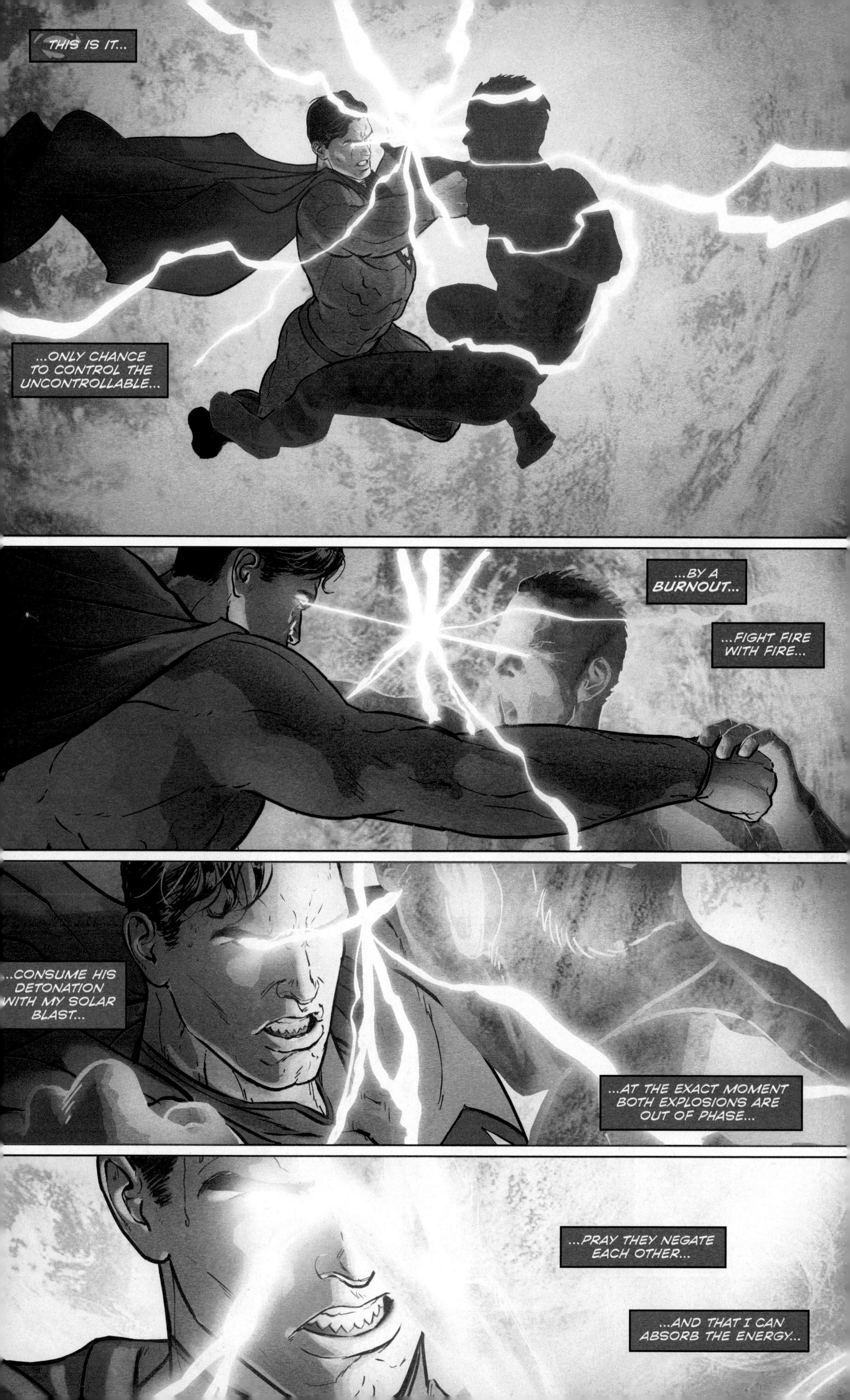
THIS IS IT...
...ONLY CHANCE TO CONTROL THE UNCONTROLLABLE...
...BY A BURNOUT...
...FIGHT FIRE WITH FIRE...
...CONSUME HIS DETONATION WITH MY SOLAR BLAST...
...AT THE EXACT MOMENT BOTH EXPLOSIONS ARE OUT OF PHASE...
...PRAY THEY NEGATE EACH OTHER...
...AND THAT I CAN ABSORB THE ENERGY...

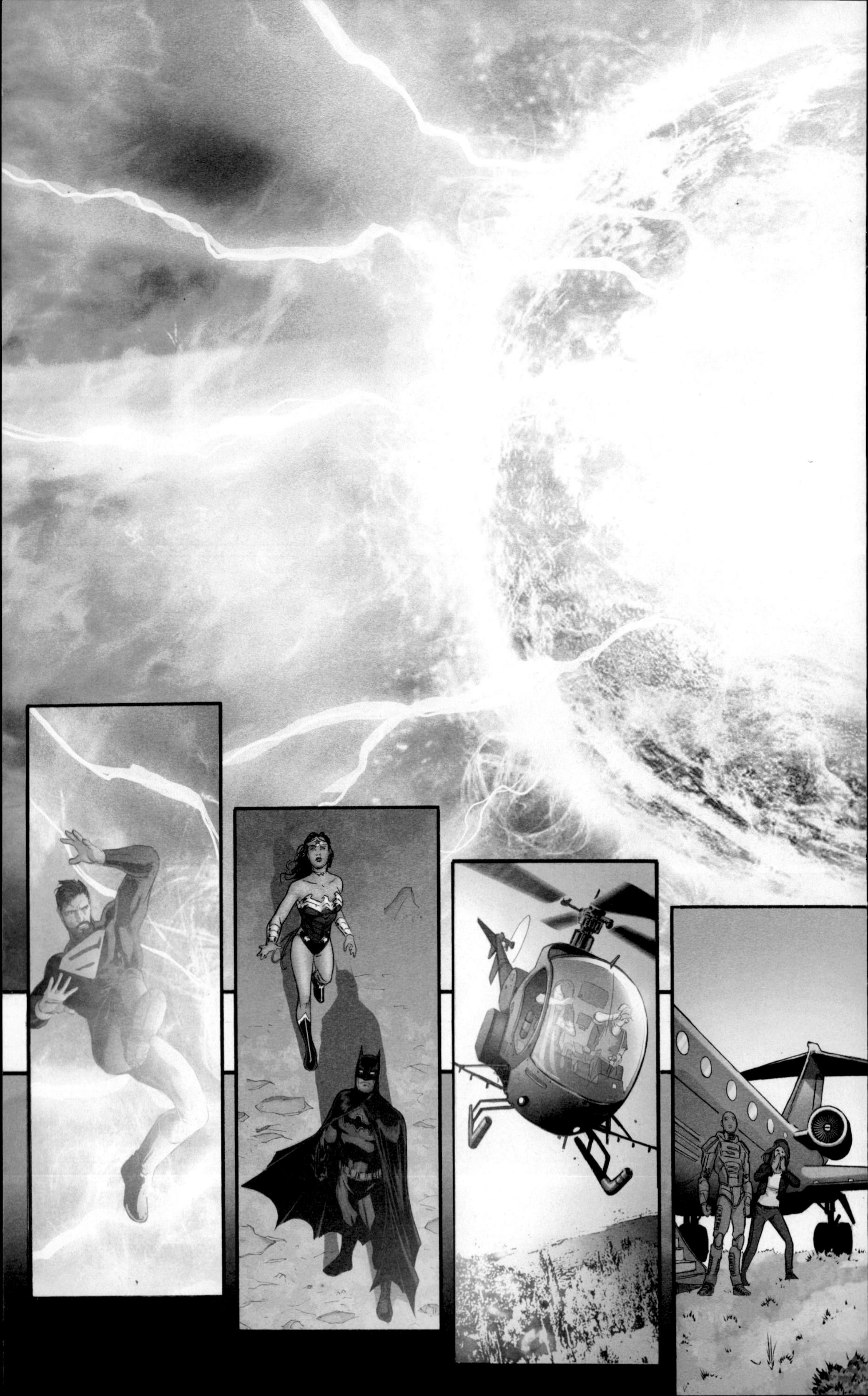

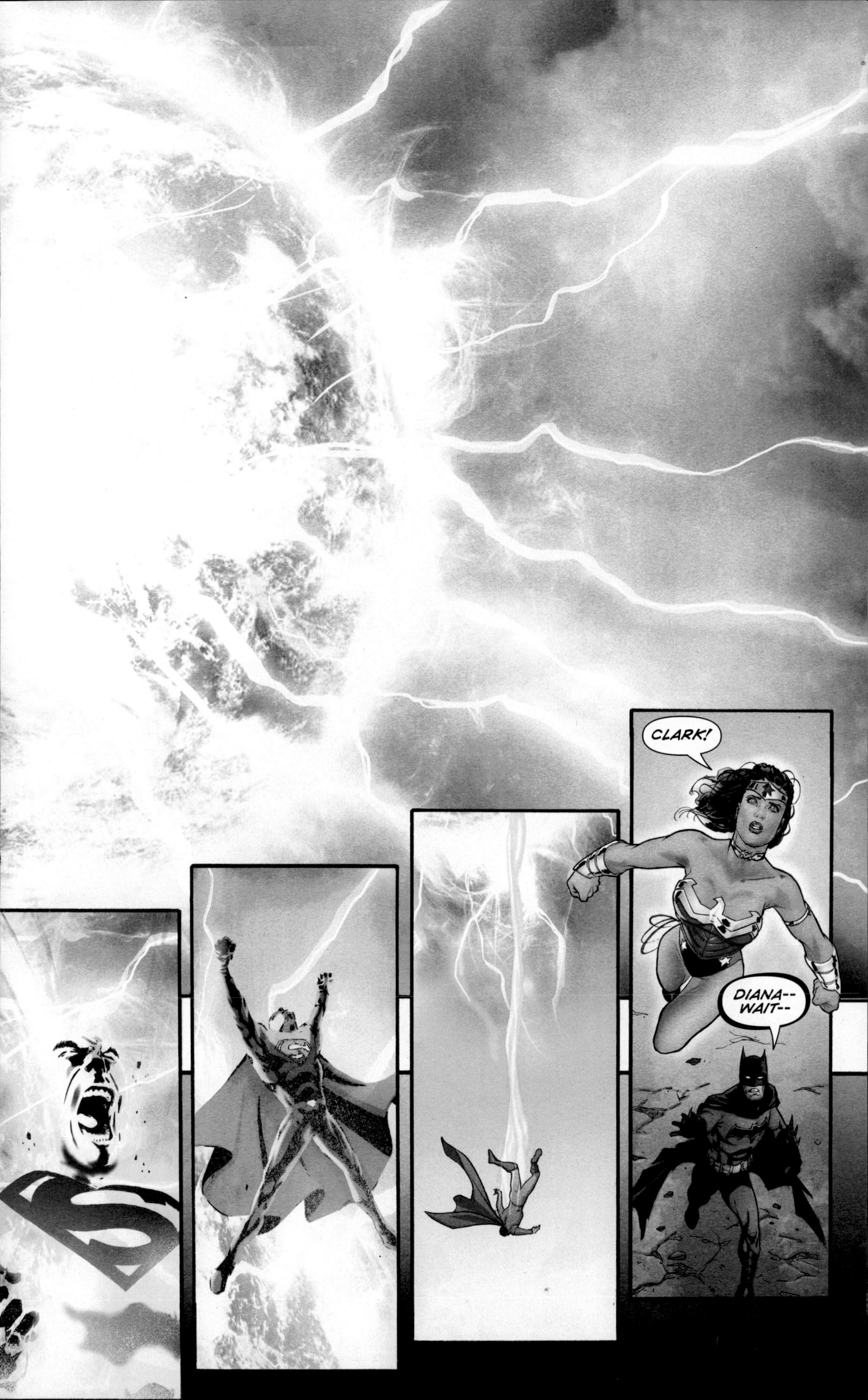
CLARK!
DIANA-- WAIT--

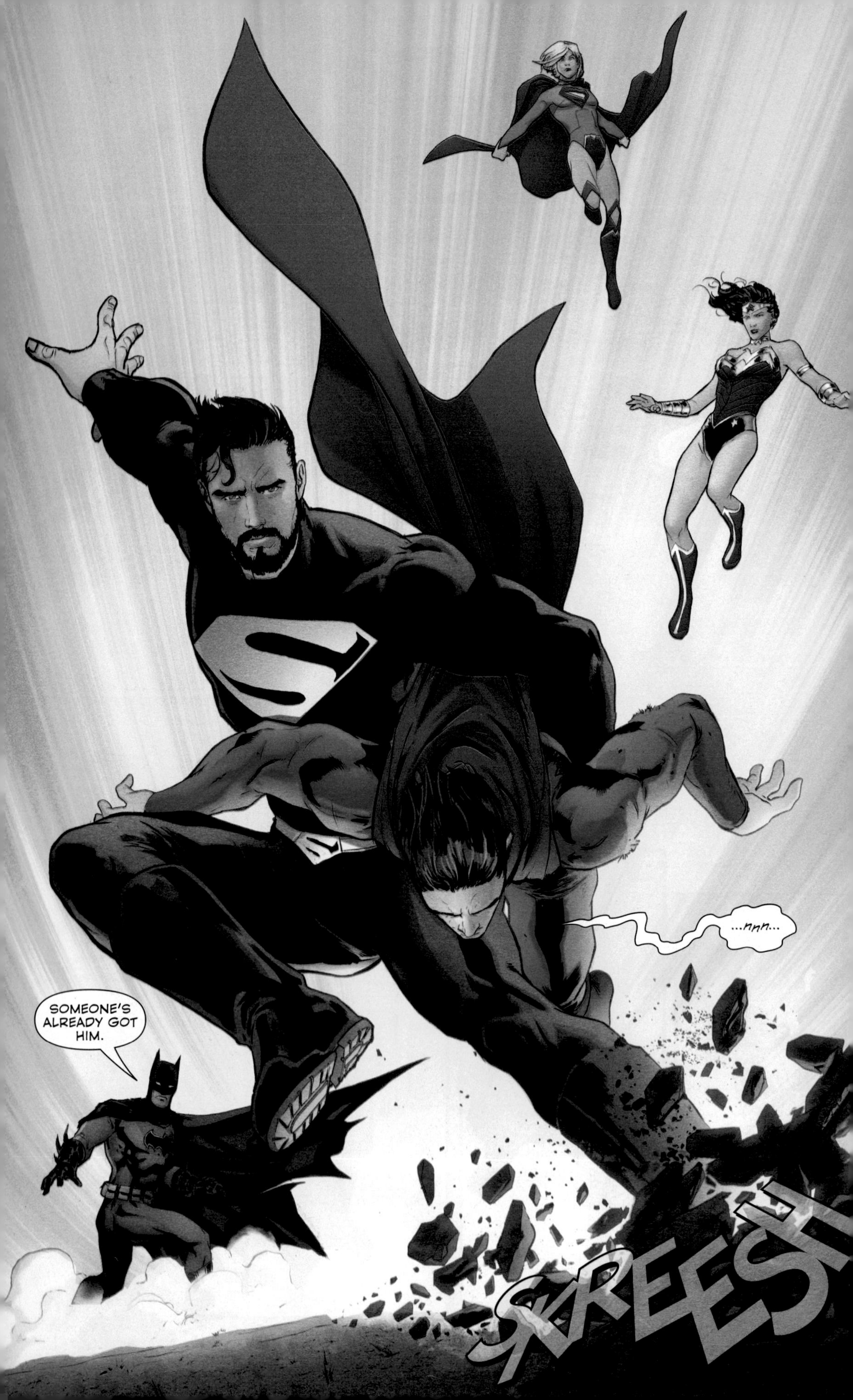
...MMM...
SOMEONE'S ALREADY GOT HIM.
SKREEEST

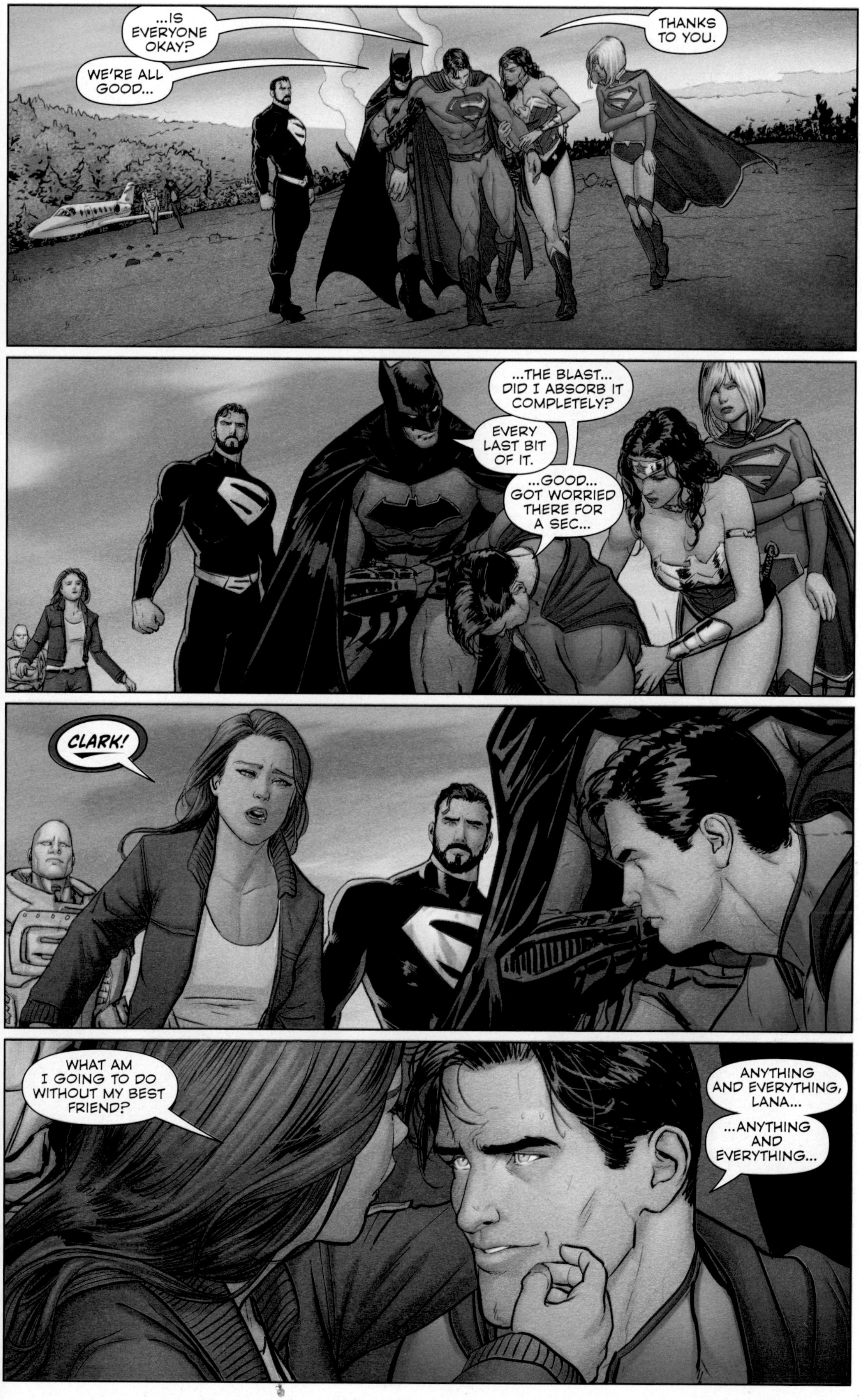
...IS EVERYONE OKAY?
WE'RE ALL GOOD...
THANKS TO YOU.
...THE BLAST... DID I ABSORB IT COMPLETELY?
EVERY LAST BIT OF IT.
...GOOD... GOT WORRIED THERE FOR A SEC...
CLARK!
WHAT AM I GOING TO DO WITHOUT MY BEST FRIEND?
ANYTHING AND EVERYTHING, LANA...
...ANYTHING AND EVERYTHING...

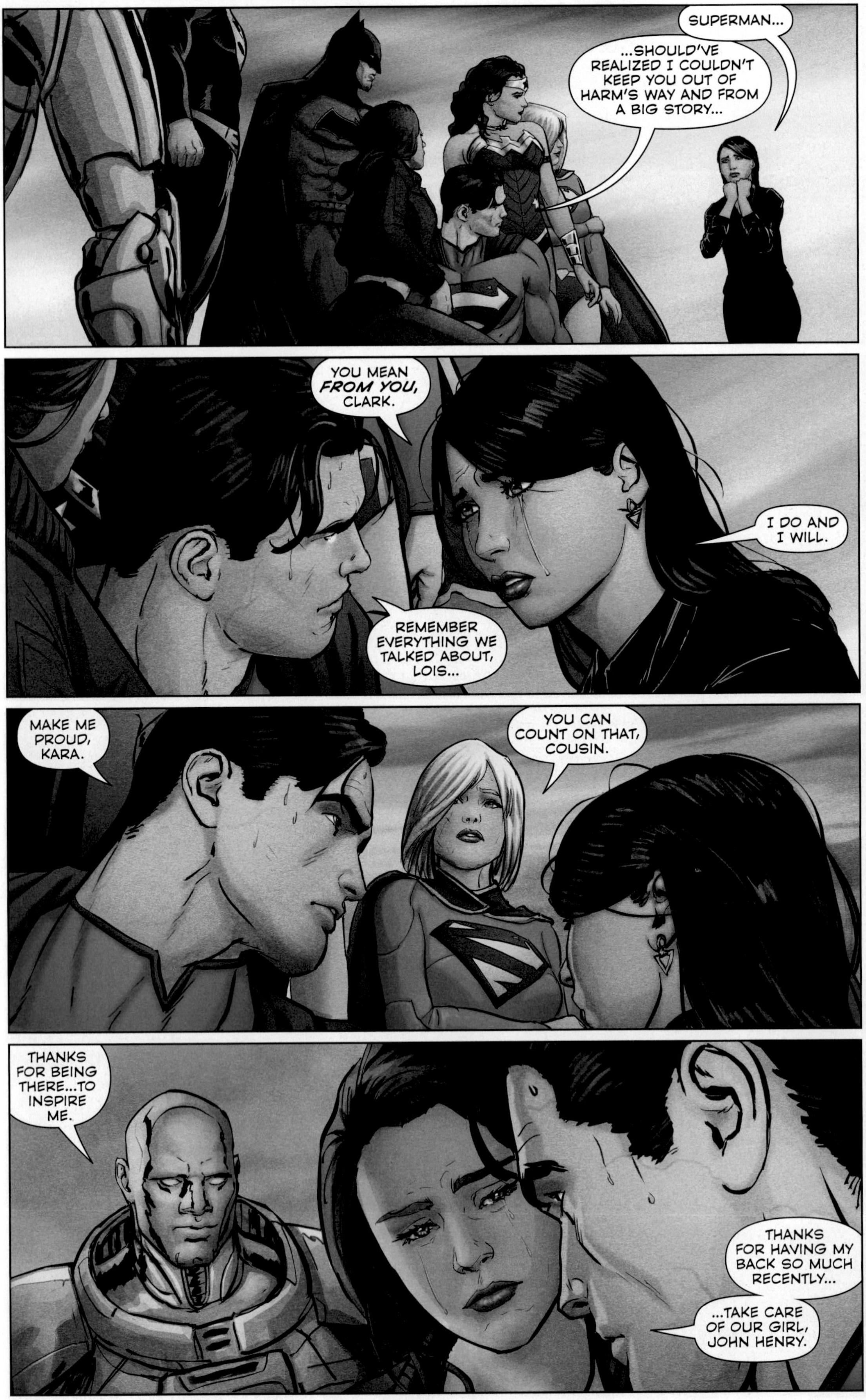
SUPERMAN...
...SHOULD'VE REALIZED I COULDN'T KEEP YOU OUT OF HARM'S WAY AND FROM A BIG STORY...
YOU MEAN *FROM YOU*, CLARK.
I DO AND I WILL.
REMEMBER EVERYTHING WE TALKED ABOUT, LOIS...
MAKE ME PROUD, KARA.
YOU CAN COUNT ON THAT, COUSIN.
THANKS FOR BEING THERE...TO INSPIRE ME.
THANKS FOR HAVING MY BACK SO MUCH RECENTLY...
...TAKE CARE OF OUR GIRL, JOHN HENRY.

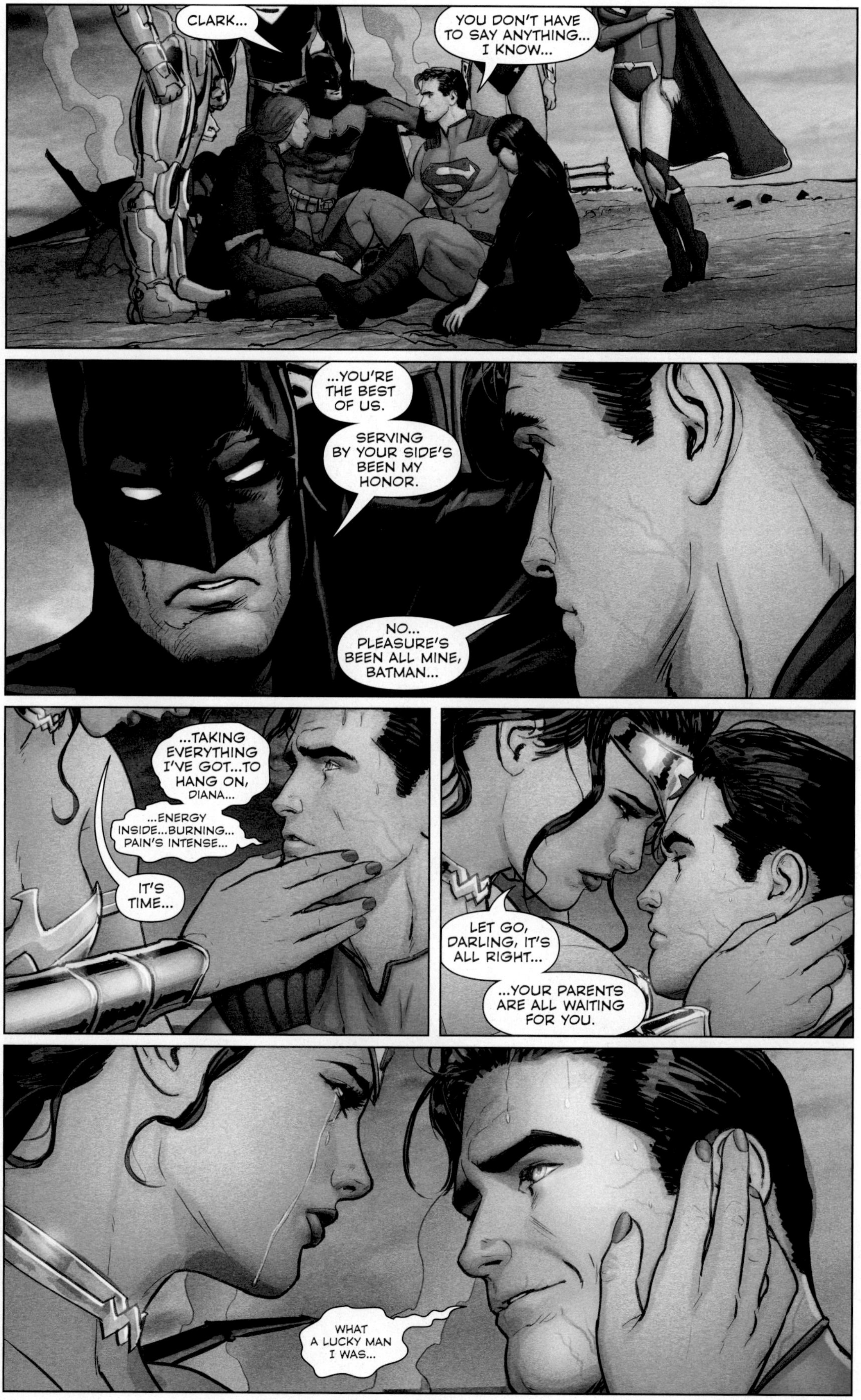
CLARK...
YOU DON'T HAVE TO SAY ANYTHING... I KNOW...
...YOU'RE THE BEST OF US.
SERVING BY YOUR SIDE'S BEEN MY HONOR.
NO... PLEASURE'S BEEN ALL MINE, BATMAN...
...TAKING EVERYTHING I'VE GOT...TO HANG ON, DIANA...
...ENERGY INSIDE...BURNING... PAIN'S INTENSE...
IT'S TIME...
LET GO, DARLING, IT'S ALL RIGHT...
...YOUR PARENTS ARE ALL WAITING FOR YOU.
WHAT A LUCKY MAN I WAS...

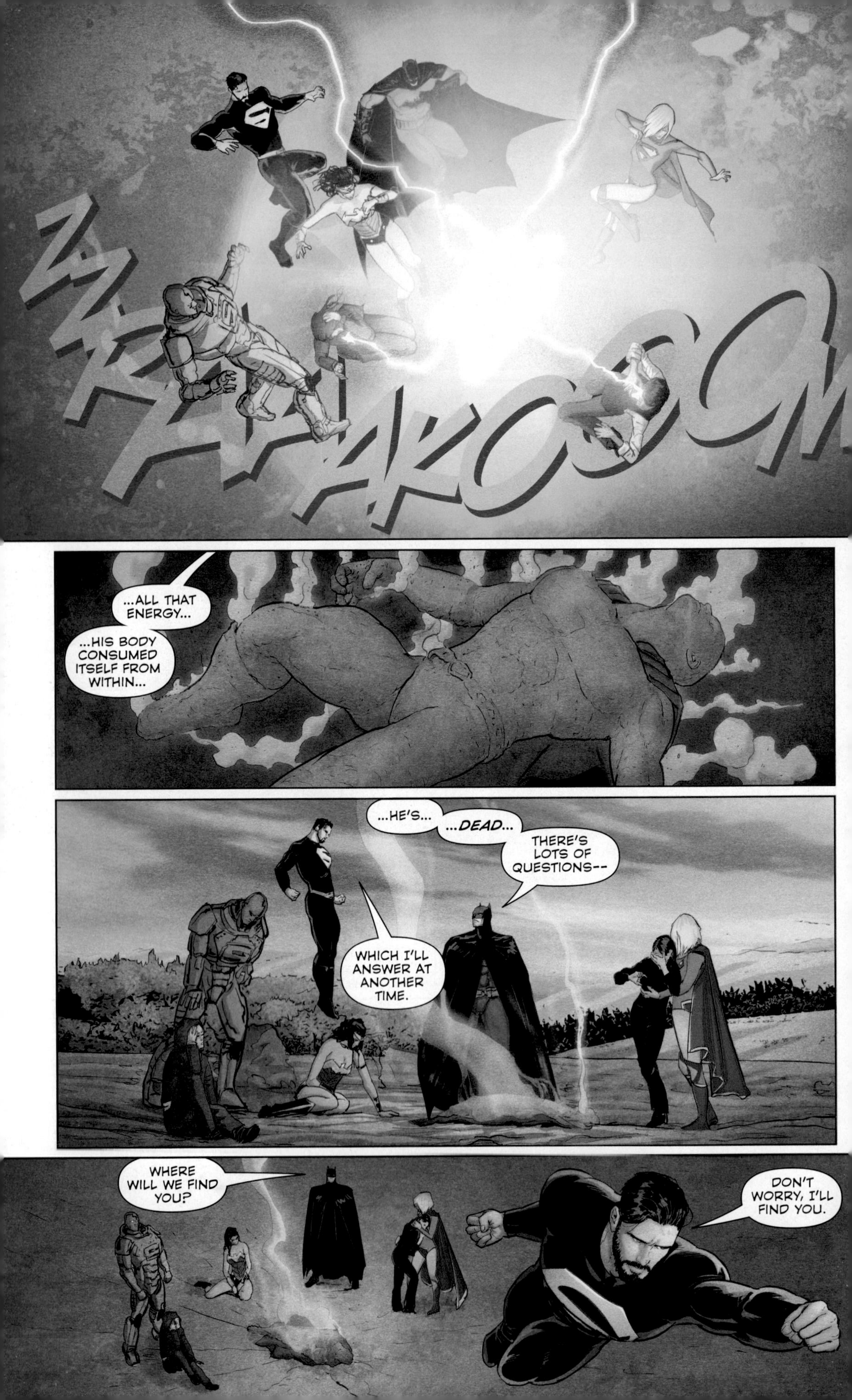

WRAKAKOOOM
...ALL THAT ENERGY...
...HIS BODY CONSUMED ITSELF FROM WITHIN...
...HE'S...
...*DEAD*...
THERE'S LOTS OF QUESTIONS--
WHICH I'LL ANSWER AT ANOTHER TIME.
WHERE WILL WE FIND YOU?
DON'T WORRY, I'LL FIND YOU.

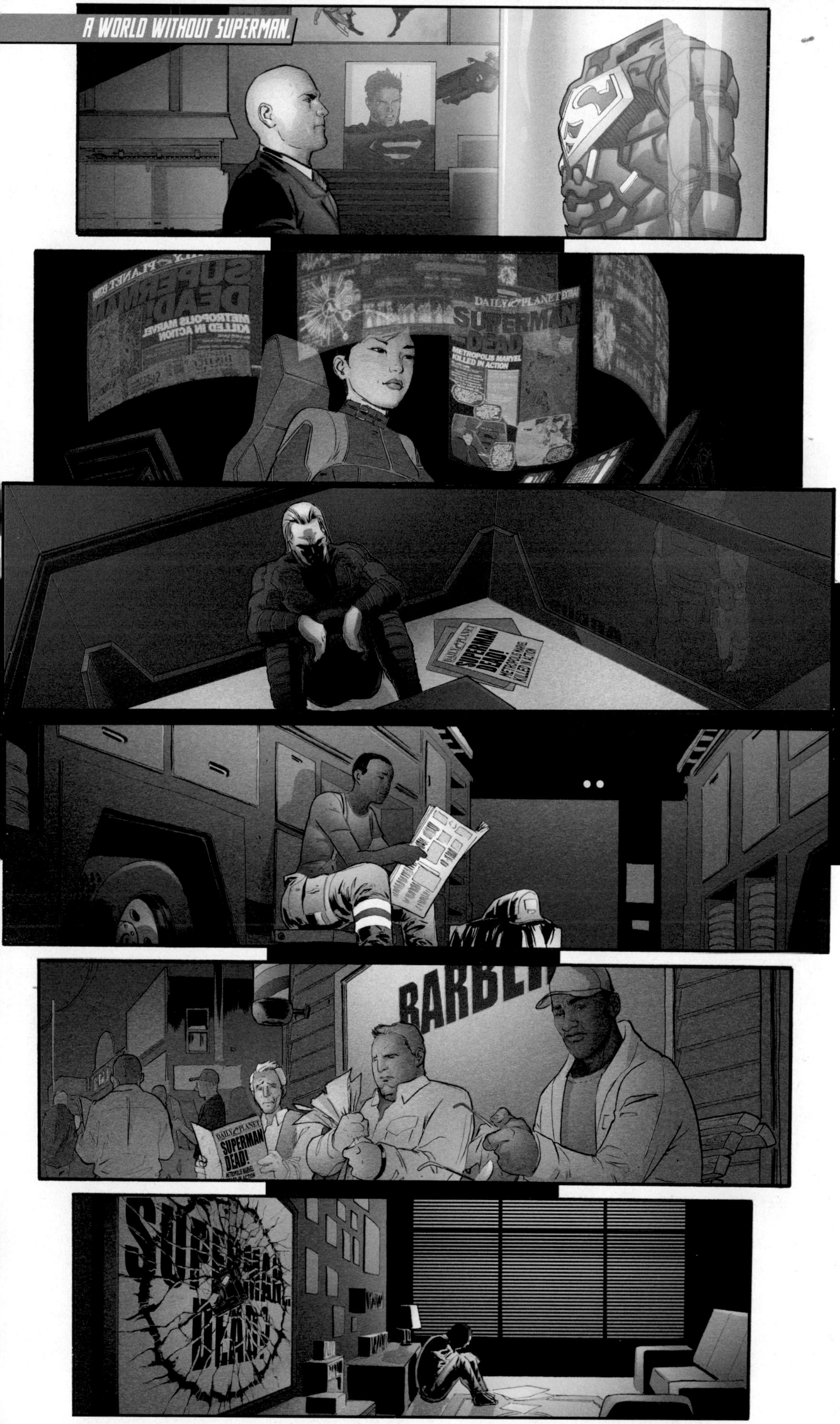
A WORLD WITHOUT SUPERMAN.
DAILY PLANET EXTRA
SUPERMAN DEAD
METROPOLIS MARVEL KILLED IN ACTION
DAILY PLANET
SUPERMAN DEAD!
METROPOLIS MARVEL KILLED IN ACTION
DAILY PLANET
SUPERMAN DEAD!
SUPERMAN DEAD

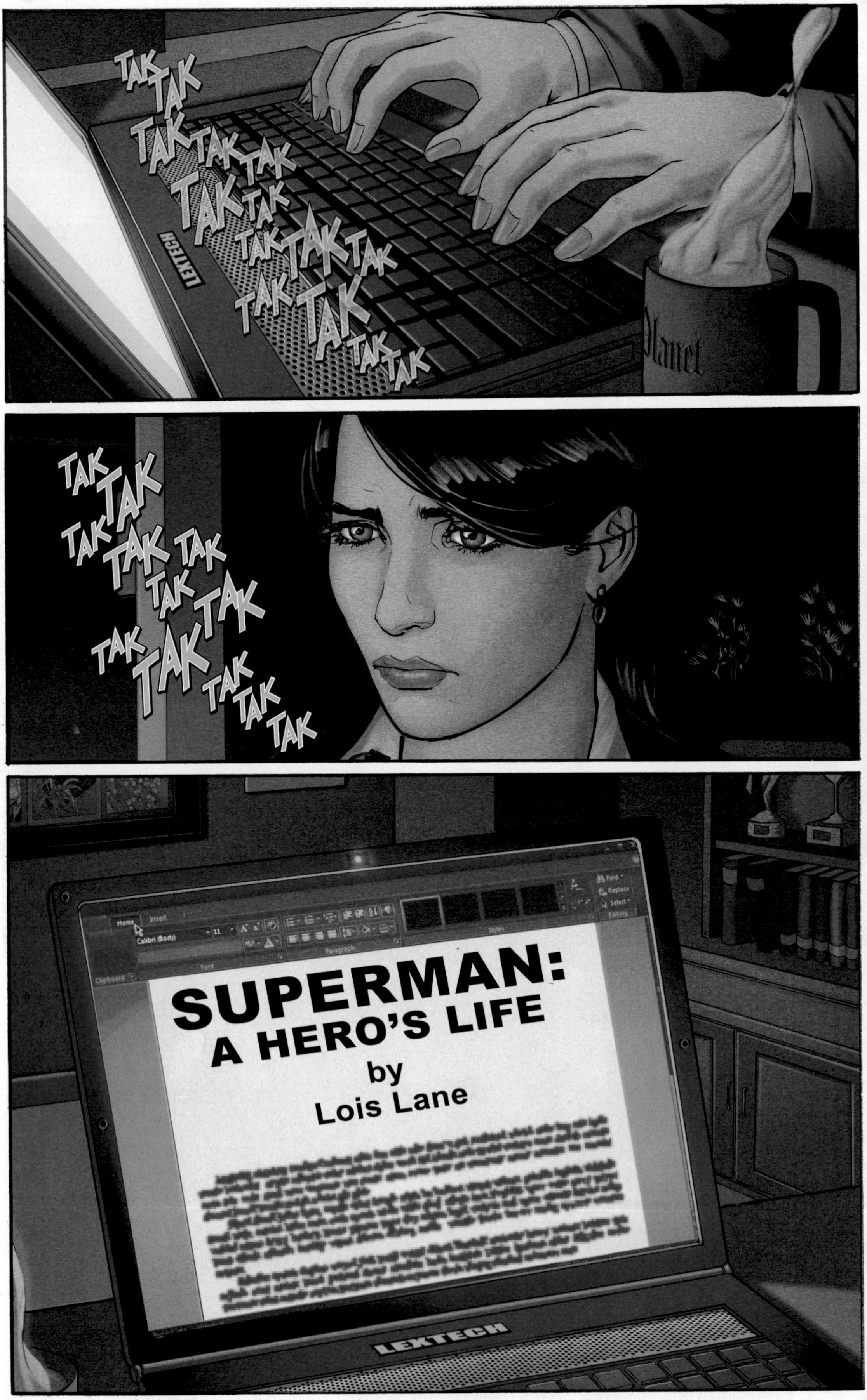
TAK TAK TAK TAK TAK TAK TAK TAK TAK TAK TAK TAK TAK TAK TAK
LEXTECH
Planet
TAK TAK TAK TAK TAK TAK TAK TAK TAK TAK TAK TAK TAK
Home
Insert
Calibri (Body)
11
Paragraph
Font
Clipboard
Styles
Find
Replace
Select
Editing
SUPERMAN:
A HERO'S LIFE
by
Lois Lane
LEXTECH

VARIANT COVER GALLERY

SUPERMAN #45
MONSTER MONTH VARIANT BY
CULLY HAMNER

SUPERMAN #46
LOONEY TUNES VARIANT BY
RYAN SOOK, SPIKE BRANDT

SUPERMAN #47
HARLEY'S LITTLE BLACK BOOK VARIANT BY
LEE BERMEJO

SUPERMAN #48
ADULT COLORING BOOK VARIANT BY
ANDY SMITH

SUPERMAN #49
NEAL ADAMS VARIANT BY
NEAL ADAMS, SIMON BISLEY, TERRY DODSON

SUPERMAN #50
VARIANT BY KAARE ANDREWS,
DAVE JOHNSON, DAVE McCRAIG

SUPERMAN #50/BATMAN #50
DCBS VARIANT BY NEAL ADAMS, JEROMY COX

SUPERMAN #50/BATMAN #50
COMIXPOSURE VARIANT BY GUILLEM MARCH

SUPERMAN #50/BATMAN #50
VARIANT BY DAVE JOHNSON

SUPERMAN #50/BATMAN #50
PULP'S COMICS AND PARIS COMICS EXPO VARIANT
BY LEE BERMEJO

SUPERMAN #50/BATMAN #50
FRIED PIE VARIANT BY RAFAEL ALBUQUERQUE

SUPERMAN #50/BATMAN #50
BULLETPROOF COMICS VARIANT BY
GABRIELE DELL'OTTO

SUPERMAN #50/BATMAN #50
MIDTOWN COMICS VARIANT BY
TERRY DODSON, RACHEL DODSON

SUPERMAN #50/BATMAN #50
DYNAMIC FORCES VARIANT BY AMANDA CONNER

SUPERMAN #50/BATMAN #50
NEWBURY COMICS VARIANT BY
TIM SALE, BRENNAN WAGNER

SUPERMAN #50/BATMAN #50
BEYOND COMICS VARIANT BY
ED BENES, TOMEU MOREY

SUPERMAN #50/BATMAN #50
COMIC CON BOX VARIANT BY
PAT GLEASON, MICK GRAY, JOHN KALISZ

SUPERMAN #50/BATMAN #50
MADNESS GAMES & COMICS VARIANT BY
JOSHUA MIDDLETON

SUPERMAN #50/BATMAN #50
FORBIDDEN PLANET LIMITED VARIANT BY
SEAN GORDON MURPHY, DAVE McCAIG

SUPERMAN #50/BATMAN #50
HASTINGS VARIANT BY
TYLER KIRKHAM, TOMEU MOREY

SUPERMAN #51
JOHN ROMITA JR. VARIANT BY
JOHN ROMITA JR., DANNY MIKI & LAURA MARTIN

SUPERMAN #52
NEW 52 VARIANT BY MIKEL JANÍN

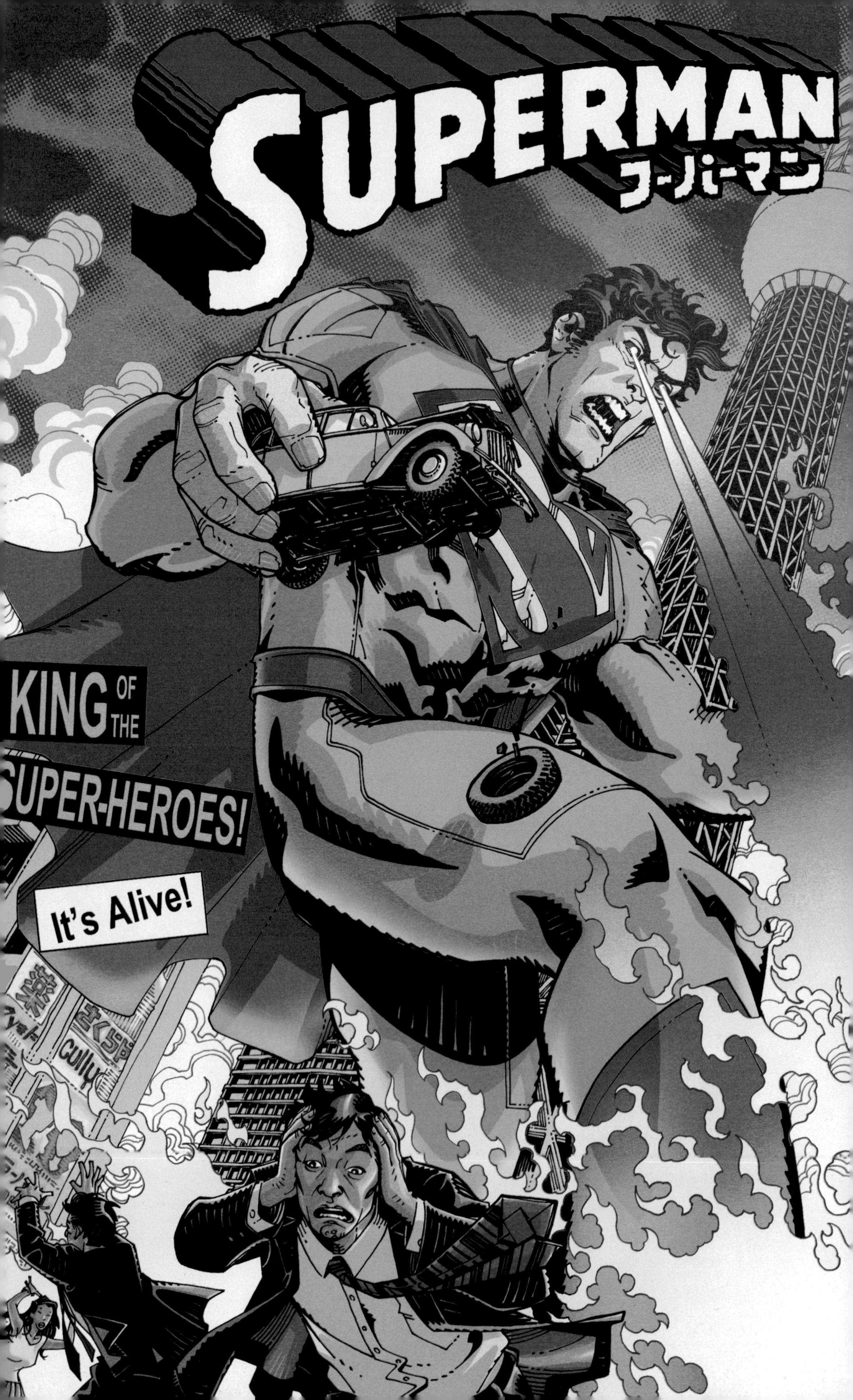
SUPERMAN
KING OF THE
SUPER-HEROES!
It's Alive!

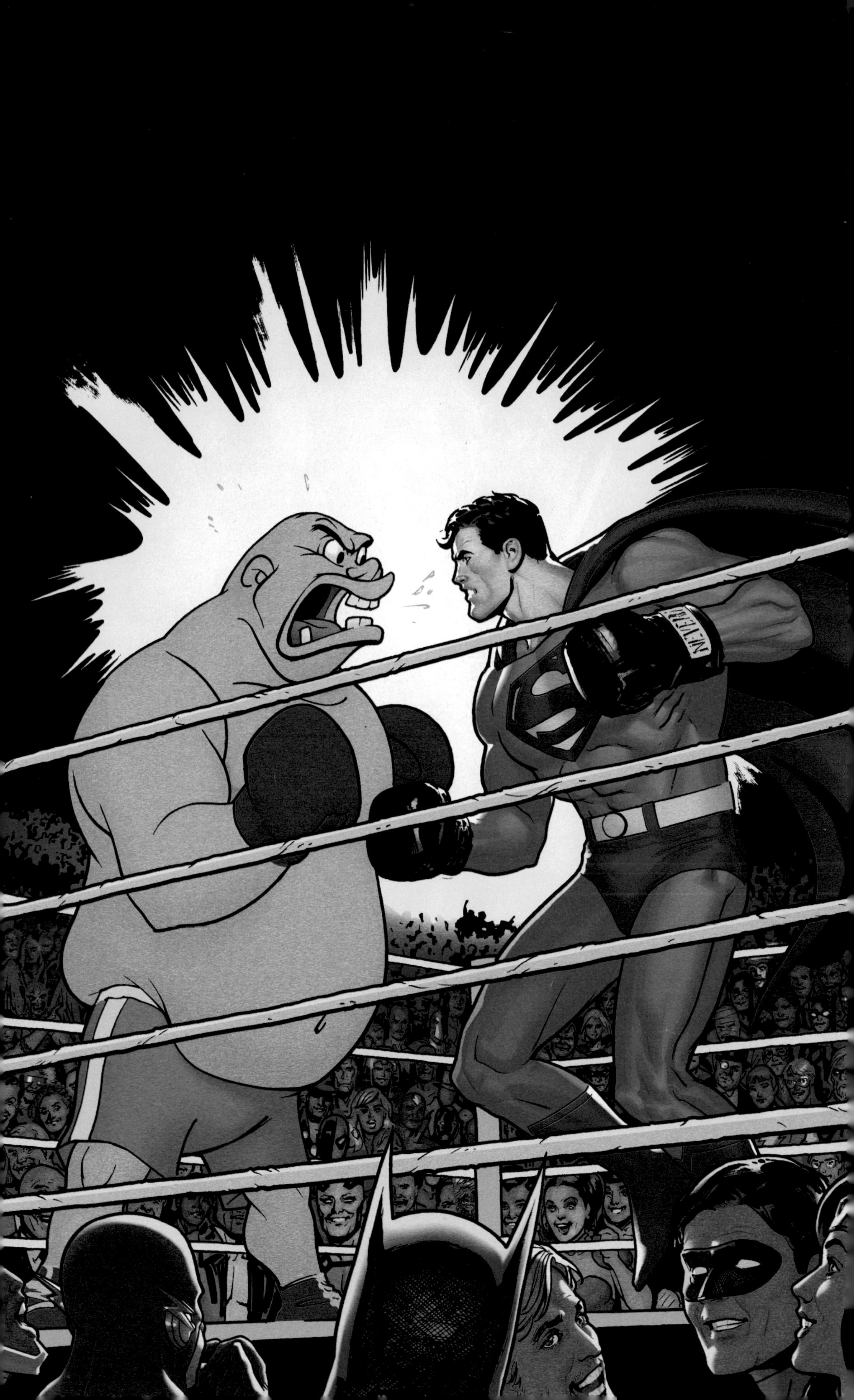

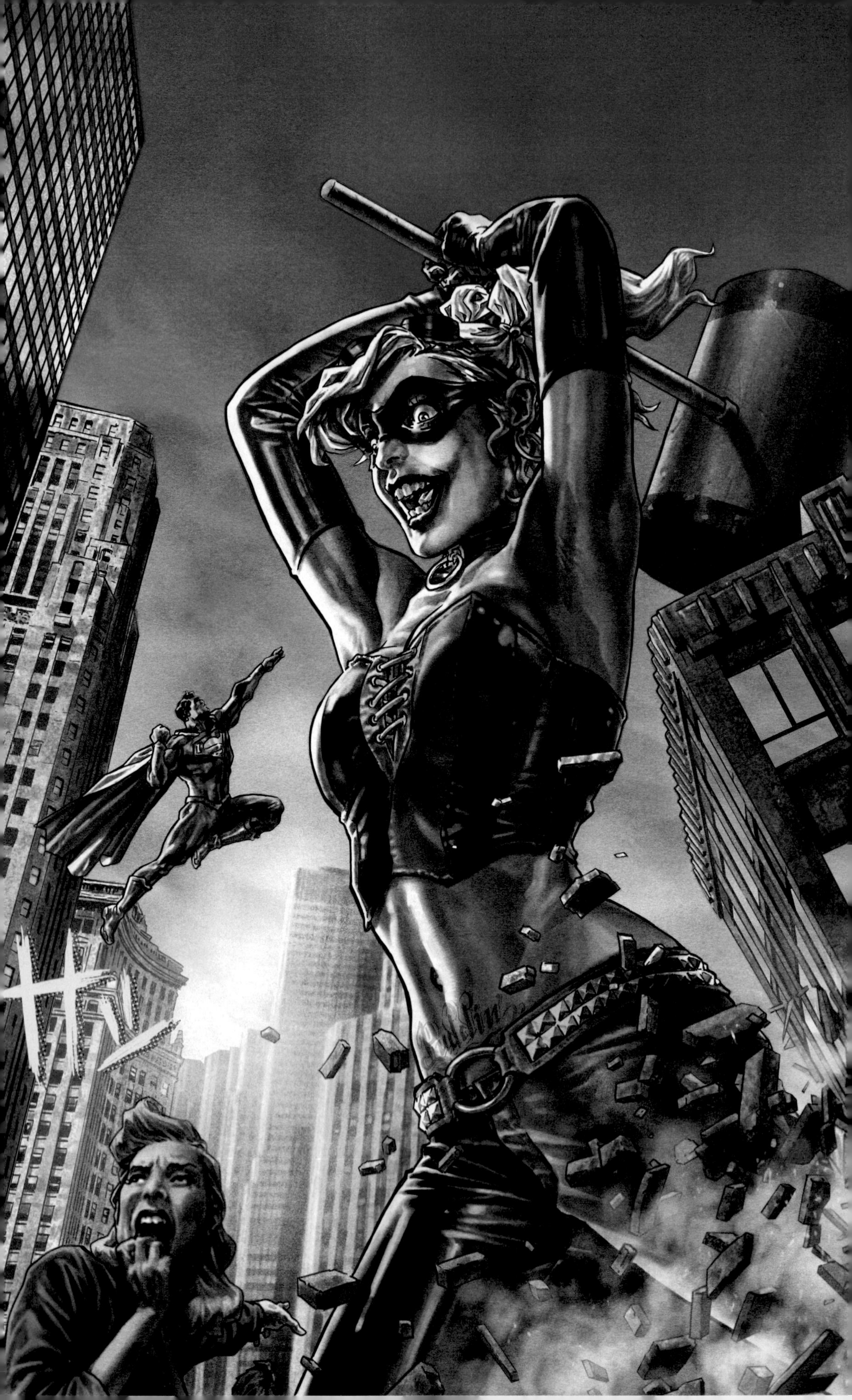

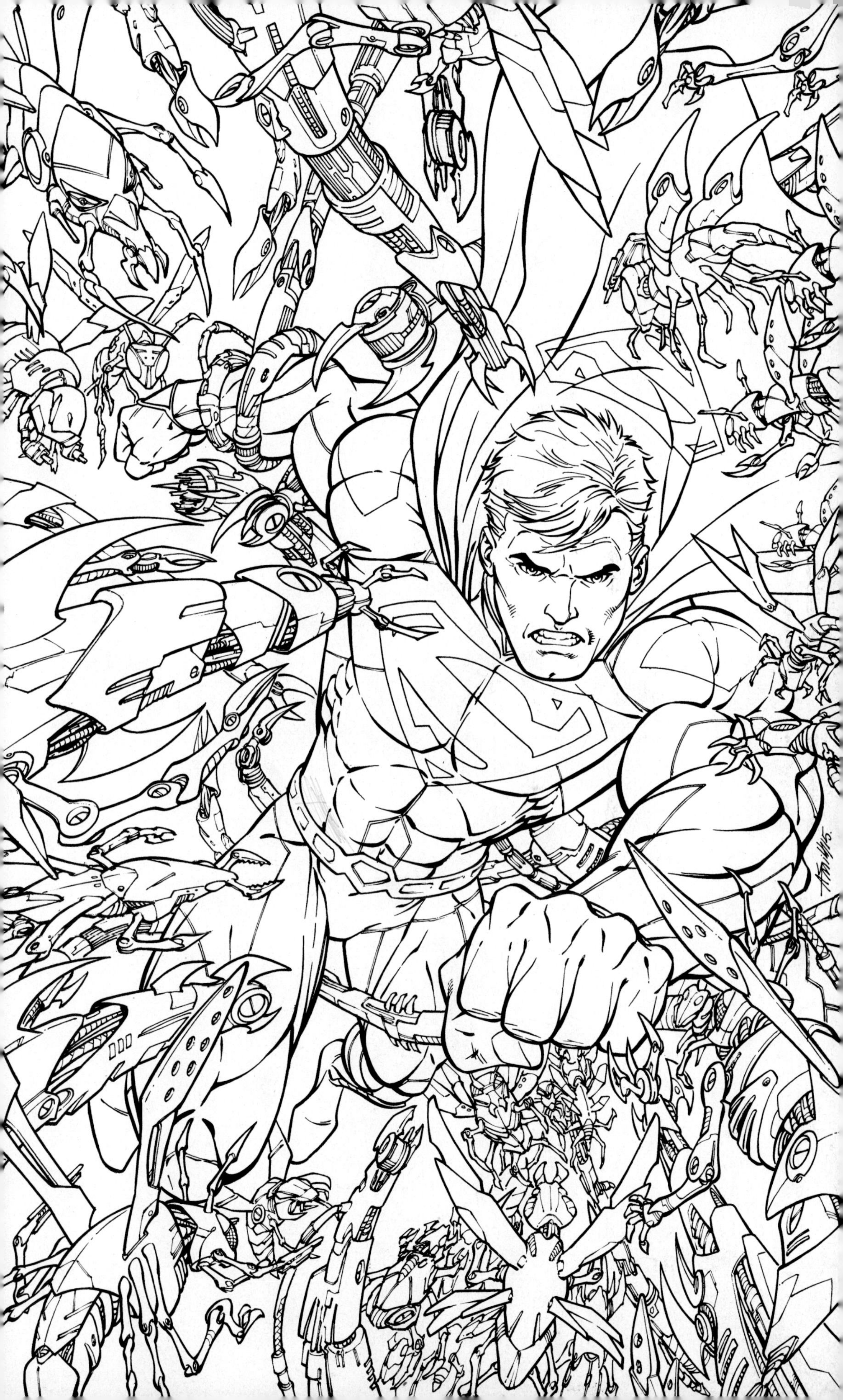

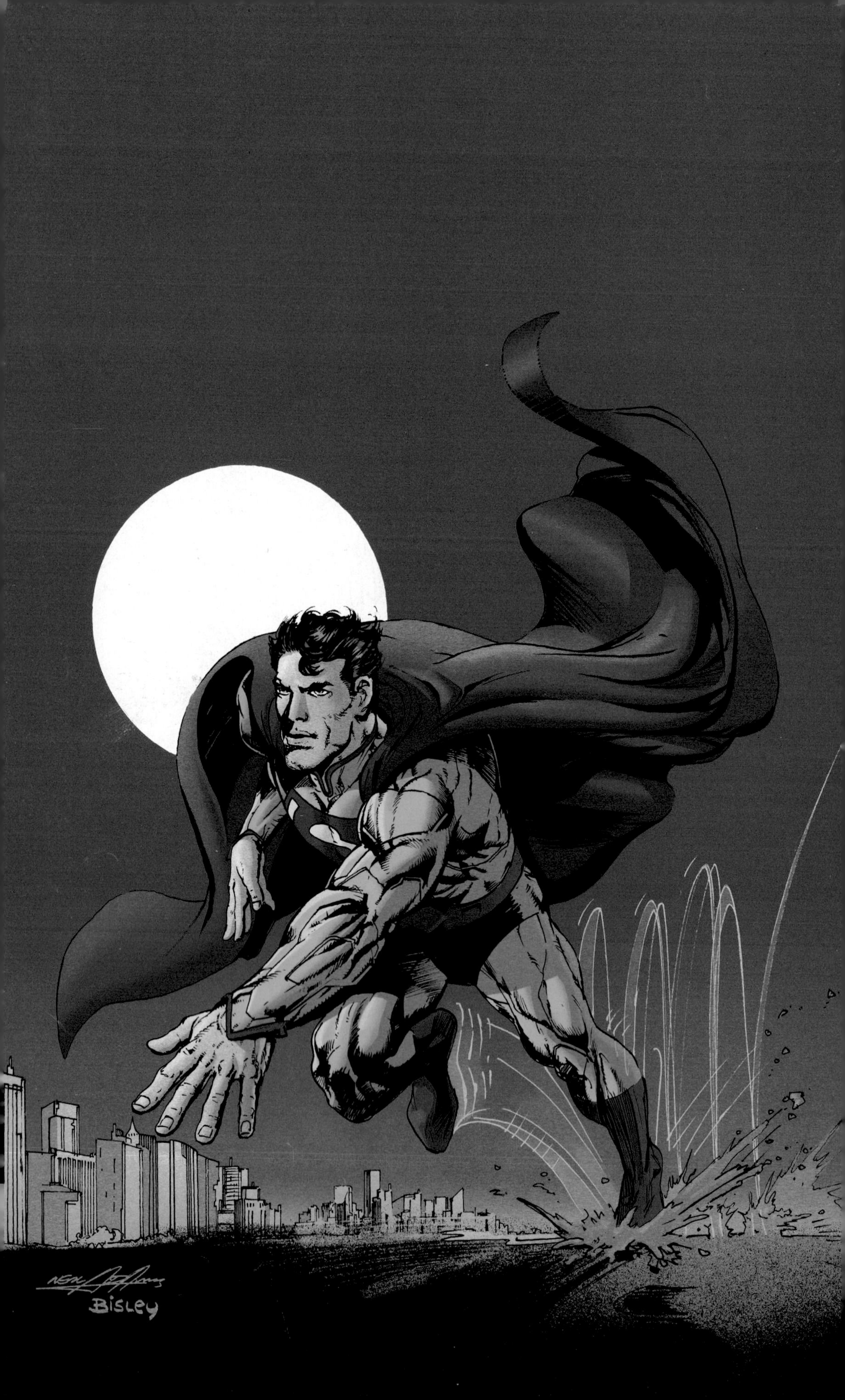
BISLEY

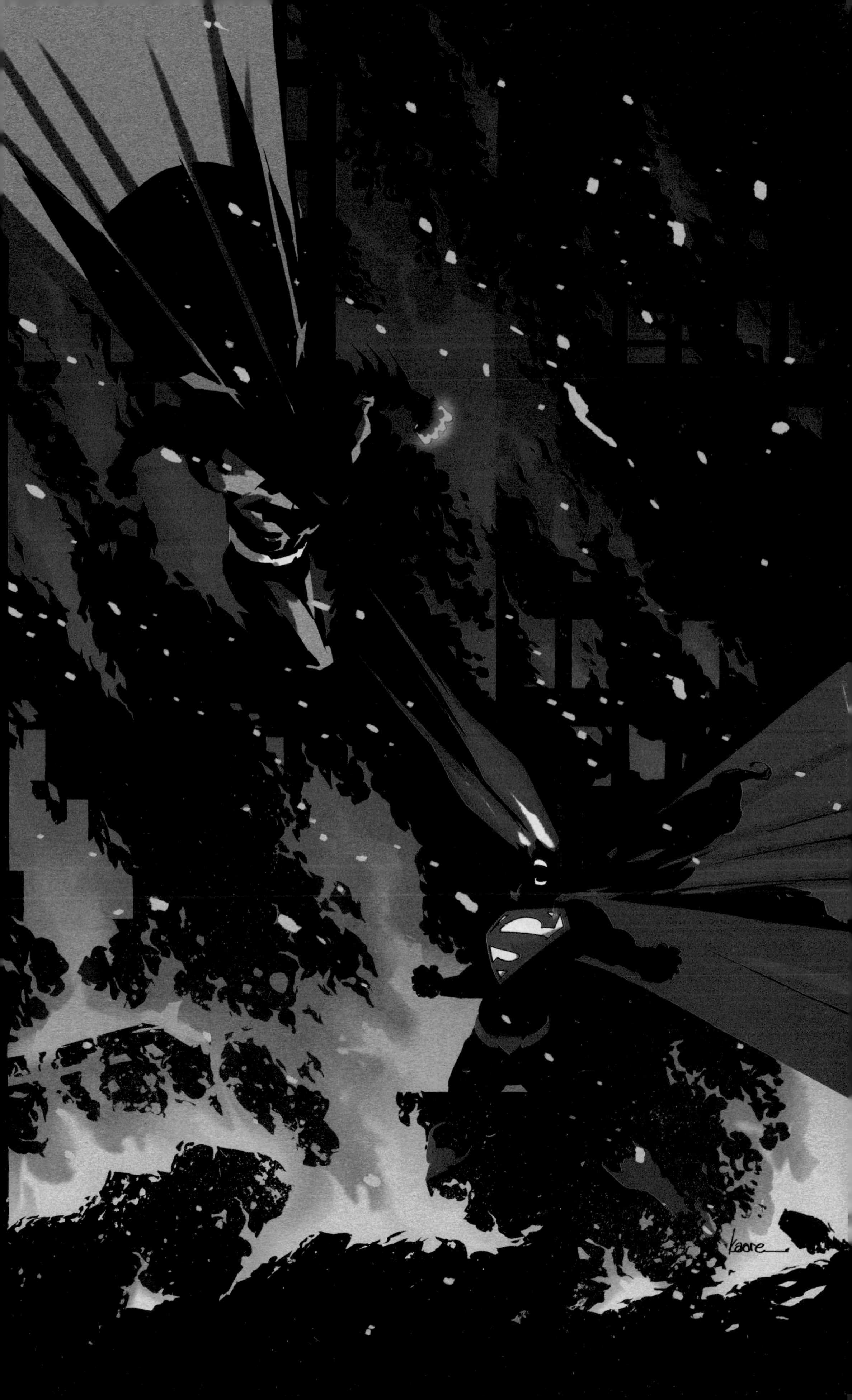

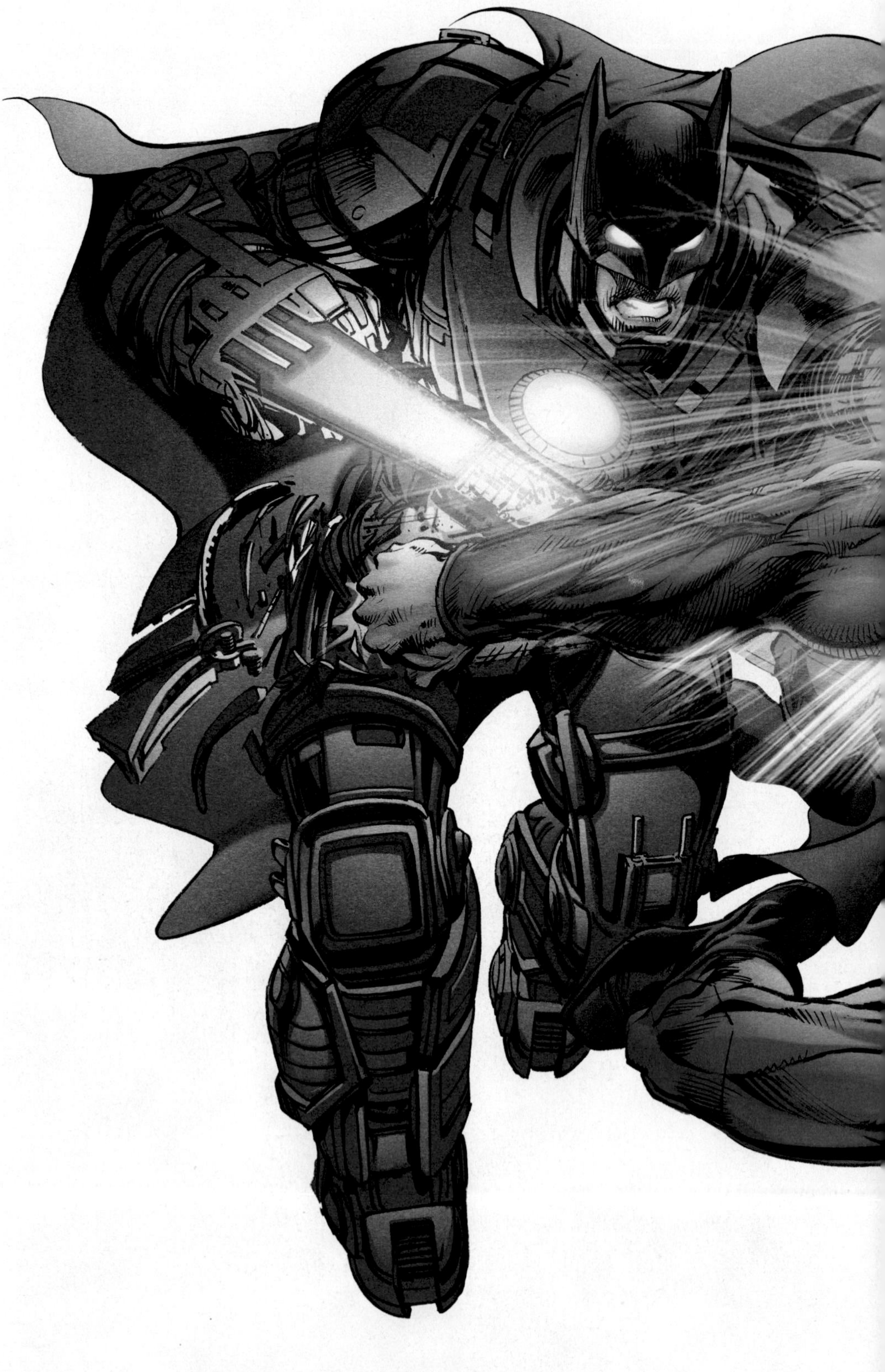

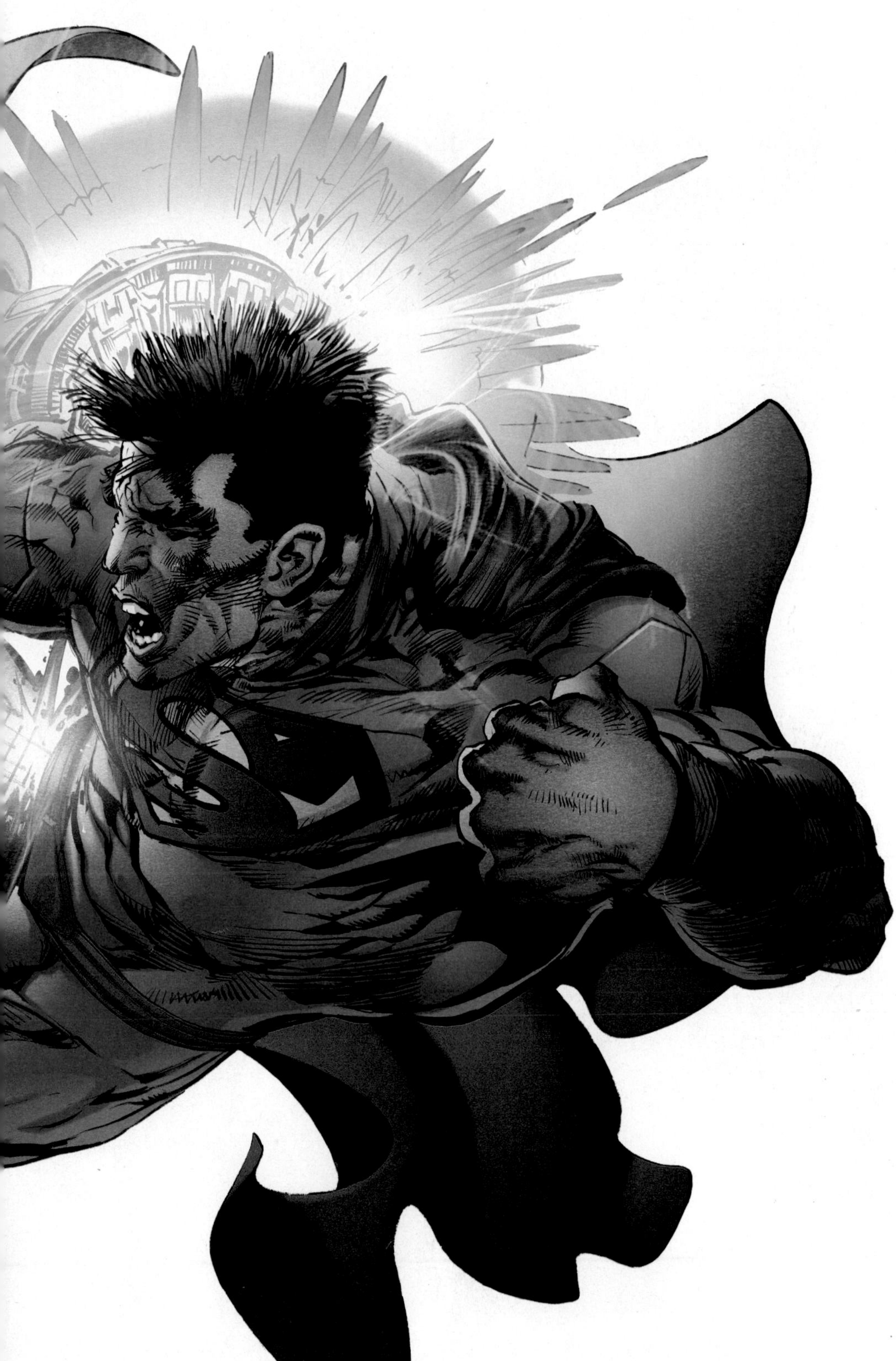

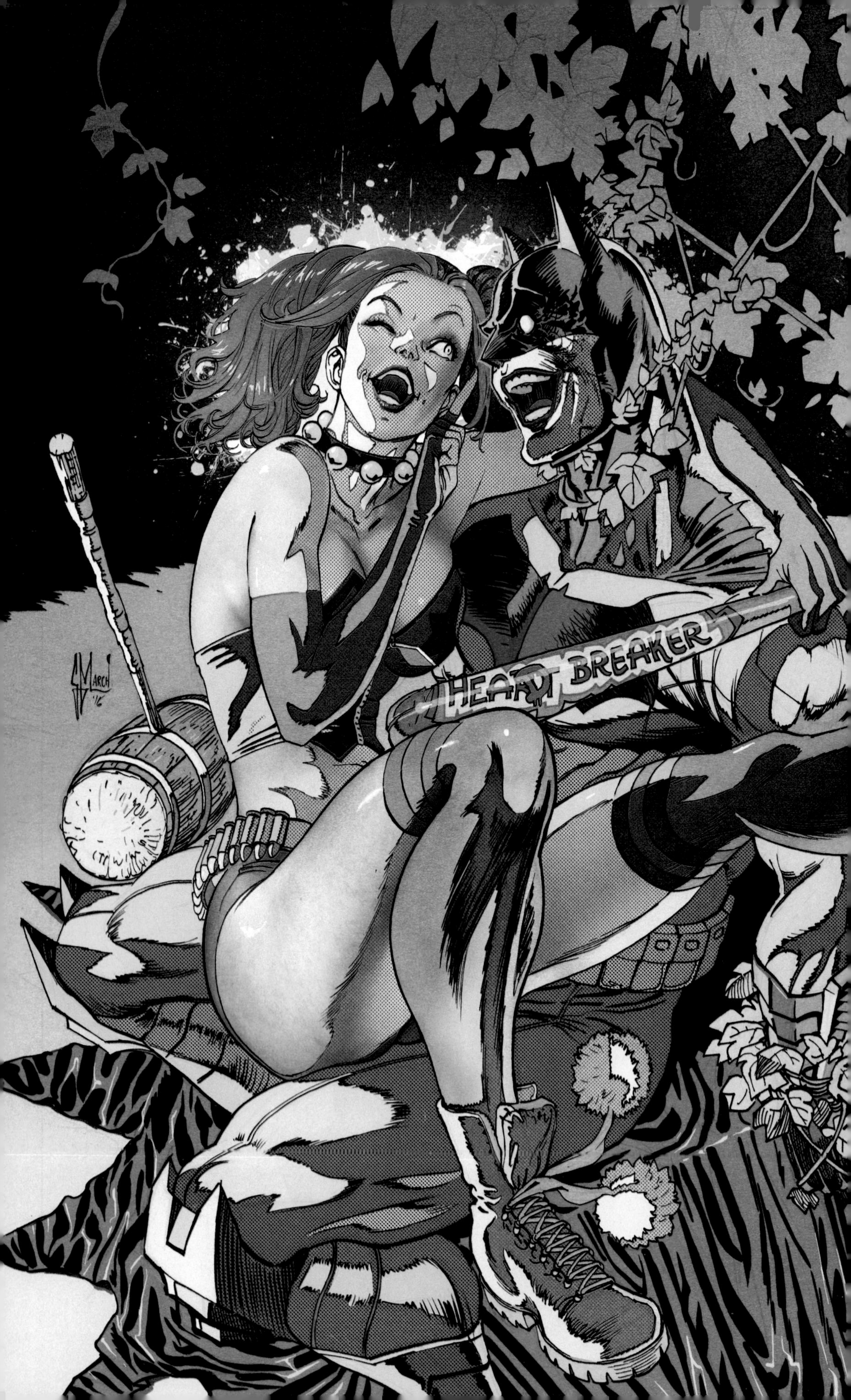
HEART BREAKER

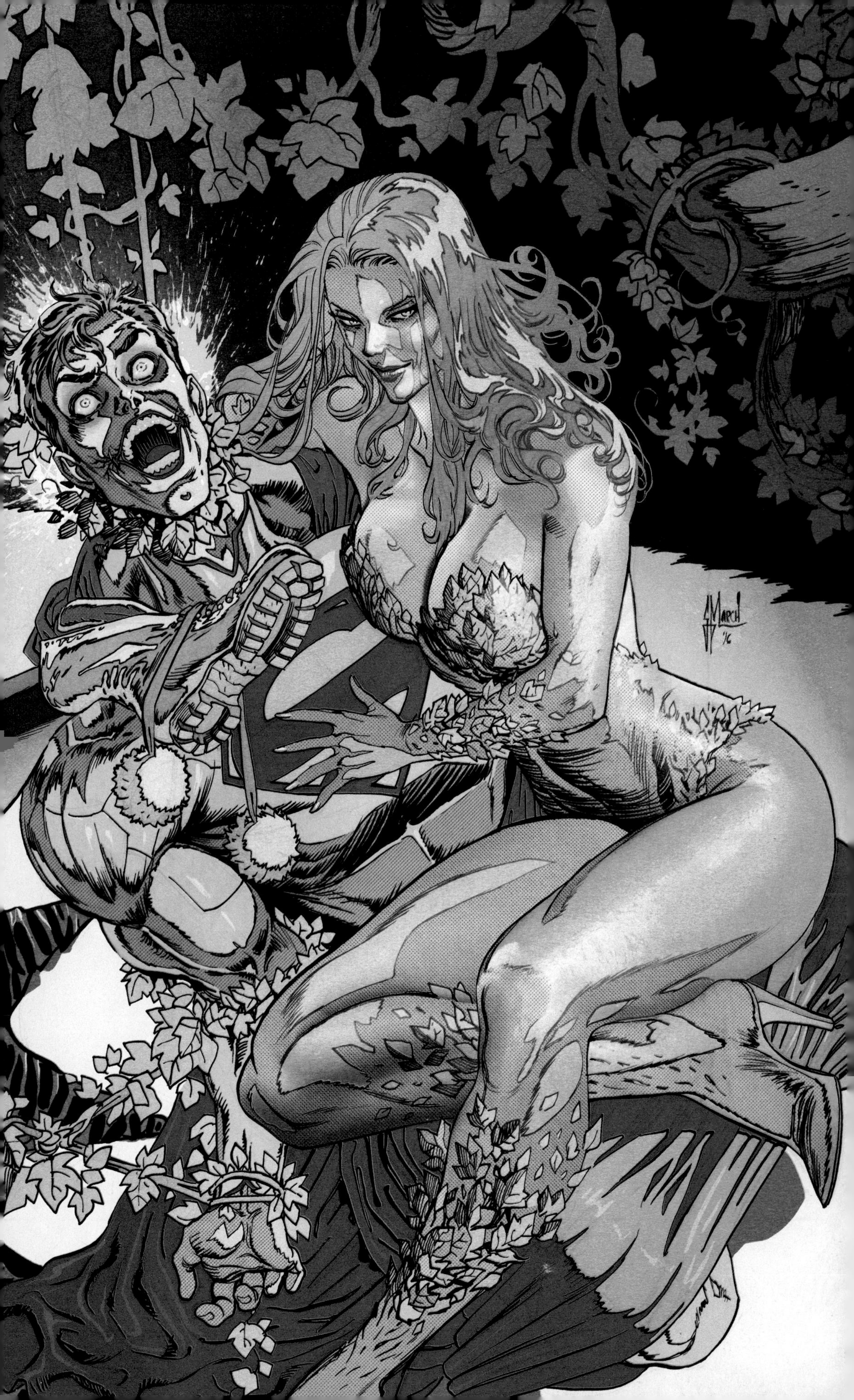

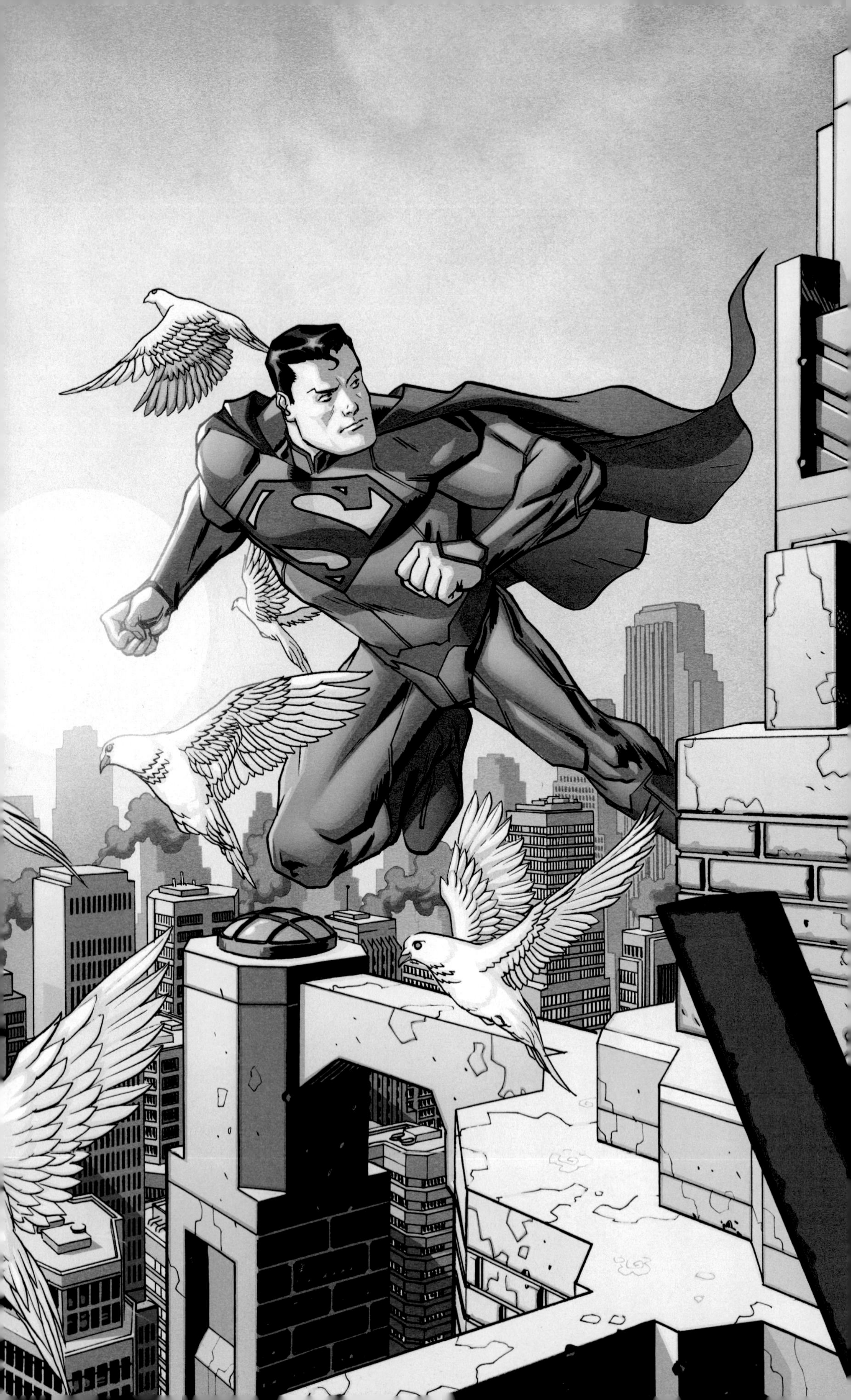

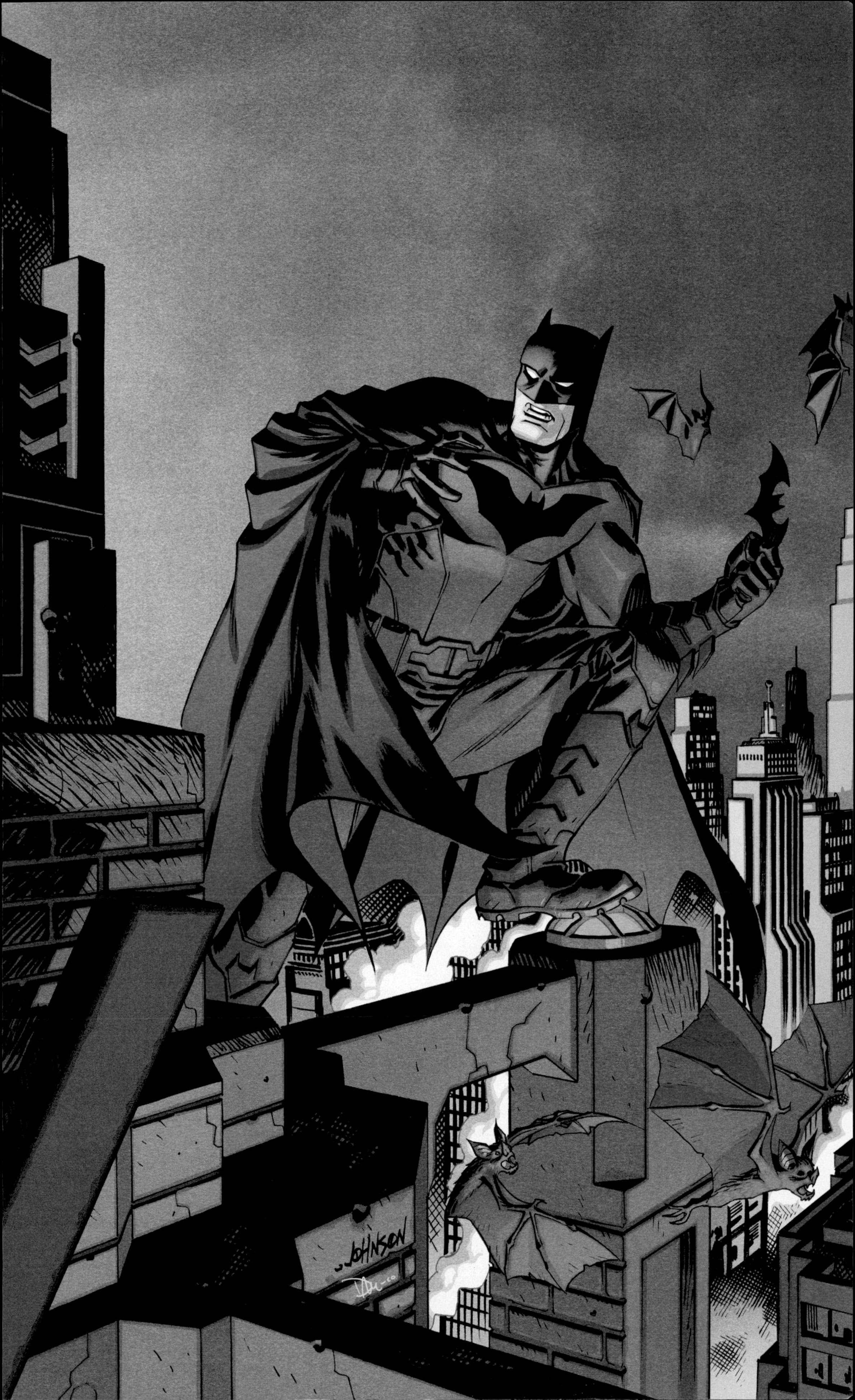
JOHNSON

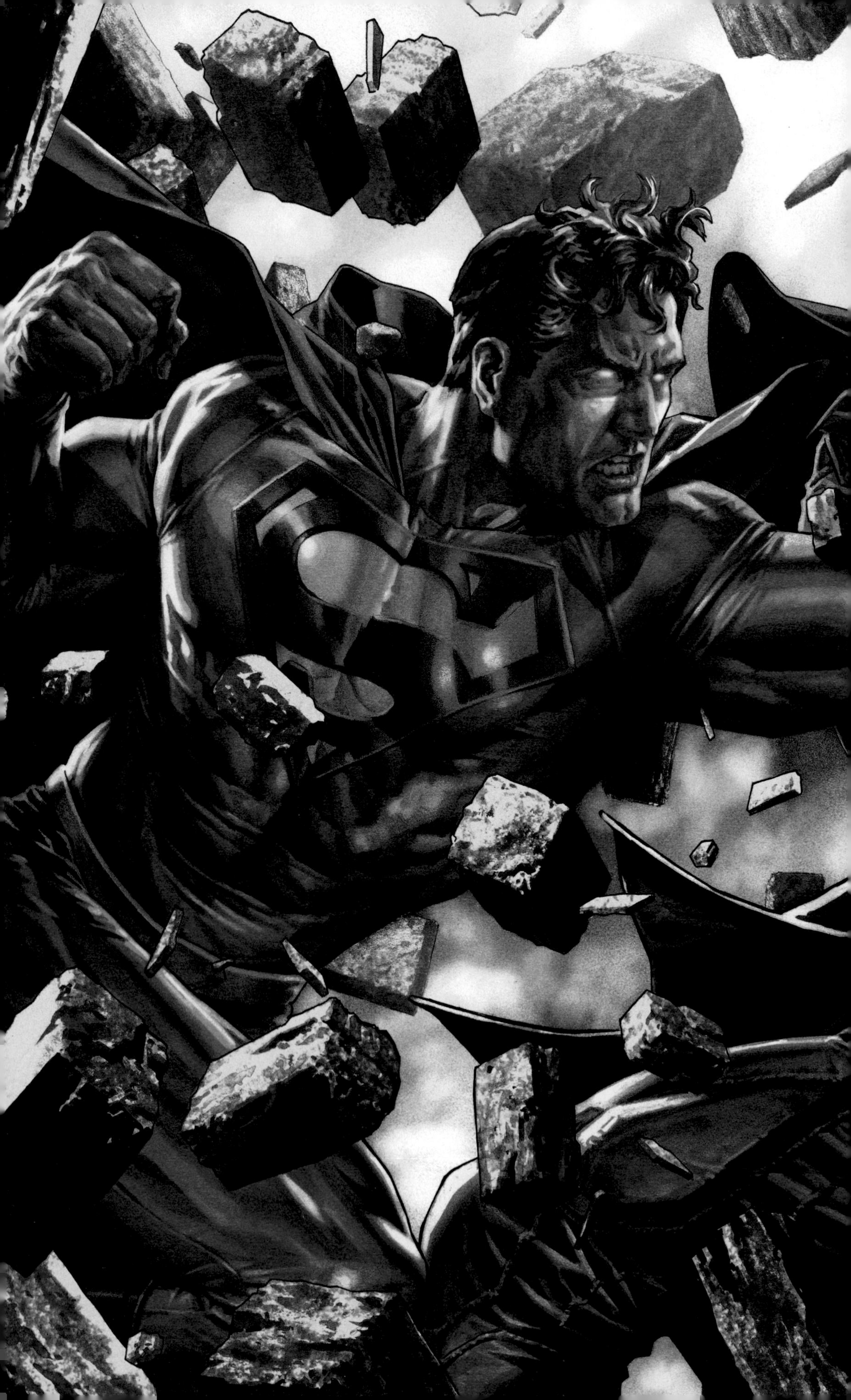

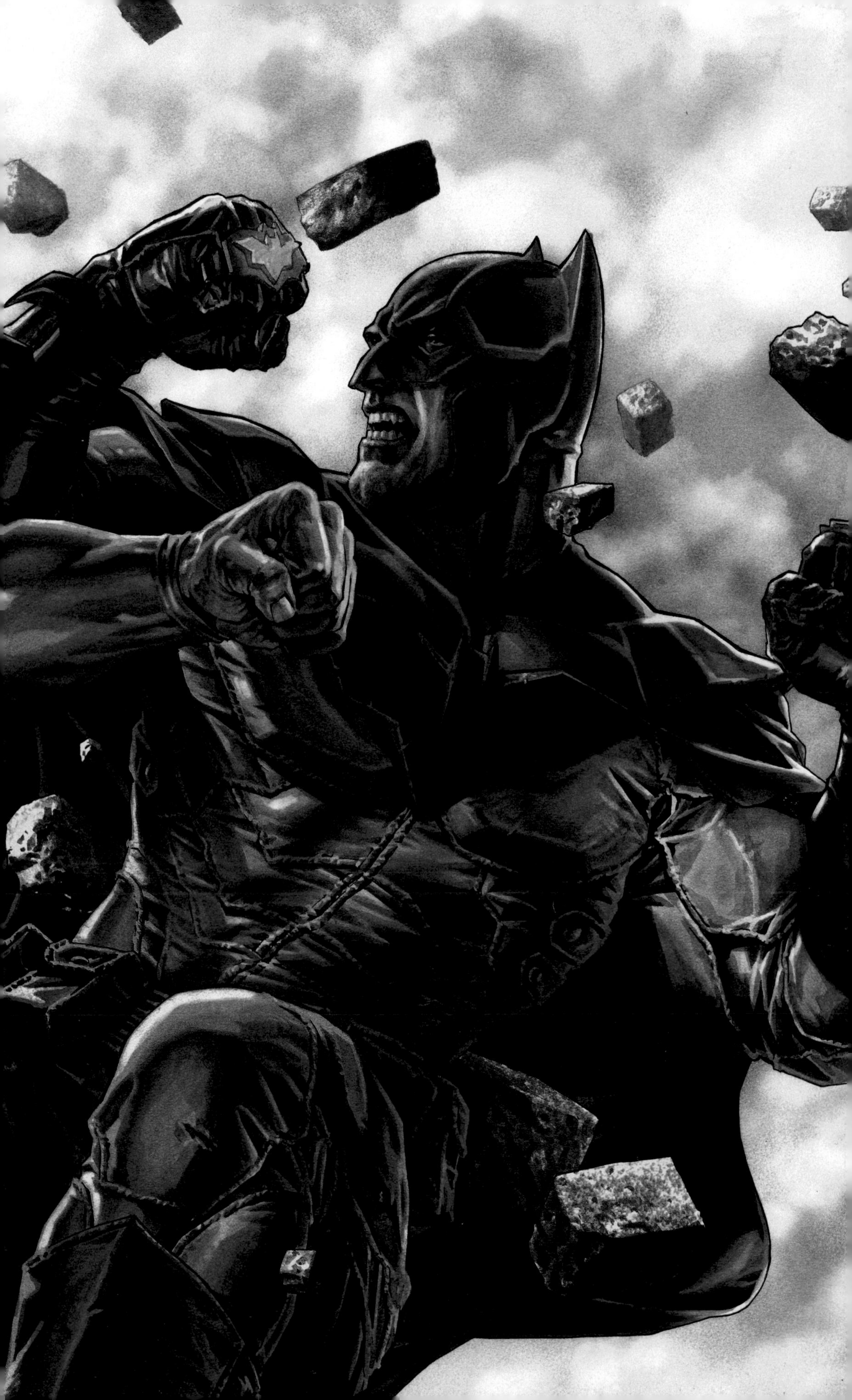

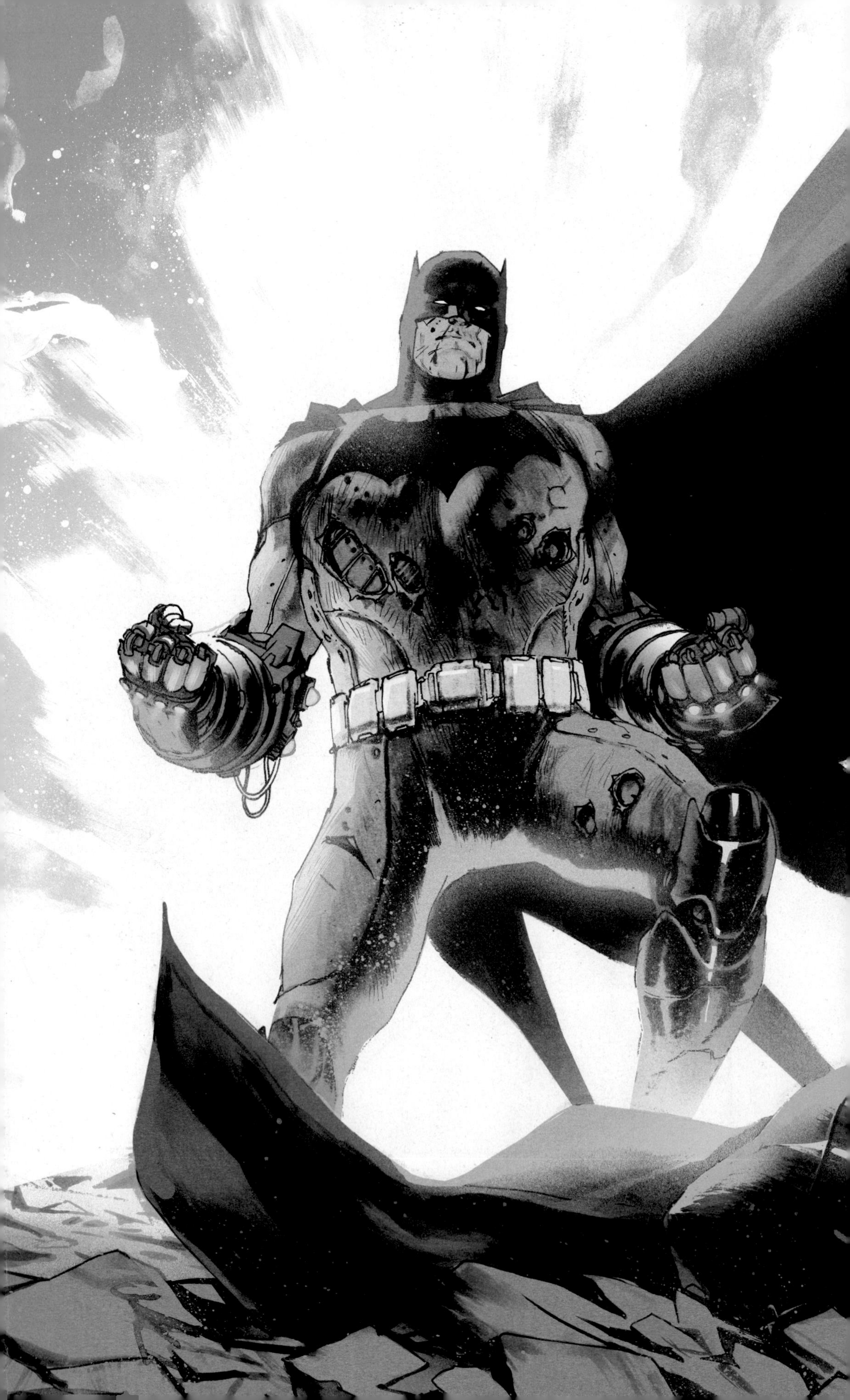

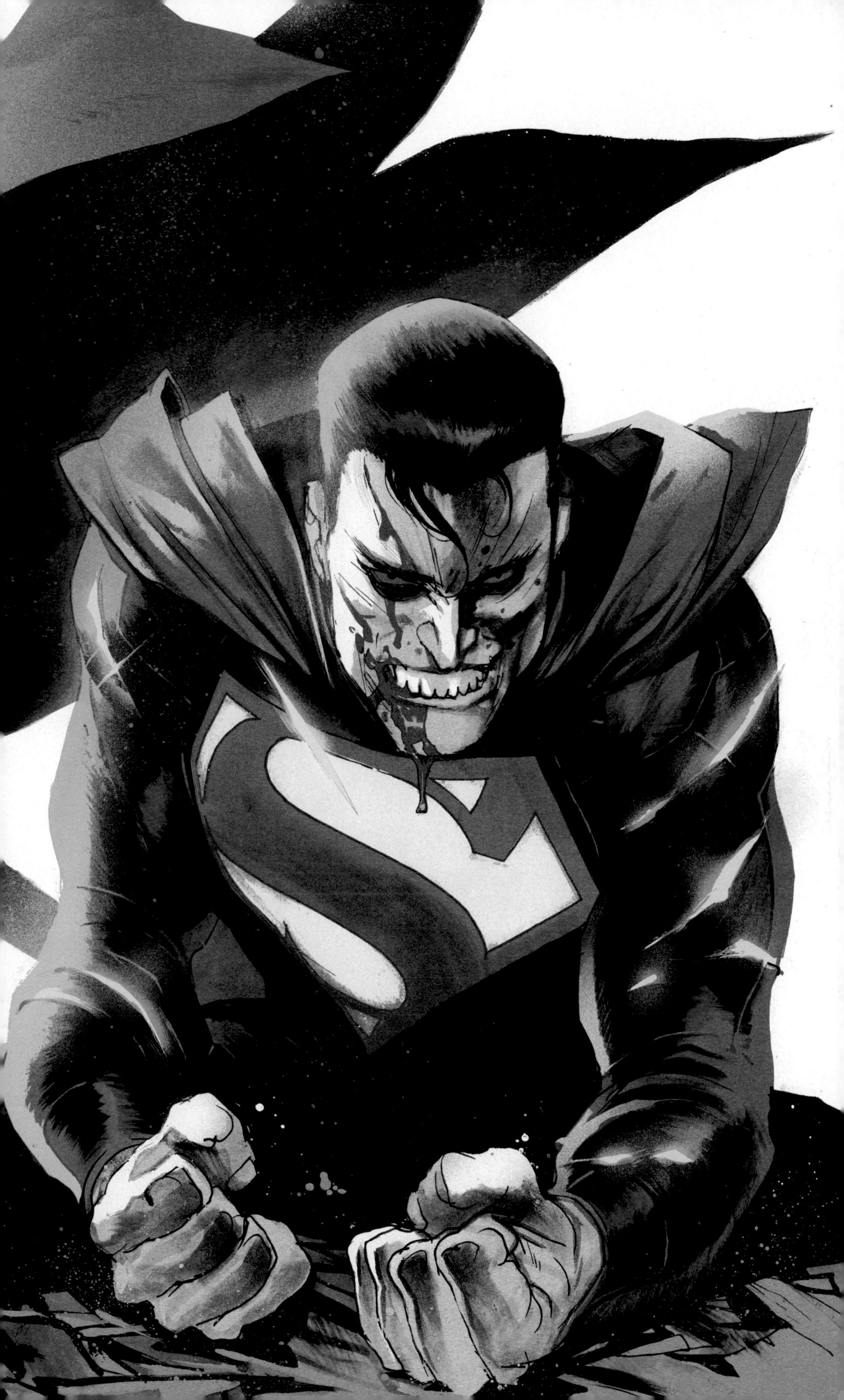

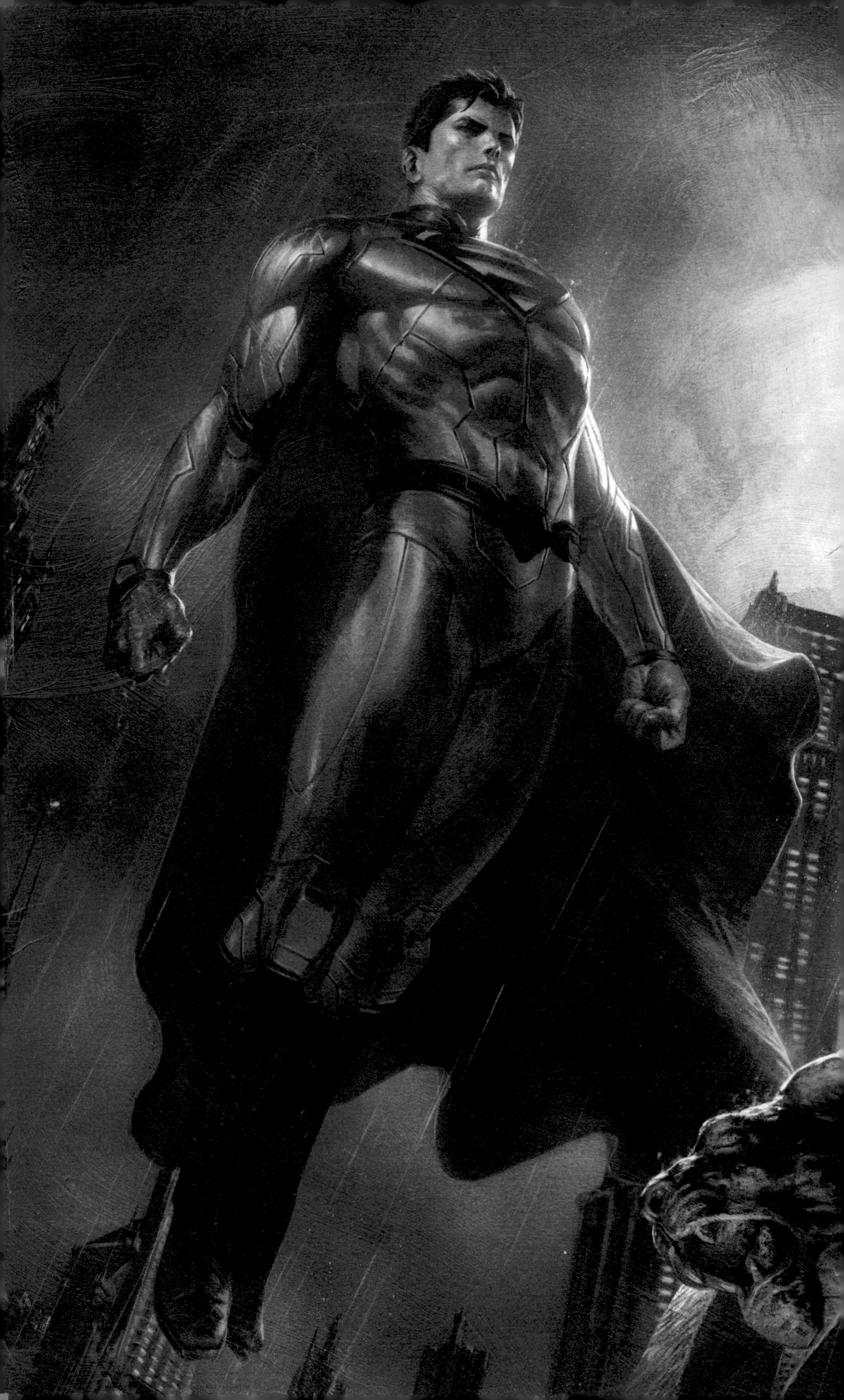

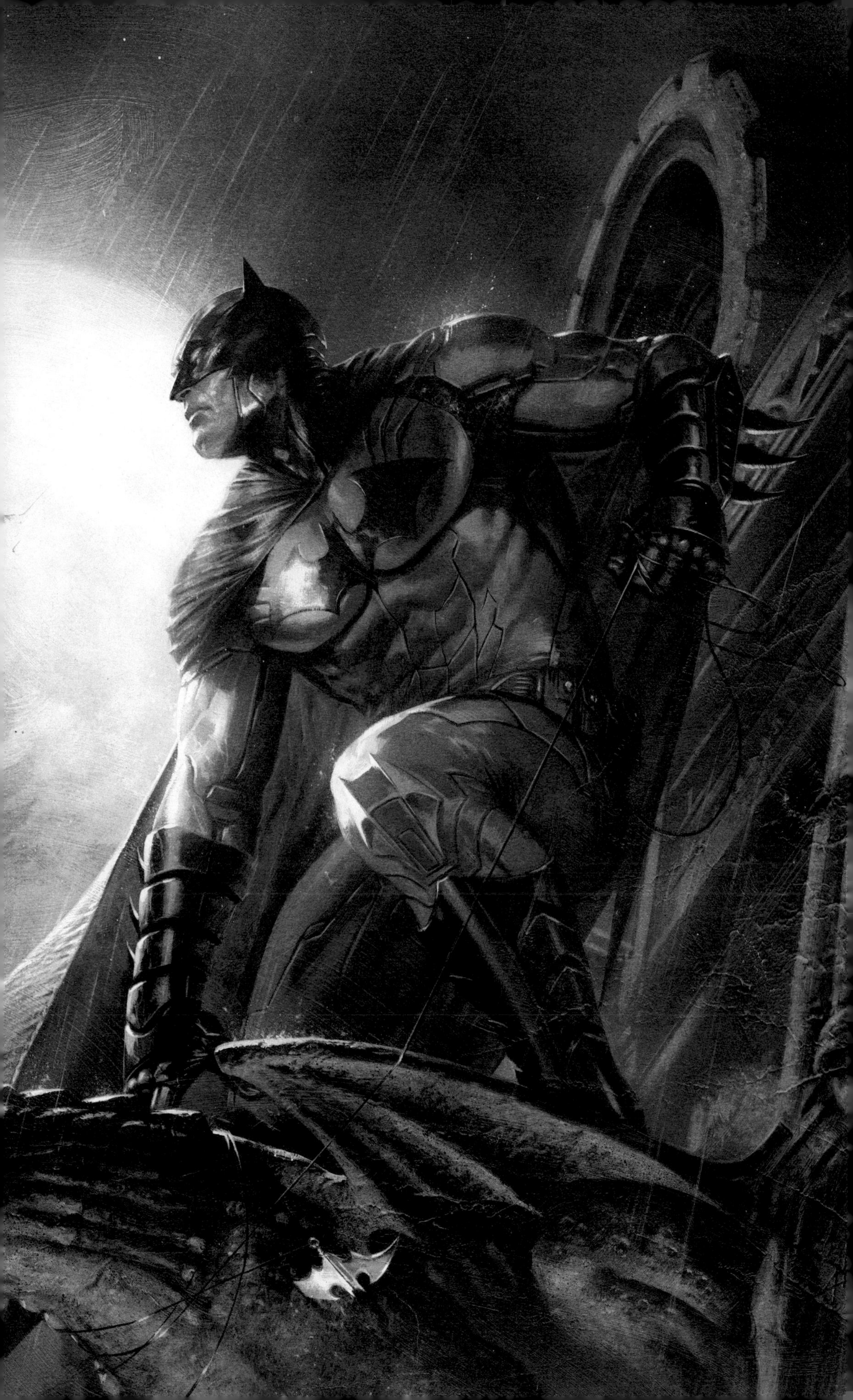

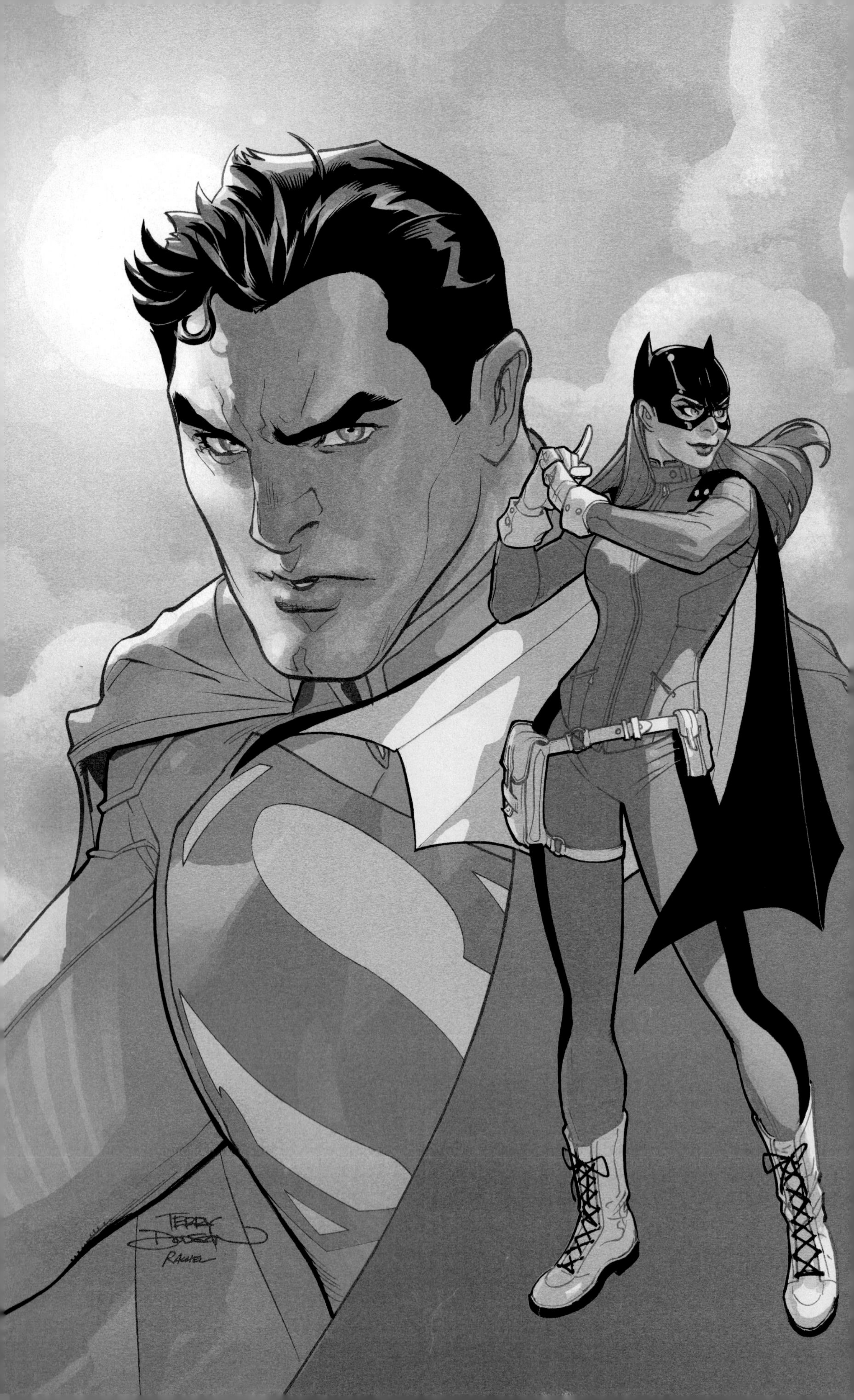
TERRY DODSON
RACHEL

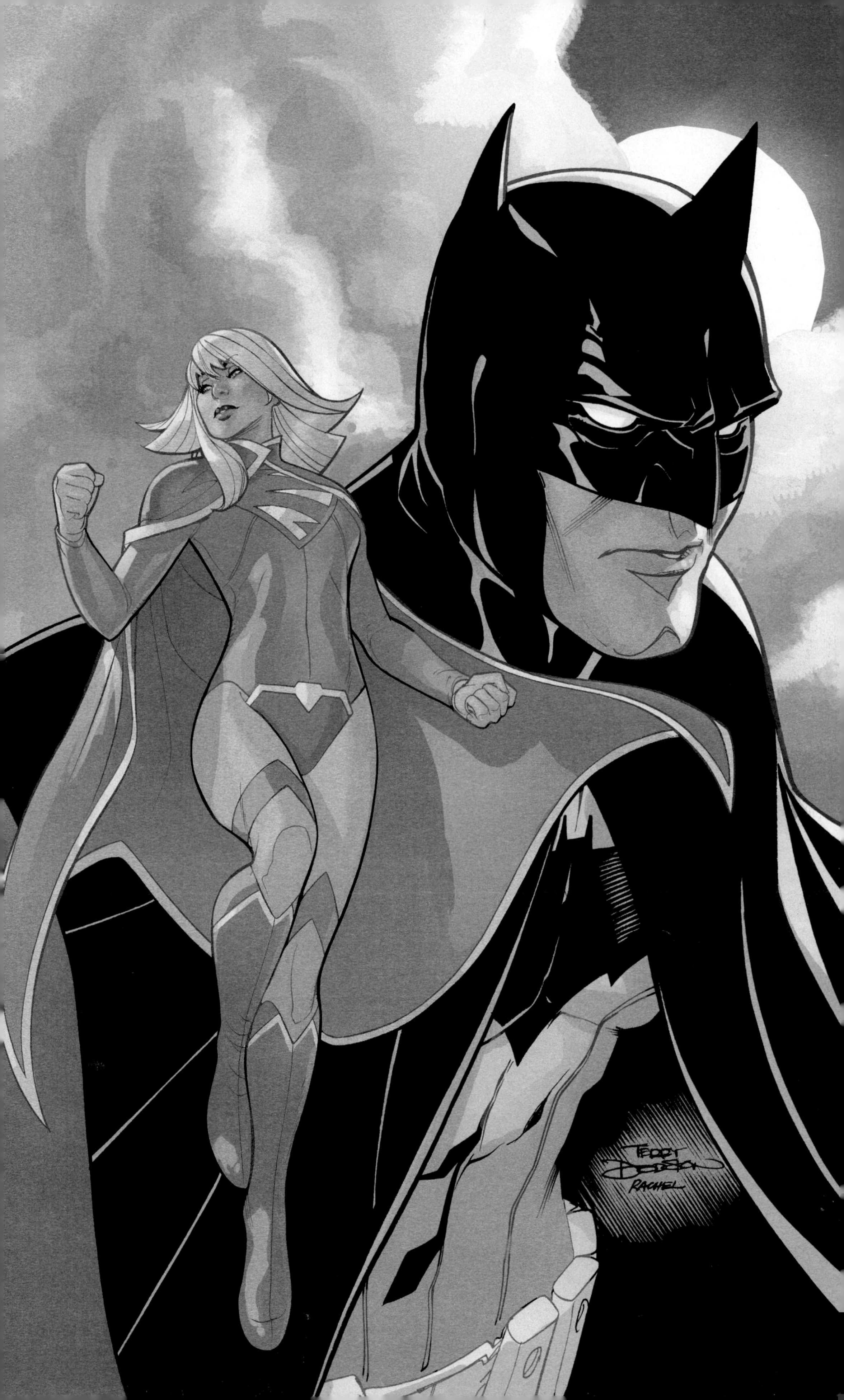

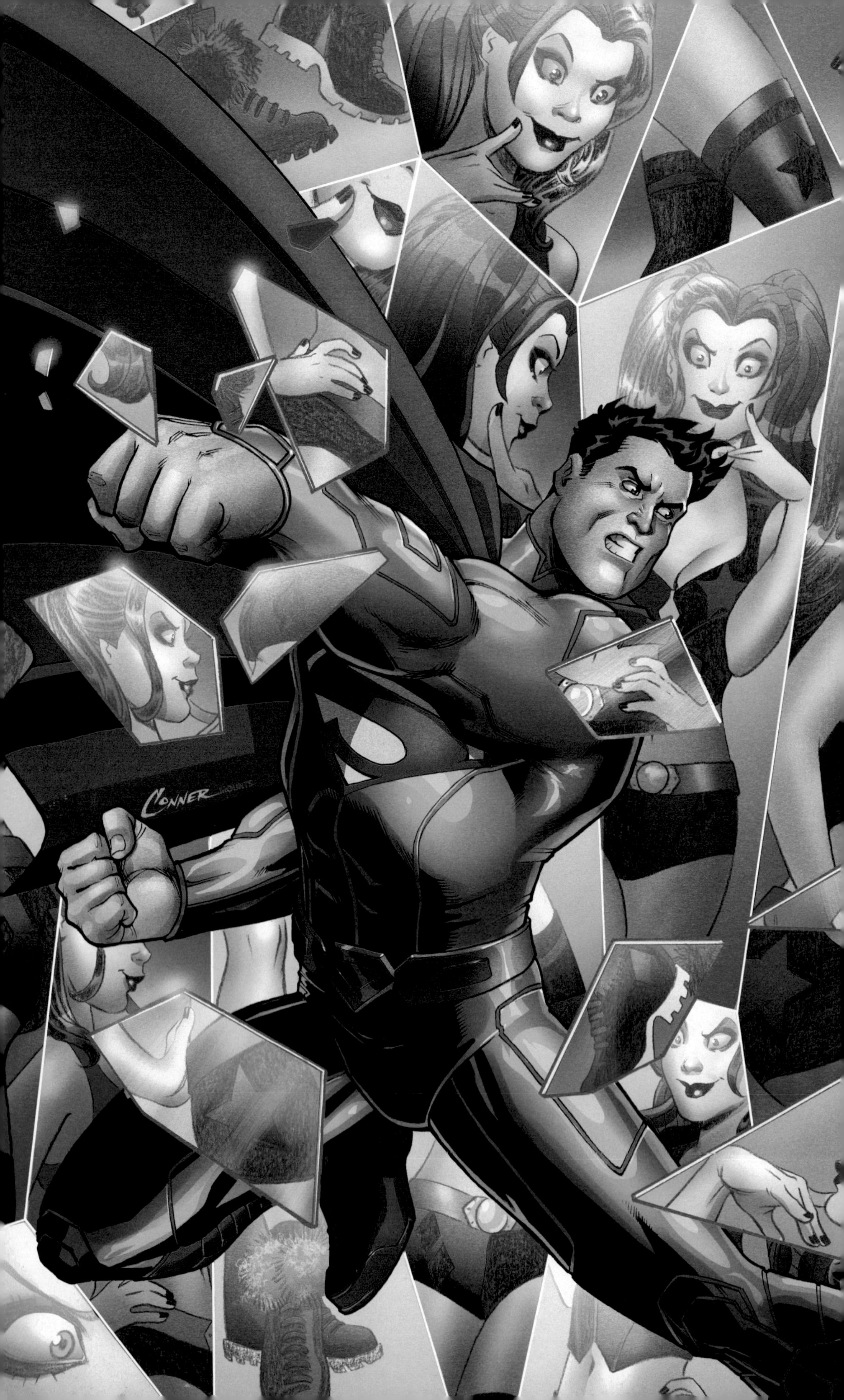
CONNER

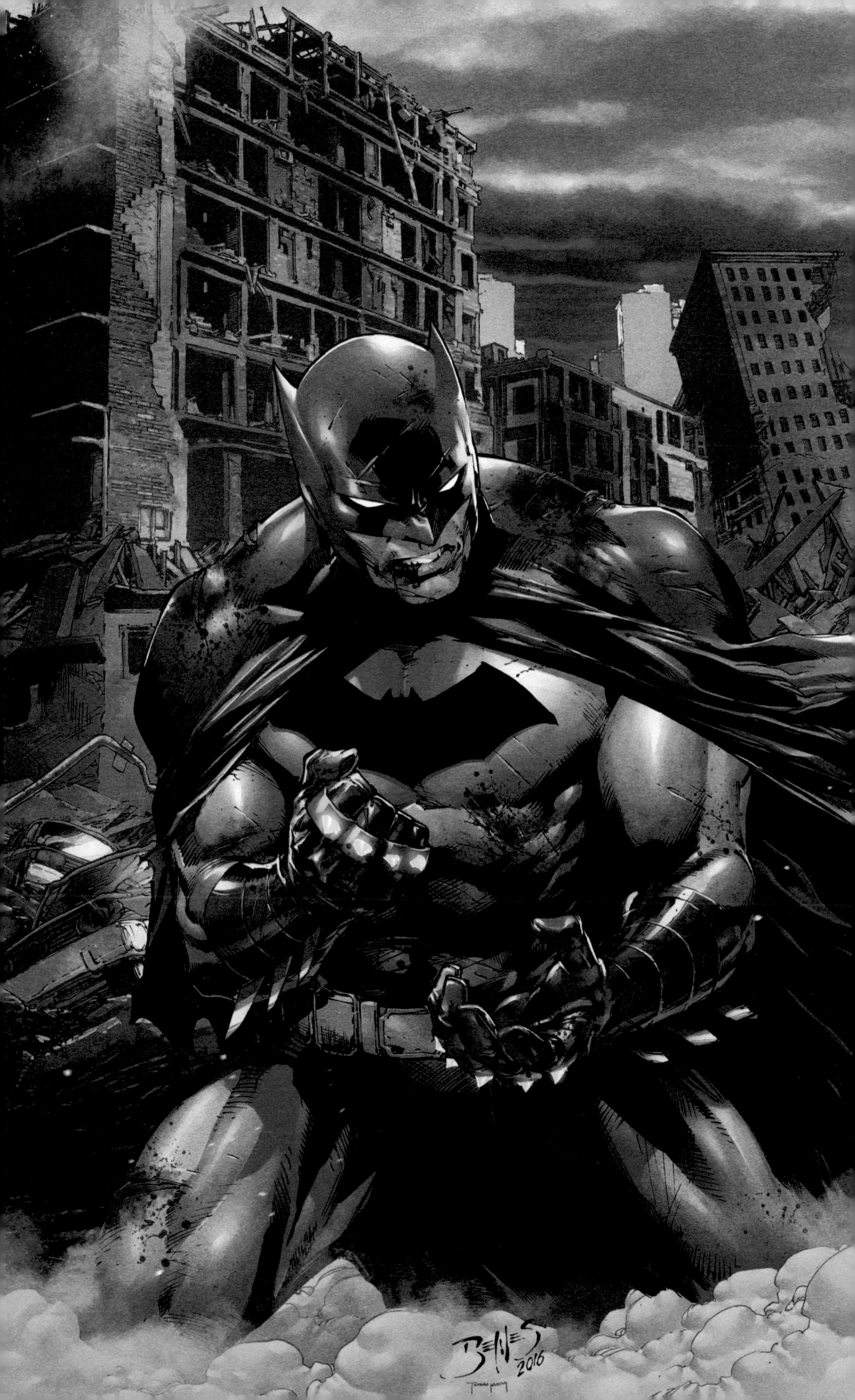
BENES
2016

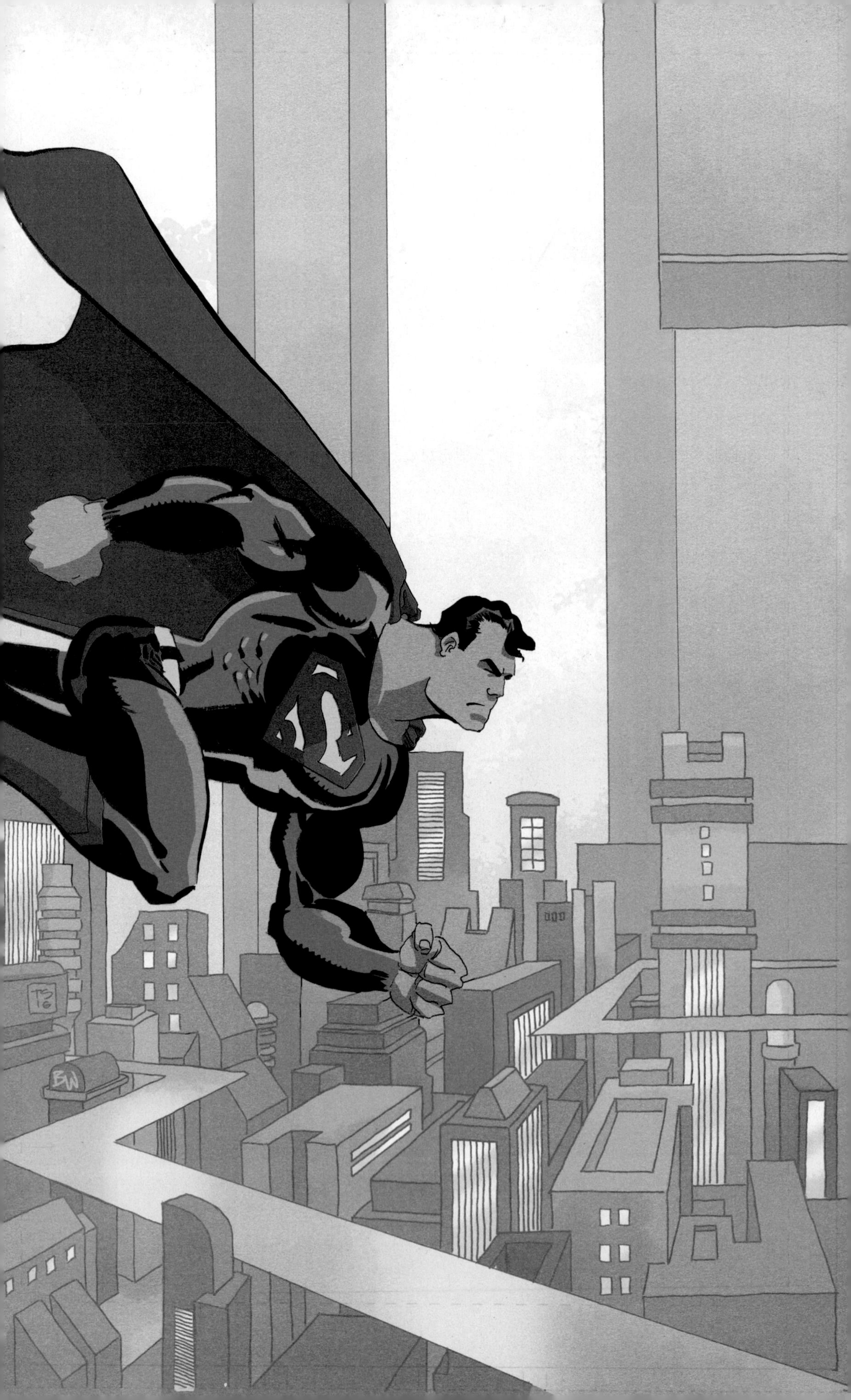

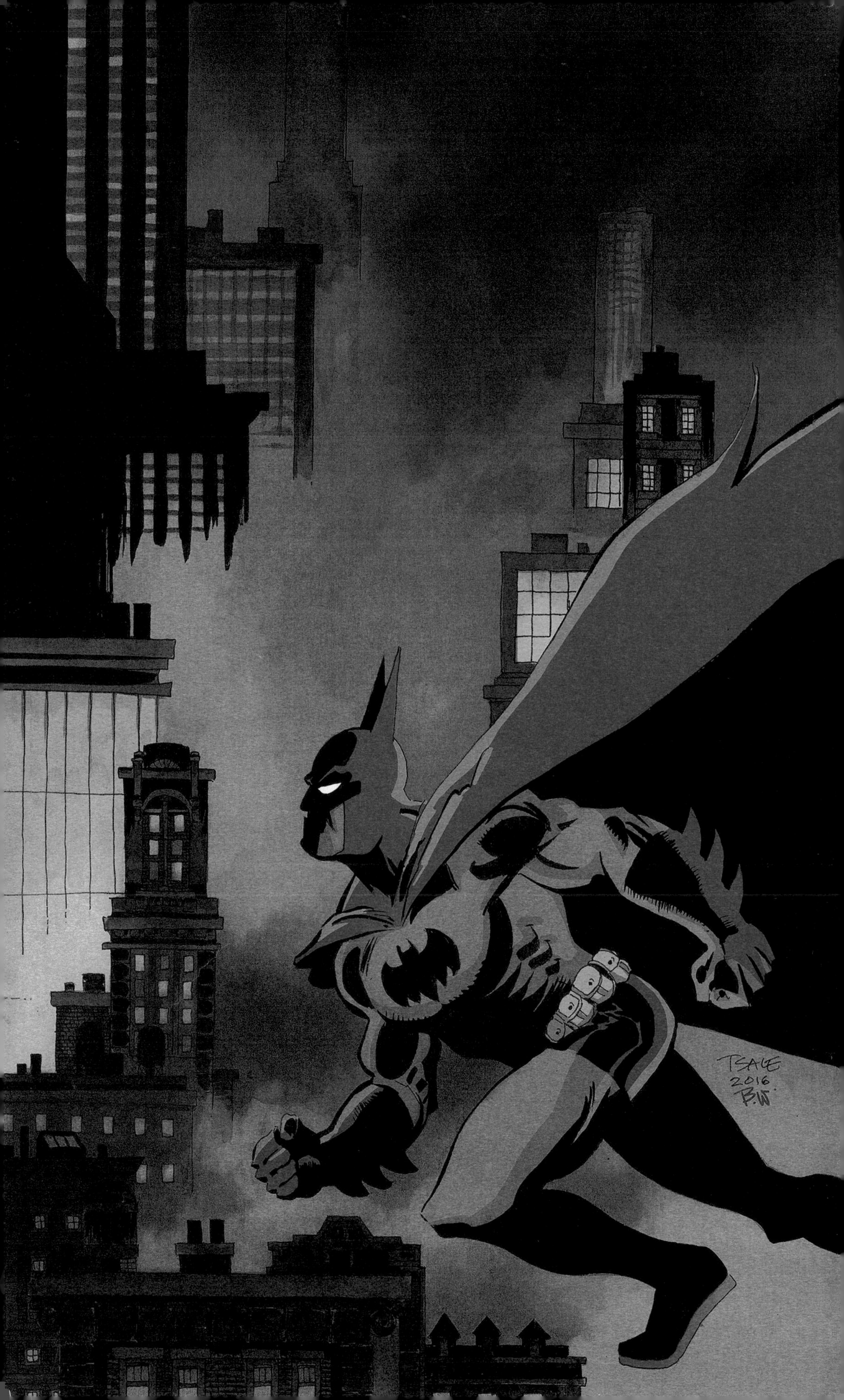
TSALE
2016
B.W.

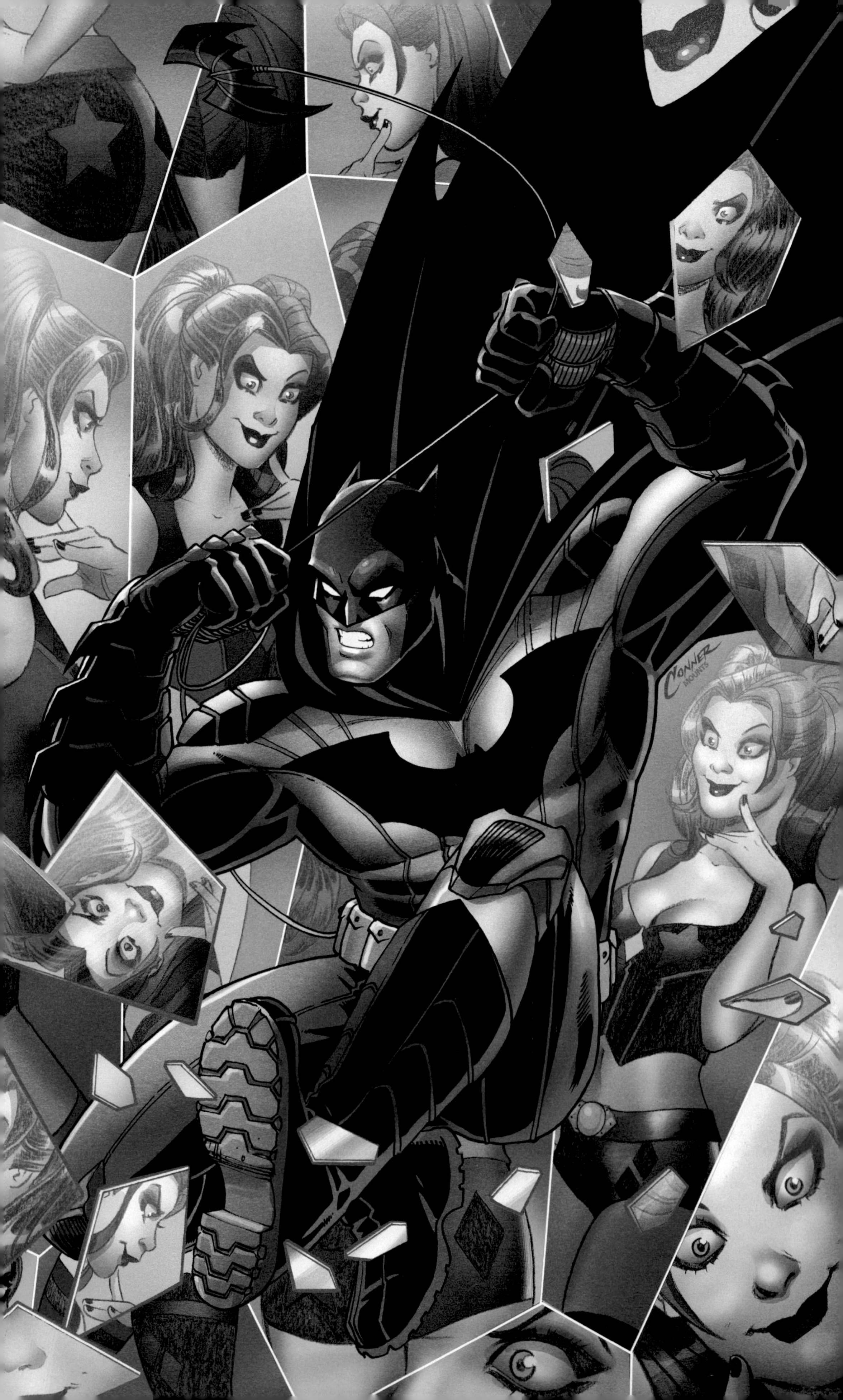
CONNER
MOUNTS

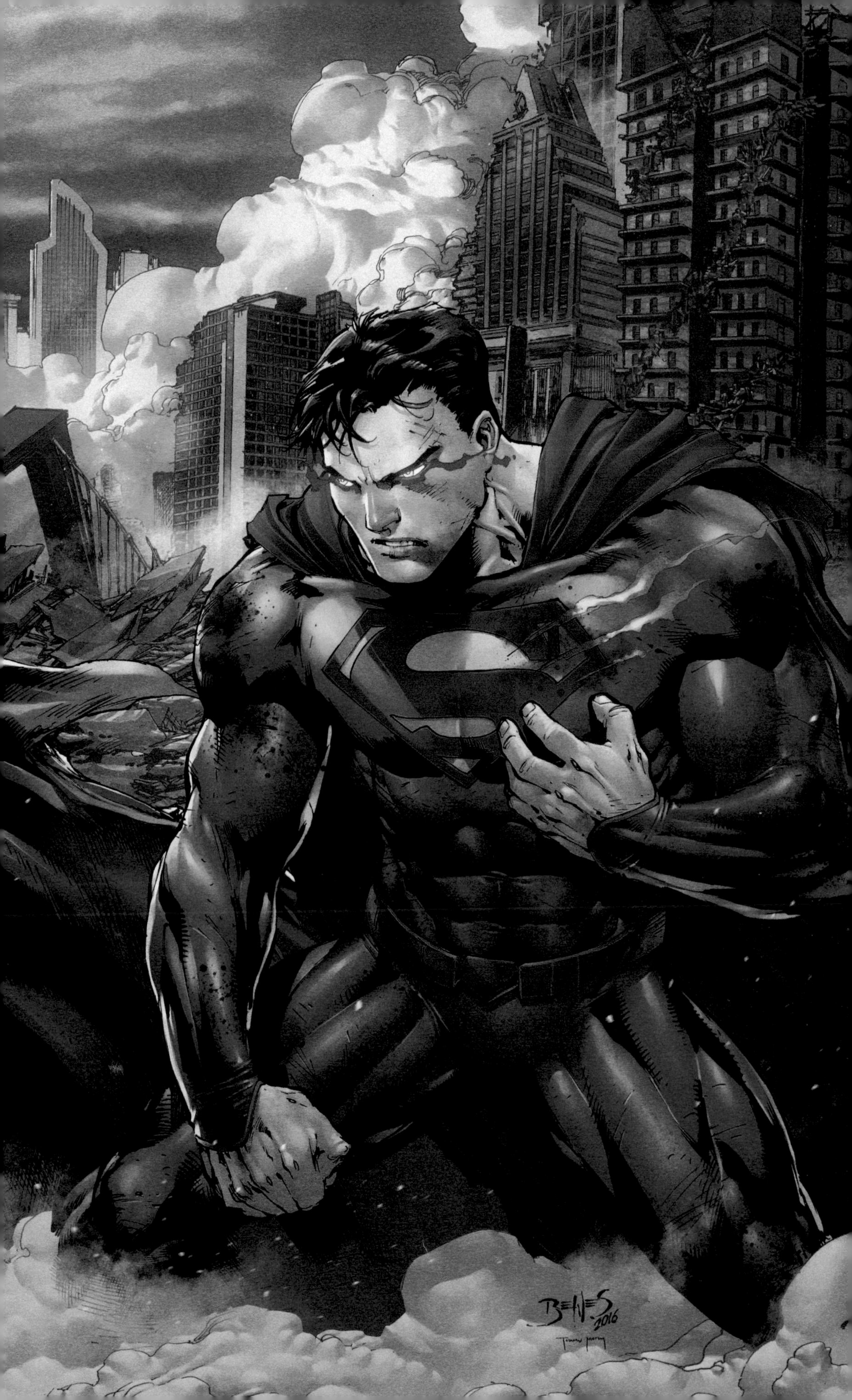

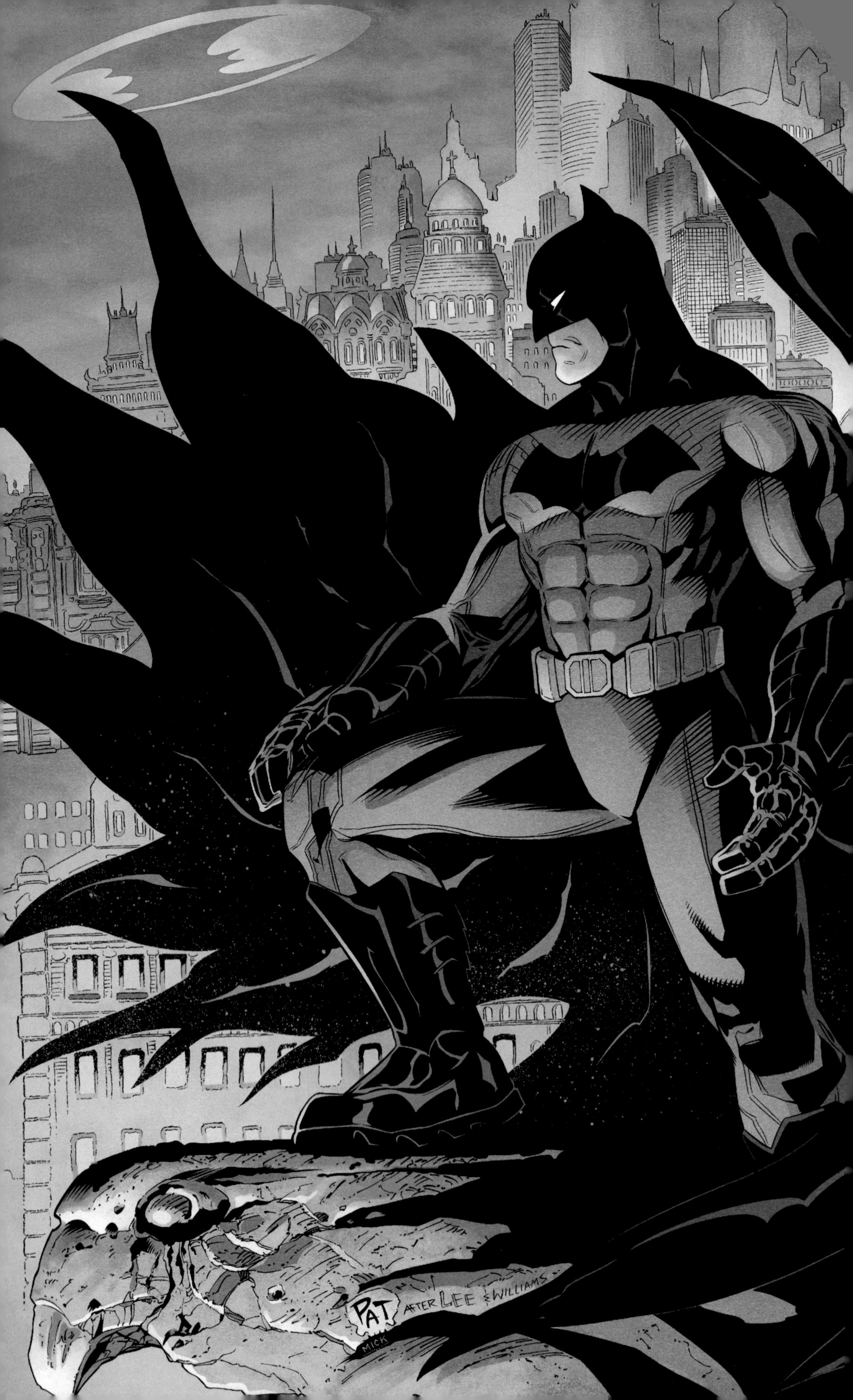
PAT
AFTER LEE & WILLIAMS
MICK

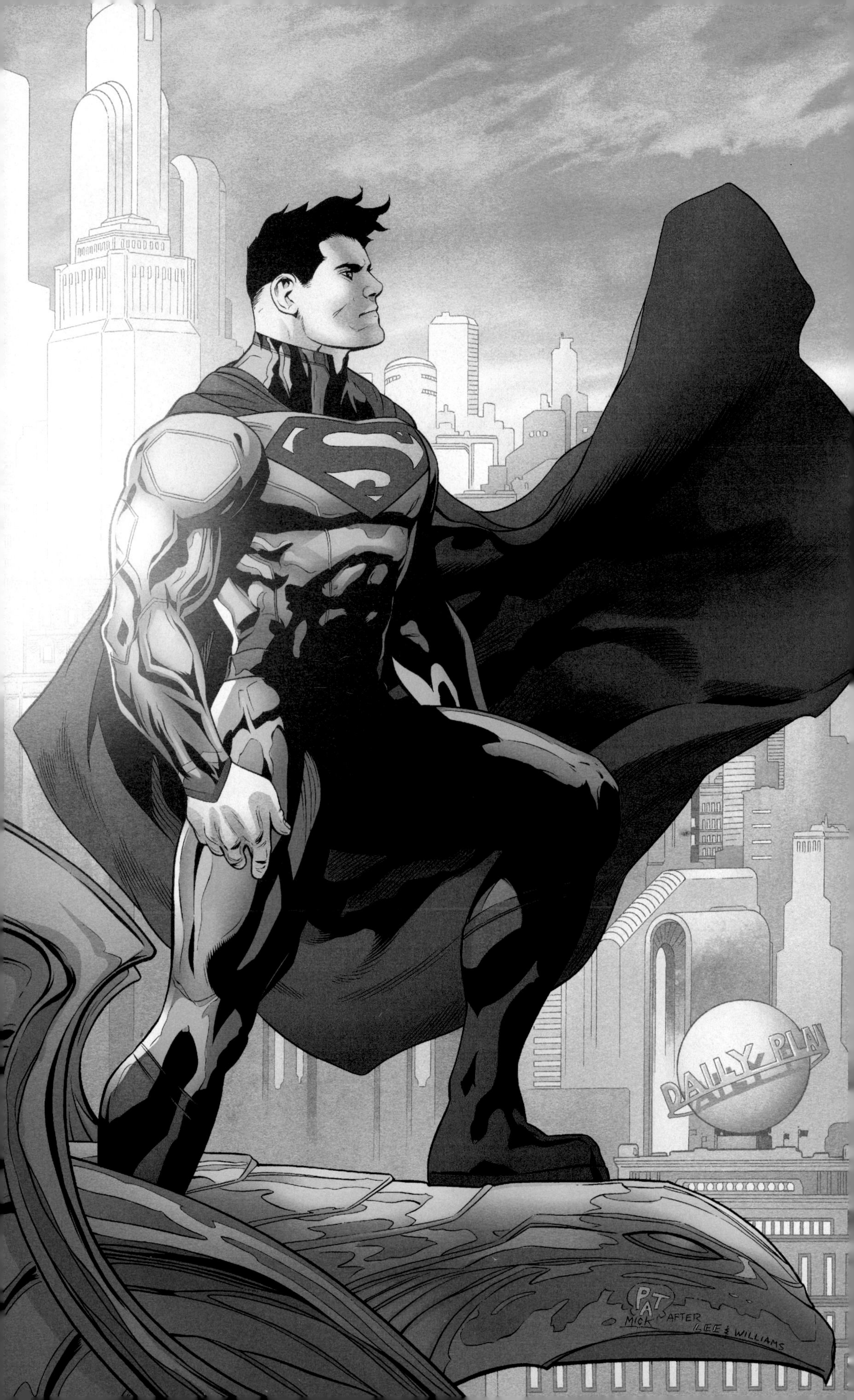
DAILY PLA
PAT MICK AFTER LEE & WILLIAMS

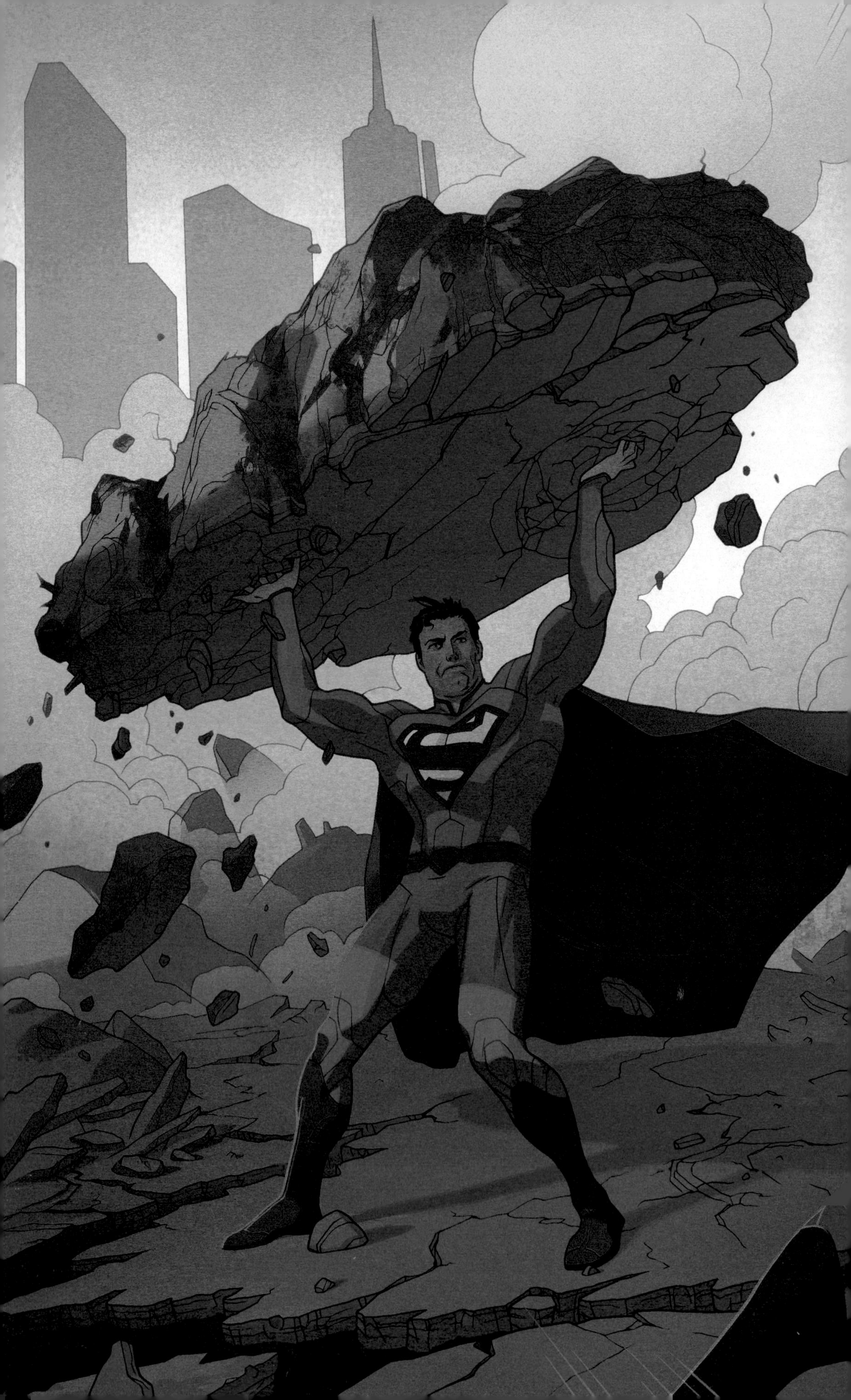

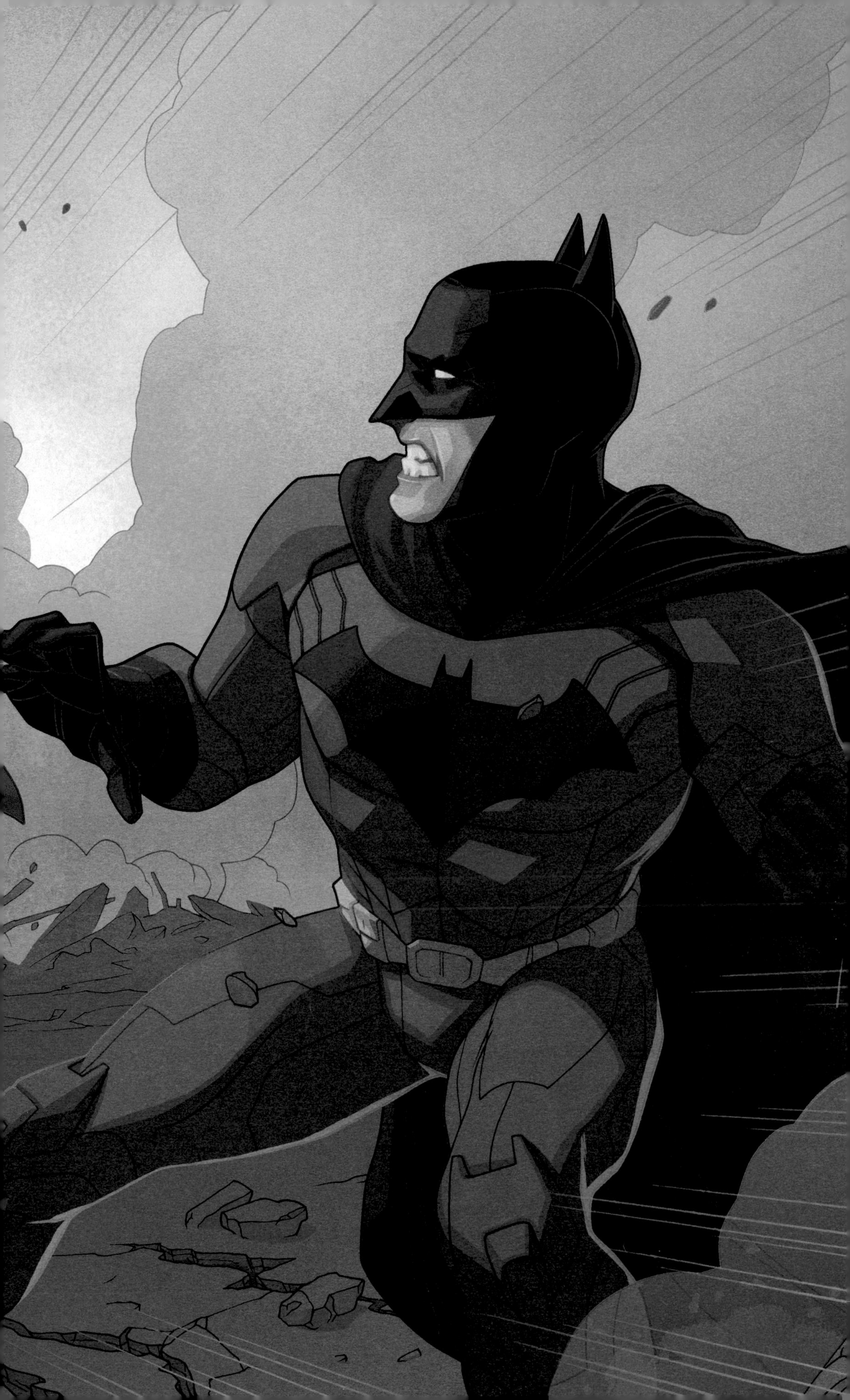

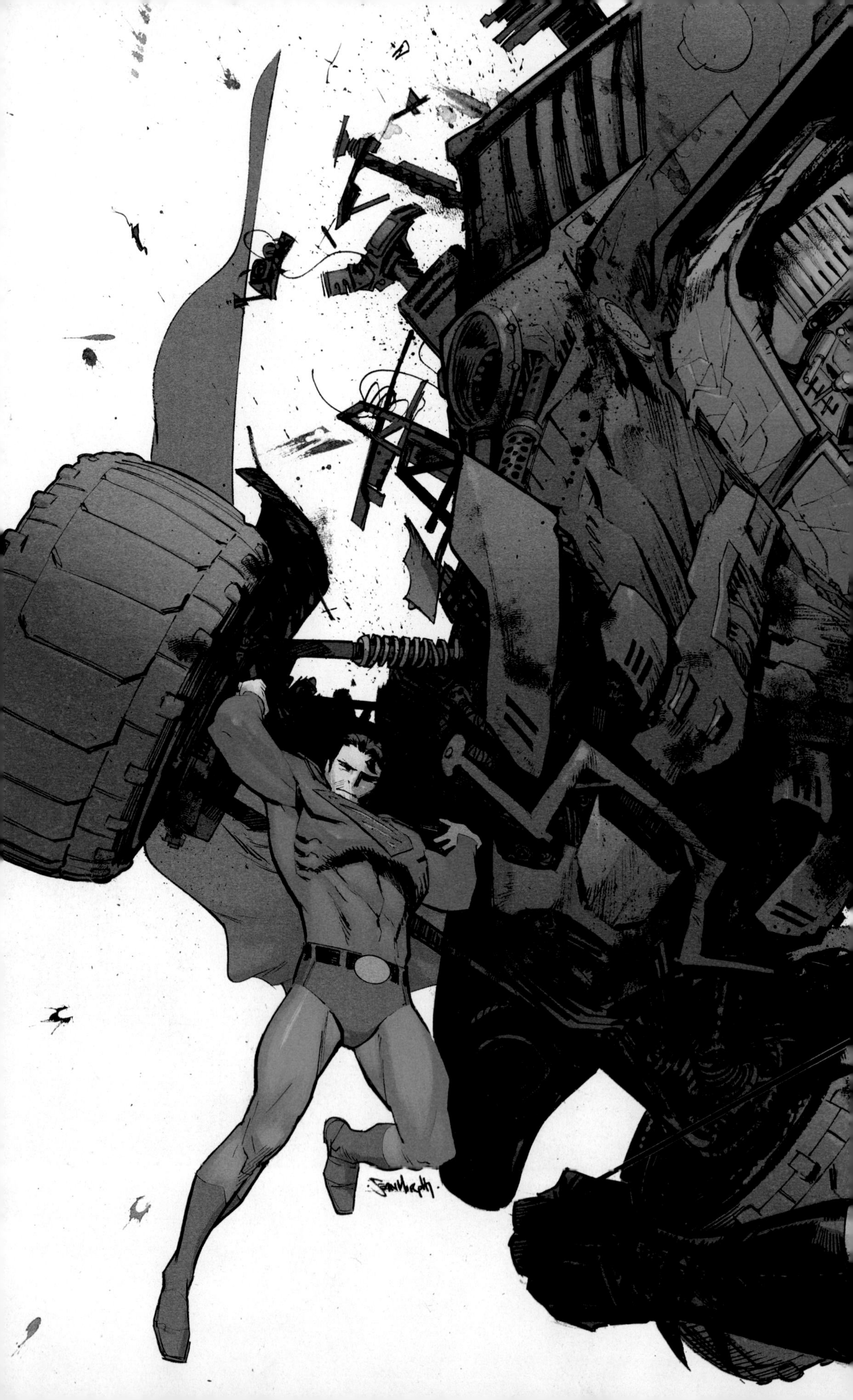

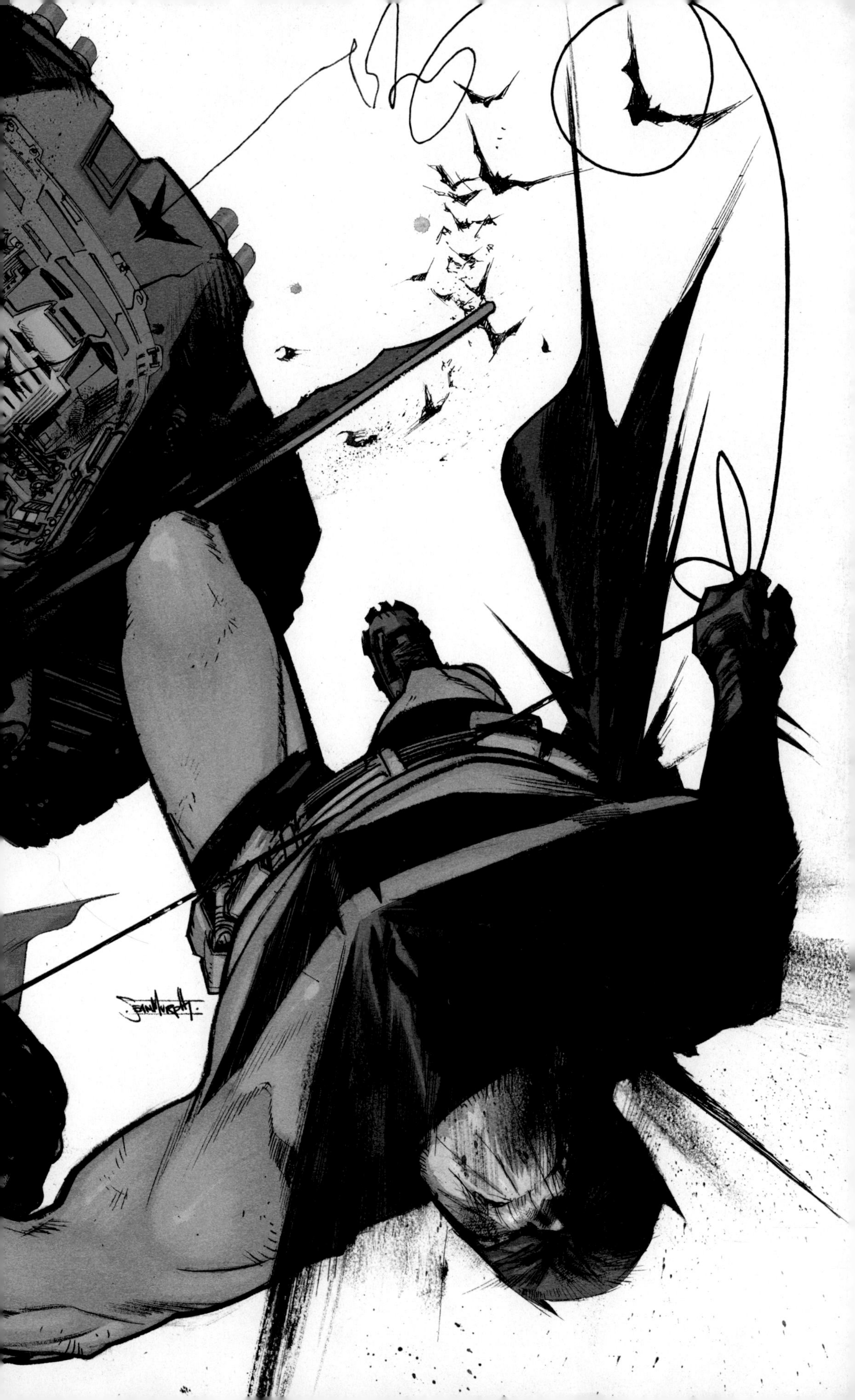

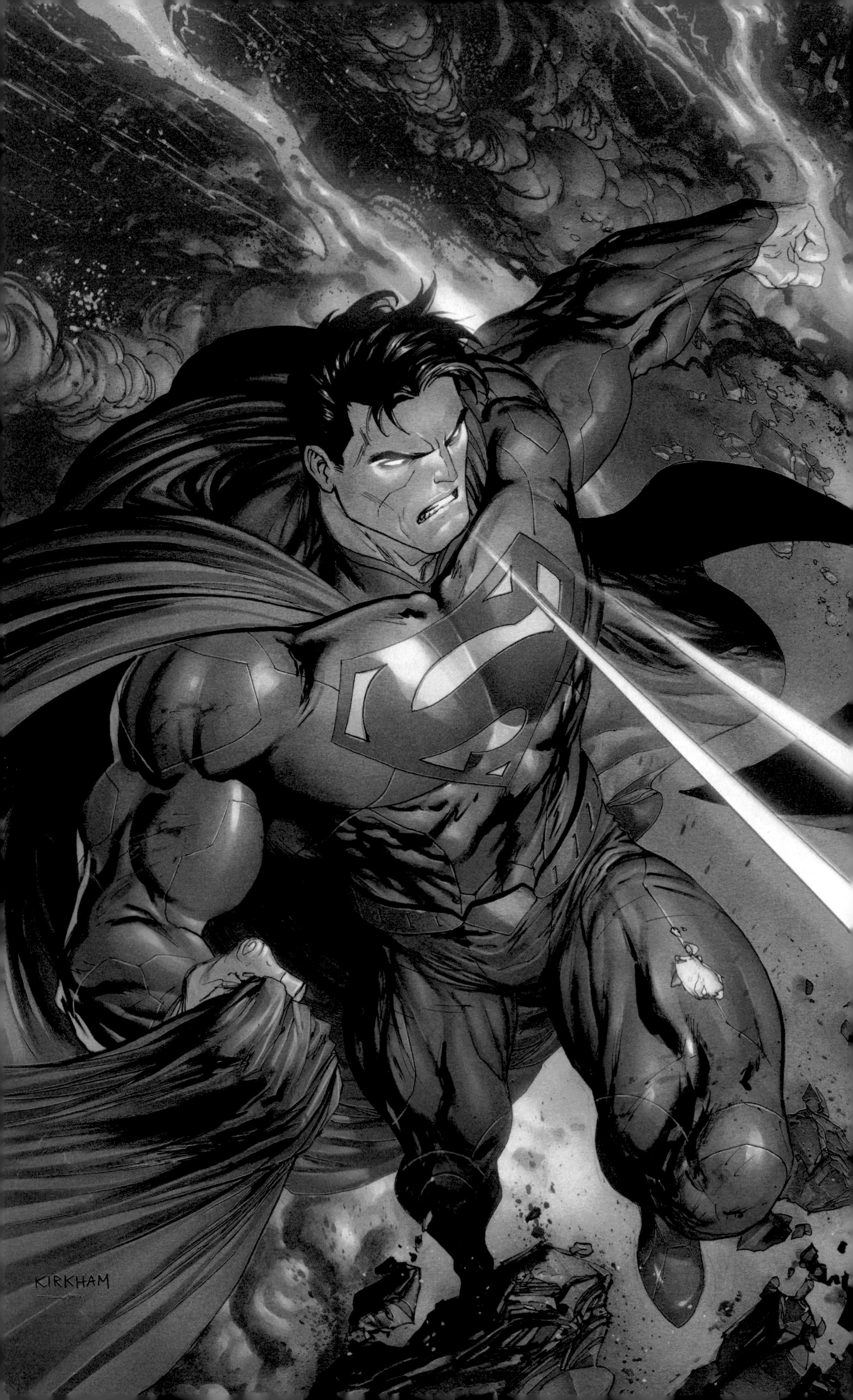
KIRKHAM

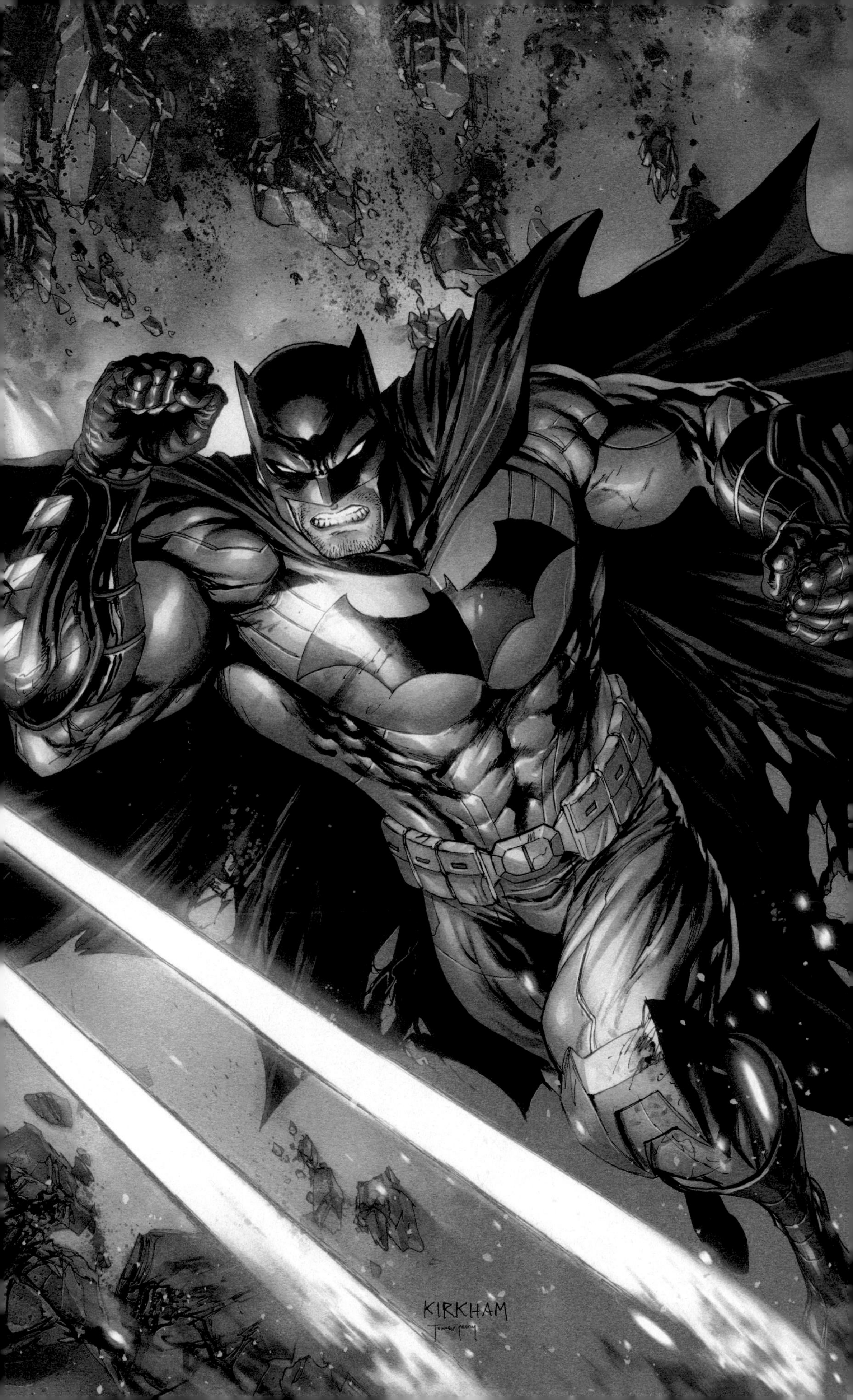
KIRKHAM

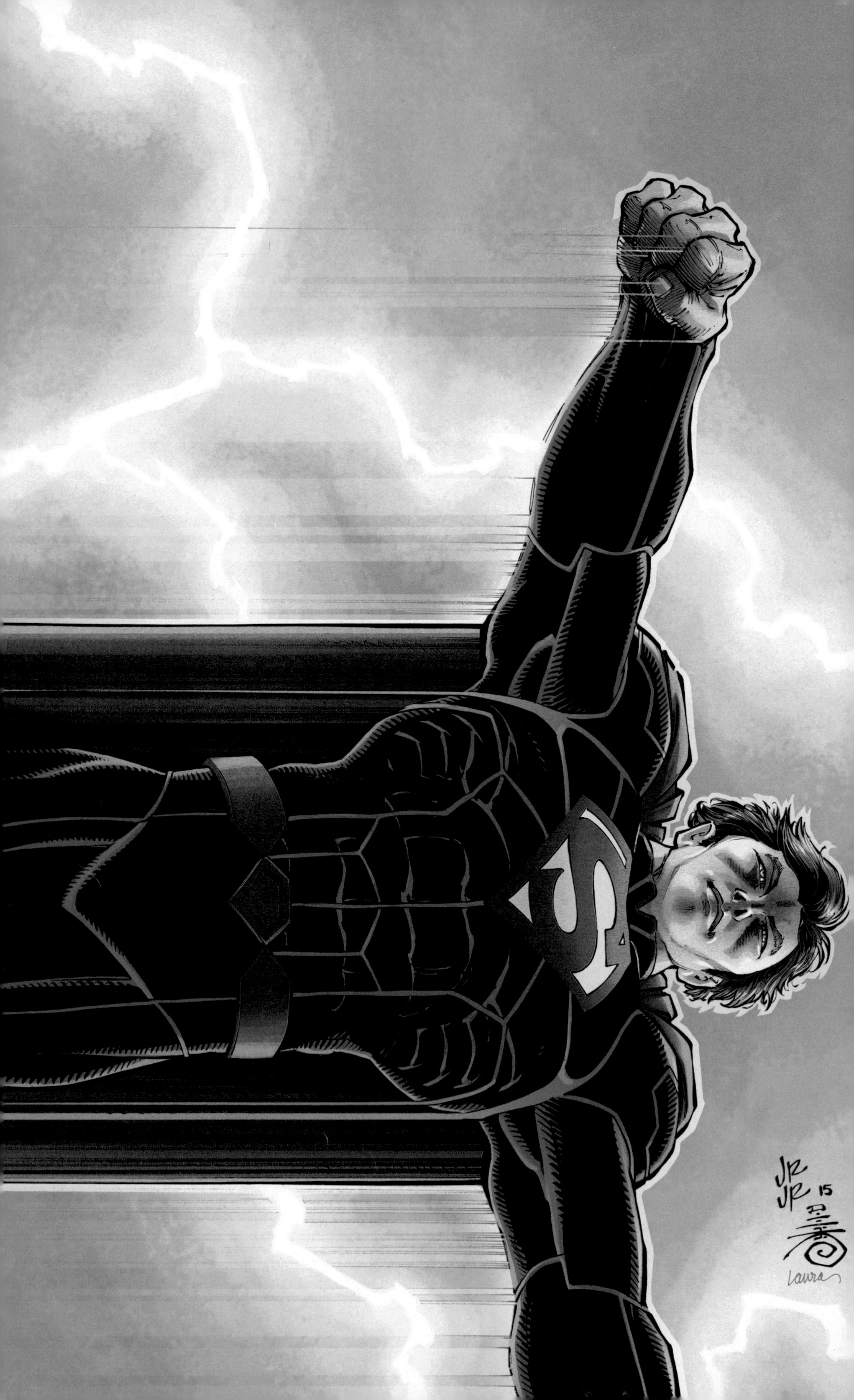
JR JR 15
Laura

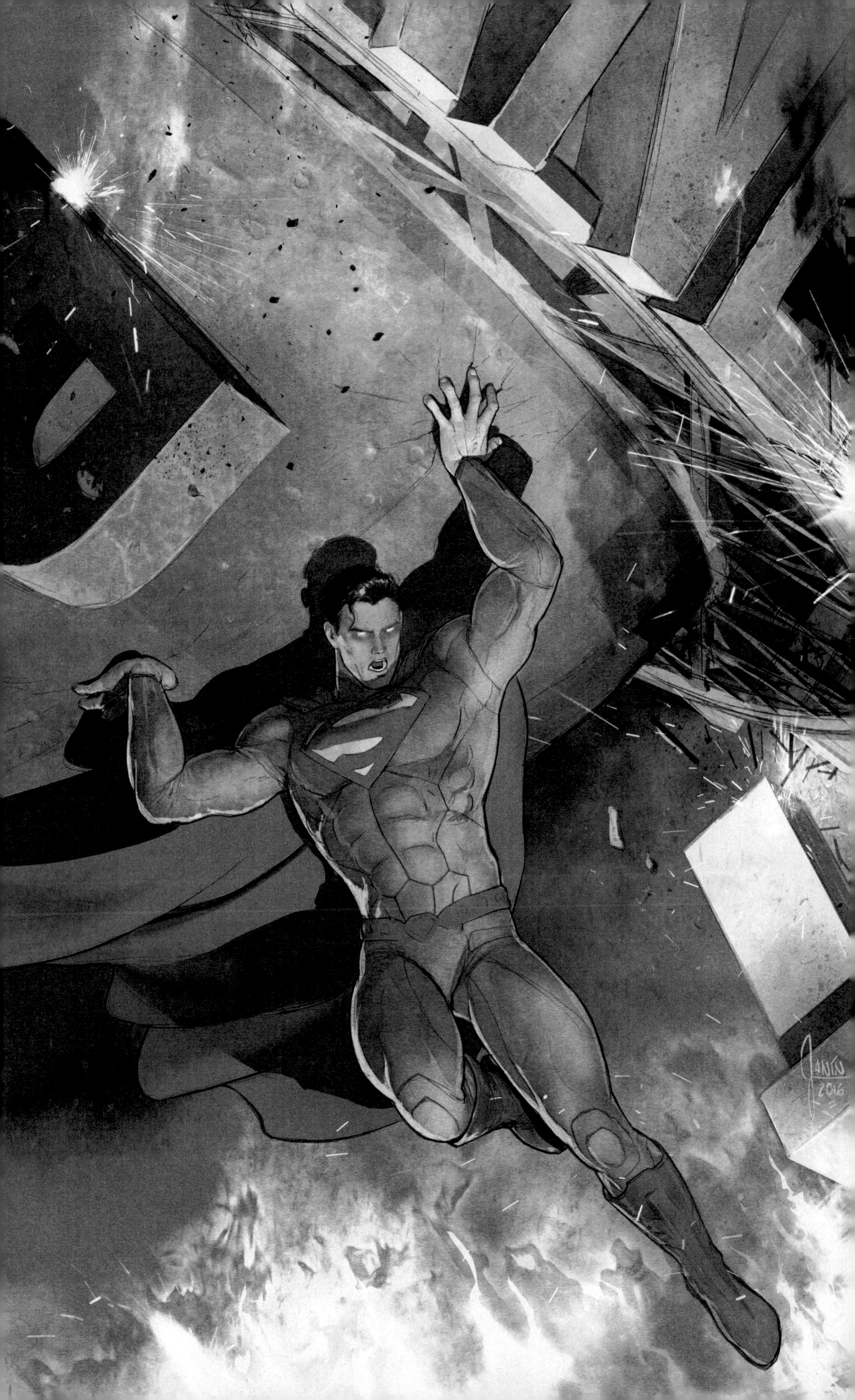
JANIN
2016

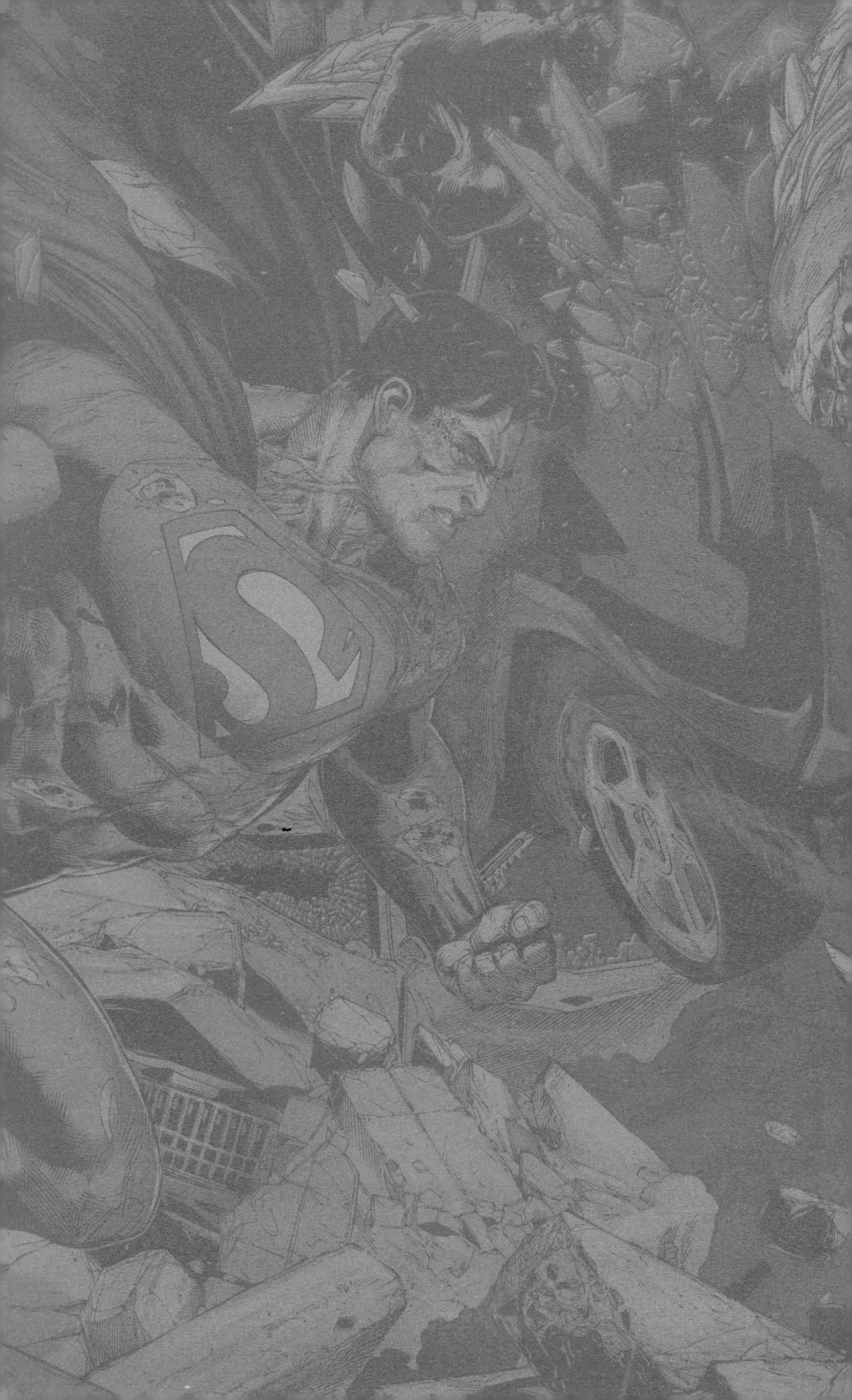

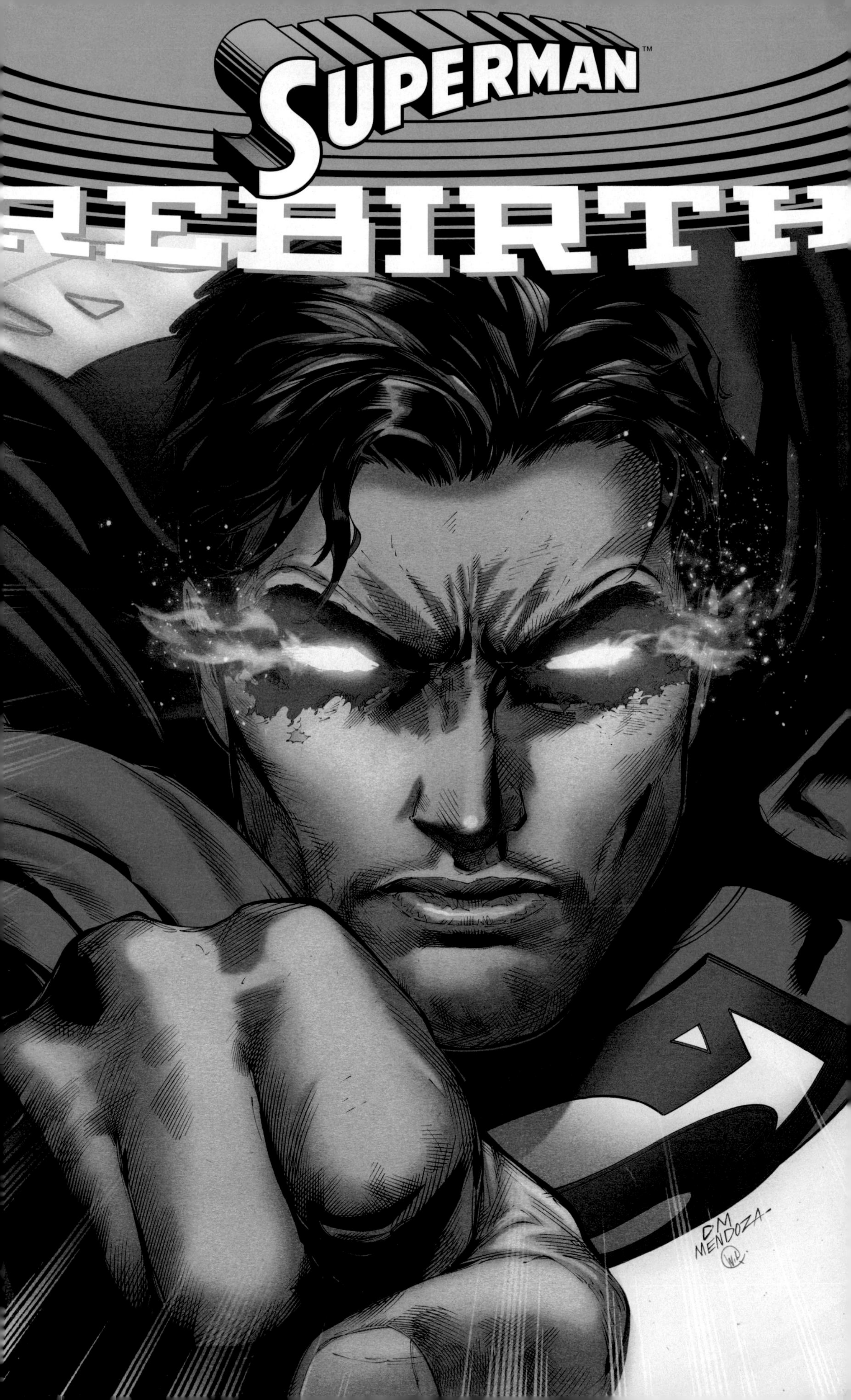
SUPERMAN™
REBIRTH
DM
MENDOZA

The future (and past) of the DC Universe starts with DC UNIVERSE: REBIRTH!

Explore the changing world of SUPERMAN in this special bonus preview of **SUPERMAN: REBIRTH #1**!

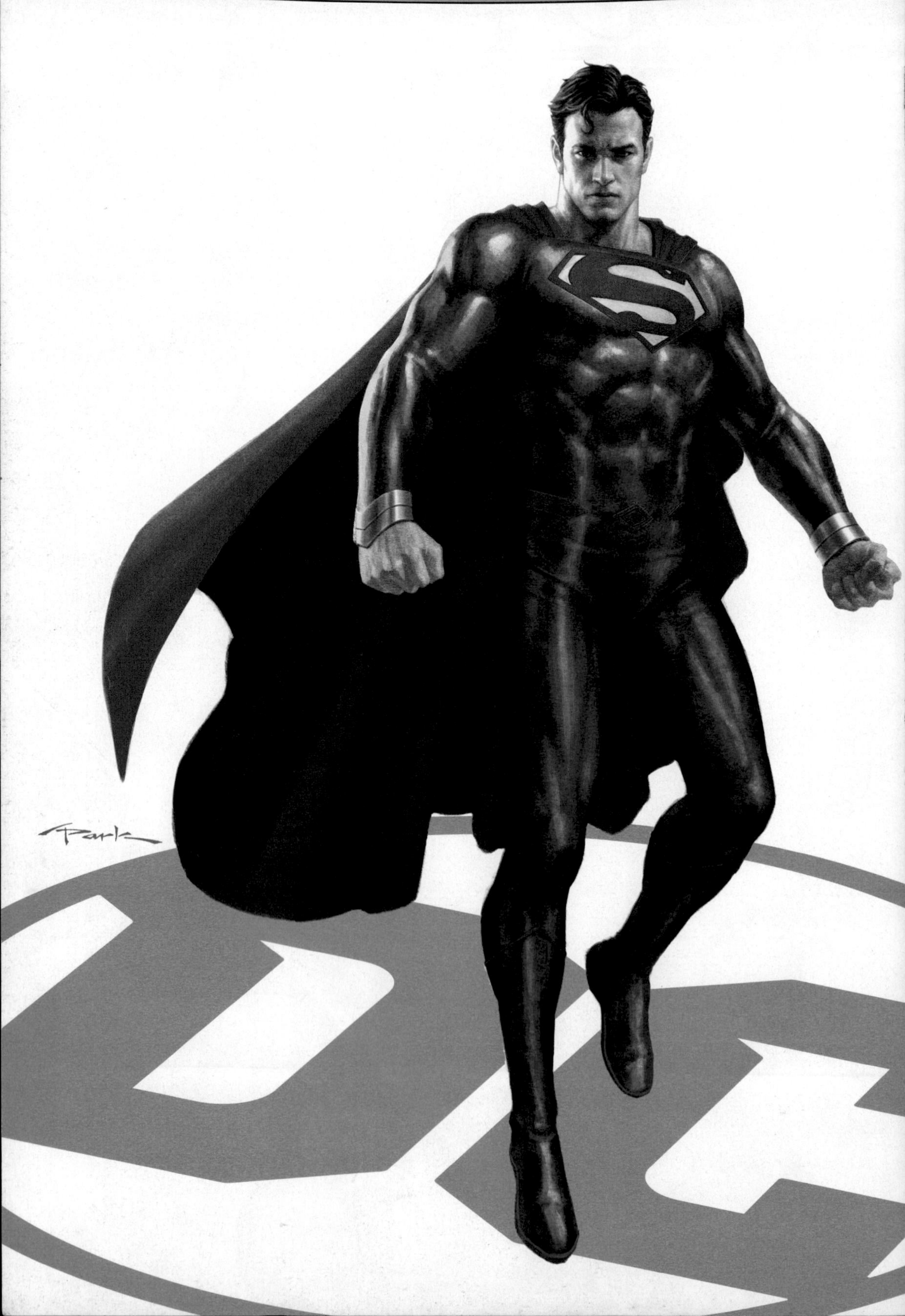

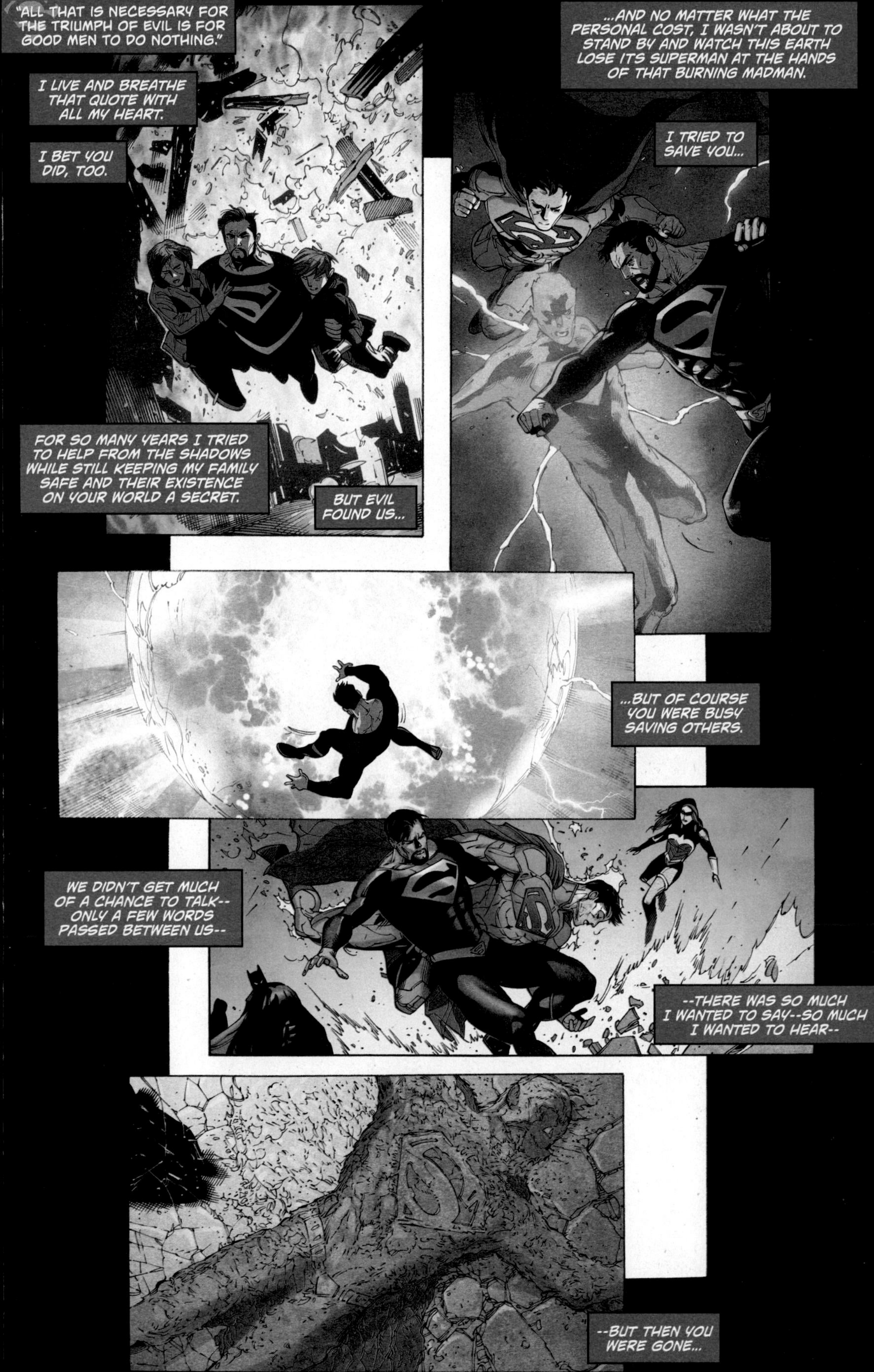
"ALL THAT IS NECESSARY FOR THE TRIUMPH OF EVIL IS FOR GOOD MEN TO DO NOTHING."
I LIVE AND BREATHE THAT QUOTE WITH ALL MY HEART.
I BET YOU DID, TOO.
FOR SO MANY YEARS I TRIED TO HELP FROM THE SHADOWS WHILE STILL KEEPING MY FAMILY SAFE AND THEIR EXISTENCE ON YOUR WORLD A SECRET.
BUT EVIL FOUND US...
...AND NO MATTER WHAT THE PERSONAL COST, I WASN'T ABOUT TO STAND BY AND WATCH THIS EARTH LOSE ITS SUPERMAN AT THE HANDS OF THAT BURNING MADMAN.
I TRIED TO SAVE YOU...
...BUT OF COURSE YOU WERE BUSY SAVING OTHERS.
WE DIDN'T GET MUCH OF A CHANCE TO TALK--ONLY A FEW WORDS PASSED BETWEEN US--
--THERE WAS SO MUCH I WANTED TO SAY--SO MUCH I WANTED TO HEAR--
--BUT THEN YOU WERE GONE...

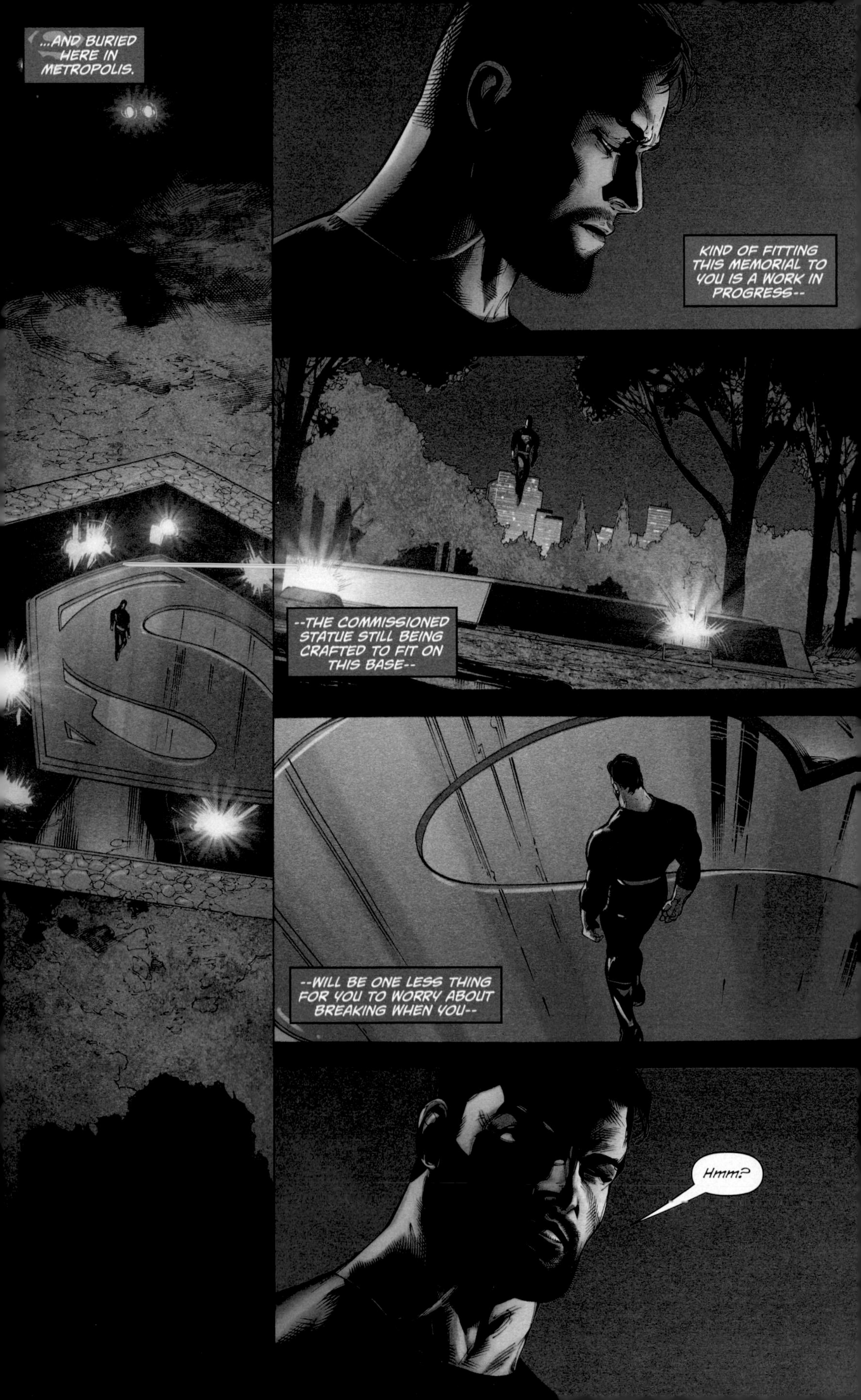
...AND BURIED HERE IN METROPOLIS.
KIND OF FITTING THIS MEMORIAL TO YOU IS A WORK IN PROGRESS--
--THE COMMISSIONED STATUE STILL BEING CRAFTED TO FIT ON THIS BASE--
--WILL BE ONE LESS THING FOR YOU TO WORRY ABOUT BREAKING WHEN YOU--
Hmm?

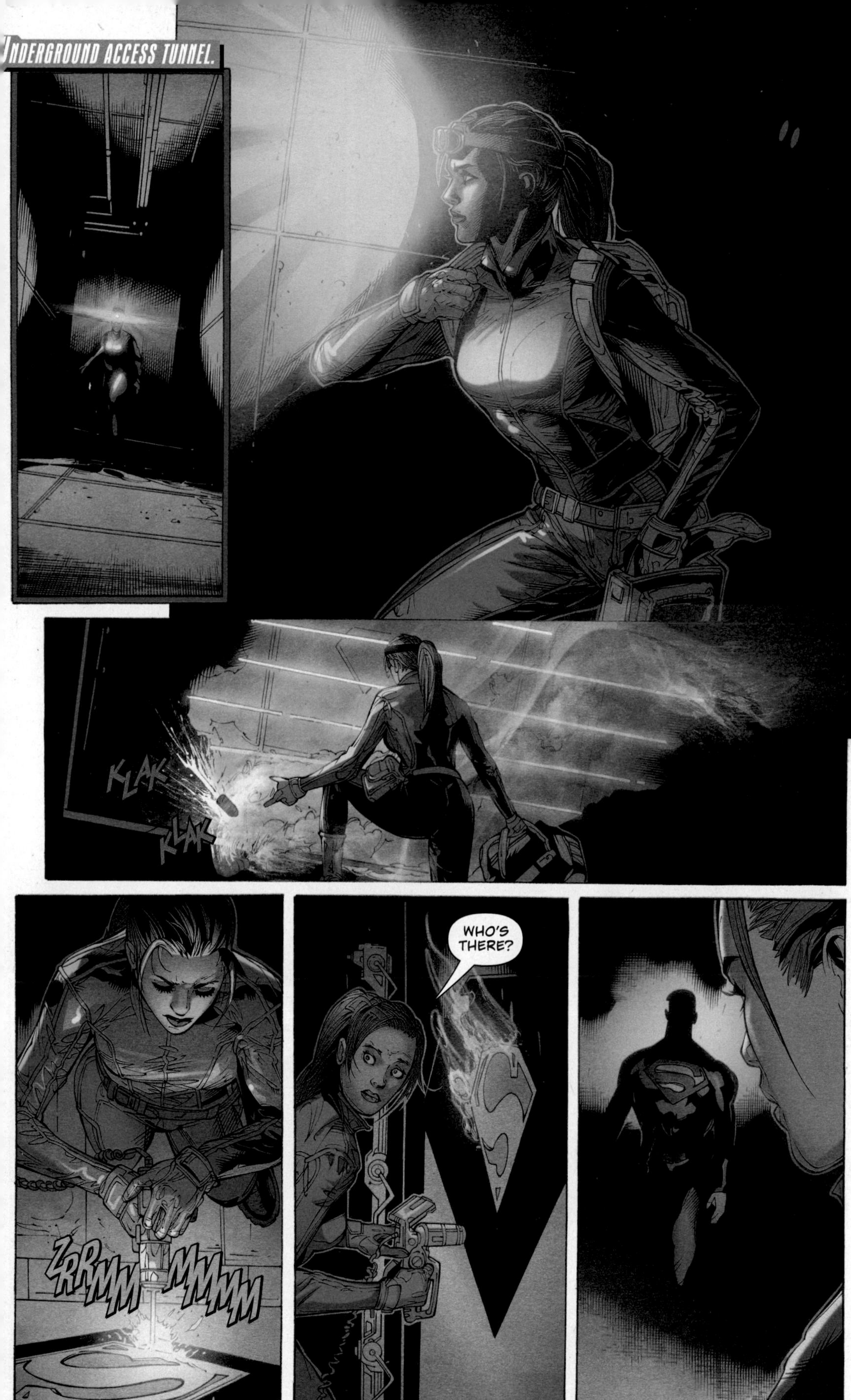
UNDERGROUND ACCESS TUNNEL.
KLAK
KLAK
ZRRMMMMMMM
WHO'S THERE?

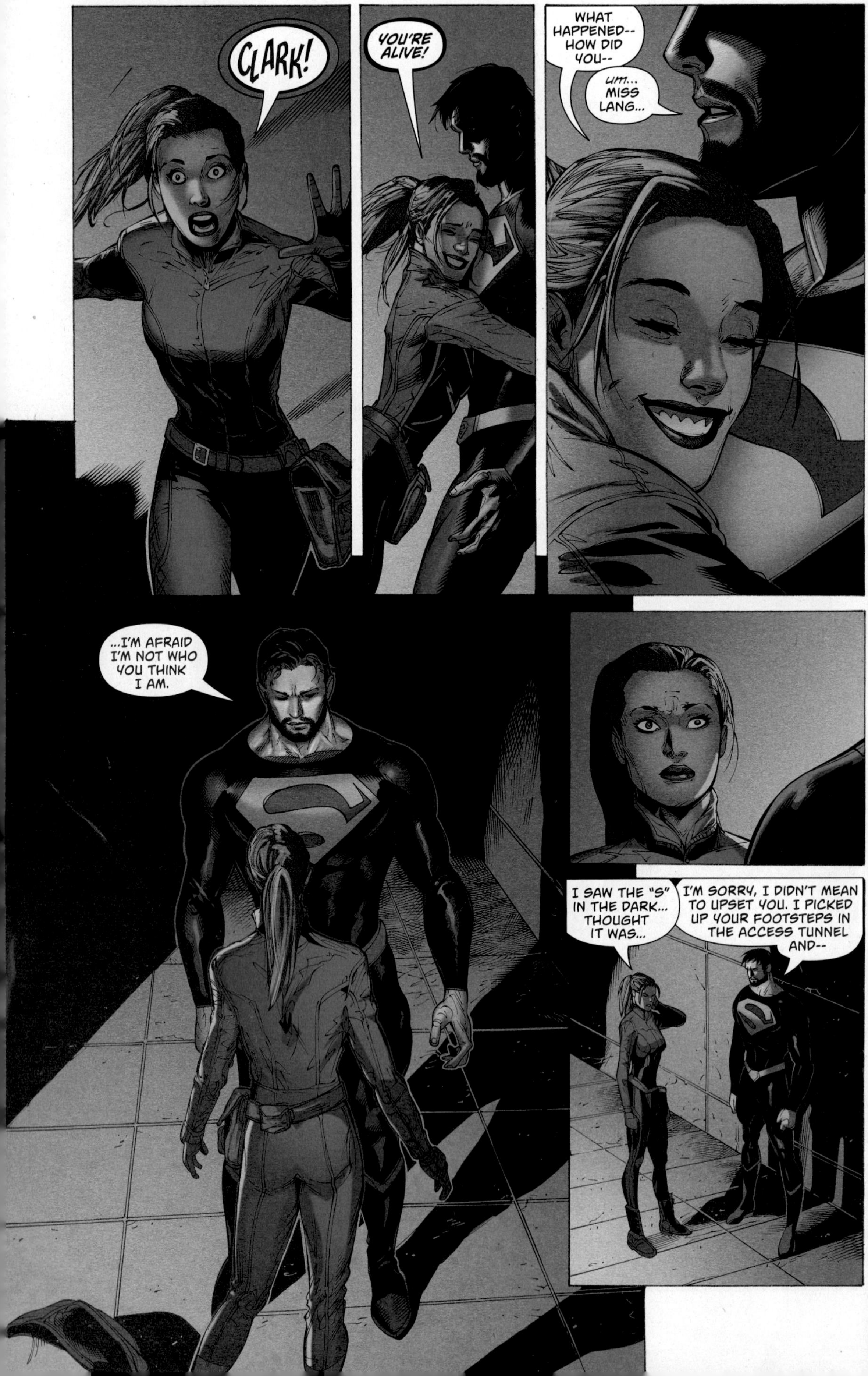
CLARK!
YOU'RE ALIVE!
WHAT HAPPENED-- HOW DID YOU--
UM... MISS LANG...
...I'M AFRAID I'M NOT WHO YOU THINK I AM.
I SAW THE "S" IN THE DARK... THOUGHT IT WAS...
I'M SORRY, I DIDN'T MEAN TO UPSET YOU. I PICKED UP YOUR FOOTSTEPS IN THE ACCESS TUNNEL AND--

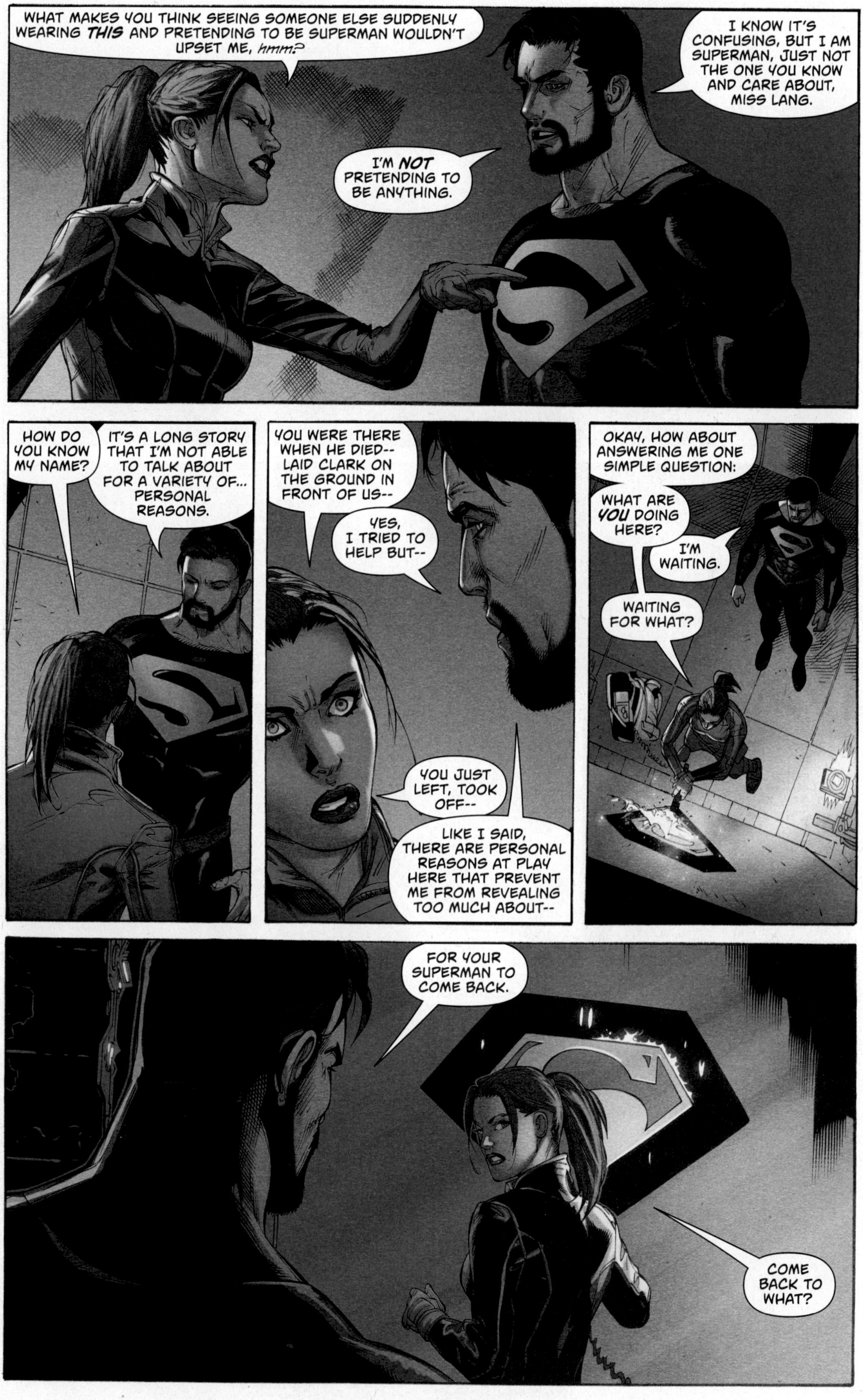
WHAT MAKES YOU THINK SEEING SOMEONE ELSE SUDDENLY WEARING THIS AND PRETENDING TO BE SUPERMAN WOULDN'T UPSET ME, hmm?
I'M NOT PRETENDING TO BE ANYTHING.
I KNOW IT'S CONFUSING, BUT I AM SUPERMAN, JUST NOT THE ONE YOU KNOW AND CARE ABOUT, MISS LANG.
HOW DO YOU KNOW MY NAME?
IT'S A LONG STORY THAT I'M NOT ABLE TO TALK ABOUT FOR A VARIETY OF... PERSONAL REASONS.
YOU WERE THERE WHEN HE DIED-- LAID CLARK ON THE GROUND IN FRONT OF US--
YES, I TRIED TO HELP BUT--
YOU JUST LEFT, TOOK OFF--
LIKE I SAID, THERE ARE PERSONAL REASONS AT PLAY HERE THAT PREVENT ME FROM REVEALING TOO MUCH ABOUT--
OKAY, HOW ABOUT ANSWERING ME ONE SIMPLE QUESTION:
WHAT ARE YOU DOING HERE?
I'M WAITING.
WAITING FOR WHAT?
FOR YOUR SUPERMAN TO COME BACK.
COME BACK TO WHAT?

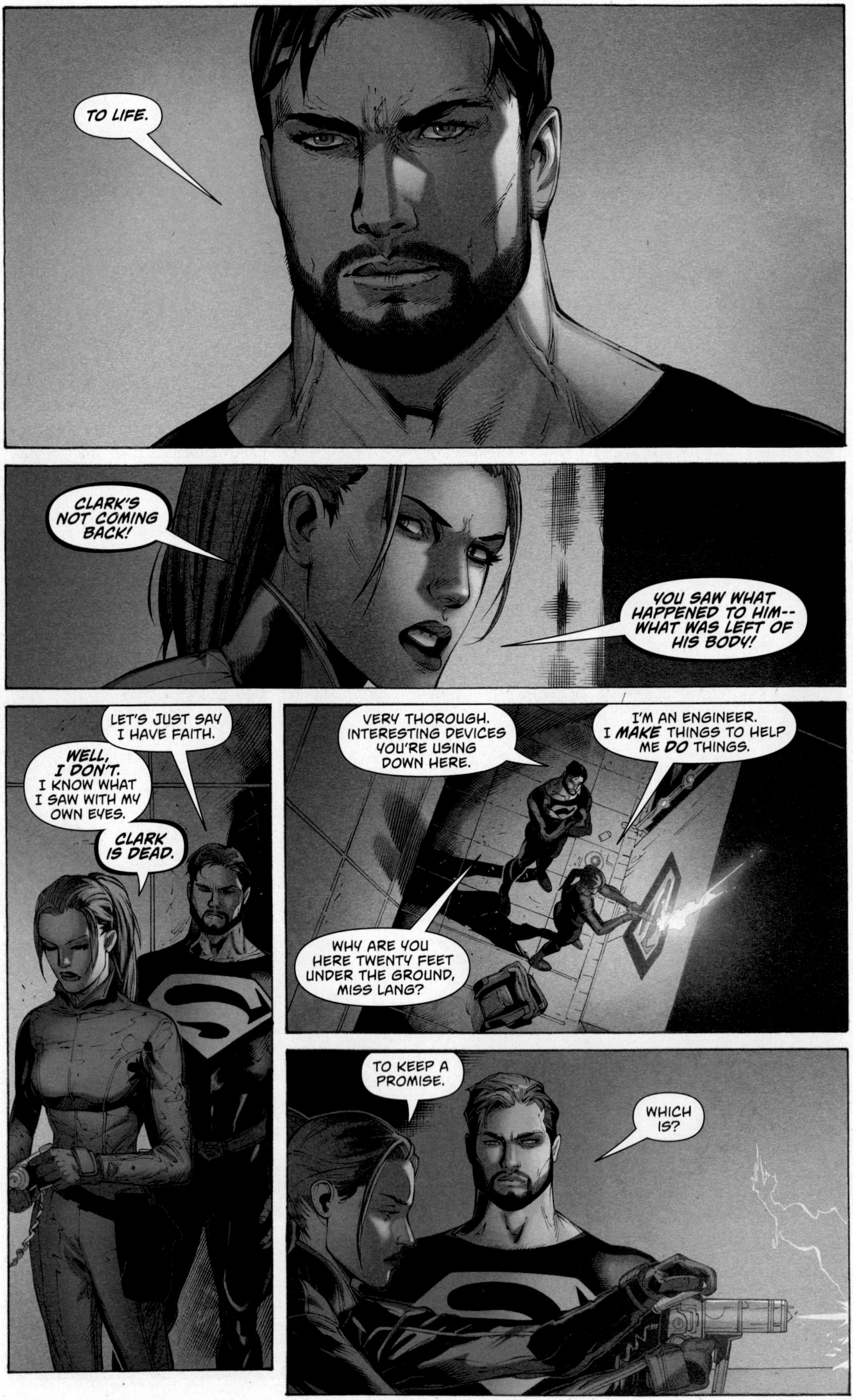
TO LIFE.
CLARK'S NOT COMING BACK!
YOU SAW WHAT HAPPENED TO HIM-- WHAT WAS LEFT OF HIS BODY!
LET'S JUST SAY I HAVE FAITH.
WELL, I DON'T. I KNOW WHAT I SAW WITH MY OWN EYES.
CLARK IS DEAD.
VERY THOROUGH. INTERESTING DEVICES YOU'RE USING DOWN HERE.
I'M AN ENGINEER. I MAKE THINGS TO HELP ME DO THINGS.
WHY ARE YOU HERE TWENTY FEET UNDER THE GROUND, MISS LANG?
TO KEEP A PROMISE.
WHICH IS?

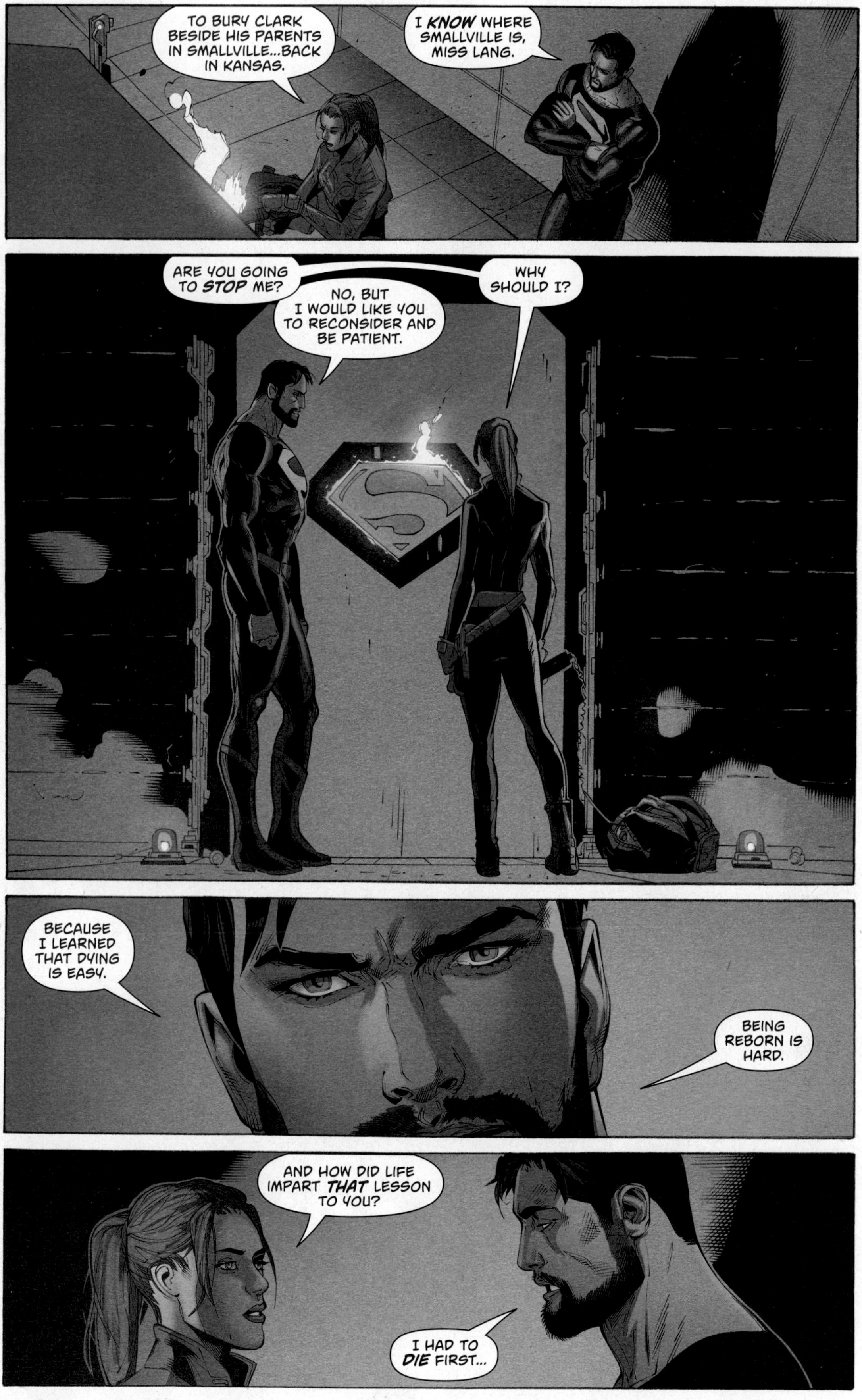
TO BURY CLARK BESIDE HIS PARENTS IN SMALLVILLE...BACK IN KANSAS.
I KNOW WHERE SMALLVILLE IS, MISS LANG.
ARE YOU GOING TO STOP ME?
WHY SHOULD I?
NO, BUT I WOULD LIKE YOU TO RECONSIDER AND BE PATIENT.
BECAUSE I LEARNED THAT DYING IS EASY.
BEING REBORN IS HARD.
AND HOW DID LIFE IMPART THAT LESSON TO YOU?
I HAD TO DIE FIRST...

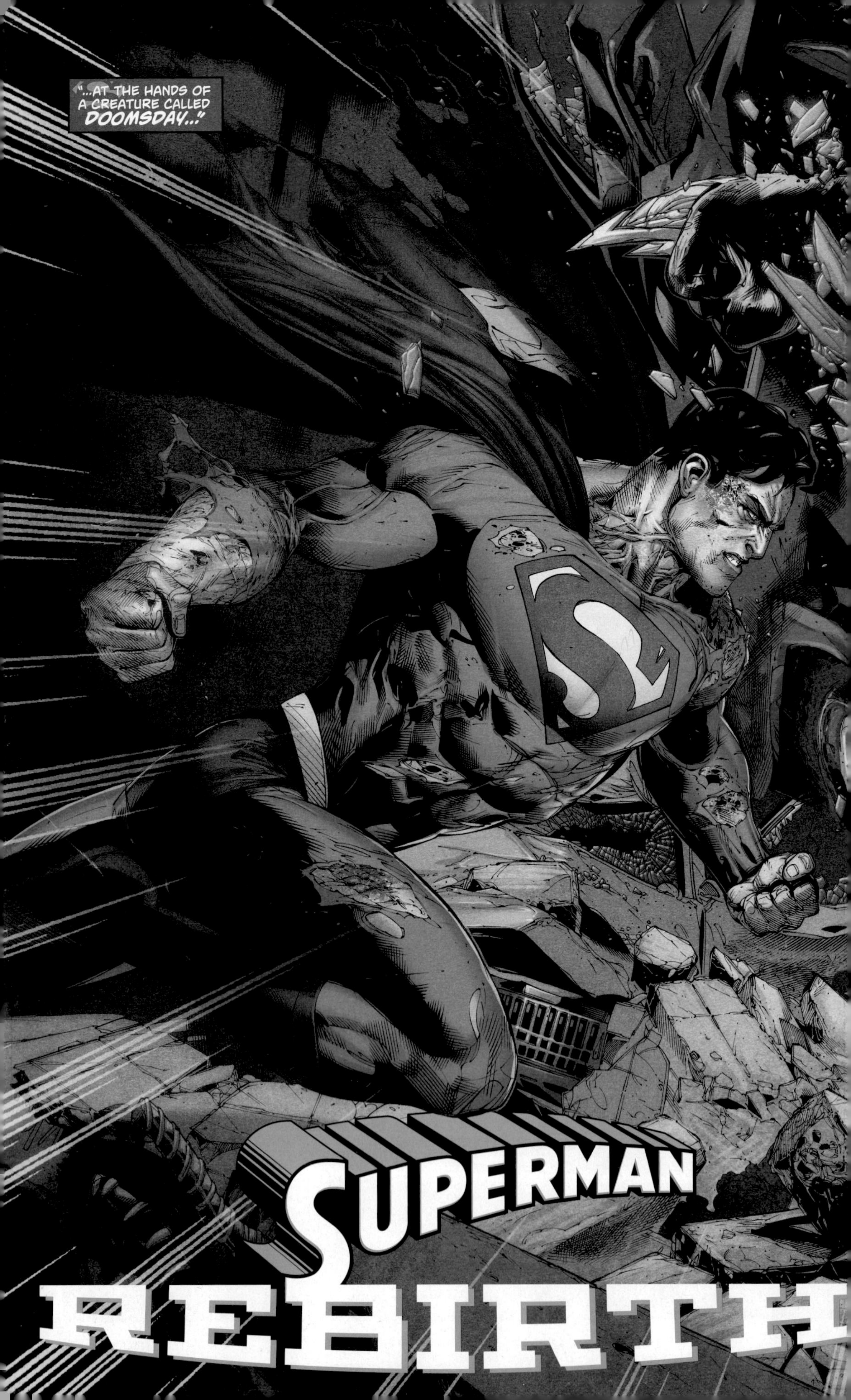
"...AT THE HANDS OF A CREATURE CALLED DOOMSDAY..."
SUPERMAN
REBIRTH

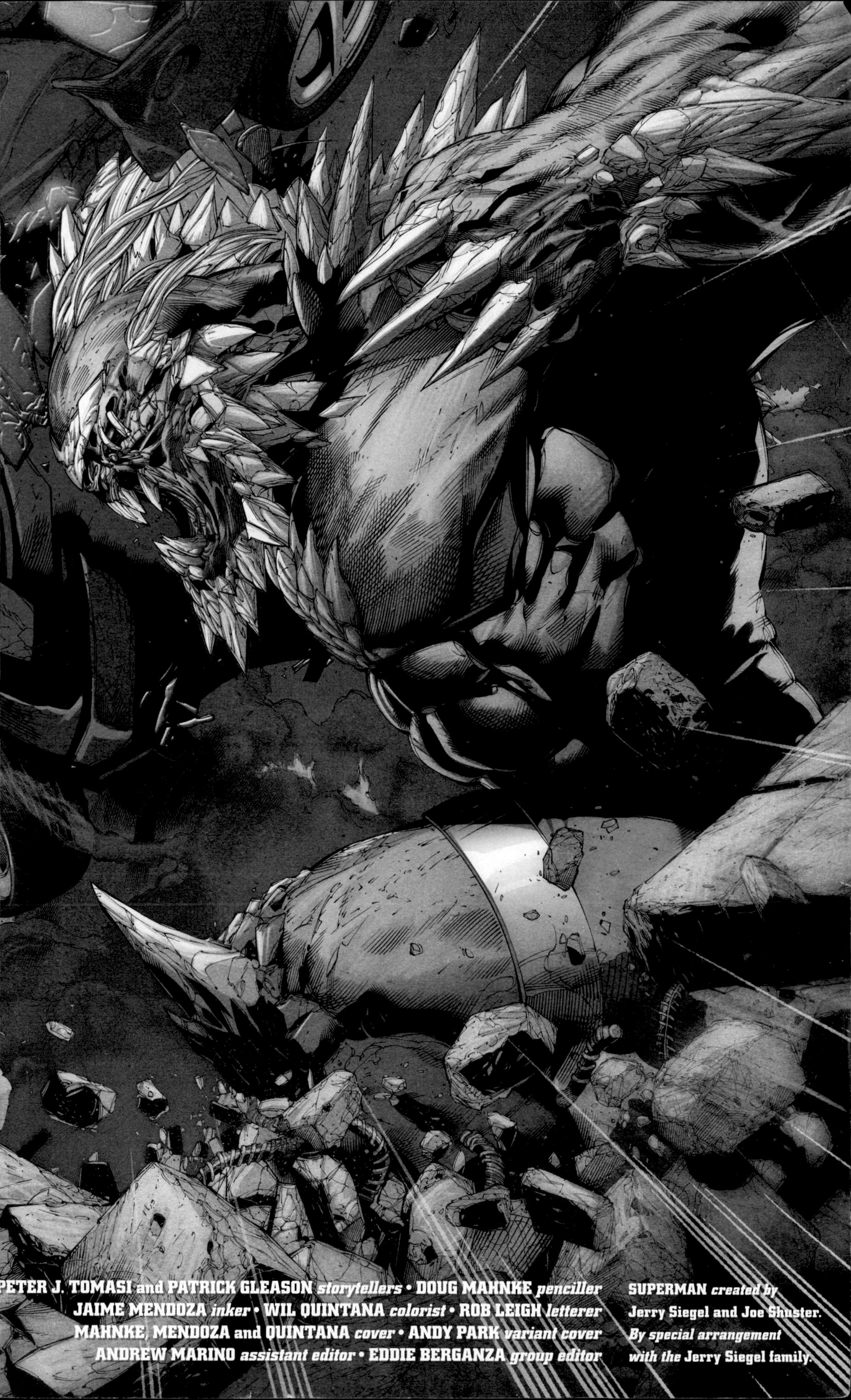
PETER J. TOMASI and PATRICK GLEASON *storytellers* • DOUG MAHNKE *penciller*
JAIME MENDOZA *inker* • WIL QUINTANA *colorist* • ROB LEIGH *letterer*
MAHNKE, MENDOZA and QUINTANA *cover* • ANDY PARK *variant cover*
ANDREW MARINO *assistant editor* • EDDIE BERGANZA *group editor*
SUPERMAN *created by* Jerry Siegel and Joe Shuster. *By special arrangement with the* Jerry Siegel family.

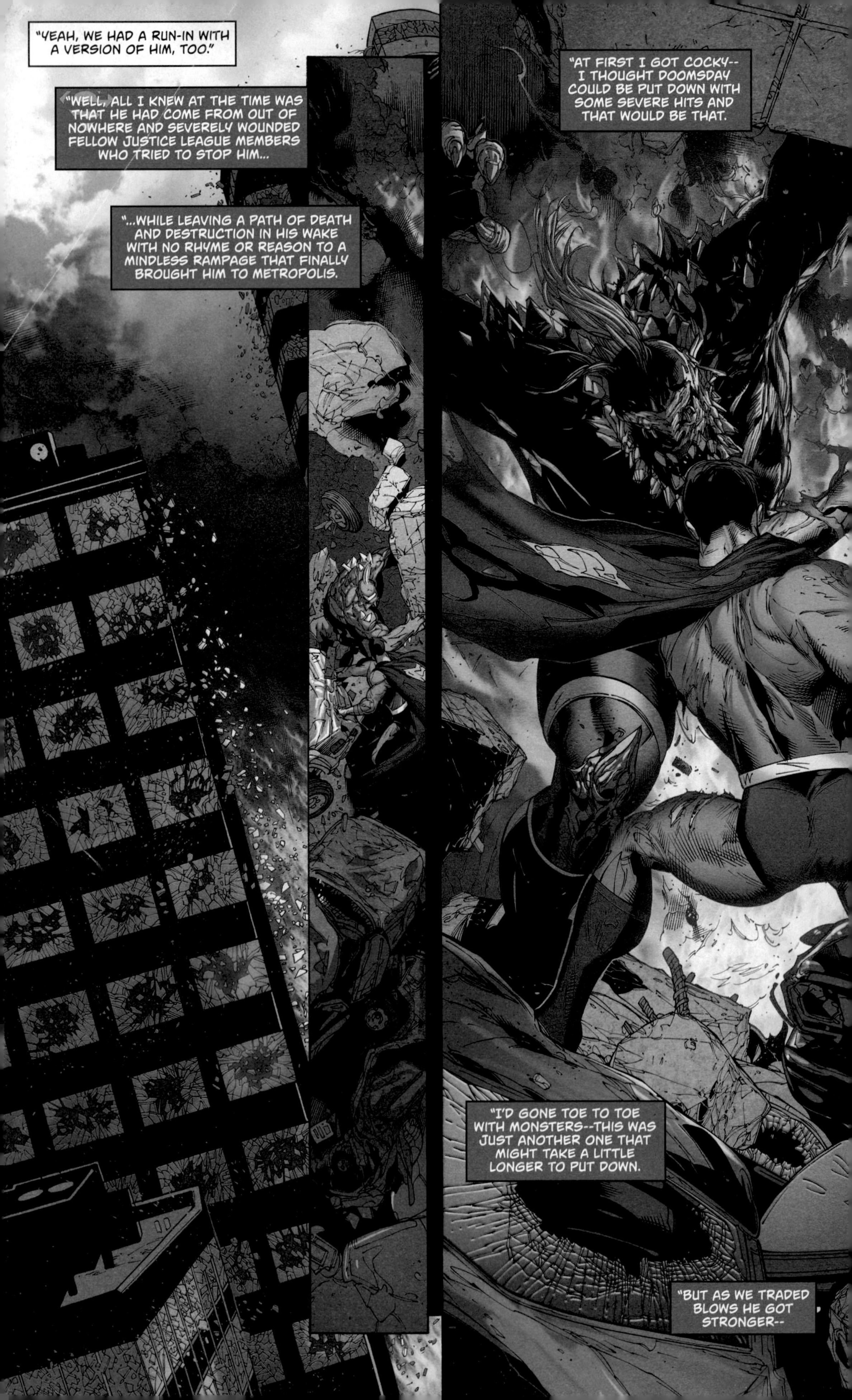
"YEAH, WE HAD A RUN-IN WITH A VERSION OF HIM, TOO."
"WELL, ALL I KNEW AT THE TIME WAS THAT HE HAD COME FROM OUT OF NOWHERE AND SEVERELY WOUNDED FELLOW JUSTICE LEAGUE MEMBERS WHO TRIED TO STOP HIM...
"...WHILE LEAVING A PATH OF DEATH AND DESTRUCTION IN HIS WAKE WITH NO RHYME OR REASON TO A MINDLESS RAMPAGE THAT FINALLY BROUGHT HIM TO METROPOLIS.
"AT FIRST I GOT COCKY-- I THOUGHT DOOMSDAY COULD BE PUT DOWN WITH SOME SEVERE HITS AND THAT WOULD BE THAT.
"I'D GONE TOE TO TOE WITH MONSTERS--THIS WAS JUST ANOTHER ONE THAT MIGHT TAKE A LITTLE LONGER TO PUT DOWN.
"BUT AS WE TRADED BLOWS HE GOT STRONGER--

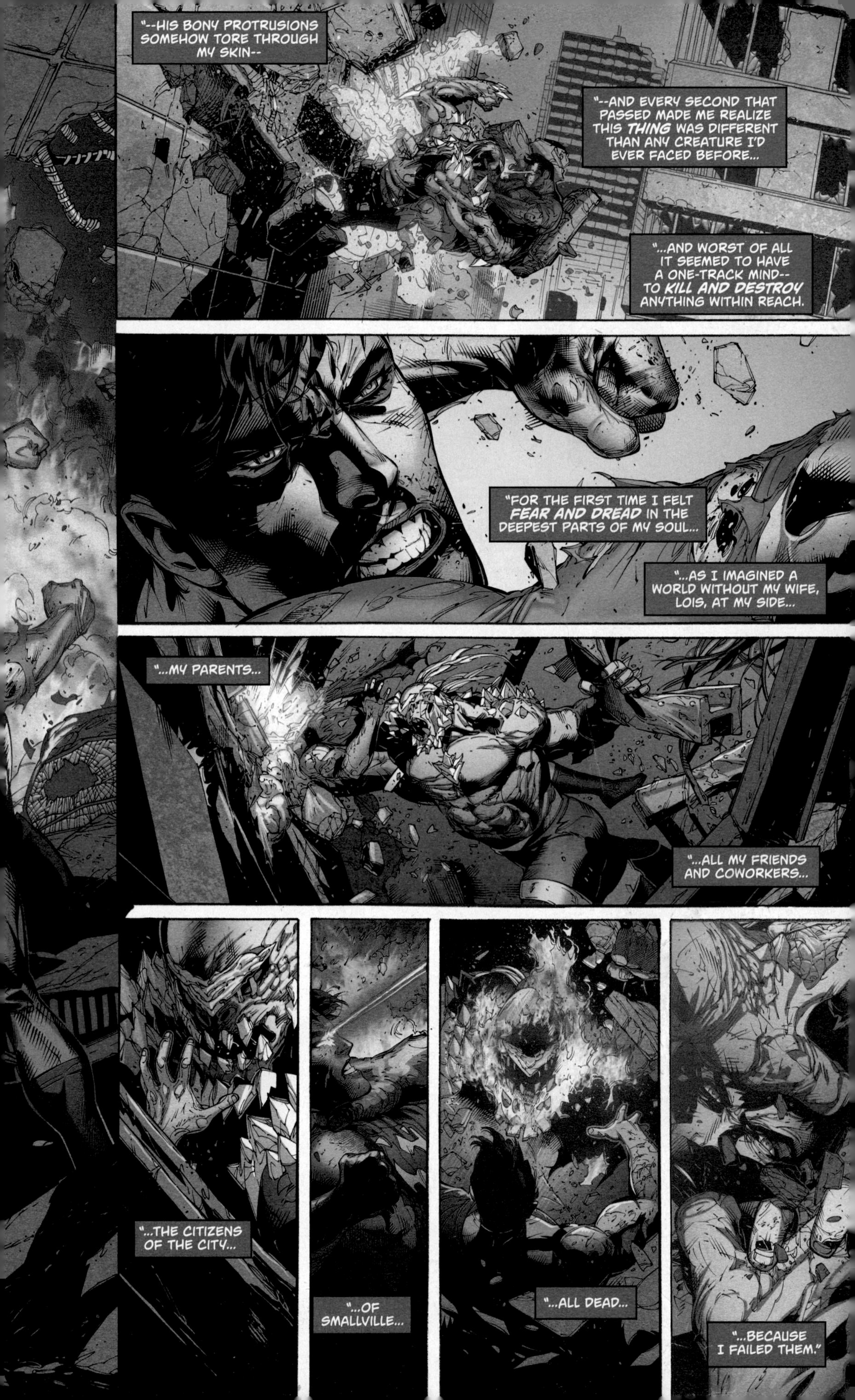
"--HIS BONY PROTRUSIONS SOMEHOW TORE THROUGH MY SKIN--
"--AND EVERY SECOND THAT PASSED MADE ME REALIZE THIS *THING* WAS DIFFERENT THAN ANY CREATURE I'D EVER FACED BEFORE...
"...AND WORST OF ALL IT SEEMED TO HAVE A ONE-TRACK MIND--TO *KILL AND DESTROY* ANYTHING WITHIN REACH.
"FOR THE FIRST TIME I FELT *FEAR AND DREAD* IN THE DEEPEST PARTS OF MY SOUL...
"...AS I IMAGINED A WORLD WITHOUT MY WIFE, LOIS, AT MY SIDE...
"...MY PARENTS...
"...ALL MY FRIENDS AND COWORKERS...
"...THE CITIZENS OF THE CITY...
"...OF SMALLVILLE...
"...ALL DEAD...
"...BECAUSE I FAILED THEM."

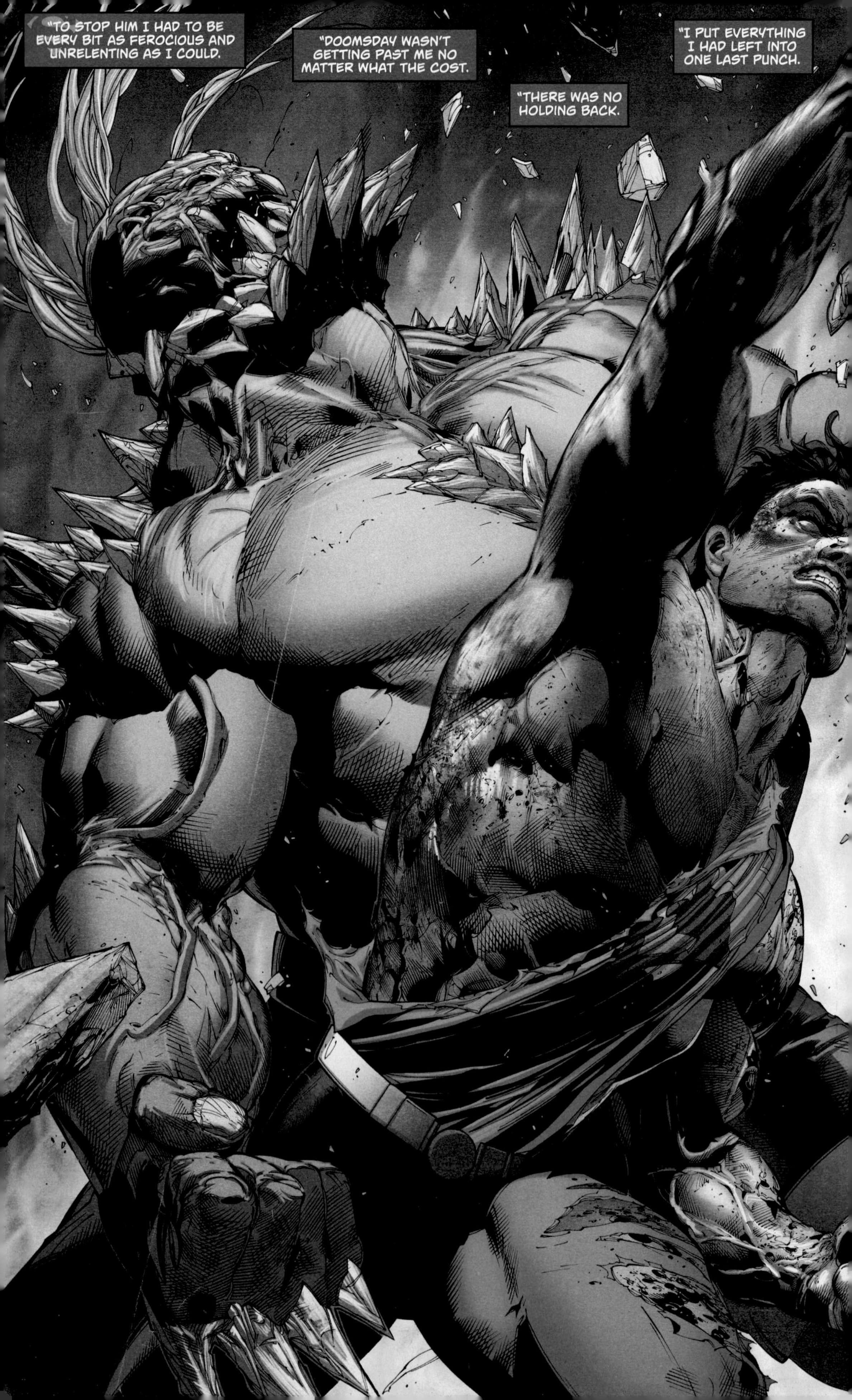
"TO STOP HIM I HAD TO BE EVERY BIT AS FEROCIOUS AND UNRELENTING AS I COULD.
"DOOMSDAY WASN'T GETTING PAST ME NO MATTER WHAT THE COST.
"THERE WAS NO HOLDING BACK.
"I PUT EVERYTHING I HAD LEFT INTO ONE LAST PUNCH.

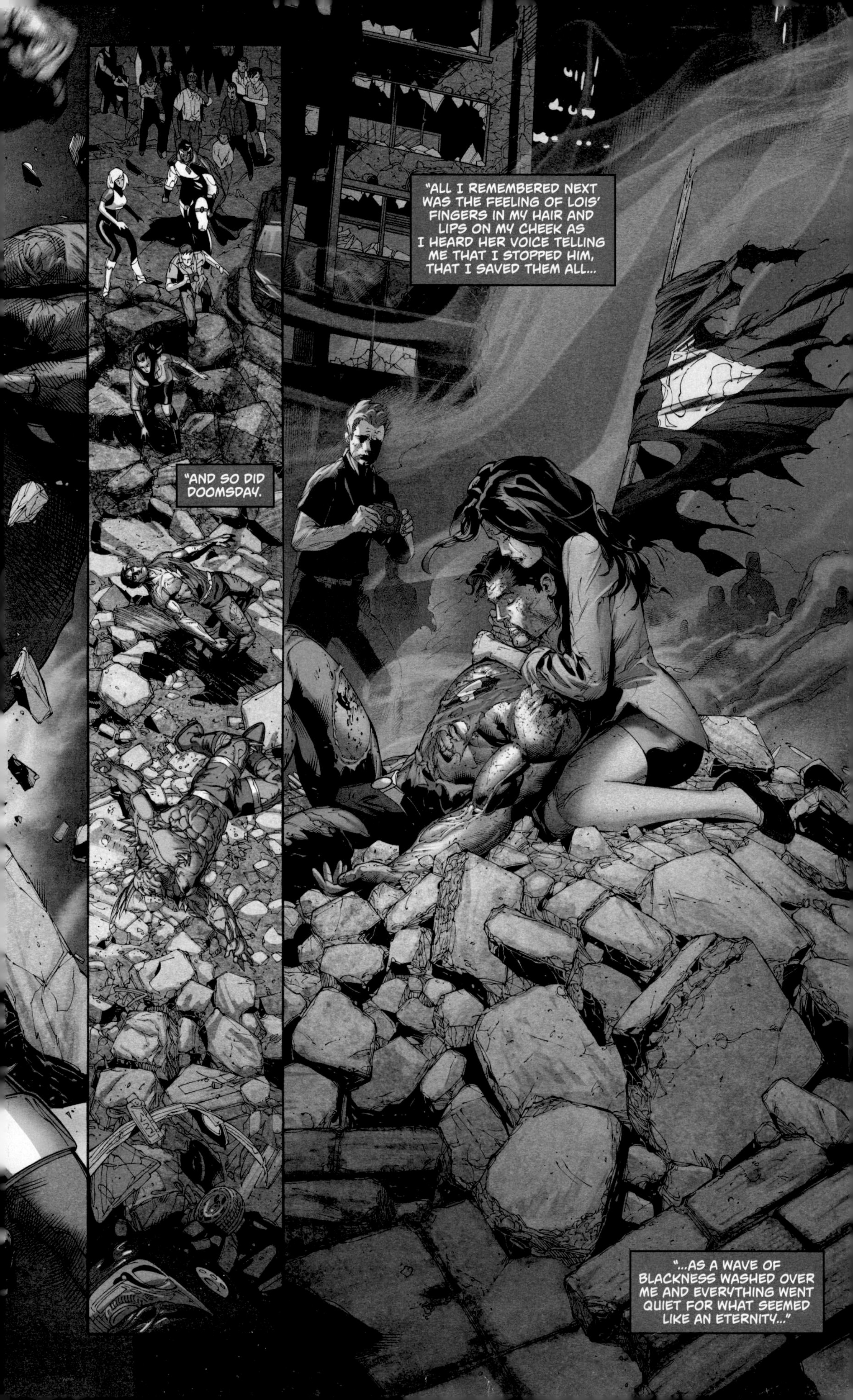
"AND SO DID DOOMSDAY.
"ALL I REMEMBERED NEXT WAS THE FEELING OF LOIS' FINGERS IN MY HAIR AND LIPS ON MY CHEEK AS I HEARD HER VOICE TELLING ME THAT I STOPPED HIM, THAT I SAVED THEM ALL...
"...AS A WAVE OF BLACKNESS WASHED OVER ME AND EVERYTHING WENT QUIET FOR WHAT SEEMED LIKE AN ETERNITY..."

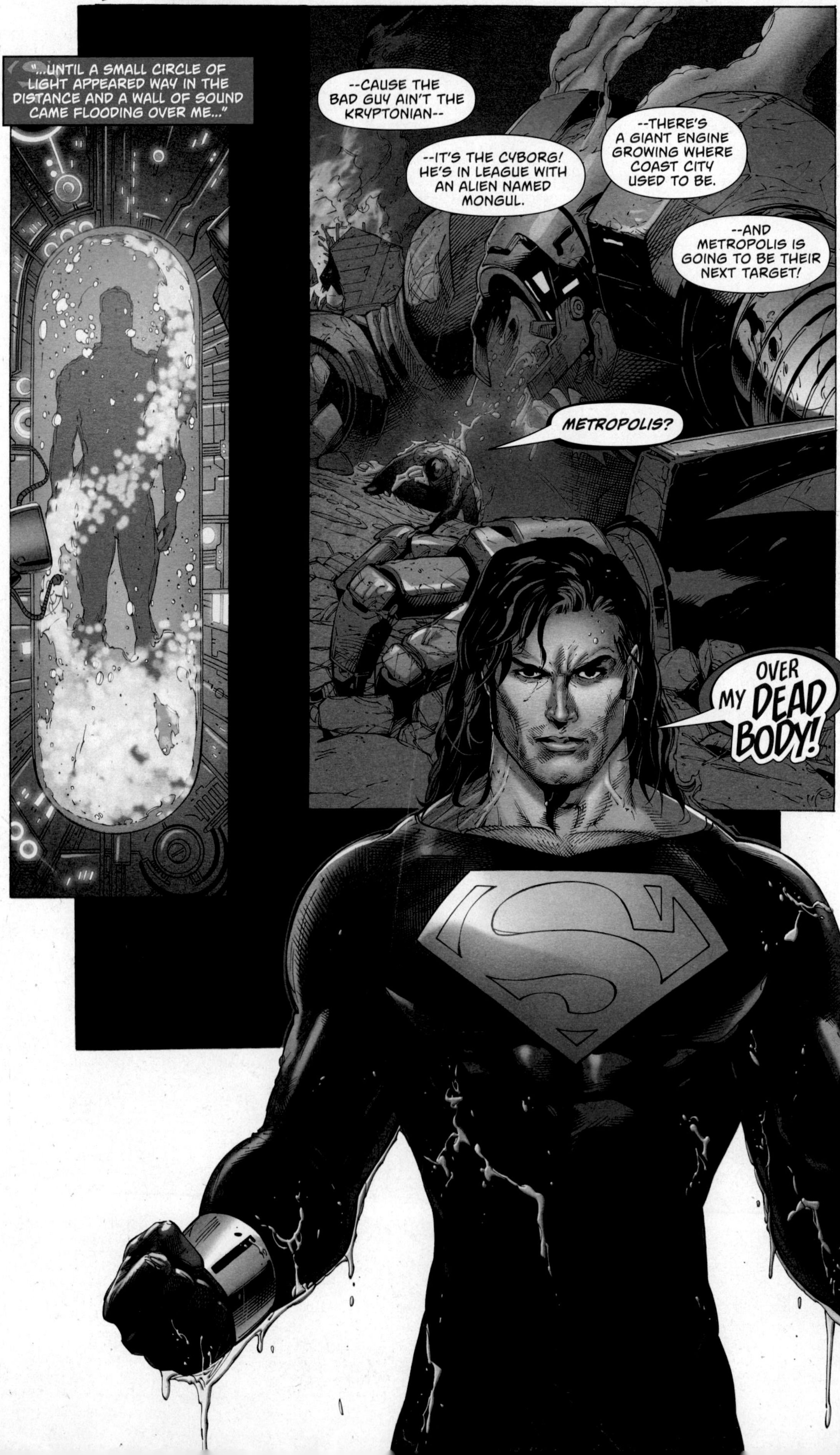
"...UNTIL A SMALL CIRCLE OF LIGHT APPEARED WAY IN THE DISTANCE AND A WALL OF SOUND CAME FLOODING OVER ME..."
--CAUSE THE BAD GUY AIN'T THE KRYPTONIAN--
--IT'S THE CYBORG! HE'S IN LEAGUE WITH AN ALIEN NAMED MONGUL.
--THERE'S A GIANT ENGINE GROWING WHERE COAST CITY USED TO BE.
--AND METROPOLIS IS GOING TO BE THEIR NEXT TARGET!
METROPOLIS?
OVER MY DEAD BODY!

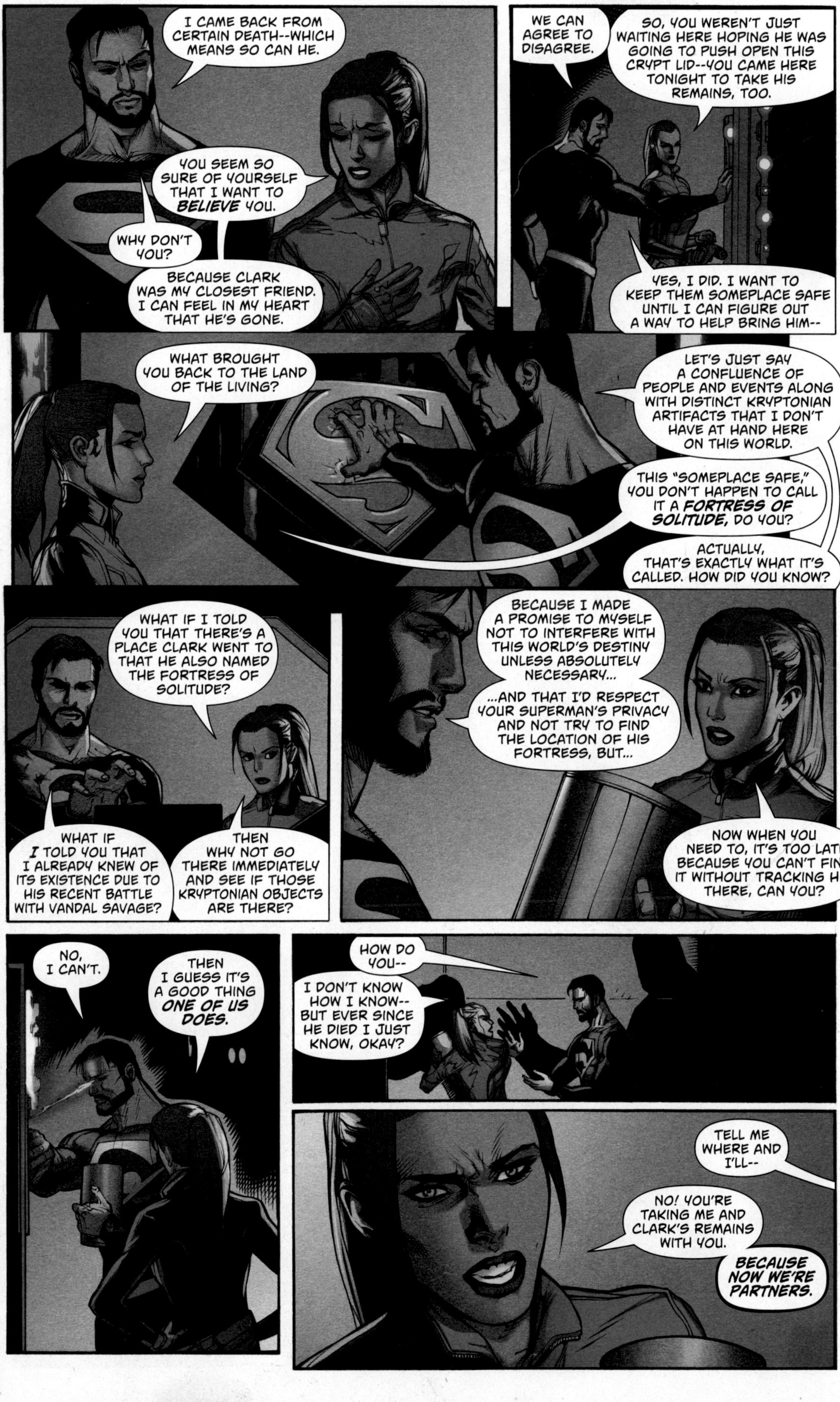
I CAME BACK FROM CERTAIN DEATH--WHICH MEANS SO CAN HE.
YOU SEEM SO SURE OF YOURSELF THAT I WANT TO **BELIEVE** YOU.
WHY DON'T YOU?
BECAUSE CLARK WAS MY CLOSEST FRIEND. I CAN FEEL IN MY HEART THAT HE'S GONE.
WE CAN AGREE TO DISAGREE.
SO, YOU WEREN'T JUST WAITING HERE HOPING HE WAS GOING TO PUSH OPEN THIS CRYPT LID--YOU CAME HERE TONIGHT TO TAKE HIS REMAINS, TOO.
YES, I DID. I WANT TO KEEP THEM SOMEPLACE SAFE UNTIL I CAN FIGURE OUT A WAY TO HELP BRING HIM--
WHAT BROUGHT YOU BACK TO THE LAND OF THE LIVING?
LET'S JUST SAY A CONFLUENCE OF PEOPLE AND EVENTS ALONG WITH DISTINCT KRYPTONIAN ARTIFACTS THAT I DON'T HAVE AT HAND HERE ON THIS WORLD.
THIS "SOMEPLACE SAFE," YOU DON'T HAPPEN TO CALL IT A **FORTRESS OF SOLITUDE,** DO YOU?
ACTUALLY, THAT'S EXACTLY WHAT IT'S CALLED. HOW DID YOU KNOW?
WHAT IF I TOLD YOU THAT THERE'S A PLACE CLARK WENT TO THAT HE ALSO NAMED THE FORTRESS OF SOLITUDE?
WHAT IF *I* TOLD YOU THAT I ALREADY KNEW OF ITS EXISTENCE DUE TO HIS RECENT BATTLE WITH VANDAL SAVAGE?
THEN WHY NOT GO THERE IMMEDIATELY AND SEE IF THOSE KRYPTONIAN OBJECTS ARE THERE?
BECAUSE I MADE A PROMISE TO MYSELF NOT TO INTERFERE WITH THIS WORLD'S DESTINY UNLESS ABSOLUTELY NECESSARY...
...AND THAT I'D RESPECT YOUR SUPERMAN'S PRIVACY AND NOT TRY TO FIND THE LOCATION OF HIS FORTRESS, BUT...
NOW WHEN YOU NEED TO, IT'S TOO LATE BECAUSE YOU CAN'T FIND IT WITHOUT TRACKING HIM THERE, CAN YOU?
NO, I CAN'T.
THEN I GUESS IT'S A GOOD THING ***ONE OF US DOES.***
HOW DO YOU--
I DON'T KNOW HOW I KNOW--BUT EVER SINCE HE DIED I JUST KNOW, OKAY?
TELL ME WHERE AND I'LL--
NO! YOU'RE TAKING ME AND CLARK'S REMAINS WITH YOU.
BECAUSE NOW WE'RE PARTNERS.

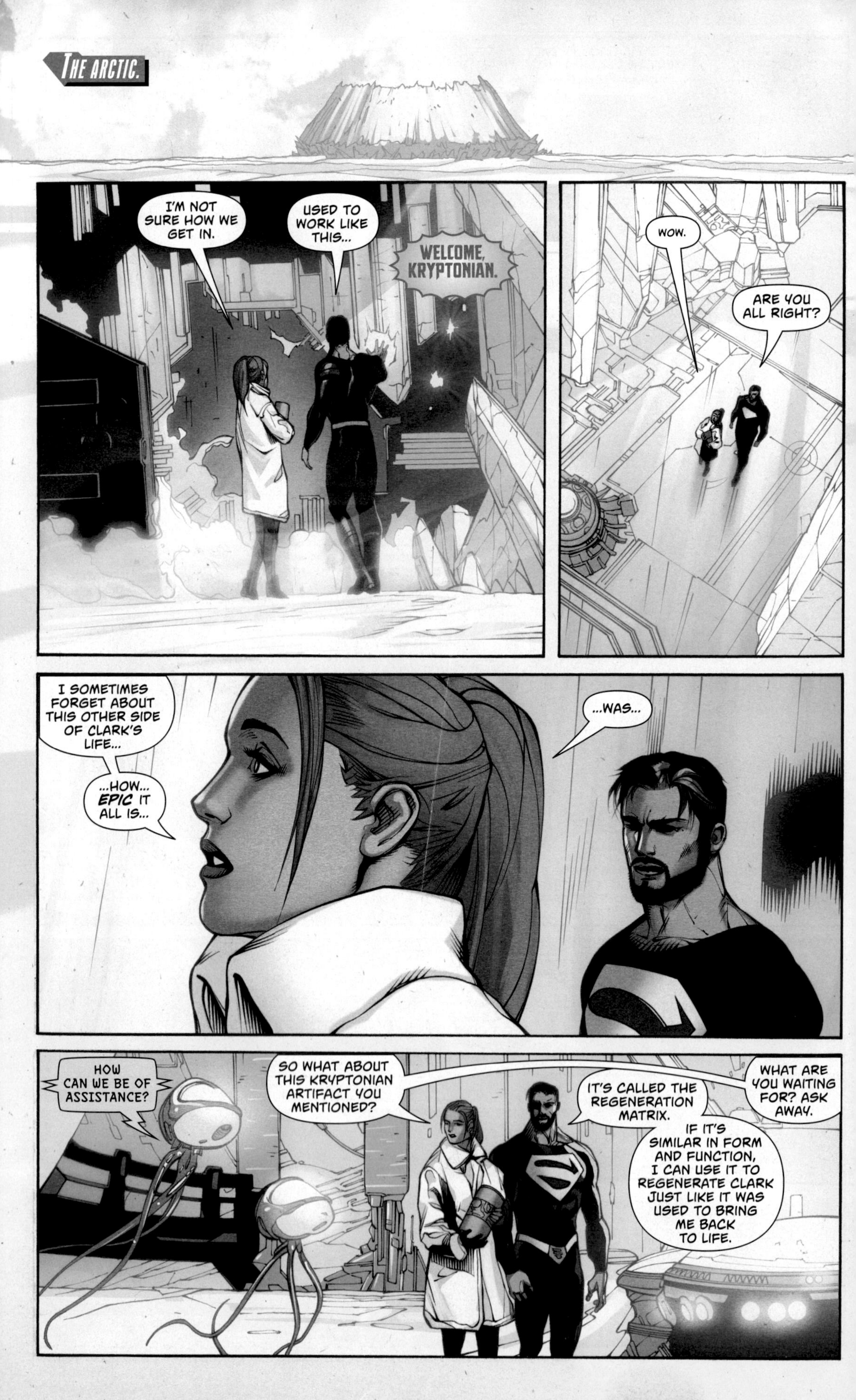
THE ARCTIC.
I'M NOT SURE HOW WE GET IN.
USED TO WORK LIKE THIS...
WELCOME, KRYPTONIAN.
WOW.
ARE YOU ALL RIGHT?
I SOMETIMES FORGET ABOUT THIS OTHER SIDE OF CLARK'S LIFE...
...HOW... EPIC IT ALL IS...
...WAS...
HOW CAN WE BE OF ASSISTANCE?
SO WHAT ABOUT THIS KRYPTONIAN ARTIFACT YOU MENTIONED?
WHAT ARE YOU WAITING FOR? ASK AWAY.
IT'S CALLED THE REGENERATION MATRIX.
IF IT'S SIMILAR IN FORM AND FUNCTION, I CAN USE IT TO REGENERATE CLARK JUST LIKE IT WAS USED TO BRING ME BACK TO LIFE.

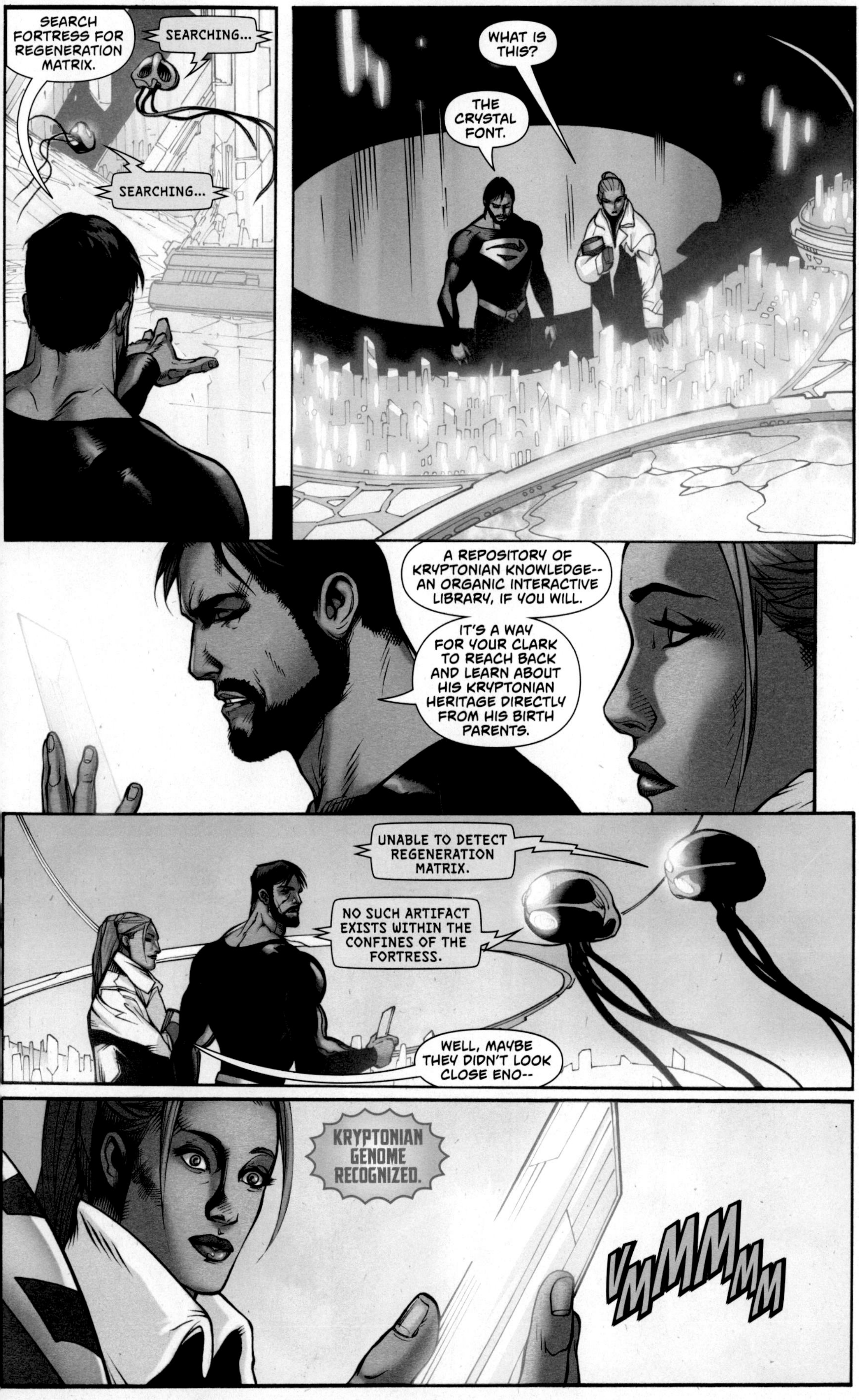
SEARCH FORTRESS FOR REGENERATION MATRIX.
SEARCHING...
SEARCHING...
WHAT IS THIS?
THE CRYSTAL FONT.
A REPOSITORY OF KRYPTONIAN KNOWLEDGE-- AN ORGANIC INTERACTIVE LIBRARY, IF YOU WILL.
IT'S A WAY FOR YOUR CLARK TO REACH BACK AND LEARN ABOUT HIS KRYPTONIAN HERITAGE DIRECTLY FROM HIS BIRTH PARENTS.
UNABLE TO DETECT REGENERATION MATRIX.
NO SUCH ARTIFACT EXISTS WITHIN THE CONFINES OF THE FORTRESS.
WELL, MAYBE THEY DIDN'T LOOK CLOSE ENO--
KRYPTONIAN GENOME RECOGNIZED.
VMMMMMM

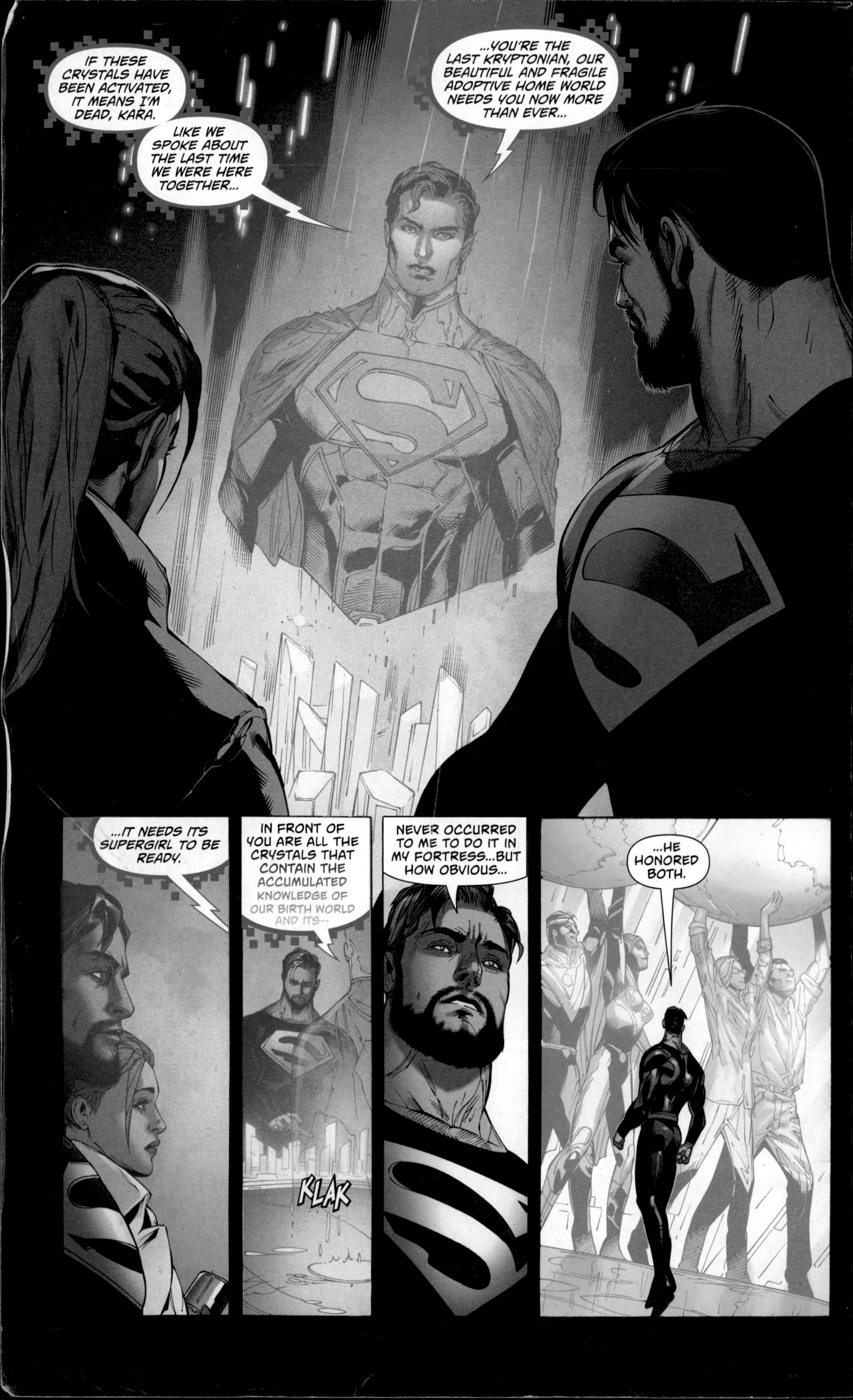
IF THESE CRYSTALS HAVE BEEN ACTIVATED, IT MEANS I'M DEAD, KARA.
LIKE WE SPOKE ABOUT THE LAST TIME WE WERE HERE TOGETHER...
...YOU'RE THE LAST KRYPTONIAN, OUR BEAUTIFUL AND FRAGILE ADOPTIVE HOME WORLD NEEDS YOU NOW MORE THAN EVER...
...IT NEEDS ITS SUPERGIRL TO BE READY.
IN FRONT OF YOU ARE ALL THE CRYSTALS THAT CONTAIN THE ACCUMULATED KNOWLEDGE OF OUR BIRTH WORLD AND ITS--
KLAK
NEVER OCCURRED TO ME TO DO IT IN MY FORTRESS...BUT HOW OBVIOUS...
...HE HONORED BOTH.